1991
TAX
GUIDE
FOR
COLLEGE
TEACHERS
AND OTHER COLLEGE PERSONNEL

For filing 1990 tax returns

Allen Bernstein, Ph.D.

Academic Information Service, Inc.

Washington, D.C. ● College Park, MD

© *1990 by Academic Information Service, Inc.*
ISBN 0-916018-44-X

This publication is designed to provide accurate and authoritative information in regard to the subject matter covered. It is sold with the understanding that the publisher is not engaged in rendering legal, accounting, or other professional service. If legal advice or other expert assistance is required, the services of a competent professional person should be sought.

From a Declaration of Principles jointly adopted by a Committee of the American Bar Association and a Committee of Publishers

Academic Information Service, Inc.
Post Office Box 929
College Park, MD 20740

*"The art of taxation consists in so plucking
the goose as to obtain the largest amount
of feathers with the least amount of hissing."*

—Jean Baptiste Colbert
Finance Minister to Louis XIV

PREFACE

This 1991 edition of the *Tax Guide for College Teachers* is designed to keep College Teachers informed about the latest tax laws and rulings that apply to them. The publication of this edition has been made possible by the continuing interest and support shown by College Teachers all across the nation.

One area of significant change this year has been the deduction for use of a home office. No less than 4 new court cases have had an impact on this deduction. In particular, the Tax Court's ruling in the *Soliman Case* has carved out a large exception to the focal point test under which many previous deductions had been denied. Using this exception, many more College Teachers will now be able to deduct their home offices. This case, along with the other new home office cases, is discussed in Chapter 3.

Another area of favorable activity has been the deduction for travel expenses. The IRS, in a surprise ruling, extended the deduction for commuting to temporary job locations to cover local destinations in addition to out-of-town destinations. This includes local libraries, other local campus locations, etc. Also, the IRS has dramatically increased the per diem meal rate which can be claimed when traveling out-of-town. This applies not just when traveling to conventions and professional meetings, but also when located out-of-town on a sabbatical, leave of absence, or temporary summer job. At the new $34 per day for most metropolitan areas, an individual on a year-long sabbatical gets an automatic meal deduction of almost $10,000. These new travel rules are discussed in Chapter 21.

The most publicized tax development of the year was the passage of the much debated (and maligned) *1990 Deficit Reduction Act* at the end of October, 1990. The tax provisions in this act do not affect 1990 returns, but will first take effect on 1991 tax returns. For tax planning purposes, we have highlighted some of the basic provisions of this act in Chapter 0.

Of course, next year's edition of this Tax Guide will contain a complete explanation of all the new rules in the *1990 Deficit Reduction Act* and other tax laws passed by the Congress in 1991. Also included will be all the new Court Cases, IRS Rulings, and Regulations of interest to College Teachers.

Remember that saving on taxes is worth more than a raise in salary. The extra salary gets ravaged by Federal and State taxes at the highest bracket your taxes reach. It may also be reduced by social security or retirement takeouts—often with little or no increase in benefits. But the money you save knowing the tax laws goes right into your pocket; nothing is taken out before it reaches you.

TABLE OF CONTENTS

Chapter 0:   1990 Deficit Reduction Act 9

Chapter 1:   Basic Rules 15

    Section 1:   Basic Steps in Computing Your Tax 15
    Section 2:   Basic Rules for Deducting Business Expenses 24
    Section 3:   Common Mistakes 25
    Section 4:   Claiming the Standard Deduction 27
    Section 5:   Tax Returns of Dependent Children 28
    Section 6:   Separate vs. Joint Returns 33
    Section 7:   Recordkeeping 41
    Section 8:   Yearend Strategies for Lowering Taxes 43
    Section 9:   IRS Matching Program 45
    Section 10:   Free or Low-Rent Housing 47

Chapter 2:   Books, Supplies, and Equipment 49

Chapter 3:   Home Office 63

    Section 1:   When Can You Deduct for a Home Office? 63
    Section 2:   Computation of Home Office Expenses 81

Chapter 4:   Expensing and Depreciation 88

    Section 1:   Introduction 88
    Section 2:   Expensing Method 91
    Section 3:   Depreciation 92

Chapter 5:   Interest 106

Chapter 6:   Medical Expenses 116

Chapter 7:   Charitable Contributions 125

Chapter 8:   Household Services and Child Care 138

Chapter 9:   Tax Deductions for Homeowners 149

    Section 1:   Interest 149
    Section 2:   Taxes 159
    Section 3:   Capital Gains on Sale of House 161
    Section 4:   Renting a Home to Others 169

Chapter 10:   Automobile Expenses 175

Chapter 11:   **Income Shifting** 190

Chapter 12:   **State and Local Taxes** 196

Chapter 13:   **Tax-Sheltered Plans** 202

     Section 1:   Benefit of Tax-Deferral 202
     Section 2:   Individual Retirement Accounts (IRAs) 204
     Section 3:   Keogh Plans 226
     Section 4:   Tax-Sheltered Annuities 233
     Section 5:   Deferred Compensation Plans 244
     Section 6:   Flexible Spending Accounts 246

Chapter 14:   **Estate and Gift Tax** 248

     Section 1:   Introduction 248
     Section 2:   Gift Tax 249
     Section 3:   Estate Tax 249

Chapter 15:   **Investing Your Money** 256

     Section 1:   Capital Gains and Losses 256
     Section 2:   Passive Loss Rules 259
     Section 3:   U.S. Treasury Securities 262
     Section 4:   Municipal Bonds 265
     Section 5:   Mutual Funds 267
     Section 6:   Special Types of Mutual Funds 275
     Section 7:   Money Market Accounts 278

Chapter 16:   **Moving Expenses** 283

Chapter 17:   **Casualty Losses** 288

Chapter 18:   **Will Your Tax Return Be Audited?** 295

     Section 1:   Audits 295
     Section 2:   Private IRS Rulings 310

Chapter 19:   **Withholding** 314

Chapter 20:   **Divorce and Separation** 318

Chapter 21:   **Travel** 324

     Section 1:   Basic Rules on Deducting Travel Expenses 324
     Section 2:   More Than One Job Location 338
     Section 3:   Commuting to a Temporary Job Near Home 342

copy

Section 4:   Temporary Job Away from Home 343
Section 5:   Travel to Look for Employment 359
Section 6:   Travel to Professional Conventions 359
Section 7:   Travel Which Combines Business With Pleasure 360
        A: Travel Within the United States 360
        B: Travel Outside the United States 361
Section 8:   Educational Travel 366
Section 9:   Discount Rates for Teachers 366

Chapter 22:   **Miscellaneous Deductions** **368**

Section 1:   Basic Rules 368
Section 2:   Employment-Related Expenses 374
Section 3:   Other Miscellaneous Deductions 375

Chapter 23:   **Expenses of Attending School** **379**

Section 1:   Basic Rules for Deducting Educational Expenses 379
Section 2:   When Do Educational Expenses
                    Qualify for Deduction? 387
Section 3:   When Are Deductions Disallowed Under Rule A?.............. 390
Section 4:   When Are Deductions Disallowed Under Rule B?.............. 393
Section 5:   Temporary vs. Indefinite Absence from Profession 395
Section 6:   Which Expenses Are Deductible? 398

Chapter 24:   **Entertainment Expenses** **402**

Chapter 25:   **Retirement Plans** **410**

Section 1:   Introduction 410
Section 2:   Payments from Retirement Plans 410
Section 3:   Contributions to Retirement Plans 414
Section 4:   Social Security 424

Chapter 26:   **Outside Business Activity** **426**

Section 1:   Basic Rules 426
Section 2:   Tax Benefits 438
Section 3:   Paying Family Members for Assistance 442
Section 4:   Outside Activities Producing a Loss 445

Chapter 27:   **Foreign Income** **451**

Chapter 28:   **Tax-Free Grants** 457

    Section 1:   Basic Rules 457
    Section 2:   New Rules for Grants Awarded on or
                  After August 17, 1986 460
    Section 3:   Grants Awarded Before August 17, 1986 466
    Section 4:   How to Claim the Income Tax Exemption 483
    Section 5:   Exemption from Social Security Tax 484

Chapter 29:   **Research Expenses of
College Teachers** 487

    Section 1:   Deduction for Research Expenses 487
    Section 2:   Research Tax Credit 491

Chapter 30:   **Alternative Minimum Tax** 493

Appendix: **Sample Tax Return**

Chapter 0

1990 Deficit Reduction Act

As you no doubt know, Congress finally passed a deficit reduction act right before it adjourned at the end of October. A significant portion of the act consists of various changes in the tax code. These changes do not affect your 1990 tax return due April 15, 1991, but rather will apply first on your 1991 tax return.

We outline below some of the tax provisions you should know about which might affect your tax planning for 1991. Next year's edition of this Tax Guide will contain further details on these and other provisions that will affect your 1991 tax return.

Change in 1991 Tax Rates

The 1990 Tax Rate Schedule [cf. Page 17] is based on 3 basic tax rates—15%, 28%, and 33%. The 33% bracket appears as a *bubble* embedded in the 28% bracket. For example, on a single person's tax return with no dependents, the 33% rate applies to income in the $47,051–$109,100 range. Above and below this range, the 28% rate applies. This idea behind this tax rate structure is that no one ever pays tax exceeding 28% of his Adjusted Gross Income less Deductions.

The 1991 Tax Rate Schedule is based upon 3 basic rates—15%, 28%, and 31%. The 31% rate starts where the 33% bracket starts on 1990 returns (adjusted for inflation). Thus, it represents a 2% tax rate reduction in this bracket. The following are the expected 1991 basic tax tables for different categories of tax returns.

1991 TAX BRACKETS

Joint Return		Head of Household	
Taxable Income	Tax Rate	Taxable Income	Tax Rate
$0-$34,000	15%	$0-$26,300	15%
$34,001-$82,150	28%	$26,301-$70,450	28%
Over $82,150	31%	Over $70,450	31%

Married Persons Filing Separate Returns		Single Persons	
Taxable Income	Tax Rate	Taxable Income	Tax Rate
$0-$17,000	15%	$0-$20,250	15%
$17,001-$41,075	28%	$20,351-$49,300	28%
Over $41,075	31%	Over $49,300	31%

For those with adjusted gross income less than $100,000 ($50,000 for marrieds filing separately), the above tables tell the full story. For others, the following 2 *phase-outs* apply:

(1) 3% Phase-Out of Certain Itemized Deductions

This phase-out applies to single and joint returns with more than $100,000 of AGI (Adjusted Gross Income). The total itemized deductions claimed on the tax return—other than medical expenses, casualty losses, and investment interest—will be reduced by 3% of AGI in excess of $100,000 ($50,000 for marrieds filing separately). However, the reduction cannot exceed 80% of this total of affected deductions.

Example

Jackson's joint tax return shows the following:

Adjusted Gross Income (AGI)	$150,000
Deductions for medical expenses, casualty losses, and investment interest	$ 6,000
Other itemized deductions	$ 7,000
Total Deduction	$ 13,000

Jackson's total of itemized deductions is reduced by 3% x ($150,000 – $100,000) = $1,500. Thus, Jackson deducts a total of $13,000 – $1,500 = $11,500 on his tax return.

Example

Same as the previous example, except that Jackson's Other itemized deductions *total $1,200 so his* Total Deductions *add up to $6,000 + $1,200 = $7,200. The basic 3% of excess AGI calculations yields $1,500 as in the previous example. However, in this example, the reduction cannot exceed 80% X $1,200 = $960. Thus, Jackson deducts a total of $7,200 – $960 = $6,240.*

(2) Phase-Out of Personal Exemptions

This phase-out applies to joint returns with AGI exceeding $150,000 on a joint return. The deduction for personal exemptions (expected to be $2,150 per dependent on 1991 tax returns) is reduced by .8% for each $1,000 of AGI exceeding $150,000. For single returns, the $150,000 is replaced by $100,000; for heads of household, $125,000; and for marrieds filing separately, $75,000. (For marrieds filing separately, the .8% figure is raised to 1.6%.)

Example

Ralph and Susan Perry have $200,000 AGI on their joint tax return. They have 2 dependent children.

On their 1991 tax return, their personal exemptions are $2,150 X 4 = $8,600.

Under the phase-out rule, this is reduced by .8% ✕ 50 = 40%. Thus, their deduction for personal exemptions is equal to $8,600 – (40% ✕ $8,600) = $5,160.

Since .8% ✕ 125 = 100%, the personal exemptions are entirely phased out over a range of $125,000 ($62,500 for married filing separately). Thus for example, on joint returns, income above $150,000 + $125,000 = $275,000 is no longer subjected to the exemption phase-out rule.

How Do the Phase-Out Rules Affect Marginal Tax Brackets?

The starting point for most tax planning is a person's *marginal tax rate*. This is the rate at which extra income earned would be taxed. For example, under the basic tax tables above, a single person with taxable income of $40,000 would be in a 28% marginal tax bracket. If he earns an extra dollar, he pays an extra 28 cents in Federal income taxes. Similarly, an extra dollar of deductions reduces Federal income taxes by 28 cents.

A person's marginal tax rate can influence whether it is worth the effort to earn more money, or whether a deductible item is worth buying. The higher the rate, the less worthwhile it is to earn more and the more worthwhile it is to purchase deductible items. Also, a higher marginal tax rate makes investing in tax-exempt securities or tax-exempt mutual funds more attractive [cf. Sections 3, 5, and 6 of the *Investing Your Money* chapter].

For the 1990 tax year, an individual's marginal tax bracket could simply be obtained from his taxable income by looking it up in the tax tables given on page 17. [Taxable income equals adjusted gross income less deductions and personal exemptions.] For example, a married couple with $85,000 in taxable income would fall into the 33% marginal tax bracket. They would pay an extra 33 cents of Federal income tax for the next dollar of income and receive a 33 cents lowering for a dollar spent on a deductible item.

For the 1991 tax year, the situation is different. Because of the disregard for simplicity shown by a Congress desperately seeking a "compromise" budget package, the 1991 picture is much more complex. There are 2 separate phase-out provisions, each starting at a different income level. And these phase-outs are based on *Adjusted Gross Income,* rather than on *Taxable Income,* which is the basis of the tax tables. Rather than consulting a simple tax table to determine the exact marginal tax rate, a more complex computation might have to be made, However, an idea of how the phase-out provisions affect tax rates can be given as follows:

Double-Bubble, Toil, and Trouble

Each of the 2 phase-out provisions can be regarded as producing a bubble superimposed on the basic 15%, 28%, 31% tax table given earlier.

The 3% itemized deduction phase-out reduces each $100 of deductions to which it applies by $3.00. In the 31% tax bracket, this amounts to a higher tax of 31% ✕ $3.00 = $.93. In other words, the itemized deduction phase-out raises the basic tax rate by about 1 percentage point. This can be viewed as an extra 1%

bubble in the tax rates over the range the phase-out is applied.

Under the personal exemption phase-out, for every $1,000 of increase in AGI to which it is applied, each personal exemption is reduced by .8% × $2,150 = $17.20. In the 31% tax bracket, this raises taxes by 31% × $17.20 = $5.33. In other words, the personal exemption phase-out raises the basic tax rate by about .5% for each exemption. This can be viewed as an extra bubble in the tax rates of .5% times the number of exemptions claimed.

The 2 bubbles operate independent of each other. One or the other or both may be present on an individual's tax return. And if both, they might overlap or they might not. It all depends on the amounts of income, deductions, and exemptions that appear on the return. A family of 4, for example, might be subject to both the 1% itemized deduction bubble and the 2% (4 × .5%) personal exemption bubble. This would produce a double-bubble tax rate of 31% + 1% + 2% = 34%.

Sad to say, this is not the end of the newly-introduced complexity. There is actually a third bubble due to the extension of the 1.45% medicare tax [discussed next] up to $125,000 of income. This third bubble will apply to more persons than the other two. While masquerading as a social security tax, this medicare levy is in fact an income tax. Unlike the basic social security tax, there will be no extra benefit received by those who pay extra tax. Note that this 1.45% bubble is only affected by *earned income* to which the tax is applied. Extra investment income or extra deductions will have no effect on this medicare tax.

New Medicare Tax Applied to Incomes Up to $125,000

In 1990, social security tax was levied on all wages up to the *social security wage base* of $51,300. The rate of tax was 7.65% paid by the employee and an additional 7.65% paid by the employer. The 7.65% rate actually consisted of 2 components—6.2% for retirement (and disability) benefits plus 1.45% for medicare.

In 1991, the *wage base* for the 6.2% retirement portion is expected to rise (because of the usual inflation adjustment) to $53,400. However the *wage base* for the 1.45% medicare portion goes all the way up to $125,000. In other words, income from $0–$53,400 will be subject to a social security tax rate of 7.65% and income from $53,401–$125,000 subject to a rate of 1.45%.

This new provision does not affect individuals with annual incomes in 1991 of $53,400 or less. On the other hand, those with wages of $125,000 or more will have to pay an extra tax of 1.45% × ($125,000 – $53,400) = $1,038. Others will pay an extra tax between these 2 extremes.

Grant recipients should consult the *Tax-Free Grants* chapter to determine if their grant qualifies for exemption from social security tax. If so, they should notify their employer. Otherwise, their employers might automatically assess the new 1.45% medicare tax on the full amount of their grants.

The 1.45% medicare tax must be paid both by the employee and by the employer. The self-employed will be required to pay both parts, 1.45%+1.45% = 2.9%.

The above "medicare tax" is expected to raise about $27 billion over 5 years for the trust fund that pays hospital bills under medicare. This trust fund is expected to go broke in about 15 years because medical costs and the elderly population are rising faster than income. According to the government, the new medicare tax will extend the date for going broke by about 3 years.

Capital Gains Rate Ceiling

The 1990 Deficit Reduction Act contains a break for capital gains on items sold after December 31, 1990. However, it is not nearly the break sought by President Bush.

Capital Gains will be taxed at a rate no higher than 28%. This will benefit those whose income reaches into the new 31% tax bracket. Also, while not clearly spelled out in the new tax act, it appears that the 28% cap applies not just to the basic tax table rate, but also serves to limit any extra tax that otherwise would be produced by the *phase-out* rules discussed earlier in this chapter.

Earned Income Tax Credit

As discussed in Chapter 1, individuals with income less than about $20,000 are entitled to a special tax credit if they have a dependent child living with them. This tax credit is being substantially increases staring in 1991. If you know a student or other low income person who might be eligible for this credit, you should alert them to the new changes. They may be able to apply to their employers to receive this credit spread out over their 1991 paychecks.

The new law (1) increases the percentage of the credit in steps over the next 5 years, (2) provides an additional credit for health insurance, and (3) provides an additional credit if there is a baby under age 1 as of the end of the year.

Cosmetic Surgery

Starting in 1991, cosmetic surgery or other procedures will not be deductible unless *"necessary to ameliorate a deformity arising from a congenital abnormality, a personal injury resulting from an accident or trauma, or disfiguring disease."* It is not yet known how strictly the IRS will interpret this restriction. For example, it's possible that some dental or orthodontic procedures will come under this restriction.

Yearend Strategies

As discussed in Section 8 of Chapter 1, there are a number of techniques that can be used to shift deductions from one year to an adjacent year. Generally, it is desirable to shift deductions to the earlier year, because the amount of tax saved can earn investment income for a longer period of time.

This benefit is magnified somewhat for those who are in the 33% tax bracket on their 1990 tax returns [cf. Page 17], but will be in the new 31% bracket under the 1991 tax rules. Shifting deductions from 1991 into 1990 will have a greater tax-lowering effect because of the higher 1990 tax rate. (The year in which a check is placed in the mail is considered to be the year of payment. The date appearing on a check is usually accepted as being the year of payment, unless there is some strong indication it was mailed in a different year [cf. Section 8 of Chapter 1].)

A greater tax discrepancy can occur with the tax on capital gains. An individual might be able to time the sale of an appreciated capital asset to occur in one year or the other. If he is in the 33% tax bracket on his 1990 tax return, delaying the sale until 1991 can reduce the tax rate on the capital gain to 28%, as discussed above.

Note: The above explanation is based on an initial reading of the law as passed by Congress. It is not known exactly how the IRS will apply the law in practice. Also, there is question as to how the new rules will be woven into next year's tax forms.

Of course, next year's edition of this Tax Guide will contain a full explanation of all the new rules. Included will be a complete set of examples which illustrate how the new law applies in varying circumstances.

Chapter 1

Basic Rules

Section 1:
Basic Steps in Computing Your Tax

The following basic procedure is used to compute your 1990 income tax:

(1) Compute your **total income** subject to tax. This consists of wages, interest, dividends, etc.

(2) Compute your **adjustments to income.** This includes alimony payments you make plus deductible contributions to tax-sheltered IRA and Keogh plans.

(3) Subtract (2) from (1). This is your **Adjusted Gross Income.**

(4) Compute your **deductions** by either:

(a) Taking the standard deduction. This is a fixed amount depending upon the type of tax return you're filing (with extra amounts for those who are at least age 65 or blind);

or

(b) Itemizing your deductions. This is done on Schedule A where you list such things as medical expenses, interest, taxes, casualty losses, charitable contributions, moving expenses, and miscellaneous deductions. Under *miscellaneous deductions* you include job-related expenses such as travel, books, supplies, professional dues, home office, etc. Certain deductions only apply after a minimum floor has been surpassed—7.5% of Adjusted Gross Income for medical expenses, 10% for casualty losses, and 2% for the sum total of miscellaneous deductions.

(5) You get a **personal exemption** for each dependent you claim, including yourself, your children, and your spouse. Multiply the number of exemptions by $2,050.

(6) Subtract (4) and (5) from (3). The net result is your **taxable income.**

(7) Compute your **tax** by looking up your taxable income in the appropriate tax table.

(8) Subtract **tax credits.** This includes the household services and child care tax credit, the credit for excess social security withheld by more than one employer, and the credit for the elderly not fully covered by social security. Observe that tax credits are much more favorable than deductions since they are subtracted directly from your tax instead of from your income.

For 1990 tax returns, the following table shows the amount of the standard deduction for different categories of individuals:

Married filing jointly	$5,450
Married filing separately	$2,725
Head of Household	$4,750
Single	$3,250

Individuals who are at least age 65 or are blind are entitled to a larger standard deduction than given above. The tax form instruction booklet contains a worksheet for computing the standard deduction for such individuals.

Example

A married couple with 2 dependent children has income of $55,000 and files a joint return. They each make a deductible $1,000 contribution to an IRA, producing a $2,000 adjustment to income. Their itemized deductions total $6,200, which exceeds their standard deduction amount of $5,450. The tax computation proceeds as follows:

(1)	Total Income	$55,000
(2)	Less: Adjustments to Income	-2,000
(3)	Adjusted Gross Income	$53,000
(4)	Less: Itemized Deductions	-6,200
(5)	Less Personal Exemptions: 4 × $2,050 =	-8,200
(6)	Taxable Income	$38,600

The tax is then computed by looking up $38,600 in the appropriate tax table. Finally, the tax credits for child care, excess social security withheld, etc. are subtracted.

Note the two places where expenses are deducted — as *adjustments to income* and as *itemized deductions*. One advantage in deducting expenses as an adjustment to income is that you can still use the standard deduction if it proves beneficial. (Self-employed persons may deduct all their business expenses on Schedule C. Thus, they are eligible to use the standard deduction and still deduct all their business expenses.)

Another advantage occurs in connection with the floors on various itemized deductions—7.5% of Adjusted Gross Income for medical expenses, 10% for casualty losses, and 2% for miscellaneous deductions. Claiming an *adjustment to income* reduces your Adjusted Gross Income, thereby lowering these floors. This in turn can raise the amounts you're entitled to deduct in the medical, casualty, or miscellaneous sections of Schedule A [cf. the *Medical Expenses, Casualty,* and *Miscellaneous Deductions* chapters].

1990 Tax Brackets

The tables below show the tax brackets for different categories of tax returns. These brackets apply only to 1990 tax returns and are scheduled to be indexed upwards in future years in line with inflation. (You may notice the peculiar feature of these tables, namely the 33% tax bracket sandwiched in between the two 28% tax brackets. This lowering of the top tax bracket was passed into law in order that no one would have to pay more than 28% of their taxable income in taxes, ignoring all personal exemptions.)

The following tables are based on *taxable income*. As discussed above, *taxable income* is equal to *adjusted gross income,* less *personal exemptions* and *deductions.*

1990 TAX BRACKETS

Joint Return		Head of Household	
Taxable Income	Tax Rate	Taxable Income	Tax Rate
$0-$32,450	15%	$0-$26,050	15%
$32,451-$78,400	28%	$26,051-$67,200	28%
$78,401-$185,730*	33%	$67,201-$157,890*	33%
Over $185,730*	28%	Over $157,890*	28%

*The $185,730 and $157,890 figures apply on tax returns claiming 2 personal exemptions. For each additional dependent, these figures are raised by $11,480.

Married Person Filing Separate Return		Single Person	
Taxable Income	Tax Rate	Taxable Income	Tax Rate
$0-$16,225	15%	$0-$19,450	15%
$16,226-$39,200	28%	$19,451-$47,050	28%
$39,201-$135,050*	33%	$47,051-$109,100*	33%
Over $135,050*	28%	Over $109,100*	28%

*The $135,050 and $109,100 figures above apply to an individual claiming one personal exemption for himself. For each additional dependent, these figures are raised by $11,480.

Dependents

You get a $2,050 exemption for each dependent, including yourself, which you claim on your tax return. You are required to list the social security numbers of all dependents who are age 2 or older on December 31, 1990. Be sure to apply for these numbers as soon as possible so you'll have them in time to file your tax return.

The instruction booklet that comes with your tax forms lists the precise rules for who qualifies as your dependent. Basically, you must furnish more than 50% of the support of a dependent and the dependent must have gross income of less than $2,050 for the year. However, the $2,050 limitation on earnings does not apply to a child of yours who is either (i) under age 19 at the close of the year or (ii) is under age 24 at the end of the year and was a full-time student during some part of each of 5 months during the year.

You count as support that you provide, the cost of food, medical expenses, health insurance, clothing, telephone, transportation, schooling, etc. You also count the fair rental value of housing that you provide for the child.

In determining whether a dependent has gross income over $2,050, tax-free scholarships or fellowships, social security payments, tax-free interest, disability payments, and other tax-free income are not counted. However, these items are taken into account when determining if an individual has provided more than 50% of another person's support. There is an exception for scholarship or fellowship payments received by a child of yours who is a full-time student in at least 5 months of the year. These payments are disregarded for purposes of the 50% requirement. This is the case even if part of the scholarship or fellowship payments is subject to tax.

In determining whether you have met the 50% support requirement, it is not necessary for the dependent to have used his earnings or savings for his own support. For example, suppose your child earns $3,000 during the year. You provide support (including food, lodging, clothing, use of auto, etc.) of $2,500. If the child saves $600 and uses the remaining $2,400 towards his own support, then you will have met the 50% support requirement.

A student loan taken out by a child to use for his support counts as support provided by the child. In some cases, it may be better for the parent to borrow money in his own name and give it to his child, in order to preserve the dependency deduction.

A 1980 court case makes it easier to claim an exemption for an elderly parent. This case decided that Medicaid payments as well as benefits from Medicare and private insurance are not counted as support. This makes it easier for a relative to show he furnished over half the parent's support. [Archer, 73 TC #78]

If a parent could be claimed as a dependent by his grown children except that no child individually provides over 50% of support, they can agree among themselves which one is entitled to the dependency exemption. The child claiming the exemption must have furnished more than 10% of support. The children each fill out Form 2120 which is attached to the tax return of the one claiming the exemption.

A non-relative must be a member of your household for the entire year in order to qualify as a dependent. But a difficulty arises with friendly, but unmarried taxpayers. If the arrangement violates a state anti-cohabitation law, then one partner cannot claim the other as a dependent. This requires some delicate decision-making when the matter is raised in court.

For example, a court recently ruled against a North Carolina unmarried couple. According to North Carolina law, *"If any man and woman, not being married to each other, shall lewdly and lasciviously associate, bed and cohabit together, they shall be guilty of a misdemeanor."* The court found their friendly cohabitation to violate this statute, thereby ruling out a dependency claim. [Ensminger, 45 AFTR 2nd 80-373]

But a Missouri judge came to a different conclusion. Missouri law forbids *"grossly lewd or lascivious behavior."* And an 1855 court case had declared *"What act can be more grossly lewd or lascivious than for a man and woman, not married to each other, to be publically living together and cohabitating with each other."* But the judge in this case ruled that times had changed. He declared unmarried cohabitation not to be grossly lewd or lascivious conduct according to today's standards. [Shackelford, 80-1 USTC 99276]

Mailing in Your Tax Return

If you have a refund coming, mail your tax return in the envelope which is enclosed with the tax return package mailed to you by the IRS. This will speed up the processing of your tax return.

Of course, if you are mailing in a check and can use extra float time before your check is cashed, you can do the opposite, using your own envelope. An extra-large envelope will especially slow down processing, because the IRS uses automatic envelope-opening machines which work only on normal-sized envelopes. Oversized envelopes will be rejected and set aside to be opened by hand, a process that takes extra time.

Don't mail more than one tax return in the same envelope, especially if a payment is enclosed. It is not uncommon for the IRS to credit a payment to the wrong tax return, resulting in unnecessary confusion that you'll have to straighten out.

When sending in your tax return, you should arrange the forms in their numerical order. Form 1040 goes on top, followed by related schedules. The remaining forms follow the *attachment sequence number* on the upper right-hand corner of the forms. You attach any supplementary information you are providing at the end.

Amending Tax Returns of Previous Years

You are permitted to amend tax returns which you filed in previous years. However, you are limited to going back three years if you wish to obtain a refund of back taxes. For example, you may amend your 1987, 1988 and 1989 tax returns if you file on or before April 15, 1991. When you amend your Federal tax return, you should amend your State tax return also.

There is a special form, 1040X, which you use for filing an amended return. You also include any applicable schedules or forms. For example, if you want to retroactively claim the child care tax credit, you would submit a Form 2441 along with your Form 1040X. Although not required, it's also a good idea to enclose a copy of the form or schedule as it was originally filed.

If you have overlooked a deduction or tax credit in a previous year, you must file an amended return to rectify the situation. You cannot claim the deduction or credit in a later year to compensate for its omission in the appropriate year.

It should be cautioned that amended returns are somewhat more likely to be audited than original returns. If there are questionable items on your original return, you are better off waiting until just before the 3-year limit is about to expire before amending your tax return. Requesting a refund on an amended return does not extend the 3-year period for auditing your original return. Thus, the amended return will not trigger an audit of other items on your original return. The IRS will pay you 3-years' interest on the amount refunded to you.

Notifying the IRS If You Move

If you move, it's a good idea to notify the IRS of your new address, especially if you're waiting for a refund. (The IRS will generally go by the last address used on a tax return of yours.) The IRS produced an optional new form in 1990, Form 8822, which you can file with the IRS, specifying your old and new addresses.

Electronic Tax Filing

The IRS now allows tax returns to be filed electronically, instead of being submitted on the usual paper forms. However, you can't use your own home computer. You must use the services of an organization that qualifies to be a mass user of the electronic filing system. Typically, the charge for such services is in the $25–$40 range per tax return.

The benefit to the IRS is that electronically-filed returns are cheaper to process. This is why they offer and promote this arrangement.

The benefit to the taxpayer is that he can get his refund about a month sooner than filing by mail. However, rarely does this benefit outweigh the cost. The refund would have to exceed about $3,000 before it became worthwhile. And the taxpayer would still be left without an exact copy of the return to refer to in case there's a problem.

Getting Copies of Tax Returns

If you need a copy of an old tax return including attachments, you can get it from the IRS. (The IRS keeps tax returns for at least 6 years.) Send in Form 4506 along with a check for $4.25 to the IRS Service Center where you filed your return. Allow 6 weeks for delivery. You can also get a copy, at no charge, of a W-2 Form by filing Form 4506 or other written request with your IRS Service Center.

You can get free of charge just an information printout of 9 basic items on your tax return including adjusted gross income and the tax due. (This information is generally kept by the IRS for more than 6 years.) This is obtained by calling or writing your local IRS office. You can also request that information be sent to a third party. This can be handy for verifying financial information to a potential lender.

If you need a current last-minute blank tax form in order to complete your tax return, try a local library. Many libraries now make available a portfolio of tax forms which can be photocopied and used in filing your tax return.

IRS Ombudsmen

The IRS has a policy of having an ombudsman, called a *Problems Resolution Officer,* in each of its district offices. The ombudsman is not there to give tax advice but rather to cut through red tape in case you're having trouble getting your refund check or straightening out some other mixup. Last year, these ombudsmen handled almost half a million cases.

If you're expecting a refund, give the IRS ten weeks before making an inquiry. After that time, phone your local IRS office. They can run a computer check to determine what happened and tell you when your refund check will be mailed. If you can't get things straightened out within a reasonable period of time, ask to speak to the Problems Resolution Officer.

IRS Telephone Error Rate

The IRS has a telephone number to "assist" taxpayers with tax questions. However, even the IRS acknowledges an error rate of about 30% by those answering the telephone lines. (For complicated questions, the error rate would be even higher.) Although not a part of the public record, you can be almost sure that the majority of mistakes err on the side of causing more tax to be due rather than less.

This high error rate is less astonishing when the composition of the workforce answering the telephones is known. Most have only a high school education and do not have extensive tax training. And during filing season, the workforce is enlarged 50% by hiring seasonal employees—most of them for annualized salaries of under $20,000. You can be sure that the IRS agents who audit tax returns are the more experienced and better-paid IRS employees—not the workers hired to give information to the public.

It should be pointed out that telephone advice from the IRS is considered to be unofficial. You cannot use it as justification for how you fill out your tax return.

Roundoff

The IRS allows you to round off all figures to the nearest dollar. Note that the detailed tax tables are broken down into bracket intervals of $50, with the same tax applying to everyone in the same bracket. Thus, a difference of 1 cent in income or deductions could, in the worst possible case, throw someone into a higher bracket and increase taxes by as much as $17. If your initial tax computation puts you just over the edge into a new bracket, changing your roundoff decision might throw you back into the next lowest bracket.

Extension of Time to File

You can get an automatic extension of 4 months to file your return. To receive this extension, you file Form 4868 with the IRS by April 15. Then file your return by August 15, accompanied by a copy of your Form 4868. However, you have to pay what you estimate your tax will be by April 15. Otherwise, you risk a penalty on the underpayment unless the underpayment is less than 10%. In addition, an interest charge will be assessed on all late payments. If you need more than 4 extra months, you can file Form 2688 explaining the reason you need more time. The IRS will accept this form if it approves of your reasons.

Two recent Tax Court cases underscore the requirements connected with filing an extension. In one case, a teacher filed an extension estimating the amount of tax due, but did not pay the amount estimated as required. This meant the extension was invalid, generating a late-filing penalty [Bacon, TC Memo 1989-90.]. And in the other case, the amount estimated was paid with the extension request, but the Court objected to the estimate. It did not object just because the estimate turned out to be way off. Rather, it ruled that the taxpayer did not utilize data (such as Forms 1099) readily available to him to generate a properly-made estimate. This meant the extension request was invalid [Crocker, 92 TC No. 57].

If you file your tax return late without the proper extension, you will be charged interest plus a penalty on the amount of tax due. However, the penalty (but not the interest) is often waived by the IRS if a valid excuse is provided. Such a valid excuse might be death or illness of yourself or family member, destruction of records in a fire, failure to receive the required forms after making a timely request from the IRS, etc.

Reporting Interest and Dividends on Your Tax Return

You report interest and dividend payments you receive on Schedule B. The IRS computer will compare the amounts you report with its own records. A mismatch may cause the IRS to seek an additional tax assessment or even conduct an audit of your tax return.

To prevent this from happening, you should report interest and dividend payments separately according to the information slips you receive from the paying institutions; otherwise the IRS computer will get confused. For example, separate accounts with the same bank should be listed separately. Dividends on stocks held in street name with a broker and reported to the IRS as a total sum received from the broker should be reported that way on your tax return; they should not be reported under the issuing corporations' names unless they were reported to the IRS that way. Dividends on money market funds should be reported as dividends rather than interest. (But income from money market accounts in a bank or savings & loan is reported as interest.) And deductible fees (not including non-deductible check-writing fees) on interest-paying accounts with a bank should be claimed as a miscellaneous deduction, not subtracted from the amount of interest you report on Schedule B.

How Married Couples Should List Their Names on a Joint Tax Return

The IRS has finally caught up with the facts of modern married life. On joint tax returns, the IRS now provides 2 separate full name lines, one for each spouse. This implicitly recognizes the fact that many wives now keep their maiden names instead of using their husbands'. It doesn't matter which name comes first as long as the first name matches the first social security number. But once a return is filed using separate names, the same order of names should generally be used on subsequent returns. Switching the order could cause the IRS computer to become confused and result in delinquent notices being sent.

However, there are times when switching the names is just the thing to do. For example, you might be in the middle of a dispute concerning payment of previous taxes. Or, you might feel last year's tax return is vulnerable to challenge. IRS computers are programmed to key off the first social security number listed. By switching the order, it's less likely that this year's refund will be held up because of association with previous returns.

Married women who use their maiden names, especially those with self employment income, are advised to check with the Social Security Administration that their earnings have been properly credited [cf. Section 4 of the *Retirement* chapter for information on how this is done]. In many cases, due to a mixup, the IRS used their husbands' last names when reporting earnings to the Social Security Administration, causing errors in properly crediting these earnings. Presumably, with the extra line now on tax returns for the listing of both spouses' names separately, this type of error has been eliminated.

Negative Income Tax for Low-Income Individuals

You may know students or other low-income individuals who are supporting a child. They might qualify for the *earned-income credit* which in some cases yields a negative income tax. That is, if subtracting the earned-income credit from their tax produces a negative result, the difference is actually paid out to them by the government.

To qualify for the earned-income credit, an individual must be either (1) a married individual filing a joint return who is entitled to a dependency deduction for a child or stepchild; (2) an unmarried individual who maintains a household for a dependent child or stepchild; or (3) a custodial parent, even if he agrees to let the noncustodial parent claim a dependency exemption for a child [cf. the *Divorce & Separation* chapter].

The credit for 1990 is equal to 14% of earned income up to a maximum of

$6,810 of income. If earned income is over $6,810, the credit is $943.40 minus 10% of the excess of adjusted gross income or earned income (whichever is larger) over $10,730. The credit is completely eliminated for those with income over $20,264. Married couples must file a joint return in order to qualify for the credit. Starting in 1991, the earned income credit will be expanded [cf. Chapter 0].

Note that the credit can produce a refund to the individual even if no tax was withheld from his salary. But a tax return must be filed in order to get this benefit. Many students and other low-income workers lose out on a refund because they are unaware that the earned-income credit exists.

Persons eligible for the credit can now arrange to have their employer make advance payments of the credit. Thus, the law provides for a negative withholding rate to go along with the negative income tax.

Section 2:
Basic Rules for Deducting
Business Expenses

You can claim a deduction for expenses which you incur in connection with your profession. These fall under the category of **business expenses.** The basic rule is that such expenses in order to be deductible, must be both **ordinary and necessary** expenses directly connected with or related to your profession.

On the other hand, not all business expenditures are deductible even though they may be ordinary and necessary. For example, commuting costs to and from work are in most cases not deductible.

What Is an "Ordinary" Expense?
The word "ordinary" refers to an expense connected with a common and accepted practice in your profession. Thus, attending a professional convention would be an ordinary expense. But buying a new suit for your boss would probably not be considered an ordinary expense since it is not the accepted practice to do so.

What Is a "Necessary" Expense?
The word "necessary" is not used here in its usual meaning of "indispensable." The best definition of a "necessary expense" is one that is **appropriate and helpful** in developing or maintaining your profession.

Fortunately, you do not generally have to interpret principles like the ordinary and necessary rule. There are specific rules and examples that apply to most of the particular business deductions you might have. These are described in the following chapters.

There is one other general restriction on deducting business expenses. You are not allowed to deduct certain expenses if they are considered to be lavish or extravagant. However, it is unlikely you would have to worry about this restriction.

Reimbursable Expenses Are Non-Deductible

If you incur expenses in connection with your employment for which you could have received a reimbursement, then these expenses are non-deductible. It makes no difference that you did not apply for the reimbursement and paid the expenses out of your own pocket. For example, a teacher in a recent court case tried to deduct expenses associated with field trips she took with her students. But the court ruled that since she could have been reimbursed by her employer, her expenses were non-deductible. [Patterson, TC Memo 1977-107]

Special Form for Deducting Business Expenses

There is a special form, Form 2106, which you use for deducting employee business expenses. You can obtain this form by calling your local IRS office. Self-employed persons deduct their business expenses on Schedule C.

Section 3:
Common Mistakes

Here's a list of the more common mistakes that are made on tax returns.

(1)   Failure to Sign Tax Return

Don't forget that two signatures are needed on a joint tax return.

(2)   Failure to Use Peel-Off Label

The IRS has issued a special request to all taxpayers to use the pre-addressed label that comes with the tax return package sent to you in the mail. This will not only save the government a little money, but it will speed up the processing of your return.

Perhaps even more important are key-punching errors that might occur. Using the pre-addressed label allows the IRS keypuncher to make 13 keystrokes instead of 85, substantially reducing the chance of error. Anyone who has tried to correct a credit card computer mistake will shudder to think of the mess that could ensue if the IRS misplaces your return due to a keypunching error. (The IRS states emphatically that the label contains no special audit codes and its use will not affect your odds of being audited.)

(3)   Use of Incorrect Tax Table

Double-check to make sure you are using the correct tax table. A common error is the failure of qualified single individuals who maintain a household for a child or dependent to use the special head-of-household table. The head-of-household rate is lower than the single rate but higher than the rate for joint returns. Note that your household needs to be the child's or dependent's *principal place of abode* only for more than half the year, instead of for the entire year as once was required. Don't overlook the fact that the head-of-household rate can apply if you supply 50% or more of the support of a dependent parent, even if the parent does not live with you. Consult the instruction booklet accompanying your tax forms for the basic rules for using the head-of-household rate.

(4) Failure to Write Information on Check

You should write your social security number on your check and note what the check is for, e.g., 1990 Form 1040 tax. That way, if your check is separated from your tax return, it will still be possible for the IRS to credit it to the appropriate account.

(5) Making Check Out to IRS

Make your check out to the Internal Revenue Service, not just to the IRS. A check made out to the IRS can be easily altered by changing IRS to MRS and writing a surname after it. Or, IRS can easily be changed to I. R. Stone or a similar name.

(6) Not Deducting Medical and Charity Travel

You can deduct travel to doctors, dentists, pharmacies, etc. as well as travel connected with charitable activities. A deduction of 12 cents per mile is allowed for autos used for charitable travel and 9 cents per mile for medical-related auto travel.

(7) Failure to Deduct Late Payment Charges

You might be assessed an extra charge for paying a mortgage or utility bill late. This charge is actually a form of interest and can be deducted as such. A survey undertaken by a New York consumer affairs office underlines the fact that this deduction is often overlooked. The office asked eleven tax preparers to fill out a tax return based on financial data which they worked up for a fictitious couple. The data submitted to the tax preparers included a charge for the late payment of a mortgage. The result was unanimous. All eleven of the tax preparers failed to claim the late charge as a tax deduction.

(8) Leaving Off Social Security Number of Spouse

If you file a joint return, you must include the social security number of yourself and your spouse. Many taxpayers believe that they do not have to include their spouse's social security number if their spouse does not earn any income. This is not the case.

(9) Filing a Joint State Tax Return

In many states, filing a joint return can be a mistake because the same rate schedule is used for joint returns as for single returns. For a married couple each having income, the only effect of filing a joint return is to shift income from a lower bracket to a higher bracket and increase your tax. To illustrate, consider the following example:

Example

A and B, a married couple, have taxable incomes of $30,000 and $20,000, respectively. On a joint return, their taxable income would be $50,000. They live in a state with the following tax rates which are used both for separate returns and for joint returns.

on first $2000 .... 2%
on next $4000 .... 3%
on next $4000 .... 4%
on next $4000 .... 5%
on next $4000 .... 6%
on next $4000 .... 7%
on next $4000 .... 8%
on next $4000 .... 9%
on next $4000 .... 10%
on next $4000 .... 11%
on next $4000 .... 12%
on next $4000 .... 13%
on next $4000 .... 14%
remainder 15%

If A and B file a joint return, their state tax is $4,120. The upper $20,000 of their joint taxable income is taxed at rates from 10% to 14%.

However, if they file separate returns, the outcome is quite different. The $20,000, which was taxed at the higher brackets in the joint return, is shifted to a separate person and is taxed at the lower range brackets of 2% to 7%. A pays the tax of $1,720 on $30,000 and B pays tax of $900 on $20,000. The total $2,620 is a net savings of $1,500 over the tax on a joint return.

If you and your spouse both have incomes, be sure to check if the joint return rate is the same as the separate return rate in your state. If so, you could save taxes by **not** filing a joint return.

Section 4:
Claiming the Standard Deduction

As explained in Section 1, the standard deduction is a fixed amount depending only upon the type of tax return being filed. The standard deduction is now equal to $5,450 for joint returns, $3,250 for single returns, $4,750 for heads of household, and $2,725 for returns of married individuals filing separately. (There is an exception, discussed in the next section, for those who can be claimed as a dependent on the tax return of a parent or other individual.) The standard deduction is increased by $650 for married persons over age 64 or blind ($1,300 if both) and by $800 for single persons over age 64 or blind ($1,600 if both).

Note that many of the chapters in this book contain information that still applies even if you claim the standard deduction.

First of all, this chapter contains general information which applies to all taxpayers, whether they use the standard deduction or itemize their deductions. Also of general applicability are the *Divorce, Withholding, Retirement, Foreign Income, Audit, Income-Shifting, Estate Tax,* and *Investing* chapters.

Second, several items can be claimed as an *adjustment to income* or *tax credit* even if the standard deduction is used. This includes household services and child care, alimony, and contributions to IRAs and Keogh plans [cf. the *Household Services & Child Care, Divorce & Separation,* and *Tax-Sheltered Plans* chapters].

Third, many items ordinarily claimed as an itemized deduction can instead be claimed as a business expense on Schedule C by those who have some self-employment income [cf. the *Miscellaneous Deductions* and *Outside Business Activities* chapters]. This would include books, supplies, equipment, home office, auto expenses, entertainment expenses, etc.

Finally, those claiming the standard deduction should also note all the other techniques for reducing tax besides just deducting expenses. For example, they may still be able to participate in a tax-sheltered annuity, deferred compensation, IRA, or Keogh plan. Or, they may be able to claim tax exemption for a grant, make tax-favored investments, shift income to a lower-bracket child, etc. [cf. the *Tax-Free Grants, Investing,* and *Income-Shifting* chapters].

Section 5:
Tax Returns of Dependent Children

You may have a dependent child with income of his own. If so, he may have to file his own tax return. The following special rules apply in this situation.

First, a child (or other individual) who is eligible to be claimed as a dependent on the tax return of a parent or other person (whether or not actually claimed) cannot use the personal exemption of $2,050 on his own tax return. This ends the situation under previous law whereby a child and parent could both claim a personal exemption for the child.

Second, a dependent child's income is divided into 2 categories for tax purposes—*earned income* and *unearned income. Earned income* is income produced by the child's own labor such as a summer or after-school job. The remainder is *unearned income,* including such items as interest, dividends, etc. Gifts and inheritances are in neither category since they are not subject to income tax. Scholarships and fellowships, to the extent subject to tax under the new law, are considered to be earned income.

Your dependent child is required to file a tax return if he has total income exceeding $500 which includes any amount of unearned income. For example, a child with $10 income from a savings account plus $500 earned income would need to file a tax return. On the other hand, if a child has no unearned income at all, he need not file a tax return unless his total income exceeds $3,250. (However, if taxes were withheld from salary he earned, a tax return should be filed to get this money refunded.)

If your child is too young to fill out his own tax return, then you as parent (or guardian) are responsible for his tax return. The IRS has specified the following format for signing the tax return for say, a child named Jane Doe:

Jane Doe by (your signature), *Parent for minor child*

Be sure to follow the above format. If, for example, you write down "Jane Doe (minor)" instead of just "Jane Doe", you could get a letter from the IRS asking who Jane Minor is. The IRS has actually been making this type of mistake, according to an article in the *Wall Street Journal.*

A dependent child with only *earned income* computes his tax in the usual way. His standard deduction as a single taxpayer is $3,250. Since a dependent child can no longer claim a personal exemption on his own tax return, amounts earned over $3,250 will be subject to tax.

Unearned income is treated differently. At most $500 of the standard deduction can be used to offset unearned income. Thus, tax will be due whenever a dependent child's unearned income exceeds $500.

If a dependent child has both earned and unearned income, then the following basic rule is applied:

The standard deduction on the 1990 tax return of a single individual who can be claimed as a dependent by another taxpayer is $3,250 except that it cannot exceed $500 or the individual's earned income, whichever is greater. (Another way to view this is that the standard deduction equals earned income, except that it cannot be less than $500 nor more than $3,250.) If an individual's total income is less than or equal to $500, then he owes no tax and is not required to file a tax return.

To illustrate, the following would be the standard deduction and taxable income (assuming no personal exemptions) of a dependent child in various situations:

Earned Income	Unearned Income	Dependent's Standard Deduction	Taxable Income
$ 300	$ 700	$ 500	$ 500
700	300	700	300
2,400	1,200	2,400	1,200
5,000	200	3,250	1,950
0	400	500	0
0	1,000	500	500

Example 1

A dependent child has $600 earned income and $1,000 unearned income during 1990—a total of $1,600. According to the rules discussed above, his standard deduction is equal to $600. Thus, his taxable income is $1,600– $600 = $1,000. This is taxed at the child's 15% tax bracket—15% X $1,000 = $150.

The above discussion assumes that the dependent child does not have itemized deductions exceeding $500. If in fact his itemized deductions do exceed $500, the tax forms will lead you through a different computation procedure, taking these deductions into account.

Children Under Age 14 with Unearned Income Exceeding $1,000

A special rule applies to a child who has not reached age 14 by the last day of the year and has unearned income exceeding $1,000. Namely, this excess is not taxed at the child's tax bracket, but rather at the parent's tax bracket, if higher. This is commonly referred to as the *Kiddie Tax*. (If the parents are married filing separate returns, the tax bracket of the spouse with the higher taxable income is used. In the case of unmarried parents, it is the tax bracket applying on the return filed by the custodial parent that counts. This is the case even if the custodial spouse files a joint return with a new spouse who is not a parent of the child.)

This proviso was enacted into law to curb the practice of transferring assets to a young child in order that income earned on these assets be taxed at the child's lower rate rather than at the parent's. However, it applies to all unearned income of the child, whether or not due to assets given to the child by his parents.

The IRS has devised **Form 8615** to be used on behalf of a child under age 14 who has unearned income in excess of $1,000. The tax on this excess amount is computed as though it had been earned by the parent on top of the income reported on the parent's tax return. The child's remaining income (i.e. earned income plus the first $1,000 of unearned income) is taxed at the child's tax rate.

Since the first $500 of income is offset by the standard deduction, the following would be the tax treatment of a child under age 14 with only unearned income:

Unearned Income	Tax Treatment
$0-$500	Exempt from Tax
$500-$1,000	Taxed at child's rate
Over $1,000	Taxed at parent's rate if higher than child's rate

Form 8615 is attached to the *child's* personal tax return, not the parent's. Form 8615 makes a *what if* calculation. It determines how much extra tax the parent would have to pay if the child's unearned income over $1,000 had been earned by the parent. However, after this computation is made, it is the child who actually owes the taxes, not the parent. If there is more than one child with unearned income over $1,000, Form 8615 calculates tax as if all the excess income were earned by the parent and it distributes the tax among the personal returns of the children.

The Form 8615 attached to the child's tax return requires the taxable income figure shown on the parent's tax return to be entered on line 6 of that form. If this figure is not available when the child's tax return is due, the IRS says you can use the figure shown on the previous year's tax return or other reasonable estimate of the parent's taxable income. You should enter *"Estimated"* on line 6 of Form 8615 next to the estimated amount. If you later determine that your estimate was so off the mark that the wrong tax bracket was used, an amended return should be filed for the child correcting the amount of tax due [cf. Section 1].

Example 2

A child has $600 in earned income and $1,300 in unearned income. His parents' highest tax bracket is 28%.

The excess of unearned income over $1,000, $1,300 − $1,000 = $300 is taxed at the parents' tax rate—$300 × 28% = $84. The remainder, $600 of earned income and $1,000 of unearned income, is subject to tax of $150 as shown in the preceding example. Thus the child's total tax would be $84 + $150 = $234.

When income on the child's return is taxed at a parent's tax rate using Form 8615, the parent's tax return is not affected. For example, the 7.5% and 2% floors on medical and miscellaneous deductions are not changed.

Unearned income of children who are age 14 or older as of the last day of the year is not taxed at the parent's tax bracket even if it exceeds $1,000. Instead, it is taxed along with earned income at the child's tax bracket in the usual way as discussed earlier.

Child's Payment of Own Medical Expenses Can Save Taxes

If your child incurs substantial medical expenses not covered by insurance, then it may save taxes for him to pay the cost out of his funds. For example, suppose your child has $2,000 of income, all unearned, and that he runs up an orthodontia bill of $1,000. Let's say that you cannot deduct this on your own tax return because 7.5% of your adjusted gross income exceeds your family's total medical bills [cf. the *Medical Expenses* chapter].

However, if your child pays the $1,000 bill out of his own funds, then the story is different. He would be entitled to a medical deduction of $1,000 − (7.5% × $2,000) = $850. Compared with the standard deduction of $500 applying to the child, this reduces taxable income by an extra $350, resulting in a lower tax bill. (You aren't supposed to directly provide the $1,000 to the child for him to turn over to the orthodontist. But there's no bar to you giving him an informal make-up gift at a later time.)

Form 8814 Eliminates Filing a Child's Tax Return

Filing a tax return for a child is a nuisance. This is especially true if he has un-earned income exceeding $1,000, requiring the inclusion of Form 8615, along with the child's Form 1040 and Schedule B.

However, in a rare flash of sympathy for the ordinary taxpayer, the IRS estab-lished a simplified procedure which allows you to include your child's unearned income on your own 1990 personal tax return. This is done by listing your child's income on Form 8814 which you attach to your own tax return. This will not change the total amount of tax due. Following the instructions to Form 8814, you will pay extra tax on your return equal to what the tax would have been had the child actually filed his own return. But the filing of an additional child's tax return is eliminated.

Not everyone can use this simplified procedure. In order to qualify to report your child's income on Form 8814 attached to your tax return, the following conditions must be satisfied:

(1) The child's income is comprised entirely of interest and dividends,

(2) The child's income is between $500 and $5,000,

and

(3) No estimated tax payments have been made in the child's name and social security number.

You fill out a separate Form 8814 for each child whose income you are in-cluding on your own tax return.

Note the strictness of Requirement (1). If your child has even one dollar of earned income, then this requirement is not satisfied. Also note that the $500 fig-ure in Requirement (2) actually has no restrictive effect. No tax is due and no tax return needs to be filed if income does not exceed this level.

If you and the child's other parent are married, but file separate returns, then only the spouse with the higher taxable income can report the child's income on Form 8814 attached to his tax return. If divorced, it is the custodial spouse who attaches Form 8814 to his tax return.

There are several disadvantages to including your child's income on your own tax return. First, under the computation procedure on Form 8814, your child's un-earned income exceeding $1,000 is added to your adjusted gross income on Form 1040 (so that it becomes taxable at your income tax rate). By increasing your ad-justed gross income, your deductions for medical expenses and miscellaneous de-ductions can be decreased since they are subjected to 7.5% and 2% of adjusted gross income subtractions [cf. the *Medical Expenses* and *Miscellaneous* chapters].

Also, there are several other provisions in the law that are negatively affected by an increase in adjusted gross income. The deduction for IRA contributions can be decreased or eliminated [cf. Section 2 of the *Tax-Sheltered Plans* chapter], the passive loss writeoff for rental property can be decreased [cf. Section 2 of the *Investing Your Money* chapter], and the Child Care Tax Credit (for those with ad-justed gross income less than $28,000) can be reduced [cf. the *Household Services and Child Care* chapter].

The above disadvantages do not apply if your child's adjusted gross income is less than $1,000, because Form 8814 computes the tax on this amount at your child's tax bracket; it is then added to your final tax bill, without affecting the adjusted gross income figure on your tax return.

Another disadvantage of using Form 8814 is that the child's itemized deductions can't be claimed. However, this disadvantage only occurs when the child's total deductions exceed $500. Otherwise, the $500 standard deduction applies.

A final disadvantage applies to those who live in States which tie their income taxes to the Federal taxes. In such States, if you file a Federal tax return which includes a child's income, you might have to do the same on your State tax return. Since your child's tax bracket will be less than yours (perhaps even zero), this will cause an increase in taxes. For example, in Maryland, a child can earn $5,000 without paying taxes. But if this $5,000 is included on the parent's Federal tax return, it must be included on the parent's State return as well. At Maryland's basic tax rate of $7^1/2$ %, this would result in an extra State tax of $5,000 \times 7^1/2$ % = $375. (In a State with a top marginal bracket of 10%, the extra tax would be $5,000 \times 10\%$ = $500.)

Why You Should Give $10,000 to Each of Your Children

As discussed above, the first $500 in investment income received by a child is exempt from tax. The next $500 is taxed at the child's rate of 15%. Thus, up to $1,000 can be received by the child with a tax of no more than $75. If the $1,000 were received by the parent instead of the child, the tax in the 28% bracket would be $280, a difference of over $200.

To take advantage of this difference in rates, parents should consider placing as much as $10,000 into the hands of each child. The income on this amount would generally be less than $1,000 and therefore be subject to the lower tax rate. [Cf. the *Income-Shifting* chapter for a discussion of the ways of placing money in the hands of minor children.]

The above discussion applies chiefly to children under the age of 14. At age 14 or older, all of a child's income is taxed at the child's rate. This means that far more than $10,000 placed in the hands of the child can produce income taxed at the lower 15% rate.

Section 6:
Separate vs. Joint Returns

As you no doubt know, there are several different tax rates depending upon your marital status. Single people may use either the ordinary single taxpayer rate or the lower head-of-household rate if they maintain a household for a child, grandchild, or other dependent and satisfy the rules as stated in the instruction booklet accompanying the tax forms.

Married people may file a joint return on which they list all their combined income. Alternatively, each of them may file his or her own return subject to a special tax rate for married people filing separate returns. This special rate is designed so that a married couple, each with X dollars of taxable income, pays the same tax by filing separate returns as by combining their income in a joint return with 2X dollars of taxable income. In theory, the graduated feature of the income tax rates would then guarantee that people with unequal amounts of taxable income pay at least as much by filing separate returns with X and Y dollars of taxable income respectively as they would by filing a joint return with X + Y dollars of taxable income.

In fact, under the tax rate schedules that applied prior to 1988, married couples earning unequal amounts of income were almost always better off filing a joint return than separate returns. Because of the graduated rate structure, income on the separate return of the higher earner would be pushed into a higher tax bracket than on a joint return. This effect almost always negated any other advantage that might be provided by filing separate returns.

However, this situation has been changed by the remarkably "flat" tax rate schedule now in effect. Many married couples will now find that the joint return tax table yields little tax advantage over the table for separate returns.

In fact, as discussed later in this section, there is a *neutral zone* where the basic tax table for a joint return yields no tax advantage at all. This would mean that if any of the following tax advantages of filing separate returns applies, then this would produce a lower total tax than filing a joint return. (This presumes that the possible disadvantages of separate returns discussed below do not outweigh the advantages.)

Advantages of Separate Returns

The following is a list of situations where filing separate returns can yield a tax advantage over filing a joint return.

(A) If one spouse pays substantial medical expenses. The reason for this is that only medical expenses in excess of 7.5% of adjusted gross income are deductible.

For example, suppose a married couple each has an adjusted gross income of $25,000. He paid medical expenses totalling $3,400, while she paid none. On a joint return showing $50,000 adjusted gross income, they would have to subtract 7.5% × $50,000 = $3,750 from the amount of medical expenses, i.e. they would get no deduction. But on a separate return, he would only have to subtract 7.5% × $25,000 (his adjusted gross income) from his medical expenses. He would then have a medical expense deduction of $3,400 − (7.5% × $25,000) = $1,525.

However, if you live in a community property state, you might be required to split all medical expenses on separate returns. This could destroy any benefit that might be obtained by separate returns. (The apportioning of income and deductions on separate returns is discussed later in this section.)

(B) If one spouse has substantial miscellaneous deductions while the other does not. The reason for this is that only miscellaneous deductions in excess of 2% of adjusted gross income are deductible.

For example, suppose a married couple each has an adjusted gross income of $30,000. She has miscellaneous deductions of $1,000 while he has none. On a joint return showing $60,000 adjusted gross income, they would have to subtract 2% × $60,000 = $1,200 from their total of miscellaneous deductions, i.e. they would get no deduction. But on a separate return, she would only have to subtract 2% × $30,000 = $600. This would leave her with a net miscellaneous deduction of $1,000 – $600 = $400.

(C) If one person sustains a substantial casualty loss. Since only casualty losses in excess of 10% of adjusted gross income can be deducted, separate returns might be advantageous for the same reason as illustrated in (A) for medical expenses or (B) for miscellaneous deductions.

(D) If you are required to file separate Federal returns to benefit from favorable State separate returns. A number of States, including New York and California, allow couples to file separate State returns only if they file separate Federal returns. And some of these states, including New York and California, have lower rates for couples who file separately [cf. the last item in Section 3]. Thus, a married couple might be better off filing separate returns if the State tax benefits exceed any Federal return disadvantage. (But don't forget that saving on State Income taxes is less valuable than saving on Federal income taxes because State income taxes are deductible on Federal tax returns, but not conversely.)

(E) If one spouse earns less than $10,000 and wishes to contribute to an IRA. If a married couple has combined income exceeding $50,000 on a joint tax return and either spouse is a participant in a retirement plan, then neither spouse can deduct for contributing to an IRA. However, on a separate return showing less than $10,000 adjusted gross income, an IRA deduction can be claimed even if one or both spouses participate in retirement plans. [cf. Section 2 of the *Tax-Sheltered Plans* chapter].

(F) If a married couple has combined adjusted gross income exceeding $185,730. In this situation, if one spouse earns at least 3 times as much as the other, separate returns can actually produce a lower total tax than a joint return, absent any other mitigating factors. (This is a peculiarity of the law caused by certain phase-out rules affecting the basic tax rate schedules.)

Disadvantages of Separate Returns

One benefit that cannot be claimed on a separate return is the tax credit for household services and child care. A married couple can generally claim this credit only if they file a joint return [cf. the *Household Services and Child Care* chapter].

Another disadvantage of separate returns applies to those who are receiving social security benefits. Their social security benefits might be taxed on a separate return but untaxed on a joint return [cf. Section 4 of the *Retirement Plans* chapter].

A third disadvantage applies to those couples who own rental property that they actively manage. On a joint return, they might be entitled to deduct up to $25,000 of net losses under the *passive loss* rules [cf. Section 2 of the *Investing Your Money* chapter]. This $25,000 allowance doesn't apply to married couples filing separate returns.

A fourth disadvantage occurs if one spouse has capital gains and the other has capital losses exceeding $1,500. On a joint return, the losses could be subtracted from the gains, producing a lower tax than on separate returns [cf. Section 1 of the *Investing Your Money* chapter].

A fifth disadvantage can apply to married couples with combined adjusted gross income less than $50,000 who wish to make a deductible IRA contribution. They can do so on a joint tax return even if one or both spouses are active participants in a retirement plan. But on separate returns, any available IRA deduction might be reduced or eliminated altogether. [Cf. Section 2 of the *Tax-Sheltered Plans* chapter.]

Reporting Income and Deductions on Separate Returns

If you and your spouse file separate returns, you must allocate your income and deductions between the two of you. You and your spouse must either both itemize your deductions or both claim the standard deduction.

Income which you earn is reported on your tax return. So is interest or dividends on securities of which you are the sole owner. Your spouse's separate return contains his or her earnings and personal investment interest. Income from investments which you own jointly with your spouse is split evenly between your 2 separate tax returns.

When you file separate returns, you must claim your own $2,050 personal exemption. If you have dependents supported by common funds of you and your spouse, you may divide their exemptions between you in any way you choose. However, you can't split the exemption of any one dependent between you. Each dependent's $2,050 personal exemption must be claimed one way or the other— either on your tax return or your spouse's.

Expenses connected with earnings must be reported on the tax return containing these earnings. For example, your job-related expenses would be claimed on your tax return. Similarly, expenses incurred to produce separate business or investment income are deducted by the spouse who owns the income, provided they're paid from that spouse's separate funds.

Expenses that are not attributable to any specific income, such as medical expenses, are deductible by the spouse who pays them. If the expenses are paid from joint funds, then the deduction is divided equally between you and your spouse. This makes it important for many couples to pay for deductible expenses in such a way that taxes are minimized when separate returns are used.

This is particularly true for medical expenses and miscellaneous expenses because they are subject to 7.5% and 2% of AGI subtractions, respectively. For example, if one spouse, preferably the lower-earning spouse, pays all the medical bills for the family, then the 7.5% of AGI subtraction will do the least harm. It may even keep from losing the entire deduction, as discussed earlier in the subsection outlining the possible advantages of filing separate returns.

Another advantage of planning can occur if spouses are in differing tax brackets on separate returns. In this case, it is generally best for the higher-bracket spouse to pay deductible items such as charitable contributions. The higher the tax bracket, the greater tax-lowering effect a deduction will produce.

If you and your spouse are splitting the income on separate returns from a joint savings account or other joint investment, you should pay attention to the Form 1099 you receive after yearend reporting this income. If all the income is reported under your Social Security number, the IRS computer matching program is likely to detect a discrepancy and kick out your return for examination. To prevent this, show the full amount of interest on your separate return as it appears on the Form 1099. Under that, subtract 1/2 of that amount, stating " 1/2 reported by spouse" followed by the name and social security number of your spouse.

There may be peculiarities in State law that affect how income and expenses are allocated to husband and wife. For example, you might be surprised to hear about the recent Massachusetts case in which the Court ruled that all income and expenses on rental property owned jointly as tenants by the entireties by a husband and wife must be reported on the husband's Federal tax return. Under Massachusetts law, property purchased prior to 1980 fell under the *"common law rule that the husband during coverture and as between himself and his wife had the absolute and exclusive right to the control use, possession, rents, issues and profits of property held as tenants by the entirety."* [Springmann, TC Memo 1987-474]

Advantage of Separate Checking Accounts

As discussed above, it can prove beneficial to control which spouse pays certain deductible expenses. The best way to accomplish this is to maintain separate checking accounts. A check drawn on an account in the sole name of one spouse is the best indication that the expenditure is attributable to that spouse alone. In contrast, a payment made by a check drawn on a joint account will generally be attributed 1/2 to each spouse and reported that way on separate tax returns.

Community Property States

Different rules apply to those who live in one of the community property States: Arizona, California, Idaho, Louisiana, Nevada, New Mexico, Texas, Washington, or Wisconsin. In these States, income earned by one spouse legally belongs 1/2 to each spouse and would be reported that way on separate tax returns. (In the last 4 of the states listed above, income from most separate investment property is similarly split between the spouses.) Expenses connected with the production of that income would similarly be divided, 1/2 on each spouse's tax return. This provides the ideal situation because the taxable income on each spouse's separate return will be comparable, likely placing them in the *neutral zone* [cf. the discussion below]. By having one spouse pay all medical or remaining miscellaneous expenses out of personal funds, tax savings might be obtained as discussed above.

Individual State laws determine which are considered community funds belonging to both spouses and which are personal funds belonging only to one spouse. Generally, personal funds are those stemming from bank accounts or investments owned prior to the marriage, or property acquired by gift or inheritance.

Estimated Taxes

The best way for a married couple to handle estimated tax payments they make [cf. the *Withholding* chapter], is to indicate they are being made as joint filers. When income tax time comes around, estimated tax payments can be allocated as you choose on separate tax returns. Any portion of the total payments can be allocated to one spouse, with the remainder allocated to the other spouse.

When Should a Married Couple File Separate Returns?

The standard advice is that married couples should compute their taxes both ways, using separate returns and a joint return, particularly when it appears that one of the advantages A-F described earlier might apply. However, to particularize this odious advice to compute multiple tax returns, we point out the likelihood of saving taxes when incomes fall within (or come close to) certain *neutral zone* limits.

The Neutral Zone

The flatness of the tax tables comes from the wide range of the 28% and 33% tax brackets. In particular, all income on a joint return in the $32,450–$78,400 bracket is taxed at the same 28% rate and all income in the $78,401–$185,730 bracket is taxed at 33%. This leads to a two segment *"neutral zone"* where the tax rate schedules produce the exact same total tax on a joint return as on separate returns. If incomes fall into the neutral zone, filing separate returns will produce a lower tax when any of the separate return advantages discussed above apply. (This presumes the possible disadvantages discussed above do not outweigh any advantages.)

Specifically, a married couple falls into the *neutral zone* if either:

(1) Each spouse's taxable income is between $16,225 and $39,200;

or

(2) Each spouse's taxable income is between $39,200 and $135,050, with their total taxable income not exceeding $185,730.

(*Taxable income* equals *Adjusted Gross Income*, less *Deductions* and *Personal Exemptions*.)

The figures in (2) above are for a married couple with no dependents. For each dependent, the $135,050 and $185,730 figures are raised by $11,480.

The following examples illustrate the effect of a married couple falling into the neutral zone.

Example 1

X and Y are a married couple with 2 children. Their income and deductions are divided as follows:

	X	Y	Joint
Adjusted Gross Income	$45,000	$30,000	$75,000
Deductions (for Charity, Interest, & Taxes)	-6,000	-6,000	-12,000
Personal Exemptions ($2,050 each)	-4,100	-4,100	-8,200
Taxable Income	$34,900	$19,900	$54,800

The taxable incomes of X and Y fall into the neutral zone. The tax computations using the rate schedules for joint and separate returns given earlier are as follows:

Tax Bracket	Separate Return of X Income	Tax	Separate Return of Y Income	Tax	Joint Return Income	Tax
15%	$16,225	$2,434	$16,225	$2,434	$32,450	$4,868
28%	18,675	5,229	3,675	1,029	22,350	6,258
	$34,900	$7,663	$19,900	$3,463	$54,800	$11,126

Thus, filing separate returns produces a total tax of $7,663 + $3,463 = $11,126, which is exactly the same tax as produced on a joint return. In effect, the 15% rate and the 28% rate are each applied to the same amount of income under either the separate returns or joint return computation, producing the same total tax either way.

In the above example, the $75,000 joint income was split $45,000/$30,000. Despite this large disparity, their taxable incomes fall into the neutral zone where the income-splitting effect of a joint return does not provide a lower basic tax than separate returns. In fact, the disparity could have been even greater had the exemptions and deductions been shifted to X, the higher earning spouse.

To illustrate, suppose in the above example that X had earned $50,000 and Y only $25,000. If on a separate return, Y claimed only 1 personal exemption, worth $2,050, and only $3,000 of the deductions (with the remaining deductions and exemptions claimed by X), then Y would have taxable income of $25,000 – $2,050 – $3,000 = $19,950. Since their total taxable income would remain $54,800, X would have taxable income of $54,800 – $19,950 = $34,850. This adjustment of deductions and exemptions places X and Y into the neutral zone, the same situation as in Example 1.

Example 2

X and Y are a married couple with no dependents. Their income and deductions are divided as follows:

	X	Y	Joint
Adjusted Gross Income	$80,000	$50,000	$130,000
Deductions (for Charity, Interest & Taxes)	-9,000	-5,000	-14,000
Personal Exemptions ($2,050 each)	-2,050	-2,050	- 4,100
Taxable Income	$68,950	$42,950	$111,900

The above taxable incomes place X and Y into the neutral zone applying to couples each with taxable income exceeding $39,200. Using the rate tables in a similar manner illustrated in Example 1, X would owe tax on a separate return of $18,684 and Y would owe tax on a separate return of $10,105. The total $18,684 + $10,105 = $28,789 is precisely the same as the tax that would be due if they filed a joint return.

As the above examples show, when incomes of a married couple are in the neutral zone, there is no difference provided by the basic tables in the amount of tax due using separate returns as compared to filing a joint return. This means that the presence of other factors favoring separate returns will yield a lower tax.

Example 3

Same as Example 2, except that Y incurred $2,600 of unreimbursed deductible job-related expenses. These are miscellaneous deductions subject to the 2% of AGI (Adjusted Gross Income) subtraction. On the Joint Return showing $130,000 AGI, the miscellaneous deduction would be equal to $2,600 – (2% × $130,000) = $0, so the tax on the Joint Return would remain the same as in Example 2. Of course, the tax for X remains the same since there are no changes on X's tax return. But the tax computation for Y improves as follows:

Separate Tax Return of Y

Adjusted Gross Income		$50,000
Deductions		
Charity, Interest & Taxes		-5,000
Miscellaneous Deductions	$2,600	
less 2% × $50,000	-1,000	-1,600
Personal Exemption		-2,050
		$41,350

Thus, the taxable income on the separate return of Y has been reduced by $42,950 – $41,350 = $1,600. This lowers Y's tax by $477. Thus, by filing separate tax returns rather than a joint return, X and Y save $477 in taxes.

The above discussion points to certain income brackets where the tax tables are neutral, i.e. they provide the same basic tax using separate returns as using a joint return. This is the situation where filing separate returns is the most likely to produce an advantage.

However, married couples with incomes falling outside the neutral zone might still be able to save taxes by filing separate returns. Here, the question becomes whether or not the advantages provided by A–F for separate returns outweigh the leveling effect of the joint return tax bracket structure. Generally speaking, the closer the incomes are to falling within the neutral zone, the more likely this is to be the case.

Section 7:
Recordkeeping

In order to substantiate your deductions, you are required to keep records of what you spend. Generally, you should retain any cancelled checks or receipts that verify expenditures. In addition, there are special recordkeeping rules which apply to certain specific types of deductions, e.g. travel expenses. These special rules are discussed in later chapters.

Except for an overall listing of your expenditures broken down into appropriate categories, you do not include your records with the income tax return which you file. It is only if your return is chosen for audit that you will be asked to produce these records.

New Recordkeeping Requirements
The 1986 Tax Reform Act brought with it a number of new recordkeeping requirements. Areas where new recordkeeping was required are listed below. (Details are provided in later chapters of this Tax Guide.)

(1) **Interest.** Interest connected with owning a home or investing your money is usually fully deductible, while personal interest (e.g. an auto loan) is only 10%-deductible. To get the full deduction to which you are entitled, you need proper records which place interest payments into the most favorable category. [Cf. the *Interest* chapter and Section 1 of the *Homeowners* chapter.]

(2) **Home Improvement Records.** You need to keep records of any improvements you make to your home. These may be needed to back up a deduction for interest secured by your home and may also be needed to figure the capital gains tax due when your home is eventually sold. [Cf. the *Homeowners* chapter.]

(3) **Tax-Free Interest.** You now have to keep track of tax-free interest from municipal bonds or municipal bond mutual funds. Even though untaxed, this interest must be reported on line 8b of your tax return. [Cf. the *Interest* chapter.]

(4) **IRAs.** If you contribute to IRAs on a non-deductible basis, you need to maintain records for the life of the IRAs. These records are needed to minimize tax due when you receive payouts from the IRAs. [Cf. Section 2 of the *Tax-Sheltered Plans* chapter.]

(5) **Travel.** You need to keep travel records which separate out your meal expenses, now only 80%-deductible on your tax return. [Cf. the *Travel* chapter.]

(6) **Carryovers.** You might be prevented from claiming a loss due to home office expenses, investment interest paid, or losses on rental property or other passive activities. These losses may be carried over to be deducted on future tax returns if you have kept records backing up your expenses. [Cf. the *Home Office, Interest*, and *Investing Your Money* chapters.]

What If You Didn't Keep Records?

You may still be able to deduct your expenses even if your return is audited. If you can establish that you are entitled to a certain business deduction, then you may be allowed to estimate your actual expenses in the absence of records. However, you can be sure that the auditor of your tax return will agree to a low estimate at best. If you should end up in Tax Court, then the court may make its own estimate of your expenses under what is called the **Cohan Rule** which permits such estimates. Once again the estimate will probably be on the low side. So you should do yourself a favor and keep records in the future if you have not done so in the past.

Exception: The Cohan Rule does not apply to travel or entertainment expenses nor to the deduction for *listed property* [cf. the *Depreciation* chapter] such as certain home computers. Charitable expenses are also now required to be substantiated. If you do not have the required substantiation, then the law permits the IRS to disallow your deduction. Even the Tax Court does not have the power to overcome this disallowance.

Loss of Records Beyond Your Control

If you lose your records due to circumstances beyond your control such as a fire or earthquake, then you will get a break. In this case, you probably will be allowed a reasonable estimate of your expenses.

How Long to Keep Records

You should keep records associated with your tax return for at least three years. Records which show how much you paid for property and the cost of improvements should be kept indefinitely.

Don't make the mistake of throwing away your records too early just because the IRS sends you a refund check. That's what Robert Wells, a college biology teacher in Florida, did as reported in the following Tax Court case. He claimed a deduction for an automobile he used to gather specimens and perform other tasks connected with his job. As the Court explained it,

"After Robert filed his tax return . . . on which he asked for a refund, further information was requested by the Internal Revenue Service about the claimed automobile depreciation. Before this matter was straightened out between Robert and the Internal Revenue Service, Robert was sent a refund check. Assuming that that was the end of the matter, Robert just disposed of all [his] literature on it and ... was grateful that I.R.S. had recommended in the favor of a legitimate taxpayer and had gone on to other matters."

But the refund check just reflected the ordinary processing procedure. It did not signify that the IRS official checking his return had accepted it as filed. Since Robert no longer had the required records, his deduction was not allowed. [Wells, T.C. Memo 1976-52]

Section 8:
Yearend Strategies for Lowering Taxes

The end of the year often presents special opportunities to adjust one's financial affairs in order to reduce taxes.

Medical Expenses

Only medical expenses exceeding 7.5% of your adjusted gross income are deductible. If your medical bills will not exceed this amount, then they do you no good this year. Instead, you should shift the expenses to the following year by delaying payment until after the first of the year. You can also delay getting optional items like new eyeglasses, etc. In this way, you will get a deduction in case your medical expenses exceed the 7.5% limitation the next year.

If your medical expenses exceeded the 7.5% limitation this year, but you are not sure they will do so the next, the opposite strategy is called for. You will want to pay all your medical bills before the end of the year to avoid losing a deduction for them the following year because of the 7.5% floor.

Miscellaneous Deductions

A 2% of Adjusted Gross Income (AGI) floor now applies to the total of miscellaneous deductions claimed on your tax return [cf. the *Miscellaneous Deductions* chapter]. The same expense-shifting maneuver discussed above with regard to the 7.5% of AGI floor on medical expenses applies with respect to the 2% floor on miscellaneous deductions.

To illustrate with a simple example, suppose you have annual AGI of $50,000. In this case, the floor on the total miscellaneous deductions is 2% × $50,000 = $1,000. If you have $1,000 of miscellaneous deductions both this year and next, you lose out on any deduction in either year. However, if you can shift, say, $300 from one year to the other, you will wind up with miscellaneous deductions totalling $1,300 in one year and $700 in the other. Applying the 2% of AGI floor, this will yield a net deduction of $300 in the year to which the expenses are shifted.

In line with the above discussion, if it looks as though you might exceed the 2% of AGI floor this year but probably not the next, then you will want to shift expenses from next year to this. On the other hand, if you will not exceed the 2% floor this year, a shift to next year when the floor might be exceeded can possibly save the deduction.

For example, you can time the purchase of job-related items such as books, supplies, equipment, journals, professional dues, etc. so they occur in the year producing the best tax result. The same for investment-related expenses like safe deposit rentals, subscriptions to financial publications, etc.

Travel expenses are also amenable to such treatment. For example, suppose you are planning a trip early in the year for which you are entitled to a deduction. You have the option of buying the airline tickets either in the year of travel or in the preceding year. The deduction belongs to the year in which you purchased the ticket.

In fact, the Tax Court ruled in a recent case that this is the only year in which you may claim the deduction. In this case, an individual claimed a deduction for a trip made in January to oversee some investment property. But because she had purchased the tickets the previous December, she was denied a deduction. By the time of the trial, it was too late to file an amended return claiming the deduction in the proper year. [Lyman, TC Memo 1984-115]

Using the Standard Deduction

Deduction-shifting may be advantageous when your deductions total near the standard deduction. For example, suppose the standard deduction to which you are entitled is $3,250. As of November 30, your deductions total $2,500 and you estimate another $400 of deductible expenses for the remainder of the year. These anticipated expenses will do you no good on this year's tax return because your total deduction of $2,900 would still be less than the standard deduction. It would be better to shift these deductions to the following year when your total deductions might exceed the standard deduction. This is accomplished by delaying payments until after the first of the year.

Conversely, if your deductions are exceeding the standard deduction one year but might not the next, transferring deductions to the earlier year might prevent their loss as a tax benefit. This is accomplished by paying early before the year's end.

When Are Payments Considered Made?

Generally, you make a payment when you write a check and place it in the mail (or deliver it in person). It does not matter that it isn't received until the next year. The deduction will be allowed for the year appearing on the date of the check unless there is some strong indication it was mailed in a different year.

Expenses charged on some credit cards are deductible in the year they're charged, not in the year the charge is paid. This applies to cards issued by third parties e.g. VISA, MasterCard, American Express, etc. Other charge arrangements are deductible in the year paid.

Sometimes, payments are made under a "pay-by-phone" arrangement whereby a bank or savings institution pays bills upon receiving telephone instructions from depositors. In the following month, the depositor receives a statement of bills paid on his account. The payment dates shown on the statement determine when payments can be deducted by the depositor. [Rev Rul 80-335]

Tax-Sheltered Plans

If you plan to take advantage of the tax-sheltered plans for which you're eligible, be sure to observe the appropriate deadlines [cf. the *The Tax-Sheltered Plans* chapter]. Note in particular that you must actually establish your Keogh Plan before December 31 even though payment does not have to be made until April 15 or extended filing date. Note also that payments to a Tax-Sheltered Annuity are only deductible in the current year if made by December 31.

Pay Interest on Personal Loans

If you have outstanding personal debt (e.g. auto loans, credit card balances, etc.), you might be better off paying any outstanding interest charges before the end of 1990. After 1990, the deduction for personal interest is being eliminated [cf. the *Interest* chapter].

Capital Gains and Losses

If you own stocks or bonds, then tax considerations may call for a sale of some of these assets prior to December 31. [Cf. the *Investing Your Money* chapter for the basic rules.] For example, you may wish to sell stocks that have decreased in value in order to offset capital gains or produce a deductible loss on your tax return.

Section 9:
IRS Matching Program

The IRS has a master computer, located in West Virginia, which matches figures reported on your tax return with Forms W-2, 1099, etc. sent to it by your employer, savings bank, etc. If a mismatch is detected, your tax return will be kicked out for examination. This will result in a letter sent to you by the IRS or a full scale audit of your tax return.

The existence of this matching program is not new. But what is new is the vastly improved implementation by the IRS.

In the past, the IRS was not able to input all the Forms W-2, 1099, etc. into the computer. In particular, most forms it received on paper, rather than on magnetic tape, were simply not processed. But now, with optical scanners for paper forms and improved efficiency overall, you can be almost certain that any discrepancy will be detected by the IRS computer.

This means that you must take care that the figures you report on your tax return agree with Forms W-2, 1099, etc. which the IRS receives from your employer, savings bank, etc. This will substantially improve the odds that your tax return won't be selected for examination.

The following is a list of items to be aware of that the matching program might pick up.

Interest and Dividends

Be sure to report your interest and dividends exactly as shown on Forms 1099 that are sent to you, because the IRS computer will be digesting the copies of these forms sent to the IRS. For example, if your stock broker sends you a 1099 Form reporting dividends on stocks which he is holding for you in "street name," then the stock broker's name should be listed as the payer on Schedule B where you report your dividends.

Also, take care if you have income from money-market or bond mutual funds. The income received from these funds is considered as dividends, not interest. If you report this income as interest, the IRS computer will think you haven't reported dividends that you received.

Married persons filing separate returns should take special care if they split income from jointly held savings accounts, stocks, etc. In this situation, you should examine each Form 1099 you receive after yearend reporting such income. If the income is reported under your social security number, the IRS computer matching program is likely to detect a discrepancy if you split the income between your tax return and that of your spouse. To prevent this, show the full amount of interest on your separate return as it appears on the Form 1099. Under that, subtract $1/2$ of that amount, stating *" $1/2$ reported by spouse"* followed by the name and social security number of your spouse.

Reimbursed Job-Related Expenses

You may have incurred job-related expenses for which you received a reimbursement from your employer. Check to see if these reimbursements were included as taxable income on your yearend W-2 Form. If so, don't just subtract this from the total income amount you report on line 7 of your Form 1040. This will cause a mismatch that the IRS computer will detect, kicking out your tax return for examination.

Instead, include the reimbursement in the total income that you report on line 7. Then, claim the expenses for which you received a reimbursement in Step 1 of Form 2106. This is discussed in more detail in the *Miscellaneous* chapter.

Moving Expenses

The same discussion above for reimbursed job-related expenses applies to reimbursed moving expenses which are included in taxable income on your W-2 Form.

Proceeds From Selling Your Home

When you sell a personal home, you are supposed to report the transaction on Form 2119, which you attach to your tax return. The information on this form will be used to calculate the amount of capital gains tax due if you ever move from a more expensive home to a less expensive home [cf. Section 3 of the *Homeowners* chapter].

In the past, this requirement was widely ignored. But now, the settlement attorney or other agent responsible for closing the sale must report the transaction to the IRS. If you don't fill out Form 2119, you'll probably hear from the IRS.

Tax-Free Grants

You may have received a scholarship, fellowship, or other grant which qualifies, in whole or in part, for tax-free treatment. [cf. the *Tax-Free Grants* chapter]. Sometimes, these grants are reported on W-2 Forms as taxable income.

In such a case, don't just omit the tax-free portion of your grant from your tax return. This will cause a discrepancy that will make the IRS computer unhappy, causing your tax return to be selected for examination.

Instead, report the full amount appearing on your W-2 Form on line 7 of your Form 1040. Then, list the tax-free portion of your grant as a negative entry on line 22, *Other Income.* This will produce the same adjusted gross income, but will not create a mismatch that makes the IRS computer unhappy. In 1987 and 1988, over 20,000 graduate students were harassed for back taxes, precisely because they were unaware of this method of avoiding a computer mismatch.

Capital Gains and Losses

On Schedule D, *Capital Gains and Losses,* you are required to report the total proceeds from the sale or redemption of stocks, bonds, etc. This should equal the total you obtain from adding up the amounts of the sales reported on 1099 Forms you receive. If it doesn't, be sure to read Section 1 of the *Investing Your Money* chapter to see if the alternate way of taking commissions into account applies.

If the totals still don't agree, you should attach an explanation of the mismatch to your tax return. The IRS computer may still kick out your return, but the human who examines the kicked-out return will be able to see the justification for the discrepancy.

Section 10:
Free or Low-Rent Housing

Some colleges and universities provide housing to faculty members or administrators either rent-free or at a reduced rent. Where the housing is a condition of employment and is used in a substantial way for college-related functions, this does not generate taxable income. This tax-free fringe benefit typically applies only to Chancellors, Presidents, or other head administrators. [IRS Private Letter Rulings 7823005, 7823007]

In other cases, the rental value of a university-supplied house is considered to be equal to 5% of its appraised value (as appraised by an independent qualified appraiser). To the extent a faculty member pays less than this amount in rent, such shortfall becomes a taxable fringe benefit. However, if the rent paid is equal to or greater than 5% of value, no extra tax is due.

Members of Religious Orders

Ordained ministers are entitled to a special tax break if they receive housing allowances provided as part of their pay. Such allowances are tax-free to the extent they are actually used for housing costs, e.g. rent or ownership costs including down payments, mortgage payments, utilities, interest, taxes, and repairs.

A 1984 court case illustrates how this can apply to faculty members who qualify. Sixteen teachers at a Christian college in the South were also ministers within the Church of Christ. The teachers owned or rented their own homes and reported their housing costs to the college. The college then designated part of their pay to cover these costs as housing allowances. The Court ruled that they could exclude from tax, housing allowances equal to their expenses. However, they could not deduct larger amounts equal to the "fair rental value" of their homes—only their actual out-of-pocket housing expenses [Reed, 82 TC No. 19]. A similar conclusion was expressed in a 1989 IRS ruling concerning ordained ministers who performed services as teachers or administrators at a church-run college. Because the college was under the control and financial stewardship of the church, the IRS ruled that the tax-free rental allowance privilege applied [IRS Private Letter Ruling 8922077].

A member of a religious order under a vow of poverty may have taxable income even if he immediately turns over his salary to his religious order. This is the conclusion of a 1986 court decision concerning a priest who taught religious studies at a publicly supported institution. His contract with the university was entered into on an "individual basis," not as a priest. The fact that payments for his services were deposited in a church-related account did not alter its status as salary.

The situation would have been different had the priest been considered an employee of the religious order rather than an outside institution. This would be the case if the school were run by the religious order or possibly if the religious order had entered into the basic contract for providing services to the outside institution. [IRS Private Letter Ruling 7917007; Rev Rul 83-127; Fogarty, 86-1 USTC 9139]

Chapter 2

Books, Supplies, and Equipment

You are entitled to a deduction for the cost of books, periodicals, supplies, equipment, home computers, and other items which you use in your profession or for other business purposes. Those items which have a definite short life span such as paper or pencils are deducted in the year they are purchased. For items which will be used for a number of years, such as a typewriter or desk, there are two options, the **expensing option** and the **depreciation option.**

Under the *expensing option,* you deduct the cost of the items, up to a total deduction of $10,000, in the year they are placed into service. Under the *depreciation option,* a specified percentage of the cost is deducted in each year of the depreciation period. The depreciation period for books, equipment, and furniture is 5 years or 7 years. For most individuals, the expensing option is preferable to depreciation. A complete discussion of the two options for deducting business items is contained in the *Expensing and Depreciation* chapter. As explained there, both options require the use of Form 4562 which you attach to your tax return. (You do not use Form 4562 for short-lived items such as periodicals, paper, or other supplies.)

Special Rules for Computers and Entertainment Items
In 1984, Congress instituted a new category of items, called *Listed Property* to which special depreciation and recordkeeping rules apply. *Listed Property* includes the following items:

Listed Property

1. Automobiles and other passenger vehicles.

2. Home Computers (except for employer-owned computers used exclusively at a regular business establishment or computers used exclusively in a home office qualifying for deduction as described in the *Home Office* chapter).

3. Property of a type generally used for entertainment, recreation, or amusement, e.g. video recorders, cameras, etc., except for such property used either (i) exclusively at your regular job location or deductible home office, or (ii) in connection with your principal job or business.

49

4. Cellular telephones first placed into service in 1990.

Special Depreciation Rules for Listed Property

Special rules apply for depreciation of listed property. Under these special rules, such items must be *required by the employer* in order for an employee to obtain any deduction. Also, if such items are used 50% or less for business purposes, a special stretched-out depreciation table must be used instead of the regular depreciation table or expensing option. Details are contained in the *Expensing and Depreciation* chapter.

Recordkeeping Rules for Listed Property

There are special recordkeeping regulations that apply to listed property. These regulations apply to all listed property for which a deduction is claimed, no matter when the property was purchased.

Formerly, listed property was subject only to the same basic rules applying to any other deduction. That is, the better your records, the more likely your deduction would stand up to IRS scrutiny. But no explicit standards applied. In fact, even in the absence of any records, taxpayers could often qualify for a deduction by making a reasonable estimate of business use.

However, now an estimate is no longer sufficient to support a deduction for an item of listed property. Instead, there must be adequate records to support your deduction. This means you must maintain a diary or similar written record which, for each job or business use of the item, contains the following information:

1. Date;

2. Business purpose (unless this is evident from the surrounding facts and circumstances);

and

3. Length of time the item was used.

Your records do not have to conform to any specific format. You can keep a diary, log book, journal, etc. Or, you can use a calendar on which you write down all the required data.

If you use an item of listed property both for personal and business purposes, you must keep track of the total amount of time the item was in use. This will enable you to substantiate the percentage of time the item was used for business purposes.

Your records should be maintained in a *timely* manner. According to the IRS, this means you write down each entry soon enough that you have *"full present knowledge"* of all the details. You are not required to make daily entries; IRS regulations state that it is all right to record your usage at the end of each week. However, even if your records are updated weekly, they should still give a daily breakdown of each separate period of use.

You do not need to maintain your records by hand. IRS regulations specifically allow you to use a home computer to keep a log of business and personal use.

If your business use percentage is relatively constant during the year, IRS regulations provide that a suitable sampling technique can be used instead of keeping records for the entire year. The following 2 examples are adapted from these regulations. [IRS Reg. #1.274-5T]

Example 1

You use a home computer during the year both for personal and business purposes. You keep adequate records for the first 3 months of the year which show that 60% of the time your computer is used, it is used for business purposes. Assuming you can establish that your business usage continues at approximately the same rate for the remainder of the year, your records support a deduction based on 60% of the cost of the computer.

Example 2

Same as Example 1 except that you keep adequate records during the first week of each month. As long as it is established that these are "representative" weeks, you can base your deduction on the business use percentage determined for the sample weeks.

Questions on Tax Return

On your 1990 tax return, the following 2 questions must be answered on Form 4562, Part III, Section A concerning your deduction for listed property:

1. Do you have evidence to support the business use percentage claimed?

2. If "Yes," is the evidence written?

Observe that it is possible to answer yes to the above questions yet not satisfy the recordkeeping requirements of the law. For example, you might create a written record at the end of the year. This would enable you to answer *yes* to the above questions so your tax return would not be spotlighted for audit. But such a record would fail the *timely* requirement described earlier. If your deduction actually were audited, it would likely be disallowed for failure to keep adequate records.

Deductible Items

The following is a list of items which are legitimate professional expenses. You may be able to think of others. Bear in mind that whether any particular item is an acceptable deduction depends on whether you use it in your professional capacity.

Books

You may deduct for the cost of books used in connection with professional duties. Those books which are only useful for a year or less are claimed as a miscellaneous deduction when purchased. Books of more lasting value are either expensed in the year of purchase or depreciated over an 8-year period [cf. the *Expensing and Depreciation* chapter].

It is generally assumed that books have lasting value unless there is some particular reason to regard them as having only short-term value, such as being an annual edition of a regularly updated publication, containing information which will soon be out-of-date, etc.

To deduct the full amount you spent during the year on books with a lasting value, the law requires you to *expense* these items on Form 4562, as described at the beginning of this chapter. If you simply deduct the cost as a miscellaneous deduction without also using Form 4562, the IRS can force you to depreciate the cost over an 8-year period. After the filing deadline (including 4-month extension) for your original tax return has expired, it is too late to elect the *expensing option*.

The importance of using Form 4562 is illustrated by the following recent 1989 court case.

Court Case

Cadwallader was a Psychology Professor at a public university in the Midwest. In addition to teaching, advising, and other university-related duties, he was actively engaged in research. During the year, he spent $747 for books connected with his professional duties. He simply claimed this amount as a miscellaneous deduction, without electing the *expensing option* on Form 4562.

The IRS did not quarrel with Cadwallader's right to a deduction for his books. However, because the *expensing option* was not elected on a Form 4562 attached to the original tax return, it was too late. Cadwallader would have to depreciate the cost over a period of years. Under the depreciation rules at the time, this meant he was entitled to a deduction in the year of purchase of only $112. The remainder, $747 – $112 = $635, could only be deducted in future years over the remaining lifetime in the depreciation period. [Cadwallader, TC Memo 1989-356]

Supplies

You may deduct the cost of pens, pencils, paper, tape, maps, records, slides, film, sheet music, staples, desk blotters, briefcases, record books, etc. These items fall into the short lifetime category and are deducted in the year of purchase.

Periodicals

You may deduct subscriptions to journals, periodicals, etc. connected with your job.

However, if you pay in advance for a subscription that extends for more than one year, the IRS states that you should spread out your deductions accordingly.

For example, suppose that in December, 1990, you paid $300 for a 3-year subscription to a job-related journal to begin in 1991. Only $100 of this amount would be deductible on your 1990 tax return. The remainder would be deducted in future years—$100 on your 1991 return and $100 on your 1992 return.

On the other hand, suppose the $300 subscription prepaid in December 1990 is not a new subscription, but rather is an extension of a subscription due to expire at the end of March, 1993. Then only $75 of the prepayment—covering the $3/4$ of the year from April to December, 1991—will be deductible for 1990. The remaining $225 will be deductible in portions for 1991 ($100), 1992 ($100), and 1993 ($25), reflecting the termination of the subscription at the end of March, 1993. [IRS News Release IR-86-169]

The above prorating of multi-year subscriptions was proclaimed by the IRS to prevent the shifting of deductions from a lower tax-rate year to a higher tax-rate year. As a practical matter, it is doubtful the IRS will single out such a deduction for examination unless the amount is substantially out-of-line, especially since tax-rates are unlikely to decline in the near future.

Newspapers and Magazines

Newspapers and magazines can be deductible if they are sufficiently connected with your job. This is illustrated by a court case involving a public relations executive. He usually bought at least two newspapers daily and magazines such as *Time* and *Newsweek*. He also purchased local newspapers and magazines when he traveled.

These magazines and newspapers were needed by him in connection with his work. No record was kept of his purchases but he estimated he spent one dollar per day for a total of $360 for the year. The Court allowed the deduction but reduced the amount to $250 because of a lack of records. [Conley, TC Memo 1977-406]

As the above case shows, a deduction for general circulation magazines can stand up in court if there is sufficient business reason to subscribe. In fact, the IRS is not likely to challenge your deduction. According to a book published by a former IRS official, *"a lot of people worry about [the deduction for professional journals] and waste time deciding what's really professional and what's just for fun. Take whatever you think can possibly qualify. The IRS doesn't much care because the amounts are relatively small."* [P.N. Strassels with R. Wool, *All You Need to Know about the IRS*, Random House]

The above advice is underscored by a 1980 court case involving a consultant who claimed a deduction for books and journals connected with his profession. The IRS allowed him a $200 deduction even though he presented no documentation to back up his deduction. [Kannas, TC Memo 1980-127]

Teachers, in particular, should take note of the above. Many teachers use current information from newspapers and magazines in their teaching. And other teachers use such information in connection with their professional research. In such cases, a deduction for these items might be justified.

In addition to job-related publications, you can deduct the cost of magazines and newspapers if they are sufficiently connected with your investment activities. This would include subscriptions to the *Wall Street Journal, Forbes Magazine,* etc.

Special Clothing

The cost of uniforms or other clothing, including their cleaning, laundering, repair, etc., is deductible if the clothing is (1) required in your job and (2) not adaptable to general wear. Such items might include athletic wear, laboratory coats and safety equipment, aprons, caps and gowns, etc. However, you cannot deduct ordinary street clothes even if you wear them only at your job.

Telephone Expenses

You can deduct your professional telephone expenses (including installation charges, repair costs, equipment fees, etc.) if you need to make business-related calls from your home.

However, there is one item connected with telephone use that you cannot deduct. Namely, you cannot deduct any portion of the monthly base charge (including related sales or excise tax) for local service on the first telephone line in your residence.

This restriction is rather limited. It does not apply to the cost of business-related long distance charges, equipment rental or purchases, optional services such as call waiting or call forwarding, or charges attributable to additional telephone lines. The restriction applies only to the basic service charge on your first telephone line.

If you have a choice of several basic telephone packages, it may pay to select the lowest priced package. This minimizes the amount that is non-deductible under the above restriction. The extra cost of additional telephone calls, above the amount provided by the basic package, would be deductible to the extent connected with business usage.

The best way to substantiate your business-related long distance calls is to go through and single them out on the listing you receive from your telephone company. If this is not possible, you'll have to make the best estimate you can.

Rather than go through your entire year's telephone bills, you might be able to use a sampling technique if you make substantial business usage of your phone. This is illustrated by a 1986 court case involving an engineer who designed and supervised rehabilitation projects of industrial offices. He made extensive use of his home telephone to call prospective employers, headhunters, and job shops throughout the U.S. and the world, chiefly in order to find work. Instead of plowing through the entire year's telephone bills, the Court agreed to use just the January bill as a representative sample of the business use percentage of his telephone. The Court estimated that 40% of the telephone calls during January were for business purposes. Since his total telephone bills for the year came to $4,216, he was allowed a deduction of 40% × $4,216 = $1,686 for the year. [Payne, TC Memo 1986-93]

Note that your telephone calls can be deductible even if you are not permitted a home office deduction for failure to satisfy the stringent rules described in the *Home Office* chapter.

As long as telephone calls are business-related, it makes no difference to whom they're made. Even if made to a relative or friend, the calls can be deductible. This is illustrated by a 1989 court case. In this case, an individual ran into financial difficulty with a farm that he owned. During the year, he made over 150 long distance calls to his sister, seeking financial and business advice regarding his continuing financial and legal difficulties. His sister was a retired Air Force cost accountant and had been raised on a farm.

The Court ruled that he could deduct $1,678 for business-related calls. According the the Court, *"If the expense was incurred for a business purpose that bears a reasonably close relationship to the taxpayer's trade or business, it will be properly deductible . . . Petitioner's contemporaneous telephone bills and other records corroborate his testimony as to a continuing course of communication with his sister regarding attempts to save his farm. He did not claim that all calls to his sister were business related, and he deducted the cost of only those identified on his monthly bills as business calls. We conclude, therefore, that there is sufficient documentation of expenses on the record to justify allowing petitioner a business expense deduction for these telephone calls."* [Lewis, TC Memo 1989-78]

Equipment and Furnishings phone answering machine

You may be able to deduct for the cost of tape recorders, cameras, projectors, home computers, typewriters, calculators, etc., which you use in connection with your job either at work or at home. In one case, the IRS even allowed a teacher to deduct for a radio used for job-related purposes [Reilly, TC Memo 1979-253] . You have to prorate the expenses if these items are also used for personal activities. You may also deduct for office furnishings such as desks, chairs, lamps, etc., which are used in a home office for which you're entitled to a deduction. [Cf. the *Expensing and Depreciation* chapter for details on how to deduct for equipment and furnishings.]

A 1984 court case shows how camera equipment can qualify for deduction. A Professor of Management spent $1731 on a Canon A-1 camera, tripod, auto bellows, and lenses. He testified that he used the equipment only in connection with his teaching duties—to take pictures and make slides to show during his lectures. He presented slides showing computer equipment and programs for use in his course in computer programming, slides of Mexico for use in his course on tourism development, and slides of Austrian coins, a passport, an international driving permit, and mountain ranges for use in his tourism course.

The Court allowed full depreciation deductions for the cost of the camera equipment. It believed the Professor that he made no personal use of the equipment, noting that he also owned a different camera, a 10-year old Mamyia Sekor, for use in taking personal or family photographs. [TC memo 1984-97]

In the above case, the ownership of a second camera was probably an important factor. In another recent case, the Tax Court denied a deduction to an elementary school teacher for the purchase of a Minolta 35-millimeter camera with wide angle lens. He used the camera to take pictures of students, to take photographs for the school yearbook, and to teach darkroom techniques to his science class. There was no evidence that the teacher owned a second "personal" camera. In this case, the Court felt that the camera was basically a personal item used only occasionally for job-related activities. Therefore, no deduction was allowed. [TC Memo 1982-453]

Home Computers

Home computers, including peripheral equipment, can be expensed or depreciated to the extent the computer is used for business rather than personal purposes. In addition, the cost of electricity to operate the computer is deductible.

Software which is bundled together with your original purchase of the computer is considered part of the original cost. Software which is itemized separately or purchased at a different time can generally be deducted in the year of purchase. Although the official IRS position is that software is an intangible item which should be amortized over a period of years, most experts disagree. And the IRS is not expected to enforce its position for the relatively small purchases of home computer software.

Home computers fall under the special rules for *listed property* described in the *Expensing and Depreciation* chapter. Unless used only in a deductible home office, the use of such a computer must be *"for the convenience of the employer and required as a condition of employment."* Otherwise, no deduction is allowed. As discussed in the *Expensing and Depreciation* chapter, IRS regulations state that in order to satisfy this requirement, the use of the computer *"must be required in order for the employee to perform the duties of his or her employment properly."* The following example illustrates a case where this requirement is not met.

Example 3

D is employed as an engineer with Z, an engineering contracting firm. D occasionally takes work home at night rather than working late in the office. D owns and uses a computer which is virtually identical to the one she uses at the office to complete her work at home. D's use of the computer is not for the convenience of her employer and is not required as a condition of employment. [IRS Reg. #1.280F-6T]

The above example taken from IRS regulations would suggest, at least implicitly, that the regular use of a home computer for valid work-related duties qualifies for deduction, provided adequate facilities are not available at work. This suggestion is also present in an official IRS Revenue Ruling issued near the beginning of 1987.

This revenue ruling concerned an individual with a doctorate in aerospace engineering who had a research position with a private corporation. His job description, like the job descriptions of all engineers and scientists who worked for the corporation, provided that he seek to accomplish the research objectives by whatever means he and the corporation determined were necessary.

He purchased a computer and kept it at home. He purchased it because the computers at work were often used by other employees during working hours and he often performed job-related work at home. He did not use the computer for any other purpose than his job-related work.

The IRS denied a deduction because of failure to satisfy the *condition of employment* test. However, the reason given for the denial was that adequate computer facilities existed at work. In the words of the IRS,

"In order to satisfy the requirement that a home computer is required as a condition of employment there must be a clear showing that the employee cannot perform properly the duties of employment without it. That clear showing is lacking in this situation because there is no evidence that the computers supplied [at work] are insufficient to enable him properly to perform the duties of his employment." [Rev. Rul. 86-129, I.R.B. 1986-45.4]

The above revenue ruling hinged its denial on the fact it was not shown that the computing facilities at work were insufficient to properly perform the job. This was the feature the IRS chose to focus upon in its official public ruling on the subject.

However, in a number of private rulings issued to inquiring taxpayers, the IRS consistently took a much harsher stance. For example, one of these rulings concerned an assistant professor who needed a home computer to work nightly on grant proposals and on technical research and publication in her field. Only inadequate limited support was available to her at the college where she worked. However, the IRS ruled she could not claim any deduction for her home computer, stating: *"The facts suggest that computer use, although work-related, is not inextricably related to proper performance of the employee's job. Further, there appears no evidence in the facts that those employees who did not purchase a computer were professionally disadvantaged."* [IRS Private Letter Ruling 8615024]

We had advised in prior editions of this Tax Guide that this position of the IRS seemed unreasonably harsh—going beyond the intent of Congress and beyond the spirit of the IRS regulations themselves. The quotation in the preceding paragraph seems to require a herculean task to justify a home computer deduction. Exactly how one could show that his home computer was *"inextricably related"* to proper performance of his job is unclear. And the requirement to provide evidence that similar employees who did not purchase a computer were *"professionally disadvantaged"* would appear to be a nearly impossible task—involving the submission of evidence not just of one's own employment activities but also other employees' performances of their jobs as well.

Consequently, we had advised our readers not to be overly deterred from claiming a deduction. We felt that future court cases might overturn such harsh IRS treatment of the home computer deduction. In the first court case on this issue since the new rules went into effect in 1984, our suggestion was borne out. A college professor whose home computer deduction was denied by the IRS had this denial overturned in a 1989 court case. Feeling strongly that his deduction was justified, he did not go to the informal small case tax court which does not establish legal precedence [cf. the *Audit* chapter], but went to the regular tax court itself. He thereby established a precedent that will prove valuable to others in a similar situation.

Court Case. Professor Wins Home Computer Victory

Thomas Cadwallader was a Professor of Psychology at a large midwestern university. His wife, Judy Douglas, was the chief transportation planner for a local governmental agency.

Cadwallader and Douglas purchased an IBM-compatible home computer costing, together with peripherals and software, $2,597. The computer was used at home, almost entirely (98% of the time) for job-related purposes.

Cadwallader used the computer in connection with his scholarly activities. He was an active researcher into the history of American psychology. He used the computer for the management of historical data connected with this research. He also used the computer for word processing and other document preparation purposes when writing papers which were published in professional journals. While there were a few computers on campus he might have had some access to, these were far from adequate. He needed to have his own home computer to accomplish the research and writing which he performed during the year.

Douglas also used the computer in connection with her job as a transportation planner. She was required to do planning which involved extensive number crunching. Much of this work previously had been done on a mainframe computer owned by the state, but the state eliminated access to this computer. Her office lacked the funds to purchase a computer of its own. And were it to ask for extra funds to make such a purchase, it would take too long a period of time even if the purchase were authorized.

The IRS objected that the purchase of the computer was not an explicit requirement of the job for either Cadwallader or Douglas. They did not need to purchase the computer either to obtain or keep either of their jobs. Neither of them had a statement from the employer stating that a computer was a necessity of the job. Thus, according to the IRS, under the listed-property rules for computers purchased by employees after June 18, 1984 [cf. the Expensing and Depreciation chapter], no deduction should be allowed.

However, Cadwallader and Douglas pointed to the IRS's own language in Rev. Rul. 86-129 [as quoted earlier in this subsection]. There did not have to be an absolute requirement to purchase the computer. It was necessary only that "there be a clear showing that the employee cannot perform properly the duties of employment without it." As he and his wife testified, this was clearly shown in both their cases. He also cleverly argued that the purchase of a microcomputer could not have been an absolute requirement of his job since microcomputers weren't even invented when he obtained his current position. (He had tenure so he couldn't be fired for not making the purchase later.)

The Court sided with Cadwallader and Douglas. It stated,

"In order for the 'condition of employment' requirement to be satisfied, petitioners' employers need not explicitly require them to use a computer. . . . Instead, it is only necessary that petitioners' use of the computers be required in order for them to properly perform the duties of their employment. . . . We conclude that this requirement is satisfied. . . .

"We also conclude that the 'convenience of employer' requirement is satis-

fied. Here the computer purchase spared petitioners' employers the cost of providing them with suitable computer equipment with which to engage in their job responsibilities."

Since the 2 basic requirements for deducting listed property were satisfied [cf. the *Expensing and Depreciation* chapter], the Court allowed a deduction for the home computer. [Cadwallader, TC Memo 1989-356]

We expect further court cases clarifying the home computer deduction to be decided in the future. Details of such cases will be contained in future editions of this Tax Guide.

Note that the above discussion only applies to computers which are **not** used in a deductible home office. If you are eligible to deduct for a home office in which you use a computer, the computer does not need to satisfy the listed property requirement that it be for the *convenience of the employer and required as a condition of employment.*

Also note that in such a case, the computer is not considered to be a fixture of the home office. Thus it can be deducted, even if the deduction exceeds the income received from the activity for which the home office is used [cf. the *Home Office* chapter].

If you can claim a deduction for your computer (purchased after June 18, 1984), *Condition 2* described in Section 1 of the *Expensing and Depreciation* chapter applies. Namely, if business use does not exceed personal use, a special stretched-out depreciation table must be used. Of course, in any event, you're only entitled to a deduction for that percentage of cost equal to the percentage of time the computer is used for business rather than personal purposes. For example, if a $2,000 computer is used 60% for business purposes and 40% for personal purposes, your deduction would be based on the cost attributable to business use — 60% × $2,000 = $1,200. However, you can still deduct the full cost of software for business or investment applications, even if the computer itself is used partly for personal purposes.

As discussed near the beginning of this chapter, special recordkeeping rules apply to use of a home computer. However, no matter what the nature of your records, the IRS may question whether your claimed business use is legitimate. Here are a number of steps you can take to safeguard your deduction:

1. Establish a clear business purpose.

To deduct a home computer, you should use it for specific business purposes — either connected with (i) your regular job, (ii) an outside business activity, or (iii) managing your investments. Of these 3 activities, the latter 2 are the safest justifications to use. As illustrated by the IRS private letter ruling described above, the IRS can be tougher about expenses incurred by an employee than it is about expenses incurred by a business owner or active investor.

It's a good idea to purchase specific business-related software in the same year you purchase your computer. Purchase of such programs as word-processing, portfolio analysis, spread sheet analysis, etc. will give credence to your claim that the computer is being used for business-related purposes. Similarly, subscriptions to data banks like the Dow Jones Information Service would point to an investment business use.

2. Don't have personal software listed on the same invoice as your computer or business software.

Of course, you should not be deducting that fraction of the cost of the computer corresponding to your use for personal purposes such as game playing. But you don't have to stir up doubts by having game software intimately connected with your computer. If your computer deduction is questioned, you would want to be able to present invoices which point to your business use of the computer, not your personal use.

3. Buy a bigger rather than a smaller computer.

Popular inexpensive computers are more questionable than higher-power, more expensive computers. The inexpensive computers are typically used for game playing while the more expensive computers are typically purchased with a business purpose in mind. There may even be a difference in image among competing brands in the same price class. Some IRS agents may be more likely to question the deduction for a computer they've seen advertised on TV by popular entertainers than they are for a less advertised brand considered more serious in purpose.

4. Buy a different computer than the one available at work.

The type of home computer most easy to deduct is one which is different than any computer available at work. This is illustrated by Example 3 discussed earlier in this chapter.

5. Save your output.

If you have a printer, save as much output as you can which illustrates your business usage. This is concrete proof that you're making substantial business use of your computer.

Insurance

You can deduct the cost of extra insurance you purchase to cover items you own. Ordinary homeowners' insurance policies usually exclude or have a special limitation on items used for business purposes. You must purchase extra insurance if you wish to cover these items. There is even special insurance you can take out on home computers to cover the extra calamities that occur such as power surges which damage equipment or software.

Where Do You Deduct Books, Supplies, & Equipment?

Items used in your professional capacity as an employee, whether deducted immediately or depreciated over their useful life, are deducted under the

Miscellaneous Deductions section of Schedule A. These items, when aggregated with your other miscellaneous deductions, are subjected to a 2% of Adjusted Gross Income floor [cf. Section 1 of the *Miscellaneous Deductions* chapter].

Items used in connection with a self-employment activity are deducted as a business expense on Schedule C. In this case, the items escape the purview of the 2% of Adjusted Gross Income floor and can be claimed even by those who use the standard deduction. In any event, if items are used partly for personal purposes, you must prorate the expenses accordingly.

Form 4562 is used to list items with a useful life of more than one year which are being expensed or depreciated. There is a special Part III on Form 4562 for computing your depreciation or expensing deduction for *listed property*. This Part III is used for all listed property for which a deduction is being claimed, no matter when the property was purchased. Under new rules for 1990, you do not need to use Form 4562 if your only depreciation deduction is for items, other than listed property, first placed into service prior to 1990. [See the *Expensing and Depreciation* chapter for further details.]

Deducting for Books or Other Items Purchased in the Past

Suppose you purchased books or other depreciable items in a prior year but did not claim a deduction. Can you get any deduction now? The answer is yes.

The key is to use an appropriate *depreciation* table rather than *expensing* the items. You cannot start at the beginning of the depreciation table, but must pick up the depreciation in the current year as though you had been claiming depreciation all along. The following example shows how this is done.

Example

You purchased $300 worth of books in 1988. You did not claim a deduction for these books, either because your combined miscellaneous deductions did not exceed 2% of adjusted gross income [cf. the *Miscellaneous* chapter], or because of simple oversight.

On your 1990 tax return, you can claim what the depreciation would have been had you been claiming depreciation all along. You can use the percentage given for 7-year property in the *straight-line* depreciation table [cf. Section 3 of the *Expensing and Depreciation* chapter] for items in the third year of use. This produces a deduction of 14.29% x $300 = $43 which you claim on your 1990 tax return.

In the future, you continue to use the depreciation table for the 4th through the 8th year. You lose out on the depreciation deductions you did not claim for the first 2 years of use. As discussed near the end of the *Expensing and Depreciation* chapter, you do not have to fill out Form 4562, unless you actually purchased depreciable items in 1990 or are claiming depreciation for listed property.

There are 2 observations to be made concerning the above example. The first concerns the use of the *straight-line* method of depreciation rather than the *accelerated* method. This was done because of the lower deductions in the first 2 years of use that had to be sacrificed. This means the total remaining deductions for years 3–8 would be larger with the *straight-line* method than with the *accelerated* method.

The second thing to point out is the possibility of amending previous tax returns to include deductions that were omitted [cf. Section 1 of Chapter 1]. This could produce the best monetary result, but might not be worth the trouble. Also, if the reason for not claiming the deduction was failure to exceed the 2% of adjusted gross income floor, then filing an amended return would do no good.

Miscellaneous Materials

The deduction for miscellaneous materials used in connection with your teaching duties might yield a sizable deduction. This is illustrated by the following court case.

Court Case

Gardner was a Professor of Education at a university in the South. The university did not provide all the supplies and educational materials which she used in her classes. As is typical with many teachers, she dug into her own pocket to pay for certain materials she felt were needed in her classroom teaching. According to the Court, *"The furnishing of supplies and materials to supplement those provided by a school may constitute an ordinary and necessary business expense."* In Gardner's case, the Court allowed a deduction of $856 for the cost of supplies and course materials purchased during the year.

Furthermore, this was not the only miscellaneous deduction allowed in connection with her duties as professor. She was allowed a deduction of $695 for depreciation, $78 for typewriter repair, and $300 for secretarial assistance. The sum of these job-related items which could be claimed as *miscellaneous deductions* was $1,929. [Gardner, TC Memo 1983-541]

If you are like most people, you haven't kept complete records of all the miscellaneous supplies you purchased for use in connection with your job. Although the keeping of records is preferred, the following court case, decided about 10 years ago, shows that the lack of such records does not necessarily rule out a deduction.

Court Case

A public school teacher claimed a deduction of $125 for miscellaneous educational materials. The IRS objected to this deduction (as well as others on his tax return) because he kept no records or receipts to back up his deduction. However, the Court believed the teacher, allowing the full $125 as a reasonable deduction for his educational materials.

Interestingly, the Court was uncertain whether the educational materials were used in the classes the teacher was teaching or in a course the teacher was taking to improve his professional skills. But, no matter. The deduction was justified whichever of the two alternatives held. [TC Memo 1978-299]

Chapter 3

Home Office

Section 1:
When Can You Deduct for a Home Office?

College faculty members often find it necessary to do a substantial amount of work at home. At one time, most of these college faculty members were able to claim a deduction on their tax returns for this use of a "home office." But a number of years ago, Congress passed tough legislation severely restricting the home office deduction. An employee must satisfy the following rules in order to claim a deduction for a portion of his home used as an office during 1990:

Rule (1). The portion of his home must be used **exclusively on a regular basis** for business purposes;

Rule (2). The home office must be the **taxpayer's principal place of business;**

and

Rule (3). The use of the home office must be for the **convenience of the employer.**

Exceptions to Rule (2). If the home office is a *"separate structure which is not attached to the dwelling unit,"* then Rule (2) does not need to be satisfied. However Rules (1) and (3) still apply. Another exception when Rule (2) does not apply is when the office is used *"by patients, clients, or customers in meeting or dealing with the taxpayer in the normal course of his trade or business."*
Let us examine the above rules separately.

Exclusive Use of Home Office on a Regular Basis
The *exclusive use* requirement of Rule (1) means that there must be a specific part of the home used solely for business or professional purposes. No deduction is allowed for a den or other area which is used both for business and personal purposes. The area set aside must be *regularly* used for business purposes. No deduction is allowed for incidental or occasional business use, even if the area is used for no other purpose.
It is not necessary for the home office to be a separate room or partitioned-off area. This is illustrated by the following court case.

63

Example 1

A college professor used a portion of his bedroom as a home office. This portion was

> *"furnished with a desk, a chair, two file cabinets, and three bookcases. In the other portion or area of the bedroom petitioner had his bed and a dresser. He insisted that although the two areas were located within a single room, they were separate and discrete areas. However, the two areas of the room were not separated by any wall, partition, curtain, or other physical demarcation."*

The IRS claimed he had not met the *exclusive use* rule because the home office was not an entire room or an area physically separated from the rest of the bedroom. But the Court found nothing in the law which supported this requirement. If the home office occupied a specific area of the home and this area was not used for other purposes, the exclusive use requirement [Rule (1)] was met, even if the area was not physically separated from the rest of the home. (The Court disallowed the home office deduction for other reasons discussed below but carefully pointed out that the *exclusive use* requirement was met in this case. [TC Memo 1981-301]

A separate court case shows that a home office need not be located in an ordinary "room." In this case, the Court ruled that a large walk-in closet would qualify as a home office, if all the other requirements for deduction were met. [TC Memo 1981-140]

Home Office as Principal Place of Business

Rule (2) which requires that a home office be the *principal place of business* is the most difficult for teachers to satisfy. In prior years, the Tax Court defined the principal place of business to be the *focal point* of a taxpayer's activities. And for an employee, the Tax Court in turn defined this focal point to be the principal place of business of his *employer*. This made it extremely difficult for an employee to claim a deduction for the office he maintained at home [cf. Examples 2 and 3].

However, in a landmark 1990 case, the Tax Court reversed its previous position. In this case, it stated that a home office need not satisfy the *focal point* test in order to be deductible. Rather, a home office could satisfy the *principal place of business* requirement if (1) the taxpayer spends a substantial amount of time in his home office, (2) the home office is essential to the taxpayer's work, and (3) no other location is available to perform the office functions. This is discussed later in this chapter in the material leading up to Example 8.

The Tax Court's change of heart did not come out of the blue. During the past few years, no less than 3 different Courts of Appeals overturned Tax Court decisions based on the focal point test. This included one college professor who did a substantial amount of research at home. These cases are discussed in Examples 4-6. [The 1990 Tax Court case discussed in Example 8 stems from these previous cases.]

Example 2

Mr. and Mrs. Chauls were music instructors, he at Valley College and she at a different nearby school. They converted 2 bedrooms in their home into offices, one for each of them. These offices were used for the preparation of classes and related duties.

The Tax Court disallowed both their home office deductions because these offices failed the *principal place of business* requirement. In disallowing Mr. Chauls' claim, it considered it immaterial that he may have spent more time working in his home office than at school. As the Court explained its decision,

> *"In our view the record is clear that the principal place of business of Mr. Chauls was Valley College. Petitioner was an instructor and he taught his classes at Valley College. He was furnished an office at Valley College and a rehearsal room at Valley College. Petitioner contends that he spent more hours working at home than he spent working at Valley College. However, in our view, the number of hours petitioner spent working at home as compared to the number of hours spent on the business premises of his employer is not the criteria for determining where his principal place of business is located. ... We take it that what Congress had in mind was the focal point of a taxpayer's activities. ... It was petitioner's teaching of classes that generated his income and, even though some or even most of his preparation for those classes was done in his home, his principal place of business was at the school where he taught."* [Chauls, TC Memo 1980-471]

Example 3

Bilenas was an engineer at an aerospace firm in New York. He also was employed as an Adjunct Professor in the Department of Mechanical Engineering at a nearby college.

The college did not provide Bilenas with an office. Rather, he set up one room of his home which he used exclusively in connection with his teaching duties. The home office was used to prepare classes, grade papers, etc. More time was spent working in his home office than was spent at the school where he taught.

The Tax Court did not allow a home office deduction. The fact that the school provided no office at work was irrelevant. So was the fact that more time was spent in the home office than at school. The school was the *'focal point'* of his activities as an Adjunct Professor. Consequently, the school rather than the home office was the *principal place of business*, ruling out a deduction. [Bilenas, TC Memo 1983-661]

Note: The preceding 2 court cases represent the Tax Court's thinking before the 1990 case discussed in Example 8 was decided. The outcome might be different were these cases to be decided today.

Example 4

Drucker was a concert violinist employed by the Metropolitan Opera. During the New York opera season, he spent about 26 hours per week at Lincoln Center performing and rehearsing. However, the Metropolitan Opera provided no individual practice *facilities. In order for Drucker to perfect his skills and master the music to be performed, he had to maintain a studio at home. During a typical week, he spent 30 hours per week working in his home studio.*

The Tax Court, following its usual line of reasoning at the time, denied Drucker a home office deduction for his studio. It held that the principal place of business of his activities was not his home studio, but rather, his employer's principal place of business where he performed.

However, the Court of Appeals overturned the Tax Court decision. Drucker spent more time in his home studio than at the Metropolitan Opera. Because he was not provided practice facilities at work, it was necessary for him to maintain a studio at home where he could practice. Furthermore, his practice was essential to the performance of his job. The work he performed at Lincoln Center, i.e. rehearsals and performances, was made possible only by his solo practice at home.

Consequently, the Court of Appeals found that his home studio satisfied the principal place of business requirement, entitling him to a home office deduction. [Drucker, 52 AFTR 2d 83-5804]

Example 5

Weissman was an Associate Professor of Philosophy at a well known University in a large northeastern city. He spent about 15 hours per week at the University, teaching his courses, meeting with students, preparing lectures, and grading examination papers.

In addition to his teaching duties, he was expected to do "an unspecified amount of research and writing in his field in order to retain his teaching position." Under the University bylaws, a candidate for promotion must possess a record of significant scholarly achievement in his field. "As in other university communities, scholarly achievement is usually measured by research, writing and publication in one's field."

Weissman lived with his family in a large 10-room apartment in the city. He used 2 rooms of the apartment, plus the bathroom between them, exclusively for research and writing. The 2 rooms were furnished with a desk, typewriter, chairs, filing cabinets and books. Weissman spent 50 to 60 hours per week in this space, doing research and writing on a book which he planned to have published.

Although the University provided Weissman with an office on campus, he was obliged to share his office with several other professors. It contained several desks, chairs and filing cabinets, but no typewriter. However, it was "not a safe place to leave teaching, writing, or researching materials and equipment."

When Weissman claimed a deduction for his home office, he wound up in Tax Court. As it had done in about a dozen other cases involving educators, the Tax Court threw out his deduction with little hesitation. Because his job was that of a teacher, the Tax Court considered the focal point of his duties to be the school where he taught, not the home office where he spent the majority of his time working on his research and writing.

However, when Weissman appealed his case to the Appeals Court in his district, he won a victory. The Appeals Court overruled the Tax Court, allowing a home office deduction.

The Appeals Court ruled that the focal point test had been misapplied in this case because Weissman's job consisted of 2 separate activities—teaching and research. In the Court's words,

> "... when a taxpayer's occupation involves two very distinct yet related activities, such as practice and performance, see Drucker v. Commissioner [cf. Example 4] or writing and teaching, the 'focal point' approach creates a risk of shifting attention to the place where a taxpayer's work is more visible, instead of the place where the dominant portion of his work is accomplished.

> "In the case of educators, the focal point approach does not always adequately distinguish between individuals with very different employment activities. No doubt many college professors spend most of their working hours teaching or engaging in teaching-related activities such as preparing for classes, meeting with students, and grading examinations and papers. Some college professors, however, spend the major share of their working hours researching and writing. Both types of employee have earned the designation 'professor,' but the title should not obscure the differences between them. In this case, the Tax Court focused too much on Professor Weissman's title and too little on his activities. ... To the extent that the Tax Court found [the] College to be the focal point of Professor Weissman's employment activities simply because he taught courses there, it erred as a matter of law by failing to consider all aspects of his activities.

> "A college professor's principal place of business is not necessarily the college at which he teaches any more than a musician's principal place of business is necessarily the concert hall at which he performs. ... Here the taxpayer is a college professor who spends the majority of his employment-related time—80% of it—researching and writing. He needs a place to read, think, and write without interruption, and it is necessary for him to work at home because his shared, unsafe office does not provide the privacy needed to undertake sustained scholarly research and writing. Though the College library is available for research, it affords Professor Weissman no working space in which his research materials may be set aside or where he may use his typewriter. The lack of a private on-campus office makes Professor Weissman's home office a practical necessity."

Not only had Weissman's home office satisfied the *principal place of business* test but also the *convenience-of-the-employer* test as well. In the Court's words,

> "The cost of maintaining his home office was almost entirely additional to nondeductible personal living expenses because it was used exclusively for employment-related activities and because such use was necessary as a practical matter if Professor Weissman was faithfully to perform his employment duties. This practical necessity negates any claim that the office was used as a matter of personal convenience rather than for the convenience of the employer. ... Although [the] College has provided some space to Professor Weissman, it has not provided space in which he can effectively carry out his employment duties. The maintenance of a home office was not a personal preference of the employee: it spared the employer the cost of providing a suitable private office and thereby served the convenience of the employer." [Weissman, CA-2, 85-1 USTC 9106]

Note the 2 requirements Weissman satisfied in order to be able to deduct his home office expenses in the above case. First of all, the research and writing performed in his home office were the most substantial part of Weissman's professional activities—he devoted more time to these activities than to his teaching duties. As shown in Example 7, the Court recently declined to use the Weissman case as a precedent where a teacher had no research duties.

Second, the office facilities at school were inadequate. It was necessary for him to do his research and writing in his home office. This meant his home office satisfied the **convenience of the employer** requirement. Weissman's office at school was inadequate because of lack of safety and lack of privacy. Other factors that make a school office inadequate might include lack of availability at night or weekends, inadequate space to store research materials, lack of air conditioning in the summer months, noise in the surrounding halls or nearby offices, etc.

The IRS has decided not to appeal the above case to the next highest court, the Supreme Court. Strictly speaking, the decision only has legal force in the area covered by the Second Circuit Court of Appeals which decided the case. (This area includes only the states of New York, Vermont, and Connecticut.) However, professors in situations similar to Professor Weissman's have a legal precedent under which to claim their home office deductions.

Much of the home office controversy concerning college faculty is due to the widespread misunderstanding of the nature of duties of faculty members at research-oriented Colleges and Universities. While the Second Court of Appeals in the above case has shown it understands the central role research and publishing play in such duties, other court opinions have not shown such perception. For example, in one footnote to another professor's home office case, a Tax Court judge indicated his opinion of why the research and publishing of scholarly articles were required as follows: *"Petitioner's research and publishing activities were required not only so that petitioner could retain his job and eventually achieve tenure (a personal reason), but also to enhance the prestige of [the] College so it could continue to attract high caliber students"* [Storzer, TC Memo 1982-328] . The fact that the 5 articles which the professor published that year might have inherent value to society which the College considered its duty to support (even if they didn't "attract" any more students) apparently did not cross the mind of the judge.

In the following case, decided by the Seventh Circuit Court of Appeals (with jurisdiction over northern midwest states), the relative length of time spent in the home office was the most important factor. Here, the *focal point* test of the Tax Court was cast aside altogether. Even though the home office was used only 2 hours per day, this constituted a majority of time spent on business. As a result, the Court found the home office to be the principal place of business, qualifying for deduction.

Example 6

John and Sally Meiers were employees of a corporation they owned, managing a laundromat in a Midwestern city. In the Court's words,

"Sally Meiers managed the laundromat and retained five part-time employees to assist the customers, make change, sell laundry products, launder customers' clothes, and clean the laundromat. Mrs. Meiers' duties as manager included drafting the work schedule for employees, collecting money from the machines and filling the coin changer, assisting customers, performing bookkeeping, and other managerial tasks. On average, Mrs. Meiers spent an hour a day at the laundromat and two hours a day in an office in her home drafting work schedules for employees and doing the laundromat's bookkeeping. The `home office' consisted of a separate room in the taxpayers' home and contained a desk, filing cabinet, safe, change counter and sofa. It is undisputed that this separate room was used exclusively for administrative work on behalf of the laundry."

When Mrs. Meiers claimed a home office deduction on her tax return, the IRS objected. And when the case wound up in Tax Court, the objection was initially upheld. As it had in other cases, the Tax Court invoked its own *focal point test*. Since the laundromat was the *focal point* of the business, the Tax Court ruled that the laundromat was the principal place of business, not the home office where she did most of her work.

After rebuff from the Tax Court, Mrs. Meiers took her case to the Seventh Court of Appeals which had jurisdiction over the midwestern region where she lived. This Court, as did the Court in the Weissman case [Example 5], did not think the focal point test to be the controlling factor. Most relevant were the length of time and importance of work done in the home office. In the Court's words,

"We, like the Second Circuit, question the usefulness of the focal point test. As Weissman points out, at least where a taxpayer's occupation involves distinct activities, the `focal point' approach shifts attention to the place where the taxpayer's work is more visible, instead of the place where the dominant portion of his work is accomplished. Here, it is undisputed that Sally Meiers' `principal place of business' in terms both of hours worked and probably of functions performed, was the home office, not the laundromat. The focal point test as applied by the Tax Court places undue emphasis upon the location where goods or services are provided to customers and income is generated, not necessarily where work is predominantly performed. The focal point test is concededly easy to apply and is less subjective than [previous] standards. Yet we do not believe this approach is fair to taxpayers or carries out in the most appropriate way the apparent intent of Congress.

"In determining the taxpayer's principal place of business, we think a major consideration ought to be the length of time the taxpayer spends in the home office as opposed to other locations. But time spent is not necessarily the only consideration. There are other factors, which may from time to time weigh in the balance, such as the importance of the business functions performed by the taxpayer in the home office; the business necessity of maintaining a home office; and the expenditures of the taxpayer to establish a home office. . . .

"In applying these standards to the present case, we conclude that the Tax Court erred in denying taxpayers a deduction for a home office. . . . Accordingly, we reverse the decision of the Tax Court. . . ." [Meiers, 57 AFTR 2d 86-642]

Example 7

Dudley was a Professor in the Business Department at a community college in the midwest. He taught 5 courses, each one consisting of a once-a-week 3-hour session. In the Court's words,

"*In addition to classroom instruction, petitioner's duties included writing various syllabi for his courses; evaluating textbooks and making choices for use in his courses; reading current periodicals, professional publications, and textbooks to stay abreast of new developments; preparing notes for classes; developing study guides; preparing, correcting, and grading examinations and homework assignments; and meeting and consulting with students. The college did not require petitioner to publish or to conduct research and writing as part of his employment.*

"*Typically, petitioner spent the morning hours from 8 a.m. to 11 a.m. reading and preparing for class. He left home for campus around 11 a.m. and returned around 4 or 5 p.m., excluding the day on which he instructed a night class. Once at home, petitioner spent 2 hours in the evening reading, writing examinations, filing, and conversing on the telephone. Petitioner also did some work in his home office on Saturdays and Sundays.*

"*The college did not require petitioner, either by contract or as a condition of employment, to maintain an office in his home. He used a room in his home for work-related activities. The room is approximately 14 feet by 12 feet and houses a desk, shelves with books from the floor to ceiling, a copier, a typewriter, and a telephone. He used his office for preparing his classroom lectures, grading and writing exams, reading, filing, and talking on the telephone with students.*"

The office facilities provided Dudley at his college were not exactly first rate. According to the Court,

"*The college provided petitioner with an on-campus room in which to perform his non-classroom duties. This room had 20 spaces and the college had approximately 100 full-time/part-time professors. The record does not show how many professors were at the college at any given time. Each space consisted of a writing shelf and locker space but no locked storage space. There was one telephone in the room designated for faculty use which could not be used for calls outside the school. Petitioner did not use this room for his non-classroom duties; he performed those duties at his home office. Some of his non-classroom duties could have been done at the library on campus.*"

Dudley, pointing to the Weissman and Meiers cases [Examples 5 and 6], claimed a deduction for his home office. However, the Court did not think the Weissman case should be applied here, stating

"*We distinguished petitioner's case from Weissman. Petitioner has not shown that research and writing were required in his case. The college did not require faculty members to conduct research or publish works, and petitioner did not spend his time in the home office doing research and writing. Petitioner's duties were limited to teaching, and he used his home office only for teaching related activities. The school, where he did his teaching, was his principal place of business.*"

The Court also ruled out the Meiers case [Example 6] as a precedent. Not only did the Court feel Dudley's preparation duties were less important than his actual classroom performance, but also that he could have done his work in the college's library or other college-provided facilities. In the Court's words,

> *"Petitioner has not shown that he meets these Meiers standards. Petitioner did not perform the most important element of his teaching job in his home office. The most important aspect of petitioner's employment was his instruction of his classes. As we have discussed, petitioner has not shown that most, if not all, of his classroom preparation could not have been done in the facilities provided by the college. Certainly, the privacy of a home office was not required for his reading of background material. There is no showing of any business necessity that petitioner performed his non-classroom activities at his home office rather than at the facilities available at the college."*

As a consequence, the Court denied Dudley any deduction for his home office.
[Dudley, TC Memo 1987—607]

1990 Tax Court Case Opens Up Home Office Deduction

In 1990, the Tax Court underwent a sharp change of heart. Since the home office rules were changed in the 1970s, the Tax Court has been extremely stingy about allowing home office deductions. Generally relying on its "focal point" criterion, the Tax Court, as discussed above, denied deductions where a distinct minority of time was spent in the home office or where the home office was not the most central place of the trade or business activity.

But in the controversial 1990 *Soliman Case,* discussed below, the Tax Court evidenced a change of view. Influenced by reversals in several Courts of Appeals, it carved out an exception to the focal point test. According to the Tax Court, a home office will now satisfy the *principal place of business* test if

1. The taxpayer spends a substantial amount of time in his home office,

2. The home office is essential to the taxpayer's work,

and

3. No other location is available to perform the office functions.

As illustrated by the following court case, this new policy considerably extends the ability to claim a home office deduction.

Example 8

Soliman was an anesthesiologist at several hospitals in the Washington, D.C. area. Because none of the hospitals provided him with an office, he used one bedroom in his 3-bedroom home as an office.

Soliman used his home office solely for activities connected with his professional duties—recordkeeping, reading medical books and journals, telephoning patients and other doctors, preparing monthly lectures he gave to nurses, etc. He didn't see any patients at his home office. Soliman spent an average of 2 to 3 hours a day working in his home office. This constituted about 30% of his total working hours.

When Soliman deducted his home office, the IRS objected. The "focal point" of his professional activities was where he administered anesthesiology to patients, not where he performed his office chores. And a distinct minority of his working time—only 30%—was spent in his office at home. According to the IRS, this meant the home office was not the *"principal place of business,"* ruling out a deduction.

But the Tax Court sided with Soliman, ruling that his home office could be deducted. The court ruled that the "focal point" test, which it had used so often in prior cases, did not apply here. It stated,

> *"The 'focal point' test looks only to the place where services are performed and income is generated. Under this test, petitioner's home office is not the 'focal point'of his business. His business activities at the house were essential to his medical practice but were ancillary to the primary income-generating services petitioner performed as an anesthesiologist at the hospitals. We believe, however, that where a taxpayer's occupation requires essential organizational and management activities that are distinct from those that generate income, the place where the business is managed can be the principal place of business."*

The Court specified 3 conditions that, if all satisfied, would mean that the "focal point" criterion would not apply: (1) The taxpayer spends a substantial amount of time in his home office; (2) the home office is essential to his work; and (3) no other location is available to perform the office functions.

If these 3 conditions are satisfied, then the home office meets the *principal place of business* requirement for deduction. As long as the home office also satisfies the *regular and exclusive use* and *convenience of the employer* requirements described at the beginning of this chapter, it qualifies for deduction.

As to Condition 1, Soliman spent about 30% of his working time in his home office. The remaining 70% was spent in the hospital. Was this usage of his home office significant?

The Court ruled that it was. This was especially true because his work was divided into 2 distinct categories—the medical work done at the hospital and the administrative work done at home. It stated,

> *"Petitioner's business required him to perform two very different functions: (1) to render medical services at hospitals, and (2) to care for administrative chores, e.g., record keeping, gathering of billing information and payments, continuing medical education. Both functions were equally essential to a successful medical practice; the second required an office while the first did not. Petitioner's business required him to devote substantial time to office chores, and, although he spent more hours at the hospitals, we believe that comparing the number of hours spent at each location is a misleading comparison because the activities are so different from each other. Such a comparison can be meaningful if the activities in the home office are similar to the activities at another place of business."*

As to Conditions 2 and 3, the Court stated,

"In this case, the activities petitioner performed in his home office, viz, book-keeping, billing, preparation for patients, and continuing medical education, were distinct from those he performed at the hospital. He maintained patient records, billed patients, collected and recorded payments, and reviewed medical procedures. These activities were essential to petitioner's work. In order to carry on his business as an anesthesiologist, it was essential for petitioner to keep abreast of the latest technology, to bill his patients, and to maintain his state certification as an anesthesiologist.

"The hospitals did not provide petitioner with office space . . . Petitioner managed and coordinated his anesthesiology work in his home office. He spent approximately 30 percent of his time in his home office. In addition to spending substantial time there, petitioner's use of the home office was important to a successful medical practice. In this case, however, petitioner had no place to manage his medical practice other than in his home."

Because the above 3 conditions were satisfied, the Court found Soliman's home office to be his *principal place of business. (*This was the case even though only 30% of his working hours were spent in the office and the focal point of his activities was in the hospital where he earned his living as an anesthesiologist.) Since the principal place of business requirement was the only one in doubt, Soliman's home office could be deducted.

Soliman also claimed a deduction for the cost of travel between his home and the hospitals where he worked. When the *principal place of business* is located in a deductible home office, then travel to and from other business locations is deductible [cf. the discussion at the end of this Section]. Since Soliman's home office was determined to be the principal place of business for his medical activities, the Court allowed his travel deduction. [Soliman, 94 TC No. 3]

Caution: The IRS is displeased with the above Soliman decision. In an action taken only every few years, it even issued a press release regarding its position. The IRS will appeal this decision to a higher court. But in the meantime, taxpayers have authority to back their home office deductions when circumstances similar to the Soliman case are present. Further information will be contained in next year's edition of this Tax Guide.

The next 1990 court case shows that even when a home office does not qualify as the *principal place of business* of an individual's business activities taken as a whole, it still might qualify as a deductible home office for one of these activities.

Example 9

Hoye was a surgeon on the staffs of 2 hospitals in the Midwest. In addition to his surgery practice, he set up a laboratory in the basement of his home. He used the laboratory to perform specialized biopsies on tissue samples from his patients and from patients of other doctors. The fees he received for his laboratory work amounted to about $9,000 per year.

The question was whether or not the laboratory qualified as a deductible home office. The laboratory was the principal place of business for the laboratory work. But, it would not be the principal place of business for his medical activities as a whole.

The Court ruled that the 2 activities could be separated. The surgical activities constituted one business and the laboratory a second distinct business. Since his laboratory satisfied the home office rules for his laboratory business, it qualified for deduction.

The IRS had objected that the surgical and laboratory work were closely related and therefore should be considered one business. But the Court did not agree. It stated, "In fact, the operation of two trades or businesses by a taxpayer is more likely to be in fields which are closely related."

Although Hoye could claim a home office deduction, he could not deduct the cost of driving between his home and the hospital where he performed surgery. To deduct the cost of traveling between a home office and a location of a different business activity, the home office must be the site of the most important activity [cf. Example 9 in Section 2 of the Travel chapter]. In Hoye's case, the most important activity was his surgical, not his laboratory work. However, he could deduct the cost of traveling between his home office and other locations directly connected with the laboratory business for which the home office was used. e.g. suppliers, the bank, etc. [Hoye, TC Memo 1990-57]

Home Office Used for Two Separate Activities

Sometimes a home office is used for 2 separate business activities. In this situation, as the next 1990 Tax Court case has established, both uses must qualify under the home office rules in order for any deduction to be allowed. In particular, the home office must be the *principal place of business* for each of the activities.

This new Court Case appears to reverse a previous case reported in prior editions of this Tax Guide [Frankel, 82 TC No. 26]. In this previous case, a deduction was allowed for shared use of a home office by a married couple, even though only the wife's use qualified under the *principal place of business* test. Although the following case concerns only a single individual using a home office for 2 different purposes, the principle involved in both cases would appear to be the same.

Example 10

Hamacher was a professional actor, working in the theatre as a well as doing radio and television commercials. In addition to his acting, he was the administrator of an acting school. The school provided office space which Hamacher could use.

Hamacher used one room in his six-room apartment as a home office. He used the office both in connection with his acting duties and his duties as school administrator.

The Court examined Hamacher's activities. He had 2 separate "business" activities—one as actor and the other as administrator. His home office was used for each of these activities.

The Court ruled that for the home office to be deductible, it must be the principal place of business for each of the business activities taking place in the home office.

In this case, it would need to be the principal place of both Hamacher's acting and administrating duties. However, Hamacher had a suitable office at the school where he was administrator. This office, not the home office, was the principal place of his administrating 'business.'

Because the home office failed the test for one of the business activities for which it was used, it did not qualify for deduction. Even if it met the basic rules to be deductible in connection with his acting activities, this would not matter. No deduction could be claimed. Nor could any travel between home and other local job locations be deducted. (The result, presumably, would have been different had the claimed home office usage been only in connection with his acting activities.) [Hamacher, 94 TC No. 21]

Home Office Used for Secondary Business Activity

For most employees, except as described in Examples 4-9, the *principal place of business* requirement rules out a deduction for a home office used in connection with their main job. But the use of a home office connected with a secondary business activity can be deducted, as long as the home office is the principal location of that activity. It does not matter that an individual's main job is located elsewhere. For example, the use of a home office for writing a book, consulting, tutoring, running a side business, etc. would qualify. However, as discussed in Section 2, the deduction for a home office used as the principal place of business for a secondary business activity cannot exceed the gross income from that activity.

Example 11

Samuel was a full-time education teacher, working on a master's degree at a nearby University. His wife was a former teacher and was also working on a master's degree at the same University. Together, they decided to develop and manage a sales business in order to earn extra money. They operated this business solely out of an office in their home and claimed a $2,500 deduction on their tax return. In the Court's words,

> *"Samuel testified that within petitioner's three-bedroom apartment, two children slept in one room, an infant child slept in petitioner's bedroom, and the third bedroom was used as an office. They also testified that there was a desk and a telephone in the third bedroom and that the closets were used to store the sales products. Samuel testified that he did not use the room to prepare for his teaching job or his university studies."*

The IRS objected that the room was not used exclusively as the principal place of their sales business. But the Court did not agree with this objection, stating,

> *"In our opinion, the evidence is sufficient to establish that petitioners exclusively used the office in their home on a regular basis as the principal place of their sales business. The room was not used for recreational purposes, and petitioners used local libraries and university facilities to study for their courses at the university. [The IRS] has presented no evidence to the contrary. Therefore, we hold that petitioners may deduct expenses incurred in maintaining the office in their home."*

> That was the good news. Had the sales business produced a reasonable amount of income, they would have obtained substantial benefit from their home office deduction. But the bad news was that they only had $46.50 in sales for the year. Not only was this a business disappointment, but under the rules described in Section 2, this meant their home office deduction could not exceed $46.50. [TC Memo 1985-49]

In the next case, decided in 1989, the Court permitted a consultant to claim a deduction for his home office. The Court focused not on the government office for which he consulted, but on his final product, namely the written report which he produced. Since this report was produced in his home office, the home office became the consultant's principal place of business. This was the case even though he spent no more than half his time working at home.

Example 12

Eastman was hired as a consultant by the Department of Energy to analyze a large computer simulation involving coal supply and the transportation industry. He was an expert in this general area, and had written a book and numerous papers in his field of expertise.

Like most consultants, Eastman was considered to be an independent contractor by the Department of Energy. He went to the Department of Energy regularly to utilize the computer and to meet with computer programmers and other employees. He had use of a desk in a room which was used also by several other consultants, and he was able to come and go at his own convenience.

Eastman maintained an office in his home which he used for research and writing reports. He spent about one-half of his time at his home office, with the remainder spent in the field or at the Department of Energy.

When Eastman claimed a deduction for his home office, the IRS objected. It asserted that the Department of Energy, not his home office, was the focus of his work and therefore his principal place of business. This would mean he violated Rule 2 stated at the beginning of this chapter, making him ineligible for the home office deduction.

However, the Court ruled that he could deduct his home office, deciding that it, not the Department of Energy, was his principal place of business during this period of time. In the Court's words,

"While under contract with the Department of Energy as a consultant, petitioner spent approximately fifty percent of his time at his home office. All of petitioner's research and writing was accomplished at his home office. This was the only reasonable place where these activities could be conducted. Furthermore, the report researched and written by petitioner in his home office was the final product for which he was being paid. Petitioner conducted his consulting business out of his home office. We therefore conclude that petitioner's principal place of business was his home office." [Eastman, TC Memo 1989-288]

You cannot get around the home office limitation by renting your home office to your employer or to an entity for which you are providing services as an independent contractor. This was ruled out by a provision in the 1986 Tax Reform Act. This loophole was eliminated in response to an accountant who, under prior law, rented his home office to the accounting firm for which he worked, converting a home office that was secondary to his job into a primary place of business of his "rental business."

Also, a home office deduction cannot be claimed for purely investment activities—reading financial periodicals, clipping bond coupons, etc. because these do not qualify as *trade or business* activities. (In order to be in the *trade or business* of investing, one must be a short-term active *trader* rather than a long-term *investor*.) But this restriction does not apply to overseeing rental properties if it involves active management duties. This is illustrated by the following court case.

Example 13

Curphey was a dermatologist, employed 40 hours per week by a hospital in Hawaii. He owned 6 single-family residential properties which he managed himself. He lived in a two bedroom condominium and

> "used one bedroom exclusively as an office for bookkeeping and other activities related to management of his rental properties. That room was furnished with a desk, a bookcase, a filing cabinet, calculators, and a `code-a-phone answering service'. There was no television, sofa, or bed in that room and petitioner did not allow guests to stay there. The closet of that room was used only to store items related to the rental properties such as lamps, carpets, and other furnishings, signs which petitioner used to advertise the units for rent, cleaning materials which he needed to prepare a rental unit for a new tenant, and a tool box."

Since Curphey was actively involved in the management of his properties, his efforts constituted a *trade or business* activity rather than just an *investment activity*. And since his home office was used regularly as the principal business location for this activity, it qualified for deduction. [Curphey 73 TC No. 61]

Home Office For Convenience of the Employer

Rule (3) requires that the home office be for the *convenience of the employer.* This requirement does not apply to self-employment activities since there is no *employer* involved. For employees, this requirement means that there must be a genuine need for you to have a home office. If you have an office at work, you will be required to show why the facilities there are inadequate.

Vacation Office Ruled Deductible

The following court case shows how a vacation home office can qualify for deduction, even when used only a small portion of the year.

Example 14

Heineman was the chief executive officer of a large corporation in Chicago. He spent his summers in Wisconsin where he owned property overlooking Lake Michigan. The property contained a vacation residence plus a separate structure which was furnished as an office. The office was used by Heineman each August for long-range corporate planning. The rest of the year, the office was unused.

The Wisconsin office was more suitable than his Chicago office because he could avoid the interruptions of daily business that would occur in Chicago. By using his Wisconsin office during August, he could find the isolation he wanted for concentrating on long-range planning.

The IRS objected to Heineman's home office deduction. It claimed that the office was simply a personal convenience, not a necessity of the job; he could have just stayed in Chicago and worked in his regular office.

The Court did not buy this objection. It found that *"there was a business reason for performing the review of the long-term plans away from the Chicago office, and the expenses of the office for performing that work are not made nondeductible because the petitioner chose to perform the work in an environment more suitable to him."*

The IRS also objected that Heineman had not asked his employer to reimburse him for the cost of constructing his home office. But the Court overruled this objection too. There was no evidence that he could have been reimbursed. And, even if he could have been reimbursed, he did not want his company to have a claim on any of his Wisconsin property.

Consequently, the Court allowed Heineman a home office deduction. This included a full year's depreciation on the cost of constructing the office, even though it was used only one month a year. [Heineman 82 TC No. 41]

The above case opens the door for individuals with summer property who perform work-related duties there. Note however that in the above case, the home office was in a separate structure not attached to the residence. This exempted it from the *principal place of business* test as described earlier in this section. Home offices which are not located in detached structures fall under the *principal place of business* requirement.

Items Used in a Home Office

As discussed in the next section, the home office deduction includes the basic cost of providing office space (including depreciation, furniture, utilities, etc.) plus the cost of auxiliary items such as equipment and telephone service. But even if you don't qualify for the home office deduction, a deduction for the auxiliary items used in the home office may still be permitted.

The cost of providing telephone service, except for the basic monthly service charge for your primary residential phone line, is an example of this [cf. the *Books, Supplies, & Equipment* chapter]. In several court cases, a deduction for business use of a home telephone was permitted at the same time the basic deduction for a home office was ruled out. [Shepherd, TC Memo 1976-48; Barry, TC Memo 1978-250]

Supplies and equipment such as a typewriter or calculator would also qualify for deduction independent of the basic home office deduction. For example, in one court case a deduction for the rental of a typewriter and calculator was permitted, even though these items were used in the person's residence at night and there was no deduction allowed for the basic cost of providing these residential facilities. [Hicks, TC Memo 1960-48]

Payments for Services

Even if you don't qualify to deduct your home office, you can still get a deduction for services performed in the office if connected with a legitimate business activity. This is shown by a recent court case concerning an individual who used a home office in connection with a real estate business he had established. His business produced no income for the year, so he was not entitled to any home office deduction under the rules that applied for that year. However, he claimed $1,300 paid to relatives for cleaning the home office, answering the telephone, and filing.

The amount paid for cleaning was considered a direct home office expense, therefore nondeductible. But answering the telephone and filing were ordinary business expenses, not direct home office expenses even though performed in the home office. As a result the Court, estimating that $1/3$ of the amounts paid to the relatives was for answering the telephone and filing, allowed a Schedule C deduction of $1/3 \times \$1,300 = \$433$. [Dollar, TC Memo 1987—346]

Office Decorating

The cost of cleaning, decorating, and furnishing your home office is deductible, as long as the home office meets the requirements described above. Pictures and other works of art do not qualify for a deduction because they do not wear out. However, in one recent court case, deductions of $445 were allowed for the cost of framing pictures which were then hung in a home office. [Fanning, TC Memo 1980-462]

But beautifying your regular office at work might not qualify for deduction. A court case disallowed a deduction to a government worker for a live plant and framed print she purchased for her office at work. Her employer had provided all the furnishings considered necessary to do her job. The cost of beautifying her office was ruled to be a personal rather than a business expense. [Henderson, TC Memo 1983-372]

Lawn Care & Landscaping

According to a 1988 court case, a portion of your lawn care and landscaping expenses might be claimed as part of your home office deduction. In this case, a couple ran an audio-visual business out of their home. Because clients regularly visited their home, the Court allowed them to deduct a portion of their expenses for lawn care, landscaping, and driveway repair corresponding to the percentage of their home used as a deductible home office. The deduction was allowed because the appearance of the residence and grounds was a factor in creating the proper impression for their clients [Hefti, TC Memo 1988—22]. (However, if a home office is used only by the owner, without regular visits by clients or customers, the cost of such items would not be deductible.)

Travel from a Home Office to Another Business Location

If you have a home office which is the principal location of a business activity, then you can deduct the cost of traveling from your home office to another location in connection with that business activity. This is illustrated by the following 1986 court case.

Example 15

Wickler was an anesthetist at a small hospital in the South. She was not considered an employee of the hospital, but rather was an independent contractor. The hospital billed patients for her fees and deducted an agreed percentage of the fees and remitted the balance to the anesthetist. In the Court's words,

"So far as this record discloses, petitioner was the only full time anesthetist practicing at the hospital. That institution, however, would not provide any office space for petitioner's use, and accordingly she maintained an office in the basement of her home, which she used exclusively for the practice of her profession. In that office, inter alia, she maintained professional books such as books and manuals on anesthesia. She also maintained a ledger of the cases in which she had served, including the patients' name[s], copies of the charges which she made with respect to each patient, medical notes related to patients which she was handling, a schedule of her appointments for operations, records of other anesthetists secured by her to perform services at the hospital, and the like. . . .

"In addition to the various records and educational materials prepared and kept by petitioner in her home office, she also conferred by telephone there with doctors at the hospital, both with regard to scheduling of appointments as well as with respect to the condition of patients, and used her office telephone to arrange for the services of other anesthetists.

"Petitioner's office in her home was the only office which she had. She traveled between her home office and the hospital in her own automobile, and frequently made several round trips a day in connection with her duties."

The Court found her home office to be her principal place of business in which a substantial part of her work was performed. In such a case, travel between her home office and another business location (in this case the hospital where she worked) is deductible. Since 90% of her automobile mileage was incurred traveling between her home and the hospital, she was permitted to deduct 90% of her automobile operating expenses and depreciation for the year. [Wickler, TC Memo 1986-1]

A similar conclusion was reached in a 1987 court case concerning an attorney associated with a law firm. He received cases referred to him by the law firm and was considered an independent contractor because of the degree of independence he had in his work. He spent most of his time working in his home office, but went to the law firm's office when he needed administrative support from the law firm's staff. Since his home office was his principal place of business, he was permitted to deduct his travel to and from the law firm. [Wollesen, TC Memo 1987—611].

Even if a home office deduction cannot be claimed because there are no expenses, a deduction may still be allowed for travel to and from the home office. That's the conclusion of the Tax Court in the following 1990 case.

> **Example**
>
> *Kahaku was a self-employed guitarist who performed 8–12 hours per week at a seafood restaurant in Honolulu. He lived in his father-in-law's house. He paid no rent to his father-in-law.*
>
> *One room in the house was set aside for Kahaku's exclusive use as an office or studio. In this room, he maintained all of his business records, practiced approximately 30 hours per week, recorded music, and listened to music.*
>
> *The IRS claimed that the restaurant where Kahaku performed was his principal place of business. But the Court did not agree. It turned to the criteria spelled out in its decision in the Soliman case [cf. Example 8]. He spent a substantial amount of time in his home office, the home office was essential to his work, and no other location was available. This meant that the home office was his principal place of business.*
>
> *Kahaku was not entitled to a deduction for his home office because he was using it rent-free. That was not the issue. Rather, because the home office met all of the basic qualifications for deduction, he could deduct the cost of driving between his home and the restaurant where he performed. Also deductible were trips to music stores and audition sites. The total deduction, including depreciation and actual expenses, amounted to $17,201 over a 2-year period. [Kahaku, TC Memo 1990-34]*

If your home is a *secondary* location of a business activity, then you cannot deduct the cost of traveling to the principal place of that business activity. Such travel is considered nondeductible commuting. A possible way around this restriction in certain cases is to make an intermediate business stop. For example, picking up business mail at a post office, making a business-related purchase, depositing business receipts at a bank, etc. might qualify. The cost of traveling between such a stop and your principal place of business for the related activity would then generally be deductible.

Section 2:
Computation of
Home Office Expenses

If you have an allowable home office deduction, then you may deduct a pro rata portion of the expenses incurred in the general maintenance of the home. The list of allowable home expenses includes:

1. rent (if residence is rented).

2. depreciation (if residence is owned).

3. cost of heat and light.

Vacuum ! 4. cleaning expenses (including salary for cleaning person).

5. painting the outside of the house.

6. premiums on home insurance.

7. general house repairs (e.g. repairing the gutters).

8. extermination and termite inspections.

9. mortgage interest.

10. property taxes.

Note that if you claim a portion of your mortgage interest and property taxes as a home office deduction, you cannot claim these same amounts again as itemized deductions elsewhere on Schedule A.

Be on the alert for any expenses which you think are relevant. For example, in one case a taxpayer was allowed to depreciate a pro rata portion of the cost of a vacuum cleaner since it was used in cleaning his home office.

Expenses relating solely to the use of your office may be deducted in full, such as the cost of painting only the office or the cost of furniture used in the office. You may not deduct expenses relating only to portions of the house excluding the office such as painting the living room.

How Is the Pro Rata Proportion Computed?

Suppose that you have a room set aside for use as a home office. There are two methods to determine what proportion of home expenses can be attributed to your home office. The first method is to divide the area occupied by the home office by the total area of the entire home. Thus, if the office occupies 140 square feet and your home has a total area of 2,500 square feet, then you can deduct 140/2,500 = 5.6% of the allowable home expenses.

The second method is to divide the number of rooms used for your home office by the total number of rooms in the home. For example, if you use one room of a five room house as your office and the rooms are about the same size, you may deduct 1/5 of the allowable home expenses [IRS Publication 587]. In general, this method will give the higher deduction. (There is a court case which indicates you don't have to count every area as a full room; in this case, a kitchen in a house was counted only as 1/2 of a room, resulting in a deduction equal to 1/5.5 of the home expenses. [Moretti, TC Memo 1982-552])

Example

You use one room of a 6 room house you own as a home office for which you are entitled to a deduction. You can deduct 1/6 of the following expenses:

Depreciation on house	$2,000
Electricity for light and air conditioning	490
Gas for heating	250
Repair of the roof	300
Fire insurance	100
Cleaning person	390
Mortgage interest	2,500
Property taxes	800
TOTAL	$6,830

Thus, your home office deduction is $1/6 \times \$6,830 = \$1,138$. In addition, you can deduct for the cost of furnishings or equipment used in the home office [cf. the Expensing and Depreciation chapter].

Home Office Can Be More Than One Room

The following court case illustrates that the home office deduction need not be limited to a single room or even two rooms.

Court Case

Greenway was a professor of anthropology, specializing in ethnomusicology. He was also an author, having written several published books and numerous articles.

He set aside 3 rooms of his house as a home office. He used 3 rooms in order to keep separate projects on which he was working simultaneously and did not use those rooms for any other purpose. Under the rules in effect at the time, he was entitled to a deduction for the use of his home office.

The IRS allowed him a deduction for the full use of all 3 rooms. The only home office question among the issues that came up at the trial was a secondary one concerning the amount of depreciation that should be allowed. [Greenway, TC Memo 1980-97]

Home Office Deduction Cannot Produce a Loss

If a home office deduction would result in a loss on your tax return, you cannot deduct this loss. The way to proceed in such a case is as follows:

Start with the gross income produced by the business activity for which you are using the home office. From this, subtract expenses other than home office— supplies, salaries, travel, etc. Next, subtract home office expenses in the following order:

(1) Interest and Taxes

(2) Operating Expenses such as repairs, utilities, insurance, cleaning, etc.

(3) Depreciation

If a loss results at any step, you must stop; in such case the business activity produces a net result of $0 for the year. (However, any unused losses can be carried over to future years as described later in this chapter.)

Of course, in the above list you only subtract that pro rata portion of interest and taxes, etc. corresponding to the percentage of the home used as an office. The remainder of interest and taxes is deducted on Schedule A in the usual way. The following illustration is adapted from an example published by the IRS. [Prop. Reg. 1.280A-2(i) (7)]

Example

X operates a consulting business out of his home office for which he is entitled to a deduction. X has a special telephone line for the office and occasionally employs secretarial assistance. X determines that his home office occupies 20% of his home. On the basis of the following figures, X determines that the sum of the allowable business deductions for the use of the office is $1,050:

Income from consulting services. $4,000

Expenses for secretary	$ 500
Business telephone	250
Supplies	350
	$1,100

Total expenses other than home office...-1,100

Net income derived from use of home office $2,900

1. Interest and Taxes:	Total	Allocable to Office
Mortgage interest	$6,000	$1,200
Real estate taxes	2,000	400
	$8,000	$1,600

Amount allowable ....-1,600

Limit on further deductions $1,300

2. Operating expenses:	Total	Allocable to Office
Insurance	$ 250	$ 50
Utilities	2,500	500
Repairs	250	50
Cleaning	500	100
		$700

Amount allowable ....-700

Limit on further deductions ....$ 600

3. Depreciation:	Total	Allocable to Office
Depreciation on house	$5,500	$1,100

Amount allowable in current year ....$ 600
Remainder (carried over to future years as described below).............................$ 500

X may claim the remaining $6,400 ($8,000 – $1,600) paid for mortgage interest and real estate taxes as itemized deductions on Schedule A.

Home Office Losses Carried Over to Future Years

As illustrated above, a home office deduction is not allowed to the extent it creates a net loss from the business activity to which it belongs. However, such a disallowed amount can be carried over to the following year to the extent it does not produce a net loss for the business activity in that year. There is no time limit on the carryover. Any amounts disallowed can continue to be carried over until there is a net profit from the business activity they can be deducted against.

Example

Smith operates a consulting business from his home office which generated gross income of $6,000 in 1990. Business expenses that are not attributable to the home office itself (e.g. secretarial services, telephone, supplies, etc.) total $4,000. Home office expenses (interest, taxes, utilities, depreciation, etc.) total $3,000. Thus, Smith has a net loss of $1,000 ($6,000 – $4,000 – $3,000) for 1990. This $1,000 loss cannot be deducted in 1990 but must be carried over to the following year.

In 1991, Smith has gross income from his consulting business of $9,000, home office expenses of $2,500, and other expenses of $3,500. The result, as reported on his 1991 Schedule C, would be as follows:

A. Gross income:	$9,000	
B. Expenses other than home office:	-3,500	
C. A - B:	5,500	
D. Home office expenses for 1991:	-2,500	
E. C - D:	3,000	
F. Carryover from 1990:	-1,000	
G. Net profit reported on Schedule C:	$2,000	

In the above example, E ($3,000) exceeded the $1,000 carryover from 1990. Had it not, any excess would continue to be carried over until there was a year in which the consulting business had a profit. For example, suppose that in the above, E equaled $600 instead of $3,000. In this case, $600 of the $1,000 carryover would be applied to reduce the net profit to $0. The remaining $400 would continue to be carried over into the future.

Sometimes it is possible to shift income or expenses in such a way that the carryover provision can be used to obtain a deduction that might otherwise be lost altogether.

Example

Jones anticipates the following income and expenses from a self-employment activity run out of his home:

Year	1990	1991
Income	$6,000	$6,000
Expenses other than Home Office	-6,000	-6,000
	0	0
Home Office Expenses	1,000	1,000
Deductible Tax Loss	0	0

The reason there was no taxable loss during either 1990 or 1991 was because of the limitation on deducting home office expenses discussed above.

But now suppose $2,000 of income is shifted from 1990 to 1991, say by delaying issuing a bill for services rendered. The result would be as follows:

Year	1990	1991
Income	$4,000	$8,000
Expenses other than Home Office	-6,000	-6,000
	-2,000	2,000
Home Office Expenses	1,000	-1,000
Home Office Expense Carryover from 1990		-1,000
		0
Deductible Tax Loss	$2,000	0

By shifting income to 1991, an extra $2,000 tax loss is achieved that would otherwise be carried over to future years or simply lost if not offset by future income from the business.

Moving Your Home Office

If you move from one residence to another, then you may deduct the cost of moving the furnishings, books, etc. in your home office. You are not restricted by the mileage limitation which applies to general moving expenses.

Where Do You Deduct Home Office Expenses?

Employees may claim a deduction for home office expenses only if they itemize their deductions. This deduction is taken under *Miscellaneous Deductions* on Schedule A. Thus it, when aggregated with other miscellaneous deductions, is subject to a 2% of Adjusted Gross Income floor [cf. the *Miscellaneous Deductions* chapter].

Home office expenses connected with a self-employment activity can be deducted even if you claim the standard deduction. And there is no 2% of Adjusted Gross Income floor. The net result of your self-employment income is reported on line 12 of Form 1040, *Business Income*.

Schedule C can be used for this purpose. However, you should be aware that Schedule C contains a specific question, *"Are you deducting expenses for business use of your home?"* If you check the "Yes" box and your return is audited, you can be almost certain that your home office deduction will be questioned.

How to Avoid Capital Gains Tax If You Sell Your Home

Ordinarily, when you sell an item that has appreciated in value, you must pay a capital gains tax on the profit. However, as discussed in the *Homeowners* chapter, there is an exception to this rule. You do not pay capital gains tax upon sale of your principal residence, provided you reinvest in another principal residence of the same or greater value. But the exception does not apply to that portion of your house used as a home office. For example, if part of your house is being used as a home office, then capital gains tax would be due on an appropriate fraction of the profit at the time of sale plus any depreciation you had claimed in prior years.

However, a 1982 IRS ruling provides a way to avoid this situation. According to this ruling, the IRS will look only at how the residence is being used at the time of sale. Thus, if your home office no longer qualifies for deduction so it is being used 100% as your principal residence, then the reinvestment rule in the preceding paragraph applies to your entire residence. As long as you invest in a principal residence of the same or greater value and no portion of the new residence qualifies for a home office deduction, then under the rules described in the *Homeowners* chapter, no capital gains tax will be due. [IRS Revenue Ruling 82-26, IRB-6 p. 5, reversing IRS Private Letter Ruling #7935003]

This ruling is especially useful because it is so easy to satisfy the required conditions. Just make some personal use of your home office during the year you sell your old home. This will disqualify you from a home office deduction that year and thereby satisfy the condition of the ruling. Then, in a later year, you can convert a room in your new residence into a deductible home office with no capital gains tax having been paid.

Chapter 4

Expensing and Depreciation

Section 1:
Introduction

This chapter concerns non-trivial job-related, business, or investment items which will be used for more than one year. Such items now generally fall into one of 3 classes.

The **real estate class** consists of houses, apartments, and other buildings. Land is not included because it generates no deduction based on its "wearing out".

The **5-year recovery** class consists of (i) automobiles and trucks, (ii) computers and peripheral equipment, calculators, typewriters, and copiers, and (iii) items used for research and experimentation.

The **7-year recovery** class includes books, furniture, and office equipment not included in the 5-year class.

For items in the real estate class, you are not allowed to deduct the cost all at once. Instead, you must apportion the cost over a period of years. This is called **depreciation.**

For items in the 5-year or 7-year recovery class (e.g. books, equipment, furniture, etc.), you can **expense** the item, that is, deduct the entire cost in the year it is first used. This option is limited to $10,000 worth of items purchased in 1990. This *expensing method* is discussed in Section 2.

You can also *depreciate* books, equipment, furniture, etc. over either 5 years or 7 years, depending upon the recovery class to which the item belongs [cf. Section 3].

Expensing is almost always preferable to depreciation because, other things being equal, a tax writeoff is more valuable the earlier it is used because of the time value of money. However, there are certain cases when the depreciation method should be used for 5-year or 7-year recovery class items.

First, an item must be used more than 50% for business purposes throughout the entire recovery class period. Otherwise, the item should be *depreciated* rather than *expensed*. If the expensing method is used for an item purchased in 1990 and then in a later year within the recovery class period, business use falls below 50%, the IRS can *recapture* a portion of the expensing deduction that was claimed [cf. Section 2].

Second, the expensing method should not be used on automobiles which cost more than $13,300. Because of special rules that apply, depreciation is superior to expensing for such automobiles [cf. the *Automobile Expenses* chapter].

Third, depreciation might be preferable to expensing in some cases where your business use percentage is expected to increase in future years.

Fourth, items used for investment purposes (e.g. a computer used just for tracking stocks) cannot be expensed, but must be depreciated.

Finally, there are special rules which apply to certain home computers, photo and video items, cellular telephones, and automobiles which are considered *listed property*. As discussed below, sometimes depreciation is the only allowable writeoff method for these items.

Form 4562 is the basic form on which the items being depreciated or expensed are listed. (However, as discussed near the end of this Chapter, Form 4562 is no longer required if all the items were purchased prior to 1990.) For employees, their total job-related depreciation or expensing deductions are included under *Miscellaneous Deductions* on Schedule A. (As discussed in Section 1 of the *Miscellaneous Deductions* chapter, a 2% of Adjusted Gross Income floor applies to the sum total of all miscellaneous deductions claimed on Schedule A.) Self-employed individuals claim these deductions on Schedule C, escaping the 2% of Adjusted Gross Income floor.

Special Rules for Autos, Computers, Cellular Telephones, and Entertainment Items

There are 2 special conditions that apply to the following items, called *Listed Property* by the IRS:

Listed Property

1. Automobiles and other passenger vehicles.

2. Home Computers (including peripherals), except for employer-owned computers used exclusively at a regular business establishment or computers used exclusively in a home office qualifying for deduction as described in the *Home Office* chapter.

3. Property of a type generally used for purposes of entertainment, recreation, or amusement (e.g. video recorders, cameras, etc.), except if used either (i) exclusively at your regular job location or deductible home office, or (ii) in connection with your principal job or business.

4. Cellular Telephones.

Condition 1: Listed Property Purchased by an Employee Must Be Required by His Employer

In order for listed property purchased by an employee in connection with his job to be deductible, the law states that its use must be *"for the convenience of the employer and required as a condition of employment."* According to IRS regulations, the phrase *"condition of employment"* refers to the proper performance of an employee's duties. Quoting from these regulations,

"In order to satisfy the 'condition of employment' requirement, the use of the property must be required in order for the employee to perform the duties of his or her employment properly. Whether the use of the property is so required depends on all the facts and circumstances. Thus, the employer need not explicitly require the employee to use the property. Similarly, a mere statement by the employer that the use of the property is a condition of employment is not sufficient."
[IRS Reg. #1.280F-6T]

The IRS has not yet similarly interpreted the phrase *"for the convenience of the employer."* However, this phrase would appear to be superfluous in this context. It is hard to produce an example where the *condition of employment* requirement would be satisfied without the *convenience of the employer* requirement being satisfied also.

The IRS regulations give 3 examples which apply to the use of automobiles or other personal transportation vehicles. In 2 cases where the employer did not provide a vehicle but the employee had to travel to various jobsites, the *condition of employment* requirement was satisfied. But in the third case the *condition of employment* standard was not satisfied where the employer made a car available to the employee, but the employee chose to use her own car and receive reimbursement instead.

The IRS regulations also contain an example concerning the use of a home computer. This example is discussed in the *Books, Supplies, and Equipment* chapter.

Condition 2: Listed Property Must Be Used More than 50% for Business Purposes—Otherwise a Special Depreciation Table Applies

Listed property which is used 50% or less for business purposes cannot be expensed. Instead, a special *listed property depreciation table* [cf. Section 3] must be used to determine the annual writeoffs. This special table stretches out the deductions over a longer period of time than under the regular depreciation table.

Listed property which is used more than 50% for business purposes is not subject to this restriction. The expensing method (or regular depreciation table) applies to these items.

However, no matter what the percentage of business use, Condition 1 above must still be satisfied. Otherwise, no expensing or depreciation deductions can be claimed.

Maximum Limitations on Autos

There are extra limitations on the amounts that can be deducted for expensing or depreciation on an automobile. These are described in the *Automobile Expenses* chapter.

Section 2:
Expensing Method

On your 1990 tax return, you can deduct in full, instead of depreciating, up to $10,000 worth of items in the 5-year or 7-year recovery classes which you placed into service during 1990. These categories include automobiles, calculators, equipment, furniture, etc. but not buildings or other real estate. However, this option does not always apply to certain *listed property* as discussed in Section 1.

The $10,000 limit applies to single or joint tax returns. For married persons filing separately, the $10,000 limit is allocated equally between the 2 separate returns unless a different allocation is elected.

The procedure of deducting the cost in the first year of use instead of depreciating is called *expensing*. To qualify for expensing, the items must be used in connection with your job or self-employment activity. Items which are used just for investment-related activities do not qualify for the expensing option but must be depreciated as discussed in Section 3.

Example 1.
You bought a $300 typewriter in 1990 which is used only for job-related purposes. Under the expensing option, you deduct the full $300 on your 1990 tax return. There are no further deductions for the typewriter in future years.

If more than $10,000 worth of items was purchased in 1990, the expensing option is limited to $10,000, with the remainder depreciated as discussed in Section 3.

Example 2.
You purchased a $200 typewriter and $11,000 worth of computer equipment during 1990, all of which are used in an outside business activity. You can use the expensing option on up to $10,000 worth of purchases, say the entire $200 typewriter and $9,800 of the computer. The remaining $1,200 of the computer is depreciated over the 6-year period 1990-1995, as described in Section 3. The total deductions in each year are as follows:

Year	Deduction
1990.................$10,000 (expensing limit) + 20% × $1,200 =	$10,240
1991 ....32% × $1,200 =	384
1992 ....19.2% × $1,200 =	230
1993 ....11.52% × $1,200 =	138
1994 ....11.52% × $1,200 =	138
1995 ....5.76% × $1,200 =	70
	$11,200

If an item is used partly for business purposes and partly for personal purposes, then the expensing option is applied to the appropriate fraction of the item's cost.

> **Example 3.**
>   You purchased a $100 calculator in 1990 which is used 90% for job-related purposes and 10% for personal purposes. You can deduct 90% × $100 = $90 of the cost on your 1990 tax return.

Election to Use Expensing Option

Technically speaking, depreciation is considered to be the "regular" method with the expensing option a secondary method which you can elect to use instead of depreciation. To elect this option, you fill out Part I of Form 4562. If you do not make the appropriate *election to expense*, the IRS could require you to use the depreciation option. This form should be included with the original tax return you file, not an amended return.

Items Converted to Personal Use

Suppose you purchase an item which is used for business purposes the first year, but is used primarily for personal purposes thereafter. Under the expensing option, you would deduct the full cost in the first year, thereby giving you a total writeoff for an item which is used overall only partly for business purposes. To prevent this "distortion," Congress enacted into law a special recapture provision affecting the expensing option.

This provision applies if the item is *not used predominantly in a trade or business* at anytime within the period of the recovery class to which the item belongs. Under this provision, the IRS is authorized to *recapture* a portion of the expensing deduction which was claimed. That is, you would be required to report as taxable income in a later year a part of the expensing deduction you claimed in the year of purchase.

Section 3:
Depreciation

This section describes the depreciation rules that apply to items placed into service in 1987-1990. For items placed into service prior to 1987, the tables described here do not generally apply. Instead, you would use the table applying to that year. For example, a typewriter purchased (and placed into service) in 1986 would be depreciated according to the percentages (15%, 22%, 21%, 21%, 21%) given by the 5-year table for the years 1986-1990 [cf. previous editions of this Tax Guide].

Depreciation Methods for 5-Year and 7-Year Property

As discussed in Section 1, items other than real estate generally fall into either the 5-year recovery class (e.g. autos, computers, typewriters, research items, etc.) or the 7-year recovery class (e.g. books, furniture, etc.). For both of these categories there are 2 choices of depreciation methods — the **accelerated** method and the **straight-line** method. (The accelerated method is sometimes referred to as the *prescribed* method, abbreviated PRE, or the *double-declining* balance method, abbreviated DDB, in IRS forms. The straight line method is abbreviated SL.) For either of these categories, you must use the same method for all items purchased during a given year. However, you may use the straight-line method for all items in one category and the accelerated method for all items in the other. You will be able to make a different choice of methods for items purchased in future years.

For items purchased in 1990, the following table shows the percentage that would be deducted each year under the accelerated and straight-line methods. The percentages are applied to full cost of an item (including sales tax, delivery charges, etc.), assuming it is used entirely for business-related purposes. Observe that the accelerated method will be the best choice for most people because it yields the most rapid write-off. (As discussed later in this section, a different table applies to certain *listed property* [cf. Section 1] used 50% or less for business purposes.)

REGULAR DEPRECIATION TABLE

5-Year Property

(autos, computers, typewriters, etc.)

Year	Accelerated Method	Straight-Line Method
1990	20 %	10%
1991	32 %	20%
1992	19.2 %	20%
1993	11.52%	20%
1994	11.52%	20%
1995	5.76%	10%
	100%	100%

7-Year Property

(books, furniture, etc.)

Year	Accelerated Method	Straight-Line Method
1990	14.29%	7.14%
1991	24.49%	14.29%
1992	17.49%	14.29%
1993	12.49%	14.28%
1994	8.93%	14.29%
1995	8.92%	14.28%
1996	8.93%	14.29%
1997	4.46%	7.14%
	100%	100%

Observe that in the above table, it makes no difference when during the year the item was placed into service. Thus, for example, the same deductions are produced by an item purchased in January as by one purchased in December. The tables are constructed on the basis of an item being placed into service at the midpoint of 1990 and being used, say in the case of 5-year property, until the midpoint of 1995—a total of 5 full years. That is why, for example, it takes an extra 6th year to fully depreciate an item in the 5-year recovery class.

Example

You purchased a typewriter in 1990 for $300. Using the first column in the table for items in the 5-year category, the following would be the annual depreciation deductions:

Year	Deduction				
1990	20	%	× $300 =	$	60
1991	32	%	× $300 =		96
1992	19.2	%	× $300 =		58
1993	11.52%		× $300 =		35
1994	11.52%		× $300 =		35
1995	5.76%		× $300 =		16
					$300

In the above example, it is assumed the typewriter was used 100% for business purposes. If used partly for personal purposes, the above deductions would be reduced accordingly. For example, if the typewriter were used 60% for business purposes and 40% for personal purposes, the basic depreciation percentages would be applied to 60% × $300 = $180. In this case, the deductions for each of the 6 years in the table would be 20% × $180 = $36, 32% × $180 = $58, etc.

Listed Property

As discussed in Section 1, special rules apply to automobiles, cellular telephones, and certain home computers or entertainment items which fall into the *Listed Property* category. If such items qualify for deduction but are used 50% or less for business purposes, neither the expensing method nor the regular depreciation table applies. Instead a special *listed property depreciation table* must be used.

The listed property depreciation table below applies to items purchased in 1990. For items purchased before 1987, different tables apply [cf. previous editions of this Tax Guide].

Depreciation begins in the year an item starts being used by you for business purposes and is based on its original cost (or market value at the time of initial business use, if lower). The percentages in the table are applied to the fraction of the cost of an item attributable to business use. You report depreciation for Listed Property in Part V of Form 4562.

LISTED PROPERTY DEPRECIATION TABLE

(Applies to Listed Property purchased in 1990 used 50% or less for business purposes)

Year	Autos	Computers	Entertainment Equipment
1990	10%	10%	4.17%
1991	20%	20%	8.33%
1992	20%	20%	8.33%
1993	20%	20%	8.33%
1994	20%	20%	8.33%
1995	10%	10%	8.33%
1996			8.34%
1997			8.33%
1998			8.34%
1999			8.33%
2000			8.34%
2001			8.33%
2002			4.17%
	100%	100%	100%

Example

A home computer was purchased for $3000 in 1990 and is used 30% of the time for job-related research required by an employer. The computer is used at home, but not in a deductible home office. Since the computer is used 30% for business purposes, the preceding Listed Property Depreciation Table is applied to 30% × $3000 = $900. Thus, the annual depreciation deductions are as follows:

Year	Deduction
1990	10% × $900 = $ 90
1991	20% × $900 = 180
1992	20% × $900 = 180
1993	20% × $900 = 180
1994	20% × $900 = 180
1995	10% × $900 = 90
	$900

Varying Percentage of Business Use

The business use of an employer-required *listed property item* purchased in 1990 may vary from year to year. In such a case, the regular depreciation table applies, provided business use exceeds personal use in each year of the write-off period indicated in the *listed property depreciation table,* i.e. 6 years for autos, 6 years for computers, and 13 years for entertainment equipment.

Example

An automobile was purchased for $10,000 in 1990. It is used for employer-required business purposes as follows: 60% during 1990, 70% during 1991, 80% during 1992 and later years until sold. The following would be the depreciation deductions according to the regular depreciation table for 5-year property described earlier in this section.

Year	Deduction
1990	20 % × 60% × $10,000 = $1,200
1991	32 % × 70% × 10,000 = 2,240
1992	19.2 % × 80% × 10,000 = 1,536
1993	11.52% × 80% × 10,000 = 922
1994	11.52% × 80% × 10,000 = 922
1995	5.76% × 80% × 10,000 = 461

For automobiles which cost more than $13,300, there are special limitations which might alter the above computation procedure. Details are contained in the *Automobile Expenses* chapter.

If listed property is not used more than 50% for business purposes in each year of use during the time period indicated in the listed property depreciation table, then the special listed property depreciation table must be used throughout the entire depreciation period.

Example

An automobile was purchased in 1990 for $10,000. It is used 60% for business purposes each year except that in 1993, it is used only 40% for business purposes. The 40% usage in one year of the 6-year period in the listed property depreciation table disqualifies it from the regular depreciation table. Thus, the special listed property depreciation table must be used as follows:

Year	Deduction
1990	10% × 60% × $10,000 = $ 600
1991	20% × 60% × $10,000 = 1200
1992	20% × 60% × $10,000 = 1200
1993	20% × 40% × $10,000 = 800
1994	20% × 60% × $10,000 = 1200
1995	10% × 60% × $10,000 = 600

As discussed above, the depreciation method to be used depends upon the business usage percentage not just in the current year but in future years as well. This means you have to predict in advance what this percentage will be in order to determine which table to use. If you use the regular table because you think your business use will remain above 50% but it turns out this is not the case, a *recapture* provision will come into play. Under this provision, you are supposed to pay back the difference between the deductions yielded by the regular table and the listed property table by including this difference in taxable income. (You may always use the listed property table for a given class of items instead of the regular table if you choose. No adjustments are made if it turns out you qualified to use the regular table because the business use percentage remained above 50%.)

Items Used for Investment Purposes

As discussed in Section 1, there is a special rule (Condition 2) which requires business use to exceed 50% in order to qualify listed property for depreciation under the regular table. In deciding if this condition is satisfied, business use does not include use in connection with investment activities. However, once the correct depreciation table is determined, investment use can be taken into account. The following example illustrates this situation.

Example

A home computer is purchased in 1990 for $3000. The computer is used at home, but not in a deductible home office. The computer is used 40% of the time for job-related research and 30% of the time for managing investments.

Not counting investment use, business use does not exceed 50%. Therefore, the listed property depreciation table must be used. However, the investment use is taken into account when applying the table. That is, the percentages in the table are applied to the cost attributable to business plus investment use, 70% × $3000 = $2100. Thus, the depreciation deductions are as follows:

Year	Deduction
1990	10% × $2100 = $210
1991	20% × 2100 = 420
1992	20% × 2100 = 420
1993	20% × 2100 = 420
1994	20% × 2100 = 420
1995	10% × 2100 = 210
	$2100

Special Recordkeeping Rules for Listed Property

There are special recordkeeping rules which apply to *listed property*. Details of these recordkeeping rules are contained in the *Automobile Expenses* and *Books, Equipment, & Supplies* chapters.

Items Purchased Late in the Year

The preceding depreciation tables provide the same deduction no matter what date during the year an item was purchased. This is because the tables treat all items as though they were purchased at the midpoint of the first year of use. For example, the 5-year regular depreciation table would yield a 20% of cost first year deduction for an auto placed into service on December 31 even if driven for only a few miles. To prevent such a "distortion," Congress has provided a special *40%-rule* when too much is purchased in the last 3 months of a given year.

The 40%-Rule

Suppose you buy one or more items during the year (other than buildings or other real estate) for which you claim depreciation. If 40% or more of the total cost is attributable to items purchased in the last 3 months of the year, the usual depreciation tables given earlier in this section cannot be used. Instead, the 40%-rule states that each item must be depreciated according to the quarter (i.e. 3-month period) during which the item was placed into service. The 40%-rule does not apply when you use the expensing option described in Section 2 instead of depreciation.

The following table gives the first three years regular or listed property depreciation percentages under this 40%-rule according to the quarter in 1990 during which an item was placed into service. (These tables cannot be used unless the 40%-rule applies.)

DEPRECIATION IN FIRST 3 YEARS WHEN 40%-RULE APPLIES

(Use column according to quarter of the first year during which the item was placed into service.)

	Year	Quarter 1	Quarter 2	Quarter 3	Quarter 4
		Regular (i.e. Non-Listed Property)			
5-year property					
accelerated	1	35%	25%	15%	5%
	2	26%	30%	34%	38%
	3	15.6%	18%	20.4%	22.8%
	4	9.4%	10.8%	12.2%	13.7%
straight line	1	17.5%	12.5%	7.5%	2.5%
	2	20%	20%	20%	20%
	3	20%	20%	20%	20%
	4	20%	20%	20%	20%
7-year property					
accelerated	1	25%	17.85%	10.71%	3.57%
	2	21.43%	23.47%	25.51%	27.55%
	3	15.31%	16.76%	18.22%	19.68%
	4	10.93%	11.98%	13.02%	14.06%
straight-line	1	12.5%	8.93%	5.36%	1.79%
	2	14.29%	14.29%	14.29%	14.29%
	3	14.28%	14.28%	14.28%	14.28%
	4	14.29%	14.29%	14.29%	14.29%
		Listed Property			
Autos or Computers	1	17.5%	12.5%	7.5%	2.5%
	2	20%	20%	20%	20%
	3	20%	20%	20%	20%
	4	20%	20%	20%	20%

Entertainment Equipment	1	8.75%	6.25%	3.75%	1.25%
	2	10%	10%	10%	10%
	3	10%	10%	10%	10%
	4	10%	10%	10%	10%

Example

An individual depreciates a computer purchased for $1,200 on March 25, 1990 and peripheral equipment purchased for $900 on December 20, 1990. These items fall into the listed property category. Over 40% of the total cost is due to purchases made in the last 3 months as is verified by the following computation:

Quarter Purchased	Item	Cost
1	Computer	$1,200
4	Peripherals	900
		$2,100

$$\$900/\$2100 = 43\%$$

Thus, the special 40%-rule tables are used—the 1st quarter column for the computer and the 4th quarter column for the peripherals.

1990 Deduction

Computer	17.5% × $1,200 =	$210
Peripherals	2.5% × 900 =	23
		$233

1991 and 1992 Deductions

Computer	20% × $1,200 =	$240
Peripherals	20% × 900 =	180
		$420

Observe that if the 40%-rule had not applied, the deduction for 1990 obtained by using the listed property depreciation table would have been 10% × $2,100 = $210 instead of $233. Thus, the 40%-rule in this case yields a higher deduction than under the ordinary rules. The reason for this is the increased deduction for the first quarter purchase of the computer. Had the computer been purchased later in the year, the 40%-rule would have produced a lower deduction than under the regular rules.

Houses and Other Real Estate

The *real estate class* is divided into 2 categories—the *residential rental category* and the *non-residential category*. The residential rental category consists of houses, apartments, etc. which are rented out as a personal residence. The non-residential category consists of other real estate such as office buildings, home offices, retail stores, etc. Land is not included because it cannot be depreciated, since it doesn't "wear out".

There are 2 depreciation tables—one for residential rental real estate and the other for non-residential real estate. These tables, given below, provide far less generous depreciation deductions than under the law prior to 1987. These tables apply to real estate which you first placed into business service in 1987, 1988, 1989 or 1990, even if purchased and used as a personal residence before 1987. (However, there is a transition rule which may allow you to apply the old rules to real estate you first contracted to buy or construct under a written contract signed on or before March 1, 1986, even if first placed into service in 1987 or later.)

RESIDENTIAL RENTAL PROPERTY

FIRST PLACED INTO BUSINESS SERVICE IN 1987, 1988, 1989 OR 1990

(Use column for the first month in the year the property is used for business purposes.)

Year	Jan	Feb	Mar	Apl	May	Jun	Jly	Aug	Sep	Oct	Nov	Dec
1	3.48	3.18	2.88	2.58	2.27	1.97	1.67	1.36	1.06	.76	.45	.15
2-27	3.64	3.64	3.64	3.64	3.64	3.64	3.64	3.64	3.64	3.64	3.64	3.64
28	1.88	2.18	2.48	2.78	3.09	3.39	3.64	3.64	3.64	3.64	3.64	3.64
29	-0-	-0-	-0-	-0-	-0-	-0-	.05	.36	.66	.96	1.27	1.57

NON-RESIDENTIAL REAL ESTATE

FIRST PLACED INTO BUSINESS SERVICE IN 1987, 1988, 1989, OR 1990

Year	Jan	Feb	Mar	Apl	May	Jun	Jly	Aug	Sep	Oct	Nov	Dec
1	3.04	2.78	2.51	2.25	1.98	1.72	1.46	1.19	.93	.66	.40	.13
2-31	3.17	3.17	3.17	3.17	3.17	3.17	3.17	3.17	3.17	3.17	3.17	3.17
32	1.86	2.12	2.39	2.65	2.92	3.17	3.17	3.17	3.17	3.17	3.17	3.17
33	-0-	-0-	-0-	-0-	-0-	.01	.27	.54	.80	1.07	1.33	1.60

Example. Residential Property

In April, 1990, you purchased a house for $100,000 (not including the price of the land) which you rent out at a fair market price. To determine the depreciation deduction each year, you use the April column in the above table. Thus, the annual depreciation deductions would be as follows:

Year	Deduction
1990	2.58% × $100,000 = $2,580
1991	3.64% × $100,000 = $3,640
1992	3.64% × $100,000 = $3,640
etc.	

If you stop using the item for business purposes before the end of a given year, then you claim depreciation for that year based on the number of months the item is used, applying a mid-month convention (i.e. the month of disposition is counted as $^1/_2$ of a month). For example, in the above calculation if you withdrew the house from the rental market on March 2, 1992, the deduction for 1992 would be $^{2.5}/_{12}$ x $3,640 = $758.

If you claim a deduction for an office in a home you own [cf. the *Home Office* chapter], then along with your other expenses, you deduct a pro rata proportion of the depreciation of your home. Similarly, you deduct depreciation for a home you rent out to others with a profit-making intent [cf. the *Homeowners* chapter]. You begin the depreciation calculation at the time you first start using the home for business purposes.

Example. Non-Residential Property

In 1984, you purchased a house for $100,000 (not including the price of the land). In March, 1988, you converted a room into a home office qualifying for deduction [cf. the Home Office *chapter]. The home office constitutes 1/7 of the home, so 1/7 x $100,000 = $14,286 is the cost eligible for depreciation. Since the room was first placed into business service in 1988, the above tables apply. You must use the table for non-residential property since you are using that particular room as a business office rather than as a residence. Since the March column applies, the following would be the annual depreciation deductions:*

Year	Depreciation		
1988	2.51%	× $14,286 =	$359
1989	3.17%	× $14,286 =	$453
1990	3.17%	× $14,286 =	$453
etc.			

As in the preceding example, if you sell the house or otherwise stop using the room as a home office, then you claim depreciation based on the number of months the item is used, applying a mid-month convention. For example, if you sold the house in September, 1990, the deduction for 1990 would be 9.5/12 × $453 = $359.

Real Estate Placed Into Service Before 1987

For real estate placed into business service prior to 1987 that you are continuing to so use, you would just continue with the same depreciation method you have been using under the old rules. The following tables show the most rapidly permitted depreciation deductions in the initial years for real estate placed into business service between January 1, 1981 and December 31, 1986. (For further information on items first placed into business service before 1987, especially if purchased before 1981, see previous editions of this Tax Guide.)

RESIDENTIAL & NON-RESIDENTIAL REAL ESTATE FIRST PLACED INTO BUSINESS SERVICE 1981-1986

Property Purchased 1/1/81-3/15/84

(Use Column for the First Month in the Year the Property is Used for Business Purposes)

Year	Jan	Feb	Mar	Apl	May	Jun	Jly	Aug	Sep	Oct	Nov	Dec
1	12	11	10	9	8	7	6	5	4	3	2	1
2	10	10	11	11	11	11	11	11	11	11	11	12
3	9	9	9	9	10	10	10	10	10	10	10	10
4	8	8	8	8	8	8	9	9	9	9	9	9
5	7	7	7	7	7	7	8	8	8	8	8	8
6	6	6	6	6	6	7	7	7	7	7	7	7
7	6	6	6	6	6	6	6	6	6	6	6	6
8	6	6	6	6	6	6	5	6	6	6	6	6
9	6	6	6	6	5	6	5	5	5	6	6	6
10	5	6	5	6	5	5	5	5	5	5	6	5

Property Purchased 3/16/84-5/8/85

(Use Column for the First Month in the Year the Propery is Used for Business Purposes)

Year	Jan	Feb	Mar	Apl	May	Jun	Jly	Aug	Sep	Oct	Nov	Dec
1	9	9	8	7	6	5	4	4	3	2	1	.4
2	9	9	9	9	9	9	9	9	9	10	10	10
3	8	8	8	8	8	8	8	8	9	9	9	9
4	7	7	7	7	7	8	8	8	8	8	8	8
5	7	7	7	7	7	7	7	7	7	7	7	7
6	6	6	6	6	6	6	6	6	6	6	6	6
7	5	5	5	5	6	6	6	6	6	6	6	6

Property Purchased 5/9/85-12/31/86

(Use Column for the First Month in the Year the Property is Used for Business Purposes)

Year	Jan	Feb	Mar	Apl	May	Jun	Jly	Aug	Sep	Oct	Nov	Dec
1	8.8	8.1	7.3	6.5	5.8	5.0	4.2	3.5	2.7	1.9	1.1	0.4
2	8.4	8.5	8.5	8.6	8.7	8.8	8.8	8.9	9.0	9.0	9.1	9.2
3	7.6	7.7	7.7	7.8	7.9	7.9	8.0	8.1	8.1	8.2	8.3	8.3
4	6.9	7.0	7.0	7.1	7.1	7.2	7.3	7.3	7.4	7.4	7.5	7.6
5	6.3	6.3	6.4	6.4	6.5	6.5	6.6	6.6	6.7	6.8	6.8	6.9
6	5.7	5.7	5.8	5.9	5.9	5.9	6.0	6.0	6.1	6.1	6.2	6.2

Example

In April, 1986, you purchased a house for $80,000 (not including the price of the land) which you rent out at a fair market price. To determine the depreciation deduction each year, you use the April column in the above table. Thus, the annual depreciation deductions would be as follows:

Year	Deduction
1986	6.5% × $80,000 = $5,200
1987	8.6% × $80,000 = $6,880
1988	7.8% × $80,000 = $6,240
1989	7.1% × $80,000 = $5,680
1990	6.4% × $80,000 = $5,120
etc.	

If you stop using the item for business purposes before the end of a given year, then you claim depreciation for that year based on the number of months the item is used, applying a mid-month convention (i.e. the month of disposition is counted as $1/2$ of a month). For example, in the above calculation if you withdrew the house from the rental market on March 2, 1990, the deduction for 1990 would be $2.5/12$ × $5,120 = $1,067.

Basis

When you compute depreciation on a used home or other building, you actually use a figure called the **basis** as the starting cost. It is used in place of "original cost" in the above examples illustrating the depreciation methods. If you start using a home for business purposes as soon as you purchase the home, then the basis is just the original price you paid for the home (including legal fees and other settlement costs that can't be deducted). However, if you start using it for business purposes in a later year than the one in which you purchased the home, then the basis is the lesser of

(1) Your original purchase price plus the cost of any improvements,

or

(2) The fair market value of the home at the time you started using it for business purposes.

The purchase price in (1) refers to the original purchase price when you bought the home. It is not dependent upon your down payment or your monthly mortgage payments.

You cannot depreciate the value of the land on which your home is situated since land doesn't wear out. Thus (1) and (2) above refer to the price of the home only, excluding the value of the land on which it is situated. You must estimate what cost was due to the home and what cost was due to the land and depreciate only the cost due to the home. Don't use a round number for estimating the cost of the house alone. Tax auditors use this as a tipoff that you haven't reduced the price by the estimated percentage attributable to the value of the land.

The same rules described above for computing the basis of a home apply to other items as well. For example, if you start using an automobile for business purposes which you purchased at an earlier date, you would use the lesser of (i) original cost, or (ii) market value as the starting cost figure. In this case, the market value would presumably be the required lesser figure.

Improvements

An improvement is a repair or addition which adds to the value or prolongs the life of the home. Ordinary maintenance or repair expenses are not improvements and cannot be depreciated. Of course, if you incur these maintenance expenses at a time when the home is being used for business purposes, then you get an appropriate deduction for these expenses.

For example, adding central air-conditioning, replacing the roof, panelling the den, installing permanent storm windows, landscaping, new plumbing, installing new shelving, etc. are improvements. But the cost of painting, cleaning, fixing a broken air-conditioner, etc. are ordinary maintenance expenses.

Form 4562

If you claim any expensing or depreciation deduction you must fill out Form 4562 and include it with your tax return. On the first page of this form, expensing is claimed in Part I while depreciation is claimed in Parts II and III. Part II of Section B calls for you to list the *"Convention"* and column (f) the "Method." When you use the accelerated method in the regular depreciation table, for 5-year or 7-year property, you would enter "HY" in column (e) [for *half-year convention*] and "200DB" in column (f) [for *200% Declining Balance Method*].

The instructions to Form 4562 have been somewhat misleading on one point. They state that the expensing deduction is limited to the *"total taxable income of your trade or business"*. However, this total includes all active trades or businesses (including those as an employee), not just the one producing the expensing deduction. Thus, an employee can use the expensing deduction in connection with an outside business activity, even if it produces a net loss for that activity.

Form 4562 May Not Be Required

If you both (1) claim depreciation only for items placed into service before 1990; and (2) do not claim depreciation for any listed property items, then the situation is different. Under new rules for 1990, you do not have to fill out Form 4562 at all. You just list the total depreciation amounts on Form 2106, Schedule C, Schedule E, or other appropriate place on your tax return, depending upon the type of business use.

Importance of Recordkeeping

The following court case illustrates the effect of inadequate recordkeeping on your home office depreciation deduction.

Example 1

Mrs. Anderson used the family room in her home as a home office. She kept no records concerning her operating expenses for utilities, insurance, etc. nor did she present any data which could be used for computing depreciation. Instead, she just deducted $500 which she felt was a "reasonable amount."

The IRS and the Court both felt she was entitled to a home office deduction. They were both willing to allow her a pro rata share of the estimated expenses of operating her home, e.g. utilities, cleaning, insurance, etc. The IRS allowed $112 which was 7.7% of the estimated operating expenses. This percentage represented the portion of her house occupied by an average size room. But the Court recognized that the room she used as her office was bigger than average. It computed that her office occupied 15.4% of her home. Since the IRS used a percentage figure exactly one-half the correct amount, the Court simply doubled the $112 allowed by the IRS and granted Mrs. Anderson a $224 deduction for her operating expenses.

However, the Court refused to estimate her depreciation deduction. While the cost of utilities, cleaning, etc. can be approximated reasonably well by an educated guess, the same is not true for depreciation. There was no way to know what she paid for the home and what she spent on improvements. In the absence of any documentation on these questions, the Court simply declined to make an estimate and allowed her no depreciation deduction whatever. [Anderson, TC Memo 1974-49]

Example 2.

This case is similar to the previous one. A doctor used part of his house as a home office but presented no financial records. Instead, he claimed a deduction of $1200 which represented the rental value of the rooms he used as an office.

However, the Court denied this "rental value" approach to calculating home office deductions. After all, even if he could be regarded as paying rent to himself, he would then have to report the rent paid as income, offsetting the deduction. As in the preceding example, the Court allowed a pro rata share of his estimated home operating costs. But it allowed no deduction for depreciation since it had no data with which to determine the cost of the house. [Tomsykoski, TC Memo 1974-105]

Chapter 5

Interest

Under the law prior to 1987, the basic tax rule for interest paid was simple—namely, all interest payments were equally deductible on your tax return. (The only major exception was for debts used to purchase tax-free investments such as municipal bonds.)

Those were the good old days. Under current law, some interest is better than others. Depending upon the use of the debt on which interest is paid, the interest might be non-deductible, partly deductible, fully deductible, or deductible in the future.

These rules apply to all debts existing in 1990, even if originated prior to January 1, 1987 when the new rules went into effect.

There are now 5 separate categories of interest—(1) *interest on your home*, (2) *personal interest*, (3) *passive interest*, (4) *trade or business interest*, and (5) *investment interest*. The basic tax treatment for each type of interest is described below.

Except for interest on a personal residence, the categorization depends upon how the proceeds of the underlying loan are *used* rather than *secured*. For example, suppose you take out a loan, secured by stocks you own, which you use to purchase an automobile. The interest you pay on the loan falls into the *personal interest* category because the loan was used for the personal purpose of buying an automobile. The fact that it was secured by stocks does not place it into the *investment interest* category.

If an interest payment is due on a loan, you can't borrow more money from the original lender to cover the payment. Otherwise, you lose out on the interest deduction. The IRS has stated that it *"will disallow any deduction claimed for interest paid on a loan if the payment was made with funds obtained from the original creditor through a second loan, an advance, or any other financial arrangement similar to a loan"* [IR-83-93] . In such a case, no actual payment is considered made—just a renewed promise to pay the original lender. However, if money is borrowed from a different lender to pay the interest due on the original loan, then a deduction is allowed. While common sense may point to this as an irrelevant distinction, the courts have upheld this distinction as a matter of law [Roberts, TC Memo 1987—235] .

(1) Interest on Your Home

This is one category of interest that survives tax reform—within limits. In particular, you can deduct interest you pay on a loan secured by your primary home or a second home. The loan can be a traditional first or second mortgage. Or, it can be a home-equity loan taken out to purchase a car or other personal item. As long as the loan is *secured* by your home, it falls into this category. The *second home* need not be an ordinary house, condominium, or cooperative, but can be a mobile home, boat, or other property as long as it contains basic living accommodations, including sleeping space, toilet, and cooking facilities.

There are limits on how much interest you can deduct on loans taken out after October 13, 1987. Generally speaking, the limit on debt used to purchase or construct a home is $1,000,000 and the limit on home-equity debt is $100,000. Details on the rules for loans secured by your home are contained in Section 1 of the *Homeowners* chapter.

Because of the new law, home-equity loans have become the debt of choice for many persons. With a typical home-equity loan arrangement, you can set up a line of credit with a bank or savings institution, secured by your equity in your house. You can then draw upon this line of credit anytime you choose. For example, if you need financing to purchase an auto, you can use a fully deductible home-equity loan. This will be better than a loan taken against the value of the auto, which would generate personal interest, not qualifying for full deduction as discussed below.

Because home-equity loans are better secured, they offer lower interest rates than most any other type of loan—typically 1 1/2% or 2% above the prime lending rate. However, the flip side of this for the borrower is the danger that ownership of his home could be jeopardized if he defaults on the loan. Also, the origination fees for a home-equity loan may offset the savings in taxes and additional interest, especially when the loan amount is on the low side.

(2) Personal Interest

The *personal interest* category includes all interest not falling into any of the 4 other categories discussed in this chapter. Thus, for example, it includes interest on credit cards, auto loans, student loans, late utility or tax payments, etc.

On your 1990 tax return, you may deduct 10% of your total personal interest. The remaining 90% is non-deductible. Starting with 1991 tax returns, the deduction for personal interest will be eliminated altogether. The total of your personal interest is reported on line 12a of Schedule A. You then multiply by 10% to obtain the deduction amount which you enter on line 12b.

Personal interest includes not just the obvious items like interest charges on bank loans and credit card purchases, but also any other payments for the "use" of money. For example, charges for the late payment of a utility bill are a form of personal interest and can be claimed as such. This deduction was missed by eleven out of eleven tax preparers in a survey taken by a New York consumer agency. However, the annual fee which most banks are now charging for credit cards is not deductible because it is considered a service charge rather than a form of interest.

Interest paid on past due Federal or State income taxes is considered *personal interest,* even if there is investment or business income reported on the tax return. However, underpayment *penalties,* such as the penalty for late filing of a tax return or underpayment of estimated tax, are not considered to be interest and yield no deductions. If the government assesses an interest charge, it will usually be listed as such on the notice it sends to you requesting payment.

Note that in order to claim any deduction for interest payments, you must be legally obligated to make the payments. For example, if your child took out a student loan on which you made payments, you get no interest deduction unless you also signed as a co-maker or had a similar legal obligation. This is illustrated by a recent court case. A father made payments totaling about $600 for interest due on his son's student loan and deducted this amount on his own income tax return. But because he was under no legal obligation to repay either the principal or interest on the debt, the Court threw out his deduction [Prendergast, TC Memo 1984-419]. Similarly, if you agreed to make payments on an automobile which your child purchased, then you will not get any interest deduction unless you had liability to pay the loan.

If you borrowed money from a relative, you can claim interest you paid on the loan. However, the loan should be as structured as possible; otherwise the IRS may challenge whether or not a bona fide loan really existed. That's what happened to a taxpayer in a 1984 court case. He borrowed money from his mother and sought to deduct interest payments he made to her on the loan. But there was no note or other documentation proving that a legitimate loan existed. Since he could not prove he had made interest payments on a valid loan, no deduction was allowed [Schiffgens, TC Memo 1984-137]. For further information on loans between relatives, see the *Income-Shifting* chapter].

(3) Interest on Passive Activities

There is a new category of human financial endeavor invented by the drafters of the 1986 Tax Reform Act, called *passive activities.* The *passive activities* category includes investments in limited partnerships or other business enterprises in which neither you nor your spouse participates on a regular, continuous, and substantial basis. It also includes investments in real estate, no matter what the extent or nature of your participation.

There is a limit on the deductibility of *passive interest,* i.e. interest connected with passive activities in which you have invested. This interest (along with other expenses) is fully deductible only against the total income produced by your passive activities.

If a net loss is produced because interest plus other expenses exceeds income, then only 10% of this loss can be deducted on your 1990 tax return. The remainder can be carried over to be deducted in future years when either there are passive profits, or your ownership of the passive activity is disposed of.

There is an exception that applies to rental real estate owned by individuals with Adjusted Gross Income not exceeding $100,000. Losses arising from such activities can be fully deducted up to $25,000, provided the individual is involved in basic decision-making connected with the rental activity. The $25,000 limit is phased out for those with income between $100,000 and $150,000.

Details on these passive activity rules are contained in Section 2 of the *Investing Your Money* chapter.

(4) Trade or Business Interest

You may deduct in full any interest you pay in connection with a trade or business activity (other than as an employee) in which you are a *material participant*. To be a *material participant*, you must perform services on a regular, continuous, and substantial basis.

For example, suppose you have a self-employment consulting practice. You would be able to deduct any interest payments you make in connection with this consulting business. This would include interest on loans for operating capital, mortgage payments on office facilities, etc. You would deduct your interest payments in the usual way as an expense item on Schedule C.

(5) Investment Interest

Income from investments that do not fall into either the *passive activity* or *trade or business* activity categories discussed above are considered to be *investment income*. This would include stock dividends, bond interest, savings account interest, etc. It would also include capital gains on the sale of stocks or bonds.

If you incur debt in order to purchase stocks, bonds, or other investments designed to provide investment income, then the interest you pay on this debt falls into the category of *investment interest* (sometimes called *portfolio interest*). Investment interest is fully deductible only against investment income, not against earnings or passive income. The way this restriction works is this.

You first determine your *net investment income* by subtracting investment losses from investment income. You can get the appropriate income and loss figures from Schedule B, Schedule D, etc. of your tax return.

Next, you total up the interest paid on any loans which were taken out to make purchases designed to produce investment income. If the total investment interest for the year is less than or equal to the total investment income, then you deduct the entire amount of interest you paid on Line 11, *Deductible Investment Interest,* of Schedule A.

If the total investment interest you paid in 1990 exceeds your total investment income, then the difference is your *excess investment interest*. In this case, you add 10% of this excess investment interest plus your total investment income. The resulting sum is deducted on Line 11 of Schedule A. The remaining 90% of excess investment interest is nondeductible on your 1990 tax return, but can be carried over to future years when there is investment income against which it can be deducted.

There is a special Form 4952 for computing your deduction for investment interest. If you have paid interest on loans used for investment purposes, you should fill out this form and attach it to your tax return.

Example 1

Cooke has a margin account with his stockbroker which he uses to purchase stocks and bonds. His 1990 investment income (including dividends, interest, etc.) totals $6,000 and he has a net capital loss for the year of $2,000. He pays $5,000 in interest during 1990 on his margin account.

Cooke's excess investment interest *is computed as follows:*

A.   Investment Interest $5,000

B.   Investment Income $6,000

C.   Less: Investment Losses.............................. -2,000

D.   Net Investment Income (B - C): $4,000

E.   Excess Investment Interest (A - D):..$1,000

Cooke may claim D plus 10% of E, i.e. $4,000 + (10% x $1,000) = $4,100, as an itemized deduction on line 11 of Schedule A. The remaining $800 is carried over to a future year in which there is investment income.

There are several exceptions to the basic rules for larger-scale investors. First, if you are able to deduct passive losses under the phase-in rule described in Section 2 of the *Investing Your Money* chapter, then you must subtract the same amount from your investment income in the computation of your excess investment interest. Second, your deduction for investment interest in 1990 cannot exceed your investment income plus $1,000 ($500 for marrieds filing separately).

Interest to Carry Tax-Free Bonds

There is one type of interest for which no deduction is allowed, even under the phase-out provisions discussed earlier in this chapter. Namely, you cannot deduct interest on a loan where the purpose of the loan is to purchase or carry tax-free municipal bonds.

For example, if you use municipal bonds as collateral for a loan, then interest on the loan would be entirely non-deductible. The same is true if you use the proceeds of a loan to purchase tax-free bonds. In these 2 situations, a direct connection can be made between the loan and the carrying of tax-free bonds.

In more indirect situations, the deductibility of the interest is a judgment call. The question becomes whether or not the *purpose* of the borrowing was to purchase or carry tax-free bonds.

For example, suppose you have 2 brokerage accounts—one a margin account which you use to purchase stocks and the other a cash account which you use to purchase tax-free bonds. The IRS would generally disallow a deduction for interest on the borrowings in the margin account to the extent you could have sold the tax-free bonds instead of borrowing to purchase the stocks [IRS Private Letter Ruling 8637061].

The situation is different for ordinary personal loans such as auto loans, credit card balances, student loans, and mortgages on personal residences. The carrying of tax-free bonds will not generally affect the deductibility of interest on these loans. The personal purpose of taking out such a loan predominates over the investment purpose of holding tax-free securities.

The above applies to the question of deductibility of interest you *pay* on loans you have taken out. No matter what the situation, you do not pay federal income tax on the interest you *receive* on tax-free municipal bonds.

While there are restrictions on borrowing to purchase or carry *tax-exempt* investments as described above, the same is not necessarily true for certain *tax-deferred* investments. For example, if you borrow money to contribute to an IRA or Keogh Plan, the IRS has informally stated that interest on such a borrowing would be *investment interest,* deductible against taxable investment earnings outside the IRA or Keogh Plan. However, the same restriction on borrowing to purchase tax-exempt investments applies to the purchase of single-premium insurance policies or annuities from insurance companies.

Allocation of Interest

As discussed above, the tax treatment of interest you paid during the year depends upon which of the 5 categories the interest falls into. According to the IRS, it is the use of the loan proceeds that determines into which category the interest is placed.

For example, suppose you borrow $10,000 from a bank, putting up stocks you own as collateral. You use the $10,000 to purchase an automobile for personal purposes. In this case, the interest paid on the loan falls into the *personal interest* category. Putting up your stocks as security did not cause the interest to fall into the investment interest category. Conversely, if you take out a personal loan and invest the proceeds, interest paid on the loan is *investment interest.* The *use* of the funds you borrowed, not the *security* for the loan, is what counts.

Exceptions

First, interest on loans secured by your primary home or a second home is fully deductible within certain basic limits. In this case, the use to which the loan is put does not matter [cf. Section 1 of the *Homeowners* chapter].

A second exception applies if you take out a loan and wait for a period of time before spending the money. Until you write the first check on the account into which you deposited the loan, the interest you pay on the loan is considered *investment interest.* For example, suppose you deposit an $8,000 loan into a checking account on February 1. The first check you write after February 1 on this account is on May 1 for $8,000 to purchase a personal auto. The interest paid on the loan from February 1 to May 1 is considered *investment interest,* fully deductible against investment income. After May 1, the interest becomes *personal interest,* only 10%-deductible on your 1990 tax return.

Tracing the Proceeds of the Loan

As described above, the category to which interest belongs depends on the use to which the borrowed money is put. This involves "tracing" the loan from the time it is received by you until the time it is put to use.

There are 3 basic ways you can control the linkage between a loan and an expenditure for purposes of placing interest into the category you want. First, you can make the purchase with the loan check, appropriately endorsed. Second, you can set up a new account into which only the loan is deposited. Or third, you can satisfy the 30-day rule discussed below by spending the proceeds of the loan for its intended purpose within 30 days of receipt.

For example, suppose you receive the loan in a check which you endorse over to another party from whom you are buying an interest in a passive activity. Or, suppose you open up a bank account into which only the loan proceeds are deposited and later, you write a check on this account to buy into a passive activity. In either case, you have a direct tracing of funds from the time of the loan to the time of purchase. Any interest on the loan belongs to the *passive interest* category.

There are rules which handle more complicated situations when there is more intermingling of funds from various sources. In this situation, you should seek accounting assistance to make the proper allocations. In general, what happens is that the loan proceeds deposited in your bank account are considered to be spent in the order you write checks [cf. Example 5], unless the 30-day rule, discussed below, can be applied.

30-Day Rule

You do not need to have a direct trace like the ones in the preceding two paragraphs. Instead, you can take advantage of the *30-day rule*.

Under the *30-day rule,* if you deposit the loan proceeds into your regular bank account, then you can make a direct connection between the loan and any expenditure made within 30 days before or 30 days after the date of deposit. The expenditure need not be made from the same bank account, but can be made with a check drawn on a different account or with cash. (The date on a check is generally considered to be the date of the expenditure, as long as an unreasonable amount of time has not elapsed between the date on the check and the date the check cleared.)

Example 2

You borrow $5,000 from a bank on September 3, which you deposit into your regular checking account. On September 26, you write a $5,000 check on this account to purchase U.S. Savings Bonds. In the meantime, you have made a number of deposits into and withdrawals from the account.

Under the *30-day rule* , you are allowed to make a direct connection between the loan and the investment in Savings Bonds. Thus, interest on the loan can be placed into the *investment interest* category.

Example 3

Same as in Example 2, except that the purchase of the Savings Bonds was made on August 10 with a check drawn on a different bank account than the one into which *the loan proceeds were deposited on September 3.*

In this case, the 30-day rule applies the same as in Example 2, even though the purchase was made prior to the loan out of a different checking account than the one used to receive the loan proceeds. Thus, the interest on the loan can be placed into the investment interest category.

Example 4

Same as in the preceding example, except that only $4,000 is used to purchase Savings Bonds. The remaining $1,000 is spent on personal items.

In this case, only $4,000 of the $5,000 loan is linked to the investment. Thus 4/5 ($4,000/$5,000) of interest payments on the loan falls into the investment interest category. The remainder is personal interest.

If the 30-day rule is not applied, then loan proceeds deposited in your bank account are considered to be spent in the order you write checks.

Example 5

There is $3,000 in your checking account. On September 3, you borrow $5,000 and deposit the funds into this checking account. On September 10, you purchase $2,000 worth of furniture. On October 25, you purchase $4,000 in U.S. Savings Bonds. These are the only transactions in your checking account during this period.

The 30-day rule does not apply to the October 25 purchase. Therefore, the $5,000 loan is considered spent $2,000 for furniture, with the remaining $3,000 spent towards the Savings Bond purchase. Thus, 2/5 ($2,000/$5,000) of interest payments on the loan constitute personal interest, with the remaining 3/5 investment interest toward the purchase of the Savings Bonds.

The above tracing rules are considerably relaxed in the case of amounts used to purchase, construct, or improve a personal residence. Details are contained in Section 1 of the *Homeowners* chapter.

How You Should Handle Future Loans

The following describes a number of steps you can take to arrange that your borrowings become deductible to the fullest extent permitted under the law.

1. Keep separate accounts for personal, business, and investment activities. Although this might entail some extra fees, this is the most surefooted way to allocate borrowings to deductible categories. For example, if you place borrowed money into your "investment account" from which all your investments are purchased, interest on the borrowings can be deductible as investment interest no matter what the timing of your borrowings and purchases.

2. If you don't maintain separate bank accounts, make sure debts incurred for investment can be connected to the investment by **observing the 30-day rule** described earlier in this chapter. Another way to make the connection is to receive the borrowings in the form of a check made out directly to your stockbroker.

3. Take out a home-equity loan and use the proceeds to pay off your auto loans, student loans, credit card balances, etc. This can convert personal interest into fully deductible home-equity interest.

4. If you purchase a home, **establish a home-equity credit line at the same time you take out a first mortgage loan** from a bank. The bank may waive its usual fees for appraisal and other services that would just duplicate services required for the first mortgage. That way, you have a low cost source of tax-deductible borrowing for your future needs.

5. Pay any interest you owe before yearend. This will not only accelerate a deduction to an earlier year, but will let you make the best of the phase-out rules as well. For example, personal interest is 10%-deductible if paid by December 31, 1990 but is not deductible at all after this date. Note that the date appearing on your check is what determines the year of payment (unless the IRS should notice an unusually long period of time between the date on the check and the date it was cashed).

6. If you purchase a new home, t**ake out the largest mortgage for which you qualify.** This initial mortgage fixes the amout of debt qualifying as fully-deductible *home acquisition debt.* Further amounts that are borrowed against your home cut into the $100,000 *home-equity debt* ceiling, unless used to substantially improve the home. While this ceiling may seem more than adequate now, who knows what future inflation in auto prices, college tuition for your children, etc. may bring.

Even if you don't need the full amount borrowed at the time of purchase it may still be worthwhile to borrow the maximum in the event of future needs. In the meantime, you can probably invest the unneeded funds, say, in a tax-free bond fund, offsetting the extra cost of the borrowed funds, after considering the tax deduction this provides. Of course, you must be willing to experience the uncertainty of favorable or unfavorable price changes in the bond fund as interest rates vary [cf. Section 5 of the *Investing Your Money* chapter].

7. Generate investment income to cover investment interest. If you have borrowed to purchase stocks or other investments, your interest is deductible as long as you have sufficient investment income, as discussed earlier in this section. It may pay to sell securities producing a capital gain or shift some investments to interest-paying taxable bonds in order to generate enough investment income to qualify your investment interest for full deduction.

8. If your employer permits you to **borrow from your retirement plan,** then you may be able to get a full deduction on the interest, even if the loan proceeds are used for personal purposes. The trick is to provide your home as additional collateral on the loan. Since the assets in your retirement plan will generally be more than enough to cover the loan you're permitted to take, there should be no additional home appraisal or other fees required. Although your employer would tap your retirement assets to cover any loan defaults, the fact that the loan is additionally "secured" by your home should establish it as fully-deductible home-equity debt. (In the case of 401(k) deferred compensation plans on tax-sheltered annuity plans [cf. the *Tax-Sheltered Plans* chapter], for the interest to be deductible, the loan should not also be secured by elective contributions made to the plan. Also, there are restrictions that apply to owners, officers, or certain other *key employees*.)

9. If you have borrowed all you can on your personal residence, **borrow additional amounts against any rental property you own.** The interest can be fully deductible as passive interest if you fall within the $25,000 exemption discussed earlier in this chapter. And, even if you don't satisfy the exemption, disallowed passive interest, unlike personal interest, can still be carried over to be deducted in future years.

10. If you own stocks or other securities, **use margin loans to make purchases.** However, you can't simply borrow against your stocks to make a personal purchase of, say, a $15,000 auto. If you do, the interest would be *personal interest* because it is the *use* to which the funds are put that determines the category of interest. But, under the law as currently written, this is how you can proceed instead.

First, sell $15,000 worth of stock and use the money to buy the auto. Then, using a margin account with your broker, repurchase the stock with funds borrowed from your broker. Interest on the margin account then becomes investment interest because the funds were used to purchase the stock.

Of course, you must take into account capital gains tax and commissions to see if this maneuver makes economic sense. Your stockbroker will be more than willing to expedite this type of transaction for obvious commercial reasons. Some even have set up special arrangements to promote this strategy. Note that the interest rate on a margin loan is probably lower than the rate on any other type of loan available to you.

Chapter 6

Medical Expenses

Schedule A includes a deduction for medical expenses that you pay for yourself, your spouse, and your dependents. This includes doctor bills, transportation, medical insurance, medical devices, etc., plus the cost of prescription medicine and insulin. You cannot deduct non-prescription medicine such as aspirin, laxatives, etc.

From your total of medical expenses, you subtract 7.5% of your Adjusted Gross Income (AGI) to arrive at your medical deduction. Schedule A leads you through the appropriate computation.

Getting Around the 7.5% of AGI Limitation

For most taxpayers, the 7.5% of AGI limitation severely restricts their medical deduction.

Here are some strategies for coping with this limitation:

1. Bunch your medical expenses into a single year.

To take a simple example, say your Adjusted Gross Income is $40,000 in each of 2 successive years, and that your family's medical expenses over this 2-year period amount to $6,000. If these expenses are spread evenly, $3,000 in each year, you lose out on any medical deduction. The medical deduction floor (7.5% × $40,000 = $3,000) wipes out the deduction in each year.

However, if expenses are shifted from one year to the other, you get a deduction. For example, if the $6,000 expenses are split up with $3,600 in the first year and $2,400 in the second, you wind up with a $600 medical deduction in the first year.

Certain elective procedures can be timed so they bunch up in one year. For example, if your family members go to the eye doctor every other year and typically need new eyeglasses, synchronize the appointments so they all occur in the same year. Similarly, non-critical elective surgery can be timed appropriately. This may be especially beneficial in the case of elective dental procedures, e.g. the pulling of wisdom teeth, because the typical medical insurance policy does not cover dental expenses.

You may also be able to arrange for a doctor or dentist to bill you all at once for work done over a period of time. For example, if your child needs $2,500 worth of orthodontia work over a 2 or 3 year period, you might be better off if you're billed for the entire amount up front rather than spreading it out over the period the work is done. However, you can't simply voluntarily pay in advance. To get a deduction, you must actually incur the financial obligation by the year you make the payment. In this example, the orthodontist would be only too happy to send you a bill showing the entire amount due in advance, and may even give you a discount for early payment.

2. Set up a medical plan under which all expenses become deductible.

This is the best idea of all because the 7.5% of AGI subtraction is totally eliminated. However, this works only if you or your spouse has income from a self-employment activity (e.g. writing, consulting, editing, reviewing, tutoring, etc.). A full deduction can be achieved by incorporating the self-employment activity and setting up a corporate medical plan to pay all expenses. Or, more simply, an individual can "employ his spouse in the business" and set up a plan which pays all the medical expenses of his spouse's family (including himself). Under either arrangement, a business deduction is obtained for the full amount of the family's medical expenses with no initial 7.5% of AGI subtraction. Also, a self-employed person might be able to set up a medical plan, without employing his spouse, which covers 25% of the cost of medical insurance for his family. [Cf. Section 2 of the *Outside Business Activity* chapter for further details.]

3. Claim medical items as a business expense.

If you can't claim a medical deduction because of the 7.5% of AGI limitation, perhaps you can claim a medical item as a business expense. For example, suppose you need special eyeglasses which you use only at work. You might be able to claim the cost of such an item as a job-related *miscellaneous deduction* rather than as a *medical deduction*.

4. Pay attention to the rules covering divorced couples.

Divorced couples should take note of the rule concerning the deduction for their children's medical expenses. Now, either spouse may claim medical expenses which he actually pays for his children. It makes no difference that the other ex-spouse may have custody of the children or that the ex-spouse is claiming dependency exemptions for them.

Because of this rule, it may be better to give an ex-spouse money to pay for your children's medical expenses rather than pay the expenses directly. This situation can occur when your total expenses do not exceed the 7.5% of AGI floor. Further details are given in the *Divorce and Separation* chapter.

Deductible Medical Expenses

(A) Doctors, Dentists, etc.

You can deduct for doctors, dentists, optometrists, chiropractors, osteopaths, podiatrists, psychiatrists, psychologists, physical therapists, and acupuncturists. The medical expense deduction also includes nursing services for a sick or disabled individual, but not for a healthy baby. The services need not be rendered by a professional nurse in order to be deductible.

(B) Medical Insurance

Deductible medical insurance includes hospital and health insurance whether paid directly by you or withheld from your paychecks. It does not include life insurance or disability insurance except for those portions specifically designated as covering medical expenses.

(C) Medical Aids and Devices

Hearing aids, dentures, eyeglasses, crutches, wheelchairs, orthopedic shoes, elastic stockings, etc. are deductible medical expenses. The IRS has also ruled that if one foot is smaller than the other because of a medical condition, the extra cost of buying 2 pairs of shoes instead of one is deductible. [IRS Private Letter Ruling 8221118]

(D) Birth Control Pills, Legal Abortions, and Vasectomies

The IRS has ruled that these items are deductible medical expenses. A deduction is also generally allowed for other birth control items when prescribed by a doctor.

(E) Medical Charge Portion of School Tuition, Retirement Home Fees, etc.

Many colleges and private schools include a charge for medical expenses as part of their tuition or fees. This is deductible, provided that the tuition bill or other statement from the school indicates the amount which is attributable to such medical fees. You should ask the school to provide you with such a statement if they do not do it automatically.

Similarly, payments to a retirement home might include a fee for health care. This fee is deductible in the year paid, even if payment is made in advance for life-time health care. If a refund is received in a later year, say because the individual leaves the retirement home, such a refund would then be includable in taxable income. [Rev. Rul. 75-302]

The IRS recently took a liberal position on how to figure the amount to be considered a health care fee in a ruling issued to a representative of a retirement community. The retirement community provided life care to its residents in return for a one-time admission fee plus a monthly service charge. This life care included access to a 31-bed medical center that was part of the facility.

The IRS ruled that the portion of the fees allocable to medically-related expenses was deductible at the time the fees were paid. In this connection, medical-related expenses included not only salaries of medical personnel and the cost of medicine plus supplies, but also *"expenses allocable to the medical facility such as housekeeping, maintenance and utilities, a proportionate share of interest on indebtedness, real estate taxes, insurance, and depreciation."* The IRS also stated that it would be appropriate to make the allocation of fees by using the financial history of a comparable facility. [IRS Private Letter Ruling 8630005] .

On the other hand, the *entire cost* of nursing home or other institutional care for an individual who requires continual medical care is a deductible medical expense. IRS regulations specify, as an example, that *"medical care includes the entire cost of institutional care for a person who is mentally ill and unsafe when left alone"* [IRS Reg 1.213-1(e)(1)(v)(a)]. Presumably, the same would apply to nursing home care for a victim of, say, Alzheimer's disease who requires continual medical care for the treatment of this disease. A doctor's statement that the nursing home care is required for the person to receive proper medical care would be helpful in protecting the deduction from challenge.

(F) Drugs and Medicine

You **can deduct** the cost of prescription medicine and insulin which you purchased. You **cannot deduct** the cost of non-prescription medicines such as aspirin, laxatives, etc. as you were once permitted to do. Even if your doctor recommends an over-the-counter drug, it is not deductible if it does not actually require a prescription to obtain.

(G) Medical Expenses of Non-Dependents

If you satisfy all the requirements of claiming a dependency for a qualifying relative, except that the relative earned more than $2,050, you may still claim a deduction for medical expenses. For example, if you furnish more than 1/2 the support for a parent, then you can deduct medical expenses which you pay on his or her behalf. This is the case even though your parent's earnings may disqualify him or her from being your dependent.

To obtain the deduction, payments must be made out of your own funds. However, it is permissible for, say, a parent to give money to a child who then pays medical expenses for the parent, thereby obtaining the deduction. This is illustrated by a recent court case in which an individual paid the medical bills of his mother out of funds she had given to him. A Court of Appeals ruled that he was entitled to the deduction because the payments were made from funds which belonged to him at the time. However, it should be clear that funds are actually given to the one making the medical payments. In this case, it was necessary to go all the way to a Court of Appeals to win the deduction. The mother had just given her son a power of attorney over her funds instead of an outright gift. The Court had to sift through State law to determine that this constituted a valid no-strings-attached gift of the funds to her son. [Ruch, 52 AFTR 2d 83-6207]

When you pay the medical expenses of a parent or other individual, be sure to make the payments directly. If you just give money to a parent who uses it to pay medical expenses, you lose the deduction.

(H) Travel

You can deduct your transportation expenses incurred in connection with obtaining medical services. Thus, you can deduct your transportation costs to and from the doctor, dentist, optician, etc. You can also deduct transportation costs to and from the drug store if you are going there in order to pick up medicine. If you use your automobile, you may deduct your actual operating expenses (such as gas, oil, tolls, and parking but not depreciation or insurance) or deduct 9 cents per mile. Medical travel can include more than just the usual trips to the doctor, dentist, or drug store. For example, the following have been ruled deductible: trips to attend meetings of Alcoholics Anonymous and trips to a swimming pool by a boy suffering from rheumatoid arthritis.

According to a recent IRS ruling, there are 2 other items you can deduct in addition to the 9 cents per mile or actual operating expenses. Namely, you can deduct a pro rata portion of taxes and interest you pay on the automobile [Rev Proc 89-66]. For example, if 15% of your annual mileage is for medical purposes, you can claim 15% of the interest and taxes as a medical deduction. However the interest amount is further reduced by the 90% factor that applies to personal interest on 1990 tax returns [cf. the *Interest* chapter].

According to two IRS rulings, transportation costs for relatives of the person receiving medical treatment are deductible when these are necessary. One ruling allowed a wife to deduct her costs in accompanying her wheelchair-confined husband to an out-of-town location to receive treatment [IRS Private Letter Ruling 7928088]. Another ruling permitted parents to deduct the cost of attending consultations at a psychiatric hospital concerning their son who was a patient there [IRS Private Letter Ruling 7931059]. However the cost of ordinary family visits to a patient in a hospital is not deductible.

If an individual travels out of town to obtain outpatient medical care at a licensed hospital or similar institution, up to $50 per day of lodging expenses (but not meals) are deductible. A separate $50 limit applies to someone who is needed to accompany the patient. For example, a parent accompanying a child could deduct up to an additional $50 per day for his lodging expenses. To obtain this lodging deduction, there can be no significant element of personal pleasure, recreation, or vacation in the away-from-home travel.

(I) Childbirth Classes

Most couples now take "childbirth classes" prior to the birth of a child. A 1989 IRS Private Letter Ruling indicates the tax status of tuition paid for these classes. Costs allocable to preparing the mother for the childbirth itself are deductible. This would include Lamaze techniques, labor and delivery procedures, birthing positions, etc. Not deductible would be instruction in feeding and newborn care, general study of prebirth developmental stages, adjusting to becoming a parent, etc. When both types of instruction are included, you are supposed to make an allocation between deductible and nondeductible items based on the number of hours devoted to each type of instruction.

Usually, the fee (if any) will cover attendance of both the prospective mother and father (or coach). In this case, the IRS asserts that only the cost of the mother is deductible (even if the father chooses not to attend). Thus, for example, if the cost of such childbirth instruction is $100, only $50 of this cost allocable to the mother would qualify for deduction. [IRS Private Letter Ruling 8919009]

(J) Special Diet

If your doctor orders you to go on a special diet, then you can deduct the excess of what the special food costs over what regular food would cost. For example, the extra cost of special food for an individual on an ulcer diet can be deducted. Also, whiskey taken for the relief of angina pains can be deducted when recommended by a doctor's prescription. [Rev. Rul. 55-261]

Two court cases illustrate the deduction for special foods. In the first case, a couple had to eat organic food because they were allergic to regular chemically-treated food. They were permitted to deduct half the cost of their food as a medical deduction. The couple used Labor Department statistics for their area to establish the extra cost of food purchased in health stores. [Randolf, 67 TC No. 35]

The second case involved an individual who was placed on a high protein diet by her doctor. She kept records of what she spent for food, compared the total with that spent by a friend, and deducted the difference. The Court allowed her a deduction for 30% of her total grocery bill as the excess amount due to her special diet. [Von Kalb, TC Memo 1978-366]

(K) Special Equipment (Including Air Conditioning)

Under doctor's orders, you might need special equipment in your house to take care of an existing medical condition or disease. This equipment can qualify for a medical deduction. For example, the IRS has ruled that the cost of a special mattress and plywood bed boards was deductible when recommended for the relief of an arthritic condition. Another IRS ruling was issued to a family with a son suffering from allergies. Upon prescription from the son's allergist, the following items were all ruled deductible: air conditioning for the home and automobile, electrostatic air cleaner, and humidifier [IRS Private Letter Ruling 8009080] . And in a 1981 case, the Tax Court allowed a deduction for health spa equipment added to the home of a Las Vegas casino dealer as a result of a doctor's advice that it would help relieve the pain of severe arthritis suffered by his wife [Keen, TC Memo 1981-313]. However, in another ruling, the IRS stated that exercise equipment could not be deducted when prescribed in order to prevent possible future heart disease, rather than to treat an existing medical condition. [IRS Private Letter Ruling 8019025]

Under special circumstances, the cost of installing a swimming pool can qualify as a medical deduction. For example, the IRS ruled in 1983 that an individual with severe osteoarthritis could deduct the cost of constructing an indoor pool in his house when his doctor prescribed a treatment of swimming several times a day [Rev Rul 83-83]. Of course, the IRS will be quite skeptical when it is claimed that the construction of a pool is primarily for medical purposes rather than for personal purposes. In the above ruling, the IRS was influenced by the fact that the pool was only 8 feet wide by 36 feet long and no deeper than 5 feet—designed for lap swimming rather than general recreational use. However, the pool need not be specially designed to warrant a deduction if all the facts and circumstances point to medical rather than personal reasons for use of the pool. [Cherry, TC Memo 1983-470]

When deducting medical equipment, you must first subtract any increase in value which the equipment adds to your house. For example, if you purchase central air conditioning for $3,000 and this adds $2,000 to the value of your house, then you can only deduct the difference, $3,000 − $2,000 = $1,000. This $1,000 is deducted in the year of purchase, not depreciated over its useful life. However, you are entitled to a full deduction for equipment added to a rented house or for portable equipment such as a room air conditioner. In any event, you can deduct the full cost of servicing and operating the equipment, e.g. electricity, repairs, service contract, etc. Note that the IRS can be tough about allowing deductions for medical equipment. You may need an appraiser's report on how much the equipment added to the value of your house. In the absence of such a report, the IRS can throw out the deduction altogether. For example, in one case, a court disallowed the full $4,000 cost of air conditioning because of the failure to get an appraiser's report. [Wallace v. U.S., 309 F. Supp. 748]

(L) Special Schooling

According to IRS Regulations, medical expenses include
"the cost of attending a special school for a mentally or physically handicapped individual, if his condition is such that the resources of the institution for alleviating such mental or physical handicap are a principal reason for his presence there. In such a case, the cost of attending such a special school will include the cost of meals and lodging, if supplied, and the cost of ordinary education furnished which is incidental to the special services furnished by the school. Thus, the cost of medical care includes the cost of attending a special school designed to compensate for or overcome a physical handicap, in order to qualify the individual for future normal education or for normal living, such as a school for the teaching of braille or lip reading. Similarly, the cost of care and supervision, or of treatment and training, of a mentally retarded or physically handicapped individual at an institution is within the meaning of the term 'medical care.'
"Where an individual is in an institution, and his condition is such that the availability of medical care in such institution is not a principal reason for his presence there, only that part of the cost of care in the institution as is attributable to medical care. . .shall be considered as a cost of medical care; meals and lodging at the institution in such a case are not considered a cost of medical care for purposes of this section."

The above regulations are illustrated by a 1984 Private IRS Ruling. This ruling allowed parents to deduct the full cost of private schooling for their daughter with a learning disability. The school was a special school attended only by children with learning disabilities. The ruling stated that the parents could deduct not only the full tuition, but also transportation to and from the school *"to the extent such transportation expenses are primarily for and essential to the medical care"* of the daughter. Presumably, this means they were allowed to deduct 9 cents per mile (or alternate actual costs as described in the *Automobile Expenses* chapter) for each day's commute to and from school. [IRS Private Letter Ruling 8401024]

In contrast, 2 other court cases have dealt with learning disabled children who attended schools which enrolled regular students, but had a separate program to aid the learning disabled. In both these cases, the extra cost of the special program was deductible, but not the regular tuition [TC Memo 1979-499, 76 TC No. 32]. But in another case, the Court allowed no deduction for the cost of a private school attended by a boy with a learning disability. The boy was sent to the school because he would benefit by the highly structured environment and the personal treatment afforded by a 4-1 student-faculty ratio. But since the school had no special program geared to the learning-disabled, the cost was non-deductible. [TC Memo 1980-572]

(M) Weight Reduction Programs and Health Spas

The IRS has ruled that a taxpayer can't deduct the cost of a weight reduction program if the purpose of the program is to improve the general health and well being of the participant. Similarly, membership in a health spa cannot be deducted (contrary to what those selling memberships may tell you) if you join just to lose weight or keep fit, rather than to combat a specific medical condition.

However, if a weight reduction program is part of the treatment of a specific medical condition or disease then it can be deducted. This was the conclusion of the IRS in a ruling issued to an individual suffering from hypertension and hearing problems. Since her doctors had recommended the weight reduction program for the alleviation of specific illnesses, the cost was deductible as a medical expense. [IRS Private Letter Ruling 8004111]

Similarly, the IRS recently allowed an individual to deduct the cost of participating in an intensive 13-day special exercise and diet program. The individual was advised to participate in the program as part of treatment for his hypertension and arteriosclerosis. [IRS Private Letter Ruling 8251045]

An IRS ruling permitted a deduction for the cost of swimming recommended by a doctor for a child who suffered from rheumatoid arthritis. This included the cost of a membership fee to use the pool plus the cost of transportation to and from the pool [IRS Private Letter Ruling 8326095]. However, the cost of swimming to maintain general health or fitness would not be deductible.

(N) Aids to the Handicapped

Individuals suffering from handicaps can claim medical deductions for expenses incurred in dealing with their handicap. For example, a blind child was permitted to deduct the cost of braille books in excess of the cost of regular editions. Similarly, the salary paid to an individual to accompany a blind child throughout the school day was ruled deductible. [Rev. Rul. 64-173]

Some recent private letter rulings indicate that the IRS will allow a wide variety of items if they are designed to aid the handicapped. For example, the cost of installing a liftgate in a van for an individual confined to a wheelchair is deductible [IRS Private Letter Ruling 8034084]. Similarly, the IRS ruled that an adapter for closed captioning of television programs could be deducted by a hearing-impaired individual [IRS Private Letter Ruling 8112030]. And in a third ruling, the IRS allowed a hearing-impaired individual to deduct the cost of maintaining a cat because the cat was trained *"to respond to unusual sounds in an instantaneous and directional manner."* [IRS Private Letter Ruling 8033038]

Expenses incurred by a handicapped person for removing structural barriers in his residence are fully deductible. These are not considered to increase the fair market value of the residence. According to a recent IRS ruling, this includes constructing entrance ramps, widening doorways or hallways to accommodate a wheelchair, making bathroom modifications, lowering kitchen cabinets, adjusting electric outlets or fixtures, modifying smoke alarms, changing door hardware, modifying entranceways and grading of ground to provide access to the residence, etc. [Rev. Rul. 87-106, IRB 1987-43, 13]

(O) Cosmetic Procedures

According to an IRS ruling, procedures which are undertaken for cosmetic rather than medical purposes are still deductible as medical expenses if they affect the *structure or function of the body*. For example, face lifts and hair transplants performed by doctors would qualify. Similarly, hair removal through electrolysis is deductible (even when performed by a technician rather than a doctor). Starting in 1991, cosmetic surgery or other procedures will not be deductible unless necessary to ameliorate a deformity arising from a congenital abnormality, a personal injury resulting from an accident or trauma, or disfiguring disease.

(P) Alcoholics Anonymous Meetings

The cost of attending meetings of Alcoholics Anonymous, pursuant to competent medical advice, is deductible. This includes the cost of transportation to and from the meetings [Rev. Rul. 63-273]. The cost of attending meetings of other similar rehabilitative organizations would also be deductible.

(Q) Disability Income

You might receive payments from your employer while sick or temporarily disabled. These payments are fully taxable even if made under a special sick pay plan. However, worker's compensation is tax exempt.

If you are permanently disabled, you may be able to exclude disability payments made from a plan to the extent you contributed to the plan. In addition there is a tax credit, computed on Form 2440, which may exclude a portion of employer-provided permanent disability payments from tax.

(R) Non-Traditional Medical Treatment

According to a 1986 court case, to be deductible, *"payments for medical care are not limited strictly to traditional medical procedures, but include payments made 'for the purpose of affecting any structure or function of the body'.... This broad view of medical care leads to the allowance of medical expense deductions for 'nontraditional' medical care"* [TC Memo 1986-138] . In accord with this policy, deductions have been allowed for holistic medical care, Navajo Indian healing ceremonies, acupuncture, etc.

Chapter 7

Charitable Contributions

You **can deduct** contributions you make to the following nonprofit agencies:

1. **Religious Organizations.** This includes annual dues, seat charges, and assessments as well as ordinary contributions.

2. **Charitable Organizations.** Examples include the Heart Fund, Salvation Army, YMCA, Travelers Aid Society, etc.

3. **Governmental Bodies** where the contribution is for some public purpose such as education, public works, civil defense, etc.

4. **Educational Organizations.** This includes colleges, universities, research organizations, etc.

5. **Civic Organizations** such as non-profit hospitals, veterans organizations (e.g. American Legion, VFW, DAV), youth organizations (e.g. Boy Scouts, Girl Scouts), volunteer fire departments, organizations to support the Olympic games and other athletic competitions, and societies for the prevention of cruelty to animals.

6. The cost of **benefit tickets** sold by charitable organizations. If these tickets are for some commercial production such as a play or concert, then you can deduct only the excess of the price of your tickets over the regular admission price. Similarly, you can deduct the excess cost of purchasing items from a charity (e.g. Christmas cards over value received). The IRS is now urging charities to state how much of the cost of a ticket or other item represents a charitable contribution, and how much represents the regular price.

7. **Contributions Required to Purchase College Athletic Tickets.** At some colleges and universities, if a person makes a specified contribution to the school or tax-exempt fund run by the school, then this qualifies the person to purchase tickets to an athletic event held in the school's facilities. Since the contribution yielded a *benefit* to the contributor (namely the right to purchase athletic tickets), it cannot be fully deducted. Instead, 80% of the specified contribution needed to qualify for the ticket-purchasing privilege can be claimed as a charitable deduction. The remaining 20% is non-deductible. (This 80%-Rule applies whether or

not the tickets are readily available for purchase by non-contributors.) No deduction is allowed for the actual cost of the tickets.

8. **Exchange Students.** The cost of maintaining an elementary or high school student (other than a dependent or relative) in your home under a program sponsored by a charity. This deduction is limited to $50 per month.

You **cannot deduct** as charitable contributions:

1. Contributions to foreign charities except as provided otherwise in treaties. However, contributions to domestic charities which distribute funds abroad are deductible.

2. Contributions to organizations which devote a substantial portion of their time in attempting to influence legislation.

3. Contributions to political organizations and candidates.

4. Contributions to homeowners associations.

5. Donations which give you a direct benefit such as tuition to a church-related school.

6. Contributions to civic leagues, social and sports clubs, labor unions, and chambers of commerce.

7. Contributions to fraternal groups except when the contribution is to be used only for charitable or other qualifying purpose.

8. The cost of raffle tickets, even if a majority of the proceeds goes to charity.

If in doubt, you can simply ask the organization in question whether they qualify for tax-free status. In questionable cases, they will probably already have received a ruling from the IRS.

Where Do You Deduct Charitable Expenses?

Charitable expenses are claimed as an itemized deduction on line 14 of Schedule A for donations of money or line 15 for donations of property. Only those who itemize their deductions can deduct their charitable contributions.

New IRS rules have made it easier to tell when a contribution will be deductible on your tax return. When tax-exempt organizations solicit you for contributions by mail, phone, TV, or radio, they must inform you in a *conspicuous and easily recognizable format* if the contributions do **not** qualify as a charitable deduction. This applies to social welfare organizations, labor unions, trade associations, social clubs, and political organizations with annual gross receipts exceeding $100,000. Thus, if you do not receive a disclaimer from such an organization, it is almost guaranteed that your donation will be tax-deductible.

New Rules for Small Items Purchased from a Charity

If you receive an item from a charity as a result of a donation you made, then you are not supposed to deduct the full amount you donated. Instead, you must subtract the market value of the item.

However, there is an exception if the value of the item is "insubstantial." In such a case, the full donation can be deducted. The IRS specified 2 rules in a 1990 ruling under which items are automatically considered to be "insubstantial.

The First Rule states that an item is considered insubstantial if its fair market value is less than 2% of the amount contributed. This rule applies to contributions up to $2,500.

The Second Rule applies when a 1990 contribution exceeds $27.25 and the only benefits received in connection with the contribution are token items (bookmarks, calendars, key chains, mugs, posters, tee shirts, etc.) bearing the charity's name or logo. In this case, if the cost to the charity of the items received is less than $5.46, then the item is considered insubstantial.

In the above rules, newsletters or program guides that are not available to the public generally are ignored unless they contain advertising or they pay for articles.

In practice, it is the charity's duty to determine if either of the above rules apply. They are supposed to inform you if any portion of a contribution you made is not deductible.

Donation of Services

You **cannot** deduct the value of services you perform for a charitable or other organization nor can you deduct for the cost or rent of property or equipment you allow a charity to use. You **can** deduct for telephone calls, materials, supplies, and the cost of operating equipment. You can also deduct the cost of ingredients or materials that go into something you donate, e.g. food cooked for a church supper. Similarly, you can deduct the cost of buying and maintaining special clothing such as choir robes or scout leader uniforms.

You can also deduct your travel costs. This includes the cost of commuting to and from the charity. It also includes expenses incurred in attending a convention of a qualified charitable organization, provided that you attend as an official delegate. (Meal expenses connected with attendance at such a convention are subject to the same 80%-rule described in Section 1 of the *Travel* chapter; that is, only 80% of the cost of such meals can be claimed as part of your charitable deduction.)

In order for travel expenses to be claimed as a charitable deduction, there must be no significant element of personal pleasure, recreation, or vacation in the travel.

The tax-writing committee of Congress described this requirement as follows:

"In determining whether travel away from home involves a significant element of personal pleasure, recreation, or vacation, the fact that a taxpayer enjoys providing services to the charitable organization will not lead to denial of the deduction. For example, a troop leader for a tax-exempt youth group who takes children belonging to the group on a camping trip may qualify for a charitable deduction *with respect to his or her own travel expenses if he or she is on duty in a genuine and substantial sense throughout the trip, even if he or she enjoys the trip or enjoys supervising children. By contrast, a taxpayer who only has nominal duties relating to the performance of services for the charity, or who for significant portions of the trip is not required to render services, is not allowed any charitable deduction for travel costs.'*

Further examples were given in a 1987 IRS notice:

"For example, a taxpayer who sails from one Caribbean Island to another and spends eight hours a day counting whales and other forms of marine life as part of a project sponsored by a charitable organization generally will not be permitted a charitable deduction. By way of further example, a taxpayer who works on an archaeological excavation sponsored by a charitable organization for several hours each morning, with the rest of the day free for recreation and sightseeing, will not be allowed a deduction even if the taxpayer works very hard during those few hours. In contrast, a member of a local chapter of a charitable organization who travels to New York City and spends an entire day attending the organization's regional meeting will not be subject to this provision even if he or she attends the theatre in the evening. This provision applies whether the travel expenses are paid directly by the taxpayer or by some indirect means such as by contribution to the charitable organization that pays for the taxpayer's travel expenses." [Notice 87-23, IRB 1987-9,6]

If your **automobile** is used, you can either deduct 12 cents per mile or compute your actual cost of operating the automobile, including gas and oil, but not insurance, depreciation, or general repairs such as tune-ups, lubrication, etc. With either method, you can deduct parking and tolls in addition.

According to a recent IRS ruling, there are 2 other items you can deduct in addition to the 12 cents per mile or actual operating expenses. Namely, you can deduct a pro rata portion of taxes and interest you pay on the automobile [Rev Proc 89-66]. For example, if 15% of your annual mileage is for charitable purposes, you can claim 15% of the interest and taxes as a charitable deduction. However the interest amount is further reduced by the 90% factor that applies to personal interest on 1990 tax returns [cf. the *Interest* chapter].

Your travel is deductible if you are actually rendering services to a charitable organization, but not if your travel is for personal purposes. For example, travel to attend church choir rehearsals or to attend scout meetings as a troop leader is generally deductible. But travel just to attend church services or drive your children to their scout meetings is not.

Gifts of Appreciated Property

The best way to make a substantial donation to charity, generally, is to give *appreciated property*, i.e. property (including stocks, bonds, etc.) that has risen in value since the time you purchased it. You can get a deduction for the full market value of the property, avoiding the capital gains tax that would be due if you were to sell the property, rather than give it away. In effect, your charitable contribution is increased by the capital gains tax that has been avoided. If you were to sell the property first, you would have that much less to give to charity after paying the capital gains tax due.

The tax advantage of giving appreciated property has been enhanced by the recent tax reform. Because capital gains are now taxed at significantly higher rates than before (up to 33% instead of 20%), more tax can be saved by ordinary taxpayers now than before. (There has been some misconception about this matter because of the negative effect of the alternative minimum tax, as discussed below, that seldom applies to ordinary taxpayers.)

There are some restrictions that apply. First of all, to deduct the full market value of appreciated property, you must have owned the property for at least 12 months. Second, *tangible property* such as furniture, art objects, jewelry, etc. must be directly related to the charitable purpose of the organization to which they were given (e.g. books given to a library). If the full market value cannot be deducted, you are allowed to deduct only the original price (or other basis) you paid for the item.

High income taxpayers who make substantial donations of appreciated property may fall under certain *minimum tax* rules [cf. the *Alternative Minimum Tax* chapter]. In such cases, professional advice should be sought.

Recordkeeping Rules

The IRS has regulations concerning the documentation you need to back up your deduction for charitable contributions. For contributions of money you need either a cancelled check, receipt, or suitably maintained record as described below.

For contributions of clothing or other property, you do not need to keep written records as was once required. Instead, you must generally have a proper receipt from the charity. As discussed below, the receipt must describe the items donated, but is **not** required to assign a monetary value to the items.

You do not include receipts or written documentation with the tax return that you file. Rather, you keep these with your own records in case your tax return is challenged by the IRS. However, as discussed later, detailed information does need to be provided as part of your tax return in the case of large contributions.

Donations of Money

For each charitable contribution of money, you are required to maintain either

   (i) a cancelled check;

  (ii) a receipt (which can be a letter or other communication) from the charity showing the name of the charity, date of the contribution, the amount, and your name. For small amounts, an emblem, button, tag, or other evidence which indicates a donation has been made will suffice;

or

(iii) in the absence of a cancelled check or receipt from the donee organization, other reliable written records showing the name of the donee, the date of the contribution, and the amount of the contribution.

No specific recordkeeping format is required by the IRS under (iii). However, the most preferable form of record would be a diary in which the information concerning each contribution is recorded *contemporaneously* (i.e. at or soon after the contribution is made). According to IRS regulations,

"The reliability of the written records . . . is to be determined on the basis of all the facts and circumstances of a particular case. In all events, however, the burden shall be on the taxpayer to establish reliability. Factors indicating that the written records are reliable include, but are not limited to:

(A) The contemporaneous nature of the writing evidencing the contribution.

(B) The regularity of the taxpayer's recordkeeping procedures. For example, a contemporaneous diary entry stating the amount and date of the donation and the name of the donee charitable organization made by a taxpayer who regularly makes such diary entries would generally be considered reliable."

Note that the above rules require each contribution to be separately documented. For example, a written diary must list each individual contribution as it is made. A monthly listing, say, just of the total amounts given that month would not satisfy the above rules.

Despite the apparent severity of the documentation rules, there is a favorable side as well. Normally, a taxpayer must be able to substantiate his itemized deductions by receipts or cancelled checks. But the regulations now specifically allow charitable deductions to be backed by an appropriate written diary in the absence of cancelled checks or other receipts. This could be a boon to those who make a large number of cash donations during the year.

For example, say, a family usually places a $20 bill in the collection plate each Sunday at church and makes other miscellaneous cash donations during the year. Under the old rules, a tax auditor would ordinarily have balked when looking at such a large total of charitable contributions unsupported by receipts or cancelled checks. But under the new rules, as long as the family has kept an appropriate written diary listing each contribution, they will have satisfied the new IRS recordkeeping requirement.

Of course, it's still best to have receipts or cancelled checks whenever possible. Even though an appropriate written diary is a permissible option, the larger the total of otherwise undocumented amounts listed in the diary, the more scrutiny will be given as to the reliability of the diary.

There is no official format specified for the written diary of charitable contributions. Even a properly kept kitchen calendar can suffice in some circumstances. This is illustrated by the following recent case.

Court Case

Burns worked as an auto assembler, earning an annual salary of over $32,000. She claimed charitable contributions of $3,462, mostly to her church.

The substantiation she had for her charitable contributions was not the best. The church didn't keep any records of the contributions nor did it issue receipts. And she didn't even have a regular checking account, so all her contributions were made with cash. However, she did keep track of her contributions by recording them on a calendar hanging in her kitchen. This was the only written substantiation she provided to the Court.

Despite the lack of receipts or cancelled checks, the Court allowed her to deduct almost the entire amount–$3,282. The Court disallowed only a few items, mainly where it was not convinced that the contributions were made to a qualified charity.

The charitable deduction was allowed despite a decided negative factor in her record. Burns had filed an initial return as a "tax protestor," claiming she owed no tax because her earnings were offset by a "Cost basis (fair market value) of labor Received as Gift from Creator." The Court usually deals harshly with persons who make such frivolous claims.

However, there were several positive features in Burns' favor. Her pastor testified that he personally observed several $150 contributions she had made which correlated with her kitchen calendar records. Also, the next year, she moved to a new church which did keep records showing that she made contributions of similar size to the ones claimed in the year at issue. These factors supported the reliability of her records.

While her records were found reliable, the Court indicated in a footnote that it was not endorsing the absence of receipts or cancelled checks in all cases. Here, it was partly influenced by the fact that the IRS had not made an objection on these grounds. [Burns, TC Memo 1988-536]

As the above case indicates, a charitable deduction can sometimes be supported just by properly kept records, even in so informal a form as notations made on a kitchen calendar. However, it is unlikely that anything less would be ruled acceptable.

This is indicated by another recent court case. In this case, a taxpayer lost a deduction for most of the charitable items she claimed. Although the Court believed she had been very involved in charitable work, including a lot of auto travel, it could not allow a deduction unsupported by any documentation. It restricted her deduction to what IRS had allowed, including a $200 estimate for cash contributions plus other items for which she had cancelled checks. [Blair, TC Memo 1988-588]

Used Clothing or Other Property

For each donation of clothing or other property except cash, you are required to have a receipt from the charitable organization. In the words of the IRS regulations, the receipt should show all of the following information:

(i) The *name* of the donee.

(ii) The *date* and location of the contribution.

and

(iii) A *description of the property* in detail reasonably sufficient *under the circumstances*. Although the fair market value of the property is one of the circumstances to be taken into account in determining the amount of detail to be included on the receipt, such value need not be stated on the receipt. A letter or other written communication from the donee acknowledging receipt of the contribution, showing the date of the contribution, and containing the required description of the property contributed constitutes a receipt for purposes of this paragraph.

Note that the above regulation explicitly states that the receipt does not need to place a value on the items donated to the charity. This means that you can assign the fair market value yourself. Of course, if the charity does agree to assign a value on the receipt, this would likely be accorded more weight should your deduction be examined.

Exception

The IRS regulations contain the following exception to the receipt-keeping requirement:

"A receipt is not required if the contribution is made in circumstances where it is impractical to obtain a receipt (e.g., by depositing property at a charity's unattended drop site). In such cases, however, the taxpayer shall maintain reliable written records with respect to each item of donated property . . ."

The written records should include the following information:

(A) The name and address of the donee organization to which the contribution was made;

(B) The date and location of the contribution;

(C) A description of the property in detail reasonable under the circumstances (including the value of the property), and, in the case of securities, the name of the issuer, the type of security, and whether or not such security is regularly traded on a stock exchange or in an over-the-counter market;
and

(D) The fair market value of the property at the time the contribution was made, the method utilized in determining the fair market value, and if the valuation was determined by appraisal, a copy of the signed report of the appraiser.

In addition to the written record of each contribution, you should also have a receipt or letter from the charity, with date and location of the contribution, which details the property contributed. However, a receipt is not required if the contribution is made in circumstances where it is impractical to obtain a receipt, e.g. where the property is deposited in a charity's unattended drop site.

Items Worth More Than $500

If you donate an item worth more than $500, you should have a written record which shows how you acquired it (e.g. by purchase, gift, inheritance, etc.), the approximate date you acquired it, and, for items other than publicly traded securities, its cost (or other basis).

If there are unusual circumstances involved in the donation of property, these must be described in the written records you keep, e.g. if you have donated only a partial interest in the property, if there are "strings attached" to the use of the donated property, if the use of the property is unrelated to the charitable activities of the recipient, or if you held the property for a year or less and are valuing it at more than you paid for it.

If you made noncash contributions totaling more than $500 in value, you must fill out Form 8283 and attach it to your tax return. You are also required to attach a qualified appraiser's report if you donated property (other than listed securities) worth more than $5,000.

Limitations

There are a number of rules which place an upper limit on the amount of charitable contributions you can deduct in any one year. If you make contributions in excess of 20% of your Adjusted Gross Income, you should check the special rules which apply. These special rules may be found in Publication 526, obtainable at no charge from your local IRS office.

Evaluating Used Items

You are entitled to deduct the *fair market value* of used clothing or other items which you donate to the Salvation Army, Goodwill, church rummage sales, etc. Most charities will give you a receipt for the donated items, but will refuse to appraise their value. This means that you must determine the value yourself.

In practice, it is difficult to assign a value based on the current *market value* because the market for used clothing and other items is so variable. However, a 1980 court case gives some guidance. An individual gave the Salvation Army 12 pairs of trousers, 3 suits, 2 coats, 2 shirts, 1 pair of cowboy boots, and 2 pairs of shoes, all less than 3 years old. These items were purchased new at a total cost of $710. The Court ruled that the individual was entitled to a charitable deduction

 of $250— about 35% of the value of the items when new.[Patch, TC Memo 1980-11]

If there is expert testimony as to the value of donated merchandise, then a larger deduction can be obtained than normally allowed. This is illustrated by a court case concerning a woman who was *"extravagant in purchasing clothing for herself and her children."* She donated much of this clothing to a local charity and claimed several thousand dollars in charitable deductions over a period of years. Ordinarily, the Court would be expected to trim the amount of deductions claimed. But the woman had worked for a period of time in the charity's clothes resale shop. Because of this, her estimate of the value of the clothing was considered expert testimony and the deduction was allowed in full. [Haseltine, TC Memo 1979-325]

Another court case, in contrast, shows that an unsubstantiated assignment of high value to used clothing can backfire. An individual claimed a deduction for 2/3 the new value for used items donated to Goodwill and the Salvation Army. The Court found the values assigned to the items to be *"clearly exaggerated to put it mildly."* Since his appraisal was so lacking in credibility, the Court simply accepted the IRS estimate and allowed the individual a deduction for only about 10% of what he had originally claimed. [TC Memo 1978-461]

As the above indicates, the IRS will disagree with an unsubstantiated high valuation based on too high a percentage of the original cost of items given to charity. However, the result may be different if a valuation is based on a large number of donated items.

This is illustrated by a 1987 court case concerning a donation to the Salvation Army. The donation consisted of a large number of used items which had been stored in an individual's garage. The individual donated the items after he and his first wife were divorced.

According to the Court, *"He had not purchased the items donated, and was unable at trial to itemize the donated property or describe it, except for a stove, which he could describe only generally. The receipt from the Salvation Army showed the donor's declared value to be $3,000 . . ."*. However, the receipt did not purport to reflect the actual value of the donated property other than petitioner's valuation, nor did it list the items contributed. Additionally, the receipt bore the notation that *"a value for contributed property could not be determined by the receiving attendant.'*

The Court did not allow a full $3,000 deduction. However, despite the meager documentation, the IRS had still allowed a rather generous deduction of $950 for the donated items. The Court accepted this figure as the proper charitable deduction [Goldstein, TC Memo 1987-47] . (However, note that under current law, you must document a donation of items to charity on Form 8283 if you claim a deduction for them of over $500.)

As the above discussion indicates, used clothing and other items usually generate a charitable deduction which is considerably less than their value when new. This is because these items are generally given away only after they are worn out, damaged, or seriously out of style. However, perhaps you donate items which are still in good condition. Maybe you are moving, have lost or gained weight, etc. If so, the value of the merchandise might be considerably higher.

There is a court case that illustrates this point. This case did not involve a charitable deduction, but rather a deduction for loss due to theft. But the identical question arises in determining both these deductions, namely deciding the fair market value of used items whose ownership has just changed hands.

The stolen items consisted of clothing, cash, a radio, and a camera. The total purchase price of these items was $1,512, with half of the total due to the clothing. The age of the items ranged from 2 years old to only a few months old. The Court placed a value of $1,054 on the items when stolen — a full 70% of the stated original price. [TC Memo 1978-332]

Court Ok's Deduction for Giving Journals and Books to Charity

In the past, there has been uncertainty surrounding the deduction for giving books to charity, in particular when the books were received free to begin with. For example, when an elementary school principal tried to claim a charity deduction in a case decided a number of years ago, he was essentially rebuffed. In a controversial interpretation of the law, it was ruled that because the principal had received the books free, his charity deduction would be cancelled out by taxable income equal to the value of the books he received free from the publishers.

However, the following recent court case changed the picture. In this case, a professor donated a collection of books and journals to a research institute. Despite the fact he had received many of these items free, the Court allowed a charity deduction based on the fair market value, with no offsetting taxable income. However, the charity deduction had to be decreased by any deductions claimed for the books and journals in previous years as job-related expenses.

Court Case

Wehausen was a Professor of Engineering Science for many years at a distinguished public university in the West. Prior to this employment, he served as the editor of *Mathematical Reviews*, a mathematics abstracting journal. Through subscriptions, gifts, and professional activities over the years, he assembled an extensive collection of mathematical journals and publications.

Nearing retirement age, he donated his collection of mathematical journals to a newly established mathematics research institute. He then claimed a charitable deduction on his tax return.

Both the IRS and the Court agreed with Wehausen that he was entitled to a deduction. And there was no disagreement as to the general method of determining the amount of the charitable deduction. Over the years, Wehausen had previously deducted a total of $1,805 in subscription fees for journals included in his donated collection. Everyone agreed that the amount of the charitable deduction should equal the *fair market value* of the journals at the time of donation, less the $1,805 total of previously claimed tax deductions.

The only dispute at trial was how to determine this *fair market value*. On hand were 2 different appraisal figures, one of $5,245 provided by the research institute to which the donation had been made, and the other of $19,900 provided by an appraiser hired by Wehausen.

The Court did not accept the methodology used in the $19,900 appraisal. The appraiser testified that for domestic journals, he *"simply looked in the backs of the journals, looked at the price of back issues and added them up."* However, the Court rejected this procedure. The main objection was the lack of evidence as to the condition of the journals donated by Wehausen.

> *"The most apparent flaw in [Wehausen's] valuation method is its failure to recognize that the demand for and value of a secondhand periodical may differ from that of a publisher's back issue (which in absence of evidence to the contrary, we presume to be unused or of a very high quality.) While we recognize that secondhand periodicals may resemble the condition and quality of back issues, and may in fact be of comparable value, petitioners bear the burden of showing this to be the case. Absent evidence of comparability, we will not assume that a publisher's back-issue subscription price represents the fair market value of a secondhand periodical. Our review of the record reveals no persuasive evidence that petitioner's donated collection of secondhand periodicals was comparable to the quality and value of the back-issue prices used as the basis for his appraisal. And as no secondhand catalog, back-issue subscription list or evaluation of the collection's quality was produced, we are unable to independently determine whether the values assigned accurately represented those of the secondhand market."*

Thus, the Court accepted the alternate appraisal for domestic journals provided by the research institute. For foreign journals, on the other hand, the appraiser's valuation was accepted. For these journals, he did not just use the back-issue price, but based his appraisal on *"his long experience of what out of print Russian, Polish, Italian or Japanese periodicals fetch on the American market."* The fact that the appraiser did not use past sale figures for the mathematical journals in question was acceptable to the Court, which stated,

> *"We recognize from the outset that foreign mathematical journals may well have an even more limited market than their domestic counterparts. Consequently, while direct evidence of actual sales of similar periodicals would furnish us with the best evidence of fair market value, it is understandable that petitioners did not produce evidence of recent sales."*

Thus for domestic journals, the Court accepted the appraisal figure provided by the research institute, while for foreign journals, it accepted the figure of the appraiser *hired by Wehausen. Putting together these 2 valuations, the Court came up with a total for the donated collection of $6,628. Subtracting the $1,805 previously deducted by Wehausen, this produced a charitable deduction of $6,628 − $1,805 = $4,815,* [Wehausen, TC Memo 1988-460]

As required in the above court case, you are supposed to reduce the value of books and journals donated to charity by any job-related deductions you claimed for these items in previous years. However, like many persons, you may not have kept sufficiently detailed records on exactly which items you have previously deducted.

In such a case, it is advised to make the best estimate you can based on your recollection. The recordkeeping requirements described earlier do not ask you to state whether a deduction has previously been claimed. In fact, your receipt or written record only needs to show the name, date, recipient, and description of the donated item. Whether you received the item free or paid and deducted for it are not part of the recordkeeping requirement. If you have the required charity records and your deduction is not unusually large, you are unlikely to be challenged.

As noted earlier, if you donate an item worth $500 or more, then you are required to record how the item was acquired. But this $500 figure applies on an item by item basis. For example, even if you donate more than $500 worth of books, you do not fall under this requirement because no single book is worth more than $500.

Chapter 8

Household Services and Child Care

You may qualify for a tax credit equal to a percentage of payments made to a babysitter, maid, housekeeper, day care center, nursery school, etc.

The exact percentage of the tax credit depends upon your adjusted gross income as explained later in this chapter. Like other tax credits, the credit for household services and child care is subtracted directly from your final tax liability instead of from taxable income. Thus, it is more valuable than a deduction of the same amount [cf. Chapter 1, Section 1].

Note that although it is required that there be dependents under 13 (or disabled dependents of any age) in the household, the tax credit still can apply when no child-watching services are performed. For example, payments to a maid or housekeeper can qualify even if no one is home the entire time services are being performed.

Qualification Rules

In order to qualify for the household services and child care tax credit, the following rules must have been satisfied.

(1) Your expenses were necessary to enable you to be gainfully employed during the period the expenses were incurred. Unpaid volunteer work or work for a nominal salary does not count. However, active search for gainful employment does qualify. If you are married and living with your husband or wife, then either (i) both of you were gainfully employed, or (ii) one of you was gainfully employed and the other was disabled or was a full-time student during 5 or more months of the year. In addition, married couples who live together must file a joint return;

(2) You maintained a household including a dependent under age 13 or a disabled spouse or disabled dependent of any age. (Qualification is determined on a daily basis. For example, if you have a child who turns age 13 on August 23, you can claim the tax credit for services rendered through August 22);

and

(3) Your payment for the service was not made to a child under age 19 of yours (or of your spouse) or to a person who can be claimed as your dependent.

138

Payments to Relatives

At one time, payments to close relatives for child care generally did not qualify for the child care tax credit. However, now the only restriction is in (3) above. In particular, payments to a child's grandparent qualify for the tax credit.

Especially with the new personal exemption and standard deduction amounts [cf. Chapter 1], many retired persons over age 65 will pay little or no income tax. The child care tax credit offers a way to transfer money to such persons and achieve a net reduction in tax. Note that there is no specific ceiling on the hourly rate that can be paid for child care, although the IRS might object if it were too far out of line. However, since this information isn't called for on the tax form, IRS objection is unlikely.

Which Expenses Qualify For the Child Care Tax Credit?

If you qualify under the preceding rules, then the following expenses qualify for the household services and child care tax credit.

(1) Expenses Within the Home

The tax credit applies to expenses for ordinary and usual household services performed in and about the home. These services must be necessary to the running of the home and must be of benefit to a qualifying dependent or disabled spouse. This includes the services of a housekeeper, maid, or babysitter, but not a gardener. The tax credit applies also to the cost of meals furnished to a qualifying household worker. But the cost of lodging is not deductible except to the extent you incur expenses beyond what you would have normally paid if you had not provided lodging. [Rev Rul 76-288]

All of your expenses for housework are eligible for the tax credit even if only part of them are for a qualifying dependent.

Example

You pay a housekeeper to care for your 9-year-old and 15-year-old children so that you can work. The housekeeper spends most of the time doing the regular household work, cleaning and cooking, and spends 30 minutes a day driving you to and from work. The entire expense of the housekeeper is a work-related expense. You do not have to subtract any amount for being driven to and from work, because the time involved is minimal. You do not have to subtract any amount for the care of the 15-year-old child (not a qualifying dependent) because the household expense is partly for the care of the 9-year-old child, who is a qualifying dependent.

In the above example, the housekeeper had some child-watching duties in addition to her main duty of taking care of the house. While this established that the housekeeper performed services of benefit to child, the law does not specify that child-watching services be performed. All that's required is that the child directly benefit from the services. This can be the case where a housekeeper, maid, or cook, at least part of the time, cleans the child's room, cooks food which the child eats, etc.

However, note the first qualification rule on the first page of this chapter, namely that the expenses must be necessary to enable you to be gainfully employed. Ordinarily, this requirement is not hard to satisfy. However, the following 1990 court case gives an example where it was not satisfied.

Court Case

Brian and Suzanne Knutson were a married couple, he an accountant and she a teacher. They had three children, all of whom were under age 15, the qualifying age during the year in question. They hired a cleaning service which sent a team of 5 or 6 workers once a week to clean the house. No direct child-care duties were performed.

When the Knutson's *household services and child care tax credit* was challenged, they wound up in Tax Court. And the Court denied the tax credit. It did not believe that the hiring of a cleaning service was necessary to enable the Knutsons to work, stating,

"Brian testified both petitioners were very busy with numerous household improvement projects and programs with the children. We find the cleaning service was employed to make life easier for petitioners and to allow them to spend their leisure time in pursuits they enjoyed rather than cleaning their home. While the Court understands petitioners' desires, we do not believe Congress intended other taxpayers to subsidize the expenses related to a cleaning service in this instance." [Knutson, TC Memo 1990-440]

There are two things to note in the above court case. First was the type of cleaning service that was employed. The cleaning was performed only once a week for a brief period of time by a team of 5 or 6 workers. This meant that the cleaners would not be available to perform extra services a housekeeper might provide, such as waiting for repairmen, accepting deliveries, letting children in the house after school, etc. Such extra services, one might argue, could not be performed personally and therefore would be beneficial in enabling one to work.

Second, the couple in the above case made the mistake of emphasizing how busy they were with household projects and activities with the children. The judge took this to mean they could have done the cleaning if they had wanted to. They did not hire the cleaning service because it was necessary in order to work, but rather because they wanted time for other activities. If the couple's spare time had been filled with work-related or essential non-discretionary activities, the result could have been different.

(2) Expenses Outside the Home

The tax credit applies to the cost of care for children under 13 outside the home, such as in a day care center, nursery school, day camp, babysitter's home, etc. Benefits incident to the care (food, education, etc.) are, strictly speaking, not child care costs. However, if a payment covers incidental benefits inseparably as part of the care, then the entire cost will ordinarily be considered as being for child care. Thus, the credit applies to the full amount paid to a day care center or nursery school even if it includes lunch or educational activities. However, tuition for a child in the first or higher grade does not qualify, nor does the cost of transportation between your home and a child care location.

The tax credit also applies to outside-the-home care of a disabled spouse or disabled dependent over 12 who regularly spends at least 8 hours per day in the taxpayer's household. Dependent care centers which care for more than 6 persons per day must comply with all applicable local regulations to qualify for the credit.

Vacation Trips

As the following court case shows, expenses connected with sending your child on an out-of-town trip can qualify for the child care tax credit.

Court Case

Mr. and Mrs. Zoltan were both employed full-time. During a span of 2 years, they sent their 11-year-old son on a school-related Easter trip to Washington, DC, and to France for 2 months to visit his older sister. The Zoltans claimed the child care tax credit for cost of the trip to Washington, D.C., and for $350 in payments made to the sister in France for taking care of the boy. The Court considered these trips separately.

Easter Trip to Washington, D.C.

The Court found that the trip to Washington, D.C. was *"primarily undertaken for the son's well-being and protection."* (It noted that the cost of hiring a housekeeper to watch over the son would have been at least as expensive as the cost of the trip.) And, although transportation costs to a child care location do not qualify for the credit, that was not pertinent here. The child care began when they delivered their son to the tour sponsor at the bus depot in their home town. Thus, the bus trip was part of the basic child care, not auxiliary transportation.

However, the Court felt that a substantial portion of the trip was for educational purposes, not just child care. Thus, an allocation had to be made between the child care services and the educational services provided by the trip. The Court ruled that only $35 of the $116 expense could be deducted. Had the trip been to a less educational place than Washington, D.C., presumably the amount allocated to child care would have been higher.

Trip to France to Visit Sister

Under the law that applied at the time, payments to close relatives did not qualify for the child care tax credit. For this reason only, the Zoltans were not entitled to a credit for the $350 they paid to their son's sister for taking care of him in France. However, this *payment to relatives* restriction no longer applies, except as provided in Rule (3) on the first page of this chapter. Presumably, the $350 would have been allowed as a child care expense had the case been decided under current law. [Zoltan, 79 TC No. 31]

As the above case shows, the cost of sending a child on an out-of-town trip can qualify for the child care tax credit. Technically, it is required that the *principal purpose* of the trip be to insure your child's *well-being and protection.* But if you need to provide child care in order to work, you could almost always claim this is your principal purpose in sending your child out of town. Since the above Court decision ruled this was the case even for an Easter trip to Washington, D.C., it is hard to conjure up a situation which would not have satisfied the *principal purpose* requirement.

In the above case, the bus trip to Washington, D.C. was considered an integral part of the child care activities qualifying for the tax credit. The key was that the work performed by the ultimate care providers started with the bus trip.

However in a recent 1989 court decision, the cost of transportation did not qualify for the child care tax credit. In this case, a married couple sent their children by airplane to visit their grandparents over a school holiday period. While payments made to the grandparents would have qualified for the child care tax credit, the cost of airplane tickets did not. Although the children were cared for on the flights by cabin attendants, the court ruled *"There is nothing in the record to indicate that the cabin attendants were under the direction of [the grandparents], the service providers in the instant case."* Presumably, had a grandparent actually accompanied the children on the plane flight, a deduction would have been allowed. [Perry, 92 TC No. 28]

Summer Camp

The cost of sending your child to overnight camp no longer qualifies for the child care tax credit. This is the case even if the camp replaces child care that would have qualified for the credit.

However, the cost of sending a child to day camp still qualifies for the child care tax credit under the same conditions that applied in prior years. Namely, if there is a significant educational component to the camp (as there would be with a computer or baseball camp), then an allocation would have to be made between non-deductible educational costs and deductible child care costs. But no allocation need be made if the day camp provides only incidental instruction (e.g. in swimming, archery, etc) in an unstructured fashion. When the educational activities are only incidental to the child care aspect of the camp, the entire cost of the camp.can be deducted. This would include the cost of food and recreational services that are *"incident to and inseparably a part of his care."* [Zoltan, 79 TC No. 31]

Similarly, out-of-town trips apart from overnight camp are not ruled out. As illustrated in the preceding court case, costs connected with an out-of-town sightseeing trip or visit with a relative can qualify for the child care tax credit.

Private Schooling

You may feel it necessary to send a child to private school in order to allow you to be gainfully employed. The following court case supports your right to a child care tax credit for a portion of the expenses you incur.

Court Case

A woman and her son moved from Maryland to Philadelphia where he was enrolled in the Wagner Junior High School. However, he was not able to adjust to his environment at Wagner. *"Unlike his Maryland school, Wagner was fraught with classroom disorders and teacher strikes. Gang fights took place after school, and petitioner was concerned for her son's safety. . . . Petitioner felt that she could not work while her son was attending Wagner because she had to remain constantly prepared to pick him up if problems arose at school."*

As a result, she enrolled her son in a private boarding school. She then claimed a tax credit for that portion of the cost which was not allocable to the cost of education. The IRS objected, claiming the private schooling was not necessary to enable her to work. Other mothers sent their children to Wagner and were able to work without incurring any child care expenses.

But the Court overruled the IRS objection. *"Petitioner considered herself unable to work while her son was at Wagner. However, no doubt many Wagner students did have working mothers. It was not objectively impossible to be employed while a child was at Wagner. However, we do not believe that the statute requires us to test the correctness of the parent's conclusion that child care is required to obtain employment, but only the sincerity of that conclusion. Different parents will apply different standards for what risks they are willing to put their children to. One parent may feel a . . . boy could be left alone at home after school hours; another would disagree. The statute requires the prescribed purpose; it does not impose a test of objective necessity."*

The IRS also objected that the dominant motive in sending her son to boarding school was not to enable her to work, but to provide for his education. But the Court tossed aside this objection also. *" . . . if the parent could not have accepted the job without having sent the child to boarding school, she is deemed to have incurred the expense in order to be able to accept gainful employment . . . Since one of petitioner's reasons for sending her son to boarding school was to be able to take a job, and since she could not have taken a job without such child care arrangement, she is entitled to a child care deduction for some part of the cost of sending him to [private school]. We adopt in other words a 'but for' test. If the care was required to permit the taxpayer to work, and if one motive for obtaining the care was to permit gainful employment, the concurrent existence of other motives will not cause the expenditure to fail the statutory test. The employment motive must be present. It need not be exclusive or even dominant."*

Thus, the Court ruled in favor of the taxpayer. The portion of the cost of the private school which went for education, tuition, books, supplies, etc., would not qualify as a child care expense. However, *"incidentals that go with providing well-being and protection such as room, board, and supervision before and after the normal school day"* would qualify for the child care tax credit. [73 TC #15]

In the above case, the cost of education did not qualify because the child was in the "first or higher grade." For younger children, the full cost may be claimed as a tax credit. For example, a 1980 court case allowed a tax credit based on the entire cost of private school because the child was only 4 years old. The school was considered a nursery school so the full cost could be claimed as described earlier in this chapter. [Christre, TC Memo 1980-64]

Interestingly, while the regulations allow a tax credit for nursery school and forbid a tax credit for education in the first or higher grades, they do not spell out the situation for kindergarten. Presumably, a tax credit could be claimed for the cost of a private kindergarten which provided more nursery school type activities than formal schooling found in the first or higher grades.

Amount of Credit

The tax credit is equal to 30% of expenses on tax returns showing an adjusted gross income of up to $10,000,decreasing to 20% for those with adjusted gross incomes over $28,000. The following table shows the exact percentage to be used at each income level, subject to the limitations described below.

Adjusted Gross Income	Applicable Percentage
Up to $10,000	30%
$10,001—$12,000	29%
$12,001—14,000	28%
$14,001—16,000	27%
$16,001—18,000	26%
$18,001—20,000	25%
$20,001—22,000	24%
$22,001—24,000	23%
$24,001—26,000	22%
$26,001—28,000	21%
$28,001 and over	20%

Limitations

1. The overall limitation

The household and child care tax credit is subject to a maximum limitation. The maximum amount of 1990 expenses to which the credit can be applied depends upon the number of *qualifying dependents* (i.e. dependents under age 13 and disabled dependents or spouse over age 12) as follows:

(a) $2,400 if there is one qualifying dependent

or

(b) $4,800 if there are 2 or more qualifying dependents.

Thus, for those with adjusted gross incomes less than $10,000, the credit cannot exceed in case (a), $720 (30% X $2,400); or in case (b), $1,440 (30% X $4,800), while for those with adjusted gross incomes greater than $28,000, the credit cannot exceed in case (a), $480 (20% × $2,400); or in case (b), $960 (20% × $4,800).

Under (b), you are entitled to the credit on up to $4,800 of expenses as long as there are at least 2 qualifying dependents, even if a majority of this amount was spent for the care of only one child. For example, if you spent $3,000 for nursery school for your 4-year old child and $300 for incidental care of your 12-year old, you would apply the credit to $3,300 of expenses. The $2,400 limit under part (a) would not apply, but rather the $4,800 limit under part (b).

2. The earned income limitation

The expenses to which the credit is applied cannot exceed your earned income. For married couples filing a joint return, the expenses to which the credit is applied cannot exceed either your earned income or your spouse's earned income, whichever is lower. Earned income includes income produced by an individual's own work, whether it be as an employee or as a self-employed person. It does not include income from investments, such as stocks, bonds, rented property, savings accounts, etc.

In some cases, it pays to "put a spouse on the payroll" in order to boost the earned income of the lower-earning spouse and obtain a larger tax credit. For example, this might be possible for an individual with an outside business activity in which the spouse can be of assistance. This is discussed more fully in Section 3 of the *Outside Business Activity* chapter.

3. Reduction for tax-free amounts received as a fringe benefit

The law allows employers to set up a *dependent care assistance program* under which employees can receive, as a tax-free fringe benefit, reimbursement for up to $5,000 of child care expenses incurred during the year. (Such reimbursements will be reported on 1990 yearend W-2 Forms.) This program is often set up as part of a larger *cafeteria plan* that allows employees to select among various available fringe benefits [cf. Section 6 of the *Tax-Sheltered Plans* chapter]. Amounts received under such a program must now be subtracted from the amount of child care expenses to which the child care tax credit is applied. If total child care expenses exceed the overall limitation of $2,400 or $4,800, then this overall limitation is reduced by the reimbursements received under a dependent care assistance program. Form 2441 will lead you through the appropriate computation.

Sometimes, dependent care assistance programs are set up under a *salary-reduction agreement*. With such an arrangement, you agree to have your salary reduced by the amount you will be receiving as a reimbursement. You wind up receiving the same total amount from your employer, but now a portion of this amount is exempt from tax. Because such dependent care reimbursements reduce the amount to which you can apply the tax credit, you essentially must choose between a reduction in taxable income and a tax credit of 20% (assuming adjusted gross income exceeds $28,000). If your income reaches into the 28% or 33% tax brackets, the salary reduction is more beneficial. In the 15% tax bracket, the

20% tax credit is more valuable.

Special Rule for Students

The preceding earned income limitation would permit no tax credit if one spouse were a student with no earned income. But since Congress wanted to make the tax credit available to married couples in which one spouse is a student, they included the following special rule:

A spouse who is a student is treated for purposes of the earned income limitation as though

(1) He earned $200 per month for each month he was a full-time student during 1990, if there was one qualifying dependent

or

(2) He earned $400 per month for each month he was a full-time student during 1990, if there were 2 or more qualifying dependents.

The above amounts only serve to raise the limit on the amount of expenses to which the household services and child care tax credit is applied. They don't affect the adjusted gross income on which the table showing what percentage to use is based.

Example

A married couple has two children under age 13 for which they incur $5,000 in child care expenses. One spouse earns $25,000 for the year, while the other has no earnings but is a full-time student for 10 months during the year. They file a joint return showing an adjusted gross income of $25,000. Thus, as determined by the table given earlier, the applicable tax credit rate is 22% of expenses. The student is deemed to have earned $400 for each of the 10 months in school, or a total of $4,000 earned income for the year. Since the amount of expenses to which the credit is applied cannot exceed this amount, their credit for the year is equal to 22% X $4,000 = $880.

Social Security Taxes

If you employ a babysitter, maid, etc. inside your home, then these are employees of yours governed by the social security laws. This means that you are supposed to pay social security tax if any of these employees earned $50 or more during any one quarter in 1990. In 1990, the social security tax rate was equal to 7.65% for the employer and for the employee. You could withhold the employee's 7.65% from his paycheck or you could pay both portions yourself. Social security taxes are paid quarterly by filing Form 942 with the IRS. You do not have to pay social security taxes for an outside contractor such as a day care center, outside babysitting service, etc.

You only pay social security tax on actual wages. Food, clothing, and lodging given to household workers aren't subject to social security tax even when the extra cost of these items qualifies for the household services and child care tax credit.

Note that any social security taxes you pay are considered to be part of your costs. That is, these taxes are included in the total expense figure on which you compute the tax credit. This was affirmed in a recent court case. [Peny, 92 TC No 28]

If you claim the household services and child care tax credit then you will want to pay any social security tax that is due. The IRS has a program for checking that those who claimed the household services and child care tax credit also filed appropriate Forms 942.

When you file your first Form 942, write *"None"* in the space provided for *employer identification number.* The IRS will assign you a number and send you each quarter a new Form 942 with your name, address, and employer identification number preprinted on it.

What If You Are Separated or Divorced?

Special provisions are made for couples who are divorced or separated under a written agreement. In this case, the household services and child care tax credit can be claimed only by that parent who has custody of a qualifying child for a longer period of time than the other parent. (This is the case even if the dependency exemption was transferred to the other spouse on Form 8332 as discussed in the *Divorce and Separation* chapter.) The child must be in the custody of one or both parents for half of the year and must receive over half of his support from his parents.

Ordinarily, married couples must file a joint return in order to claim the household services and child care tax credit. However, there are the following exceptions to this rule for separated couples.

An individual who is legally separated from his spouse under a decree of divorce or of separate maintenance can claim the credit on a separate tax return. An individual who simply does not live with a spouse for the last 6 months of the year can also claim the household services and child care tax credit on a separate tax return. In this case, the qualifying child's principal home must have been with the individual for more than half of the year and the individual must have furnished over half the cost of maintaining the home.

Where is the Tax Credit Claimed?

You use Form 2441 to claim your Household Services and Child Care expenses. This form will lead you through a step by step computation of the appropriate tax credit.

Reporting Requirement

There is a reporting requirement for 1990 tax returns. You must report the name, address, and SSN (Social Security Number) or TIN (Taxpayer Identification Number) of any provider of child care or household services for which you're claiming a tax credit. You list these 3 items on the Form 2441 which you use to claim the tax credit. If the provider is a tax-exempt organization (charity, church, etc.) no identification number needs to be reported. You would just enter *"tax exempt"* in the space provided for the identification number.

There is a special form, Form W-10, which the child care provider can fill out giving the required information. This form is not filed with the IRS. Rather, you keep this form with your records to back up your tax credit claim in case of IRS challenge. This form is obtainable form your local IRS office or by calling 1-800-424-3676. It is best to have the provider fill out this form when hired. If you wait until tax preparation time, you might not be able to track down a provider you are no longer using.

The use of Form W-10 is not mandatory. In its place, the IRS permits you to have either

(1) a photocopy of the provider's social security card or driver's license showing the social security number,

(2) a recently printed letterhead or printed invoice that has on it the provider's name, address, and social security or taxpayer identification number,

or

(3) a copy of a completed Form W-4 (Employee's Withholding Allowance Certificate) if the provider is the individual's household employee.

Note that the child care provider is actually required by law to furnish you with a correct social security or taxpayer identification number. The provider is liable for a $50 penalty for each failure to furnish a correct number.

Chapter 9

Tax Deductions for Homeowners

We have discussed in a separate chapter how to deduct expenses connected with using a home office. The purpose of this chapter is to discuss the other deductions to which a homeowner is entitled simply through the use of a house as a personal residence. Throughout this chapter, the word *house* or the word *home* refers not just to a free-standing structure, but includes cooperative apartments, condominiums, etc. which you own.

In order to deduct interest or taxes on a home, you must actually own the home. Otherwise, the deduction is lost. For example, suppose you live in a home owned by your parents and you make the mortgage payments which include interest and taxes. Then neither you nor your parents can claim a deduction. If you had paid your parents rent and they had made the payments, then they would have been entitled to the deductions.

Section 1:
Interest

As described in the *Interest* chapter, some interest is no longer fully deductible. For example, interest on consumer purchases is only 10%-deductible on your 1990 tax return and completely nondeductible on 1991 tax returns.

However, the deduction for interest on loans secured by your home remains fully deductible—within certain basic limits described below. This is the case even if the proceeds of the loan are used for consumer purchases or any other purpose. This special treatment applies to loans on your primary home and on a second home. The loans can be first or second mortgages, home-equity loans, or any other loans secured by your primary or second home. Also, late payment charges on such loans are considered to be interest on the loans since they are payments for the "use" of money.

The second home need not be an ordinary home, condominium, or cooperative, but can be a mobile home, boat, or other property as long as it contains basic living accommodations, including sleeping space, toilet, and cooking facilities. If you rented out the second home during part of the year and also made personal use of it, the home will qualify if your personal use of it is both (i) more than 14 days and (ii) more than 10 percent of the number of days during the year that the home was rented out at a fair rental. (If the home was not rented out at all, it can qualify as a second home no matter what personal use you made of it. This includes rent-free use by a close relative.)

If you have more than one possible second home, you can choose any one you wish to be your *second home* for the year. Next year, you can make a different choice of *second home*.

A married couple filing separate returns can claim home interest only on 2 homes between them. Each one can take into account only one residence unless they both consent in writing to one of them taking into account both residences.

To qualify under the home interest rules, the debt must be secured by the home under a legally binding agreement. If a loan is used to make payments on a home but is not actually secured by the home, it does not qualify.

This is illustrated by several recent IRS Private Letter Rulings. In one ruling, an individual took out a loan from a savings and loan association, using funds on deposit as collateral. He then used the loan proceeds to make payments on the mortgage on his home. The IRS ruled that interest on the loan from the savings and loan association was not deductible as home mortgage interest (but rather only partially-deductible as consumer interest). Even though the loan was used to make payments on a home, it was not *secured* by the home and therefore could not generate fully deductible home interest [IRS Private Letter Ruling 88 02056]. In another ruling issued in 1989, the IRS vetoed a full deduction for interest on a loan used to purchase a personal residence because the debt was secured only by stocks and bonds, not by the residence itself [IRS Private Letter Ruling 8906031].

In most cases, a portion of your monthly mortgage payment goes toward paying interest on a home loan while another portion goes toward paying off the principal. Only the interest portion can qualify for deduction. You cannot deduct the portion which goes toward paying off the principal. Most lenders provide an annual statement which shows what portion of your payments is attributable to interest costs.

If an interest payment is due on a loan, you can't borrow more money from the original lender to cover the payment. Otherwise, you lose out on the interest deduction [IR-83-93]. In such a case, no actual payment is considered made—just a renewed promise to pay the original lender. However, if money is borrowed from a different lender to pay the interest due on the original loan, then a deduction is allowed. While common sense may point to this as an irrelevant distinction, the courts have upheld this distinction as a matter of law. [Roberts, TC Memo 1987-235]

Limit on Deductible Home Mortgage Interest

Debt secured by a home is divided into 2 categories—*acquisition debt* and *home-equity debt*. The following shows the maximum amount of each type of debt that generates fully deductible home interest. These limits apply to the combined debt on a primary and second home.

Acquisition Debt:	$ 1,000,000
Home Equity Debt:	$100,000

The above amounts are halved for married persons filing separate returns.

Acquisition debt consists of debt incurred to purchase, construct or substantially improve a residence. If such debt is later refinanced, then the new debt is still considered acquisition debt to the extent it does not exceed the balance of the old debt at the time of refinancing. (If you refinance for a larger amount, taking out the extra amount in cash, this extra amount is not considered *acquisition debt* but becomes *home-equity* debt as discussed below.)

However, under a grandfathering provision, debt on a home incurred before October 14, 1987 is considered acquisition debt (and the $1,000,000 limit not applied to such debt), no matter for what purpose the debt was incurred. For example, even a home-equity loan taken out before October 14, 1987 is considered *acquisition debt* rather than *home-equity debt*. As such, it is not counted against the $100,000 limitation that applies to *home-equity debt* taken out after this date. Furthermore, the grandfathering rule still applies if such debt is refinanced on or after October 14, 1987, to the extent the new debt does not exceed the old debt at the time of refinancing. Under this grandfathering provision only, the final payment date of the new debt cannot extend beyond the final payment date of the old debt. (In the case of a "balloon" mortgage acquisition debt that is not amortized over its term, the grandfathering provision applies for the term of the first refinancing, but not for more than 30 years after that first refinancing.)

For determining whether or not a loan is considered *acquisition debt,* the tracing rules described in the *Interest* chapter are relaxed. If you take out a loan within 90 days before or after you purchase a home, then you may treat the loan as *acquisition debt* to the extent of amounts spent to purchase the home. Or, if you construct or substantially improve a residence, then loans taken out during the period from 24 months before completion of the construction to 90 days after may similarly be considered acquisition debt.

You may treat a loan as "taken out" on the date you make a written application to incur the debt, provided the debt proceeds are actually disbursed within a reasonable time (30 days is a reasonable time) after approval of the application. In particular, these new rules allow you to purchase or construct a house for all cash and still have *acquisition debt* when you proceed to finance the house within 90 days after purchase or construction.

If you borrow money under the above rules to purchase, construct, or improve a residence, then the debt does not become *acquisition debt* until it is actually secured by the residence via a deed of trust or other legal document. Before that time, it is generally *personal interest* (cf. the *Interest* chapter). [IRS Notice 88-74]

Home-equity debt consists of all other debt secured by your primary or second home other than acquisition debt. Note that it makes no difference to what purpose the home-equity debt is put. To the extent the debt does not exceed the $100,000 limit, all interest on such debt is fully deductible as home mortgage interest, no matter how the debt proceeds are spent.

Example 1

Kramer bought a personal residence in 1984 for $90,000, putting down $25,000 cash and taking out a first mortgage for $65,000. By July 1, 1990, his home had appreciated in value to $200,000.

Case 1: On July 1, 1990, Kramer took out a second loan secured by the home (second mortgage, home-equity loan etc.) for $80,000.

The initial $65,000 loan is *acquisition debt* and the $80,000 loan taken out on July 1, 1990 is *home-equity debt*. Since the home equity debt of $80,000 does not exceed the $100,000 home-equity limit, all interest payments on both loans are fully deductible as home interest.

Case 2: Kramer took out a second loan in 1990 with an average 1990 balance of $120,000.

Since this loan exceeds the $100,000 limit, only $5/6$ ($100,000/$120,000) of the loan is considered home-equity debt. Thus, Kramer can deduct as *home interest* all the interest on his first mortgage (acquisition debt) plus $5/6$ of the interest on the second loan (home-equity debt). The remaining $1/6$ of the interest on the second loan is only 10%-deductible as *personal interest,* unless qualifying as investment or business interest as discussed in the *Interest* chapter. (See the text following Example 2 for the definition of the term *average balance.*)

Case 3: Kramer took a second loan for $120,000 before October 14, 1987.

In this case, the second loan comes under the grandfathering rule and is considered *acquisition debt*. Thus, Kramer can deduct the full interest on both the first and second loans as home interest. Furthermore, interest on any additional home loans up to $100,000, taken out after October 14, 1987, will be fully deductible home-equity interest.

Example 2

Cooper purchased a home for $60,000 in 1980, putting down $10,000 and taking out a first mortgage for $50,000. On January 1, 1990, the house had risen in value to $180,000 and the first mortgage balance paid down to $30,000. On this date, Cooper refinanced the first mortgage for $155,000. The *average balance* of this refinanced loan during 1990 was $150,000.

Since the balance of the first mortgage on the date of refinancing was $30,000, then $30,000 of the new mortgage is considered to be acquisition debt. The remaining $120,000 ($150,000 − $30,000) is home-equity debt. Of this $120,000, $100,000 falls within the home-equity limit. Thus $130,000 of the refinanced loan ($30,000 + $100,000) qualifies for deduction. That is, $13/15$ ($130,000/$150,000) of the interest on the loan is fully deductible as home interest. The remaining $2/15$ of interest is 10%-deductible as personal interest unless it falls into the investment or business interest category as described in the *Interest* chapter.

In the preceding example, the **average balance** of the refinanced loan during 1990 was compared to the balance of the old loan just before refinancing to see if the $100,000 limitation on home-equity debt was satisfied. Most mortgage lenders now provide this *average balance* figure on the statement they send to you after yearend reporting the taxes and interest you paid during the year. Or, there are a number of methods for computing an average balance figure yourself which are described in the instructions to Form 1040. For example, one method that can be used under the appropriate circumstances is to add the 1989 yearend balance plus the 1990 yearend balance and divide by 2.

Example 3

Wilson bought a home on February 15, 1987 for $200,000. He paid all cash, taking out no loans on the home at the time of purchase because he expected interest rates to fall. On September 1, 1990, he took out a first mortgage which had an average balance during 1990 of $150,000.

Case 1: None of this money was used to substantially improve the home.

Wilson has no acquisition debt on the home, since the first mortgage was taken out more than 90 days after purchase. The $150,000 is considered to be home-equity debt. Only $100,000 of this debt generates fully deductible home interest. Thus, Wilson deducts $2/3$ ($100,000/$150,000) of the interest payments on the loan as home interest. The remainder is 10%-deductible as personal interest unless it qualifies as investment or business interest as discussed in the *Interest* chapter.

Case 2: Out of the proceeds of the loan, $20,000 is used for making substantial improvements to the home. The remainder is used for personal purposes.

In this case, there is acquisition debt of $20,000. The remaining $130,000 ($150,000-$20,000) is considered home-equity debt, $100,000 of which generates fully deductible home interest. Thus, Wilson deducts $12/15$ [($20,000 + $100,000)/$150,000] of his interest payments as fully deductible home interest. The remaining $3/15$ is 10%-deductible as personal interest.

Warning to Homebuyers— Take Out Large Mortgage at Time of Purchase

If you are planning to buy a home, pay particular attention to Example 3. You should take out as large a loan as you will need at the time of purchase. This will establish the loan amount as a fully deductible acquisition debt. As Example 3 illustrates, a loan taken out at a later time might not qualify for a full deduction if the deductible limit for home-equity debt is exceeded. In effect, the tax law encourages home buyers to take out the largest initial mortgage with the smallest down payment possible.

Similarly, it may be unwise to prematurely "pay off" your existing mortgage. A refinancing of your existing mortgage is generally considered to be acquisition debt. But once all debt is paid off, any new loan is considered home-equity debt, subject to the $100,000 limitation.

Example 4

You have a primary home and a second home, both of which you own debt-free because you have paid off your mortgages. On December 1, 1987, you borrowed $60,000 on your primary home and on January 1, 1990 you borrowed $80,000 on your second home. (Both loans were balloon mortgages.) The proceeds of these loans were used for personal purposes.

You are limited to a $100,000 total on the amount of home-equity debt qualifying for deduction. You can deduct in full interest on the earlier $60,000 loan and 1/2 [$40,000/$80,000] of the second loan. Or you can lump the 2 loans together and deduct in full $10/14$ [$100,000/($60,000 + $80,000)] of the total interest paid on the 2 loans during the year. In either case, the remaining interest is 10%-deductible as personal interest on your 1990 tax return.

What to Look for in a Home-Equity Loan

As the above shows, the tax code enshrines home-equity loans as a privileged borrowing vehicle, no matter what the status of the borrower or purpose to which the loan is used. A millionaire who takes out a $100,000 home-equity loan to throw an African Safari party for his close friends gets a full deduction for interest on the loan. Meanwhile, the less affluent individual who takes out a student loan or borrows on an automobile needed to get to work can only get a 10%-deduction on his 1990 tax return for personal interest. And next year, even the 10%-deduction will disappear altogether.

If you are a homeowner, then you need to take cognizance of this bias in the law. You should lean toward taking out a home-equity loan rather than use other forms of consumer credit such as auto loans, credit card debt, etc.

Of course, factors other than tax treatment must also be considered when comparing a home-equity loan with other types of debt. On the plus side is the fact that home-equity loans generally offer a lower interest rate than other types of consumer loans—often significantly lower.

On the negative side are the fees that may be required to take out a home-equity loan. Such fees might include origination fees, appraisal fees, legal fees, insurance, annual maintenance fees, etc. Because of the competitive nature of the home-equity market, shopping around for the best deal might save considerable amounts on such fees.

Starting in 1990, lenders have been required to hold cash reserves to cover the value of credit lines that borrowers have not yet drawn upon. Because of this, most banks will charge a fee based on the total line of credit which you obtain, not just on the amount currently borrowed. Even before this reserves requirement went into effect, many banks had been charging a closing fee of 1%-3% (sometimes termed "points") on the total credit line. Now, this type of fee or an "inactivity fee" is widespread. In the presence of such fees, you should not establish a credit line in excess of the amount you actually anticipate borrowing.

You should also beware of "teaser rates" much lower than normal. When you read the fine print, these teaser rates only apply for a short period of time, with a higher rate applying thereafter.

One last caveat is to remember that home-equity loans are secured by your home. In case of default, ownership of your home could be jeopardized. Particular care should be taken with floating interest rates under which required payments can increase if certain benchmark interest rates rise.

Points

When you buy a house, you might have to pay "points" in order to be able to obtain the loan. Since these points represent money you are paying to a lender in order to borrow money, they are really a form of interest and are deductible as such. An exception occurs in the case of VA points or any portion of FHA points which represent a service charge to these agencies. Also, *fees* incurred in obtaining the loan such as appraisal fees, settlement fees, notary fees, etc. are not considered to be interest and cannot be deducted as such.

When you obtain your mortgage loan, the lender can tell you about the tax status of any points being charged. Only points which are paid to purchase your *principal* residence and which do not exceed what is generally paid in your area can be deducted immediately. Other points must be deducted over the period of the loan.

To be deducted immediately when a home is purchased, you must actually *pay* the points to the lender. If the lender *withholds* the points from the mortgage loan, the points are not deductible but must be prorated over the life of the loan. This distinction is illustrated by a recent court case in which an individual borrowed $55,000 from a bank to finance a house. The bank subtracted 2 points, $1,100, from the $55,000 and disbursed the remaining $53,900 (less an origination fee which we will ignore for purposes of this illustration).

The Court ruled that the individual could not deduct the $1,100, but must prorate it over the life of the loan. Essentially, they required the transaction to be treated, partially, as a discount loan of $53,900 with $55,000 to be paid at maturity as described in the next subsection.

Instead of structuring the transaction in the above manner, the bank should have turned over the full $55,000 to the title attorney. With a separate check, the individual would have paid the bank $1,100. Then he could have obtained an immediate deduction of $1,100 on his tax return. While common sense may indicate that this is no different than having the bank withhold the $1,100 from the loan, the Tax Court has ruled that the two situations are treated differently under the law. [Schubel, 77 TC No. 51]

If a loan was taken out in connection with improving your principal residence, then points charged on the loan are similarly deductible. However, points on a loan taken out to *refinance* your home are not deductible when paid, but must be deducted ratably over the period of the loan. For example, if you pay $2,400 in points on a 20-year loan involving 240 monthly payments, then you deduct $10 for each payment that was due during the tax year. [Rev. Rule. 87-22]

An exception occurs when a refinancing is undertaken *in connection with* the purchase or improvement of the home. An example of this is given in a 1990 court case. In this case, an individual purchased a house, financed by a 3-year first mortgage of $122,000. Before this mortgage expired, he refinanced with a 30-year mortgage, paying off the previous loan. As part of the refinancing, he paid a total of $4,440 in points.

Because the original loan expired in only 3 years, it was obviously contemplated at the time that it would be refinanced within the 3-year period. For this reason, the court ruled that the refinancing was sufficiently connected with the original purchase of the home. The same would be true with a refinancing of a bridge loan, construction loan, or similar short-term loan. [Huntsman, 66 AFTR 2d 90-5020, reversing Huntsman, 91 TC No. 57]

If you are required to deduct points ratably over the period of the loan, then any undeducted points become deductible if the loan is paid off early via a refinancing or otherwise. For example, if the $2,400 loan discussed above were paid off after 40 months, then you would deduct the remaining points, $2,400 − (40 × $10) = $2,000 in the year of pay-off. [IRS Private Letter Ruling 8637058]

If a new loan is taken out on a personal residence in part to refinance an existing loan and in part to pay for improvements, then points allocable to the part used for improvements can be deducted immediately. The amount allocable to the refinancing is prorated over the lifespan of the loan.

Example

Jacoby has an existing long-term mortgage on his home with a current balance of $80,000. He refinances in 1990 with a new 25-year $100,000 loan, using the extra $20,000 to pay for improvements to the home. He is required to pay $4,000 in points when he takes out the new loan.

Of the $100,000 new loan, 20% is used to pay for improvements. This means that 20% of the points, 20% × $4,000 = $800, can be deducted in 1990. The remaining $3,200 is prorated over the 25-year lifespan of the loan at the rate of $3,200/25 = $128 per year. Thus, Jacoby deducts $800 + $128 = $928 in points on his 1990 tax return, with $128 deducted in each of the remaining 24 years of the loan.

Points To Be Reported to IRS by Lender

Starting with loans taken out in 1991, a new reporting requirement comes into effect. The lending institution will generally report the amount of points you paid on the interest-reporting form it sends the IRS after yearend. The form will specify whether you paid the points from separate funds as opposed to the points being withheld from the loan disbursement. The IRS plans to use this reporting to uncover home buyers who are deducting points which were not handled properly.

Discount Loans

Sometimes, loans are issued under a discount arrangement under which you receive less than the face amount of the loan, with the difference representing the interest. FHA mortgage loans and home improvement loans are common examples of this. The following example shows how to treat this type of loan.

> **Example**
>
> You borrow money from a bank in order to make a home improvement. The face amount of the loan is $10,000. However, you receive only $8,000 and are required to pay back the face amount of $10,000 in 40 equal monthly installments of $250 each. The interest on the loan is the difference between the $10,000 you pay back and the $8,000 you received, namely $2,000. This is prorated evenly over the 40 monthly payments. Thus, $2,000/40 = $50 of each monthly payment is deductible as interest. If you made 12 such payments during the year, you would have a $50 × 12 = $600 interest deduction for the year.

In the above example, the $10,000 which you paid back all went to the lender as payment for the loan. However, often the loan will include mandatory insurance payments. These insurance payments are not deductible except in connection with home office or other business expenses. In the above example, if each of the 40 monthly payments had included $5 for insurance, then you would really be paying $200 in insurance and only $9,800 back to the lender. Thus, your interest deduction would be $9,800 – $8,000 prorated over the 40 month period. Your loan agreement will state any insurance charges that are included in your monthly payments.

Graduated Payment and Adjustable Rate Mortgages

Some mortgages are structured so that payments in early years are artificially low, increasing during later years. That is, the early payments do not cover all the interest due on the mortgage; the principal due on the loan increases by an amount equal to the unpaid interest. A similar situation can arise on certain adjustable rate mortgages when the interest rate is adjusted upward but mortgage payments remain fixed below the amount required to cover the total interest due.

In such cases, you can only deduct the amount of interest actually paid. You cannot deduct the unpaid interest which was added to your mortgage balance. (The statement received from the bank or mortgage company holding your mortgage will generally show the amount actually paid.)

However, a recent IRS ruling contains a little-known fact. If you pay off or refinance the loan with another institution, you can then deduct the deferred interest which increased the principal balance on your mortgage. In this ruling, an individual borrowed $55,400 on his home under a graduated payment mortgage. Since his payments for the first few years did not cover the amount of interest on the loan, his principal balance had grown by $3,300 to $58,700 after two years. He then refinanced his house with another lending institution, paying off the $58,700 balance with the original lender. The IRS ruled that he could deduct the $3,300 at the time he refinanced the loan as a payment of deferred interest on the original loan.

The IRS noted that had he refinanced with the same institution, the $3,300 could not have been deducted at that time. In such a case, he has made no actual payment but just promised to pay again. While this may seem a distinction without a real difference, the courts have upheld this distinction. [IRS Private Letter Ruling 8347015]

Seller Financing Restricted

Often, when a house or other real estate property is sold, the seller will help the buyer finance the purchase by lending at a below-market rate. The seller must charge an annual interest rate of at least 9% (assuming compounding semi-annually) unless the going rate for U.S. Treasury securities of comparable maturity is less than 9%, in which case this lesser rate may be charged. (For land sales to family members which do not total more than $500,000 during a given year, the 9% requirement is reduced to 6%.) If the required minimum interest rate is not charged, the IRS will tax part of the principal as interest income to the seller.

Similar restrictions apply to most other types of loans, whether or not used to finance a house. Extra restrictions apply to loans in excess of $2.8 million. There is a special exception to the minimum interest requirement for certain upfront payments of $90,000 or less made to certain *continuing-care facilities* by a taxpayer age 65 or older, or on behalf of a spouse who is age 65 or older.

Penalty Payments for Prepayment of Mortgages

Many mortgage contracts provide for a penalty payment if you prepay part or all of your mortgage. These payments are deductible as interest.

Deducting 13 Monthly Interest Payments Instead of 12

Typically, the 1990 statement from the institution holding your home mortgage will reflect the 12 monthly payments due on the first day of each month during the year. You would then be entitled to deduct the total interest portion of these payments.

However, there is a way to squeeze an extra month's interest deduction on your 1990 tax return. This is done simply by sending in your January 1, 1991 mortgage payment early so it's received by the lender during December, 1990. Since this payment is actually for the use of money during December, 1990, you're entitled to deduct this on your 1990 tax return.

It's possible that the statement you receive from the lender might not show this extra payment, even if received prior to yearend. In such a case, it's best to request the lender to issue a corrected statement to be sent to you and the IRS. This will eliminate the possibility of an IRS computer letter asking you to explain a discrepancy.

Where Do You Deduct Interest Payments?

Interest payments on a primary or second home are deducted on line 9 of Schedule A. You cannot deduct interest payments on a personal residence if you claim the standard deduction.

If you make interest payments on a home mortgage to an individual rather than a bank or other lending institution, Schedule A requires you to list that individual's name and address. In theory, this can be used to check that the individual receiving the payments reports them on his tax return. However, in practice, this is more in the nature of a reminder that such payments must be reported. Without requiring the social security number of the recipient, the IRS has no way of making a general crosscheck.

Section 2:
Taxes

The real estate taxes which you pay on your home are deductible, the same as under prior law. Often, you do not pay these directly to the local government, but instead pay them as part of your monthly mortgage payment. What usually happens to these tax payments is this. The mortgage company accumulates these payments during the year in an escrow account. Then, when a year's worth of payments has been accumulated, the mortgage company pays your real estate taxes for the next year to the local government.

You can deduct the real estate taxes only when they are actually paid to the local government. The mortgage company which places your payments into escrow is considered to be acting as your agent. Thus, the IRS does not consider that you have paid your taxes by sending money to the mortgage company. They must actually be delivered to the taxing agency.

Example
Your local tax year begins on July 1 and runs through June 30 of the following year. From July, 1989 through June, 1990, you pay $100 per month for local property tax as part of your mortgage payment to your bank. The bank accumulates these payments into an escrow account and pays your real estate tax bill of $1,200 on July 1, 1990. You can deduct this $1,200 on your 1990 tax return. The tax portion of your mortgage payments from July through December, 1990 is not deductible on your 1990 return. These amounts are being placed in escrow and will become deductible on your 1991 return when the bank pays your July 1, 1991 tax bill.

In its yearly statement to you, the institution holding your mortgage will state how much real estate tax it paid on your account the previous year. This is the figure you use in deducting your taxes. Do not simply multiply your current tax payments by 12 because the tax rate might have been changed recently.

Your taxes are deducted on Schedule A along with the rest of your itemized deductions. You cannot claim a deduction for taxes on your personal residence if you claim the standard deduction.

Special Assessments
If an assessment is paid for the purpose of building or improving some facility then it is a non-deductible item. For example, assessments for sewers, street

paving, etc. are non-deductible. The law regards such items as capital expenditures, that is, expenditures which tend to increase the value of your property. Even if you could show that no increase in value actually took place, it would do you no good. It would not change the non-deductible category into which the IRS places these expenditures.

If a portion of an assessment represents a maintenance charge or interest expense associated with an improvement, then this portion is deductible if it is levied *against an interest in real property,* as opposed to being a *user charge* for some service or benefit. While this distinction is not always easy to make, an IRS ruling has described 3 situations which illustrate the difference. In situation 1, the city assesses a front-foot benefit charge against abutting property that is benefited by the construction of a water system. In situation 2, a city water authority imposes a 2-part charge upon its customers, one part being a metered per-gallon fee and the other a flat uniform charge for maintenance and interest on the water system facilities. And in situation 3, a sewer authority imposes a flat charge per unit for each year on all residential customers. In situations 2 and 3, no deduction is permitted because the charges are considered to be merely fees paid for receipt of water and sewer services. But in situation 1, the charge is considered to be an assessment *"imposed because of and measured by some benefit inuring directly to the property against which the assessment is levied."* Thus it is an assessment *"against the property"* and the portion representing interest and maintenance is deductible. [Rev. Rul 79-201]

Observe that in situation 3, had the sewer services been paid from revenue derived from a general local tax such as a property tax, the entire tax would still be deductible. It is only when the charges are singled out as user fees for services that they become non-deductible.

You will have to check with your local government to determine if any percentage of your water or sewer bill is attributable to deductible assessments. Sometimes this information will be distributed to all city residents. However, in surprisingly many cases, the local government is unfamiliar with the tax law and cannot give this breakdown. All you can do in such a case is to refer the appropriate government official to the above cited revenue ruling and pressure for this information to be provided.

How Do You Apportion Taxes When a House Is Sold?

When a house is sold, the real estate taxes are considered apportioned according to the date the property is transferred to the new owner. The following example illustrates how this is done.

Example

You buy a house and sign the final settlement papers on February 1, 1991. The real estate tax year in your locality runs from July 1 through the following June 30.

The settlement sheet includes real estate taxes in two places. First of all, the previous owner had paid one year's taxes in advance on July 1, 1990. (This payment was actually paid by the mortgage company from money placed into escrow taken *from monthly payments from July, 1989 through June, 1990.) Since you are occupying the house from February 1, 1991 through June 30, 1991, you must reimburse the previous owner for this 5-month portion of the tax bill which he already paid for.*

The second place where real estate taxes appear is in compensating the previous owner for the tax portion of his mortgage payments which was placed into escrow from July, 1990 through January, 1991. In effect, you are purchasing this escrow account from the previous owner. The tax portion of your mortgage payments from February, 1991 through June, 1991 will then be added to this escrow account so that by July 1, 1991, a full year's taxes will have been accumulated. This will be used to pay your taxes for the next year, July 1, 1991—June 30, 1992.

The taxes for the period July 1, 1990 through January 31, 1991 belong to the seller of the house. Since he paid these taxes in advance on July 1, 1990, his deduction is claimed on his 1990 tax return. The purchaser of the house deducts on his 1991 return, the taxes from February 1, 1991 through June 30, 1991 which he paid at settlement plus the full next year's taxes paid on July 1, 1991 by the mortgage company out of the escrow account.

The preceding example shows how taxes are divided for the purpose of determining how much tax deduction goes to the seller and how much to the buyer. The actual settlement sheet may not reflect this division correctly. For example, the seller may have paid part of the taxes attributable to the period after transfer. However, this does not count. The IRS considers this as a disguised way of reducing the price of the house. The seller can only deduct the taxes for the period when he owned the house. The buyer deducts the taxes for his period of ownership, even if he did not actually pay them.

Transfer Taxes

When you buy a house or other real estate, the settlement charges include various transfer and recordation taxes. These taxes can add up to several thousand dollars in some localities. These taxes are **not** deductible. Only those local taxes which are specifically designated in the tax code can be deducted. And this does not include real estate transfer or recordation taxes.

Under the 1986 Tax Reform Act, transfer and recordation taxes are considered to be part of the cost of the property. If the property is used for business or investment purposes (e. g. rental real estate, home office, etc.), then those taxes will be written off over a period of years as part of the depreciation on the property [cf. the *Expensing and Depreciation* chapter].

Section 3:
Capital Gains on Sale of a House

If you sell your house for a higher price than the one at which it was purchased, then you may have a capital gain. This capital gain is computed by subtracting the original purchase price of the house and the cost of any improvements from the amount realized by the sale. You also add back any deductions you have claimed for casualty losses.

The **amount realized by the sale** means the actual sales price less the cost of expenses directly connected with making the sale. Such expenses include the cost of advertising, commissions, legal fees, transfer taxes, and points or loan placement fees charged to the seller.

You do not include the cost of furnishings such as rugs, drapes, washing machine, etc. in the price of the house. You are supposed to pay capital gains tax in the unlikely event you receive more for these items than you paid. However, you cannot claim a capital loss if you sell these items at a lower price.

The **purchase price** of a house includes not only the cost of the house itself, but also expenses connected with buying the house such as legal fees, title fees, transfer and deed-recording fees, etc.

An **improvement** is a replacement or addition which adds to the value or prolongs the life of your house. This is distinguished from an ordinary maintenance or repair expense. For example, adding central air-conditioning, replacing the roof, panelling the den, new plumbing, new furnace, installing permanent storm windows, landscaping, assessments for capital items, etc. are improvements. Similarly, the cost of blacktopping a driveway, replacing gutters, new doors, waterproofing the basement, installing built-in shelving, etc. can generally be regarded as improvements. But the cost of painting, cleaning, fixing a broken air-conditioner, etc. are ordinary maintenance expenses.

Sometimes a repair can be converted into an improvement by working it into a major remodeling project. This can provide a tax advantage because improvements reduce the capital gains tax that might become due when the house is sold. For example, the cost of wallpapering and painting can be included as part of an overall improvement plan of remodeling or renovation. But independent of such a plan, wallpapering and painting do not constitute improvements. [Bayly, TC Memo 1981-549]

The above capital gain is subject to tax according to the usual rules for taxing capital gains (cf. the *Investing Your Money* chapter) unless you reinvest the proceeds in a new personal residence as described in the following paragraphs. If you wind up with a capital loss on the sale of a house used strictly as a personal residence, you cannot deduct the loss.

Exemption from Capital Gains Tax When a New House is Purchased

If you sell your personal residence and buy a new personal residence, then you do not have to pay capital gains tax, providing you satisfy all of the following three rules.

Rule 1. Both houses must be your principal residence. Vacation houses, second homes, etc. do not qualify.

Rule 2. The purchase price of the new house must be at least as much as the adjusted sales price of your old house.

Rule 3. You must occupy the new house within 2 years before or after the sale of your old house.

If you move into your new house before actually selling your old house, you might temporarily rent out your old house while continuing your efforts to find a buyer. This does not violate Rule 1. Your old house is still considered to be your principal residence during a reasonable period you are trying to sell it.

Furthermore, if the rental activity produces a loss, you may be able to deduct this loss on your tax return [cf. Section 4]. This was the conclusion in a recent Court of Appeals decision, reversing a previous Tax Court opinion. In this case, a couple moved out of their old residence into a new home that had just been constructed. They put their old residence up for sale, but it took about a year to find a qualified buyer. During most of this period, they found a tenant to rent the old residence. They charged the going rate for such a rental property even though the rental payments did not entirely cover the mortgage payments the couple was making on the old house.

The Court of Appeals ruled that since they had abandoned the old house as a residence and were charging a fair market rental rate, their rental activity was a legitimate business activity with a profit motive. This meant they could deduct the loss produced by the rental activity according to the rules discussed in Section 4. [Bolaris, 56 AFTR 2d 85-6472]

Note however, that if a profit motive is lacking, no rental loss can be claimed. This was the conclusion of a 1986 Court case in which a prospective tenant was allowed to occupy a house rent-free, rather than being charged market rent. [Madan, TC Memo 1986-7]

Adjusted Sales Price

To determine the adjusted sales price in Rule 2 above, you subtract expenses directly connected with the sale from the actual sales price. This includes broker fees, advertising costs, legal fees, etc. You also subtract any expenses incurred for fixing up the house to make it more salable, provided the work is done within 90 days before you sign the contract to sell. You should pay the bill for this work no later than 30 days after the sale.

Fix-up costs include such things as painting, cleaning, and repairs. They do not include capital improvements such as buying a new furnace, replacing the roof, etc.

Note the peculiar treatment of fix-up costs. You take them into consideration when determining if you satisfy the rules for avoiding current payment of capital gains tax. But you do not deduct these fix-up costs when determining the actual amount of the capital gain.

Observe that Rule 2 does not state that you must invest as much cash in the new house as you had equity in the old house. It only compares the two selling prices. Thus, you could take out a larger mortgage on the new house and wind up with an excess of cash. This would make no difference as long as the cost of the new house was larger than the adjusted sales price of the old one.

You can use the above capital gains avoidance rule only once in any 2-year period. However, this restriction does not apply if you move because of a change of employment and your move qualifies for the moving expense deduction [cf. the *Moving Expenses* chapter].

If, by the time you file your return, you have not yet purchased a new house, but plan to do so and thereby qualify to avoid capital gains tax, you should attach a statement to that effect showing the computation of the gain on your old house. You do not have to pay any capital gains tax at the time you file. Later, when you do purchase your new house, you should notify in writing the Internal Revenue Service Center where you filed your return that you have replaced your old residence, giving the dates of purchase and occupancy of the new residence and its cost. If your plans change and it turns out you should have paid a capital gains tax, then you should file an amended return.

There are rules that deal with various husband and wife ownership circumstances when a marriage or separation is involved. For example, suppose 2 single persons marry, sell their separate personal residences, and each contribute 1/2 of the purchase price for a new jointly-held home. As long as the 2-year deadline is met and the purchase price of the new home exceeds the combined adjusted sales prices of the old homes, the tax-free rollover privilege applies.

Similarly, if a husband and wife divorce and sell their family home, they can each rollover his or her share of the profit tax-free into the purchase of separate residences. In this case, the purchase price of each individual's new home must exceed only the individual's share of the adjusted sales price of the old family residence.

Specific tax advice should be sought in complicated cases. This applies in particular to a married couple who sell an old residence and purchase another, but change the nature of their ownership (e.g. one individual owns the old residence in his individual name but the new residence is owned jointly).

Extending the 2-Year Rollover Period

Rule 3 gives you 2 years to sell your old house after moving into your new house. However, if you want to rent out the old house or are having difficulty selling it, there's a way to salvage the situation if the 2-year time period for selling your old home is about to expire. Namely, you can form a personally-owned corporation and sell your old home to this corporation before expiration of the 2-year time period. That way, you can avoid paying capital gains tax as long as the purchase price of your new home exceeds the price for which you sold your old home to the corporation you own. When the corporation later sells your old home, it will have to pay capital gains tax if the sale price exceeds the price for which you sold the home to your corporation.

The best type of corporation to set up for purchasing your home will probably be an S-Corporation, a simplified type of corporation that pays no tax itself, but passes income or expenses along to be reported on your personal tax return [cf. Section 1 of the *Outside Business Activity* chapter]. This type of corporation can offer an extra tax benefit if your old home is being rented out. The basis for computing depreciation on the home becomes the price paid by the corporation, rather than the original price you paid for the home [cf. the *Depreciation* chapter]. This can produce a tax loss which the S-Corporation passes along to be claimed on your personal tax return. To set up this type of arrangement for getting around the 2-year limitation, you should seek legal assistance.

Tax Deferred — Not Eliminated

Suppose you incur a capital gain which is not taxed because you purchase a new residence in accord with the provisions of the preceding subsections. Actually, the tax on this gain is not eliminated, just deferred. Eventually, if you sell a personal residence without purchasing a new personal residence, you may have to pay tax on the gain. The way it works is this. You subtract the capital gains on your first house from the purchase price of your second house to obtain a figure called the **basis** of your second house. If you then sell the second house and purchase a third house, the basis of the third house is equal to the purchase price of the third less the difference between the selling price of the second house and the basis of the second house. After the sale of your final house, you are liable for capital gains tax on the difference between the sales price and the basis of the final house. In effect, this computation produces a tax on the sum of all the capital gains realized on the purchase and sale of each of the houses you have owned.

If you suffer a capital loss on the sale of a house, you do not subtract the loss in making the preceding calculation. However, you get credit for any capital gains tax you paid on any of the sales because of failure to satisfy Rule 2.

What If You Don't Satisfy Rule 2?

If the purchase price of your new house is less than the adjusted sales price of your old house, then the difference between these amounts is not protected from capital gains tax. If you have a capital gain on your old residence exceeding this difference then you pay tax on the difference. Otherwise, you pay tax on the entire capital gain if there is one.

Example

You sell your old house and purchase a less expensive new house. The following computation illustrates the capital gains computation:

A	Sales price of old house (less selling costs)	$80,000
B	less Purchase price	-60,000
C	less Improvements	- 3,000
D	Capital gain on old house	17,000
E	Purchase price of new house	75,000
F	Capital gains on which tax is due (A-E)	5,000
G	Amount of capital gains not taxed (D-F)	12,000
H	Basis of new house (E-G)	$63,000

In the above, the purchase price of the new home in E can be increased by the cost of any improvements made to the new home within 2 years of the sale of the old one.

Form 2119

When you sell a personal residence, you are required to file Form 2119 with your tax return for the year during which the sale occurred. By filing a Form 2119 whenever you sell a personal residence, the appropriate computation of tax will be made if you ever fail to purchase a new residence which costs at least as much as the adjusted sales price of the previous residence. Form 2119 will lead you through the appropriate computation according to the general rules described above. You are required to file this form even if you do not have to pay capital gains tax.

If you have not yet purchased a new home by tax-filing time, but plan to do so within the 2-year limit, attach a note to your tax return to that effect. Then, when you do purchase a new home, fill out Form 2119 and mail it into the IRS.

In the past, many taxpayers did not bother to fill out Form 2119 when they sold a personal home. Since the IRS had no independent information showing that a sale had been made, no problem occurred. However, this situation has been changed.

Now, whenever a home is sold, the IRS receives a Form 1099-S reporting the proceeds of the sale. This form is required to be filed by the settlement attorney or other agent responsible for closing (and reporting) the transaction. Presumably, the IRS will double check to see that a Form 2119 is filed by the taxpayer corresponding to each 1099-S that is received. The settlement attorney or other agent is required to send you by February 28, 1991 a copy of any Form 1099-S filed with the IRS during 1990.

Special Break for Those Age 55 or Older

If you sell your home after you reach age 55 (or your spouse reaches age 55 if the home is owned in joint tenancy), then up to $125,000 of profit realized from the sale is exempt from capital gains tax. The home must have been your principal residence for at least 3 out of the 5 years preceding the sale. (The 3-year requirement is generally reduced to 1 year for handicapped persons who move into a nursing home or other similar institution.) This break is available on only one sale in your lifetime after July 26, 1978, even if less than $125,000 of profit on the sale is exempted.

If the $125,000 exemption is used while a couple is married, then both spouses are forbidden from using the exemption in the future, even if the home was only in one of the spouse's names. Because of this, couples planning to get married and move into a new home are best advised to sell their old homes before marriage if planning to use the $125,000 exemption.

This is illustrated by a recent IRS Private Letter Ruling. A man sold his home using the $125,000 exemption and later in the year got married. He and his new wife then bought a new home. After he died, she was able to get another $125,000 exemption when she sold the new home. Since she wasn't married on the date the first home was sold, she had not used up her one-time $125,000 exemption. In contrast, had the first home been sold after they had married, then her exemption would have been used up and she would have no exemption to apply to the sale of the new home. [Rev. Rul. 87-104, IRS 1987-43, 12]

As discussed above, the $125,000 exemption can be used only once in a lifetime, and not even once if one's spouse used it previously. Because of this, the master IRS computer keeps a file of all taxpayers that have claimed this exemption. If an attempt to claim this exemption again is made in a future year, the computer will kick out the tax return for examination.

Joint Tenancy vs. Individual Ownership

Most married couples own their homes (or other property) in joint tenancy, each spouse effectively being a 1/2 owner. Under this type of ownership, when one of the co-owners dies, the property passes automatically to the other co-owner. It cannot be willed to another individual.

There is a special type of joint tenancy available only to husband and wife, called *tenancy-by-the-entireties*. Under ordinary joint tenancy, one party alone can demand to dissolve the tenancy and retrieve his share. But under tenancy-by-the-entireties, generally, both parties must agree on any dissolution of the ownership. As far as tax laws are concerned, ordinary joint tenancy and tenancy-by-the-entireties are treated identically.

Joint tenancy is the prevalent form of ownership among married couples mostly for personal reasons — the sense of partnership and family unity that it suggests. Also, joint tenancy provides a simple way for property to be passed on to an heir. Ownership is automatically transferred to the surviving spouse without having to go through probate proceedings. However, there are tax aspects to owning property in joint tenancy which bear upon the choice of ownership for many married couples. In fact, it is wise for a married couple to periodically review the manner in which property is owned.

For married couples filing a joint return, it makes no current tax difference whether a house (or other assets) are owned jointly or individually by one of the spouses. It is only when property is transferred after the death of one spouse that a tax difference arises.

There are two separate taxes to consider. First, there is an estate tax which is levied, when an individual dies, against the total value of his assets which are passed on to his heirs by will or automatic transfer under joint tenancy. Under current law, any amount of property which one spouse inherits from the other is totally exempt from estate tax. Also, one spouse can give any amount of property to the other without incurring any gift tax. This means that for married couples who remain together until death do them part, the estate and gift taxes do not directly bear upon the form of ownership chosen. Furthermore, married couples can change the type of ownership from joint to individual or conversely, without any gift tax complications. (However, more well-to-do individuals should seek professional advice on how various forms of ownership affect the estate tax that becomes due when the longer-living spouse dies.)

The second type of tax, namely income tax on capital gains, is affected by what form of ownership is chosen. The basic rule is this. When property is inherited by one individual from another, it is given a *fresh start* basis. That is, for purposes of future capital gains computations, it is treated as though it were purchased at its market value at the time of inheritance. When the property is later sold, tax is due only on the appreciation in value since the time it was inherited. No tax is ever paid on the increase in value that took place when the property belonged to the previous owner.

From this point of view, it is better for the spouse who dies first to own the property in his name only. That way any pre-death increase in value escapes capital gains tax. If the property is owned jointly, then only $1/2$ the property gets the fresh start basis.

Example

John and Mary purchased a house for $50,000. John dies and the house is inherited by Mary who sells it later for $125,000. At the time of John's death, the house was worth $100,000.

Case 1. John owned the house in his name only.
The house gets a stepped-up basis of $100,000 when it is inherited by Mary. When she sells it, her capital gain is $125,000 – $100,000 = $25,000.

Case 2. Mary owned the house in her name only.
Mary's capital gain is simply the selling price minus the purchase price, $125,000 – $50,000 = $75,000.

Case 3. John and Mary owned the house in joint tenancy.
The house is treated as though it were owned $1/2$ by each of them. John's half gets a stepped-up basis of $50,000 ($1/2$ the market value at his death) and is sold for $62,500 ($1/2 \times \$125,000$), a capital gain of $62,500 – $50,000 = $12,500. Mary's half was purchased for $25,000 ($1/2 \times \$50,000$) and sold for $62,500 ($1/2 \times \$125,000$), a capital gain of $62,500 – $25,000 = $37,500. The total capital gain is $12,500 + $37,500 = $50,000.

The above example shows that capital gains are lowest when the spouse who dies first owned the property in his name only and highest when the surviving spouse was the sole owner. This difference may not lead to a tax difference because of the exemptions from capital gains tax described earlier in this Section. But for those who will not qualify under these exemptions or wish to conserve their once-in-a-lifetime $125,000 exemption for those age 55 or over, the difference can be substantial. In such a case it might be advisable to shift jointly-owned property to the spouse most likely to die first, the husband in most cases. This will benefit the wife by lowering her tax upon sale after her husband's death. (However, shifts made within the one year period prior to the husband's death do not count.) If the wife does not wish to give up the security of her ownership position, a local attorney may be able to find a solution under the law such as her retention of the right to live in the house.

The above only touches upon the basic considerations involved in choosing the proper form of ownership. A qualified attorney should be consulted before making any major decisions. This is especially true in common law states where the rules governing ownership transfers between spouses are more complicated.

Section 4:
Renting a Home to Others

If you rent out a home you own, then you report the rent as income and you take the expenses associated with the rental as a deduction against the income. Special rules cover the situation when expenses exceed income. As discussed later in this section, these rules may prevent you from claiming a loss in this situation.

There are also special *passive loss* rules that can restrict the ability to deduct losses on rental activities. However, these passive loss rules do not apply to losses up to $25,000 incurred by persons with income under $100,000, provided they sufficiently participate in managing the rental. This $25,000 limit is phased out for those with income in the $100,000 — $150,000 range. [cf. Section 2 of the *Investing Your Money* chapter for details on these *passive loss* rules.] In the remainder of this section, we assume that these passive loss rules do **not** affect your total deduction because of this $25,000 exemption or the existence of offsetting passive profits.

Deductible expenses include advertising costs, legal fees, utility bills you pay, homeowner's insurance, management fees, interest, and taxes. You can also deduct depreciation according to the rules described in the *Expensing and Depreciation* chapter. You compute your depreciation starting from the point you first rent your home as described in the *Expensing and Depreciation* chapter. That is, your depreciation is based on the original purchase price of the house plus the cost of improvements (less any casualty losses you have claimed) or else on the fair market value of the house when you start renting it out, whichever is lower.

Depreciating Your Furniture

If you rent out your home furnished, then you can deduct depreciation on the furnishings and appliances. Since used furniture and appliances are usually worth less than their original purchase price, you will have to estimate their current fair market value and use this as the basis for depreciation. You can use either the straight-line or accelerated depreciation method for 7-year property as described in the *Expensing and Depreciation* chapter.

How are Rental Income and Expenses Reported?

You report your rental income and expenses on Schedule E. Note that expenses connected with renting a home are not considered itemized deductions. Thus, they may be deducted even if the standard deduction is claimed.

Example

Jones rents out a house from September 1, 1990 until December 31, 1991, a total of 16 months.

Depreciation Calculation on House

Jones originally paid $80,000 for the house when he purchased it in 1981 and later added central air conditioning at a cost of $4,000. Since the sum of these two amounts, $84,000, is less than the current fair market value, this sum is used as the basis for depreciation.

The following depreciation calculation is made according to the procedure explained in the Expensing and Depreciation chapter.

(1) Depreciation for 4 months from
   9/1/90 to 12/31/90..1.06% × $84,000 = $ 890
(2) Depreciation for year from
   1/1/91 to 12/31/91 ....3.64% × $84,000 = $3,058

Depreciation Calculation on Furniture

Jones estimates that the furnishings and appliances in the house have a current value of $6,000. Since $6,000 is less than his original cost, it is used as the basis for depreciation. He uses the accelerated method for 7-year property, as described in the Expensing and Depreciation chapter.

(1) Depreciation for 1990...14.29% × $6,000 = $ 858
(2) Depreciation for 1991...24.49% × $6,000 = $1,470

Total Expenses

Jones pays $500 per month in mortgage interest. He also pays $1,200 per year in property taxes and $120 per year in insurance. In order to make the appropriate allocations to 1990, these latter two amounts are prorated on a monthly basis— $100 per month for taxes and $10 per month for insurance.

Expense Summary

	1990	1991
Depreciation on house:	$ 890	$3,058
Depreciation on furniture:	858	1,470
Interest:	$500 × 4 mo. =2,000	$500 x 12 mo. = 6,000
Taxes:	$100 × 4 mo. = 400	$100 x 12 mo. = 1,200
Insurance:	$ 10 × 4 mo. = 40	$10 x 12 mo. = 120
Advertising:	25	0
Legal expenses:	40	137
Totals:	$4,253	$11,985

Rent

Jones rents out his house for $625 per month. The tenants pay the cost of utilities. Thus Jones receives rent of $625 × 4 months = $2,500 in 1990 and $625 × 12 months = $7,500 in 1991.

Net Result

For 1990, Jones has rental income of $2,500 and expenses of $4,253, a net loss of $1,753 for 1990.

For 1991, Jones has rental income of $7,500 and expenses of $11,985, a net loss of $4,485 for 1991.

The depreciation deductions illustrated in the above example apply to houses placed into rental service after 1986. Houses placed into rental service in 1986 or earlier, come under more generous rules [cf. the 1987 edition of this Tax Guide], even if the rental period extended into 1987 and beyond.

Profit Motive Needed to Establish Loss

As in the above example, it may turn out that your expenses exceed the rental income, producing a net loss. In order to deduct the loss on your tax return, you should have a profit motive when you rent out the house. To begin with, you must charge the going rate for rent in your locality. But even if you charge this "fair market rate," the IRS may still question your profit motive.

This is confirmed by an IRS Private Letter Ruling (#7826006) concerning a College Professor who rented out his house when he went away on leave of absence. The Professor had listed his house with a rental agency and charged the fair market value for rent in his area. A local IRS office had apparently sought advice from the National Office on what additional factors should be considered in deciding whether a loss should be allowed

The IRS ruling stressed that the Professor must have a profit motive. If he was just renting out his house to lessen the loss that would occur if the house were left unrented, this would not suffice. He must have actually intended to make a profit on the transaction. Beyond this, the IRS ruling did not give much further guidance, telling the local IRS office that, *"The question of whether the taxpayer had a profit-making objective is a determination to be made by you based upon all the surrounding facts and circumstances."*

According to letters we have received from readers of prior editions, the IRS has in fact been challenging the profit motive of individuals when they rent out their personal residences while temporarily located away from home. Since there is often no chance that the rental income will exceed the taxes, interest, and other expenses, the IRS simply claims that there could be no profit motive. The taxpayer is often stymied as to how to counter this logically simple objection.

However, there is a strong argument that can be made by the taxpayer in this situation. Namely, the profit motive in owning a rental house comes from the appreciation in the value of the house that will occur over the period of time the house is rented out. In fact, investors who buy houses for the sole purpose of renting them out are often in precisely this situation. Their expenses exceed their rental income but they look to the profit that will be made eventually when the house is sold for more than its purchase price.

There is a Tax Court case that supports this position. An individual owned some property which he rented out at substantial annual losses. The IRS challenged the deduction of his losses, claiming that these large losses showed there could be no profit motive present.

But the Tax Court permitted the losses to be deducted. It ruled that considering the anticipated appreciation of value of the property, a profit motive was present. In permitting the eventual increase in property value to be considered, it quoted the Income Tax Regulations as follows:

> *"The term 'income for [these purposes] includes not merely income of the taxable year but also income which the taxpayer has realized in a prior taxable year or may realize in subsequent taxable years, and is not confined to recurring income but applies as well to gains from the disposition of property. For example, if defaulted bonds, the interest from which if received would be includable in income, are purchased with the expectation of realizing capital gain on their resale, even though no current yield thereon is anticipated, ordinary and necessary expenses thereafter paid or incurred in connection with such bonds are deductible. Similarly, ordinary and necessary expenses paid or incurred in the management, conservation, or maintenance of a building devoted to rental purposes are deductible notwithstanding that there is actually no income therefrom in the taxable year, and regardless of the manner in which or the purpose for which the property in question was acquired."* [TC Memo 1978-85]

Home Rented Out for Part of the Year

If you rent out a home for less than 15 days during the year, then it is considered that no business transaction took place. In this case, you neither report the rental income nor deduct any expenses. You deduct your taxes and interest on Schedule A as though no rental had taken place.

If you rent out your home for at least 15 days during the year, and use it for personal purposes part of the year, then you cannot deduct a rental loss if the following condition is satisfied:

> *The home was used for personal purposes both:*
> *(i) more than 14 days*
>
>   *and*
>
> *(ii) more than 10% of the number of days during the year on which the home is rented out.*

However, if the above condition applies, then the home qualifies as a *primary* or *second home* under the rules discussed in Section 1. This means that all interest attributed to your personal use of the home can be deducted as *home interest* on line 9 of Schedule A.

However, if you do not satisfy the above condition, then you have not used the home enough to qualify it as your *primary* or *second* home. This means that the interest attributed to your personal use of the home is considered *personal interest,* only 10%-deductible as described in the *Interest* chapter. However in this case, because of your minimal personal use, you would qualify to deduct a loss from the rental activity.

Exception

For a home which is rented out for part of the year and used as your principal residence the remainder of the year, the above restriction on deducting rental losses does not apply if either:

(1) The rental period consisted of at least 12 consecutive months (not necessarily all in the same calendar year)

or

(2) The rental period was a consecutive period of less than 12 months ending in the sale of the residence.

For example, if you rent out your home from June 1, 1990 through May 31, 1991 and use it as your principal residence the remainder of 1990 and 1991, then the consecutive 12-month rental period satisfies the above exception.

If you are planning to be out of town for an extended period of time, you should take careful note of the above exception. By making sure you rent out your house for at least 12 consecutive months, you might become eligible to deduct a rental loss on your tax return. As shown by the preceding example, this could make a significant difference in your taxes. (This exception permitting losses on rental houses to be deducted can be used on a *primary or second home* [cf. Section 1] even if the passive loss rules, as discussed in Section 2 of the *Investing Your Money* chapter, would otherwise apply. More specifically, any interest disallowed under the passive loss rules can be claimed as primary or second home interest on line 9 of Schedule A. To qualify, you must use the home during the year for personal purposes both (i) more than 14 days, and (ii) more than 10% of the number of days during the year for which the home is rented out.)

What Happens If a Loss Cannot Be Deducted?

If you are prevented from deducting a loss on a rental house for the reasons above, you must use the following procedure for offsetting your rental income with your expenses: Start with the *gross rental income*. This equals the rent you receive from tenants less the costs of obtaining these tenants (advertising, rental agency fees, etc.). From this amount, (a) first subtract taxes and interest, (b) second, subtract rental expenses such as maintenance, insurance, utilities, etc., and (c) third, subtract depreciation. If a loss results, you cannot deduct the loss. The rental simply produces no tax result — neither a gain nor a loss. Of course in (a), (b), (c), you deduct only that proportion of the annual expense which corresponds to the proportion of time the house is rented out.

Note that the above order of deducting expenses forces you to deduct taxes and interest first. This prevents you from using the other expenses in (b) and (c) first to offset the rental income and then claiming the full amount of taxes and interest as an ordinary itemized deduction on Schedule A. However, if the allowable tax and interest expenses should exceed your rental income, then the excess is deductible in the usual place on Schedule A. In any event, you still deduct on Schedule A that proportion of interest and taxes corresponding to the percentage of time the home is used for personal purposes.

Any rental losses on a residence rented out for part of a year which cannot be deducted as described above can be carried over to a future year. That is, these losses can be deducted against any rental income you receive on the residence in a future year.

Example Revisited

In the preceding example, net losses resulted both in 1990 and 1991. Since the home was not used for personal purposes in 1991, the full loss of $4,485 is reported on the 1991 tax return. According to the 12-month exception described above, the $1,753 loss is also deductible on the 1990 tax return, provided the home is used as a principal residence for the period preceding the rental.

However, let us now suppose that the home was rented out only for the 4-month period Sept. 1, 1990–Dec. 31, 1990 and used for personal purposes the remainder of 1990. In such a case, the restriction on deducting losses would apply. The rental would produce neither a net gain nor a net loss on the 1990 tax return. However, the $1,753 loss that cannot be deducted in 1990 can be carried over to a future year.

Note that since the $2,000 interest and $400 taxes attributable to the rental period total less than the $2,475 gross rental income ($2,500 rent less $25 advertising cost), these amounts are used up in offsetting the rental income according to the (a), (b), (c) priority described above. Thus, these amounts cannot be deducted in the Interest or Taxes Sections on Schedule A. However, the interest and taxes attributable to the period the house was used for personal purposes can be deducted as itemized deductions on Schedule A.

Note: The above discussion is meant to give general guidance on the proper treatment of homes that are used both for personal and rental purposes. Because of pending IRS regulations, there is currently a lack of certainty as to the exact treatment that applies in every case. Especially if the passive loss rules come into play [cf. Section 2 of the *Investing Your Money* chapter], professional assistance should be sought to handle your writeoffs in the proper way. Next year's edition of this Tax Guide will contain further information on this issue.

Renting to Relatives

Rental of a residence by an individual to a family member can be treated the same as rental to any other individual provided a fair market value is charged and the dwelling is the principal residence of the person to whom it is rented.

The *fair market rental* means the amount generally being charged in your locality for similar accommodations. However, a recent court case shows that it is all right to give a suitable discount to a family member. In this case, an individual rented a house he owned to his parents. The fair market rent that could have been charged a stranger was $450. But the Court ruled that this could be reduced by 20% to $360 because a management fee was avoided and the parents were trustworthy tenants. [Bindsell, TC Memo 1983-411].

Chapter 10

Automobile Expenses

Many types of auto travel can be deducted as described in the *Travel* chapter—convention trips, travel to and at a temporary job, travel between two jobs, travel to obtain education, etc. In addition, you can deduct for miscellaneous automobile travel connected with your employment such as travel from your office to libraries to do research, travel to pick up official visitors at an airport, etc.

There are two basic methods to deduct for business use of an automobile which you own. The first method is to deduct a *standard rate* per mile plus parking and tolls. The second method is to compute your *actual expenses*. As discussed below, the second method can prove superior because it includes a write-off for the cost of the automobile in addition to operating costs.

There are special rules for automobiles purchased after June 18, 1984. Under these rules [cf. the *Expensing and Depreciation* chapter] illustrated later in this chapter, a special depreciation table applies if business use does not exceed 50%. And an employee must use the standard mileage rate unless the use of his auto is required by his employer.

Where on the Income Tax Form Do You Deduct Auto Expenses?

An employee uses Part II of Form 2106, *Employee Business Expenses*, on which to list his automobile expenses. The total of automobile expenses is then entered as a *miscellaneous deduction* on Schedule A of the 1990 tax return. As discussed in the *Miscellaneous Deductions* chapter, the sum total of travel expenses plus other miscellaneous deductions is subjected to a 2% of Adjusted Gross Income floor.

Self-employed persons claim auto expenses on Schedule C the same as any other business expense related to their self-employment activity. Thus, these expenses escape the 2% of Adjusted Gross Income floor that applies to miscellaneous deductions; also, non-itemizers as well as itemizers get to deduct their auto expenses on Schedule C.

If, as discussed later, expensing or depreciation is claimed for an auto, then Form 4562 must be filled out also [cf. the *Expensing and Depreciation* chapter]. Also, if a person claims auto expenses in connection with a self-employment activity, then Part III of Form 4562 must be filled out whether or not expensing or depreciation is claimed.

Recordkeeping Rules

You are required to maintain adequate records to support your deduction for auto expenses.

In general, this means you must maintain a diary or similar written record which, for each job or business use of your auto, contains the following information:

1.   Date;

2.   Business purpose of trip;

       and

3.   Business mileage traveled.

You should also keep track of the total mileage your auto was driven during the year by, say, writing down the odometer readings at the beginning and end of each year.

If you are deducting your actual expenses rather than using the standard mileage rate, you must also record the date and amount of each expenditure for gasoline, repairs, etc. You can take the sum of such expenses and prorate this sum based on the percentage your auto was driven for business purposes. For example, if your auto was used 60% for business purposes and you spent $1,000 for gasoline during the year, you would be entitled to a deduction of 60% × $1,000 = $600 for gasoline (assuming you are deducting your actual expenses rather than using the standard mileage rate).

Your records should be maintained in a *timely* manner. This means you write down each entry soon enough that you have full recall of all the details. However, it is no longer required that your records be contemporaneous with business use. According to the IRS, it is acceptable to record your usage or expenses at the end of each week. However, even if your records are kept weekly, they should still give a daily breakdown of each separate period of business use.

It is not necessary to write down information in a diary (or other record) which duplicates information reflected on a receipt as long as your diary and receipts complement each other in an orderly manner. And you do not have to write down the business purpose of your travel if it is evident from the surrounding facts and circumstances.

On the next page is a suggested recordkeeping format for an auto for which you use the standard mileage rate. You can use a different format as long as the requisite information is recorded.

AUTO MILEAGE & EXPENSE RECORD

Date	Destination/Business Purpose	Odometer Start	End	(Round Trip) Mileage Bus.	Invest.	Med.	Char.	Parking/ Tolls
1/1	Beginning Odometer Reading	7168						
1/5	Dr. Jones—appointment	7216	7237			21		
1/6	Drop off Goodwill donation	7237	7259				22	
1/10	Seminar at State Univ.	7342	7371	29				$3.00
1/12	Pick up Dr. Smith (Visiting Consultant) at Airport	7410	7462	52				
1/16	Church Choir Rehearsal	7531	7543				12	
1/18	Pick up Medicine at Drug Store	7571	7579			8		
1/20	Consult with Stockbroker	7612	7632		20			
12/31	Ending Odometer Reading		15,641					
	TOTALS			1,264	124	212	314	$146
	CENTS/MILE ALLOWED			26	26	9	12	
	TOTAL DEDUCTIONS			$329	$32	$19	$38	$146

Sampling Rule for Local Auto Travel

The type of detailed records normally expected for out-of-town travel do not have to be kept for local auto travel of a recurring nature. According to a 1986 IRS regulation, it is permissible to use a "sampling technique" for deducting such travel on your tax return [IRS Reg. 1.274-5T]. The following examples are adapted from this regulation.

Example 1.

You work at 2 different business locations and often drive from one location to the other on the same day. You should record the date of each trip at or near the time of each trip. However, you need to record the distance between the 2 business locations only once, not each time you drive. You also should record the total number of miles your auto is driven overall. This will satisfy the recordkeeping requirement for this travel.

> ### Example 2.
>
> *You use your auto during the year for miscellaneous business travel, e.g. travel between job locations, to seminars, to libraries, etc. You keep adequate records for the first 3 months of the year which show that this business mileage is 15% of the total mileage put on your auto. You also record the beginning and final odometer readings for the year which show your auto was driven for 10,000 miles during the year. Assuming it is established that your business usage continues at approximately the same rate for the remainder of the year, your records support a deduction for 1,500 miles (15% × 10,000 miles) of business auto travel for the year.*

> ### Example 3.
>
> *Same as Example 2 except that you keep adequate records during the first week of each month which show your auto is used 15% for business travel. As long as it is established that these are "representative" weeks, your records support a deduction for 15% of the total mileage for the year.*

Observe that in both Examples 2 and 3, the sampling period constitutes about $1/4$ of the year. The IRS specifically states that this can be an adequate sampling period. However, the IRS has not stated what the shortest acceptable sampling period would be. For example, if records were kept only during 1 or 2 months of the year, there is no current guidance as to whether or not this would constitute an acceptable sampling period.

Information Required on Tax Return

You do not include your mileage or expense records when you send in your tax return. Rather, you keep these records in case your tax return is audited. However, on your 1990 tax return, the following questions (stated in slightly different words) must be answered for all auto travel (local and out-of-town) either on Form 2106 for employees or on Part III of Form 4562 for self-employment travel:

1. When was the vehicle first placed into service?
2. What was the total number of miles driven during the year?
3. Was the vehicle used for commuting? If so, what was the total commuting mileage for the year?
4. How many miles was the vehicle driven for non-commuting personal purposes?
5. Was another vehicle available for personal use?
6. Do you have evidence to support your deduction? If so, is the evidence written?

Note that the purpose of asking the above questions on tax returns is twofold. First, the existence of these questions (in particular question number 6) will discourage carelessly made estimates, rather than more careful recordkeeping. Second, if the IRS examines the answers to these questions, indication of an unjustified deduction may be spotlighted. For example, if the answer to question 3 indicates the auto was used a large percentage for non-deductible commuting, this may be inconsistent with the percentage of business use claimed. Or, if the answer to question 6 is "no," this will raise a red flag concerning the ability to justify the auto deduction claimed.

Note that a written re-creation of your business travel made at the end of the year might entitle you to answer "yes" to question 6 above, thereby avoiding spotlighting your return for audit. However, should your return actually be audited, such a re-creation would not actually satisfy the recordkeeping requirement discussed earlier in this chapter.

The Standard Mileage Rate

Under the standard rate method, you deduct 26 cents per mile for each mile of business use. In addition, you may deduct parking fees and tolls.

The standard mileage rate is not meant to cover interest or taxes on the auto. These might be able to be deducted separately according to the rules discussed in the *Interest* and *Taxes* chapters. However, note that sales tax can no longer be claimed as an itemized deduction. Instead, it is now considered a part of the purchase price, perhaps boosting an expensing or depreciation calculation based on the cost of the auto.

There are some restrictions which the IRS has placed on the use of the standard mileage rate [Rev. Proc. 82-61]. First of all, if you use the standard rate, it must be used right from the beginning of business use. That is, you cannot use the standard rate on an automobile for which you have deducted your actual expenses in a prior year. This restriction applies to automobiles first placed into service for business purposes in 1981 or later years. For automobiles placed into service before 1981, you cannot now use the standard rate if either the accelerated depreciation method or extra 20% first year allowance which applied before 1981 was used. Instead, you must make a computation of your actual automobile expenses and base your deduction on that amount.

Secondly, once you use the standard rate on an automobile you cannot use the usual depreciation method on that automobile in a later year. Instead, you must continue to use the standard rate, or else compute your actual expenses using an appropriate straight-line depreciation method. This restriction does not apply to automobiles placed into service before 1981.

Extras in Addition to the Standard Rate

According to the IRS, the standard rate is used *"in lieu of all operating and fixed costs of the automobile allocable to business purposes. Such items as depreciation, maintenance and repairs, tires, gasoline (including all taxes thereon), oil, insurance, and registration fees are included in operating and fixed costs. However, parking fees and tolls attributable to use for business purposes may be deducted as separate items."* [Rev. Proc. 82-61]

According to a 1984 court case, the above quote is not interpreted as restricting the extras that may be deducted to the *parking fees and tolls* described in the third sentence above. Other items not covered by the first two sentences can be deducted also. In this case, an individual used his automobile 50% for business purposes for which he claimed the standard mileage rate. During the year, he incurred towing expenses of $173.25.

The Court ruled that these towing costs were not part of the operating and fixed costs covered by the standard mileage rate. It ruled,

"*. .under the standard rate method, petitioners are also entitled to deduct certain additional amounts actually incurred, such as parking and tolls. We believe that petitioners' towing costs which respondent has conceded were substantiated fall within this category.*"

Since the individual's automobile was used 50% for business purposes, the Court allowed a deduction of 50% × $173.25 = $86.62 for towing costs. The allocation was not based on the nature of auto use when the towing costs were actually incurred. [Alcorden, TC Memo 1984-334]

No indication is given as to what items besides towing costs would be allowed in addition to the standard rate covering *"operating and fixed"* costs. Clearly, garage rental fees could be considered parking fees. But other extras (e.g. auxiliary auto supplies) are neither clearly included or excluded. What the above court case suggests, for the first time, is that an individual can use the standard rate and still be entitled to deduct extras besides parking and tolls which can also be considered neither *operating* nor *fixed* costs.

Computing Your Actual Auto Expenses

Instead of the standard mileage rate, you can deduct your actual automobile expenses. This includes gas, oil, repairs, insurance, etc. — plus parking and tolls. It also includes a portion of the cost of the automobile. It is here that a substantial deduction can be claimed.

To write off the cost of the automobile, you use the appropriate expensing or depreciation procedure as described in the *Expensing and Depreciation* chapter. However, there are special maximum limitations, described below, that apply only to automobiles.

Also, as described in Section 1 of that chapter, expensing or depreciation can be claimed by an employee for job-related use of an auto purchased after June 18, 1984 only if such use is required by his employer. Otherwise, the standard mileage rate must be used.

Interest on an auto owned by an employee is considered personal interest even if the auto is used for job-related purposes. As such, it can only be claimed as an itemized deduction on line 12a of Schedule A, subject to the 10%-reduction rule for personal interest [cf. the *Interest* chapter].

Expensing and Depreciation Rules for Autos

There are special **maximum limitations** on the total of expensing plus depreciation deductions that can be claimed for a given automobile in any one year. The following table gives the maximum limits on annual deductions that can be claimed for an automobile placed into service in 1987–1990. (For autos placed into service before 1987, different limitations apply [cf. previous editions of this Tax Guide]. Also, after 1990, the limits will be raised according to the increase in the automobile component of the Consumer Price Index.) These limits were designed to affect only "luxury" automobiles costing more than $13,300 in 1990. However, because of the expensing option, the initial first year limit can affect the deduction for any automobile purchased in 1990 costing more than $2,660.

Maximum Annual Deductions for Autos Placed into Service in 1987 or 1988

Year	Maximum Deduction
1	$2,560
2	4,100
3	2,450
each succeeding year	1,475

Maximum Annual Deductions for Autos Placed into Service in 1989 or 1990

Year	Maximum Deduction
1	$2,660
2	4,200
3	2,550
each succeeding year	1,475

The above limitations apply to an auto used 100% for business purposes. They are reduced proportionately for autos used partly for personal purposes. For example, the upper limit on an auto used 60% for business purposes would be 60% of the above amounts.

If the maximum limitations come into play, the full value of the automobile can still be written off—the writeoff period is just extended. Examples 3 and 4 illustrate this situation.

When the expensing method is used, the remainder not expensed is depreciated according to the usual 5-year table [cf. the *Expensing and Depreciation* chapter]. However, the total expensing plus depreciation deductions for a given year are subject to the maximum limitations described above. This can lead to an unexpected pitfall. [Temp. Reg. 1.280F-2T]

To illustrate, suppose that an automobile was purchased for $10,060 in 1990 and the maximum expensing deduction of $2,660 is claimed in the first year. The remainder, $10,600 – $2,660 = $7,400, would then be depreciated according to the 20%, 32%, 19.2%, 11.52%, 11.52%, 5.76% percentages provided by the 5-year depreciation table. Since the maximum $2,660 writeoff has been used up by the expensing deduction, no depreciation deduction is allowed for the first year. The depreciation deductions for the remaining years are as provided in the following table. Observe that an extra 7th year is now required to achieve the full $10,060 writeoff for the cost of the auto.

Year		Deduction
1990		$2,660 expensing
1991	32% × $7,400 =	2,368 depreciation
1992	19.2% × $7,400 =	1,421 depreciation
1993	11.52% × $7,400 =	852 depreciation
1994	11.52% × $7,400 =	852 depreciation
1995	5.76% × $7,400 =	436 depreciation
1996	Remainder =	1,471 depreciation
		$10,060

It is possible to avoid the above pitfall of spilling over the auto writeoff into a 7th year. The key is to claim an expensing deduction of less than $2,660, with the remaining depreciation deductions filling out the normal depreciation period for 5-year items. This can generally be done for automobiles costing less than $13,300 by using the following formula to compute the optimal Expensing amount E:

$$E = \frac{\$13,300 - \text{Cost of Auto}}{4}$$

For autos costing $13,300 or more, the depreciation method alone should be used, with no expensing deduction.

Example 1. Auto Costing Less than $13,300

An auto is purchased in 1990 for $9,060 and is used entirely for business purposes. According to the formula above, the following amount E should be expensed:

$$E = \frac{\$13,300 - \$9,060}{4} = \$1,060$$

The remainder, $9,060 – $1,060 = $8,000, is depreciated via the usual 5-year depreciation table.

Year	Expensing		Depreciation	Deduction
1990	$1,060	+	20% × $8,000 =	$2,660
1991			32% × $8,000 =	2,560
1992			19.2% × $8,000 =	1,536
1993			11.52% × $8,000 =	921
1994			11.52% × $8,000 =	921
1995			5.76% × $8,000 =	462
				$9,060

Example 2.

Same as Example 1 except that the auto is used 60% for business purposes. In this case the amount to be written off is 60% of the cost, namely 60% × $9,060 = $5,436. In the formula for E, the $13,300 is similarly multiplied by 60%: 60% × $13,300 = $7,980. Thus, the expensing deduction E in this situation is:

$$E = \frac{\$7,980 - \$5,436}{4} = \$636$$

The remainder, $5,436 – $636 = $4,800, is depreciated via the usual depreciation table for 5-year property.

Year	Expensing		Depreciation	Deduction
1990	$636	+	20% × $4,800 =	$1,596
1991			32% × $4,800 =	1,536
1992			19.2% × $4,800 =	922
1993			11.52% × $4,800 =	553
1994			11.52% × $4,800 =	553
1995			5.76% × $4,800 =	276
				$5,436

Note that the deduction for 1990 is equal to the maximum limitation that applies, namely 60% × $2,660 = $1,596.

Example 3. Auto Costing $13,300 or More

An auto is purchased in 1990 for $16,000 and is used 100% for business purposes. Because the auto costs more than $13,300, the deduction produced by the 5-year depreciation table would exceed the maximum limitations ($2,660 is less than 20% × $16,000 = $3,200; $4,200 is less than 32% × $16,000 = $5,120, etc.). Thus, the depreciation deductions for each year are equal to the maximum limitations *until the final year, when the amount used is chosen to fully depreciate the $16,000 cost:*

Year	Deduction
1990	$2,660
1991	4,200
1992	2,550
1993	1,475
1994	1,475
1995	1,475
1996	1,475
1997	690
	$16,000

In the above example it is presumed that the automobile continues to be owned through the end of 1997. Under any depreciation method, for items in the 5-year or 7-year category placed into service in 1990, half a year's depreciation is allowed in the year of disposition. Thus, in the above example, if the automobile were disposed of in 1995, the depreciation deduction for 1995 would be $1/2 \times \$1,475 = \$738$. The automobile would produce no further deductions after 1995, the year of disposition.

Also, in the above example, it was assumed the automobile is used 100% for business purposes. The following example illustrates a situation where business usage is less than 100%.

Example 4.

Same as the previous example, except that instead of 100%, the business use percentage is 60% for 1990–1993, and 55% for 1994–1997. In this case, the amounts in the previous example are multiplied by these percentages to arrive at the depreciation deductions for each year.

Year	Depreciation Deduction
1990	60% × $2,660 = $1,596
1991	60% × $4,200 = 2,520
1992	60% × $2,550 = 1,530
1993	60% × $1,475 = 885
1994	55% × $1,475 = 811
1995	55% × $1,475 = 811
1996	55% × $1,475 = 811
1997	55% × $ 690 = 380

Comparing the Actual Expenses Method with the Standard Mileage Rate

The following examples illustrate the use of the actual expenses method and compare the results with the standard mileage rate.

Example 5.

You purchased an automobile in February, 1990 for $9,060. You drive the automobile 10,000 miles per year for each of the years 1990–1995. Of these 10,000 miles, 6,000 (60% of the total) are for business purposes.

Actual Cost Method

Your operating expenses per year are as follows:

Repairs and parts	*$650*
Insurance	*250*
Car washing	*50*
Gas and oil	*700*
License (including driver's license)	*75*
Motor club membership	*40*
Garage rent	*150*
Total	*$1,915*

Since your auto is being used 60% for business purposes, the amount of operating expenses attributable to business use is 60% × $1,915 = $1,149.

The expensing and depreciation deductions for this situation have already been calculated in Example 2. Thus, the total deductions for each year are as follows:

Year	Expensing/ Depreciation		Operating Expenses		Total Deduction
1990	$1,596	+	$1,149	=	$2,745
1991	1,536	+	1,149	=	2,685
1992	922	+	1,149	=	2,071
1993	553	+	1,149	=	1,702
1994	553	+	1,149	=	1,702
1995	276	+	1,149	=	1,425
					$12,330

(In addition to the above amounts, parking fees and tolls incurred in business-related travel are deductible.)

On a per business mile basis, the figures above become:

1990:	$	2,745/6,000 business miles =	46 cents per mile
1991:	$	2,685/6,000 business miles =	45 cents per mile
1992:	$	2,071/6,000 business miles =	35 cents per mile
1993:	$	1,702/6,000 business miles =	28 cents per mile
1994:	$	1,702/6,000 business miles =	28 cents per mile
1995:	$	1,425/6,000 business miles =	24 cents per mile
Overall:		$12,330/36,000 business miles =	34 cents per mile

(The above figures were based on a purchase price of $9,060 and will change according to any change in purchase price. For example, for an auto costing $13,300 or more, the overall cents per mile figure in this example for the period 1990–1995 would be 41 cents instead of 34 cents.)

Standard Mileage Rate

The standard mileage rate is 26 cents per mile. This is less than the amount computed under the actual cost method. However, when an employee uses an auto purchased after June 18, 1984 for job-related travel, such use must be required by his employer in order for the actual cost method to be used [cf. the Depreciation *chapter]. Otherwise, the standard mileage rate must be used.*

Comment. Observe that under the depreciation option, the higher the percentage of business use, the higher will be the deduction. Thus, it pays you to limit your personal use of an auto which is used for business purposes in order to increase the percentage of business use. For example, if you own two automobiles, use one of them (as much as possible) for business purposes and the other (as much as possible) for your personal activities.

As described in Section 1 of the *Depreciation* chapter, special rules apply to automobiles purchased after June 18, 1984 which are not used more than 50% for business purposes in each of the first 6 years of ownership. For such automobiles, the special *Listed Property Depreciation Table* must be used [cf. Section 3 of the *Depreciation* chapter].

Example 6.

You purchased an automobile in March, 1990 for $12,000. You drive the automobile 10,000 miles during each of 1990–1995. Of these miles, 30% are for business purposes each year. Since the automobile is used 30% for business purposes, the cost attributable to business use is 30% × $12,000 = $3,600.

Your operating expenses (not including expensing or depreciation) total $1,200 per year. Since your auto is being used 30% for business purposes, the amount of operating expenses attributable to business use each year is 30% × $1,200 = $360.

Actual Cost Method

Since business use does not exceed 50% in each of the first 6 years, the expensing method cannot be used. And depreciation is limited to the amounts in the Listed Property Depreciation Table given in the Depreciation chapter. Thus, the annual deductions for 1990–1995 are as follows:

	Depreciation		Operating Expenses	Total Deduction
1990:	10% × $3,600	+	$360 =	$ 720
1991:	20% × 3,600	+	360 =	1,080
1992:	20% × 3,600	+	360 =	1,080
1993:	20% × 3,600	+	360 =	1,080
1994:	20% × 3,600	+	360 =	1,080
1995:	10% × 3,600	+	360 =	720
				$5,760

(In addition to the above amounts, parking fees and tolls incurred in business-related travel are deductible.)

To see how this works out on a per mile basis, the calculation is as follows:

Total mileage, 1990–1995:	60,000 miles
Business miles:	30% × 60,000 = 18,000 miles
Total expenses, 1990-1995:	$5,760
Per mile deduction:	$5,760/18,000 = 32 cents per mile

Standard Mileage Rate

As in the preceding example, the standard mileage rate of 26 cents per mile can be used instead of the actual cost method. (The standard rate is mandatory if the use of the auto is not required by the employer.)

Taxes and Registration Fees

The annual fee you pay to register your automobile and receive your new license plate or sticker is deductible to the extent the automobile is used for business purposes.

For an automobile used for personal purposes, this annual fee is generally not deductible. However, in some states, part of the fee is based on the value of the automobile and constitutes a form of personal property tax. In such a case, the part of the fee that qualifies as a personal property tax is deductible under *Taxes* on Schedule A. States that qualify include Arizona, California, Colorado, Indiana, Iowa, Maine, Massachusetts, Nevada, New Hampshire, Oklahoma, Washington, and Wyoming.

Interest

If you borrow money to purchase a personal automobile, then interest on the loan is considered personal interest—10% deductible on your 1990 tax return [cf. the *Interest* chapter]. The same situation applies to an *employee* who uses his automobile for deductible job-related travel, whether he deducts his actual auto expenses or uses the standard mileage rate. That is, all interest paid on the automobile is still considered 10%-deductible personal interest. (An exception would occur if the auto was financed by a home-equity loan, in which case the interest could be fully deducted as discussed in Section 1 of the *Homeowners* chapter).

The opposite is true if the auto is used in connection with a self-employment activity. In this case, any interest attributable to such use is fully deductible on Schedule C as interest paid in connection with a trade or business. This interest is deductible in addition to the regular automobile deduction computed under either the actual expenses or standard mileage rate method.

For example, suppose you use an auto 30% for self-employment activities and that you paid $1,000 interest on an auto loan during 1990. You would claim $300 as a *business interest* deduction on Schedule C. The remaining $700 would yield a personal interest deduction of 10% × $700 = $70 on Schedule A.

Allocating Repair Expenses

A 1980 court case shows how to allocate repair expenses when an auto is used both for personal and for deductible purposes. You do not have to establish which repairs are directly attributable to your deductible travel. Instead, just multiply the total of your repair bills for the year by the fraction: deductible mileage/total mileage for the year. [Goodman, TC Memo 1980-122]

Trading In Your Old Automobile

Suppose that you trade in or sell your old automobile when you purchase a new one. If you did not claim a deduction for your old automobile, then your old automobile does not enter into the computation of depreciation for your new automobile. Thus, you use the full price of your new automobile (without subtracting the trade-in value of your old automobile) in calculating your depreciation the same way as if you had no trade-in.

If you sell or trade-in an automobile on which you have claimed depreciation, then you must take this into account in depreciating your new automobile. The following example illustrates how this is done:

Example

You owned an automobile which was used two-thirds for business and one-third for pleasure. It originally cost $7,200, which had been allocated $4,800 to business use and $2,400 to personal use. $2,700 of depreciation (and/or expensing) had been claimed and allowed in prior years. You trade it in on a new one that sells for $12,000, and were given a trade-in allowance of $2,400. The new automobile is also to be used two-thirds for business. The depreciable portion of the basis of the new automobile is computed as follows:

1. Cost of old car allocable to business use, 2/3 of $7,200 .... $4,800
2. Less:
(a) Trade-in allowance applicable to business
    portion, 2/3 of $2,400 1,600
(b) Total depreciation allowed on old car. 2,700   4,300
3. Unrecognized loss applicable to business portion ....(500)
4. Purchase price of new car. 12,000
5. Portion of new car allocable to business use, 2/3 of $12,000 8,000
6. Plus: Unrecognized loss on trade-in (from line 3) 500
7. Depreciable portion of basis of new car $8,500

If the amount on line 3 were a gain instead of a loss, you would subtract it on line 6 rather than add it.

Chapter 11

Income-Shifting

Basic Principle

The basic principle behind income-shifting is simple. You are in a certain tax bracket and your child is in a lower (usually zero) tax bracket. If you can shift some of your income from yourself to your child, then you will have reduced or eliminated altogether the income tax due on such amounts.

Actually the beneficiary need not be your child, but could be a parent, relative, or other person to whom you desire to transfer property or money. However, you generally cannot use the methods described here to shift money to your spouse.

What Kind of Income Can Be Shifted?

You cannot transfer income you earn as a salary to someone else and relieve yourself of tax. You are always liable for the tax on your own earned income. But unearned income produced by investments such as stocks, bonds, savings accounts, and royalties can be shifted. However, you can't just assign the income on such investments to someone else. In order to shift the tax burden, you must also transfer the property (real estate, stocks, bonds, royalty contract, money, etc.) which produces such income.

If you wish to transfer income-producing property to someone else, you can make an outright gift of that property. However, if the recipient of your gift is a minor child, an outright gift can cause difficulty. Because your child lacks legal responsibility, it may be impossible to control the property. For example, a broker may be unwilling to sell a security and buy another, because he is concerned about the lack of legal obligation of the minor to pay.

Gifts to Minors

Gifts to minors have generally been made under the Uniform Gifts to Minors Act. This Act provides a simple way to transfer securities (or life insurance policies or money) to a minor and still retain the power to buy, sell, and reinvest these items on behalf of the minor. You buy the securities in your child's name with yourself or your spouse declared as custodian. (Your broker or banker will know how to handle such a transaction.) You then have the power to reinvest (into other securities, savings accounts, etc.) as you choose, providing you do so for the benefit of the child. When the child reaches majority age, he or she then assumes complete ownership and control over the investment and your custodianship ends.

Recently, many states have switched over from the *Uniform Gifts to Minors Act (UGMA)* to the *Uniform Transfers to Minors Act (UTMA)*. The UGMA and UTMA are basically the same, except for 2 provisions. In most states, under the UGMA, the assets automatically come under control of the child when he reaches 18, the age of majority. Under the UTMA, distribution of the assets to the child can be delayed to a later age, generally 21. Also, the UTMA permits the custodianship to own a wider array of properties such as real estate, partnerships, royalties, etc.

Under either the UGMA or UTMA, the income earned on the investments is taxed to the child. (Make sure you obtain a separate social security number for your child so the income won't be taxed to you.) But there is one important exception. If the income is used to discharge your legal obligation to support the child, then you must pay the tax on the amounts so used. See the subsection later in this chapter on what constitutes support.

Tax on Children's Income

Special rules now apply to children under the age of 14. Under these rules, discussed in Section 5 of Chapter 1, unearned income in excess of $1,000 is taxed at the parent's tax rate rather than at the child's. These rules were designed by Congress to prevent large scale income-shifting to young children. As a result, current taxes are no longer saved to the extent property producing income in excess of $1,000 is transferred to a child under age 14.

Another feature of the current law is that a child cannot claim a personal exemption if he is eligible to be claimed as a dependent on a parent's tax return. This means that lower levels of income will be subject to tax than before. In particular, only the first $500 of unearned income is now exempt from tax. Amounts between $500 and $1,000 are taxed at the child's rate (15% for 1990). The remainder of unearned income may be subject to tax at the parent's rate, depending upon whether or not the child is under age 14.

Although large scale income-shifting to young children has been eliminated, this does not mean income-shifting is dead. For one thing, the first $1,000 of unearned income each year is taxed to the child. Under the 1990 tax tables, the tax on this amount would be only $75, no doubt less than if taxed at the parent's top tax bracket.

Second, the income of a child age 14 or older is still taxed at the child's rate. Only children under age 14 are affected by the rule taxing unearned income at the parent's rate. Thus, income-shifting to an older child or other relative remains intact. Furthermore, by choosing appropriate investments, advantage can be taken of the potential for income-shifting to an older child, even if the child is currently under age 14. This is done by choosing investments which pay off in a future year in which the child will be at least age 14.

One example of such an investment would be U.S. Series EE savings bonds. The interest on these bonds need not be reported until the year in which the bonds are redeemed, which can be arranged to occur after the child has reached age 14.

A second example would be stocks chosen for growth rather than for dividends. If the stocks are sold after the child has reached age 14, the entire capital gain will be taxed at the child's tax bracket. (However a stock mutual fund would not serve the same purpose because it would declare periodic capital gains distributions.)

Further examples of investments which delay income to future years would be real estate, deeply discounted bonds, insurance policies, and gold or other precious metals.

Trusts

Another way to shift income is to set up a *trust* for the benefit of your child. You then transfer money or other assets into the trust. The trust can then accumulate the income produced by these assets.

This income earned by the trust enjoys a tax advantage. Namely, the first $5,000 in income is taxed at the lowest 15% rate. This assumes the income is accumulated by the trust rather than being distributed to a beneficiary.

The trust can be set up to distribute money to a child at some later time, e.g. when the child goes to college. Or, arrangements can be made to delay distributions of remaining funds until the child reaches age 21 or some later age. These distributions are taxed at the child's rate as long the child is at least age 14 and the distributions are not used to discharge your legal obligation to support the child.

In addition to allowing income-shifting on earnings up to $5,000, setting up a trust has another advantage over making an ordinary gift. Namely, a trust allows you to maintain control over the funds until your child reaches an age you regard as being sufficiently mature. In contrast, under the Uniform Gifts to Minors Act, the child gets automatic control over all the funds when he reaches the relevant age of majority, typically age 18.

For example, suppose an individual wishes to set aside $20,000 for a child's college education. He is reluctant to make a gift under the Uniform Gifts to Minors Act because the money would come under the complete control of the child when he reaches age 18. He is not sure he can adequately predict how his child will use so large a sum of money received at a relatively young age.

Instead, the individual could set up a trust with his spouse as trustee. The money in the trust can be spent for the child's benefit, but only at the direction of his spouse, the trustee. Eventually, when the child reaches a sufficiently mature age any remaining funds in the trust can be turned over to him.

What Constitutes Support?

As stated above, tax shifting isn't allowed on amounts used to discharge your legal obligation to provide support. But the definition of what is included in this legal obligation depends upon the state where you live. In most states, only the necessities such as food, shelter, and clothing are considered support so that income-shifting can be used for the cost of private school, music lessons, summer camp, etc. In other states, support includes all that is commensurate with the parents' wealth and social position, possibly including a college education. However, in most states, a child reaches majority at age 18, after which there may be no support obligation.

Hiring a Child or Spouse

One of the best ways to shift income to a child (or spouse) is to hire him in connection with an outside business activity. A dependent child can earn up to the amount of the standard deduction ($3,250 in 1990) before any tax is due. Earned income above this amount is taxed at the child's tax bracket [cf. Chapter 1].

Examples of work he might do include operating a computer, clerical work, cleaning a home office, etc. This type of arrangement is discussed more fully in Section 3 of the *Outside Business Activity* chapter.

Stock Investment Plans

A number of companies offer special *dividend reinvestment plans* under which dividends are automatically invested to purchase additional shares of stock. These plans are particularly useful for investing funds held in your child's name because the dividends are automatically reinvested without any action required on your part. Furthermore, under some of these plans, the reinvested dividends purchase additional shares at a 3% or 5% discount. Your stockbroker won't tell you about these plans because the purchases are made directly through the companies with no commission costs whatever. Many plans even permit further purchase of stock to be made still with no commission charges. Ordinarily the charge for purchasing a small number of shares of stock would be quite high.

Most of the dividend reinvestment plans have the following features. First of all, in order to participate, an individual must already be a stockholder in the Company. However, you do not have to own any specific amount of stock. Ownership of just one share entitles you to full participation in the plan.

There are two features to the plan. The first feature is that you can choose to have all or a portion of your dividends on Company stock automatically reinvested to purchase further shares of the Company. These shares are purchased with little or no commissions or service charges. Also, there may be a discount of up to 5% of market price. Full reinvestment of dividends is made possible because the plan permits fractions of shares to be issued.

The other feature of the plan is that at any time, additional funds can be mailed in to purchase further shares of the Company at the full market price. Once again, no commissions are charged and the issuance of fractional shares allows the full amount to be invested. However, there is an upper limit, typically $3,000–$5,000 that can be invested in any one quarter (3-month period).

Recordkeeping is all done by the Company. Unless you request otherwise, no certificates will be issued. Instead, purchases will be credited to your account with statements mailed to you periodically. At any time, you can request to have certificates issued to you in the amount of your account.

You can get a free list of about 600 companies on the N.Y. Stock Exchange with dividend reinvestment plans by writing to: *NY Stock Exchange Marketing Group; 20 Broad St., 18th Floor; New York, NY 10005*. Also, the May 1990 issue of *Money Magazine* contains a list of 67 high-yielding large companies which have dividend reinvestment plans. In addition, the *Value Line* advisory service, found in many libraries, can be used to check whether a given company offers a stock purchase plan. If a company does have such a plan, this fact will be noted at the bottom of the page description of that company. If a discount on reinvested dividends is offered, this will be indicated in the note. You can then write to the company itself for full details of the plan.

Dividend Reinvestment Plans should be considered especially when accounts are maintained for children or other dependents. The automatic reinvestment feature, the simplified recordkeeping, the ability to invest small amounts, and the up to 5% discount all combine to make these plans very attractive.

Rules for Interest-Free Loans

At one time, interest-free loans could be used as a means of income-shifting between family members. For example, a child could have received an interest-free loan from a parent and then earned interest on the money. The interest would have been taxed at the child's lower tax bracket rather than at the parent's higher bracket.

But Congress eliminated this technique. Now, if an individual makes an interest-free loan to another person who invests it at a lower tax bracket, the IRS will "impute" interest to the lender at the going interest rate. For example, suppose a parent makes an interest-free loan of $5,000, payable on demand, to a child who invests the money in his name in a certificate of deposit. If the short-term U.S. Treasury interest rate is 7%, then the IRS will impute interest to the parent of 7% × $5,000 = $350. This amount will have to be included in the taxable income of the parent and is deductible by the child. Effectively, this undoes the tax-shifting of the interest-free loan.

For loans made at a below-market interest rate, a similar provision applies. In this case, the difference between the going Treasury rate and the interest actually charged will be imputed to the lender.

The above rules apply to interest-free loans made in order to shift income to a lower tax bracket. For other interest-free loans, where the avoidance of tax is not *"one of the principal purposes,"* the rules are different. In such a case, you can make up to $100,000 of loans to an individual without the imputed interest rules corning into play. (For example, parents could loan money interest-free to a child to buy a home, attend school, etc.). In this situation, if the recipient does earn some income on the money, interest can still be imputed to the lender. The amount imputed is either the going Treasury rate or the actual amount of income earned, whichever is lower. However, no interest is imputed if the recipient's net investment income (from all sources) for the year is less than $1,000. This $1,000 exemption as well as the use of actual income earned instead of the Treasury rate only applies if tax-avoidance is not one of the principal purposes of the loan.

Also, if the total balance of amounts you loaned to an individual does not exceed $10,000 and the loans are *not directly attributable to the purchase or carrying of income-producing assets,* then no income is imputed to you. This $10,000 limit and the $1,000 limit in the preceding paragraph are the same for married couples as for individuals; they are not doubled.

The above rules apply to loans made after June 6, 1984. However, for demand loans (i.e. loans without a predetermined maturity date), the above rules apply no matter when the loans were made.

Turning Your Child's Purchases into a "Tax Shelter"

One way to utilize the $10,000 exemption for income-shifting purposes occurs if you have a child with his own money from a part-time job or gifts from relatives. Say the child was planning to spend this money on "extras" such as a car, stereo, home computer, jewelry, etc. Instead, you can lend your child the money to make the purchase. He keeps the money he would otherwise have spent and places it in an income-producing account or investment. The first $500 of investment income is exempt from tax and the next $500 is taxed at the child's tax bracket [cf. Chapter 1, Section 5]. At some later date, he returns the money you have lent him, i.e. he repays the loan. In the meantime, income earned on the money saved by the child might be taxed at his tax bracket instead of yours.

In the above manner, you can lend up to a total of $10,000 per child or other recipient, apparently without running afoul of the imputed interest rules. Technically speaking, you are making *interest-free, payable-on-demand* loans to your child which should be documented by a simple promissory note signed by the child (and custodian, if applicable). In practice, since the loan transaction does not appear on any tax form, the IRS is not likely to find out about the transaction, even in the event of an audit. This is especially true since the amounts loaned are not large.

Chapter 12

State and Local Taxes

You **can deduct** the following taxes on your 1990 tax return, imposed by a State or local government:

Property tax [cf. the *Homeowners* chapter]

 Income tax

Personal property tax

You **cannot** deduct:

Sales tax

Beverage tax

Cigarette tax

Admission tax

Gasoline tax

Driver's license fee

Dog license

Fishing or hunting license

Also, you cannot deduct a passport fee unless qualifying as a legitimate business expense. (For example, a passport fee for a business-related trip would be deductible, but not for a pleasure trip.) Automobile registration fees are deductible only to the extent the auto is used for business purposes or the fees are based on the value of the automobile and, therefore, qualify as a personal property tax [cf. the *Automobile Expenses* chapter].

Generally, the deduction for State and local taxes is only available to the taxpayer who incurs the taxes. For example, a child may have a State tax liability on income he receives. Even if the parents pay the tax, they get no deduction on their Federal tax return. Such a payment is considered to be a gift to the child followed by payment of the tax by the child. Thus the child, not the parents, gets

196

the deduction for State taxes paid.

In most cases, the child will not be able to use the deduction for State and local taxes paid. Now, a dependent child is entitled to a 1990 standard deduction of at least $500, even if he has only unearned income. Thus, unless a child has at least $500 in deductions, including the deduction for State and local taxes, he will use the standard deduction instead of itemizing—thus the deduction for State and local taxes will not be usable [cf. Section 5 of Chapter 1].

Payroll Taxes

In some places, contributions to unemployment or disability funds are deducted from employees' paychecks. The IRS will allow contributions to state disability funds in New York, California, New Jersey, and Rhode Island to be deducted as a tax on Schedule A. (Contributions to private disability funds remain nondeductible.) Also, the IRS ruled in 1989 that amounts withheld from wages for contribution to the West Virginia unemployment fund are deductible taxes [Rev Rul 89-16].

Transfer Taxes

When you buy stocks, bonds, real estate, etc., you may have to pay a transfer tax. Under prior law, such a transfer tax could generally be deducted when paid in the year of the purchase. But now, these taxes are no longer deductible expenses. Instead, they are considered to be part of the purchase price. As such, they reduce any capital gains (or increase losses) in the year of sale and increase annual depreciation write-offs in the case of investment real estate [cf. the *Expensing and Depreciation* chapter].

Sales Tax

Prior to 1987, you were permitted to claim a deduction for State and local sales tax you paid during the year. Generally, this deduction was obtained from an IRS-provided table, based on your income and the state where you lived. But this deduction was eliminated.

However, sales tax is still deductible on items for which you are claiming a deduction, say as a trade or business expense. For example, if you are deducting for supplies purchased in connection with your job, you would deduct the full amount you paid for the supplies, including any sales tax charged. Similarly, if you purchase an item such as an automobile or typewriter which you are deducting as described in the *Expensing and Depreciation* chapter, then you use the full cost of the item, including any sales tax charged, as the basis for your expensing or depreciation deduction.

State and Local Income Taxes

Schedule A includes a deduction for State and local income taxes which you pay. These taxes are deductible in the year in which they are paid by being withheld from your paychecks or by direct payment. For example, amounts withheld during 1989 from your paychecks and credited toward your State income tax due

April, 1990 were deductible on your 1989 Federal tax return. If you made an additional direct payment toward these taxes in 1990, then this amount becomes deductible on your 1990 tax return.

On the other hand, you may have received a State or local tax refund during 1990 because of overwithholding during 1989. In this case, the full amount withheld during 1989 should have been deducted on your 1989 tax return and you report the refund as income on line 10 of your 1990 tax return. (The 1989 refund is still reported as income even if you have it credited against your current tax rather than having a refund check mailed to you.)

An exception to this has been described in an IRS ruling. You do **not** have to report a 1990 tax refund as income to the extent it was due to overwithholding during 1989 from which you derived no Federal tax benefit.

For example, suppose you claimed the standard deduction on your 1989 tax return. This means that you did not get any Federal tax benefit from the **deduction** for State taxes withheld from your paychecks. In such a case, you would not have to report a 1990 tax refund as income. This is illustrated in Example 2 below.

Example 1

In 1989, $2,000 in State income tax was withheld from your paychecks which you deducted on your 1989 Federal tax return along with $6,000 in other deductions. When you filled out your 1989 State tax return, you computed $1,500 as the amount of State income tax for the year. Since $500 too much was withheld during 1989, the State sent you a refund check for that amount in 1990. Since you deducted the $2,000 withheld on your 1989 Federal tax return but received $500 of this amount back, you're really entitled only to a net $1,500 deduction. To compensate for the extra benefit you obtained by deducting $2,000 instead of the $1,500, you report the $500 refund as income on your 1990 Federal tax return.

In the above example, the $500 State tax refund received in 1990 was due to overwithholding in 1989. Because the overwithholding produced an extra tax benefit on your 1989 tax return—a $2,000 deduction instead of a $1,500 deduction—the $500 refund had to be included as income on your 1990 return to offset the extra benefit.

However, if a State tax refund is the result of overwithholding from which no extra benefit was obtained, then the refund check does not have to be included in income. The following example illustrates this situation.

Example 2

In 1989, $1,000 in State tax was withheld from Smith's paychecks. His other deductions amounted to $800. Since $1,000 + $800 = $1,800 was less than the standard deduction, Smith did not itemize his deductions on his Federal tax return but used the standard deduction instead. Smith received no Federal tax benefit from the $1,000 withheld in State taxes because he didn't itemize his deductions.

Now suppose Smith received a State tax refund in 1990. This refund resulted from the fact that the $1,000 withheld in 1989 was too much. But, because he claimed the standard deduction, this overwithholding produced no Federal tax benefit on his 1989 return. Therefore, he does not have to include the refund in income on his 1990 Federal tax return.

In the above example, Smith received no Federal tax benefit from the State tax overwithheld from his paychecks because he used the standard deduction. Therefore, the State tax refund which resulted from this overwithholding did not have to be reported as income in the following year.

However, sometimes an individual receives a **partial** benefit from State tax overwithholding. This can occur only when an individual's other deductions are less than the standard deduction, but when the State tax is added in, the total exceeds the standard deduction. In this situation, you report as income on line 10 of your 1990 tax return that portion of the overwithholding during 1989 (which you received in 1990 as a refund of State tax) from which you derived a tax benefit.

In practice, you compute this amount by filling out the worksheet in the instructions to Form 1040. However, the following illustrates the basis behind this computation.

Example 3

C and D filed joint Federal income tax returns for 1989 and 1990. For 1989, their State income tax deduction (equal to the amounts withheld from their 1989 paychecks) was $1,000 and their other itemized deductions were $2,700. On their 1989 State tax return, they computed their State tax to be $600. This meant that $400 of State tax had been overwithheld during 1989 resulting in a $400 State tax refund received in 1990. However, only a portion of this $400 overwithholding had actually produced a tax benefit on their 1989 Federal tax return. This portion is computed as follows:

(1) Total deductions actually claimed on 1989 Federal tax return: $2,700 + $1,000 = **$3,700**

(2) Total deductions that would have been claimed on 1989 Federal tax return had there been no State tax overwithholding. [The greater of (i) $2,700 + $600 = $3,300 or (ii) the Standard deduction for 1989, $3,540]: **$3,540**

(3) Tax benefit on 1989 Federal tax return resulting from State tax overwithholding, (1) – (2): **$3,700 – $3,540 = $160**

The amount computed in (3) above, $160, is the portion of the $400 refund which yielded a tax benefit the preceding year. Thus $160 is reported on line 10 of their 1990 Federal tax return.

The above examples concern refunds of State or local income taxes. However, the same principle would apply to refunds of property taxes. Thus, a 1991 refund of property taxes overpaid in 1990 would be reportable as income only to the extent it pushes deductions over the standard deduction as illustrated in the above examples. IRS instructions have been misleading on this matter.

Tax Refunds Reported on Form 1099-G

If you received a State or local income tax refund during 1990, you may receive a statement of this amount on Form 1099-G which is mailed to you by the payer of the refund. The IRS will also receive a copy of the Form 1099-G.

Don't make the mistake of automatically including the amount reported on Form 1099-G on your tax return. If this amount is exempt from tax according to the discussion above, then you do not report any of this amount on your return. If partially exempt, you only report the amount that is taxable on line 10 of Form 1040. It is alright if this amount does not agree with the amount reported on Form 1099-G.

However, it is advisable to attach a statement to your tax return explaining any discrepancy. This will protect against being questioned on this issue should the IRS matching program kick out your tax return because of the discrepancy.

Some States allow you to contribute, by means of a check-off on your State income tax return, to one or more special funds for certain public purposes. Examples include funds for veterans' benefits, food and housing aid to the poor, wildlife conservation, etc. These check-offs might reduce the amount of the State tax refund you receive. In such a case, the amount reported on Form 1099-G will probably exceed your actual refund—it will report the refund you would have received in the absence of any check-offs. You would then use the higher amount reported on Form 1099-G as the basis for reporting your tax refund on line 10. You would then deduct the amounts contributed via check-offs as a charitable contribution on your Federal tax return.

1990 Taxes Paid in 1991

Ordinarily, deductible items belong on the tax return only for the year payment is actually made. However, suppose you pay 1990 State or local taxes in early 1991. According to a recent court case, you might actually be entitled to deduct such a payment on your 1990 tax return.

In this case, an individual made a $1,000 estimated State tax payment in January. He could have deducted this $1,000 in the year it was paid. However, this $1,000 payment was for State taxes estimated to be owed for the preceding year. Therefore, he wanted to be able to claim the $1,000 payment on the Federal tax return for this preceding year.

The Court ruled that this was permissible. In essence, it allowed him to use the *accrual system* of accounting for non-business income and deductions. Under the *accrual system,* income and deductions are credited to the year in which they are produced, even if actual payment is made in a later year. Since the $1,000 payment was for a tax liability "accrued" in the preceding year, it could be deducted in that year instead of in the next year when the payment was actually made. [Flagg. 53 AFTR 2d 84-1321]

The above court case concerned the payment of State income taxes. But the same reasoning would apply to other types of taxes such as property taxes. For example, a payment made in early 1991 for property taxes incurred in 1990 could presumably be deducted on your 1990 tax return.

Chapter 13

Tax-Sheltered Plans

Section 1:
Benefit of Tax-Deferral

A number of different types of tax-sheltered plans are available under the current tax laws, including IRAs, Keogh Plans, tax-sheltered annuities, flexible spending accounts, and deferred compensation plans. Of particular note are the remarkable *Defined-Benefit Keogh Plans* discussed in Section 3. With such plans, those with self-employment income can often **shelter up to 100% of this income from tax.**

The principle behind most of these tax-sheltered plans is the same. First, you place a certain amount of money which you earn this year into one of these plans. You do not generally pay any current tax on this money. That is, it is subtracted from your adjusted gross income on this year's tax return. (A major exception to this is non-deductible payments made to an IRA, as discussed in Section 2.)

Second, after the money is placed into the plan, it is invested in savings certificates, stocks, bonds, or other securities depending upon the type of plan it is. As income is earned on the investment, no tax is paid. Year after year, the interest or other investment income compounds without the interference of any amount being taken out to pay taxes. If instead of placing an amount of money into such a plan, you were to invest it yourself, you would have to pay the tax as you went along. Any amount taken out in tax would no longer be available to earn investment income for you. In effect, the tax-sheltered plan is letting you use these amounts you would have to pay in tax as an interest-free loan to invest for your benefit.

Finally, when you start withdrawing the income earned by the plan, then you must pay tax as the money is withdrawn. Thus, you have not avoided tax but simply deferred it. But this deferral can result in a tremendous benefit because of all the extra interest, interest on interest, etc. you have earned on that amount of money not taken out in tax.

The table below illustrates the monetary advantage of a tax-sheltered plan. It examines the options of an individual with $1,000 he wishes to invest at the end of year 1. The table assumes that the individual's highest Federal tax bracket remains at 28% and that there is an additional effective marginal state tax rate of 9%.

202

Column A shows the yearly total accumulation of original investment plus all income earned, assuming that the individual first pays the tax due on $1,000 ($370) and invests the remainder ($630) himself. Column B shows the yearly total, assuming the $1,000 is placed in a tax-sheltered plan. Column C shows the amount the individual would receive if distribution of the accumulated funds were subject to tax at the same rate used throughout the table. All three columns assume the funds earn 9% annual interest.

Year	Column A Invested by individual; all taxes paid	Column B Invested in tax-sheltered plan; tax not paid	Column C Invested in tax-sheltered plan; all taxes paid
1	$ 630	$ 1,000	$ 630
5	786	1,412	889
10	1,035	2,172	1,368
15	1,364	3,342	2,105
20	1,796	5,142	3,239
25	2,367	7,911	4,984
30	3,118	12,172	7,668
35	4,108	18,728	11,799
40	5,413	28,816	18,154

For some, the above table understates the advantage of tax-sheltering. If a person's income tax rate rises through the years, the Column A accumulations might decrease markedly. The Column C distribution would not be affected nearly as much because there is no compounding effect caused by the annual application of a higher tax rate. Also, the Column C distribution might be greater than indicated if the individual's tax rate drops after retirement, if he elects an annuity option which further defers tax, or if he can use the special lump sum averaging provision discussed later in this chapter.

Contributing to Tax-Sheltered Plans Can Raise Other Deductions

Generally, contributions to tax-sheltered plans reduce your AGI (Adjusted Gross Income). This happens directly when wages are reduced by the amount of the contributions [cf. Sections 4-6] or when contributions can be claimed as an Adjustment to Income [cf. Sections 2 and 3].

This reduction in AGI can have a favorable secondary effect of raising certain other deductions. In particular, the deduction for miscellaneous expenses is reduced by 2% of AGI [cf. the *Miscellaneous Deductions* chapter]; thus, reducing AGI raises the deduction for miscellaneous deductions. The same situation applies to the deductions for medical expenses and casualty losses since these are subject to 7.5% and 10% of AGI income subtractions, respectively [cf. the *Medical Expenses* and *Casualty Losses* chapters].

Another benefit of lowering AGI is to permit deductible IRA contributions to be made by some individuals. For example, as discussed in Section 2, a married individual who is a participant in a retirement plan cannot make a deductible contribution to an IRA if his AGI is $50,000 or more. And he can obtain only a partial deduction if his AGI falls into the $40,000-$50,000 phase-out range. Thus, for example, if a married individual with AGI of $50,000 reduces his AGI by making a $5,000 contribution to a Keogh plan, tax-sheltered annuity, deferred compensation, or other tax-sheltered plan, his AGI would be reduced to $45,000. This would give him an additional $1,000 deduction if this amount is contributed to an IRA. The same benefit would apply if his AGI initially were in the $45,000-$50,000 range [cf. Section 2 for further details].

Section 2:
Individual Retirement Accounts

The 1986 Tax Reform Act changed the basic rules governing Individual Retirement Accounts (IRAs). These are individual tax-sheltered savings plans set up with a mutual fund, savings institution, insurance company, etc. Under prior law, any person could deduct up to $2,000 of his earned income contributed to an IRA. But now, some persons will be denied a deduction and others will be allowed a deduction of less than $2,000. Only those who are not covered by another retirement plan or whose income does not exceed certain limits will qualify for the full $2,000 deduction. However, even if an individual does not qualify for an IRA **deduction**, he can still contribute up to $2,000 to an IRA on a **non-deductible** basis.

Other than the rules for deducting contributions, IRAs operate the same basic way as in prior years. That is, funds in one or more IRAs can be invested as an individual wishes, with all investment income exempt from tax. Only upon withdrawal is tax paid on any of the income accumulated by the IRA. It is this ability to compound income over a period of time in a tax-free manner that may make contributing to an IRA desirable, even if no initial deduction is received for the contribution.

Who Can Deduct Contributions to an IRA?

Some persons will still be able to fully deduct their contributions to an IRA. To qualify for a full deduction of $2,000 contributed to an IRA, you must satisfy **either** of the following conditions:

Condition A: Neither you nor your spouse is covered by another retirement plan.

or

Condition B: The total Adjusted Gross Income (ignoring IRA contributions) on your tax return is less than $40,000 on a joint return or $25,000 on a single person's return.

To satisfy Condition A, you must not be an *active participant* at any time during the year in a *retirement plan*. Here, the term *retirement plan* includes tax-favored plans run by your employer such as a pension, profit-sharing, deferred compensation, or stock bonus plan. It also includes tax-sheltered annuities [sometimes called 403(b) plans] and Keogh plans. However, it does not include social security, nor does it include unfunded deferred compensation plans established by a government or tax-exempt organization.

Your employer will determine whether or not you are an *active participant* in a retirement plan which it sponsors. In some cases, this determination can rest upon certain technical factors. However, in general, you are an *active participant* in a plan if any contributions were made **to** the plan on your behalf during the year. (Receipt of annuity payments **from** the retirement plan does not cause an individual to be classified as an active participant.) However, if you are covered by a retirement plan with a specific defined benefit (e.g. an amount based on salary and length of service), then you are automatically considered to be an *active participant,* even if no contributions were made on your behalf that year. Furthermore, you can be an *active participant* in a plan even if you have not been in the plan long enough to be vested. Your employer is required to inform you on your yearend W-2 Form, by marking the *Pension Plan* checkbox, if you were an *active participant* in one of its plans during the year.

If you satisfy either Condition A or Condition B, then you can deduct any IRA contributions totalling up to $2,000 for the year, provided the total does not exceed your own *earned income*. In this situation, your spouse can also be eligible to deduct up to $2,000 of his or her earned income contributed to a separate IRA, for a total of $4,000.

Earned Income means income produced by your own work, whether as an employee or as a self-employed person. It does not include income on investments such as stocks, bonds, savings accounts, rental property, etc., nor does it include income which is exempt from tax.

Tainted Spouse Rule

To satisfy Condition A, both you and your spouse cannot be an active participant in a retirement plan. This is colorfully called the *tainted spouse rule*. Even if you are not an active participant in any plan, you can still fail Condition A because of the taint of your spouse's participation. This is the case even if you and your spouse file separate tax returns.

There is a loophole in the tainted spouse rule for married couples filing separate returns where one spouse earns less than $10,000. That spouse can make a deductible contribution under the phase-out rules described on the next page, no matter what the earnings amount or retirement plan status of his spouse [cf. Example 6 for an illustration of this situation].

There is also a special rule for married couples who live apart for the entire year. On a separate return, either spouse can choose to ignore the other spouse's earnings or retirement plan status and choose to apply the IRA rules for single persons. Under these rules, a deductible $2,000 IRA contribution can be made by a person if either he alone is not covered by a retirement plan or has AGI on his separate return of $25,000 or less [cf. Example 6].

If you divorce during the year, then the tainted spouse rule does not apply. Since the basic tax rules look to your marital status as of the end of the year, you are considered a single person for the entire year. As such, you file a single tax return under the rules applying to single taxpayers.

Spousal IRAs

If your spouse has no earned income, then you can deduct contributions totalling up to $2,250 to IRAs in each of your names, provided Condition A or Condition B is satisfied. (A spouse with earnings of less than $250 can be treated here as though he had no earned income.) You set up two separate accounts, one in each name, and divide the total between these accounts any way you choose, as long as the contribution credited to any one individual for the year does not exceed $2,000.

For example, you can contribute $2,000 to your IRA and $250 to your spouse's IRA, or vice versa. Or, you can divide the total in another manner e.g. $1,125 to each IRA. However, the working spouse should open at least a token account in his name, even if he wishes to put the maximum possible into his spouse's account. Also, a joint return should be filed.

The decision on how to divide up the $2,250 each year could be an important one. From a tax-saving point of view, it is best to put the most funds into the account of the younger spouse. That way, the funds will have a longer period of time to accumulate tax-free interest before distribution is required to begin at age $70^1/_2$.

For example, suppose a 60-year-old husband has a non-working wife age 50. If he contributes $2,000 to his wife's account, then this $2,000 can accumulate tax-free income for as long as 20 years before distribution begins, instead of the 10 years if placed into the husband's account. (On the other hand, if earlier withdrawal of IRA funds is desired, the opposite strategy might be called for. That is, the maximum level of funds might be placed into the older spouse's account.)

Phase-Out Range

The $2,000 individual limit for deductible IRA contributions is phased out if Adjusted Gross Income (ignoring IRA contributions) falls into the *phase-out range*. The phase-out range is $40,000–$50,000 for joint filers and $25,000-$35,000 for singles.

For joint filers in the $40,000–$50,000 phase-out range, the maximum amount that can be deducted is given by the formula: 20% × ($50,000 — AGI). As can be seen from the formula, the maximum IRA deduction for joint filers is $2,000 if AGI (Adjusted Gross Income) is $40,000, and $0 if AGI is $50,000, with an intermediate amount between the phase-out endpoints of $40,000 and $50,000.

Analogous formulas apply to singles and marrieds filing separately. The following table gives the formulas and phase-out ranges for these formulas:

PHASE-OUT TABLE

COLUMN I Type of Tax Return	COLUMN II Maximum Deduction for IRA Contributions	COLUMN III Phase-Out Range for which Column H Applies
Joint	20% × ($50,000 - AGI)	$40,000-$50,000
Single	20% × ($35,000 - AGI)	$25,000-$35,000
Married filing separately	20% × ($10,000 - AGI)	$0-$10,000

You round up to a multiple of $10 after using Column II to determine the maximum IRA deduction that applies. For example, if you compute $1,488 using Column II, you round this up to $1,490. Also, if you compute a deduction limit of less than $200 but more than $0, you are allowed to use $200 as the deduction limit.

As discussed earlier, the $2,000 individual IRA deduction limit is raised to $2,250—an increase of 12^1/2%—when you also contribute to a separate *spousal IRA* for a non-working spouse. In the phase-out range ($40,000-$50,000 for joint filers), the maximum deduction computed using the Phase-Out Table is similarly increased by 12^1/2%, when contributions are made to a spousal IRA. This is illustrated by Example 5.

Example 1

Morgan files a joint tax return showing AGI of $70,000. Neither he nor his wife is covered by a retirement plan.

In this case, Condition A applies. Morgan can deduct a contribution to his IRA of any amount of his earned income up to $2,000. His spouse can also deduct a contribution to a separate IRA of any amount of the spouse's earned income up to $2,000.

Example 2

Scott files a joint tax return showing AGI of $70,000. He is covered by a retirement plan provided by his employer.

Scott can get no deduction for contributing to an IRA. Neither Condition A nor Condition B applies. Furthermore, his AGI is above the $40,000-$50,000 phase-out range given in the preceding Phase-Out Table.

Example 3

Farley files a single tax return showing AGI (ignoring IRA contributions) of $28,560.

Case 1. Farley is covered by his employer's retirement plan. Using the appropriate formula in Column II of the Phase-Out Table, Farley's IRA deduction cannot exceed 20% × ($35,000 − $28,560) = $1,288, which is rounded up to $1,290.

Case 2. Farley is not covered by any retirement plan. In this case, Condition A applies. This means that Farley can deduct any amount up to $2,000, when contributed to an IRA.

Example 4

John and Mary file a joint tax return with AGI of $42,000 (ignoring IRA contributions). Mary is covered by her employer's retirement plan.

Case 1. John and Mary each earn $21,000. To compute the maximum IRA deduction for each spouse, the Column II formula for joint returns is applied:

$$20\% \times (\$50,000 - \$42,000) = \$1,600.$$

Thus, each spouse can deduct an IRA contribution of up to $1,600—a total of $3,200 for the couple.

Case 2. John earned $1,500 and Mary earned $40,500. In this case, Mary can deduct an IRA contribution of up to $1,600, the same as in Case 1. But John's deductible IRA contribution is limited to $1,500, the amount of his earned income.

Example 5

You and your spouse file a joint tax return with AGI (ignoring IRA contributions) of $42,000. Your spouse has no earned income.

You use the Phase-Out Table to compute your own deduction limit:

$$20\% \times (\$50,000 - \$42,000) = \$1,600.$$

If there is a spousal IRA, an additional deduction of $12^1/2\% \times \$1,600 = \$200$ is permitted—a total deduction of $1,600 + $200 = $1,800. You can divide the $1,800 between your IRA and your spouse's IRA any way you choose, as long as each IRA is allocated a deduction no less than $200 and no more than $1,600.

Example 6

Sam and Jane, a married couple, have earned income of $60,000 and $6,000, respectively. They have no unearned income. Sam is covered by a retirement plan, but Jane is not. If they file a joint tax return, then the fact that their combined AGI exceeds $50,000 and that Sam is an active participant in a retirement plan rules out a deductible IRA contribution both for Sam and for Jane (because of the tainted spouse rule).

If they file separately, then Sam still cannot deduct an IRA contribution on his separate tax return. But the situation for Jane is different. She is still covered by the tainted spouse rule which rules out a full $2,000 deduction. But because the income shown on her tax return lies in the $0-$10,000 phase-out range for separate returns, she can make a deductible IRA contribution of the following amount [cf. Column II of the Phase-Out Table]:

$$\text{Deduction} = 20\% \times (\$10,000 - \$6,000) = \$800$$

The above assumes that Sam and Jane lived together. If they did not live together at any time during the year, then Jane could apply the IRA rules for single individuals. Since the AGI on her separate return is under $25,000, she could make a $2,000 contribution to an IRA, fully deductible on her separate return.

Where Is the Deduction for IRA Contributions Claimed?

The deduction for IRA contributions is claimed as an adjustment to income on line 24 of Form 1040. Because it is an *adjustment to income* rather than an *itemized deduction*, it can be claimed by those who use the standard deduction as well as by those who itemize.

Non-Deductible Contributions

If you do not qualify for the full $2,000 IRA deduction, you can make *non-deductible contributions* to an IRA. Although these IRA contributions are not deductible, all *earnings* on these funds compound entirely free from tax until distributions are made.

The total of all your IRA contributions (deductible and non-deductible) for the year cannot exceed $2,000 ($2,250 if there is a spousal IRA), nor can it exceed earned income. For example, if you were allowed no deductible IRA contribution, you can make a $2,000 non-deductible contribution; if you were allowed an $800 deductible IRA contribution, you can make an additional $1,200 non-deductible contribution.

On the other hand, if you make a $2,000 *deductible* contribution to your IRA, you cannot make any *non-deductible* contribution for the year to the same or different IRA in your name. (However, if you wanted to designate part or all of the $2,000 contribution as being non-deductible, this would be allowed. You might wish to do this, say, if your tax rate in a given year was unusually low and you intended to make distributions in the near future.)

You make non-deductible contributions to an IRA in exactly the same way you make deductible contributions—i.e. you just deposit funds into the IRA account. You can mingle deductible and non-deductible contributions in the same IRA. No purpose is served by segregating these 2 different types of contributions into different IRAs.

At the time you contribute to an IRA, you do not need to specify to the institution running your IRA what the tax nature of the contribution is. Only when you fill out your tax return, do you need to specify what percentage of your total contribution for the year is deductible and what percentage is non-deductible.

For example, you can make a $2,000 contribution to your IRA at the beginning of the year, even if you don't know what your tax situation will be for the year. You will determine what percentage is deductible when you fill out your tax return after the end of the year. And, as discussed later, you can even undo any contributions for the year you wish to retract by making withdrawals before the tax-filing deadline.

To illustrate the rules for making non-deductible contributions, let us revisit the previous examples in this section. In Example 1, if Morgan makes the maximum deductible IRA contribution of $2,000, then no non-deductible contribution can be made to an IRA in his name. On the other hand, in Example 2, since no deductible contribution is allowed, a $2,000 non-deductible contribution could be made.

In Case 1 of Example 4, if each spouse makes the permitted $1,600 deductible contribution to his own IRA, then each spouse could make an additional $400 non-deductible contribution; in Case 2, only the higher-earning spouse could make a $400 non-deductible contribution.

And in Example 5, if $1,800 in deductible contributions were divided between your IRA and a spousal IRA for your non-working spouse, then an additional $450 ($2,250 — $1,800) in non-deductible contributions could be made. The division must be made so that the total contribution for the year made to each of these IRAs is between $250 and $2,000.

Form 8606

If you make a non-deductible contribution to an IRA in 1990 (or in 1991 for the year 1990), you must fill out Form 8606 and include it as part of your 1990 tax return. Only a few lines on this form need to be filled out. Basically, you list the value of all your IRAs on December 31, 1990 and the amount of non-deductible contributions you made for the 1990 tax year. You will automatically receive this information from the institution running your IRA. They are required by law to send you a Form 5498 reporting the December 31, 1990 balance of your IRA account and any contributions you made during 1990.

Your spouse must file a separate Form 8606 if any non-deductible contributions were made to an IRA in her name.

If you made a non-deductible contribution to an IRA for 1990, then you are supposed to keep a copy of your 1990 tax return until you no longer have an IRA in your name. You are also supposed to retain the Form 5498 sent to you by the institution running your IRA for each year you either make a contribution to or receive a distribution from an IRA.

The maintenance of these records may be required to back up your claim of non-taxability for a portion of IRA distributions received in later years. When you withdraw funds from your IRA(s), the more non-deductible contributions you have made, the larger the portion of the withdrawal that is exempt from tax [cf. Example 7]. Without any records, you would not be able to back up the fact you have made non-deductible contributions to your IRA. This would mean that if challenged by the IRS, all distributions received from your IRA might be subject to tax as if you had made no non-deductible contributions.

When Are Your IRA Contributions Due?

You can choose any schedule you want for making contributions. You can make periodic contributions or make one big contribution. You are under no obligation as to the amount you contribute in any given year, as long as your contributions do not exceed the maximum allowable amount. You have until the filing date of your tax return to establish or make contributions to an IRA. Thus, contributions for 1990 can be made up until April 15, 1991. You don't need to have made your contribution when you file your tax return as long as the contribution is made by April 15. However, the April 15 deadline applies even if you have an extension to file after this date.

According to a 1986 IRS ruling, if you mail in your IRA contribution, the postmark date is what counts. In this ruling, a person mailed a $2,000 contribution on April 11 which the bank did not receive until April 16, one day after the deadline. The IRS ruled that since the envelope was postmarked April 12, three days before the April 15 deadline, the $2,000 payment could be deducted as an IRA contribution. [IRS Private Letter Ruling 8611090]

If you make an IRA contribution and later change your mind, you can withdraw the contribution before the due date of your tax return, with no penalty. You should also withdraw any investment income earned by the withdrawn funds while in the IRA. However, this withdrawal privilege does not apply to lump-sum distributions rolled over into an IRA as described at the end of this Section.

Contributing After Age 59 1/2

Suppose you don't want to contribute to an IRA because you want to have the funds readily available to spend if you need them. However, if you are age 59¹/2 or older, an IRA is generally a no-lose proposition, because you can withdraw funds at any time with no IRS penalty. You can use the IRA simply as a tax-free savings account in which you want to keep readily available emergency funds.

Can IRA Contributions Be Made After Age 70 1/2?

The general rule is that you cannot contribute to an IRA for the year you reach age 70¹/2 or any year hereafter. However, if you have reached age 70¹/2 and are still working, you may contribute to an IRA for your non-working spouse as long as your spouse is less than age 70¹/2 at the end of the tax year. Also, you can roll over a lump sum distribution from a pension plan (see below), even though you have reached age 70¹/2, provided you begin distributions as required.

When Is Money Withdrawn from an IRA?

You may start withdrawing money from your IRA anytime after the age of 59¹/2. After that age, you may take as much money out of your IRA each year as you choose.

However, you must begin the distribution of money by April 1 of the year following the year in which you reach age 70¹/2. You don't have to retire from your ordinary job in order to receive payments. You can choose to receive the entire account in one lump sum or receive the amount in periodic payments spread out over a number of years.

If you turn 70¹/2, say, during 1991, then you must make your initial withdrawal for the 1991 tax year by April 1, 1992. This distribution is taxable in the year received. Distributions for each future year must be made by December 31 of that year. In particular, your distribution for the 1992 tax year must be made by December 31, 1992. This means that distributions for both years 1991 and 1992, if received in 1992, are taxed in the same year. If this bunching would shift you into a higher tax bracket, then you should advance the 1991 distribution so it's received before December 31, 1991. That way, it will be reported as income on your 1991 tax return instead of on your 1992 tax return.

If you have more than one IRA when you reach age 70^1/$_2$, then application of the basic rules would require minimum annual distributions to be made out of each IRA. However instead of making withdrawals out of each IRA, you may choose to make a withdrawal from just one of the IRAs, as long as the total amount withdrawn is at least as much as the sum total required to be distributed under the basic rules [IRS Notice 88-38, IRB 1988-15]. This is of particular benefit if one of the IRAs consists of a long term CD or other investment that would produce a financial penalty if cashed in early.

It is permissible for you to withdraw money from an IRA before reaching age 59^1/$_2$. However, as discussed later in this section, an extra 10% penalty tax may apply to such early withdrawals.

How Are IRA Distributions Taxed?

If you have never made any non-deductible contributions to an IRA, then the taxation rules for distributions are simple. Namely, any withdrawal of funds from the IRA is taxed at your ordinary income tax rate along with your other income. Thus, you will probably want to spread out payments over a number of years instead of receiving a lump-sum distribution. Note that lump-sum distributions do not qualify for the special averaging rule that applies to regular retirement plans or to Keogh Plans [cf. the *Retirement Plans* chapter].

Distributions of Non-Deductible Contributions

If you have made non-deductible contributions to an IRA, then a portion of any distributions you later make from the same or a different IRA in your name is not taxed. (You have already paid tax when you earned the money to make the non-deductible contribution.) Also, the 10% penalty tax on early withdrawals before age 59^1/$_2$, discussed later, does not apply to a return of non-deductible contributions. Thus, the portion of a distribution attributed to non-deductible contributions escapes not only the ordinary tax, but the additional 10% penalty tax as well.

To determine the non-taxable percentage of a distribution, you divide the total non-deductible contributions you have made over the years by the value of your IRA at the end of the year of distribution. The *value* of your IRA is the yearend account balance, adding back any distributions made during the year. If you have more than one IRA in your name, you group them together and treat them as if they were all part of one big IRA.

Example 7

You made the following contributions to an IRA:

	Deductible	Non-Deductible
1986	$2,000	
1987	1,500	
1988	1,000	$1,000
1989	1,000	1,000
	$5,500	$2,000

On October 31, 1990, you make a withdrawal of $3,000. Let's say that at the end of 1990, the total in the IRA account is $7,000.

The percentage of your account that is due to non-deductible contributions is:

$$\frac{\$2,000}{\$3,000 + \$7,000} = 20\%.$$

Thus, 20% of the $3,000 distribution is tax-free: 20% × $3,000 = $600. The remaining $2,400 ($3,000 - $600) is included in taxable income on your 1990 tax return.

As can be seen from the above example, the tax treatment of a distribution depends upon the percentage of your IRA due to non-deductible contributions—the higher the percentage, the larger the portion of the distribution that is exempt from tax.

If you have a choice, you are better off concentrating non-deductible contributions in one spouse's IRA and deductible contributions in the other's. That way, if you want to make a withdrawal, you can do so from the IRA in which the non-deductible contributions are concentrated. Since amounts attributable to non-deductible contributions are not taxed upon withdrawal, this will maximize the amount of the withdrawal that is exempt from tax.

Example 8

You have one IRA in your name, and your spouse, who also works, has none. The account balance in your IRA at the end of the year (due to contributions in previous years plus interest) is $10,500. You wish to make a $1,500 non-deductible contribution on this date and intend to make a $1,000 distribution one year later. We will assume an interest rate of 10% for this one-year period.

Case 1.   You make a $1,500 non-deductible contribution to your own IRA.

This brings your account balance to $10,500 + $1,500 = $12,000. Under the 10% interest assumption, this rises to $13,200 by the end of the next year when you make the $1,000 distribution. Under the rules illustrated in Example 7, the percentage of the distribution that is untaxed (as a partial return of non-deductible contributions) is $1,500 ÷ $13,200 = 11%. Thus 11% × $1,000 = $110 is untaxed, with the remaining $890 subject to tax in the year of distribution.

Case 2.   You make the $1,500 non-deductible contribution into an IRA set up in your spouse's name.

Under the 10% interest assumption, the account balance of $1,500 rises to $1,650 by the end of the next year when the $1,000 distribution is made. Following the method illustrated in Example 7, the percentage of the distribution that is untaxed is $1,500 ÷ $1,650 = 91%. Thus 91% × $1,000 = $910 is untaxed, with only $90 remaining to be taxed in the year of distribution. When compared with Case 1, this is a decrease in current taxable income of $890 – $90 = $800.

In the preceding example, each spouse had earned income of his own, so they could choose into whose IRA the $1,500 would be placed. The same situation occurs when there is a non-working spouse. Under the *Spousal IRA* rules discussed earlier, among your choices are to contribute $2,000 to your IRA and $250 to your spouse's, or the reverse—$250 to your IRA and $2,000 to your spouse's.

As in the preceding example, you are better off placing the $2,000 non-deductible contribution into your spouse's IRA if your existing IRA balance is greater than your spouse's. This will generally minimize tax if a partial distribution is made in the future. Conversely, if your spouse's existing IRA is greater than yours, you would be better off contributing the $2,000 to your IRA.

Are Non-Deductible Contributions Worthwhile?

Before making non-deductible contributions to an IRA, you should exhaust all the tax-deductible plans for which you are eligible—Keogh plans, tax-sheltered annuities, and deferred compensation plans [cf. the remaining sections in this chapter]. If you still have money left that you wish to invest on a long-term basis, then non-deductible contributions to an IRA make sense. The ability of the IRA to compound earnings without paying current tax is valuable, especially over a long period of time.

However, if you expect to make withdrawals from your IRA before many years have passed, you should be careful about making non-deductible IRA contributions when you already have an existing IRA.

The reason for this is illustrated in Case 1 of the preceding example. In that case, a non-deductible contribution of $1,500 was followed the next year by a $1,000 withdrawal—leaving a net $500 addition to the IRA. Because there was a substantial amount already in an IRA, a tax was triggered on $890 of the withdrawal. If we assume the tax on this $890 amounts to $300, the withdrawal would yield $700 in after-tax money.

However, instead of making the full $1,500 contribution, it would have been better to hold on to $700 and contribute the remaining $800 to the IRA. This leaves you with the same in-pocket $700, but the IRA winds up with an extra $800—$300 more than the net $500 addition in the preceding paragraph. (Investment income was ignored in the preceding analysis because its inclusion would not affect the basic comparison.)

Can Money Be Withdrawn Before Age 59½?

Yes. However, the purpose of the legislation creating the IRAs was to provide a retirement vehicle. Thus, there is a penalty for early withdrawals. If you do withdraw money before age 59½, and you have never made any non-deductible contributions to an IRA, then there is a 10% penalty tax on the amount of the distribution. This is in addition to the ordinary income tax that applies.

If you have ever made a non-deductible contribution to an IRA, then as discussed above, only a portion of any distribution is subject to ordinary income tax. The 10% penalty tax only applies to this taxable portion. The remaining portion of the distribution attributed to non-deductible contributions is not subject to ordinary income tax nor to the 10% penalty tax.

Note that the 10% penalty is not so severe as to absolutely limit the use of an IRA to those seeking a retirement vehicle. You still might be better off setting up an IRA and making a premature withdrawal than you would had you invested the money outside an IRA.

For example, suppose you could make a $1,000 deductible contribution to an IRA or invest without tax protection. If you were in the 28% tax bracket, then investing the funds yourself would mean you could put $720 to work earning interest or other income. But the IRA would have an extra $280. Over a period of years, the extra income earned on the $280 would be sufficient to compensate for the 10% penalty. In addition, the fact that your money is compounding entirely tax-free in an IRA instead of being taxed each year provides a further advantage.

Assuming no non-deductible contributions have been made, the breakeven point is generally around 7 years. That is, you are generally better off with an IRA if the money is left in for about 7 years or more and then withdrawn prematurely (with 10% penalty) than you would have been with a comparable investment outside the IRA. However, the exact breakeven point depends upon the interest rate earned by funds in the IRA and your upper tax bracket (Federal plus state and local). For example, assuming an 8% interest rate and 33% tax bracket, the breakeven point is 7 years; but assuming a 10% interest rate and 40% tax bracket, the breakeven point is reduced to 5 years.

In the case of non-deductible contributions, the breakeven point is about twice as long. For example, assuming an 8% interest rate and 33% tax bracket, the breakeven point is 13 years. This presumes there have been no deductible contributions made to IRAs over the years. Otherwise, because of the complex distribution tax rules, the breakeven point is even longer.

For example, if substantial deductible contributions have been made, the breakeven point can be as much as 23 years under the previous assumptions. The reason for this increased breakeven period is that in this case, a small distribution from an IRA can be almost fully taxable, whereas with only non-deductible contributions, a significant part of the distribution is exempt from tax.

Because of the extended breakeven point, it is not generally advisable to make non-deductible contributions to an IRA if you plan to withdraw funds before reaching age $59^1/2$.

Exception

There is a case when the 10% penalty tax does not apply to distributions received before age $59^1/2$. Under a special provision in the law, you can start annuity distributions from your IRA, prorated over your lifetime, at anytime you wish. In such a case, the 10% penalty does not apply, even if you are under age $59^1/2$. If you wish, the annuity payments can be stopped after 5 years, provided you are at least age $59^1/2$ at that time. You can also make penalty-free early withdrawals in the event of permanent disability.

The IRS recently issued a ruling indicating the appropriate methods that are permissible in determining how much can be paid out under this annuity provision. The institution running your IRA can advise you of the exact amount in your situation, depending upon your age, the age of the beneficiary you name, and the prevailing interest rate. However, an example in the IRS ruling gives an indication of what to expect.

In this example, a 50-year old individual with a $100,000 account balance was permitted to receive annual distributions of $9,002 per year. This amount was based upon using a current *"reasonable interest rate"* of 8% and a life expectancy of about 33 years [IRS Notice 88-25]

If the individual in the above example continued this payout rate over a 5-year time period, he would receive a total of about $45,000—45% of the original $100,000 account balance. After reaching age 59¹/₂, he could either continue with the payments or halt them, letting the income continue to compound inside the IRA.

In the above example, a "reasonable" interest rate of 8% was used. However, in a number of recent private letter rulings, the IRS approved higher interest rates. Several of these rulings permitted a 9% interest rate to be used in the calculations [IRS Private Letter Rulings 8919052, 8916047]. And one ruling approved an interest rate that was to be set at 120% of the *long-term applicable federal rate*. Under rates prevailing in 1990, this would place the interest rate at about 12% [IRS Private Letter Ruling 8946045]. Of course, the higher the interest rate assumption, the greater can be the withdrawals from the IRA. Under a 12% interest rate assumption, for example, about 60% of the IRA could be withdrawn over a 5-year period.

It should be pointed out that in the above example, the payout each year was exactly the same. However, this is not the only type of payout method that is permitted. It is permissible to make an annual recomputation based on the new remaining account balance and a new life expectancy figure. This recomputation procedure permits payments to continue until death, instead of possibly running out as can happen with a fixed payout schedule.

IRA Contribution Based on Alimony Payments

A special rule applies to alimony payments. As long as these payments qualify as alimony [cf. the *Divorce & Separation* chapter], taxable to the recipient, they can be considered the same as *earned income* for purposes of the IRA rules. The person paying the alimony still gets to make his normal IRA contribution based on his earned income.

Custodial Fees

Many institutions charge a set-up fee or an annual maintenance fee. If these fees are separately billed, they can be deducted in addition to the maximum allowable IRA contribution which you make. For example, suppose you are eligible to make a $2,000 deductible IRA contribution with an institution charging a $25 custodial fee. You could pay the institution $2,000 for the IRA contribution which you deduct on line 24 of Form 1040, plus the $25 fee which you deduct as a Miscellaneous Deduction on Schedule A. You should pay the fee with a separate check so you're not accidentally credited with an excess contribution.

However, you can't separately deduct brokerage commissions connected with the purchase and sale of securities in your IRA.

Hidden IRA Bonus

When contemplating how much to contribute to your IRA, take note of the extra bonus you get if you also are claiming a medical deduction. Only medical expenses in excess of 7.5% of your Adjusted Gross Income (AGI) are deductible on your 1990 tax return. But your IRA contribution is an "above the line" *adjustment to income* which reduces your AGI, thereby raising your medical deduction.

For example, if you make a deductible contribution of $2,000 to an IRA, your AGI is reduced by $2,000 which in turn can raise your medical deduction by 7.5% × $2,000 = $150—a 7.5% bonus.

A similar situation occurs with the 2% of AGI floor discussed in the *Miscellaneous Deductions* chapter. A $2,000 deduction for an IRA contribution can raise the deduction for miscellaneous expenses by $40.

What Kinds of IRA Plans Are Available?

Most financial institutions have set up IRA plans in which you can invest your money. The following is a general discussion of the types of plans being offered by different institutions.

Banks and Savings & Loans

Generally, IRAs run by *banks* or *savings & loans* place your money into a certificate of deposit. Most of these institutions give you a choice of several types of certificates. The choice will usually include both fixed-rate certificates and variable-rate certificates. The rate on a *fixed-rate certificate* is set at the time of purchase and remains the same during the entire certificate period. The rate on a *variable-rate certificate* is adjusted periodically, usually once a month, based on a formula tied to the going rate on Treasury bills or other standard. Some institutions set a floor below which the interest on a variable-rate certificate cannot fall. This can be a valuable feature if short-term interest rates drop a significant amount.

Each institution is free to set its own interest rate according to any method it chooses and to select which kinds of certificates it will offer. This means that you will have to shop among your local banks and savings institutions if you want to get the best deal. When you inquire about the interest rate being offered, be sure to ask for the **effective annual yield.** This takes into account the effect of the compounding method used by the institution, e.g. daily, monthly, etc., and therefore is an accurate standard of comparison. Also, be sure to inquire whether money can be added to an existing account and whether there are any fees for opening or maintaining an account.

Many institutions allow you to add funds to an existing IRA account, with the maturity date remaining the same. This is a particularly useful feature because it avoids the unwieldy situation of having numerous different IRA accounts, each with a separate maturity date.

A number of institutions allow additional funds to be added at the original interest rate, regardless of rates being paid on new IRA accounts. This can be a valuable feature if interest rates fall.

IRA accounts with a bank or Federal savings & loan are backed by the same Federal Deposit Insurance applying to regular accounts. The minimum amount which can be invested varies among institutions from as little as $1 to as much as $1000 or more. Most banks and savings & loans do not charge a fee to open or maintain an IRA account.

Like regular certificates of deposit, there is generally an interest penalty if funds are withdrawn prior to maturity. However, an institution may waive the penalty if funds are withdrawn early from a certificate of deposit at age 59½ or thereafter or upon death or disability. A majority of institutions (but not all) will make such a waiver as a general policy.

If you receive a promotional item such as a toaster or free checking account when you deposit money into an IRA, then you need not worry. The IRS had been claiming that the receipt of such items could be considered as "prohibited transactions" causing a penalty tax to be assessed. But in 1990, the IRS announced that it would find such promotional items acceptable and would not assess any penalty. This assumes that the promotional items are reasonable in value and the interest rate paid on the IRA account is within normal range. [IRS Announcement 90-1, IRB 1990-2]

Money-Market and Other Mutual Funds

Nearly every money-market or other mutual fund can be used as an IRA by filling out the appropriate form with the fund's sponsor. You make all investment and other transactions through the mail. The typical minimum investment to open an IRA account with a mutual fund is $500, although some have lower minimums. There is generally an annual custodial fee of about $10 charged by the mutual fund for running your IRA.

There are mutual funds which concentrate in virtually any type of investment, e.g. long-term bonds, growth stocks, money-market instruments, etc. If you invest in a no-load mutual fund run by one of the major fund institutions, you can switch money from one type of fund to another just by making a toll-free telephone call. See Sections 4-6 of the *Investing Your Money* chapter for further information on investing in mutual funds.

Stockbrokers

Most stockbrokers offer *self-directed IRA accounts*. These are used like ordinary brokerage accounts to buy stocks, bonds, etc. You can also make more esoteric purchases such as limited partnerships in real estate or oil drilling ventures. You instruct your broker which securities to buy and sell with the money in your account. There are usually fees connected with self-directed IRA accounts. These vary widely from one brokerage house to another, but a typical fee structure might be a one-time $50 set-up charge plus an annual $50 maintenance charge. (However, at least one discount brokerage house, the nation's largest, charges no set-up or maintenance fees: Charles Schwab & Co.; One Second Street; San Francisco, CA 94105.) In addition, the usual brokerage commissions would apply.

Because of the custodial fees and commission charges, self-directed plans are not suitable for most individuals with less than $5000 in an IRA. Unless they have a particular investment strategy in mind, they are better off with an IRA run by a bank, savings institution, or a no-load mutual fund.

In addition to self-directed accounts, many stockbrokers offer IRAs which place money into mutual funds. The custodial fees may be lower for this type of account than for a self-directed account. However, most of the mutual funds used by stockbrokers are *load funds* which impose a sales charge of up to 8%. If you want to invest in a mutual fund, you would be better off with a no-load fund offered directly by the sponsoring organization, with no sales fee imposed.

Insurance Companies

Insurance companies offer annuity plans into which you can place your IRA money. Many of these plans offer a choice of several investments including money-market or other mutual funds. Other plans may guarantee a certain rate of return for a short period of time but after that, the rate could drop substantially.

Insurance company IRAs usually have significant fees associated with their use. These fees can include an "up-front" sales charge or a "back-loaded" fee for withdrawing money within 7-10 years after investment. Or, the "fee" could take the form of a lower interest rate or lower payout calculation than would be justified by market conditions or actuarial calculations. Because of the fees which are charged by insurance company IRAs, most individuals will be better off with an IRA run by a bank, savings & loan, or mutual fund.

Gold and Silver Coins

Under prior law, IRA contributions could not be invested in *collectibles* such as art, coins, antiques, stamps, etc. But now, there is an exception for certain U.S. minted gold and silver coins and for certain coins issued under the laws of individual states. These coins can be purchased for an IRA, provided they are held for you by a trustee such as a broker, banker, etc.

If you are planning on holding coins over a long period of time, it may not be worthwhile to hold them as part of your IRA portfolio. Since coins yield no income until they are sold, there is no need to hold them in a tax-deferred plan. On the other hand, if you think you will buy and sell your coins over time, the ability to keep capital gains tax-deferred will be of value.

Switching Funds from One IRA to Another

The IRS allows you to switch your funds from one IRA into another. There are two ways to make such a switch — by direct transfer or by rollover.

A *direct transfer* is accomplished by having the institutions running the IRAs transfer the funds between them. You do not take possession of the funds at any time. There is no limit on the number of direct transfers that can be made during any period of time.

A *rollover* is an investment switch which you make yourself. You withdraw the funds out of your existing IRA account which you then invest in your new IRA. As long as the reinvestment is made within 60 days after receipt of the funds, no tax is paid. You must notify the institution from which you are withdrawing funds that you're planning to make a rollover.

You are limited to one such rollover of an existing IRA account during any 12-month period. You keep and pay tax on any income earned on funds during the period the funds have been removed from the first IRA and not yet rolled into the second IRA.

You can make more than one rollover during a 12-month period if different funds from different IRAs are involved. For example, if you have 2 separate IRAs, you may consolidate by rolling over the funds from each of these IRAs into a third IRA. [IRS Private Letter Ruling 8731041]

Partial rollovers of amounts withdrawn from an IRA are permitted. This enables you to defer tax on that portion which is rolled over. The portion withdrawn which is not rolled over is includible in your ordinary income.

Most (but not all) institutions will permit you to switch out of their IRAs at any time. If you want the switch made with dispatch, a rollover may be better than a direct transfer. Institutions often take several months to complete a direct transfer because of delays in processing the paperwork.

There may or may not be a small switchover fee, depending upon the institution. And if your money is invested with a bank in a certificate of deposit, there will usually be a penalty (typically 3 or 6 months loss of interest) if a switch is made before the certificate matures.

You can avoid the bother of making a direct transfer or rollover by investing with a large no-load family of funds. Typically, you will then be allowed to switch between funds just by making a toll-free telephone call whenever you wish. You can also divide up your IRA among several different funds as you choose.

Borrowing from Your IRA

You might need to borrow money for a short time to meet an unexpected emergency. Your IRA can come in handy for this purpose. Even though your IRA cannot make a formal loan to you, the same effect can be obtained by using the rollover privilege.

Under the rollover privilege described above, you can withdraw funds from your IRA anytime you choose. You then have 60 days in which to deposit the funds in a new IRA. This gives you 60 days use of the money to cover a temporary emergency. Of course, the money should be redeposited in an IRA within the 60-day period, otherwise tax (plus 10% penalty if under age $59^1/2$) will be triggered on the withdrawn amount. According to a 1990 IRS ruling, you do not need to set up a new IRA, but can simply redeposit the money in the same IRA from which it was withdrawn [IRS National Office Advice Memorandum 9010007]. As mentioned above, these funds cannot be rolled out again until 12 months have elapsed since the previous rollout.

What If You're Short of Cash to Fund Your IRA?

You may want to contribute to an IRA for 1990 but are temporarily short of cash to contribute as much as you wish. Here are some ways to get around this difficulty.

1. Borrow from a bank or savings institution

You are permitted to borrow funds to make your IRA contribution. You get a deduction for the IRA contribution and can still deduct the interest as *investment interest* under the rules described in the *Interest* chapter. Ordinarily, you can't deduct interest on any loan if the proceeds are used directly to make a tax-exempt investment. But the IRS has ruled that this restriction does not apply to IRAs because the income earned by IRA funds is not strictly *exempt* from tax as with, say, municipal bonds. Rather, this income is tax-deferred because tax does have to be paid on IRA earnings when money is withdrawn at some later date [IRS Private Letter Ruling 8527082]. It is best to borrow from a different institution than the one with which your account is established so the IRS can't construe that you're using your IRA as collateral for the loan.

2. "Borrow" from an existing IRA

As discussed in the previous subsection, you can "borrow" from an existing IRA for a period of 60 days or less. If you are short of funds, you can use this 60-day turnover period to pay this year's IRA contribution out of an existing IRA account from a previous year. For example, suppose you file a tax return on March 15, 1991 showing that you're due a refund of $1,000. Let's say you listed a $1,000 IRA deduction on the tax return but didn't have the money to make the contribution (which is due by April 15).

On April 10, you roll $1,000 out of an existing IRA and deposit it in your checking account. You then write a $1,000 check to open a new IRA for the 1990 tax year. When you receive your $1,000 tax refund, you can write a $1,000 check to your new IRA which is regarded as completing the rollover started on April 10.

The period from March 15 to 60 days after April 10 (when the rollover must be completed) is sufficient time to receive your refund unless there is a foul-up. However, since the rollover needs to be completed within 60 days, you might want to have a backup source of emergency funds to avoid the situation of making a premature withdrawal should your refund be inordinately delayed.

3. Contribute your tax refund to your IRA

You must make your IRA contribution by April 15, 1991 in order for it to be deductible on your 1990 tax return. However, you may take the deduction on your 1990 tax return even if you have not yet contributed to or even opened your IRA account. As long as your contribution is eventually made by the April 15 deadline, you're alright.

For example, suppose you want to make a $2,000 deductible contribution to your 1990 IRA but only have $1,200 on hand. Let's say you fill out your tax return by February 10, 1991 which shows a large refund due to you. In this situation, you can do the following:

Contribute the $1,200 to your IRA, but claim a $2,000 IRA deduction on your tax return. Then mail in your tax return promptly. Since the IRS usually sends refunds within 6-8 weeks, you should receive your refund before April 15, 1991. You then contribute the remaining $800 to your IRA out of the refund money you receive from the IRS.

This procedure has been officially approved by the IRS. Your IRA account does not even have to be opened at the time you mail in your tax return. As long as you eventually contribute by April 15, 1991 the amount claimed on your 1990 tax return, your deduction is proper. [Rev. Rul. 84-18]

However, if April 15, 1991 rolls around and you don't have enough money to make the contribution claimed on your 1990 tax return, you'll have to file an amended tax return. This is done by filling out Form 1040X [cf. Chapter 1, Section 1] on which you report the actual IRA contribution made and recompute your taxes with this new lower figure as your IRA deduction instead of the old one. You should enclose a check for the extra tax due when you mail in your Form 1040X to the IRS.

Why Two IRAs Can Be Better than One
There are several reasons why an individual might want to have his money split into two (or more) IRAs instead of one.

One consideration is the ability to use your IRA as a short-term source of money as described earlier in this Section. With one IRA, you can borrow money in this manner only once in any 12-month period. But, under regulations proposed by the IRS, each IRA is considered separately for purposes of this 12-month rule. For example, suppose you have two IRAs, IRA 1 and IRA 2. If you roll over IRA 1 into a new IRA 3, you cannot roll out this money until 12 months have elapsed. But this does not restrict withdrawals from IRA 2. You can use the rollover privilege to withdraw funds from IRA 2 without regard to the rollover of funds from IRA 1. In effect, you have had the use of IRA money for two 60-day periods instead of one.

If you contemplate an IRA as a backup source of emergency cash, you might want to have 2 IRAs for a different reason. You would want one IRA in a liquid investment such as a mutual fund required to disburse funds upon request with no penalty. The remainder of your money could be placed in a less liquid investment such as a bank C.D. requiring an interest penalty on premature withdrawals.

Finally, of course, is investment diversification. Spreading money out in different investments is typically recommended to lessen market risk. This benefit alone, however, may not be sufficient to outweigh the extra bother of maintaining more than one account, especially if the amounts are small relative to your overall financial picture.

Placing a Spouse on the Payroll

In some cases, it pays to "put a spouse on the payroll" in order to obtain the maximum $4,000 IRA deduction for married couples. This might be possible, for example, for those with an outside business activity in which the spouse could be of assistance. This is discussed more fully in the *Outside Business Activity* chapter.

Choosing a Beneficiary

When you set up your IRA, you will be asked to choose a beneficiary in case you die before all funds are distributed to you. Several years ago, Congress altered the tax consequences of such a choice. Formerly, only if the beneficiary were a spouse could the funds remain in a tax-sheltered IRA. Other beneficiaries had to draw out all the funds within 5 years, paying tax upon withdrawal.

But now, tax-sheltering can continue over the life of a non-spouse beneficiary. In fact, some individuals will want to change their beneficiary from a spouse to a child to take advantage of these rules. If distributions from the IRA have not begun, the options permitted by the IRS are as follows:

(1) Starting within one year of death, annual payments can begin to the beneficiary based on his life expectancy. For example, a beneficiary with a life expectancy of 60 years would receive at least 1/60 of the value of the IRA the first year, 1/59 (approximately) the second, etc. The remaining funds continue to earn tax-free income in the IRA.

(2) If payments do not begin within one year, the entire balance must be distributed to the beneficiary within 5 years after death. However, if the beneficiary is a spouse, payments do not have to begin until the year the deceased would have reached age 70$1/2$ and they can be spread out over the life of the spouse.

(3) In any event, income tax is due on any payments received by beneficiaries from the IRA.

According to (1) above, naming a young child as beneficiary allows the IRA to continue sheltering funds from tax for a long period of time. But under (2) above, naming a spouse as beneficiary means distributions need not begin until a later time. Which option has a stronger tax-savings effect depends upon the ages of the various people involved.

There is a pitfall to be cognizant of when a non-spouse is named beneficiary of an IRA. The existing IRA should simply be renamed to reflect the new ownership. It should not be rolled over or transferred into a new IRA in the beneficiary's name. And no further contributions should be made to that IRA. Otherwise, a tax could be triggered. [Rev Proc 89-52, IRB 1989-37, 17]

This is illustrated by a 1990 IRS private letter ruling. In this ruling, an individual took an IRA which she inherited (not from a spouse) and rolled it over into a new IRA in her name. According to the IRS, this simple shift caused the entire IRA to be taxed to the beneficiary [IRS Private Letter Ruling 9014071]. If you have named a non-spouse as beneficiary of your IRA, it is important to inform that beneficiary of this pitfall.

The above only refers to the *income tax* consequence of inherited IRAs, not to the *estate tax* consequence. If your estate will be large enough to fall under the estate tax rules [cf. the *Estate Tax* chapter], professional estate planning should be sought to minimize that tax also.

Rolling Over a Pension Plan Distribution into an IRA

Let us say you leave your current job at which you have been working for a number of years. If you have been participating in a retirement plan, then a certain portion, perhaps all, of your employer's contributions to this plan will have become **vested.** This means that these amounts now belong to you and do not revert back to your employer when you change jobs. If you elect to receive these amounts plus investment income thereon when you leave the job, then you must pay tax on such amounts at that time. The special averaging rule and capital gains treatment [cf. Section 2 of the *Retirement Plans* chapter] lessen this tax burden substantially but your money is no longer sheltered. Any future investment income is subject to tax.

The *rollover* provision of the IRA legislation allows you to avoid the above situation. If a lump-sum distribution [cf. Section 2 of the Retirement Plans chapter] of the money in your retirement plan is received after leaving your job (including death or disability) or after reaching age 59$1/2$, then this sum or a portion of this sum can be transferred into an IRA. (Employee contributions on which you have paid tax are excluded as are *minimum distribution amounts* that must be made if you are over age 70$1/2$ when the distribution is made.) You should complete the rollover within 60 days and should inform in writing the institution with which you set up the IRA that you're making a lump-sum rollover.

When funds are taken out of an IRA, you may be issued a Form 1099-R or other form reporting the withdrawal to the IRS—even if you later make a tax-free rollover to a new IRA. To prevent the IRS computer from kicking out your tax return, this is what you should do. Report the amount shown on Form 1099-R on line 17a of your tax return. Then, on line 17b, report *zero* as the amount of the distribution that was taxable (assuming you roll over the entire distribution).

According to a 1990 IRS private letter ruling, *double-dipping* is permissible for those who have reached the retirement age specified in a retirement plan but continue working. Since they will be at least age 59$1/2$, they can roll over a distribution into an IRA. And according to this ruling, they can continue to participate in the retirement plan as long as they are eligible do to so. [IRS Private Letter Ruling 9009055]

You can divide the rolled over funds among 2 or more IRAs if you choose. The money and all investment income on this money then continues to be exempt from tax until withdrawn from the IRA according to the regular rules. However, the averaging rule and capital gains treatment will no longer apply. If you roll over only part of the distribution into an IRA, the remainder (less employee contributions on which you have already paid tax) is taxed in the year of receipt and is not eligible for the averaging rule and capital gains treatment.

If you receive a lump-sum distribution from a tax-sheltered annuity after leaving your job or after you are age 59$1/2$, then you can similarly roll over all or a portion of this distribution into an IRA [cf. Section 4 for further details].

If you have rolled over a retirement distribution into an IRA, you can place part or all of this IRA into the retirement plan of a new employer, if he permits it. If this is done, the special averaging rule and capital gains treatment will become applicable again. Similarly, tax-sheltered annuity distributions rolled over into an IRA can be rolled back into a tax-sheltered annuity plan provided by a new employer. However, it may pay to transfer a retirement distribution directly to your new employer's plan if permitted, rather than use an intermediate rollover IRA. When this is done, service with the old employer counts when determining if you later satisfy the 5-year participation rule for using one of the special lump-sum averaging rules [cf. the *Retirement Plans* chapter]. If you roll it over through an IRA, then you need 5 years of participation with the new employer before becoming eligible to use a lump-sum averaging rule.

Partial Distributions

To qualify for the tax-free rollover privilege, it is not necessary to receive a total distribution of the amount credited to your account. It is only necessary that you receive a partial distribution of at least 50% of a given pension or tax-sheltered annuity plan. This 50% requirement only applies to one plan at a time. For example, if you have several tax-sheltered annuities in your name, you need receive only 50% of the funds in one of them in order to make a tax-free rollover into an IRA. The funds in the other tax-sheltered annuities need not be distributed.

The rules for partial distributions are stricter than for total distributions in one respect. A partial distribution from a plan qualifies for tax-free rollover only after an individual has terminated his employment (including death or disability) with the employer maintaining the plan. In contrast, total distributions can qualify for tax-free rollover if the employee is over age 59$1/2$, even if he does not leave his job.

If a partial distribution of less than 100% is made, then future distributions from the same plan (or similar plans maintained by the same employer) are disqualified from the special averaging rule or capital gains treatment. Also, amounts from a partial distribution which are rolled over into an IRA cannot be rolled tax-free back into a new retirement plan or tax-sheltered annuity.

Lump-sum distributions are subject to withholding unless you elect otherwise by filling out an appropriate form your employer will provide. If you are planning to roll over a distribution into an IRA, you should elect to avoid this withholding.

You should place rolled-over funds into separate IRAs distinct from any other IRAs which you may use. Otherwise, you may lose the right to roll back the funds into a new employer's retirement plan. Tax-free rollovers of lump-sum distributions are made by receiving funds and placing them into an IRA within 60 days of receipt.

Spouses of employees may also benefit from rollover IRAs. If an employee dies and his spouse receives a lump-sum retirement fund distribution, all or part of this distribution can be placed into an IRA and continue to grow tax-sheltered.

Note that the contribution limits do not apply to IRA rollover contributions nor do the active participant or earnings tests (Conditions A and B) discussed at the beginning of this section. Any amount may be rolled over without paying tax. However, you cannot include your own non-deductible contributions which you made to your retirement plan. These amounts must be subtracted from the total distribution before being transferred to the IRA. Of course, no tax is due on the return of your own contributions to you since you have already paid tax on these amounts when they were earned [cf. the *Retirement Plans* chapter].

Before deciding to use the rollover feature of an IRA, be sure to examine whether or not the loss of the special averaging rule and capital gains treatment will make such use unwise. However, the ability to continue a tax-free shelter for a number of years often outweighs the loss of the averaging rule and capital gains treatment.

Also, if a new employer will accept the distribution into his retirement plan, then the rollover feature probably should be used. Similarly, if your original employer allows you to leave your money in his plan even though you terminate employment, then this may be the best arrangement of all. This is especially true because your own contributions to the plan remain tax-sheltered.

However, there are cases when people will prefer to have their money in an IRA rather than a regular retirement plan. The flexibility of being able to make premature withdrawals (although subject to a 10% penalty tax), the ability to choose your own investment vehicle, and the ability to precisely determine the payout rate during retirement may create such cases.

Due to the complexity of the rules, professional advice should be sought before making any lump-sum distribution decisions.

Section 3:
Keogh Plans

A Keogh Plan (named after a congressman) is a tax-sheltered retirement plan which can be used to shelter self-employment income from tax. Self-employment income includes earnings resulting from personal services which are not employee wages (i.e. the type from which social security is withheld).

This might include income from consulting, royalties from writing a book, fees for editing or reviewing, sales from an invention, income from tutoring, honorariums for lecturing, commissions from real estate sales, director's fees, or any other income earned from a side business or as a private contractor. Sometimes an employee can rearrange his agreement with a current employer so as to become a self-employed private contractor. Self-employment income does not include investment income such as interest and dividends.

Each year, you can contribute a certain portion of your self-employment income into your Keogh Plan. These contributed amounts are not taxed in the year of contribution. You get this benefit even if you claim the standard deduction. Furthermore, no tax is paid on the investment income as it is earned by the amounts you contribute. Only when money is withdrawn from the Keogh Plan is any tax paid.

Note that you do not have to specifically withhold your contributions from the earnings you receive. You can contribute any funds you have to a Keogh Plan within the maximum limitations described below. For example, you can make a contribution by taking money out of a savings account and placing it in your Keogh Plan. You still get a tax deduction for the amount shifted to the Keogh Plan and furthermore, your savings are now shielded by the umbrella of a tax-sheltered plan.

The same types of plans can be set up for a Keogh Plan as for an IRA as discussed in Section 2. The chief differences between Keogh Plans and IRAs are the eligibility requirements and contribution limitations. In addition, there is a special averaging rule that applies to lower the tax on lump-sum distributions from Keogh Plans, but not from IRAs. Also, if your self-employment activity requires you to hire other employees who work either more hours than you or at least one thousand hours per year, you may have to make contributions to your Keogh Plan on their behalf.

How Much Can Be Contributed?

You can contribute up to 20% of your earned self-employment income up to a maximum contribution of $30,000. For example, if your 1990 self-employment income is $10,000, you can contribute 20% × $10,000 = $2,000. The 20% figure applies to your **net** self-employment earnings. That is, you must subtract business expenses from income before multiplying by 20%.

The 20% limit applies in full only if you owe no social security tax on your self-employment income. (This will be the case if you have wages exceeding the Social Security base, $51,300 for 1990.) Otherwise, the upper limit is reduced to take into account the new deduction for self-employment tax claimed on line 25 of Form 1040 [cf. Section 1 of the *Outside Business Activity* chapter]. There will be a special table for calculating the Keogh ceiling for 1990 in Publication 560, which should be available from the IRS around January 1, 1991.

The above limits apply to regular Keogh Plans. There is a special type of plan, called a *Defined-Benefit Keogh Plan,* to which far more can be contributed—in many cases, **up to 100% of a person's net self-employment earnings.** This type of plan is discussed later in this section.

The above limitations are maximum levels of contribution. You may contribute any amount not exceeding these maximums. Furthermore, you do not have to be consistent from year to year. You might contribute the maximum one year and nothing the next.

In order to make a Keogh Plan contribution for the 1990 tax year, the Keogh Plan must be in existence on December 31, 1990. If your Keogh Plan has been established by December 31, you have until April 15 of the following year to make contributions. If you obtain an extension of time to file your tax return [cf. Chapter 1], you have until the extended due date to make a contribution. Of course, the earlier you make a contribution, the sooner your funds are put to work earning tax-free income.

Those with incomes in 1989 from both a regular job and an outside business activity should apportion their expenses judiciously if they want to make full use of the Keogh Plan limitations. Swing items, such as professional books, may best be taken as a miscellaneous employee deduction connected with the regular job rather than as a business expense against self-employment income. (This assumes that the 2% of AGI floor discussed in the *Miscellaneous Deductions* chapter has already been exceeded.) This will keep net self-employment income as high as possible, maximizing the contributions that can be made to a Keogh Plan. (However, if extra social security tax is triggered by an increase in self- employment income, this may not be the best strategy. This would happen if total earnings do not exceed the social security wage base, $51,300 in 1990.)

What if You Missed the December 31 Deadline?

If you missed the December 31, 1990 deadline for opening a Keogh Plan to shelter your 1990 earnings, all is not lost. There is another type of plan, called a SEP (Simplified Employee Pension) which is similar to a Keogh Plan but which can be opened up until April 15, 1991. SEPs were designed to be simplified pension systems for small businesses with more than one employee but can be used by individual self-employed persons as well. Ordinarily, a Keogh Plan is preferable to a SEP because the contribution limitations are more generous and the lump-sum averaging privilege applies. However, in the case where the Keogh Plan deadline is missed, a SEP can be the remedy. (There is no continuing funding requirement for a SEP, and a Keogh Plan can be set up starting the next year.) Most banks, mutual funds, etc. can set up a SEP for you upon request.

How Is a Regular Keogh Plan Established?

The simplest procedure is to choose a mutual fund, bank, or savings institution of your choice. They will have the appropriate forms you need to establish your plan. All investment income will then be automatically reinvested in the mutual fund, savings account, etc. Insurance companies also sell plans which combine investment features with insurance features.

When you set up your Keogh Plan, you will probably be asked to specify what percentage of self-employment income you wish to contribute. Keogh Plans which specify such a percentage are sometimes called *money-purchase* plans. If in a later year, you wish to change the percentage, you can make a simple "amendment," specifying the new percentage. However, if you do not want to contribute more than about 13% of your net self-employment income, you can set up your Keogh Plan as a *profit-sharing* plan. Profit-sharing plans let you contribute any amount you wish each year within the legal limits, without specifying a particular percentage.

To achieve maximum flexibility without the need of making any "amend-ments," some persons set up both types of plans, one *money-purchase* plan and one *profit-sharing* plan. This type of arrangement can specify that each year, 8% of net self-employment income be contributed to the money-purchase plan and that any desired amount up to 12% of self-employment income be contributed to the profit-sharing plan. An individual with this arrangement can then contribute any amount between 8% and the upper limit (about 20%) of net self-employment income each year, without any amendment provision coming into play.

Keogh Plans set up with banks or savings institutions generally invest money in higher-paying certificates of deposit rather than in passbook accounts. With most institutions, the waiting period before such certificates can be cashed in does not apply when money is withdrawn after an individual is age 59½ or over.

Individuals should shop around before choosing a Keogh Plan. There are even differences between plans set up with savings institutions or banks. Some require an annual service charge while others do not. And the top interest rate can vary depending upon the manner in which the interest is compounded. According to the IRS, you can have your Keogh Plan funds transferred from one institution to another without incurring any tax penalty.

It is also possible to set up a Keogh Plan in such a way that you control the investment of the funds. One way to maintain indirect control is to set up a *self-directed* Keogh Plan with a bank or stockbroker. The bank or stockbroker acts as custodian and agrees to invest the funds as you direct. You can deduct any custodial fees you pay as a separate business expense in addition to the actual contributions to the plan which you make.

At one time, a Form 5500 or 5500-EZ had to be filed with the IRS each year the plan was in force. But the IRS has been steadily reducing this requirement. Now, Keogh Plans covering only one person do not have to file any form as long as the assets in the plan do not exceed $100,000. If your Keogh Plan does not meet this condition, check with the institution running your plan to give you information for filing the proper form.

Defined-Benefit Keogh Plans

Because of a change in the law a few years ago, a tremendous opportunity has become available to those with self-employment income. Instead of being bound by the limitations on a regular Keogh Plan as described above, they can set up a more generous *Defined-Benefit Keogh Plan.*

Defined-Benefit Keogh Plans, in their present form, came into being in 1984 after a new "pension parity" law went into effect. Congress decided that persons with self-employment income should be placed on a par with individuals operating under the shell of a corporation (e.g. physicians who list the initials P.A. or P.C. after their name). Because the laws for corporations allow for the funding of such generous pensions, those with even a modest amount of self-employment income have now been handed this big tax break.

Defined-Benefit Keogh Plans work like other tax-sheltered plans, e.g. IRAs, tax-sheltered annuities, or regular Keogh Plans. You get a full deduction on your tax return for any contributions made to your Plan. And the money in your Plan is invested, with all interest, dividends, etc. compounding entirely exempt from tax until withdrawn from the Plan. Also, the same special averaging break that applies to lump sum distributions from regular Keogh Plans applies to Defined-Benefit Keogh Plans as well.

The chief advantage of Defined-Benefit Keogh Plans is that far more can be contributed (and deducted) than to a regular Keogh Plan. The exact amount is based on a person's age, sex, marital status, and self-employment earnings. (As with regular Keogh Plans, *self-employment earnings* here means *net self-employment earnings* after related business expenses have been subtracted.) As an illustration, here's a rough estimate of the maximum contribution range for a married man if the plan is set up the right way:

Age	Maximum Deductible Contributions as a Percentage of Self-Employment Earnings
40	40%- 70%
45	50%- 75%
50	55%-100%
55	55%-100%

A history of prior self-employment earnings will place the maximum allowable contribution in the upper end of the range in the table above, in many cases 100% of self-employment earnings. For example, suppose a 50-year old married man anticipates self-employment earnings during 1991 of $10,000. Let's say he had self-employment earnings during each of 1988-1990 which averaged $4,000 or more. In such a case, he could generally contribute (and deduct) any amount up to 100% of these earnings, namely $10,000.

Note that under a regular Keogh Plan, the above individual would be limited to a contribution of no more than 20% × $10,000 = $2,000. Thus, the Defined-Benefit Keogh Plan in this case permits a deduction of 5 times as much as a regular Keogh Plan.

A person with no self-employment earnings prior to 1991 might be restricted to the lower percentage figure in the table for his age. However, this percentage can be boosted—perhaps up to 100%—if the person "employs his spouse" in the business activity. Any legitimate employee activity will do, e.g. clerical work, typing, answering business calls, etc., as long as wages are actually paid to the spouse. Because of a special provision in the law for employees, even a small wage paid to a spouse can dramatically increase the percentage of earnings that can be contributed to the Plan.

Employing a spouse to perform some business activities can have another beneficial effect. This might enable you to set up a plan to pay all medical and dental expenses of your employee-spouse and family (including yourself). In this way, you get a full medical deduction for your family's medical expenses, with no initial 7.5% of adjusted gross income subtraction. [Cf. the *Outside Business Activity* chapter for further details.]

The figures in the above table represent the **maximum amounts** that can be contributed. With a properly structured plan, you have the option of making any contribution amount you choose as long as it doesn't exceed the maximum allowable. Each succeeding year, you can contribute any portion of your self-employment income you choose that year, as long as the maximum contribution level is not exceeded. If there are contributions to a tax-sheltered annuity or other Keogh Plan, these may, in certain circumstances, lower the contributions you are permitted to make to your Defined-Benefit Keogh Plan.

An important extra benefit is that you can serve as manager of your Defined-Benefit Keogh Plan, in complete charge of all the money in your Plan. You directly control the investments in and disbursements from the Plan. On the other hand, you may prefer to delegate investment responsibility to a professional investment advisor, stock broker, etc. The choice depends upon you.

To take advantage of a Defined-Benefit Keogh Plan to shelter 1991 earnings, you must set up your Plan before the end of 1991. (However, the earlier in the year you set up such a Plan, the better.) These Plans are more complicated to set up and run than regular Keogh Plans because an actuary must be involved in making the appropriate calculations and sending in the appropriate certification forms each year to the IRS. Fees for such services are tax-deductible as a business expense.

How Do You Set Up a Defined-Benefit Keogh Plan?

To get further information on how to set up a Defined-Benefit Keogh Plan, write to *Academic Information Service, Inc.* at the address on the back cover of this book with the envelope marked *Attention: David Harry.* This information will include the name of an actuarial firm to whom we have referred many readers of previous editions of this Tax Guide with favorable results. If you wish, this firm can handle all the details of setting up and maintaining your Plan.

When May Funds Be Withdrawn?

You may start withdrawing money from your Keogh Plan anytime after the age of 59½. However, you must begin withdrawing money by April 1 of the year following the year in which you reach age 70½. It is possible to contribute to a Keogh Plan after age 70½ even though, as required, you are withdrawing funds at the same time.

If you withdraw any funds prior to age 59½, then such funds are taxed along with your other income that year. In addition, an extra 10% tax is imposed on the amount of the early withdrawal, except in the case of death or disability. The 10% penalty tax will be waived if either (i) the withdrawal is used to pay medical expenses in excess of 7.5% of your adjusted gross income, (ii) the distribution is made after you stopped working and is part of a series of substantially equal periodic payments intended to extend over your lifetime or the joint lives of you and your spouse, or (iii) you have retired after reaching age 55.

As a general rule of thumb, even if you have to pay the extra 10% tax prior to age 59½, the tax advantage of sheltering your savings under a Keogh Plan puts you ahead if the funds withdrawn were in the Plan for 7 years or more.

How Are the Proceeds of Your Keogh Plan Taxed?

You can take your money out of a Keogh Plan in the form of a lump-sum distribution. Lump-sum settlements can receive favorable tax treatment provided that you have been a plan participant for at least 5 tax years before the tax year of the distribution.

This favorable tax treatment is provided by a special averaging rule that applies to most or all of the lump-sum distribution. For example, this rule applied to $100,000 of distribution yields a tax rate of about 15%. Furthermore, the tax rate is totally independent of your other taxable income. This averaging rule is described in Section 2 of the *Retirement Plans* chapter.

Except in the case of death or disability, you can use the averaging rule for a Keogh Plan you maintain only after reaching age 59½ and then can use it only once. If you withdraw any money from your Keogh Plan prior to age 59½, this might destroy your right to use averaging at a later time when you otherwise would qualify [IRS Private Letter Ruling 7726047]. Also, if you have made contributions to a Keogh Plan prior to 1974, special capital gains rules may apply to a portion of the lump-sum distribution [cf. the *Retirement Plans* chapter].

You do not need to take a lump-sum settlement. It is often advantageous to elect to receive the distribution over one of the following periods:

(a) your lifetime
(b) the joint lifetime of you and your spouse
(c) a period not extending beyond your life expectancy
                                    or
(d) a period not extending beyond the joint life expectancies of you and your spouse.

The advantage of receiving the distribution over an extended period of time, say the joint life expectancy of you and your spouse, is that the balance of the funds remains in the Plan, compounding investment income entirely free from tax. The distributions you take out from the Plan this way are taxed as ordinary income.

Can You Combine a Keogh Plan with Other Plans?

Yes. You can contribute to a Keogh Plan even if you participate in some other type of retirement plan, IRA, or tax-sheltered annuity. Of course, your contributions to the Keogh Plan are based only on your self-employment income. And your combined contributions to an IRA and a Keogh Plan cannot exceed your earned income.

Comparing Keogh Plans with IRAs

If an individual with self-employment income does not wish to contribute the maximum amounts to both a regular individual Keogh Plan and an IRA, he will have to make a choice. Which is better? Operationally, there is little difference—the usual investment choices can be made with either type of plan. And the requirement to begin distributions between age 59¹/₂ and 70¹/₂ applies to both types of plans. However, there is one distinguishing feature, namely the special lump-sum averaging rule described above. This feature applies to Keogh Plans but not to IRAs. Because of this, a Keogh Plan is generally preferable to an IRA. (Of course, a Keogh Plan is much preferable to an IRA if contributions to the IRA are non-deductible, as discussed in Section 2.)

Where Do You Deduct Payments to Your Keogh Plan?

Payments on your behalf to your Keogh Plan are deducted on line 27 of Form 1040 as an *Adjustment to Income*. Contributions made on behalf of any employees covered under your Keogh Plan are deducted on line 19 of Schedule C.

Section 4:
Tax-Sheltered Annuities

A *Tax-Sheltered Annuity* is a special type of plan available only to employees of educational institutions and certain other non-profit organizations. (Tax sheltered annuities are often called *"403(b) plans"* after the Tax Code section under which they are authorized.) Most of these institutions maintain a list of one or more of these plans which are available to their employees. Generally, all employees are eligible to participate including principals, librarians, clerical help, etc. In fact, under new nondiscrimination rules, tax-sheltered annuity plans must be available to employees generally (except students working less than 20 hours per week), rather than just to higher paid employees.

Employees of State or local departments of education are also eligible unless they are holding a public office such as a trustee or board of education member. For example, the IRS has ruled that an electrical engineer qualified for a tax-sheltered annuity because he worked for a State Department of Education. [IRS Private Letter Ruling 8137067]

The actual rule is that only an employer's contribution to such a plan is not taxable. However, the usual policy is to permit an employee to reduce his current or next year's salary by an amount equal to that being contributed to the annuity plan. Thus the employer incurs no cost but the employee may still take advantage of the tax-saving feature of the plan.

For example, suppose a teacher's annual salary is $45,000 and he wishes to contribute $1,000 toward the purchase of an annuity. He would agree with his school to take a reduction of $1,000 in his salary. His annual salary would then officially be $44,000 and his school would contribute $1,000 toward the purchase of an annuity. The teacher would pay tax based on his $44,000 salary but not on the amount contributed to his annuity until he retired and started receiving annuity payments.

Note that an institution may have a regular retirement plan and still provide their employees the opportunity to participate in tax-sheltered annuities.

In order to get a tax break for contributions to a tax-sheltered annuity, the appropriate *reduction-in-salary* agreement must be signed in advance. Failure to sign the appropriate form can ruin the entire arrangement. This was learned the hard way by a New Jersey teacher in a recent court case.

The teacher authorized her employer to withhold part of her salary and place it into a tax-sheltered annuity. But she failed to sign the appropriate reduction-in-salary agreement. This meant that the contributions to the annuity plan were not technically made from her employer's funds, but rather from her funds. The court was sympathetic but ruled against the teacher as a matter of law. As the written court opinion stated,

> *"The Court recognizes that the myriad of statutory and administrative provisions may be confusing. Nevertheless, plaintiff did not comply with the base provision that the contributions be made 'by' the employer."* [Bollotin vs U.S., 38 AFTR 2nd 76-5712]

The IRS permits you to start a tax-sheltered annuity anytime during the year you choose. But once a contribution agreement is signed with your employer, you cannot alter the agreement later in the year except to terminate payments for the remainder of the year. The following year, you can sign a new agreement if you choose.

For example, if you sign an agreement on January 15, 1991 to contribute 10% of your salary to a tax-sheltered annuity, you can't reduce contributions to 5% on November 1, 1991 because, say, you're running short of funds. The IRS would consider payments made after November 1 to be taxable. Instead, provided your employer agrees, you could terminate payments altogether on November 1 and start a new contribution agreement the following January 1.

However, according to a recent IRS Ruling, an agreement signed in one year can now be altered in a succeeding year. Thus, in the example in the preceding paragraph, you could sign an agreement to reduce contributions to 5% at anytime during 1992. This new percentage could not then be changed until 1993 or later, except that contributions can be terminated at any time you choose. [Rev. Rule. 87-114, IRB1987-45,7]

The above only restricts changes in tax-sheltered annuity contributions with a given employer. You can institute a different tax-sheltered annuity agreement with a second employer anytime you choose.

Withdrawals from Tax-Sheltered Annuities

Previous law did not require there to be any restrictions on when you were first allowed to withdraw funds from a tax-sheltered annuity. However, now an extra 10% penalty tax applies to withdrawals made from a tax-sheltered annuity prior to the date an individual reaches age $59^{1}/_{2}$, dies, or becomes disabled. The 10% penalty tax will be waived if either (i) the withdrawal is used to pay medical expenses in excess of 7.5% of adjusted gross income, (ii) the individual has retired from his job after reaching age 55, or (iii) the distribution is part of a series of substantially equal periodic payments intended to extend over the life of the employee or the joint lives of the employee and a beneficiary.

The exception in (iii) can be used to withdraw amounts before age 59^1/$_2$ and escape the 10% penalty tax. For example, an individual could begin receiving his annuity payments at age 50. As long as the distribution method provides for substantially equal lifetime payments as described in (iii), the 10% penalty tax does not apply.

Furthermore, the individual can alter the distribution agreement after reaching age 59^1/$_2$ as long as no change is made in the first 5 years other than by reason of death or disability. For example, an individual can start receiving payments at age 50 and alter or stop the payments after reaching age 59^1/$_2$. Or, he could start receiving payments at age 57, continuing for 5 years until he reached 62. In either case, the 10% penalty tax is waived. (However, observe the rules below for years after 1988 under which the ability to receive distributions prior to age 59^1/$_2$ is restricted.)

There is an exemption from the 10% penalty tax for individuals who, as of March 1, 1986, had separated from service and elected to start receiving a scheduled series of specified benefit payments.

There is also a mandatory distribution rule that applies to benefits accruing in 1987 or later years. Distribution of such benefits must start by April 1 of the year following the year in which you reached age 70^1/$_2$. (However some employees, including those who reached age 70^1/$_2$ before 1988, may continue to defer the receipt of benefits until April 1 of the year following the year of actual retirement, if they wish.) This mandatory distribution rule does not apply to benefits accrued before 1987. (However, there may be a mandatory distribution requirement imposed by the particular tax-sheltered annuity plan to which you have contributed.)

If you have more than one tax-sheltered annuity, then annual distributions need not be made out of each separate annuity. You can determine the total amount required to be distributed that year from all your tax-sheltered annuities under the basic rules described later in this section and withdraw this amount out of just one (or more) of the tax-sheltered annuities as you choose [IRS Notice 88-38, IRB 1988-15].

There is a special restriction on the ability to withdraw funds from a tax-sheltered annuity, with or without the 10% penalty. Specifically, withdrawals from tax-sheltered annuities can be made only after an employee leaves his job, attains age 59^1/$_2$, becomes disabled, dies, or encounters *financial hardship*. However, this restriction only applies to voluntary contributions (under a reduction-in-salary arrangement) made after 1988 and to earnings both on those contributions and on amounts held as of December 31, 1988. Hardship withdrawals will be restricted to contributions invested in the annuity under a reduction-in-salary agreement, excluding any earnings earned by the investments. An employee will be considered to encounter a *financial hardship* only to the extent he has *"an immediate and heavy bonafide financial need and does not have other resources reasonably available to satisfy the need."*

Borrowing From Your Tax-Sheltered Annuity

There is a way to tap the funds in your tax-sheltered annuity early without running into the new restrictions on withdrawals made before age 59$\frac{1}{2}$. Namely, you may be able to borrow money from your tax-sheltered annuity account.

The IRS has specifically allowed tax-sheltered plans to offer loan privileges to its participants, subject to certain limitations on the amount and duration of the loan. The basic maximum loan amount is $50,000. However, this limitation may be reduced by previous loan balances during the preceding 12 months. And the duration of the loan cannot exceed 5 years unless used to purchase the employee's personal residence.

Interest on loans secured by your elective deferral amounts in your tax-sheltered annuity plans is not deductible. This is the case even if the loan is used for normally deductible purposes such as purchasing a residence, making investments, etc. [cf. the *Interest* chapter]. Congress did not want an employee to be able to earn tax-free interest on money in a tax-sheltered annuity plan at the same time he was deducting interest payments on amounts borrowed from the plan.

Note that the above information only describes possible loan rules permitted by the IRS. A given tax-sheltered annuity plan may or may not offer loan privileges to its participants. If you want to be able to borrow money from a tax-sheltered annuity, it may be necessary (if possible) to transfer your funds to an annuity plan which in fact does offer these privileges.

What Types of Tax-Sheltered Annuity Plans Are Available?

Many different types of plans exist. Most eligible non-profit institutions select several different plans which they make available to their employees. Some of them provide investment in fixed income securities such as bonds, and others provide investment in common stocks as well. Some plans require that you wait until retirement whereupon the amount accumulated in your account is used to purchase an annuity. Others allow you to withdraw the cash value of your account before retirement. This latter feature is attractive for those who wish to put aside money to be received in an otherwise low income year.

To get further information on the plans available to you, contact the personnel office where you work. They will have a list of those plans in which you can participate and either provide you with descriptive brochures or give you the addresses of where to write for these brochures. Be sure to obtain and read these brochures carefully. Different plans have different combinations of features. You will want to select the plan which best meets your own personal objectives.

Some institutions allow their employees to choose any commercially available plan. In this case, a way to get a sampling of available plans would be to contact a few of the large mutual fund organizations [cf. Section 5 of the *Investing Your Money* chapter for addresses and toll-free telephone numbers], write to TIAA/CREF [cf. the discussion later in this section], and check with some major insurance companies.

When selecting which tax-sheltered annuity plan to invest in, be sure to examine the options available for the withdrawal of funds. Some plans allow more withdrawal opportunities than others. And some plans provide for a fixed annuity payout after retirement while others gear the payout to the performance of stocks or other securities in their portfolio. Also, different options may be offered governing the period during which payments are made, as well as different survivorship options under which payments continue to a beneficiary after the death of the individual.

It is possible to have part or all of your funds in one tax-sheltered annuity plan transferred to another plan with no tax consequence, provided the two plans permit such a transfer. A new IRS ruling, issued in 1990, governs this situation. According to this ruling, such a transfer can be made as long as the new plan has as stringent distribution restrictions as the original plan. In particular, this applies to the restriction on withdrawals before age 59½ that applies to post-1988 contributions and earnings [cf. the discussion earlier in this Section]. The ability to have one's funds transferred from one tax-sheltered annuity into another applies not just to current employees, but to retirees and beneficiaries as well [Rev. Rul 90-24, IRB 1990-11]. An individual who wishes to make such a transfer should contact his employer or the organization providing the tax-sheltered annuities to arrange the transfer without having any funds pass through his hands.

If you can't arrange a direct transfer, it's possible to receive a distribution check from the first plan and sign it over to the second. In this case, the IRS prefers you *"immediately surrender the proceeds of the first plan pursuant to a binding agreement you have previously signed to turn over the funds to the second plan."* [Rev. Rul. 73-124, 1973-1 C.B. 200; IRS Private Letter Rulings 8322101, 8628053, 8628058]

However, according to a recent court case, it may not be mandatory to make a binding agreement in advance to purchase the second annuity. In this case, a teacher received a check closing out her existing annuity and, a few days later, filled out the application for the new annuity accompanied by the close-out check which she endorsed over to the new annuity company. Despite IRS objection, the Court ruled this to be a valid tax-free shift even though she had previously not made a binding agreement. [Greene, 85 TC #9]

Choosing a Beneficiary

When you set up a tax-sheltered annuity, you will be asked to name a beneficiary in case you die before funds are distributed to you. The tax rules are the same as for beneficiaries of an IRA. Under existing rules, naming a child rather than a spouse as a beneficiary can save on taxes in some situations [cf. Section 2 of this chapter].

Rolling Over Your Tax-Sheltered Annuity into an IRA

There is one further option which some plans may provide, namely the right to receive the funds credited to an individual's account in a lump sum payment. Due to a little known provision in the law, this could be the most beneficial option of all. Here's why.

Lump-sum distributions from tax-sheltered annuities can now be rolled over into an Individual Retirement Account (IRA). This is a special type of account set up with a mutual fund, savings institution, or brokerage house. The funds placed into an IRA continue to earn income entirely free from tax. Only when funds are withdrawn is income tax paid.

The rollover privilege for tax-sheltered annuities is basically the same as for pension plans discussed in Section 2 of this chapter. It applies to lump-sum distributions received after leaving your current employer, or after you are age 59$^{1}/_{2}$. It also generally applies to a partial distribution, received upon leaving your job, of at least 50% of the total amounts in your tax-sheltered annuity. (Before making a rollover, you must subtract any contributions on which tax was already paid as would be the case, for example, if contributions exceeded the allowable limits or if a proper reduction-in-salary agreement was not in force. Such contribution amounts cannot be rolled over into the IRA.)

There are several requirements that must be met for a lump-sum distribution from a tax-sheltered annuity to qualify for rollover into an IRA. Check with your employer for the exact rules that apply. [Also see Section 2 of this chapter.] Note that in particular, the payouts constituting the distribution must be made within the same calendar year and the rollover made within 60 days after the final payout.

The advantage of an IRA over an annuity is in the flexibility and individual control it provides. Your funds can be placed into virtually any type of investment you choose. Often, funds can earn a higher interest rate than would be credited to your account under a fixed annuity arrangement. And you can switch your funds from one type of investment to another as your goals change.

Finally, you can control the payout of funds from an IRA. Each year, you can withdraw any portion of the funds you choose. Or, you can leave the funds alone and let the tax-free income build up, subject to the following restrictions: (i) Funds withdrawn prior to age 59$^{1}/_{2}$ are subject to a 10% penalty tax in addition to the regular income tax, and (ii) You must start withdrawing funds no later than April 1 of the year following the year in which you reach age 70$^{1}/_{2}$ with the rate of withdrawal high enough that the funds would be entirely paid out based on life expectancies. [Cf. Section 2 for further information on IRAs.]

TIAA/CREF Supplemental Retirement Annuities

A Supplemental Retirement Annuity (abbreviated SRA) is a type of tax-sheltered annuity plan run by TIAA/CREF (Teachers Insurance and Annuity Association/College Retirement Equities Fund, a pair of non-profit foundations; address: 730 Third Avenue, New York, NY 10017). An attractive feature of SRAs is the low annual fee charged by TIAA/CREF—about $^{1}/_{4}$ of 1% of assets in your account. Note that your institution does not have to be part of the TIAA/CREF regular retirement program in order for you to purchase an SRA.

SRAs have the same general features as the regular TIAA/CREF plans. Currently, there are 5 choices you can make on how your money will be invested. See the *Retirement Plans* chapter for information concerning the investment choices, withdrawal privileges, and tax treatment of TIAA/CREF plans.

Unisex Mortality Tables

Because of a Court decision, TIAA/CREF will use a unisex mortality table to compute pensions for individuals retiring after May 1, 1980. This decreases benefits for men in some cases with a corresponding increase for women [cf. the discussion in the *Retirement Plans* chapter]. However, only those annuity payments which are an integral part of the plan are affected. If you receive the benefits in a lump sum which you then use to purchase a commercial annuity, then the Court ruling does not apply. Unless the law is changed, the commercial annuity can generally be based on mortality tables which are differentiated by sex.

Women, on the other hand, benefit from plans based on unisex mortality tables if they are planning to select a single-life annuity at retirement [cf. the *Retirement Plans* chapter]. For example, TIAA/CREF, which will pay the same annuities to men and women per dollar invested, becomes more attractive than a plan which lets the individual select only a commercial annuity paying less to women than to men. For women, unisex annuities can also be more attractive than the do-it-yourself withdrawals provided by rolling over a tax-sheltered annuity into an IRA. This is because they are based on a life-expectancy assumption which is shorter than that expected by the average woman.

Social Security Tax

Amounts contributed to a tax-sheltered annuity under a reduction-in-salary agreement are subject to Social Security tax. The Social Security tax is withheld from the employee and matched by an employer's contribution.

Contribution Limits for Tax-Sheltered Annuities

There are 3 basic limitations on how much can be contributed to a tax-sheltered annuity, the *elective deferral limitation,* the *annual limitation,* and the *overall limitation.*

The **elective deferral limitation** requires that the total voluntary contributions made by an individual to tax-sheltered annuities under a reduction in salary agreement cannot exceed $9,500 per year. The $9,500 limit is reduced by deductible contributions made to a SEP [cf. Section 3] or by amounts deferred under a 401(k) deferred compensation plan [cf. Section 5].

The $9,500 limit will be raised to as much as $12,500 for individuals who have worked for their current employer for at least 15 years, provided their previous contributions to tax-sheltered annuities with their current employer averaged less than $5,000 per year. Precisely, for such long-term employees, the $9,500 limit is raised by the lesser of (i) $3,000, or (ii) the excess of $5,000 multiplied by the number of years of service with the current employer over the total voluntary contributions made in prior years to tax-sheltered annuities with that employer.

The extra amounts provided by this rule cannot total more than $15,000 over a lifetime. Thus, if a person voluntarily contributes $12,500 under this rule for each of 5 years, his lifetime maximum of $15,000 would be used up. His voluntary contributions for future years could then not exceed $9,500 per year.

Example

Smith has worked for his current employer for 20 years. During each of the first 10 of these years, he made voluntary contributions of $3,000 to his tax- sheltered annuity, and during the last 10, $6,000 per year. His total voluntary contributions for these 20 years add up to (10 × $3,000) + (10 × $6,000) = $90,000. This is subtracted from 20 × $5,000 = $100,000 as required in (ii) in the above discussion: $100,000 – $90,000 = $10,000. Since this exceeds the $3,000 figure in (i), the maximum allowable voluntary contribution under the *elective deferral limitation* is $9,500 + $3,000 = $12,500.

The above $9,500 (or $12,500) limit applies only to *voluntary* contributions that you elect to have made to your tax-sheltered annuities. It does not apply, for example, to contributions which are a fixed percentage of compensation that are required to be made as a condition of employment.

In contrast, the next 2 limitations, the *annual limitation* and the *overall limitation,* apply to the *total* contributions made during any one year, whether the contributions are voluntary or required. Thus, contributions which are required to be made to a pension plan set up under the tax-sheltered annuity rules (and thereby exempted from current tax) are included in computing the *annual limitation* and the *overall limitation,* but not included in the *elective deferral limitation.*

The **annual limitation** states that contributions in any given year cannot exceed 25% of your reduced salary. Your reduced salary is the amount you are paid after the annuity contribution is deducted from your original salary.

Example

Your annual salary is $40,000 before any contributions to tax-sheltered annuities are made. The annual limitation in this case would be $8,000. This yields a reduced salary of $40,000 – $8,000 = $32,000. Then $8,000 = 25% × $32,000, verifying that $8,000 is the annual limitation. (Observe that $8,000 is equal to 20% of the unreduced salary of $40,000; this same 20% percentage would apply in general no matter what the actual salary figure.)

To determine if this year's contributions to your tax-sheltered annuity satisfy the **overall limitation** you perform the following steps:

(1) Subtract this year's contributions (voluntary and required) to your tax-sheltered annuities from your salary to obtain your *reduced salary.*

(2) Take 20% of your reduced salary and multiply this by the number of years you have worked for your current employer. (Count part-time work in proportion to the fraction of the full-time load you worked.)

(3) Under your current employer, add up the total of all amounts that have been contributed to your tax-sheltered annuity plus the amounts contributed by your employer to your regular retirement plan, including this year's contribution. Also, add in salary which your employer deferred under a Governmental deferred compensation plan.

(4) If (3) does not exceed (2), you have satisfied the overall limitation.

Example

You have worked for your current employer for 5 years. Your initial salary was $30,000 and you received a $2,000 raise in each of the succeeding years. In each of these years, your employer contributed 6% of your salary to your regular retirement plan. In addition, you arranged to have $4,000 of your salary contributed to a tax-sheltered annuity in each of the first 4 years. For the 5th year, the overall limitation restricts your tax-sheltered contribution to $5,900. This is verified according to the following computation.

Year	Salary	Employer's Contribution to Retirement Plan	Contribution to Tax-Sheltered Annuity	Reduced Salary
1	$30,000	$1,800	$4,000	$26,000
2	32,000	1,920	4,000	28,000
3	34,000	2,040	4,000	30,000
4	36,000	2,160	4,000	32,000
5	38,000	2,280	5,900	32,100
		$10,200	$21,900	

To verify that the $5,900 contribution in year 5 falls within the overall limit, note that $10,200 (Retirement Plan Contributions) + $21,900 (Annuity Contributions) = $32,100 does not exceed 20% × $32,100 (reduced salary) × 5 (number of years on job) = $32,100.

We have presented the above rules for your information in planning for the future. In actual practice, your employer will, at your request, compute for you the maximum amount that can be placed tax-free into your tax-sheltered annuity for any given year.

Reduction of the Annual Limitation

This reduction rule only applies if you are covered by a "defined contribution" pension plan with the same employer under which you are having contributions made to your tax-sheltered annuity. A **defined contribution** plan is one that computes your retirement benefit strictly on the basis of how much was contributed to your account. If your retirement plan provides a pension based on a percentage of your salary during a certain period of time, then it is **not** a defined contribution plan. Most governmental and private pension plans are not defined contribution plans. However, pension plans run by TIAA/CREF are defined contribution plans so the reduction rule would apply.

The reduction rule states that in computing the 25% annual limitation, you must add in your employer's contribution to your retirement plan plus certain other amounts such as forfeitures credited to your account. If you are covered by a defined contribution plan, you'll have to check with your employer to determine the precise limitation in your case.

Options Which Permit an Increase in the Annual or Overall Limitations

Believe it or not, the above are only basic rules which apply. The law provides several options you are permitted to adopt which may increase the contributions that can be made to your tax-sheltered annuity. (If you don't wish to contribute more than the regular rules allow, you don't have to concern yourself with these options.) These options provide alternatives to either the annual limitation or the overall limitation. They do not affect the elective deferral limitation. In all cases, your annual voluntary contributions to a tax-sheltered annuity cannot exceed $9,500 (or $12,500 for certain 15-year employees as described earlier).

Each of the following three options may serve to increase the amount you can have contributed to your tax-sheltered annuity with the tax-exempt educational, charitable, or religious organization for which you work. Once you utilize one of these options, you cannot use any of the other options in a later year.

Option #1. You can choose to forget entirely about the overall limitation. You would still be restricted by the annual limitation which provides a 25% ceiling on contributions as well as by the $9,500 (or $12,500) elective deferral limitation.

Option #2. You can raise the annual limitation by $4,000. If you adopt this option, your annual contributions are still subject to the overall limitation plus a third limitation of $15,000. Also, the elective deferral limitation would still apply.

Option #3. For your final year of employment, you can disregard the annual limitation altogether and be restricted by the overall limitation where you take into account only the last ten years. However, the $9,500 (or $12,500) elective deferral limitation would still apply.

Discussion of the Options

Option #1 is of little use to the average individual. It would only come into use if someone wishes to make consistently high contributions to a tax-sheltered annuity during his entire employment period. Most people would not be able to afford such contributions in their earlier years so that the overall limitation does not come into force. However, those switching to a new job late in their careers might be benefited by this option.

Example

Jones obtains a new position three years from retirement age. He wishes to contribute the maximum possible amount to a tax-sheltered annuity. Jones adopts Option 1. He can then have 25% of his reduced salary contributed each year (provided the elective deferral limitation is satisfied). Under the basic rules or the other options he would be restricted to 20%. However, note that Option 3 provides a limitation based on 20% of the *final* year's salary. Thus, if his salary were to go up substantially, this could turn out to be the best choice.

Option #2 might be chosen if you wish to make large contributions now but have made low contributions in the past.

Example

Stirling has 5 years left until retirement and will earn $25,000 in each of these years. He has held his current job for the past 15 years and has not participated in a tax-sheltered annuity to date. During these 15 years, his total salary has added up to $200,000. By selecting Option 2, he could have $8,200 per year contributed to a tax-sheltered annuity for his remaining 5 years with the remainder, $25,000 – $8,200 = $16,800 being his reduced salary. Since he is in no danger of exceeding the overall limitation, the 25% + $4,000 limitation of Option 2 applies: $8,200 = $4,200 + $4,000 where $4,200 is 25% of the reduced salary of $16,800.

Option #3 represents an opportunity for anyone who wishes to defer tax on a substantial portion of his final salary and spread it out via an annuity over his lower-bracket retirement years.

Example

Rodgers has been working for the same employer for 20 years and decides to quit. His employer has annually contributed $1,000 to his regular retirement plan. In addition, during the last 10 years, he had a total of $14,000 contributed to a tax-sheltered annuity. His final salary was $30,000. Under Option 3, Rodgers can have $12,000 contributed to a tax-sheltered annuity in his final year (assuming the elective deferral limitation is satisfied). This is verified as follows:

Salary in final year	$30,000
Contribution to tax-sheltered annuity	$12,000
Reduced Salary	$18,000
Allowable total contributions:	
$18,000 × 20% × 10 years =	$36,000

The total contributions made by his employer to the regular retirement plan plus the total of all contributions to a tax-sheltered annuity do not exceed this allowance as is verified by the following computation:

Employer's contribution to retirement plan:	
$1,000 × 10 =	$10,000
Previous contributions to tax-sheltered annuity	$14,000
Final year contribution to tax-sheltered annuity	$12,000
Total	$36,000

There is no special form to file with the IRS to elect one of the above options. You just arrange with your employer to withhold the appropriate amount. You are considered to have elected an option when it is needed to justify the extra amounts being contributed to your tax-sheltered annuity. In following years you can elect the same option or apply the regular limitations, but not elect a different option.

If you contribute to a regular Keogh plan or participate in another pension plan of a company you own, then there is a $30,000 upper limit on the total annual contributions to tax-sheltered plans made on your behalf.

Section 5:
Deferred Compensation Plans

Some employers permit deferral of income under a *Deferred Compensation Plan*. Under such a plan, typically, salary is set aside instead of being paid out currently. The money set aside is invested on behalf of the employee, with the accumulated funds paid out after retirement, usually in the form of an annuity.

Deferred compensation plans may not have the same legal status as regular retirement plans or tax-sheltered annuities. In particular, they may be *unfunded* instead of *funded* plans. This means that the employee's claim to the funds owed him has the same status as any other creditor's claim instead of having the preferred status that applies to regular retirement plans.

Deferred compensation plans offered by private companies vary from organization to organization. Each organization sets its own limits (within IRS guidelines) on how much pay can be deferred. Many private companies will match part of their employees' contributions, making these plans particularly attractive. The special lump-sum averaging rule [cf. the *Retirement Plans* chapter] can apply to plans run by private companies. Details should be available from the personnel office where you work.

Note that the 1986 Tax Reform Act placed a ceiling on contributions to deferred compensation plans known as 401(k) plans run by private companies. This ceiling is reduced by deductible contributions to an IRA and by an individual's contributions to a tax-sheltered annuity made under a salary reduction agreement. The ceiling for 1990 was $7,979 and is adjusted annually for inflation. However, the IRS may require particular company plans to have a lower ceiling if not enough lower paid company employees participate in the plan.

Withdrawal Rules

The IRS has issued new rules concerning the ability to withdraw funds from deferred compensation plans (called 401(k) plans after the relevant section of the Tax Code) maintained by private companies. These rules affect so-called *hardship withdrawals*.

Ordinarily, the same general withdrawal rules that apply to other types of retirement plans also apply to 401(k) deferred compensation plans. That is, withdrawals attributable to contributions you elected to make can be made only upon separation from service (including retirement, death, or disability) or after reaching age $59^1/2$. However, there is an extra provision that allows you to make such withdrawals if you need the money because you have a *financial hardship*.

The IRS recently spelled out what qualifies as a hardship distribution. The basic requirement is that it must have been made because of *an immediate and heavy financial need*. The following are examples of such financial needs:

1. Medical expenses of the employee, spouse, or dependents,

2. Purchase of a principal residence (not including mortgage payments),

3. Tuition for the next term of college education for the employee, spouse, or dependents,

or

4. Payments to stave off eviction from or foreclosure on a principal residence.

To demonstrate a need for the funds, the general requirement is that you weren't able to obtain the funds elsewhere such as from insurance, reasonable liquidation of assets, other distributions or nontaxable loans from other retirement plans, or borrowing from commercial sources on reasonable commercial terms. However, the new rules provide for an exception to this general rule if your deferred compensation plan has written into it certain *safe harbor* rules. These safe harbor rules are satisfied if:

1. The distribution does not exceed the amount of the need,

2. The employee has obtained all available distributions and nontaxable loans from other plans maintained by the employer,

and

3. The employee cannot make further elective contributions to the plan for a period of between 1 and 2 years, according to IRS regulations.

If the above safe harbor rules are satisfied, the employee need not exhaust his other resources before making a hardship withdrawal.

Loans

Many deferred compensation plans have a provision under which you can borrow a certain percentage of your account balance. Generally, such loans are secured by the funds in your account. However, this can be a tax mistake. If the loan is secured by the elective contributions you chose to make to the plan, then you cannot deduct any interest you pay on the loan, no matter what the purpose of the loan. You can't even deduct the 10% of interest allowed under the phase-out rules for personal interest [cf. the *Interest* chapter].

However, the law permits you to secure such loans by assets other than the funds in your account. If such assets are the only security, the absolute prohibition against deducting interest does not apply. For example, if your employer permits, you can secure the loan by your automobile, home, etc. In particular, if you can secure the loan solely by your principal or second residence, then you can deduct *all* the interest, provided the $100,000 ceiling has not been exceeded [cf. Section 1 of the *Homeowners* chapter]. (However, there are extra restrictions that apply to full or partial (1% or more) owners of the company maintaining the plan.)

Tax-Exempt Organizations

Different rules apply to deferred compensation plans run by tax-exempt organizations. The basic rule for such plans is as follows:

> *During any given year, the amount of salary set aside cannot exceed either $7,500 or 25% of an individual's full salary before reduction. If the employee participates in a tax-sheltered annuity, then this limitation applies to the total amount contributed to both plans.*

There is an exception to the above limitation which allows catch-up contributions to be made. During each of the 3 years prior to normal retirement age, an employee may defer up to $15,000 per year. However, this catch-up provision only applies to the extent that full utilization was not made of the full limitations in prior years going back to 1979. In other words, the total amounts set aside over the life of the plan still cannot exceed the total amounts that would have been set aside had the individual made full use of the $7,500 or 25% of salary contribution each year starting in 1979.

Details concerning any deferred compensation plans available to you should be obtained from the personnel office where you work.

Section 6:
Flexible Spending Accounts

The tax-sheltered plan that is rapidly becoming one of the most popular is the so-called *Flexible Spending Account* (FSA) (sometimes called a *cafeteria plan*). The name comes from the fact that under this type of plan, you can choose from a selection of different tax-sheltered benefits according to your needs. Although these types of plans have been in existence for several years, the IRS has just recently issued clarifying rules. Because of this, many more companies and institutions are expected to set up plans in the near future.

The way a typical FSA plan works is this. You are permitted to set aside a certain portion of your salary—which goes untaxed—to go towards paying certain benefits you select from a list provided under the plan. Such benefits can include:

1. medical and dental expenses (other than health insurance)

2. child care expenses (for dependents under age 13)

3. deferred compensation arrangement

4. group term life insurance

5. extra vacation days

To illustrate, let's take the example of a FSA plan that includes the first 2 benefits listed above and that permits you to set aside up to $2,000 of your salary towards these expenses. At the beginning of the year, you designate how to apportion this $2,000 (assuming you choose to set aside the maximum amount). For example, let's say you designate $500 towards child care expenses and $1,500 towards medical expenses of yourself, your spouse, and dependents. As you incur these expenses during the year, you submit the bills to your employer who will reimburse you up to the $500 maximum for child care expenses and $1,500 maximum for medical expenses.

To pay for these reimbursements, your employer will withhold the $2,000 from your paychecks during the year. However, you do not have to wait until sufficient amounts have been withheld. For example, you could get reimbursed for $2,000 worth of expenses incurred in January even though only a fraction of the $2,000 had been withheld up until that point.

The advantage comes from the tax treatment. The $2,000 withheld from your paychecks is exempt from tax. Thus, your taxable income is reduced by $2,000. If you had received this amount in salary and then paid the expenses directly yourself, you would have had to pay both income tax and social security taxes as well. In particular, this is an inferior outcome if you can't otherwise get a tax deduction or tax credit for these expenses because of the limitations that apply [cf. the *Medical Expenses* and *Child Care* chapters].

Under many FSA plans, you would have complete flexibility as to the allocation of the $2,000 each year. You could choose an allocation like that illustrated above, or you could choose to receive part or all of this amount in salary instead.

The main catch in FSA plans is the *use it or lose it* rule. That is, if you do not use up the initially designated amounts before the end of the year, then these amounts are lost to you. You cannot receive a refund nor carry over the amounts to the following year.

Thus, in the above example, if you incurred only $400 in child care expenses and $1,000 in uninsured medical expenses, you would be reimbursed for these amounts only. The remaining $600 would revert to the employer or be spread out among all the participants in the plan. Thus, you will not want to allocate funds unless you are fairly certain expenses will be incurred. This is usually not a problem for families which can count on a certain minimum of medical (including dental) expenses, child care expenses, etc.

FSA plans are of particular benefit to working couples. Often, there is a duplication of benefits under typical fringe benefit arrangements. For example, one spouse's medical insurance plan may be just a duplication of the other spouse's plan—causing a loss of benefits. However, under a FSA plan which included medical insurance as only one of several options, there would be no loss of benefit. The funds could be allocated towards paying for other benefits such as uninsured medical or dental expenses, child care, or perhaps contributed to a deferred compensation plan instead.

It pays to check into any FSA plan for which you might be eligible. Because FSA plans are relatively new, many employees are still unaware of how beneficial they can be. In fact, fewer than 25% of employees whose employers offer FSAs take advantage of them.

Chapter 14

Estate and Gift Tax

Section 1:
Introduction

Basic Gift and Estate Tax Law

Prior to 1977, there were two separate taxes, one on estates and one on gifts. The estate tax was levied on property passing from one individual to another upon death of the first individual. And to prevent an individual from escaping estate tax simply by giving away his property before death, a separate gift tax applied to the **giver** of substantial amounts.

The 1976 Tax Reform Act combined these two taxes into a new Unified Estate and Gift Tax. The way it works is this.

To determine the amount of gift tax due, a cumulative total of all gifts made by an individual during his lifetime is kept. When this total exceeds a certain minimum amount, then gift tax becomes due. Excluded from this cumulative total are gifts totalling less than $10,000 per year per recipient and gifts made in any amount to a spouse.

The tax rate is graduated with the rate determined by the cumulative lifetime total of gifts. For example, if a person has made gifts worth X amount in prior years and gives Y amount of gifts this year, then the gift tax rate that applies is the one in the X to X + Y bracket.

To determine the amount of estate tax due, the deceased's taxable estate is first computed by subtracting certain adjustments (as explained in Section 3) from the sum total of all property passing to his heirs. The tax on this estate is then obtained by using the same tax schedule that applies to gifts. And the cumulative total of all gifts made during the individual's lifetime determines which tax bracket applies. For example, if a person has made gifts worth G during his lifetime and his taxable estate is worth E, then the tax rate used is the one that applies to the bracket G to G + E.

In summary then, the Unified Estate and Gift Tax applies to the sum total of all taxable gifts made during one's lifetime plus the value of the taxable estate. However, no tax is due unless this total exceeds $600,000.

Section 2:
Gift Tax

If one person makes a substantial gift to another, then the giver may have to pay a gift tax. The recipient pays no tax. The gift tax is computed by adding up the cumulative total of all gifts made during an individual's lifetime to other individuals. There are two exemptions which are excluded from this cumulative total.

(1) Each year you may exempt gifts totalling $10,000 to any one person. You get a separate $10,000 exemption for each person to whom you make a gift. If your spouse consents, you can regard a gift to a third person as being 1/2 from each of you and give $20,000 tax-free to each person.

(2) In addition to (1), you may exempt any gifts made during your lifetime to your spouse. Also, you can exempt any amounts paid on behalf of any donee directly to a school for tuition or to a health care provider for medical services.

The following is a sampling of the 1990 tax rates that would apply to different amounts of lifetime gifts:

Lifetime Total of Taxable Gifts	Tax
$ 600,000	$ 0
$ 750,000	$ 55,500
$1,000,000	$153,000
$2,000,000	$588,000

The above schedule is not applied separately to each year's gifts, but instead is applied to the sum total of all gifts you have made in your lifetime. For example, suppose that (after subtracting exclusions) you have made taxable gifts totalling $200,000 in previous years and have paid gift tax (under prior law) totalling $7,800. If you now make a taxable gift of $550,000, this will bring your lifetime total of gifts up to $750,000. Since the tax on $750,000 is $55,500 and you have already paid $7,800 tax in previous years, you must now pay the difference, $55,500 − $7,800 = $47,700.

Section 3:
Estate Tax

The Gross Estate
The first step in computing the estate tax of a deceased person is to determine the gross estate. The gross estate includes the value of the following items:

• Home and other owned real estate

• Cash and debts owed to the deceased

• Stocks and bonds

• Personal belongings and household furnishings (including automobiles)

• Life insurance

• Annuities and death benefits

In order for you to estimate the size of your estate, let us consider the above items separately.

Your Home and Real Estate

Include the value of all your real estate holdings, including your own home and real estate in other countries. If you have a mortgage on your property, then the amount of the unpaid balance will be subtracted from the value of the property. If you own property jointly, see the subsection on jointly-held property.

Cash and Amounts Owed to You

Include money you have in banks and savings accounts as well as currency on hand. Also include any amounts which others owe to you via a note, mortgage, etc. which you hold.

Stocks and Bonds

All stocks and bonds you own are subject to estate tax. This includes U.S. savings bonds, income-tax-free municipal bonds, stocks in foreign countries, etc. These are valued at their current market value. If you own a piece of a small business, then the IRS will, at your death, evaluate your shares more or less according to what it thinks a willing buyer would pay for it.

Life Insurance

If you own a life insurance policy on your life, then the face amount of the insurance is included in your estate. However, there is a way to avoid having this insurance included in your estate. If the insurance goes to a beneficiary and if that beneficiary or other individual owns the policy, then the insurance is not included in your estate. However, that person must have complete control of the policy. You must not possess any "incident of ownership" in the policy such as the right to borrow on the policy, to surrender it for cash, or change the beneficiary. There is also a problem if the policy was transferred to the beneficiary within 3 years prior to the death of the insured.

There is another restriction which forbids you having a "reversionary interest" in the policy. Roughly speaking, this restriction states that you should have less than a 5% chance of getting back the policy or its proceeds because of your beneficiary dying before you. This restriction can be satisfied by having your beneficiary name someone other than yourself to inherit the policy in the event the beneficiary dies before you.

Jointly-Owned Property

There are two basic ways in which property can be jointly owned. The first way, called tenancy-in-common, means that each of the owners has a share of the property and can dispose of that share as he chooses. Upon death, his share passes to whomever is named in his will. If there is no will, it, together with his other property, passes according to the inheritance laws of the state.

Under tenancy-in-common, your share of the ownership would be included in your estate. For example, if you own an equal share of a house under tenancy-in-common with another person, then your estate would include 1/2 the value of the house. It would make no difference who had contributed the funds to buy the house.

The second and more prevalent type of co-ownership is called joint tenancy. Under this type, when one of the co-owners dies, the property passes automatically to the other co-owner. It cannot be willed to another individual.

Your estate includes 1/2 the value of any property held in joint tenancy with your spouse. For property held in joint tenancy with a non-spouse, your estate includes that portion of the joint property which represents the fraction you paid for.

There is a special type of joint tenancy available only to husband and wife, called **tenancy-by-the-entireties.** Under ordinary joint tenancy, one party alone can demand to dissolve the tenancy and retrieve his share. But under tenancy-by-the-entireties, generally, husband and wife must agree on any dissolution of the ownership. In most states, tenancy-by-the-entireties is available only in joint ownership of real estate. There is no difference between ordinary joint tenancy and tenancy-by-the-entireties as far as estate tax is concerned.

Annuities and Death Benefits

Many annuities and pension plans have a survivorship feature which pays a beneficiary either a lump sum or periodic payments upon the death of the original participant. Also, tax-sheltered annuities, Keogh plans, and IRAs may make payments to survivors. The value of such payments is generally included in the estate.

Deductions from the Gross Estate

To compute the taxable estate, the following deductions are subtracted from the gross estate:

(1) The marital deduction

The full value of all property left to a spouse is deductible from the estate. Thus, if the entire estate is left to a spouse, no estate tax is due. Special rules apply if the spouse is not a U.S. citizen.

(2) Funeral expenses, administration expenses, and debts

This includes undertaker charges, cost of burial plot and tombstone, and any personal debts that must be settled by the estate. Also deductible are the costs of settling the estate—attorney fees, court costs, executor fees, and appraiser fees.

(3) Charitable contributions

The full market value of any bequest made to charity is deductible. Sometimes, bequests are made in a form other than an outright donation. For example, income-producing property might be left in trust with the provision that the income from such property be paid to a child, upon whose death the property is given to charity. In such a case, an actuarial computation is made to determine how to allocate the benefits between the child and the charity. The estate would get a deduction for the value allocated to charity.

Computation of the Estate Tax

The estate tax is computed as follows: First, the taxable estate is computed by subtracting allowable deductions from the gross estate. Then, the total of lifetime taxable gifts is added in and the tax computed on this amount. Next, any gift taxes that have already been paid are subtracted from the tax bill. Last, there are several tax credits which are subtracted to reduce the tax bill further.

Tax Credits
(1) State death tax credit

You can subtract state death taxes up to a certain maximum amount. There is also a credit for death taxes paid to a foreign country on property in that country.

(2) Credit for prior Federal estate tax

Suppose one person inherits part of an estate on which estate tax was paid and then dies soon after the inheritance. The estate of the second person to die might then be hit by a second estate tax. To reduce the effect of this double taxation, a credit is allowed on the estate tax of the second person to die if death occurs within ten years of the first death — the longer the time, the less credit allowed.

State Inheritance Taxes

Virtually all states have some type of inheritance tax. These taxes differ widely from state to state both in the size of the tax and the manner in which they are applied. Many states vary the rates according to the relationship between the deceased and the beneficiary—the closer the relationship, the lower the tax.

How Is the Estate Settled?

The rules differ according to state law but the basic procedure is the same. Property which is owned in joint tenancy passes directly to the surviving owner. Property in certain types of trusts remains governed by the trust agreement. Other property is distributed to the heirs as provided in the will. If there is no will, then State law governs how the property is distributed.

A court will be responsible for supervising the distribution of the estate. In the will, an executor is named who has the responsibility of evaluating the assets, paying the appropriate taxes, and distributing the property according to the will. If there is no will, an executor will be appointed by the court. If the estate is simple, a family member or friend may be named as executor. Complicated estates are often executed by an individual or bank trust department specializing in such matters. In such cases, executor fees typically range in the neighborhood of 5% of the value of the estate governed by the will.

Making a Will

Anyone with even a modest amount of assets should have a will. In the absence of a will, your assets will be distributed according to an arbitrary formula given by State law. The distribution formula may not be what you think. For example, in some states, the estate of a married individual with no children would be distributed 50% to the individual's parents and 50% to the spouse. Elsewhere, the estate of a married individual with children might be distributed 1/3 to the spouse and 2/3 to the children. This could impose a hardship on the spouse who might actually have to go to court to get permission to use the children's share for their benefit.

If there are children, a will should be drawn up which includes the appointment of a guardian in case both the parents die. Otherwise, the court would be in charge of appointing a guardian. Even if there are no children and all property is held in joint tenancy, a will may be called for. To illustrate what can happen without a will, suppose an individual with no children owns all property in joint tenancy with a spouse. If the two of them die in a joint accident, without a will the property would pass from the first to die to the second to die and then to, say, the parents of the second party. The family of the first to die would get nothing.

You should have your will reviewed by a qualified attorney whenever your circumstances change significantly—for example if you divorce or change permanent residence to another state.

Note that the cost of drawing up a will isn't deductible as such. However, if your will includes provisions designed to reduce estate tax, the cost of working out these provisions is deductible. Ask your lawyer to itemize on his bill that portion of his fee attributable to estate tax planning.

What Can Be Done to Minimize Estate Tax?

There are many strategies for reducing estate tax. If your estate will be sizable, then you should consult one of the many lawyers specializing in such matters to design a plan to minimize your estate tax. In fact, many people claim that the main effect of the estate tax is not to raise significant amounts of money for the Treasury, but to force people to arrange their affairs in such a way as to avoid or minimize the tax.

Here are just three of the basic techniques used for reducing estate tax:

(A) Give property away before death.

The annual exemptions of $10,000 per recipient per year ($20,000 if married) can be used to transfer a substantial amount over a period of years. Gifts of income-producing property can also have the advantage of reducing income tax by shifting income to a lower-bracket taxpayer.

Sizable gifts made to minors are usually made under the Uniform Gifts to Minors Act [cf. the *Income-Shifting* chapter]. Under this act, a custodian is named who controls and invests the funds until the minor reaches majority age whereupon he assumes control of the funds. You or your spouse can serve as custodian. However, if you serve as custodian of funds you gave and you die before the minor reaches majority age, then the value of the funds held as custodian would be included in your estate. Thus, it might be better to name your spouse or someone else as custodian to avoid this possibility.

(B) Use trusts to avoid double estate tax.

A common device used in estate-planning for large estates is to place funds in a trust. Typically the situation is this: An individual wants to leave funds first to his spouse and, after the death of his spouse, to his children. If the funds were left outright to the spouse, these funds would escape estate tax at that time but would be subjected to estate tax at the death of the spouse. The second estate tax is usually more severe than the first because the second estate does not qualify for the marital deduction (unless the surviving spouse remarried) and is generally larger in amount.

To lessen the taxation of the spouse's estate, most planned estates leave a certain portion of the funds to a trust. For example, the trust might be directed to pay the interest earned by the funds to the spouse as long as the spouse is living. Upon death of the spouse the funds would be transmitted to the children. The trust could also provide that in case of emergencies, the trustees are directed to pay to the spouse part of the principal in addition to the interest.

The value of the funds placed in such a trust is included in the estate. But, since the spouse never has control of the funds, there is no second estate tax upon the death of the spouse. The principal simply passes automatically over to the children without a second estate tax being paid.

(C) Make charitable gifts.

There is an estate tax deduction for any funds left to charity. However, an individual may want to benefit a charity, but is worried that an outright bequest would leave a surviving spouse or child without adequate support.

A common approach is to leave funds to a charitable trust. For example, a trust might be directed to pay all annual income earned by the funds to a spouse or child. Upon death of the spouse or child, the remaining principal is given to charity. The estate gets a charitable deduction based on an actuarial computation of the present value of the future gift to charity.

Sometimes, instead of leaving funds directly to charity, it is better to leave the funds to someone else with the express understanding that this person will donate the funds to charity. This second person will then get an income tax deduction for the charitable gift. This income tax deduction might save more taxes than the corresponding estate tax deduction if the funds were donated directly.

Caution

We have only briefly touched upon some of the basic principles involved in estate planning. The only proper way to plan an estate is to consult with a lawyer who specializes in such matters and is familiar with the intricacies of Federal and State law.

Chapter 15

Investing Your Money

Section 1:
Capital Gains and Losses

Most of the income you receive, whether salary from your job, stock dividends, interest on a savings account or bond, rent from property you own, etc. is considered **ordinary income.**

But, if you buy an item at one price and sell it at a higher price, then the resulting profit is not considered ordinary income but falls into a special category called a **capital gain.** The item could be a bond, stock, real estate, or any other type of property or security.

The same distinction exists with respect to losses. If you lose money in a business venture, or rental property because expenses exceed income, etc., then you have an **ordinary loss.** This ordinary loss is generally just subtracted from your ordinary income when you compute your tax. But if you sustain a loss because you sell an investment item at a lower price than the one at which you purchased it, then you have a **capital loss.** This capital loss cannot always just be subtracted from your income, but is treated according to the special rules below.

Before 1988, long-term capital gains were taxed at a lower rate than ordinary income. But now, capital gains are taxed at the same rate as ordinary income. This means that long-term capital gains can be subject to as high a tax rate as 33%, a 67% rise from the maximum 20% rate under the old law.

Although capital gains and ordinary income are taxed alike, you still report capital gains on your tax return in the same manner as before. That is, you fill out Schedule D, on which short-term gains and losses are kept separate from long- term gains and losses as discussed below.

If you are undecided whether or not to sell an asset which will produce a long-term capital gain, you may be better off waiting. If the maximum tax brackets are raised in a future tax bill (a likely possibility), then the capital gains rate may well be lowered again as part of a compromise package. It is not considered as likely that the rate on capital gains will rise in the near future. Congress specifically provided that if the basic tax rates are changed in a future tax bill, the rate on long-term capital gains would not rise, but instead remain capped at the 33% rate. It is probably with this potential change in mind that the IRS continues to require that short-term gains and losses be segregated from long-term gains and losses on Schedule D.

Short vs. Long-Term

If you owned an item for more than 12 months, then you are considered to have owned it for a **long term.** Less than or equal to 12 months is a **short term.** The capital gain or loss resulting from a sale in 1990 is then either a long-term or short-term gain or loss accordingly. A sale is considered made on the *trade date* (rather than the *settlement date* which is generally 5 days later.)

Capital Gains and Losses

Your first step is to subtract the total of your long-term losses from the total of your long-term gains for 1990. If you have more gains than losses, the result is your **net long-term gain.** On the other hand, if you have more losses than gains, the difference is your **net long-term loss** for the year.

You perform a similar operation on your short-term gains and losses. If you have more short-term gains than losses, then the difference between the two is your **net short-term gain.** If the losses exceed your gains then the difference is your **net short-term loss.**

The above losses and gains are computed on page 1 of Schedule D. (There is also a Schedule D-1 for listing transactions if you should run out of room on Schedule D.) On page 2 of schedule D, you combine your net gains and net losses together, both short and long term. If your gains are more than your losses, you wind up with a net capital gain for the year. This net gain is then transferred to line 13 of Form 1040. Here, it gets added to your other income and taxed on your 1990 tax return at the same rate that applies to all ordinary income. (However, special rules apply to capital gains produced by the sale of your personal residence [cf. the *Homeowners* chapter].)

On the other hand, if your losses are more than your gains, you wind up with a net capital loss for the year. In this case, you deduct it from your ordinary income up to a maximum of $3,000 ($1,500 for a married person filing separately). If your total net loss for 1990 exceeds this amount, then you deduct $3,000 ($1,500 for a married person filing separately) from ordinary income on your 1990 tax return and carry over the excess into the future. Capital losses are deducted from ordinary income by entering a negative entry on line 13 of Form 1040.

Example

On a joint return you have a net short-term gain of $2,000 and a net long-term loss of $9,000. These combine to produce a net loss of $7,000. Of this, you deduct $3,000 on your 1990 tax return and carry over $7,000 - $3,000 = $4,000 to be deducted on future tax returns.

Reconciliation with Broker's Statements

If you sold stocks, bonds, etc. during the year, you will receive a Form 1099-B at the end of the year from your broker, mutual fund, etc. reporting the proceeds from the sales. The total of all amounts reported on Forms 1099-B you receive, other than for real estate transactions, is reported on Line 1, Schedule D. You must attach a statement to your tax return explaining any discrepancy between the amount reported on Line I and the total sales prices shown in the sections on Schedule D where you compute your capital gains and losses on stocks, bonds, etc.

The Form 1099-B which you receive from your stock broker reporting 1990 transactions will show the amount being reported to the IRS as the *total proceeds* from your sales of securities. It will also indicate whether these proceeds are the *gross proceeds* or the *gross proceeds less commissions* you paid on the sales.

If your broker reported the *gross proceeds* to the IRS, you list the gross amounts received on each sale before commissions are subtracted in Column d, *Sales price,* on Schedule D. You then add the commissions to the amount reported in Column e, *Cost or other basis.* Thus, the amount reported in Column e will include your purchase price plus the commissions paid both on the purchase and the sale of the security. In this way, when the amount in Column e is subtracted from the amount in Column d, your true monetary gain or loss will be calculated, including the effect of the commissions you have paid.

If your broker reported the *gross proceeds less commissions* to the IRS, then these are the amounts you report in Column d. The amount in Column e will then be your purchase price plus the commissions you paid on the purchase, but not including the commissions you paid on the sale which were already taken into account in the figure reported in Column d.

Wash Sales

You may own stocks or other securities which are selling at a lower price than when purchased. Tax considerations might call for a sale of such securities in order to create a currently deductible tax loss. However, if it is desired to still own the securities while producing a tax loss, you can't just sell securities at a loss and then buy them right back. Any purchase of the same securities within 30 days before or after the sale negates any losses. To get around this restriction, you can purchase similar but not identical securities to the ones sold. Or, in the case of bonds, you can achieve the same result by making a swap through a brokerage house. They can also advise you of more exotic methods of achieving the same result such as using appropriate short sales or options transactions.

Brokerage Fees

You cannot deduct brokerage commissions or other charges related to the purchase or sale of securities or other assets. Instead, as discussed above, these fees serve to lower the capital gain or increase the capital loss computed on Schedule D when you make a sale.

Custodial or management fees you pay on investments are deductible as a *miscellaneous deduction* on your 1990 tax return. For example, a fee charged by a bank for management of a money-market account would be deductible (unless it represented a normal check-processing fee).

Special Treatment for Inherited Property

Inherited property such as real estate, stocks, bonds, etc. is given a *fresh start* basis when inherited. That is, for purposes of future capital gains tax computations, it is treated as though it were purchased at its market value at the time of inheritance. Thus, when you sell property which was acquired by inheritance, tax is due only on the appreciation in value since the time it was inherited. No tax is ever paid on the increase in value that took place when the property belonged to the previous owner.

Shifting Profits to Different Years

When you sell property on which you have a profit, you may wish to shift some or all of this profit to later years. This can be done by making an *installment sale*. That is, you agree to receive part or all of the money due you in one or more future years. Then, you would report the proportionate profit in the years you receive the various payments from the buyer. There are no restrictions on the number of payments or on the size of the initial payment.

The installment sale reporting procedure does not apply to the sales of stocks or securities that are traded in an established marketplace. Also, there are restrictions that apply to the sale of real estate for more than $150,000 when the seller owes any business-related debts. These restrictions do not generally apply to the sale of a personal home even if for more than $150,000.

If you receive delayed payments, you must charge interest. You can't simply regard all money received as part of the selling price and thereby convert interest into capital gains. Check with the IRS to determine the minimum acceptable interest rate to charge at the time of sale.

The law prevents tax reduction by using an installment sale to a very close relative as an intermediate step. For example, suppose you sell property on which you have a profit to your father with payments to be made in future years and he immediately resells it for the same price. You would have to include the entire profit on your tax return in the year of sale, not as you received the payments from your father.

You do not have to use the installment reporting procedure described above. If you wish, you may elect to report the entire profit in the year the sale is consummated, even if payments are to be made in future years. In such a case, you should check the appropriate box in Part VI of Schedule D.

Section 2:
Passive Loss Rules

In the past, many high-earning individuals sought *tax-shelter* investments that were designed to produce a current loss rather than a profit. This loss could then be used on the individual's tax return to cancel out earnings which otherwise would be taxed at a high-bracket rate of as much as 50%. Ideally, a tax-shelter investment would mostly generate "paper losses" produced by the tax law rather than an actual cash loss.

For example, the most common of these tax shelters has been investments in rental real estate. The paper losses in real estate come from the annual depreciation allowances permitted under the law. (Depreciation can be claimed as a deduction even if the property is increasing in value.)

The 1986 Tax Reform Act cracked down on tax-shelter investments by restricting losses produced by *passive activities*. The basic idea is that losses produced by a *passive activity* cannot be used to offset either *earned income* or *investment income* from stocks, savings accounts, etc. These losses can only be used to offset income from other passive activities. As enacted by Congress, the rules apply not just to passive activities which produce a paper loss, but also to activities which produce cash losses as well.

What is a Passive Activity?

A *passive activity* is a limited partnership or other business activity in which neither you nor your spouse participate on a regular, continuous, and substantial basis. However, any rental activity is automatically considered to be a passive activity no matter what the level of personal participation.

In contrast to *business* activities, *investing* in stocks, bonds, savings accounts, etc. is not considered to be a *passive activity*. Also, there is a special exception for oil and gas working interests in which there is no limit on the taxpayer's liability.

Limit on Passive Losses

Losses produced by a passive activity cannot be used to offset income from active sources such as salary from a job or profits from a business run by the taxpayer. And it cannot be used to offset *investment income* such as dividends or interest. Rather, losses from passive activities can only be used to offset income from the same or other passive activities.

The way this restriction on passive losses works is as follows. You first total up the profits and losses from all your passive activities. This includes any capital gains or losses generated by the sale of a passive activity. It also includes interest on debt used to buy into the passive activity as well as interest expenses incurred by the activity itself. It does not include any portfolio income such as dividends or interest on securities, even if connected with a passive activity.

Next, you compare the total profits with the total losses produced by the passive activities. If the total profits exceed the total losses, then you have a net *passive profit* for the year. In this case, the passive loss rules do not apply. The profits and losses from your passive activities are treated in the same manner as other income.

However, if the losses exceed the profits, then you have a *net passive loss* for the year, which cannot be deducted on your tax return. However, losses not currently deductible may be carried over to future years, as discussed later in this section.

Exceptions

There are 2 basic exceptions to the above disallowance rule for passive losses. First, there is an exception for rental real estate losses that applies to anyone whose adjusted gross income does not exceed $100,000 (ignoring IRA contributions, taxable social security benefits, and passive activity losses). Such an individual can exempt up to $25,000 of his net losses produced by rental real estate from the passive loss disallowance rule. To qualify for this exception, the individual (together with his spouse) must own at least 10% of the rental real estate and must be an *active participant* in the rental activity. To qualify as an *active participant,* the individual need not manage the property himself. But he needs to be involved in basic decision-making activities such as choosing tenants, approving repairs, etc. (The rental property exception also can apply to a vacation home which is rented out, on average, for periods of 7 days or less. Here the $100,000 and $25,000 limitations do not apply. However in this case, the owner must either be the only one performing services connected with the rental or meet a *material participation* standard requiring a minimum number of hours of service of at least 100 hours.)

Second, there is a *phase-in* provision that applies to interests in passive activities acquired before October 23, 1986. For net losses produced by these activities, 90% is disallowed on 1990 tax returns. The remaining 10% is deductible.

The $25,000 passive loss exemption for rental real estate is phased out at the rate of 50 cents for each dollar of income over $100,000. For example, an individual with adjusted gross income of $110,000 could exempt $20,000 of rental real estate losses. The exemption is entirely phased out for those with adjusted gross income of $150,000 or more.

For married persons filing separately, the $25,000, $100,000, and $150,000 figures above are halved, provided they lived apart for the entire year. If they did live together and are filing separately, the $25,000 exemption is eliminated altogether.

Carry-Over Provisions

There are 2 carry-over provisions which cushion the passive loss rules. First, any passive losses which are disallowed in a given year may be carried over to be deducted against passive profits in future years. Second, in the year you sell your entire remaining interest in a passive activity to an unrelated party, any unused passive losses connected with this activity can be deducted. Thus, the passive loss rules do not really *deny* deductions, so much as *delay* these deductions until a future time.

What Should You Do If You Have Disallowed Passive Losses?

Seek help. You will need professional assistance if you are caught in the web of the passive loss rules. For one thing, you may be able to negate the effect of these rules by investing in other suitable passive activities which produce a profit. Or, you may want to sell a passive activity in order to be able to claim any unused losses under the carry-over provisions.

There is a Form 8582 to be filled out if there are passive activities with net losses. This form will carry you through the appropriate computation. In addition, there are special instructions on Schedules A, C, D, and E of Form 1040 that may apply if you have passive losses.

You are exempted from the requirement to file Form 8582 if you satisfy the first exception for rental real estate losses described above. For this filing exemption, your adjusted gross income must actually be less than $100,000, not in the phase-out range above $100,000. Also, your only passive losses must be from rental real estate activities.

If you own a home you rent out for part of the year and live in for part of the year, then the passive loss rules may result in disallowance of interest expenses on your 1990 tax return. If this is the case, any interest disallowed in connection with the passive activity may still be deductible as interest on a primary or second home [cf. Section 4 of the *Homeowners* chapter].

Section 3:
U.S. Treasury Securities

When you purchase U.S. Treasury Securities (sometimes just called *U.S. Treasuries),* you are making a loan to the U.S. Government. These securities fall into one of three categories according to their maturity lengths. *Treasury Bills* have maturity lengths of 3 to 12 months; *Treasury Notes* from 2 to 10 years, and *Treasury Bonds* of 30 years. The minimum purchase amount for Treasury Bills is $10,000; for Treasury Notes with maturities less than 4 years, $5,000; and for Treasury Notes and Bonds with maturities 4 years or longer, $1,000.

U.S. Treasuries offer the following advantages:

1. Safety

U.S. Treasuries are the safest securities you can own, being backed by the full credit of the U.S. Government. You are guaranteed to receive all interest payments due in addition to the full principal upon maturity.

This guarantee is stronger than the one backing bank and S & L deposits up to $100,000 per account. When a bank or S & L goes under, an agency of the U.S. government will assure that your deposits are returned to you plus interest earned up to the date of default. However, you may have to wait a period of time before receiving any money and can lose interest on your funds for the duration of this period.

U.S. Treasuries, of course, are subject to the same market risks as other securities. That is, if the prevailing market interest rate goes up, the value of the securities goes down. This risk is the strongest for long-term securities like 30-year Treasury Bonds and the smallest for short-term securities like 3-month Treasury Bills.

2. Competitive Interest Rates

Interest rates on short-term U.S. Treasuries are competitive with interest rates paid on Certificates of Deposit. In fact, sometimes the yield on a U.S. Treasury will exceed the rate you can get from your bank or S & L on a C.D. with the same maturity. For example, this was the case in Fall, 1990 for 3-month Treasury bills. As discussed later in this section, you can use the U.S. Treasury rates reported in the newspaper to make an exact comparison with the rates paid by your local bank or S & L.

Because they are guaranteed by the Government, long-term U.S. Treasuries do not pay as high an interest rate as bonds issued by private corporations. However, the spread is not as great as one might expect. For example, in Fall 1990, long-term U.S. Treasuries were paying interest rates of about 1/2% less than high quality corporate bonds.

3. Liquidity

Because there is a huge market in U.S. Treasuries, they are very easy to buy or sell. *The Wall Street Journal* and major daily newspapers contain a listing of the prices each day and most any bank or stockbroker can execute a purchase or sale at the going rate. (Also, there is a lower spread between bid and ask prices than on stocks or bonds traded on major stock exchanges.)

4. No Unwanted Calls

Many corporate and municipal bonds have a "call" provision which allows the issuer to buy back your bond. This comes into play if market interest rates go down. In this case, if the issuer calls your bond, you are unable to earn the same interest rate as you have been receiving. In contrast, U.S. Treasuries cannot be called early. If interest rates go down, you continue earning the higher interest rate until the date of maturity.

A similar comparison can be made with federally-backed mortgage securities like GNMAs. When interest rates fall, more people pay off their mortgages causing a larger payout of principal. Once again, you are unable to earn as high an interest rate as you were before.

5. Freedom from State and Local Income Tax

Interest you receive on Treasury securities is exempt from State and local income tax (but not from Federal income tax). This gives it an advantage over competing investments, such as certificates of deposit and corporate bonds, which are subject to State and local income tax.

Income from mutual funds which invest only in Treasury securities is also free of State and local income tax in most States. However, there are some States which do tax such income.

How to Purchase Treasury Securities

There are 2 basic ways to purchase Treasury securities:

1. Purchase Through a Bank or Stockbroker

You can purchase existing securities through a bank or stockbroker. The commission on such a transaction is about $50. This is a prohibitive 5% commission on a $1,000 purchase, but only a 1/10 of one percent commission on a $50,000 purchase. You can sell Treasuries before maturity through a bank or stockbroker also.

You can find a listing in the *Wall Street Journal* or other daily newspaper of the Treasury yields for various maturities. The *yield* column is the one you want to look at. It shows the annualized yield to maturity, which is the figure that should be used to compare competing investments.

The *yield* should not be confused with the *coupon rate*. The coupon rate is based on the rate at the time of issuance. When buying a Treasury security after issuance, you are paying that price which will produce the quoted yield. This price will be more or less than the original cost depending on which way interest rates have moved.

Treasury Bills have the peculiarity of being purchased on a *discount basis*. This means for example, that a 10% one-year bill with face value $10,000 would actually be purchased for $9,000 and redeemed one year later for $10,000. This produces an annualized yield of ($10,000 − $9,000)/$9,000 = 11.11%, a higher rate than the quoted 10% rate. This is the general situation. When purchasing a Treasury Bill, you need to check out the *annualized yield* figure in the newspaper if you want to make a comparison with other investments.

2. Purchase Directly from U.S. Government

Treasury Securities can be purchased directly from the Government without paying any commissions. This is done through a *Treasury-Direct* account which you can open up with the Government by mail. When you open up this account, you must designate a checking or savings account at a financial institution into which interest and principal payments are deposited. Once deposited, these funds are fully available to you by writing checks or making cash withdrawals. The Government does not send any checks directly to you.

A convenient feature of the Treasury Direct system is the ease with which part or all of the money received at maturity can be reinvested. Well before maturity, a letter will be sent to remind you that your securities are coming due. The letter will explain your reinvestment options, and you indicate your choice by return mail.

In some cases you are allowed to indicate future automatic investments. For example, with 3-month bills, you can designate that automatic reinvestments be made every 3 months over a 2-year period. You can cancel the reinvestment designation by giving notice at least 20 days prior to any of the maturity dates.

You can purchase U.S. Treasury Notes or Bonds by mailing in a cashiers check or a personal check. For Treasury Bills, a personal check must be certified. This means you will have to lose a few days interest until the purchase is officially consummated. If you prefer, you can deliver cash or check to a Federal Reserve Bank in person.

When individuals purchase U.S. Treasuries directly from the Government, they usually do so on a *noncompetitive* basis. This means that they will accept the market yield determined when the Government auctions the bills. This will be the lowest yield needed to sell all the securities to meet the Government's needs. If you wish, you can also make a competitive bid specifying the yield you wish to receive. If the market yield set by the auction equals or exceeds the yield you have specified, your purchase will go through. Otherwise, your money will be returned to you.

To set up a Treasury-Direct account for the purchase of U.S. Government securities, you can write to: *Bureau of Public Debt; Division of Customer Services; 300 13th Street, S.W.; Washington D.C. 20239.* They will send you an application form plus the appropriate informational material. According to this material, thousands of Government checks are lost or stolen in the mail each year. But with Treasury-Direct, this is not a problem because funds are transferred electronically.

Instead of writing, you can call 202-287-4113 instead. You will get a recording which gives you a menu of options for listening to various informational tapes. As the recording will indicate, when you press "3" on a touch tone telephone, you will be connected to a human being if you call during regular business hours. This person can answer questions you may have and will mail application forms and informational material you need.

Instead of contacting Washington, D.C., you can call, write, or visit the Federal Reserve Bank servicing your area. You can even make purchases in person at one of these banks, if you don't want to transact business by mail. Your local bank should be able to give you the address and telephone number of the nearest Federal Reserve Bank.

Section 4:
Municipal Bonds

Municipal Bonds are issued by cities, states, counties, or other local governments. The chief feature of such bonds is that the interest they pay is entirely exempt from Federal Income Tax. If the bond is issued by a governmental body in the purchaser's home state, then the interest is also exempt from State Income Tax.

A bond is simply a loan. The **purchaser** of a bond is lending the issuer a fixed amount of money called the **principal** of the loan. In return, the issuer pays periodic interest at a fixed rate for a certain length of time. After this length of time, the bond reaches its **maturity date** and the issuer returns the principal to the purchaser. Municipal bonds are issued in denominations of $1,000.

General Obligation Bonds are fully guaranteed by the issuing municipality. That is, the full taxing authority of the municipality stands behind the bond. **Revenue Bonds** are guaranteed only by the revenue of some income-producing facility. A typical example of this is a toll road bond which is backed by the income which that toll road produces. If the toll road operates at a deficit, the bondholders will suffer because there will not be enough revenue to make the required interest payments.

Certain *private activity* municipal bonds issued after August 7, 1986 might be subjected to a minimum tax provision of the new law [cf. the *Alternative Minimum Tax* chapter]. An individual should seek professional advice before purchasing a sizable amount of such bonds.

How Bonds Are Purchased

When they are issued, bonds are usually sold through brokerage houses. After that, the bonds may be traded on the open market. That is, the original purchaser can sell to someone else who in turn can sell when he wishes, etc. Typically, bonds are resold through brokerage houses. That is, brokerage houses will keep an inventory of certain bonds. They will be willing to buy your bonds from you or sell bonds to you from their inventory. They make their profit by keeping a spread between the price they are willing to pay for a bond and the price at which they are willing to sell.

Due to the large number of different types of municipal bonds, they are not as liquid an investment as stocks or corporate bonds. This is particularly true for small numbers of bonds or bonds issued by obscure municipalities.

The interest rate paid by a bond depends upon the maturity date, the financial strength of the issuer, and the general level of interest rates in the economy. The current market value of a bond rises and falls as the general interest level varies. When interest rates rise, the value of a bond will fall and when interest rates fall the bond value will rise. However, this effect is muted as the maturity date draws close because a bond is worth precisely its face value on the maturity date.

There are also no-load mutual funds which invest in municipal bonds and pass along the tax-free feature to the individual investors. These mutual funds are useful because they provide instant liquidity with no sales or redemption charges. Further discussion of these funds is contained in Section 6.

Reporting Tax-Free Income on Your Tax Return

You are now required to report tax-free interest you receive from municipal bonds on line 8b of your Form 1040. The amount you report on this line is not subject to tax. And, currently, the IRS does not match the amount you report against any other information it receives as it does with taxable wages, dividends, interest, etc. Rather, Congress wants data on tax-free income mainly to use in designing future tax bills.

However, there are 2 situations in which the IRS might possibly use the information reported on line 8b. First, this amount might affect the amount of tax due if you are receiving Social Security income [cf. Section 4 of the *Retirement Plans* chapter]. And second, it might be used to see if you're wrongly deducting interest on loans used to buy or carry tax-free municipal bonds [cf. the *Interest* chapter].

Section 5:
Mutual Funds

A mutual fund is an easy way to invest in securities. The fund maintains a diversified portfolio of securities and sells shares in the fund to the general public. When you purchase a share in the fund, you are simply purchasing a proportionate piece of all its securities. The securities held by the fund do not remain constant. The management of the fund will buy and sell securities as it feels such a change will be advantageous.

There are hundreds of different funds. Almost any type of investment philosophy is represented by some fund. The majority of funds maintain a portfolio of common stocks. Some of these stock funds aim at high growth, some at high current yield, and some aim in the middle. Whatever their basic objective, most invest in a wide number of different industries. But there are exceptions to this. For example, you can invest in a fund which only purchases stocks involved in the energy industry.

While mutual funds investing in common stocks have been around a long time, a number of different types of funds have been developed within the past decade. These new funds invest in tax-free municipal bonds, money-market instruments, high-yielding bonds, etc., depending upon their objective. And these newer funds permit money to be withdrawn much easier than the old type funds — by telephone, telegram, or even by writing a check against the funds in one's account. Further discussion is contained in the next section.

Load vs. No-Load Funds

A *load fund* is one for which you must pay a sales commission (up to as much as 8 or 9 percent) in order to purchase shares. A *no-load fund* charges no sales commission. Most funds are load funds which testifies to the salesmanship ability of the investment industry. There is no reason to believe that by charging a sales commission a fund will be better able to decide what stocks to purchase. In fact, studies show that, on the average, no-load and load funds perform about the same.

No-load funds are typically sold through the mail and a number are advertised in newspapers and financial publications such as the *Wall Street Journal*. A directory of no-load mutual funds can be obtained for $2 from the *No-Load Mutual Fund Association* [address: 11 Penn Plaza, Suite 2204, NY, NY 10001].

There is a middle category, sometimes called *hidden-load* funds, which are basically akin to load funds. However, instead of charging an up-front sales commission, these funds bury their extra charges in some other manner, e.g. by charging a redemption fee or by levying extra annual *distribution fees* (sometimes referred to as *12b-1* fees).

The change to hidden-load funds was a huge marketing success for brokerage houses because investors couldn't spot the hidden fees like they could the up-front sales fees on regular load funds. But now, as discussed below, the Securities and Exchange Commission has made it much easier to detect the existence of such "hidden" fees.

SEC Requirements Make it Easier to Compare Mutual Funds

There are 3 disclosure requirements, put into effect in mid-1988, which make it easier to compare mutual funds with respect to yields, overall performance, and fees.

1. Newspaper Listings of Mutual Funds Must Indicate the Existence of Extra Fees.

As discussed above, there are many hidden-load mutual funds which attempt to camouflage extra fees by charging redemption fees, extra annual distribution fees, etc. In the past, these extra fees could not be detected just by looking at a newspaper's daily listing of mutual funds prices. Rather, the only sure-fire way of detecting extra fees was to examine the fund's prospectus.

But this situation has changed. Now, the existence of extra charges is indicated in newspaper listings—by the letter *p* for extra distribution fees or the letter *r* for redemption fees.

For example, a newspaper listing might contain the following information:

	NAV	Offer Price
AAA Fund r	6.71	6.71
BBB Fund	p 9.10	N.L.
CCC Fund r	p 10.53	10.53
DDD Fund	11.10	11.56
EEE Fund	8.73	N.L.

In the above, only the last *EEE Fund* is a true no-load fund. This can be spotted by the designation *N.L.* in the *Offer price* column plus the absence of the letters *r, p,* or *t* (*t* is sometimes used when both *r* and *p* apply). The existence of a load charge in the first 3 funds is indicated by the letters *r* and/or *p*. The load in the fourth *DDD Fund* is indicated by the discrepancy between the figure in the NAV column (the *Net Asset Value*, i.e. price you would receive if selling a share) and the *Offer price* which you would pay if buying a share.

To get a more precise picture of the fees charged by a fund, you need to look at the prospectus. This is discussed below.

2. Mutual Funds Must Spell Out All Fees in a Standard Format.

In the past, it was often difficult to get a direct comparison between mutual funds on their fee structures. Sometimes, information on fees would be buried in various places on the inside of a formidable looking prospectus.

But the SEC (Securities and Exchange Commission) changed this situation. Now, Mutual Funds are required to lay out their fees in a standardized tabular form and to compute what these fees would add up to on a $1,000 investment over several time periods. This information must be reported on one of the first few pages of the mutual fund's prospectus.

The following is an example of how the fee schedule would look for a typical no-load mutual fund.

A. Shareholder Transaction Expenses

Sales Load Imposed on Purchases	None
Sales Load Imposed on Reinvested Dividends	None
Redemption Fees	None
Exchange Fees	None

B. Annual Fund Operating Expenses

Management and Advisory Expenses	.32%
Investment Advisory Fees	.26%
Shareholder Accounting Costs	None
12b-1 Fees	.10%
Distribution Costs	None
Other Expenses	.06%
Total Operating Expenses	.74%

C. Example
You should pay the following expenses on a $1,000 investment, assuming (i) a 5% annual return, and (ii) redemption at the end of each time period:

1 year	$7
3 years	$24
5 years	$42
10 years	$94

The are several things to observe in the above example. First, Section A has "None" listed on each line for sales and redemption fees. If there are expenses listed on any of these lines, you're not looking at a true *no-load* fund.

Second, Section B contains a listing of the various operating expenses. The significant figure here is the bottom line—total operating expenses. (The breakdown into different kinds of operating expenses is basically accounting mumbo-jumbo.) In the above example, the total operating expenses are.74%. This means that for every $100 you have invested, the fund management company takes 74 cents for profit and expenses.

Section C in the above example is basically a restatement of the total operating fees figure summed over various time periods, assuming a 5% increase in value with all dividends reinvested. The only case where this section gives an extra standard of comparison is for load funds, where the sales and redemptions fees can be factored in over various time periods.

The table in the above example reflects all expenses which the fund charges for its services. However, it does not include brokerage fees which the fund pays when it buys or sells securities. These brokerage fees are built into the price performance and are not itemized separately in the prospectus.

3. Mutual Funds Must Advertise Yields the Same Way.
The SEC has instituted uniform reporting rules for advertising in newspapers or other print media. For example, income funds must use a 30-day yield figure computed in a uniform manner if they advertise their returns. And if a stock or bond fund advertises a total return figure (distributions plus increase in value), it

must include its average annual total return for the past 1, 5, and 10- year periods. In theory, this makes it possible to compare funds on a uniform basis. (In the past, funds would use the method producing the highest yield or return figure and tout that figure in its ads.) In practice, this has caused most mutual funds to delete any numerical figures from their ads.

You can call a mutual fund to ask for yield or total return figures. If you wind up conversing with a talking computer, then the above rules for print advertising apply. That is, the uniform 30-day yield must be the one quoted and if total return is given, the 1-year, 5-year and 10-year total returns must be provided.

However, if you end up conversing with a human, then anything goes. That is, the human can quote a yield or total return figure which puts the mutual fund in the best light. The uniform 30-day yield figure and the 1, 5, and 10-year total return figures are required to be provided only if you specifically ask for them.

Open-End Funds

Most funds are *open-end* funds. This means that you can always buy shares directly from the fund itself. The purchase price you pay is determined by evaluating the market value of all the securities and assigning a proportionate value to each share. This is called the *net asset value* of the share.

Similarly, you can redeem your shares in the fund any time you wish by selling them back to the fund at the current net asset value. When more people buy than redeem shares, the fund invests the excess cash in new securities. Conversely, when more shares are redeemed than purchased, the fund must sell some of its holdings to meet the excess redemption.

Closed-End Funds

A *closed-end* fund does not sell or redeem shares. It just invests and reinvests the money it already has, without receiving any input of new capital or experiencing any withdrawals. If you wish to buy a share of such a fund, you must find someone who will sell it to you. Similarly, to sell a share you must find a buyer. In practice these funds are sold on a stock exchange or through brokerage houses which make a market in them. Thus you don't have to look for a buyer or seller yourself.

The market value of a closed-end fund is determined by the law of supply and demand. It need not be the same as the net asset value (the proportionate share of the market value of the stocks in the fund). In fact, the market price of closed-end funds often differs from the net asset value. Generally, closed-end funds sell at a discount, that is, at a price less than the net asset value. One partial explanation for this is that since they do not guarantee redemption at net asset value as do open-end funds, the lack of this feature makes them less attractive to investors.

One might think that this discount represents a bargain. But this bargain is in the most part illusory. Unless the discount narrows in the future for some reason, the shares in the fund will not appreciate in price any faster than the value of the securities in the fund. However, you will be receiving a greater portion of the dividends than you would receive if you bought shares of the stocks themselves instead of shares in the fund.

Over the past few years, over 10 billion dollars worth of new closed-end funds have been sold by stockbrokers. When issued, these funds sell at their net asset value rather than at a discount. After a while, a discount generally appears in a loss of value, even if the stocks themselves do not change in price. This loss, when combined with commissions brokers get for selling these funds, generally makes it an unwise move to be an initial purchaser of a closed-end fund.

Tax Aspects of Mutual Funds

As with the purchase of individual shares of common stock, there are two types of taxation that occur with mutual funds. First of all, the stocks in the portfolio of the fund may pay dividends (or interest in the case of bonds). Usually, the fund allows you to receive your proportionate share of these dividends in cash or else it automatically reinvests these dividends in more shares of the fund. Either way, the value of these dividends is ordinary income to you and is taxed at your usual rate. The fund will provide you with an annual statement as to the amount of dividends on which you must pay tax.

The second type of taxation is the tax on capital gains. This can occur in two ways. First of all, the fund itself realizes a capital gain or loss as it sells shares of some securities in order to purchase others. If the fund sells stock at a higher price than the purchase price, then a capital gain is created. The opposite situation produces a capital loss. At least once a year, usually in December, the fund will make a distribution if it has realized a net capital gain on the shares it sold during the year. It may distribute this gain in cash or may automatically reinvest it for you in more shares of the fund. In either event, you must report this capital gain on your tax return.

Of course, a mutual fund may realize a net capital loss in a given year instead of a capital gain. In such a case, you are not allowed to deduct the loss on your own tax return. Instead, the mutual fund is allowed to carry over these losses up to 5 years into the future in order to cancel out future capital gains. For example, if the fund incurs a $50,000 capital loss in one year followed by a $70,000 capital gain in the next year, then the outcome would be a $20,000 capital gains distribution to be reported on shareholders' tax returns the second year.

In addition to tax paid on annual capital gains distributions, you must also pay tax on capital gains if you sell your shares in the mutual fund at a higher price than your purchase price. This is treated the same way as a capital gain arising from the purchase and sale of any other asset. Of course, if you sell at a lower price than the purchase price, then you have a capital loss which can be deducted according to the usual rules for capital losses [cf. Section 1].

If you purchased shares of the same fund on different dates, when you sell some of these shares you will be presumed to have sold the earliest purchase shares. However, there are exceptions to this rule. If you can identify certain shares as having been purchased on a particular date, then you can use the purchase price on that date as the original cost. Or, you can use the *average cost method* to determine the purchase price. Under this method your purchase price is considered to be the average price paid for all the shares you own. There is another *double-category averaging method* under which you take 2 such averages, one for purchases resulting in long-term gains and another for short-term gains. Shares sold are considered to be taken first from the long-term category unless you specify otherwise to the mutual fund at the time of sale. With either averaging method, you have to indicate on your tax return what you're doing. Consult your mutual fund for further information on electing one of these alternate methods.

If the mutual fund has been reinvesting your dividends or capital gains distributions, the following example shows how to avoid overpaying tax on capital gains when you sell your shares.

Example

You purchase $5,000 worth of shares in a mutual fund. Over a period of years, your shares are credited with $1,000 in dividends and $2,000 in capital gains distributions which are automatically reinvested to purchase more shares of the fund. You pay tax on these dividends and distributions in the years in which they are declared and reinvested. After 5 years, you sell all your shares in the fund (both the original shares and the shares obtained by reinvestment of dividends and capital gains) for $10,000. To determine your final capital gain you subtract from this $10,000 your original purchase price, $5,000, as well as all dividends and capital gains on which you have already paid tax, $3,000. Thus you must pay a tax on the capital gain of $10,000 – $5,000 – $3,000 = $2,000.

If you had sold your shares for $7,000, then this computation would yield $7,000 – $5,000 – $3,000 = – $1,000. Thus, you would have a long-term capital loss of $1,000 in the year of sale which you deduct according to the usual rules for deducting capital losses.

Tax Considerations in Buying Mutual Funds

The tax rules regarding capital gains distributions suggest a number of important considerations. First of all, you should **not** buy mutual funds shortly before a capital gains distribution is about to be declared. Otherwise, you're simply buying a tax liability.

Example

On November 1, you purchase shares in a mutual fund for $5.00 per share. One month later, a capital gains distribution of 50 cents per share is declared. The price of the mutual fund will automatically decline a corresponding amount so that you now have shares worth $4.50 per share plus the 50 cents per share distribution. But you must now pay tax on this 50 cents per share. Had you purchased your shares after the distribution was declared, you would not have paid any tax. Of course, in the first case, the decline from $5.00 per share to $4.50 per share produces an unrealized capital loss. But until you sell your shares in the fund, this loss gives you no tax benefit. In the meantime, you lose all the interest you could earn on the tax you paid.

Before purchasing a mutual fund, you can check to see if they have realized any capital gains so far that year. This information should be contained in their quarterly reports.

The disadvantage in buying a tax liability corresponds to an advantage in the opposite situation. That is, you may be able to buy a tax credit. For example, suppose that a mutual fund has incurred capital losses in the past few years. These losses can be carried over into the future to offset capital gains. Thus, if the mutual fund realizes capital gains after you purchase it, no capital gains distribution will be declared until the gains exceed the carried-over losses. In effect, you have bought into a tax credit situation. You will be delaying the payment of capital gains tax until you sell your shares of the mutual fund.

In addition, you should consider not only the *realized* capital gain or loss situation of a mutual fund, but also its *unrealized* capital gains or losses. For example, the current portfolio may have a market price which is lower than the total prices at which the stocks were purchased, so that the fund has a net unrealized loss.

It is better to purchase mutual funds with an unrealized loss than an unrealized gain. As the mutual fund changes its portfolio by selling stocks it owns, these unrealized losses become realized and produce a capital loss. Thus any capital gains the mutual fund achieves will be reduced by these losses. Conversely, if a fund has unrealized gains, then capital gains are produced when the fund sells their stocks, even if their value is no higher than when you bought into the fund. You may wind up with a capital gains distribution even though you haven't made any profit. You can find out the extent of any unrealized capital gains or losses listed in the prospectus or annual report of the mutual fund.

We have seen in the above discussion that it is better to buy mutual funds with realized or unrealized capital losses. In the case of open-end funds, the tax advantage of such funds costs nothing extra because the price of shares in the fund is simply determined by the prices of the stocks in the portfolio. The tax situation of the fund plays no part in determining the price of its shares. This is one of the rare cases of getting something for nothing that exists in the investment world.

How Do You Choose a Mutual Fund?

We have already touched upon the various criteria which are important in selecting a fund in which to invest. You should purchase a no-load fund which invests in the type of securities meeting your general objective, whether it be high current income, long-term capital growth, speculation, etc. You should also look for a fund with unrealized or realized capital losses.

Next, you should check to see what the expense rate of the fund is. All funds deduct a certain percentage of the net asset value to cover operating expenses, investment advice, and provide a profit to the fund operators. This percentage is generally in the 1% range. However, even among large comparable no-load funds, there can be a substantial difference in the amount of fees charged.

There are no indications that higher fees correlate with better fund performance. This is particularly evident with money-market funds which all invest in basically the same type of securities. For example, the Vanguard money-market fund with a low expense charge has shown one of the greatest returns over the past few years. And the funds with the highest fees did poorly.

Note that the expense rate of a mutual fund does not include brokerage commissions. These are considered a "capital expense" and serve to reduce any capital gains or enlarge capital losses incurred as the fund changes its portfolio. Therefore, you should also check the turnover rate of the fund, that is, the percent of the portfolio which gets changed during the year. For example, a fund with a turnover rate of 20% during a given year has bought and sold stocks representing 20% of its portfolio. The other 80% has not changed. Turnover rates vary widely among funds. By selecting a fund with a low turnover rate, you will in effect be paying less brokerage costs. This could amount to an advantage of several percentage points a year. Also, a lower turnover rate generally produces less realized capital gains producing taxable income.

Finally, you might want to examine the past performance of the funds in which you are interested. However, this information may be of dubious value. Frankly, there is no good evidence that funds which have performed well in the past will continue to perform well in the future.

Selected Mutual Fund Companies

The following is a list of some of the largest mutual fund companies. Each of these companies offers a wide range of different types of no-load mutual funds, including money-market funds, bond funds, stock funds, etc. Section 6 contains a discussion of some of the different types of mutual funds.

T. Rowe Price Funds	**Vanguard Investment Group**	**Dreyfus Funds**
100 East Pratt Street	P.O. Box 2600	600 Madison Ave.
Baltimore, MD 21202	Valley Forge, PA 19482	New York, NY 10022
800-638-5660	800-662-7447	800-645-6561
(In MD: 301-547-2308)	(In PA: 800-362-0530)	(In NY: 212-715-5000)
Fidelity Group	**Scudder Funds**	
82 Devonshire St.	175 Federal St.	
Boston, MA 02109	Boston, MA 02110	
800-544-6666	800-225-2470	
(In MA: 617-523-1919)	(In MA: 617-439-4640)	

The large no-load fund companies are probably the best place to look if you wish to invest in a mutual fund. To start with, no-load funds are a much better deal then load funds. The sales or redemption fee which rewards a stock broker or sales agent for selling you the fund does not make the fund any smarter in picking investments. In fact, studies show that load and no-load funds perform the same on average, not counting the extra fees.

Among no-load funds, bigger is better when it comes to fees. On average, the larger the total assets in the fund, the lower the operating fees. This means that the large no-load funds run by the mammoth no-load organizations generally have the lowest fees.

In fact, the larger no-load organizations have other advantages as well. For one thing, there is safety in numbers. A large mutual fund run by a major no-load institution does not have the same risk from incompetent or dishonest management that might be present with an isolated mutual fund.

For another, the large no-load funds generally get high marks for service. In particular, Vanguard, Fidelity, and T. Rowe Price have all scored near the top in several recent surveys of investors concerning the quality of services provided.

Where Do You Find Information about Mutual Funds?

It is possible to get information on mutual funds without contacting each mutual fund company directly. In particular, a number of services provide annual data on mutual funds, including their past performance, investment philosophy, expense rate, and turnover rate. These services can be found in the financial reference section of your library. If your library does not have an adequate financial section, then you should check through back issues of *Forbes Magazine* to which most libraries subscribe. Each August, it publishes statistics on all mutual funds currently available.

The Wall Street Journal and major local newspapers report the prices of mutual funds each day. Strangely, they do not report the most important piece of information needed to evaluate bond funds — namely their yield. Some information can be found in *Money Magazine* which publishes each month a list of the yields paid by the larger bond funds.

One piece of information that is not likely to be found in general reference material is the extent of unrealized or realized capital gains or losses. You will probably have to get this information from the mutual fund prospectus or annual report itself.

Section 6:
Special Types of Mutual Funds

Municipal Bond Funds

These funds invest in bonds issued by State and local governments. As interest income is distributed to investors, this income is exempt from Federal income tax. Most of these funds are set up to provide maximum liquidity. Interest is credited on a daily basis from the date of investment to the date of withdrawal. Usually, this interest is automatically reinvested to purchase additional shares in the fund. If you prefer, you can have monthly interest checks mailed to you.

Investments are made by mailing in a check or having your bank wire money to the fund. A number of options are available when it comes to withdrawal. The slowest way to withdraw funds is to request the fund to mail the money to you. More speedy withdrawal methods are provided by most funds. For example, you can call a toll-free number and request that money be wired to your bank account by the next day.

The best withdrawal system, offered by a number of the funds, is a checkwriting privilege. These funds have a special arrangement with a bank. The bank issues you checks which you write against the balance in your municipal bond fund. The checks must exceed a specified minimum, typically $500.

This check-writing arrangement has the extra advantage that your funds are earning interest up until the day your check clears. This can be especially useful when paying taxes. Often, governmental agencies will take a long time before they cash checks. You can be earning interest on your money in the meantime.

Opening an account with a municipal bond fund is easy. You fill out a short application form and mail in a check to open your account. Monthly statements are mailed to you showing the activity in your account. Each fund has a minimum amount which must be exceeded in order to open an account and a smaller minimum figure for additional contributions.

Of course, you should realize that the value of your investment will be subject to fluctuation. This is due to the fact that the municipal bonds in the fund rise and fall in value as the general level of interest rates changes in the economy.

Most municipal bond funds invest primarily in bonds with a high quality rating. This means there is minimal likelihood the bond will default on any interest payments. But higher quality bonds pay a lower interest rate than lesser quality bonds. Those willing to accept more risk can invest in a high-yield municipal bond fund. This type of fund invests in lower-rated bonds and therefore can pay higher interest than other bond funds. An example of such a fund is the *Fidelity High-Yield Municipal Bond Fund.* A prospectus and further information can be obtained by calling their toll-free telephone number, 800-544-6666.

Actually, the chance of substantial loss due to default is low. For one thing, even medium quality municipal bonds have a good record of meeting their interest payments. And the portfolio diversity offers substantial protection against serious default loss.

Just as there are bond funds which offer a higher risk coupled with a higher yield, there are also lower risk-lower yield funds. In this case it is not the risk of default but the risk of falling prices that is protected against. Shorter-term bonds fall less in value when interest rates rise (and rise less in value when interest rates fall). Thus, municipal bond funds investing in shorter-term bonds carry a lower risk than regular municipal bond funds.

The *Vanguard Municipal Bond Fund* provides an attractive opportunity for those who wish to shift their investment according to changes in the market and changes in their own personal circumstances. This fund maintains three separate regular portfolios — short-term, medium-term, and long-term. The shorter the term, the lesser the market risk and the lesser the yield. In addition, there is a high-yield portfolio investing in lower quality bonds. An investor can choose to have his funds apportioned among any of the portfolios he chooses. Then, at any time he chooses, a toll-free telephone call will cause funds to be switched from one of the portfolios to another. The Vanguard Municipal Bond Fund provides check-writing privileges and a lower than average management fee. Further information can be obtained by calling their toll-free telephone number, 800-662-7447.

Those who live in one of the larger states can find mutual funds which contain only in-state bonds. Income from such funds is exempt not just from Federal income tax, but from state income tax as well. For example, Fidelity (800-544-6666) offers single-state funds for the following states: California, Connecticut, Massachusetts, Michigan, Minnesota, New Jersey, New York, Ohio, Pennsylvania, and Texas. Other mutual fund companies offering a number of single-state funds are Dreyfus (800-645-6561) and Scudder (800-225-2470).

Municipal Bond Trusts

A Municipal Bond Trust is a second type of investment which provides tax-free interest through the purchase of municipal bonds. However, in contrast to mutual funds, these trusts do not buy and sell municipal bonds as market conditions change or as more money is invested. Instead, these trusts purchase a single portfolio of bonds which are kept until maturity. Shares of the trust are sold until the full portfolio is paid for, after which no further investments or withdrawals can be made. It is possible to sell one's shares in the trust, although this is not as easily done as withdrawing funds from a Mutual Fund.

These trusts generally pay a higher interest rate than Municipal Bond Mutual Funds because they invest in somewhat lesser quality bonds and charge a lower annual expense fee. However, they are subject to an initial sales charge of about 4%. Because of the initial sales charge and relative illiquidity, these trusts are only suitable for the longer range investor. The portfolios of some Municipal Bond Trusts are insured against default by an insurance company. Municipal Bond Trusts are sold by most stockbrokers who will be pleased to give you further information upon request.

To escape state and local tax as well as Federal tax, there might be a trust investing only in bonds issued in your state. Otherwise, investments in a different state's municipal bonds are subject to your state's income tax. Such trusts are available in a number of states including NY, CA, MD, MA, MI, NJ, CT, FL, OH, OR, PA, and VA.

High-Yield Corporate Bond Funds

Mutual funds which invest in corporate bonds have been around a long time. But recently, there has been considerable interest in mutual funds which invest in lesser quality bonds (often called junk bonds) because these funds make it practical for an individual to earn high interest rates on his money. Since these funds invest in a wide portfolio of bonds, the risk of significant loss due to default is much less than if only a few of these bonds were purchased individually. However, individual bond defaults can lower the total return. And in the past few years, junk bond funds have had significant decreases in value.

Most mutual funds which specialize in higher-yielding bonds are load funds. One high-yielding no-load fund is the *Vanguard High Yield Bond Fund* (800-662-7447). There is no fee charged upon investment or upon withdrawal.

Of course, the value of shares in a bond fund is affected by changes in the interest rate. If interest rates fall, the shares will rise in value and if interest rates rise, the share price will fall.

Short-Term Funds

Money-market funds invest in very short-term debt securities, typically with maturities in the 30-60 day range, offered by the nation's leading banks and corporations. These funds operate similarly to an interest-bearing checking account, except that only large-denomination checks can be written. Further details on money-market funds are contained in the next section.

As an alternative to money-market funds, some people keep their money in a *short-term* or *limited-term* bond fund. These funds generally invest in bonds with an average maturity of 2-5 years. This tends to produce a higher interest rate than money-market funds, with substantially less market risk than long-term bond funds.

Also, many fund companies offer *intermediate-term* bond funds. However, these funds generally are similar to long-term funds, with a somewhat lesser yield and lesser market risk.

Section 7:
Money-Market Accounts

Money-market accounts are special accounts which pay interest based on the going short-term market rate. These accounts are liquid, allowing you to withdraw your funds at any time. Since the funds pay interest on a short-term basis, there is no market risk. That is, you can't experience a loss of principal because the underlying investment goes down in value as can happen with longer-term bonds or with stocks.

The going money-market interest rate can vary widely during the course of the year depending upon conditions in the economy.

There are now four basic different types of money-market accounts. Two of these are offered by banks and savings & loans. The other two are offered by mutual funds and stockbrokers. These 4 types of money-market accounts are discussed below.

Bank and Savings & Loan Money-Market Accounts

These accounts have been in existence for less than 10 years but have become enormously popular. You can make an unlimited number of deposits or withdrawals in person or by mail. You can also make up to 6 additional transactions per month including telephone transfers to another account, third party transfers, and check-writing against your account. There is no minimum amount for which checks must be written. However, no more than 3 checks per month can be written without penalty. The same $100,000 Federal insurance that applies to regular accounts applies to these accounts as well.

Each bank or savings & loan is allowed to set its own interest rate that it pays on money-market accounts. Some institutions impose various fees while others impose no fees at all. And the method of computing whether the minimum balance has been breached may vary. Only by exploring these features in addition to the stated interest rates can one account be compared with another.

Fees charged on a money-market account for investment management are deductible as a *miscellaneous deduction* on your 1990 tax return. But ordinary checking account charges are not deductible [IRS Private Letter Ruling 8345067]. The institution running your money-market account should inform you of any deductible fees charged against your account in the yearend statement it mails to you.

NOW Accounts

These accounts, sometimes called *Super-NOW* accounts, offered by banks and savings & loans, are similar to money-market accounts as described above. However, there is no limitation upon the number of checks that can be written. And the interest rate paid by NOW accounts is lower because of government-imposed reserve requirements and the cost of check-processing.

Most NOW accounts have a minimum balance requirement, generally in the $1,000-$5,000 range. If your balance falls below the minimum, you may be hit with a monthly fee and/or checkwriting fees. If your account is likely to remain below the minimum for a period of time, you will probably be better off with an ordinary checking account instead of a NOW account.

Cash Management Accounts

A *cash management account* is basically a checking account opened with a stock brokerage house. But unlike ordinary checking accounts, your money is invested in a special money-market fund, earning daily interest on your entire balance. Unlike ordinary money-market funds, there is no minimum denomination on the amount for which the checks may be written nor is there a limitation on the number of checks that may be written each month.

One of the chief advantages of cash management accounts is that they provide instant borrowing power to those who own securities. The way it works is this. You deposit with the brokerage company a combination of securities and cash. The cash is deposited in a money-market fund and interest and dividends received on the securities in your account also go into the money-market fund automatically. As checks are written, money is withdrawn from the money-market fund to cover the checks. If that is depleted, you can continue to write checks against the borrowing power of the securities (generally 50%-70% of their value). These are considered loans and interest is charged at a rate based on the going rate for brokerage margin accounts. This rate is lower than the rate charged on typical bank loans. As cash is deposited into your account, your loan is automatically paid down and interest charges reduced.

In addition to check-writing privileges, you are issued a VISA (or other) charge card. You can use this card to charge purchases in the usual way. You can also use this card to obtain immediate cash at any of the 100,000 bank locations in the world connected with VISA. Many banks will permit you to obtain the full value of your account on the spot. Others place a $5,000 or other daily limit on how much can be withdrawn in this way. The VISA (or other) card is usually a *debit card* rather than a true *credit card*. With such cards, there is no one-month billing period on charge purchases, as is the case with ordinary credit cards. As soon as the charge slip reaches the bank, the amount is subtracted from your account. Also, there are stricter reporting requirements should your card be lost, in order for you to avoid liability for unauthorized purchases.

Merrill Lynch was the pioneer in instituting cash management accounts followed by *Dean Witter*. The plans operated by these two brokerage houses are virtually identical. Both require stiff minimum initial deposits — securities and/or cash with a combined value of at least $20,000. It is not necessary that the account value remain this high although if it falls below $10,000, there is a possibility your account will be terminated. Both plans allow you to choose a tax- exempt money-market fund as a substitute for an ordinary money-market fund. These pay interest at a lower rate than ordinary money-market funds but might still be advantageous for high bracket taxpayers.

There is an annual fee, generally $50-$100 for maintaining a cash management account. There are no further bank charges, check printing charges, annual credit card fees, etc. The *Dean Witter* plan also allows you to designate which checks are for tax-deductible expenses as you write them. At the end of the year, you are provided a complete computerized listing of all your tax-deductible expenditures made by check. The *Dean Witter* plan also gives you check-cashing privileges at any of 850 Sears department stores, many open until 9:30 PM.

Cash management accounts are a good deal for the consumer. The brokerage houses do not offer them in order to profit from their operation. The annual fees serve only to defray the cost of the checking services (they pay 10 cents or more to a clearing bank for each check or VISA entry) and bookkeeping expenses. And the money-market management fees are, if anything, lower than average. Rather, the chief motivation of the brokerage houses is to get your money and securities under their wing. That way, when you buy or sell securities generating lucrative commission revenues, you are likely to do it through them.

Merrill Lynch has more than half of the cash management market. By now, most major brokerage houses have set up cash management accounts to remain competitive. And many banks offering brokerage services have set up such plans also.

Charles Schwab & Co., the nation's largest discount brokerage house, has introduced a cash management account which is of interest to those who cannot meet the minimum deposit requirements of most brokerage houses. The *Schwab* account can be opened with a minimum cash deposit of only $5,000 instead of the $20,000 required by *Merrill Lynch* or *Dean Witter.* And there is no annual fee.

Money-Market Funds

Money-market funds are mutual funds which pay money-market interest rates. These funds bear a similarity to money-market accounts offered by banks and savings & loans, the principal difference being that you do not transact your business in person. Instead, you mail in your deposits or have them wired by telephone transfer. Your funds earn daily interest from date of deposit to date of withdrawal.

You can write checks against your account any time you choose. There is no limit on the number of checks that can be written nor upon the number of transactions you can make per month. However, money-market funds usually set a minimum amount for which a check can be written or a telephone transfer can be made — typically $250 or $500.

Money-market funds also have a minimum amount which you need to open an account. This varies from fund to fund but there are a number of prominent funds requiring only a $1,000 minimum deposit. Unlike most bank money-market accounts, you earn full money-market interest on your entire balance even if it falls below the minimum amount necessary to open an account.

There is no Federal deposit insurance on money-market funds. However, they are virtually risk-free because they invest only in short-term securities offered by the most financially secure institutions.

If you are seeking the highest rate, you will have to check out individual institutions to see what rates are currently being offered. A listing of the current rates paid by the major money-market funds is published once a week in the *Wall Street Journal* (on Mondays) and in other newspapers. The published interest rates are net rates after expenses have been deducted.

When comparing interest rates, be sure to take into account the difference in the way the interest rates are quoted. Banks and savings & loans may quote you the effective annual rate — the actual rate you would earn on funds left in a full year with the result of interest-compounding figured in. Money-market funds, however, generally publish a daily rate which does not include the effect of compounding.

If the daily rate is known, there is a way to approximate the effective annual yield produced by compounding the daily rate over a full year. The extra effective annual yield produced by the daily compounding is approximately equal to $i \times i/2$, where i is the quoted uncompounded interest rate. For example, 8% annual interest yields approximately $8\% + (8\% \times 8\%/2) = 8\% + .32\% = 8.32\%$ when compounded daily. (The mathematically trained may observe that this approximation works because $i \times i/2$ is the 3d term in the Taylor series expansion for $\exp(i)$ which is the end result of continuously compounding interest rate i for one year, starting with an initial investment of one dollar.) Because the extra compounding effect is proportional to the *square* of the interest rate, it becomes more significant the higher the interest rate. For example, if the 8% interest were to rise by 1/4 to 10%, the extra compounding effect would be about $10\% \times 10\%/2 = .5\%$. This is an increase of over 1/2 in the .32% extra compounding term for 8% interest.

Income received from a money-market mutual fund is technically considered a *dividend* rather than *interest* and should be reported as such on your tax return. If you report it as interest, the IRS computer may become confused and send you a dunning notice. Income from bank or S&L money-market accounts is considered *interest*.

The table that follows lists a number of leading money-market funds. You can obtain further information and an application blank by writing to the fund or calling the telephone number listed in the table.

Most of the organizations which run the regular money-market funds listed in the table also run 2 other types of special money-market funds — tax-exempt funds and government-securities funds. *Tax-exempt money-market funds* invest in short-term securities issued by State and local governments which are exempt from Federal income tax. These funds pay less interest than regular money-market funds and are suitable only for those in the highest tax bracket. *Government securities money-market funds* invest in short-term securities issued by the Federal government.

Comparing the Different Types of Money-Market Investments

Money-market funds are convenient for those who want the ability to switch into other types of mutual funds via telephone and for those who want to write more than 3 checks per month. Bank money-market accounts, on the other hand, have several advantages of their own. There is no minimum denomination on the three checks per month that can be written, they are convenient for those who prefer in-person rather than mail transactions, and they are insured by the FDIC.

NOW accounts and cash-management accounts are the choice for those who want full checking services. Between these two, NOW accounts are generally the more convenient because of the ability to make in-person transactions and the typically lower minimum for opening an account. However, cash management accounts pay a higher rate of interest (even when fees are subtracted) and have other features such as instant borrowing power that may make them attractive to those who meet the minimum requirements.

SELECTED MONEY-MARKET FUNDS

Fund	Minimum Initial Deposit	Minimum Subsequent Deposit	Minimum Check Redemption	Telephone Number for Information
Dreyfus Liquid Assets, Inc. 600 Madison Ave. New York, NY 10022	$2,500	$100	$500	(800) 645-6561 in NY (212) 715-5000
Fidelity Cash Reserves P.O. Box 193 Boston, MA 02101	1,000	250	500	(800) 544-6666 in Mass. (617) 523-1919
T. Rowe Price Prime Reserve Fund 100 E. Pratt St. Baltimore, MD 21202	1,000	100	500	(800) 638-5660 in Md. (301) 547-2308
Scudder Cash Investment Trust 175 Federal St. Boston, MA 02110	1,000	None	500	(800) 225-2470 in Mass. (617) 426-8300
Vanguard Money Market Trust P.O. Box 2600 Valley Forge. PA 19482	1,000	100	250	(800) 662-7447 in Penn. (800) 362-0530

Chapter 16

Moving Expenses

If you moved to a new residence because you went to work for a new employer or transferred to a new place of employment, then you may deduct your moving costs, provided you meet the following two requirements:

1. The distance between your new principal place of work and your old residence must be at least 35 miles farther than the distance between your old place of work and your old residence. (The distance between two points is measured by the shortest of the more commonly traveled routes between the two points.) If you went to work for the first time or went back to full- time work after a substantial period of part-time work or unemployment, then your new principal place of work must be at least 35 miles from your old residence.

2. You must work full-time for at least 39 weeks during the first 12 months following your arrival in the general location of your new place of employment. (Self-employed persons must also work full-time for at least 78 weeks during the first 24 months after arrival in the new job location.)

The 39 weeks of employment need not be consecutive, nor do they have to be for the same employer. It is necessary only that you be employed on a full- time basis within the same general commuting area. Any week during which you work on a full-time basis counts in satisfying the 39-week test. The requirement that your work be full-time is judged by the customary practices in your job. For example, a teacher with a full schedule is working full-time even if the school day is 5 hours or less.

If the work is seasonal, then off-season weeks count as weeks of employment as long as your work agreement covers an off-season period of less than 6 months. For example, teachers are not excluded from a moving expense deduction merely because their academic year is less than 39 weeks. Also, you will be considered as working during any week that you are out through no fault of your own. This refers to a temporary absence from work because of illness, strike, shutout, layoff, natural disaster, etc.

If you paid the moving expense in 1990 but have not met the 39-week test by the time your 1990 return is due, you should take a 1990 deduction for the moving expense if it appears that you will later meet the 39-week test. However, if you later fail the test, you must report an amount equal to the 1990 moving expense deduction as 1991 taxable income on your 1991 tax return or on an amended 1990 tax return. If you leave the deduction off your 1990 return and later meet the 39-week test during 1991, you will have to amend your 1990 return to get your refund.

A recent court case emphasizes the fact that you must deduct the moving expenses in the year the move takes place. A nurse, who had not yet worked the required number of weeks at her new job when filing time came along, waited until a later year, after she had worked the required amount of time, to claim the moving expense deduction. But the Court overruled her deduction. It said she should have claimed the deduction in the year of the move. The only thing she could do now is amend her original return. [Meadows, 66 TC 51]

If you are married and file a joint return and if both you and your spouse are employees, then either of you may satisfy the full-time work requirement. However, you may not add the weeks your spouse works to those you work to satisfy the 39-week requirement.

Moving expenses are deductible if paid in connection with the commencement of work at a new principal place of work. It is not necessary that you have a contract or commitment of employment prior to moving to the new location— the moving expense deduction is allowable if employment actually does occur.

Moving expenses are deductible only if reasonable under the circumstances of the particular move. Travel should be by the shortest and most direct route available from your former residence to your new residence by the conventional mode of transportation actually used and in the shortest period of time required to make the move. Additional expenses for circuitous scenic routes or sidetrip stopovers are not deductible.

Which Moving Expenses Can You Deduct?

If you qualify to deduct moving expenses as described above, you may deduct reasonable amounts for the items listed below.

(Note that the cost of meals included in the items below is subject to the same 80%-Rule that applies to travel-related meals as discussed in Section 1 of the *Travel* chapter. That is, only 80% of the cost of meals can be claimed as a moving expense. The basic treatment of reimbursed meal expenses is similar to that discussed in Section 1 of the *Miscellaneous Deductions* chapter.)

1. **Travel expenses** including meals and lodging for yourself and your family while en route from your old residence to your new residence. This deduction is allowable for only one trip made by you and members of your household; however, it is not necessary that you and all members of your household travel together or at the same time. Members of your household include your spouse and your dependents for tax purposes; economically independent relatives or others are not included.

2. The cost of **moving household goods** including automobiles, personal ef- fects, and household pets of both you and members of your family. This includes the cost of transportation from your old to your new residence, plus packing, crating, insurance, and 30 days worth of storage, as well as connect- ing and disconnecting utilities (but not a telephone). It does not include the cost of automobile registration, driver's license, carpet installation, or appliance installation.

Transportation of goods to your new residence from some place other than your old residence is deductible to the extent that it does not exceed the cost of transportation from your old residence. But you cannot deduct the cost of transporting goods purchased en route from your old to your new residence.

3. Provided you have already obtained employment at the new location, your travel costs (including meals and lodging) of **premove house-hunting trips** from your former residence to the area of your new employment and back.

4. The cost of **temporary quarters** (including meals and lodging) at the new location of work during any period of 30 consecutive days after obtaining work.

5. The **cost of selling your residence** or settling your lease at the old location and purchasing a residence or acquiring a lease at the new location. This includes:

- Real estate commissions
- Attorney's fees
- Title and escrow fees
- Points (to the extent not deducted elsewhere as interest)
- State transfer taxes
- Advertising expenses of selling your old residence
- Payments for release of a lease
- Expenses of obtaining a sublessee
- Excess of rent paid under a lease over that received under a sublease.

The above expenses may not then be used a second time to reduce any capital gains tax you might pay on the sale of either your old or new residence.

If you use your automobile to transport yourself, your family, or your goods, then you may take either of these options: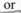

1. Deduct your actual expenses such as gasoline, oil, repairs, etc. but not depreciation. (You must keep a record of each expense in this case.)

or

2. Deduct 9 cents per mile.

According to a recent IRS ruling, there are 2 other items you can deduct in addition to the 9 cents per mile or actual operating expenses. Namely, you can deduct a pro rata portion of taxes and interest you pay on the automobile [Rev Proc 89-66]. For example, if 20% of your annual mileage is for moving, you can claim 20% of the interest and taxes as a moving expense. However the interest amount is further reduced by the 90% factor that applies to personal interest on 1990 tax returns [cf. the *Interest* chapter].

Limitations

A. The move should be within 1 year from the time you first report to your new job. If the move does not take place within that time, the expenses will not be deductible unless there are extenuating circumstances the IRS finds acceptable (e.g., a child needs to finish school at the old location).

B. The deduction for the combined expenses of house-hunting trips, temporary quarters, and selling your residence is limited to $3,000 overall. No more than $1,500 of this may be used for house-hunting trips and temporary quarters.

The above dollar limitations apply to the taxable unit, regardless of whether it is a single individual or a family. Thus, husband and wife filing separate returns would each be limited to half the above amounts. No dollar limitations are placed on en route travel expenses and moving of household goods.

Exceptions

1. If, after you move to your new residence, you are farther from your new job than if you had stayed in your old residence, then your moving expense deduction may be disallowed unless you can give a suitable justification for your move, such as lower commuting time or costs.

2. The 39-week full-time employment requirement is waived if you are involuntarily discharged (other than for willful misconduct), transferred because of a request initiated by your employer, or become disabled. However, you must show that you would have satisfied the 39-week test except for being discharged, transferred, or disabled.

3. The 39-week employment requirement need not be met to the extent that you receive reimbursement by your employer for an item of moving expense. In this case, you claim a moving expense deduction to offset your employer's reimbursement included in your gross income.

Reimbursements Received from Employer

You may have received a reimbursement from your employer for moving expenses which you incurred. Your employer is supposed to include these reimbursements (including amounts paid directly to a mover or other third party) in the amount of taxable income reported on your yearend W-2 Form. He should also provide you with a completed Form 4782 showing a detailed breakdown of all payments that were made for moving expenses.

It is then up to you to claim your moving expenses as an itemized deduction to offset the reimbursement included on your W-2 Form. Don't just subtract your reimbursements from taxable income you report on Line 7 of Form 1040. This will cause the IRS computer to kick out your tax return when it compares the income reported on your W-2 Form with the amount you report on Line 7.

If you don't itemize your deductions you're out of luck. You'll just wind up paying taxes on the reimbursement received from your employer without getting an offsetting deduction.

Where Do You Report Moving Expenses?

Moving expenses are claimed as an itemized deduction on line 19 of Schedule A. The 2% of Adjusted Gross Income floor that applies to miscellaneous deductions [cf. the *Miscellaneous Deductions* chapter] does *not* apply to moving expenses.

Form 3903 is used to compute the moving expense deduction to which you are entitled. It will lead you through the 80%-Rule that applies to meal expenses, as well as the treatment of reimbursements received from your employer. The total moving expense deduction is then entered on line 19 of Schedule A.

Foreign Moves

The limits are higher for moves to a foreign location. First, the cost of temporary quarters qualifies for deduction for a 90-day period after obtaining work instead of just 30 days. Second, the $3,000 and $1,500 limitations under item B given earlier are raised to $6,000 and $4,500, respectively. Finally, costs associated with the storage of furniture and other effects are eligible to be deducted.

Moving to a Temporary job

If you move to obtain a temporary post away from home, you cannot deduct both moving costs and the travel costs described in the *Travel* chapter.

Example

A professor at a midwestern university accepted a one-year temporary appointment with a government agency in Washington, D.C. He returned to his teaching post at the end of the year. There was no quarrel with his deduction for the cost of his meals and lodging during the stay in Washington, D. C. These were legitimate deductions while at a temporary position away from home as described in the Travel chapter. Also, he could deduct the cost of his transportation to and from his temporary post for the same reason.

But he was not allowed to deduct, as a moving expense, the cost of transporting his family and his household goods to and from Washington. It was inconsistent with the IRS regulations to allow a moving expense deduction to a place where the taxpayer has been allowed deductions for travel, meals, and lodging while at a temporary post away from home. [Goldman, 34 AFTR 2nd 74-5046]

Chapter 17

Casualty Losses

If you suffered a casualty or theft loss, then you might be entitled to a deduction.

At one time, you could deduct all but $100 of each loss that occurred. But now, you must also subtract 10% of your adjusted gross income from your total losses when computing the deduction. In particular, only a large amount of losses will yield any deduction at all. The exact procedure for computing your casualty deduction is discussed later in this chapter.

What Is a Casualty?

A **casualty** is the complete or partial destruction or loss of property resulting from an identifiable event that is sudden, unexpected, or unusual in nature.

Note that the elements of suddenness and unexpectedness must be present to justify a deduction. For example, damage to tropical plants caused by a freeze would be deductible in an area where freezes are practically unknown. But if you live in an area where a freeze is not abnormal, the deduction would be disallowed. Similarly, if your driveway is damaged by an unusual freeze or hot spell, then this would be deductible. However, the event should be sudden. Damage caused by *progressive deterioration* is not deductible.

Similarly, termite damage is not generally deductible because it is not considered to be a sudden misfortune. Another example occurs with diseases affecting your trees or shrubbery such as Dutch Elm disease. The Court ruled in 1981 that damage caused by a disease does not qualify for the casualty deduction [Coleman, 76 TC No. 49]. But a sudden insect invasion might cause a deductible casualty loss if the damage is caused by the insects themselves, rather than a disease they are carrying. For example, in a 1979 IRS ruling, a deduction was allowed for damage to trees caused by an invasion of pine beetles.

Further illustration of the *suddenness* requirement is given by two cases involving damage due to heavy rainfall. In one case, a deduction was allowed because the rain was concentrated in a short period of time—14.5 inches in a single week [Clapp, 321 F 2d 12]. But in another 1983 case, a deduction was denied because the damage was caused by excessive precipitation over a 4-month period. Since the damage was not caused by a *sudden event* but rather by *progressive deterioration,* a deduction was disallowed [Forrest, TC Memo 1983-177].

Examples of deductible casualty losses include:

Damage from a natural disaster, e.g. hurricane, tornado, flood, storm, fire, accident, heavy rains, landslides, extreme dry and wet spells, sudden sinking of land, etc.

Damage from an auto accident to your own automobile. This is deductible even if the accident was your own fault, provided it was not caused on purpose or by willful negligence. You do not deduct payments you make to the owner of another car you damaged in an accident.

Loss from vandalism.

Sonic boom damage.

Damage to your house from boiler explosion, water pipe break, etc.

Smog damage from an unusual, severe concentration of chemicals in the atmosphere. Progressive damage from a long term smog problem is not deductible.

Loss to personal property caused by accident. For example, one court case allowed a deduction for the loss of a diamond ring jarred loose by a car accident in the person's driveway. Another case allowed a deduction for a ring demolished by a garbage disposal.

Damage from snow, ice, and freezing. Court cases have allowed deductions for damage due to icy road, freezing of an automobile motor, garage wall collapse due to unusual freeze, collapse of eaves due to ice and snow, damage to driveway and brickwork from severe freeze, damage to a house from thawing of collected ice and snow, and damage to trees, shrubs, plants, etc. from extreme winter weather.

Loss from severe drought. Unusual droughts can cause deductible casualty losses. This is illustrated by a 1981 court case involving a married couple who lived in Marin County, California. Because of an unusually severe drought, residents were limited to using only 148 gallons of water a day. As a result, the couple could not water the trees, shrubs, and lawn they had planted on their property, resulting in the complete destruction of these items. Because the Court felt the drought to be unusually sudden and unexpected, it allowed a $2,000 deduction for the decline in property value caused by the destruction of the landscaping.

In another case, decided in 1984, a homeowner claimed a deduction for $10,500 worth of damage caused by drought. The drought had caused the house to settle, producing cracks in the interior walls, ceiling, and driveway. Because the damage was caused by an identifiable event (severe drought) rather than progressive deterioration, the Court allowed the deduction. His case was probably helped by the fact that his part of the country had been declared a national disaster area. [Stevens, TC Memo 1984-365]

If you own property that was damaged in 1990, be sure to claim any damage on your 1990 tax return. If you wait until a later year, your deduction will probably be disallowed. This is illustrated by a 1988 court case concerning a married couple whose house had been damaged by a severe drought that occurred in 1981. Some fine cracks were noticed in 1981 but nothing was done until 1982 when more severe damage was noticed—cracks in the front porch, patio, driveway and walls, gaps between the walls and ceilings, loosened mortar in a brick wall etc. According to an engineering report, the initial cause for all the damage was due to the soil starting to dry out during the original drought. As the soil dried further, it shrank, causing $30,000 of structural damage to the house.

Their claim of a deduction on their 1982 tax return was disallowed by the Court. The lapse of time between the occurrence of the drought and the damage done in 1982 was *"sufficiently prolonged that it can be said that the loss stemmed from intervening causes, in this case dryness and soil erosion, and consequently should be characterized as progressive deterioration."* This meant the requirement of suddenness necessary to produce a deductible casualty loss was missing. Had a loss been claimed for the damage done in 1981, the story could have been different. According to the Court,

"Perhaps petitioners' situation would have been stronger if they had claimed their loss in 1981 when there were visible signs of damage. At that point, the lapse of time would have been much shorter and the impact of the drought clearer so that there would have been a lessened potential for a 'progressive deterioration' characterization of the cause of the loss. But the fact that a loss might have been allowable in another year, not before us, does not support the allowance of the loss in 1982." [Short, TC Memo 1988-40]

You cannot deduct common, ordinary household misfortunes. For example, you cannot deduct breakage of china or glassware that you drop, the loss of a pet which has run away, or the loss of a ring which has been misplaced.

You can deduct a casualty loss even if you were at fault. In one case, a court allowed a deduction for damage to a lawn due to careless use of a weed poison.

A court case has established that you don't necessarily have to identify the event that caused the casualty loss. In this case, a supermarket cashier noticed that the diamond was missing from a woman's ring as she went through the checkout counter. The woman was sure the diamond was still in the ring earlier that morning when she polished her nails. Apparently it had been dislodged when the woman was doing various chores that morning.

When the ring was examined after the diamond was lost, two of the prongs were missing and the claws on the opposite side of the ring were forced upward. According to expert testimony, this could only have happened if a fairly strong blow had struck the side of the ring. The Court concluded that the *"cause of such a loss was not an ordinary, common, or easily predicted occurrence"* but rather that *"there was a sudden, unexpected, destructive blow to the ring that, although unnoticed by petitioner in her rush to perform her morning's chores, caused damage to the ring's setting and the resulting loss of the diamond."* Even though the precise incident causing the loss could not be pinpointed, the Court allowed a deduction of over $10,000 for the loss of the diamond. [Kielts, TC Memo 1981-329]

Theft Losses

To claim a theft loss, you must establish that an actual robbery, burglary, embezzlement, etc. took place. The mere disappearance of money or property from your person or home is not sufficient proof. You might have misplaced the item, dropped the money, etc. Usually, you need some evidence that another person took the property in question. Of course, if you return home to find your grand piano missing, no one would dispute that a theft had occurred.

You should always report a theft to the police. The first thing the IRS will ask for if it questions a theft deduction on your return is a copy of the report you made to the police.

However, lack of a police report does not automatically rule out a deduction. In a recent court case, an individual claimed a $1,700 deduction for the value of a stereo, TV, and diamond ring stolen when his apartment was burglarized. He had not reported the burglary to the police because he did not believe they would be able to recover the property. He felt this way because the police had been unsuccessful in recovering property stolen in a previous burglary. Because the Court believed his testimony that the items were stolen, it allowed a deduction despite the lack of a corroborating police report. [Novik, TC Memo 1981-446]

How to Compute Your Loss

The amount of your casualty or theft loss is defined to be the decrease in the value of your property caused by the loss. If you incur expenses for restoring the property back to its original condition, then this will usually be accepted as being equal to the loss. However, you do not have to replace or repair the damaged property in order to deduct the loss.

The value of your property before the casualty loss would be its resale market value if there is a realistic market for the item. This would be the case for a house, automobile, jewelry, etc. But using the resale value is not always a reasonable way to set the value of items. For example, used clothing is worth quite a bit more to an individual than its value in the secondhand market.

This is illustrated by a Tax Court case involving a couple whose home and contents were destroyed by fire. The Court rejected the IRS method of evaluating the destroyed property by what it *"would have brought if hawked off by a secondhand dealer or at a forced sale."* Instead it accepted the insurance industry's general valuation method of using the original cost of the items less a depreciation factor of 20% to 25%. [56 TC 976]

You cannot deduct the cost of repairs or replacements to the extent they represent an improvement over the condition of the property before the casualty or theft. For example, if your watch is stolen, your loss is equal to its used price value. You cannot deduct the cost of a new watch you buy to replace it. Similarly, if your furnace is ruined by a flood, you cannot deduct the cost of a new furnace—only the value of the old furnace.

If you suffer casualty damage, you can establish the amount of the loss by ob-taining an appraisal from an experienced and reliable appraiser. You can then deduct the appraiser's fee as a miscellaneous deduction. You should also take photographs where appropriate before the damaged property is repaired.

Your loss cannot exceed the actual price you paid. For example, suppose you purchased your house for $30,000 a number of years ago and then it is totally de-stroyed by fire. At the time of destruction, the house was worth $75,000. Your casualty loss would be limited to $30,000 plus the cost of any improvements you had made.

You treat your house, land, shrubbery, and other items on your property as one unit. For example, suppose your trees sustain $2,000 worth of damage in a hurri-cane. You planted these trees yourself many years ago at a cost of $10. You do not have to limit your casualty loss to this $10. Since you are treating the entire property as one unit, the entire $2,000 is the amount of your casualty loss since it doesn't exceed the price you paid for the entire property.

Damage to Trees, Shrubs, and Plants

You are entitled to a casualty deduction for damage due to unexpected ice, snow storms, drought, fire, wind, rain, vandalism, smog, or damage from vehi-cles. You can deduct the costs of removing damaged trees or shrubs, pruning, bracing, and replanting in order to eventually restore the property to its original state.

However, if there has been extensive damage, another computation procedure may be better. Namely, you can deduct the difference in the value of your proper-ty before and after the casualty. This computation procedure may give a larger deduction because damage to landscaping can cause a reduction in property val-ue far greater than the cost of repairing and replanting. You will need to get a qualified appraiser's report to substantiate your claim of decrease in property value.

Casualty deductions for trees and other plant life can be substantial because of the extra value they contribute to property. For example, a recent court decision granted a Florida homeowner a $15,000 deduction for damage to landscaping caused by an unexpected freeze. [Thebaut, TC Memo 1983-699]

The Tax Court, as illustrated by several cases, has been quite sympathetic when trees are destroyed. In one case, a $3,500 deduction was allowed for the loss of 5 cypress trees located 90 feet away from a house after the trees were blown down during a storm. The Court indicated the deduction might have been even higher had there been better testimony as to the loss incurred. [Zardo, TC Memo 1982-84]

In another case, 12 trees were blown down by a tornado. The IRS had denied any deduction whatever because the property contained 10 acres filled with trees and it felt the loss of only 12 of them would cause no measurable decrease in the value of the property. But the Court noted that 7 of the destroyed trees were on the cleared portion of the lot near the home and therefore contributed extra value to the property as shade trees. Consequently, it allowed a deduction of over

$19,000 for the loss of the trees. [Bowers, TC Memo 1981-658]

And a third case is the most striking of all. In this case, the Court allowed a deduction of $14,900 for the loss of a single prominent oak tree which was done in by a sudden attack of woodborers. [McKean. TC Memo 1981-670]

Insurance Payments Reduce Loss

You must reduce your loss by any reimbursements you receive from your insurance company. However, you only have to subtract insurance payments which are direct compensation for the loss. Indirect payments for living expenses after a house has been damaged or for a rental car after your automobile has been stolen, for example, are not subtracted in computing your loss.

You must reduce your loss by the amount covered by your insurance policy even if you don't file a claim.

The $100 and 10% of Adjusted Gross Income Limitations

After computing your casualty and theft losses, you must make two subtractions in order to obtain your deduction. First, you subtract $100 from the loss caused by each individual incident and total up the remainders. Then, you subtract 10% of your adjusted gross income from the total to obtain your deduction.

Example

The adjusted gross income on your tax return is $50,000. During 1990, you had a theft loss of $4,000 of which $1,000 was covered by insurance. Also, a windstorm caused $1,600 damage to your roof, $550 to your fence, and $700 to your shrubbery, none of which was covered by insurance.

	Windstorm		**Theft**	
Roof	$1,600		$4,000	
Fence	550		– 1,000	insurance
Shrubbery	700		$3,000	net loss
	$2,850		– 100	exclusion
	– 100	exclusion	$2,900	
	$2,750			

Total losses ($2,750 + $2,900) $5,650
Less 10% of Adjusted Gross Income (10% × $50,000) ....–5,000
Amount of your deduction ....$ 650

Business Casualties Fully Deductible

The $100 per event and 10% of adjusted gross income subtractions only apply to casualties involving property used for personal purposes. If you suffer a casualty to an item used for professional or business purposes, these subtractions do not apply. Instead, you can deduct the full casualty loss up to your *adjusted basis* in the item. Your *adjusted basis* is equal to the price you paid less any depreciation you were entitled to claim.

Example

You purchased a typewriter in 1989 for $200 which you used entirely for job-related purposes. During 1990, the typewriter was stolen. Your adjusted basis in the typewriter is $160 ($160 = the purchase price, $200, less the depreciation deduction of $40 that was allowable in 1989, $200 x 20% = $40).

The entire $160 can be claimed as a casualty deduction. Neither the $100 per casualty subtraction nor the 10% of adjusted gross income subtraction applies since the casualty occurred to business property rather than to personal property.

When to Deduct Your Casualty Losses

You deduct your loss in the year the casualty or theft actually occurred. If you anticipate that you will be reimbursed by insurance, you subtract the amount of the expected reimbursement from your loss in computing your tax. If the reimbursement does not turn out to be what you expected, then you adjust your next year's tax return accordingly. If you suffer a disaster loss in an area declared by the President as qualifying for Federal assistance, you can deduct the loss either in the year the disaster occurred or in the prior year.

Casualty and Collision Insurance

You cannot deduct premiums you pay on insurance against fire, theft, or other casualties. Only actual losses due to such casualties are deductible.

Free Inventory Book From the IRS

You can obtain a free inventory workbook from your local IRS office. This workbook is used to make an inventory of all your personal possessions, including their cost, current value, description, location, etc. The workbook has separate sheets for listing the contents of each room along with pre-printed entries of items typically found in these rooms.

If you should suffer a casualty or theft loss, this inventory workbook will be a valuable document in establishing your loss. You should keep this workbook in your office or a safe deposit box so that it will not disappear in a theft or major disaster. To request this workbook, call your local IRS office and ask for Publication 584.

To complement the workbook, the IRS suggests you keep a file of pictures of both your home and its contents. Note that the workbook and picture file are also valuable in establishing your loss for insurance purposes. It's also a good idea to take pictures immediately after a casualty. For example, photographs of a house ransacked by burglars or damaged by fire would support your claim to a deduction.

Where Do You Deduct Your Losses?

There is a special line on Schedule A for listing your total casualty losses. You also attach Form 4684 on which the amount of your deduction is computed.

Chapter 18

Will Your Tax Return Be Audited?

Section 1:
Audits

At one time, IRS procedures for checking tax returns were kept top secret. But now, a number of documents give a considerable amount of insight into the inner workings of the IRS. Most important are various IRS manuals which it issues for general guidance to its Tax Auditors. These documents were forced into public view by suits brought under the Freedom of Information Act. Another elucidating document is a report prepared several years ago by the GAO (General Accounting Office), a watchdog agency of the Congress. The GAO report provides an independent outside look into how the IRS behaves in its dealings with taxpayers.

Basic Procedures

After you fill out your tax return, you send it to one of the 10 IRS Service Centers. At the Service Center, your tax return is subjected to an initial inspection both by a human being and by a computer. One of the purposes of this initial inspection is to determine if the return contains any of a number of designated Unallowable Items. The GAO report contains a list of these Unallowable Items. If you have one of these items on your tax return, the IRS will send you a notice to that effect. The most pertinent of these IRS notices are given below.

Personal Legal Expenses

Your deduction of legal expenses, reported on Schedule A, has been disallowed. Deductions for personal, living, or family expenses are allowable only if expressly provided for in the law. Personal legal expenses for wills, trusts, adoption, divorce, and other items not connected with the production of income are not provided for, and are therefore not deductible.

Educational Expenses for Other Than Taxpayer or Spouse

Your deduction of educational expenses for someone other than yourself or your spouse, reported on Schedule A, has been disallowed. Deductions for per-

sonal, living or family expenses are allowable only if expressly provided for in
the law. Educational expenses for someone other than yourself or your spouse
are not provided for, and are therefore not deductible.

Automobile Expenses—Donated Services

Your deduction for automobile expenses incurred in donating your services to
a qualified charitable organization, reported on Schedule A, has been adjusted
because you used an unallowable mileage rate to compute your automobile expenses. When using a mileage rate to determine automobile expenses for donated services, you are limited to 12 cents a mile, which is the rate we used in determining your deduction.

Contributions—Nonqualifying

Your charitable contributions deduction, reported on Schedule A, has been
adjusted because contributions to individuals or to other nonqualifying recipients, such as lobbying organizations and foreign charities (except Canadian
charities), are not deductible by law.

Federal Taxes

The deductions you claimed on Schedule A for Federal taxes have been disallowed. The law denies a deduction for Federal income tax; social security and
railroad retirement taxes; social security tax you paid for a personal or domestic
employee; Federal excise taxes on automobiles, tires, telephone service, and air
transportation; customs duties; and Federal estate and gift taxes.

Utility Taxes

Your deduction for taxes, reported on Schedule A, has been adjusted. . . .
Utility taxes with respect to sewers, water, phones, and garbage collection are
not. . . deductible by law.

Automobile License, Registration, and Tag Fees or Taxes

Your deduction for automobile license, registration, tag fees, or taxes, reported on Schedule A, has been adjusted. The law provides that such amounts may
be deductible as personal property taxes only if they are imposed by your State
annually, and in an amount based on the value of your automobile. Because your
State does not impose the fees and taxes in this manner, they do not qualify as
personal property taxes and are therefore not deductible.

Sale or Purchase of Personal Residence

Your deduction of expenses incurred in the sale or purchase of your residence,
reported on Schedule A, has been disallowed. Deductions for personal, living, or
family expenses are allowable only if expressly provided for in the law. Closing
expenses, settlement fees, legal fees, or realtor commissions are not provided for,
and are therefore not deductible.

Matching Program

The income you report on your return is matched against the W-2, interest, and dividend forms which were sent to the IRS by your employer, bank, companies whose shares you own, etc. If the computer discovers that you did not report all your income, it will tag your return for examination.

In practice, the IRS matches your tax return against virtually all information sent to it on magnetic tape. This includes most wage information forms because the Social Security Administration now converts this data to magnetic tape and passes it on to the IRS. Also, stockbrokers and financial institutions which send out more than 50 dividend or interest information forms must now report this information to the IRS on magnetic tape. At one time, relatively few interest and dividend forms sent to the IRS on paper were fed into the matching program because of the extra cost of processing such forms. But now, the IRS expects to process over 95% of these paper forms with new optical scanning equipment.

Matching usually starts early in the year after the tax return is filed. Thus, for example, matching on 1990 tax returns which are filed in 1991 will probably begin early in 1992. The IRS has a tough new policy when the matching program turns up unreported dividend and interest income—an automatic negligence penalty will be assessed. To escape the penalty, the taxpayer will have to provide evidence that he was not intentionally or carelessly omitting the income, but rather that there was justification for the omission.

Because the matching program is so effective, you should take care that income and deductions are reported the right way on your tax return. Otherwise, the matching program will kick out your return for examination. Section 9 of Chapter 1 contains a description of how to avoid the most common pitfalls that can trigger the computer to declare a mismatch.

After your return is checked for routine omissions, it is fed into the master computer in West Virginia. All tax returns are classified into categories, depending upon the total income reported and whether it is a *business* return or a *personal* return. For each category, the computer assigns to each return in that category a number called the DIF (Discriminate Function) number. This number indicates the likelihood that an audit of the return will result in an additional tax assessment. The higher the DIF number, the greater is the potential additional tax assessment.

The formula used by the computer program to assign the DIF number to a tax return is a highly guarded secret. It is based on the experience of the IRS in previous audits and is regularly updated.

According to a declassified IRS audit manual, it is not just the items which appear on your tax return that can produce a high DIF score. The **absence** of certain items can raise the DIF score and cause your return to be targeted for examination. [MT 41(12)0-1:310]

For example, the absence of dividend income when Schedule D shows sales of stock you've owned may be an examination trigger [IRM 41(12)0-1:330]. Or, the absence of a deduction for real estate taxes when a mortgage interest deduction is claimed may cause suspicion. If there is a suspicious inconsistency on your tax return, it would be wise to attach an explanation of the reason for such inconsistency to your tax return, in order to deflect the possibility of an audit.

The DIF program is highly effective in singling out tax returns which are filled out incorrectly. Only about 17% of audits of taxpayers in the $25,000—$50,000 income category result in no change in the amount of tax due.

Middle-Income Taxpayers Over-Audited

The GAO has criticized the IRS for auditing too many middle-income taxpayers. These individuals have shown the greatest level of compliance with the tax laws of any category of taxpayers. In contrast, the tax returns of small businesses exhibit a much lower level of compliance. Yet, the audit rate of these small business returns is about the same as the audit rate for middle-income individuals.

The reason there is little difference in the audit rates is that individual tax returns can be audited in much less time than business returns so that the yield per manhour of IRS time becomes higher. But the GAO feels that this is a shortsighted approach. The purpose of conducting audits is not just to extract money from the most vulnerable taxpayers, but also to encourage a high level of compliance from others out of a fear of audit. In fact, it has been shown that as the audit frequency increases among a given class of taxpayers, the general compliance level among all taxpayers in that class rises. Thus, the GAO recommended that more audits be directed to those taxpayers with a history of lower compliance than middle-income taxpayers. However, recent figures show that middle-income taxpayers continue to be significantly over-audited.

How to Reduce the Odds of an Audit

After the computer assigns DIF numbers to all the tax returns, the local IRS offices request from the computer those returns in each category showing the higher DIF numbers. When these returns arrive at the local office, an experienced IRS classifying officer reviews these returns to see if there is an auditable issue involved in the return. The officer may accept the return as submitted or he may send it to an IRS examiner who will contact you for the purpose of setting up an audit. Of tax returns that the computer has kicked out, about 50% are selected for audit with the remaining 50% accepted as filed.

It's here that you have a chance to lessen the odds you will be audited. Your tax return should be filled out in such a way that the examining officer is encouraged not to select it for audit.

The first thing you can do is to avoid suspiciously rounded figures. According to the GAO, this is one of the first things an examiner is trained to look for. Figures of $200, $350, $600 will arouse suspicion which $213, $371, $594 will not. If your figures represent a guess, then at least guess an odd amount. And if your return accidentally contains too many round numbers, you might even want to go back and "unround" a few of these numbers to be on the safe side.

The second thing is to avoid having identical numbers appear on a return for two different items. This is an indication you may have miscopied a number in the wrong /

place. According to one tax newsletter, the IRS uses a quality control procedure to kick out such returns for examination. For example, if your return shows a $2,000 IRA deduction and a $2,000 credit for estimated tax, the processing of your return is halted. At the least, you then could be sent a letter asking for an explanation.

The third thing you can do is to attach documentation to your return which substantiates any large or unusual deduction that is likely to kick out your return for audit. When the classifying officer reviews your return, this attached evidence may convince him that an audit is not likely enough to produce additional revenue. If so, then you have prevented an audit.

If the problem is an unusually high deduction, you can attach copies of supporting documents such as bills or checks. An example of this kind would be unusually large medical expenses. In this case, you should show in an attached statement that you have subtracted any amounts of insurance payments you received. A common mistake that the IRS looks for when a large medical deduction is claimed is the failure to subtract insurance reimbursements.

On the other hand, if the problem is mainly one of understanding the law, you might just write a short statement proving you understand the law. For example, to support a home office deduction [cf. the *Home Office* chapter], you might include the following statement:

"The home office is the principal place of business for the taxpayer's job or business activity of _____. It is used exclusively on a regular basis for business purposes. The home office deduction does not exceed the gross income from this activity after deducting other business expenses attributable to the activity."

The attaching of documentation to a tax return is confirmed by the GAO Report as being of great importance in influencing the examiner not to choose your return for audit. In fact, the IRS has agreed to lessen the arbitrary manner with which classifying officers choose returns for audit after the computer has kicked them out with high DIF scores. This means that appropriate documentation attached to your tax return may become virtually the only way a classifying officer will accept your return without audit. The IRS asks that supporting statements not be attached directly to their related forms. Rather, all supporting statements should be assembled in the same sequence as the forms they support and placed at the end of the tax return.

Another helpful factor is for your tax return to include some income which would not show up unless you reported it. This is an indication to the examiner that you are an honest and careful taxpayer.

You should be careful when you fill out the *occupation* lines for yourself and your spouse that appear on your tax return. This information is likely to be the first thing an examining officer looks at. An occupation of mostly salaried individuals will arouse less suspicion than an occupation of mostly self-employed individuals because there is less opportunity to hide income or exaggerate deductions. Thus, a consulting engineer should list his occupation as *engineer* rather than *consultant*. Similarly, a music teacher should list his occupation as *teacher* rather than *musician*.

Not all audited tax returns are computer-selected under the DIF program. A significant number are selected because the IRS has special reason to think they might contain errors. The most common of these special reasons is that the return was prepared by a professional tax preparer whom the IRS has on its list as preparing erroneous returns in the past.

The number of returns each IRS office requests depends upon the availability of personnel in that office to examine such returns. Thus, a return with a given DIF number might be sent to one local office for examination, while in a different locality, another return with the same DIF number might escape examination because the office in that locality is understaffed. In fact, there is a wide discrepancy in the percentage of returns audited in various districts. This variation is due partly to a geographic maldistribution of questionable returns and partly to a maldistribution of agents across the country. There is also a wide discrepancy in the extra tax collected by various IRS offices from those taxpayers that are audited.

Each year, the IRS selects a certain number of tax returns at random under its Taxpayer Compliance Measurement Program, or TCMP. The purpose of this program is to obtain a detailed statistical profile of taxpayers in various income categories. Using this profile, the IRS constructs its general DIF program for auditing tax returns with high adjustment potential. If your tax return is selected under the TCMP program, it's bad news. Your return will be subjected to an exhaustive audit, much more detailed than an ordinary audit. The entire tax return must be verified and documented, line by line. For example, if an "over 65 standard deduction" is claimed, it must be backed up by a birth certificate or other record of birth.

What If There Is Only One Questionable Item on Your Tax Return?

Suppose your tax return contains only one questionable deduction. Is this sufficient to cause your tax return to be audited? According to a declassified IRS Audit Manual, the answer is generally "no." This manual advises its examiners that,

> "Single issues should generally not be examined, as experience has shown that such examinations frequently result in insignificant or no tax change when other questionable items are not present on the return." [MT 41(12)0-1:510(4)(b)]

If there is one large item on your tax return which is susceptible to IRS challenge, take note of the above suggested IRS policy. Avoid including any other questionable items if they do not significantly lower your taxes. Or, if there are other unusually large deductions, attach documentation to your tax return which removes them from the questionable category. That way, the "questionable items" on your tax return will consist only of the one large susceptible item you're concerned about. According to the above quote, this will place your tax return in the category the IRS suggests not generally be audited.

Make Sure Your State Tax Return Agrees with Your Federal Return

The IRS has entered into a cooperative arrangement with a number of different States. Entries on Federal and State tax returns are checked against each other for consistency. In case of discrepancy, both returns could be flagged for audit. Be sure your tax returns agree with each other to avoid triggering an unnecessary audit.

Average Deductions

Although the formula used by the IRS computer to select returns for audit is a closely guarded secret, the basic principle behind the formula is not. The formula is based primarily on the amount and relationship between the deductions claimed. If a person's deductions are significantly higher than the average of those with the same income, then the computer is likely to select his return for audit. However, it is not just the total of all deductions which counts. If a person's deductions in any one category are high enough, the computer may tag his return for audit, even if the total of all deductions is in line with the average. For this reason, it is interesting to know what the average deductions in various categories are in relation to income. The table below lists the average deductions on 1988 returns claiming such deductions, as related to the adjusted gross income listed on such returns. (Data for 1989 returns won't be available until later in 1991.)

Adjusted Gross Income	Medical	Taxes	Charity	Interest
$ 20,000-25,000	$ 2,793	1,696	1,083	3,759
25,000-30,000	2,462	1,830	1,075	4,150
30,000-40,000	2,687	2,306	1,091	4,667
40,000-50,000	3,079	2,844	1,282	5,153
50,000-75,000	4,281	3,853	1,524	6,129
75,000-100,000	5,580	5,659	2,083	8,562
100,000-200,000	12,967	8,725	3,402	11,507

We caution that the average deductions listed in the table are for informative use only in assessing the likelihood you will be audited. You are not allowed to use the average amounts in these tables on your own return in place of the actual amounts to which you are entitled. In fact, the IRS computer selects a certain number of returns at random, so simply filing an "average return" will not guarantee that you won't be audited.

Types of Audits

There are 3 types of audits.

(1) Correspondence Audit. Here, the IRS will write you a letter asking for further information. All dealings are conducted through the mail. This is the most convenient type of audit because you do not have to travel to the IRS office. Furthermore, you are not faced with making on-the-spot reactions or decisions as you might be in a face-to-face interview.

(2) Office Audit. In this type of audit, you will be requested to pay a visit to your local IRS office and discuss your return with an IRS auditor. The letter requesting such a visit may ask you to bring documentation to support items on your return.

You may be able to avoid an office audit if it is chiefly a matter of verifying that you actually paid deductions claimed on your tax return. Contact the auditor and ask if you can send in copies of the cancelled checks or other evidence of payment. Then if he agrees, mail in the information so that it reaches him before the scheduled time of examination. If everything is in order, you will have saved yourself a trip to the IRS office.

(3) Field Audit. In this type of audit, the IRS agent comes to your home or office. Field audits will usually occur only if you operate a business or live in a remote area.

The IRS Manual lists the following deductions as suitable for examination by correspondence audit: *"interest, taxes, contributions, medical expenses, and simple miscellaneous deductions such as union dues and small tools."* More complicated issues such as travel expenses, educational expenses, etc., fall into the office audit category.

The letter informing you of an audit will specify certain items on your return in which the IRS is interested. These are usually the only items that will be questioned.

IRS Cutoff Figures Made Public

Amended returns are subjected to a special audit procedure. These returns are classified into categories depending upon the kind and amounts of the deductions being amended. All the tax returns in one category are examined while only a small percentage of returns in the other category are subject to examination.

An IRS Agents Manual makes a surprising revelation of just what the cutoff numbers are for placement into the must-examine category. Usually, this type of data is withheld to prevent individuals from claiming just below the cutoffs. In addition to providing data on amended returns, these cutoff numbers give insight into the audit policy on regular returns because they illustrate the relative weights that the IRS assigns when comparing the questionability of one deduction versus another.

The following IRS list shows the amount of change in various items on an amended tax return which will place it into the must-examine category.

(1) Schedule B (Interest & Dividend Income)—Decrease of $2,000 or more.

(2) Schedule D (Capital Gains or Losses)—Decrease in gain or increase in loss of $10,000 or more.

(3) Education Expense—Increase in excess of $400.

(4) Travel Expense—Increase in excess of $2,000.

(5) Moving Expenses—Increase in excess of $5,000.

What to Do If You Are Audited

The letter informing you of an office audit will list the items being challenged and the time and place of the audit. If the time is not convenient, you have the right to rearrange the time to fit in with your schedule although you can't make extensive delays. The best time to schedule an audit is in the time-slot before lunch or before the end of the day. The auditor will be less likely to prolong the audit to examine an extra secondary issue. Also, the end of the month is a good time to schedule an audit. If the auditor has not "closed" enough cases that month, he may be anxious to get a quick agreement with you without venturing into grey areas.

You can also request the audit be moved to a different IRS district office if you have a sufficient reason (e.g. you moved outside the original district or you work in a different district). Making such a request is a good idea. A substantial delay can occur in transferring your file from one office to another. And your file might go to the bottom of the stack when assigned to a new agent. Meanwhile, the statute of limitations for auditing your return can expire.

You can have a lawyer, CPA, or enrolled agent (who has passed a special IRS exam) argue your case for you (in your absence if you wish). If you are presenting your own case, you can bring with you one other friend or relative. Representatives from commercial preparation firms may accompany you to the audit, but they usually can't argue your case.

Note that you are entitled to bring up deductions you overlooked in addition to defending those the IRS is challenging. About 5% of all audits result in refunds to the taxpayer for this reason. The best time to bring up such unclaimed deductions is right after the auditor has gone over all his proposed adjustments with you. Otherwise, he might be tempted to offset your new deductions by being tougher on other items.

The notification letter from the IRS will contain a checklist of the items being questioned on your tax return. Normally, these will be the only items discussed at the audit. You should bring documentation to support your deductions for these items. However, you should not bring supporting documents for other items not mentioned in the IRS notification. If the auditor's curiosity is aroused by another item, he will be deterred by the fact you haven't brought documents to examine. He will be more likely to let the matter drop and close the examination than to force you to come back with the extra documents.

There are two different types of examiners—Revenue Agents and Tax Auditors. Revenue agents usually have a college education with a major in accounting and are used to audit more complicated tax returns. Tax auditors, on the other hand, are not required to have taken any accounting or business courses, although they must take some training in accounting before advancing to the journeyman level.

Taxpayer Bill of Rights

As part of the *1988 Tax Revision Act,*Congress included a *Taxpayer Bill of Rights*. This was designed to protect against IRS abuses and give the average citizen a reasonable shot when there is a tax dispute with the government.

The following are some of the more important provisions in this *Taxpayer Bill of Rights*.

1. Audits can be tape recorded.

"A taxpayer is permitted, upon advance notice to the IRS, to make an audio recording of an in-person interview at the taxpayer's own expense. IRS employees also are authorized to record taxpayer interviews, provided the taxpayer receives prior notice of such recording and is supplied a copy or a transcript of the recording upon request and payment of the costs of the copy or transcript."

The IRS issued an "administrative pronouncement" in 1989 describing how this provision will work in practice. According to this pronouncement, the taxpayer must give advance notice to the IRS auditor that he intends to make a recording. This notice must be received by the IRS at least 10 calendar days before the audit is scheduled to take place. The taxpayer must provide the equipment with which the recording is made. [IRS Notice 89-51]

2. Taxpayer can call a halt in the middle of an audit.

"If a taxpayer clearly states during an interview with the IRS (other than an interview pursuant to an administrative summons) that the taxpayer wishes to consult with [a] representative [e.g. lawyer or CPA], *the interview must be suspended to afford the taxpayer a reasonable opportunity to consult with the representative. . . .*

"The suspension procedure provided by the provision is to be available to facilitate taxpayers' access to their representatives and not to delay needlessly the interview process. It is intended that in instances of abuse of this process (such as repeated suspensions of interviews to contact different representatives) the IRS may issue an administrative summons."

3. Taxpayer isn't required to appear in person at an audit.

"The bill provides that a taxpayer may be represented during a taxpayer interview by any attorney, certified public accountant, enrolled agent, enrolled actuary, or any other person permitted to represent a taxpayer before the IRS, who is not disbarred or suspended from practice before the IRS and who has a properly executed power of attorney from the taxpayer. . . . Absent an administrative summons, a taxpayer cannot be required to accompany the representative to an interview."

4. Ombudsmen in each IRS office get wide latitude to help taxpayers.

"The Taxpayer Ombudsman (or any designee of the Ombudsman) is provided statutory authority to issue a taxpayer assistance order if, in the determination of the Ombudsman, the taxpayer is suffering or about to suffer a significant hardship as a result of the manner in which the IRS is administering the internal revenue laws. The Ombudsman may take action whether or not a taxpayer has filed an application requesting relief. A taxpayer assistance order may require remedial actions, such as release from levy of property of the taxpayer. A taxpayer assistance order is binding on the IRS unless modified or rescinded by the

Ombudsman, a district director, a service center director, a compliance center director, a regional director of appeals, or any superior of any such person."

5. Taxpayers can be awarded costs if the IRS is wrong.

"Any person who substantially prevails in any action brought by or against the United States in connection with the determination, collection, or refund of any tax, interest, or penalty may be awarded reasonable litigation costs plus reasonable administrative costs incurred after the earlier of (1) the date of the receipt by the taxpayer of the notice of the decision of the IRS Office of Appeals, or (2) the date of the notice of deficiency."

How to Get the IRS to Call Off Repeat Audits

Few things are more irritating than to be audited, to convince the auditor that you're correct, and then to be audited on the very same issue the next year. To prevent this from happening, the IRS has adopted a special policy. Namely, a taxpayer is generally not supposed to be audited on any issue on which he was audited in either of the two preceding years—provided the taxpayer was cleared on that issue in the previous audit. (However, if he was cleared in one of the preceding years and had to pay tax in the other, the current audit can proceed.)

Note that the IRS does not generally check for previous audits. It is up to you to tell the IRS agent about a preceding no-change audit. He should then call off the audit after verifying your story.

The IRS Agents Manual

The manual which the IRS issues to its own agents offers some interesting glimpses into how agents are instructed to treat taxpayers. Below are some excerpts from this manual. We have added underlining for emphasis.

Office Interview Examination

A. Direct contact with a taxpayer is a more satisfactory way to determine the proper depth and scope of an audit. Thus the office interview technique should be used when selected returns contain issues which require an analytical approach and individual judgment. The following types of issues should. . . be initiated for examination by office interview.

1. Dependency exemptions unless they clearly meet the criteria for the correspondence method [e.g. the dependent is a spouse, child, or parent.]

2. Income from tips, pensions, annuities, rents and royalties.

3. Deductions for employee's business expenses.

4. Deductions for bad debts.

5. Determination of basis of property.

6. Complex miscellaneous deductions such as casualty and theft losses requiring determinations of fair market value and education expenses; and fellowships and scholarships.

7. Salaried employees whose occupations lend themselves to possible outside employment.

B. Regardless of issue, this technique will be used if needed to ensure the rights of taxpayers under the law. Aside from tax issue, other factors, such as those below, may indicate that an office interview examination is necessary:

1. Taxpayer's income is low in relation to his financial responsibilities as indicated by entries on the return (number of dependents, interest expense, etc.)

2. Taxpayer's occupation is of the type that requires only a limited formal education.

3. The appearance of the tax return (writing, grammar, neatness, etc.) indicates the taxpayer may not be able to effectively correspond with us.

Instructions For Examining Officer

Evaluation of Evidence

(a) Oral statements—The principal method of introducing evidence in a court case is through the testimony of a witness. Therefore, oral statements made by taxpayers to examining officers represent direct evidence which must be thoroughly considered. Uncontradicted statements which are not improbable or unreasonable cannot be disregarded even if made by an interested party. The degree of reliability placed by an examining officer on oral statements must be based on the credibility of the taxpayer as supported by surrounding circumstantial evidence. If the issue involves specific recordkeeping required by law and regulations,. . . then of course, oral evidence alone cannot be substituted for necessary written documentation.

(b) Credibility:

1. It is the responsibility of the examining officer to establish the degree of credibility of the taxpayer. It is here that the examining officer must exercise to the fullest his skill and judgment. He should take into account the demeanor of the taxpayer, his manner of making the statement and the extent of subject knowledge demonstrated. These first impressions should be carefully tested by skillful questioning to bring out all pertinent surrounding circumstances. Corroborative or contradictory details will have an important bearing on determining the reasonableness and probability of the statements.

2. If the statements of the taxpayer, although self-serving, are not improbable or unreasonable, self-contradictory, or inconsistent with surrounding facts and circumstances, they should be accepted. If the statements of the taxpayer, in the judgment of the examining officer, reveal some degree of unreliability, his findings should take this into account. Unless the taxpayer's statements have been found to be wholly unreliable, they must be given some weight in the conclusion reached.

3. In considering issues susceptible to abuse by taxpayers, the examining officer should assess the credibility of the taxpayer with caution. Since oral statements with strained constructions of fact are more likely to be encountered in these cases, the examining officer's skill and judgment in developing the surrounding circumstances are especially important, so that the taxpayer does not profit from his failure to maintain documentation substantiating his income and deductions. Some examples of such issues are personal expenses disguised as business, convention or education expenses and determination of income from tips, prizes, awards, gambling, or miscellaneous independent activities.

Soliciting Agreements

(1) Upon completion of an examination, the examining officer will explain the basis of the proposed adjustments to the taxpayer or his representative, and make an effort to obtain an agreement to the proposed tax liability. If necessary, the examining officer will cite the provisions of the law, regulations, published rulings, Tax Court and other court decisions on which he has based his conclusions. If the taxpayer indicates disagreement with any of the proposed adjustments, he should be informed of his appeal rights, as well as his right to pay any deficiency and file claim for refund. If agreement can be reached on one or more, but not all issues or years, the taxpayer should be encouraged to enter into a partial agreement by executing a waiver of restrictions covering the agreed issues or years. In attempting to reach agreement, however, Audit personnel must recognize that they are not authorized to settle cases in the same sense that a settlement may be negotiated by Appellate Division.

(2) If a taxpayer specifically requests a written record of what has been agreed to at the time a partial agreement is entered into, an appropriate letter or statement may be furnished covering such agreed issues or years. The issuance of such a letter or statement will be subject to the same review procedures as a regular report.

Will the IRS Bother with Small Amounts?

Officially, "*The primary objective in selection of tax returns will be the highest possible revenue yield from the examination manhours expended, and the examination of as many returns of all classes as is feasible for the maintenance of a high degree of voluntary taxpayer compliance.*"

The average office audit results in a recommended tax increase of about $1,000 and takes about 90 minutes.

The IRS Manual also states,

"*The Service recognizes that many accounts outstanding on the books are so small that the expenses of collection are out of proportion to the amount to be realized from further collection effort. In the interest of efficient and economical utilization of available manpower and other resources, small balance accounts may be written off when it is determined in accordance with Manual instructions that the collection costs involved do not warrant attempting to collect.*"

IRS Tells Its Agents: Be Reasonable

Often, taxpayers are put into a no-win situation when challenged by the IRS. The trouble and expense of fighting the IRS in court leads the taxpayer to give in even when the law is on his side. IRS agents sometimes take advantage of this by disallowing legitimate deductions, figuring that the taxpayer will not fight back.

To lessen the incentive for government abuse, Congress passed a law under which the IRS can be forced to reimburse taxpayers for court and attorney's fees when they lose in court. Because of the danger of having to reimburse taxpayers when the IRS acts in bad faith, agents are instructed to be reasonable. Instead of trying to twist the law, IRS agents are instructed to apply the law in a reasonable way as it was intended to be applied.

> "... it is the responsibility of each person in the Service, charged with the duty of interpreting the law, to try to find the true meaning of the statutory provision and not to adopt a strained construction in the belief that he is 'protecting the revenue.' The revenue is properly protected only when we ascertain and apply the true meaning of the statute.
>
> "The Service also has the responsibility of applying and administering the law in a reasonable, practical manner. Issues should only be raised by examining officers when they have merit, never arbitrarily or for trading purposes. At the same time, the examining officer should never hesitate to raise a meritorious issue. It is also important that care be exercised not to raise an issue or to ask a court to adopt a position inconsistent with established Service position.
>
> "Administration should be both reasonable and vigorous. It should be conducted with as little delay as possible and with great courtesy and consideration. It should never try to overreach and should be reasonable within the bounds of law and sound administration...." [Internal Revenue Manual supplement 42G-369]

How Long Does the IRS Have to Audit Your Return?

The general rule is that the IRS has 3 years from the due date of your return in which to make an audit. There are several exceptions to this general rule. If you file late, then the IRS has 3 years from your actual filing date. If the IRS can prove that at least 25% of gross income was omitted from your tax return, the time span is 6 years. However, if the government can prove fraud, there is no time limit on auditing a return, although it generally destroys returns after 7 years. But if the government wishes to prosecute for criminal fraud, it must do so within 6 years. Criminal prosecution for fraud is a rare occurrence—about 1/50,000 of all tax returns filed.

Although the IRS has 3 years in which to conduct an audit, the IRS Manual instructs its agents to do so in a shorter period of time. Except when a return is suspected of fraud or covered under some special audit program, the examination and disposition of income tax returns will be completed within 26 months after the due date of the return (or the date filed in the case of returns filed late). The IRS ordinarily allows 6 months for the examination process. Thus, to complete the examination within 26 months, the IRS must usually initiate examination no later than 20 months after the filing date. Thus, if you haven't heard from the IRS by late 1992, your 1990 return will be safe from audit except in unusual circumstances.

Appealing Within the IRS

If you feel an auditor is taking an unreasonable position, you can ask to speak to his supervisor right then. The supervisor can change the auditor's determination if he agrees with you that the position is unreasonable. Otherwise, if you can't come to an agreement at the audit, you can appeal to the Appellate Division of the IRS. The auditor will explain your rights under this appeals procedure.

An IRS directive issued to the Appeals Division makes it easier to reach a settlement. Formerly, the Appeals officer was not allowed to suggest what would be acceptable as a settlement. Instead, all offers had to come from the taxpayer. But now, if you make a reasonable offer of settlement, the Appeals agent *"should give an evaluation of the case in such a manner as to enable the taxpayer to ascertain the kind of settlement that would be recommended for acceptance."* In plain English, this means that they will make a counteroffer. This negotiation policy makes settlements easier to reach, especially if the amounts involved are not large. In more than 80% of appeals cases, the taxpayer achieves a reduction or elimination of extra taxes or penalties.

One situation where an appeal is particularly effective is when the auditor imposes a negligence penalty. Such penalties are often mistakenly assessed by tax auditors in routine cases, rather than in the *"clearly erroneous"* type of case for which they are intended. The Appeals Officer will often cancel such negligence penalties.

Small Case Tax Court

There is a way to contest the IRS without having to get a lawyer or incur beyond a small charge. Disputes involving less than $10,000 may be submitted to the Small Case Tax Court. Here, cases are decided by an impartial judge who will keep the proceeding informal, explaining it as he goes along. You do not need a lawyer and the decision of the judge is final—neither you nor the IRS can appeal and the decision does not set legal precedent.

The procedure for taking a case to Small Case Tax Court is relatively simple. You file a petition asking for a hearing and pay a $60 filing fee. A free booklet describing the procedure can be obtained by writing to Clerk of the Court, U.S. Tax Court, 400 Second Street, N.W., Washington, D.C. 20217.

Note that even if you don't want to appear in court, it pays to submit the petition anyhow. The IRS does not want to send their lawyers into court to adjudicate small issues in a forum that does not involve setting legal precedent. Some time after you file a petition, the IRS will contact you to arrange a settlement. About 90% of small tax cases are settled without going to trial, with the IRS settling for about 50% of the amounts it claimed were due. And if you have a reasonably good case, you might even be able to beat this average.

Section 2:
Private IRS Rulings

You might want to learn in advance the tax consequences of an action you contemplate taking. Many times, the question of whether or not a particular activity falls under the rules for tax-free treatment becomes a matter of judgment. This is especially true when the issue involves determining whether the primary purpose of an activity is for business or personal purposes.

In order to determine how the IRS will treat a particular matter, you can solicit a *Private Letter Ruling* from the IRS. This written opinion, which you attach to your tax return, will then govern the treatment of your particular case by the IRS.

Soliciting a written opinion from the IRS is completely different from merely phoning the information number the IRS provides. It is well established that you cannot legally rely on oral advice from IRS personnel. Past surveys have found substantial error rates in such advice. The error rate is no doubt even higher on specialized or complicated matters. After all, it is unreasonable to expect any given individual to be familiar with all the tax laws as they apply to people in all professions.

What Kind of Questions Will the IRS Rule On?

The IRS has the option of deciding whether or not to issue a ruling. Basically they will issue a ruling on most matters with the following major exceptions:

1. The IRS will not issue a ruling to specify how much a certain property is worth, to specify the building/land ratio of property for depreciation purposes, or to specify other such "numerical" issues.

2. The IRS will not rule on a hypothetical question nor on one involving several alternatives. They will not rule on a transaction to be consummated at some indefinite future time. They must be presented with a single definite course of action which is seriously being considered.

3. The IRS will not rule on a transaction or matter having as a major purpose the reduction of Federal taxes. In other words, they won't issue a ruling if they feel they are simply being presented with a tax-dodging scheme.

If the ruling request deals with a matter on which the IRS will not issue a ruling, the taxpayer will be so advised. However, the request may be forwarded to the district IRS office for association with the taxpayer's return. The IRS is also reluctant to issue rulings applying changes in the Tax Code until the IRS has had time to issue regulations interpreting the changes.

Preliminary Contact

The National Office of the IRS ordinarily won't discuss a "substantive tax issue" prior to receipt of a written ruling request. However, you can always inquire whether the IRS will rule on a particular question. Any such written inquiry must contain your name and social security number. You can also make inquiries as to procedural questions concerning the request for a ruling.

A ruling request may be withdrawn at any time before the ruling is issued. However, withdrawal won't necessarily prevent the IRS from furnishing its views to the local IRS office where your tax return is filed.

How to Request a Ruling

To request a ruling, you write a letter describing all the circumstances addressed to: Internal Revenue Service, Associate Chief Counsel (Technical and International), Attn: CC: IND: D:C, PO. Box 7604, Ben Franklin Station, Washington, D. C. 20004. Ordinarily, either you or your attorney, accountant, or enrolled agent will sign the letter.

The request for a ruling should include the following:

1. The names, addresses, and social security or taxpayer account numbers of all interested parties.

2. Location of the IRS district office having audit jurisdiction over the tax return in question.

3. A carefully detailed description of the transaction including a full and precise statement of the business reasons for the transaction.

4. Copies of all relevant documents. Photocopies will usually be accepted as true copies of the original documents. Originals should not be sent since they won't be returned.

5. A description of how the attached documents or exhibits bear on the issue in question.

6. A statement whether, to the best of the knowledge of the taxpayer or his representative, the identical issue is pending before any other IRS office and if so, the office involved.

7. If the request pertains to only one step of a larger transaction, the facts concerning the larger transaction.

8. A statement of the taxpayer's view as to what the tax outcome should be, including reference to relevant authorities in support of this view.

9. A statement whether or not the identical issue is being or has been examined in an IRS audit of a prior tax return which has not yet been finally resolved.

10. Any regulations, rulings, etc. which are contrary to the taxpayer's position, or a statement that none are known.

11. A separate signed declaration as follows: *"Under penalties of perjury, I have examined this request, including accompanying documents, and to the best of my knowledge and belief, the facts presented in support of the requested ruling or determination letter are true, correct and complete."* This statement does not have to be notarized.

If a ruling request does not contain all the needed information, the IRS will write back and request the missing information. Only one copy of the ruling needs to be sent unless more than one issue is presented. In such a case, duplicate requests should be mailed.

The IRS now charges a fee for issuing a private letter ruling. The fee schedules range from $50 to $1,000 depending upon the nature of the ruling request. The fee for a typical ruling issued to an individual would generally be about $200.

Optional Statement of Controlling Facts

If you request a ruling, your request might include some information on future actions which you are not certain will take place. If you feel this information is not critical to your case, you would not want the ruling invalidated because of an irrelevant change in plans. In your ruling request you can make a statement as to what you feel are the "controlling facts." That is, you feel these controlling facts alone should determine the tax outcome. In their ruling, the IRS can then agree with your list of controlling facts or they can make their own list. Any change in facts or circumstances not on the list of controlling facts would then not invalidate the ruling.

Rulings Made Public

The IRS is required to make public all private letter rulings which it issues. Before making a ruling public, the IRS deletes the name of the taxpayer as well as any identifying details or confidential information.

If there is any confidential information which you do not want revealed, you should send a statement to this effect along with your original ruling request. Attached to the statement should be a copy of your ruling request with the material you wish to be kept private indicated by brackets. If there is no information you wish kept confidential, you must attach a separate statement to your ruling request which states that no information needs to be deleted other than your name, address, and social security number.

The release of IRS rulings is of great assistance to the taxpaying public. At one time, the only information that was made public was contained in rulings which the IRS chose to issue and in reports of cases which wound up in court. Now, it is possible to find out the IRS position on any question about which some taxpayer was concerned enough to request a ruling.

Future editions of this Tax Guide will contain reports of all pertinent rulings issued in the future. This provides new information on many issues for which there is currently no clear guidance.

Rulings on Completed Transactions

In addition to obtaining a ruling on future transactions, you can also obtain a ruling on completed transactions if you wish. If the issue concerns clearly established rules, such a request is directed to your local IRS District Director. He will issue a judgment called a determination letter. If the issue involved is novel, the ruling request should go to the address in Washington, D.C. given earlier. If the ruling request is misdirected to either Washington, D.C. or your local District Director, it will be forwarded to the appropriate office.

Ordinarily, it is not recommended that you seek a ruling on a completed transaction. Nor is it advisable to seek a ruling concerning a future course of action which you are planning to take regardless of the tax consequences. In such cases, you are usually best advised just to treat the transaction in the most favorable manner you consider reasonable.

Can You Rely on Rulings?

If you request and receive a ruling concerning your own tax situation then you can safely rely on that ruling as long as the facts you have described are correct. The IRS won't change its mind in your case. However, you cannot absolutely rely on rulings issued to other people even if the circumstances are the same. That is, the IRS can treat two taxpayers in the same situation differently. However, they do attempt to maintain a consistent policy whenever possible. You must attach to your return a copy of any ruling you have received which is relevant to that return. The IRS wants to make sure that rulings are complied with.

Speedy Action

The IRS has a procedure for processing ruling requests in a speedy fashion. If the subject matter of the request falls into one of the categories set up for fast processing, then the taxpayer will generally be contacted within 3 weeks by an official of the IRS. This official will inform the taxpayer if he will recommend to the IRS that the ruling be approved or disapproved or whether any additional information is needed. If he is not recommending a fully favorable ruling, the official may suggest how the situation covered in the request can be altered so as to warrant a favorable ruling.

Chapter 19

Withholding

Withholding from Salary

Every employee is required to have a completed Form W-4 on file with his employer. This form is used by the employer in computing the amount of taxes to be withheld from the employee's paychecks. You need to fill out a new W-4 with your current employer only if you wish to change your withholding. You can probably best determine this after you fill out your tax return. A large refund indicates too much being withheld, while a large amount of tax due indicates that too little tax is being withheld. In such a case where your withholding is off the mark, you should file a new W-4 Form with your employer.

On Form W-4, allowances are claimed based on your dependents, deductions, adjustments to income, child care expenses, and the amount of non-wage income such as dividends and interest that you anticipate receiving. There are 2 components to the form—a worksheet for computing the number of withholding allowances you are entitled to claim, and the shorter actual W-4 itself, which is what you file with your employer. You do not file the worksheet, but rather keep it for your own records.

There is also a separate section on the Form W-4 entitled *"Two Earner/Two-Job Worksheet."* This section is used if there are 2 separate incomes (either because an individual has 2 jobs or because a married couple each have jobs) and the total income exceeds a threshold amount—$25,000 for singles or $40,000 for married couples. Under this section, tables are provided which subtract allowances based on income level and marital status. If these allowances are not subtracted, then too little will probably be withheld.

Married couples should use only one worksheet based on their combined exemptions, deductions, etc. The total number of allowances computed on this worksheet is then divided between the husband and wife who file individual W-4 Forms with their respective employers. The IRS recommends that the higher-earning spouse claim all the withholding allowances on his W-4 Form, while the other spouse claims none. Married couples who choose a different allocation method will usually experience overwithholding.

Similarly, if you work for more than one employer during the year, you cannot claim the same allowance twice. You should use one worksheet on which you report all your income and allocate the allowances among the W-4's filed with each of your employers.

Individuals whose tax picture is expected to materially change are supposed to file a new withholding form with their employer. (As discussed below, a penalty can apply unless the total withholding plus estimated taxes paid during 1990 is at least either (i) 90% of the actual 1990 tax liability, or (ii) 100% of the 1989 tax liability.)

If you claim 10 or more withholding allowances, your employer is required to report this fact to the IRS. In such a case, the IRS may write you, asking for your computation of the allowances to which you claim you're entitled.

Check out your state tax situation also. Some states have not revised their tax structure in line with Federal tax reform. This means that your withholding might come out right for your Federal tax return, but be too high for your state tax return. In such a case, you should adjust your state withholding allowances separately from your Federal withholding allowances.

Students with summer jobs may be able to avoid any withholding on their wages. Any student (or other individual) who owed no tax the previous year and expects to owe no tax for the current year qualifies. The exemption from withholding is claimed by writing *"exempt"* on the appropriate line of Form W-4. However, exempt status cannot be claimed by any person who (1) can be claimed as a dependent by a parent or someone else; (2) expects his total income to be more than $500; and (3) has some interest, dividends, or other nonwage income. A person satisfying all 3 of these conditions will generally owe income tax. For example, a dependent student who earns $1,500 on a summer job and has $400 in interest income would owe $60 tax. (However, he could *earn* up to $3,250 in wage income and be exempt from tax, as long as he had no *nonwage* income.)

George Bush Had Too Much Withheld

A good example of excessive withholding is provided by President Bush's 1988 tax return. He had over $65,000 withheld, but owed taxes for the year of only $32,778. This means his overwithholding came to over $32,000. This patriotic assist toward solving the nation's cash flow problem cost George Bush over $2,500 in interest he could have earned had his withholding been more accurate.

IRS Says You Can Disregard W-4 Worksheet

In keeping the W-4 down to only 2 pages (at one time it ran 4 pages), the IRS had to compromise some accuracy for the sake of simplicity. That is, for some persons (in particular, working couples and higher-income persons), withholding based on the new W-4 may still be off the mark—producing either too large a refund or too much tax due.

The IRS issued an unusual pronouncement about what you can do in such a case. Namely, you can choose to ignore the W-4 worksheet section altogether and make your own computation, as long as it more accurately reflects the amount of tax due. [IRS Notice 98-42, IRB 1988-15]

Thus, the IRS has thrown in the towel on trying to come up with a reasonable

W-4 Form that gives an accurate estimate of the amount of tax due in all circumstances. The current tax law is just too complicated to make it possible. The approach of adjusting your withholding up or down depending upon your tax refund or amount due may well be the most workable approach for many people.

Backup Withholding on Interest and Dividends

If you fail to furnish a correct social security number to a bank, savings & loan, stock broker, or other financial institution, this could subject you to backup withholding. This backup withholding consists of 20% of the interest, dividends, etc. paid to you. Upon your furnishing of a correct social security account number, the withholding ceases. This is not a penalty, just extra withholding. You get credit for this withholding when you file your tax return, the same as for amounts withheld from your paychecks.

Estimated Tax Payments

If you have taxable income which is not subject to withholding, then you may be required to make quarterly estimated tax payments throughout the year. Generally, you are required to prepay (through withholding and/or estimated tax payments) the lesser of

(i) 90% of your total tax liability for the year

or

(ii) 100% of the tax shown on the preceding year's tax return.

If salary withholding equals either (i) or (ii), then no estimated tax payments are required. Also, no estimated tax payments are required if the total amounts due for the year are $500 or less.

You don't have to verify on your tax return that you have paid the appropriate amount of estimated tax; the IRS computers will check this automatically. If you have not, you will be sent a bill for amount of penalty due.

Your estimated tax is paid in four installments, the first one being due April 15. You use Form 1040-ES to make your estimated tax payments. This form contains a worksheet for computing the amount due plus four vouchers which you send in with your payments. You do not send in your computation worksheet — only the vouchers indicating the amounts you are paying.

There is an exception which applies if your income is irregular, with more being earned toward the end of the year than toward the beginning. You will escape penalty if your estimated taxes at each quarterly payment date meet the 90% test for your income through the end of the corresponding quarter—i.e. your estimated taxes are computed as though your income would continue to be earned at the same rate for the rest of the year. To use this exception, you file Form 2210 with your tax return for the year. The IRS can also waive the penalty for an underpayment due to an unexpected calamity such as loss of records in a fire or serious illness.

If your 1990 tax return shows a refund due, you can indicate on the tax form to have part or all of this refund treated as an estimated tax payment made on April 15, 1991, rather than being paid out to you.

There is a penalty for underpayment of estimated tax. This penalty is adjusted periodically, based on the prime interest rate. This penalty is not deductible.

Don't overlook the following remedy if you discover towards the end of the year that you did not make sufficient estimated tax payments. You can request your employer to withhold extra amounts from your yearend paychecks. Form W-4 is used to make this request. This enables you to move the total prepayment (withholding plus estimated tax) towards the required amount. Under IRS regulations, your employer is *required* to honor your request. He must withhold any extra amounts you request after being given reasonable advance notice to make the adjustment. [Reg. section 31.3402(1)-2]

Having extra amounts withheld from your yearend paychecks is better than making an extra estimated tax payment near yearend. Your estimated tax payments are generally supposed to be made evenly throughout the year. Even if the total is sufficient to cover your liability, you could be penalized because the early payments were less than the later payments.

But withholding can be considered spread out evenly no matter when it occurs. This means that amounts withheld late in the year are treated exactly the same as if they were withheld earlier. There is no penalty unless the total for the year is insufficient.

Withholding on Pension and Annuity Payments

Under current law, income tax will be withheld on payments from pension plans, annuities, IRAs and Keogh plans. However, any individual can exempt himself from this withholding (for any reason) by filing an appropriate form with the payer. Payers are required to notify you in advance of your right to elect out of the withholding rules. In any event, even if no election is made, nothing will be withheld from payments which do not exceed a certain minimum amount.

Chapter 20

Divorce and Separation

Filing Status

Your marital status on December 31 determines the type of tax return you can file for the year. If, on December 31, you are married and not legally separated under a decree of divorce or separate maintenance, then you may file a joint return. If you are divorced or legally separated, then you may not file a joint return. Instead, you file as a single person. In this case, you may use the lower head-of-household rate if you meet the usual requirements for using this special rate.

A separated couple must have a legal separation under a court decree in order to file as single persons. An informal separation, even under a written agreement, does not count with the following exception:

Exception

Even if you are not divorced or legally separated, you may file as a single person (including as a head-of-household) if you meet **all** of the following tests:

(1) You do not file a joint return,

(2) You paid more than half the cost to keep up your home for the year,

(3) Your spouse did not live in your home at any time during the last 6 months of the year,

and

(4) For over six months of the year, your home was the principal residence of your child or stepchild whom you are entitled to claim as a dependent (or would be entitled except that you relinquished the exemption to your spouse on Form 8332 as described later in this chapter).

Note that the above tests apply to your tax return only. Your spouse must also meet the above tests in order to file as a single person. Otherwise, he or she must file using the high rates for married individuals filing separately. Of course, you both could file a joint return together if that is preferable, provided you are not divorced or legally separated on December 31.

318

A couple might be better off taxwise if a joint return is used, especially if only one of them has a significant amount of income. Or, they might be better off filing as single persons. In accord with the above tax rules, this consideration may play a role in deciding whether to turn a separation agreement into a legal separation.

Alimony

When a married couple is separated or divorced, one of them may make "alimony" payments to the other. If these payments are made on an informal basis, then there is no tax consequence. The payer does not claim the payments as a tax deduction nor does the recipient treat the payments as taxable income. However, if all of the following conditions are met, then the alimony payments are deducted by the payer and reported as income to the recipient. (This often reduces the total tax bill since the payer is usually in a higher tax bracket than the recipient.)

Conditions Under Which Alimony Is Deducted by Payer and Reported as Income by Recipient

Pre-1985 Rules

Divorce or separation agreements executed prior to 1985 must satisfy the following rules in order for alimony to be deductible:

(1) Payments are required by an official agreement. This agreement could be part of a divorce, legal separation, or other court decree, or it could simply be a written agreement between the two parties without any court proceedings.

(2) The couple lives separately.

(3) The payments are periodic. They could be fixed monthly amounts, a percentage of annual income, etc. There are several additional requirements that need to be checked out to make sure this periodic condition is satisfied.

and

(4) The payments are for the general support of the recipient. Amounts designated specifically for child support do not qualify. Neither do payments to settle loans or other obligations.

Post-1984 Rules

Divorce or separation agreements executed after 1984 must satisfy the following rules in order for alimony to be deductible:

(1) Alimony payments must be required by an official agreement. This agreement could be part of a divorce, legal separation, or other court decree. Or, it could simply be a written agreement between the two parties without any court proceedings.

(2) Alimony payments must be made in cash, check, or money order and there must be no liability to make payments after the death of the recipient spouse. Payments made to a third party on behalf of the spouse (e.g. tuition, medical expenses, etc.) can count as alimony if they are made under the terms of the divorce or separation instrument. However, an individual cannot count payments he makes to maintain property he owns (e.g. mortgage payments, taxes, insurance) even if such payments are made pursuant to the terms of the divorce or separation instrument.

(3) Alimony payments cannot be scheduled to decrease upon a child marrying, leaving school, moving out of the house, getting a job, or similar contingency. For example, if the agreement provides for payments of $800 per month, decreasing to $600 after a child marries, only $600 per month will be considered alimony. The remaining $200 per month will be considered nondeductible child support. Similarly, payments cannot be scheduled to decrease upon a child reaching age 18, 21, or local age of majority (give or take 6 months).

Amounts designated specifically for child support do not qualify as alimony. According to a recent court case, if the full amounts specified in a court decree are not paid, an allocation is made first to child support. For example, suppose you are required to pay $2,000 in child support and $3,000 in alimony for the year, but only pay a total of $2,500. In such a case, $2,000 of the $2,500 would be child support and $500 alimony. This is the case even if you and your spouse were to agree to the lower amount as a reduction in child support, without a modification in the court decree. [Blair, TC Memo 1988-581]

(4) Alimony payments for the first 3 years must not be excessively *front-loaded*. The exact requirement is rather complicated to state. However, in all cases, if alimony payments do not decrease by more than $10,000 from either of the first 2 years to the next, this requirement will be satisfied. Also, for agreements executed in 1985 or 1986 only, alimony payments must generally continue for at least 6 years unless all payments are less than $10,000. However, this 6-year requirement ceases to apply upon the death of either spouse or the remarriage of the recipient spouse.

This rule (4) applies to payments made under a divorce decree or separation decree or agreement. It does not apply to payments made under only a temporary support decree. The purpose of this rule is to discourage property settlements which typically have a large initial payment from being treated as alimony.

(5) Once a divorce or separation decree is entered, the spouses cannot live in the same dwelling. Payments made while living in the same dwelling after a decree is entered do not qualify as alimony, except for a 1-month grace period allowed for the spouses to separate. This restriction does not apply to payments made under a written separation agreement, rather than a divorce or separate maintenance decree.

If payments satisfy the above rules, they can be deducted by the payer and become taxable income to the recipient. However, the spouses may designate that payments otherwise qualifying as alimony shall be nondeductible by the payer and nontaxable to the recipient by so providing in a divorce or separation instrument. An existing instrument can be legally amended to make this provision. The recipient should attach a copy of such a designation to the tax return for each year to which the designation applies.

Alimony Can Be Claimed Even If You Use the Standard Deduction

Alimony payments are claimed as an *adjustment to income* on line 29, Form 1040, rather than as an itemized deduction. This means that you can deduct alimony payments whether you claim the standard deduction or itemize your deductions.

Reporting Requirements

There is a special reporting requirement that applies. If you deduct alimony payments on your tax return, you are required to list the recipient's social security number on your return. The IRS can use this to crosscheck that the recipient reports these amounts as taxable income. This reporting requirement applies to all alimony payments, even if made under divorce or separation agreements executed before 1985.

IRA Deduction Based on Alimony Payments

Contributions to an IRA for 1990 can be based on alimony income. Individuals may be able to contribute up to $2,000 of alimony income to an IRA and deduct this amount on their 1990 tax returns [cf. Section 2 of the *Tax-Sheltered Plans* chapter].

Dependency Exemptions

When separate returns are filed, it must be determined which parent is entitled to claim a child as a dependent. The current rule is that the parent (called the *custodial spouse*) having custody of a child for the greater portion of the year is entitled to the dependency exemption. (This assumes that the parents together would have been entitled to the dependency exemption had they been married and filing a joint return.) It makes no difference that the other parent may have furnished most or all of the funds for support of the child.

However, the custodial spouse may release the right to a dependency exemption, in which case the non-custodial spouse can claim the exemption. This release is made by the custodial spouse on Form 8332 which the non-custodial spouse attaches to his return. The exemption may be released for a single year, for a number of specified years (for example, alternate years), or permanently. A copy of the release form must be attached to the tax return of the non-custodial spouse each year he claims the exemption.

Exception: The non-custodial spouse is entitled to the dependency exemption if so specified under a decree or written agreement executed before 1985. In such a case, no release form is needed. This exception only applies if the noncustodial spouse furnishes at least $600 towards the support of the child.

According to a 1986 IRS ruling, the pre-1985 agreement must **explicitly** assign the dependency exemption to the non-custodial spouse. In this ruling, a man was ordered to pay $300 per month child support in a 1973 divorce agreement. Since the divorce, he had been providing more than half the support of his 3 children and had been claiming dependency exemptions for them. However, even though he had been entitled to the dependency exemptions under the law existing at the time, the divorce agreement did not explicitly specify that he was entitled to the dependency exemptions. Thus, under the new law starting with 1985, since the children lived with their mother, she was now entitled to the dependency exemptions. This could not even be changed by amending the language of the old divorce agreement. The only way he could now claim the exemptions would be for her to release her claim on Form 8332 which he would attach to his tax return each year he claimed the exemptions. [IRS Private Letter Ruling 8609034]

Altering Old Agreements

You may have a divorce or separation agreement with an ex-spouse that results in a total tax bill which is higher than necessary. This is especially true because of the changes in the law governing divorce and alimony. If so, you should seek legal advice to straighten matters out. In many cases, you can amend a pre-1985 divorce or separation agreement so that it comes under the new rules, should that be advantageous. Sometimes, only a wording change will suffice, with no change in the underlying specifics of the agreement.

Medical Expenses

Either spouse may claim medical expenses which he actually pays for his child. It makes no difference that the other spouse may be claiming the dependency exemption. This assumes that the child receives over half of his total support from his parents.

Because of the 7.5% of income floor on deductible medical expenses [cf. the *Medical Expenses* chapter], divorced spouses should take care who actually pays the medical bills for a child. For example, suppose the ex-wife earned $20,000 and the ex-husband $50,000. For simplicity, let's say their child ran up a $3,000 bill at the orthodontist and that there are no other medical expenses involved. If the ex-husband paid the bill directly, there is no deduction because his medical expenses floor, $7.5\% \times \$50,000 = \$3,750$, exceeds the $3,000 expense. But the ex-wife's medical expense floor is $7.5\% \times \$20,000 = \$1,500$. If he gave his ex-wife $3,000 and let her pay the bill, she gets a deduction of $\$3,000 - \$1,500 = \$1,500$ while he has lost nothing in the transaction.

Property Transfer

A house or other property such as stocks or bonds may be transferred from one spouse to another as part of a divorce settlement. At one time, the IRS could treat such a transfer as a sale subject to capital gains tax. For example, a husband who transferred a house worth $85,000, but which he purchased for $45,000, to a spouse was liable for capital gains tax on the $40,000 increase in value.

But now, divorce-related property settlements no longer trigger a capital gains tax at the time of transfer. However, the spouse who receives the property must treat it as acquired at the original purchase price. When sold, the difference between the sale price and original purchase price will be subject to capital gains tax. In the example in the preceding paragraph, if the wife were to sell the house for $95,000 in a later year, she would have a capital gain of $50,000. This $50,000 profit would be subject to capital gains tax, unless the usual exemption for purchasing a new house of greater value or the exemption for those over 55 applies [cf. the *Homeowner's* chapter].

Legal Fees

The legal fees involved in obtaining a divorce are not generally deductible. However, the portion of such fees which covered tax advice to the individual can be deducted. Also, a spouse may deduct legal costs associated with obtaining or collecting taxable alimony. In any divorce or separation proceeding, your lawyer should provide an itemization which indicates any portion of his fee that is deductible.

Chapter 21

Travel

Section 1:
Basic Rules on Deducting Travel Expenses

You can deduct the cost of travel connected with your job or other income-producing activity. This includes travel between two or more job locations the same day, travel to professional or union meetings, travel related to a temporary job away from home, travel to obtain education, travel in connection with an outside business activity, etc. An exception is ordinary commuting expenses which cannot be deducted except as discussed in Sections 2-4.

There are special rules which apply to various types of deductible travel. These are discussed in later sections. The remainder of this introductory section concerns those general rules which apply to all types of travel.

Where on the Income Tax Form Do You Claim Travel Expenses?

An employee reports his job-related travel expenses on Form 2106, *Employee Business Expenses.* The total of such expenses is then transferred to Schedule A as a *miscellaneous deduction.* As discussed in the *Miscellaneous Deductions* chapter, this total of travel expenses plus other miscellaneous deductions is subjected to a 2% of Adjusted Gross Income floor.

Self-employed persons claim travel expenses on Schedule C, the same as any other business expense related to their self-employment activity. Thus, these expenses escape the 2% of Adjusted Gross Income floor that applies to miscellaneous deductions; also, non-itemizers as well as itemizers get to deduct their travel expenses.

An employee with an outside business activity should take note of the more favorable treatment accorded self-employed persons when deciding how to treat his travel expenses. For example, suppose a college professor incurs unreimbursed travel expenses in attending a convention in his field of expertise. If the professor has self-employment income from consulting or writing, then he may have a choice. Instead of treating travel expenses as a miscellaneous deduction connected with his college duties, he may be able to treat these expenses as a Schedule C writeoff connected with his self-employment activity. [Cf. Section 1 of the *Miscellaneous Deductions* chapter for further discussion.]

Which Expenses Are Deductible?

The first point to note is the distinction between travel and transportation expenses. Transportation refers to the task of getting from one place to another. But travel expenses may include, in addition to transportation expenses, certain living costs.

Let's assume that your travel meets the requirements for deductibility. Then if you are **away from home overnight,** the following are deductible travel expenses:

- Air, rail, or bus fares both en route and at your destination
- Lodging both en route and at your destination
- Meals both en route and at your destination (subject to the 80%-Rule discussed later in this section)
- Transportation costs to and from your destination
- Baggage charges
- Reasonable cleaning and laundry expenses
- Transportation between the airport and your hotel
- Transportation between where you obtain meals and lodging and a temporary work assignment
- Telephone and fax expenses (non-personal)
- Reasonable tips connected with the above expenses

If, on the other hand, you are not away from home overnight, then only your transportation costs are deductible. You cannot deduct the cost of meals, lodging, or laundry. For example, if you drove from Washington, D.C. to New York and back all in one day, you would not be permitted any deduction for meals. Several courts felt this rule was unreasonable until the Supreme Court upheld it as a fair and workable administrative approach.

A special limitation applies to travel by ocean liner or other water transportation. The deduction for such travel cannot exceed twice the highest per diem travel amount allowable to employees of the executive branch of the U.S. government. The cost of meals and entertainment is included in this limitation. However, this limitation does not apply to conventions, seminars, or other meetings held on a cruise ship.

What Does "Away From Home" Mean?

"Home" has a special meaning to the IRS. It means the general area of your principal place of employment, regardless of where you maintain your family residence. For example, if your family residence is in Chicago but you work in Milwaukee, then your *"tax home"* is the Milwaukee area. If you stay overnight in Milwaukee, then you are not considered to be away from home overnight. Of course, you probably live and work in the same general area. Then this general area is considered to be your tax home.

Exactly how much territory the "general area" includes is not well specified. Distinct cities at a distance of 50 miles apart would probably be considered in different areas. However, two points in the same metropolitan area would be considered in the same general area, even if those points were considerably far apart. [Harris, TC Memo 1980-56]

What About Commuting Costs?

In general, the cost of commuting between your residence and your work is not deductible. However, there are two exceptions relating to temporary assignments away from your home.

(1) If you are on a business trip out of town or if you are on a temporary assignment out of town, you may deduct all your transportation costs between your temporary lodgings and your business destination. You may also deduct all transportation costs from one business destination to another.

(2) If you are required to work at a temporary location outside the general area of your home city, you may deduct transportation expenses for daily round trips from your home to the temporary business location. For example, if your home is in Baltimore and you are required to work in Washington, D.C. for a month, then you can deduct your commuting expenses.

See Sections 2-4 for further details.

80%-Rule for Meal Expenses

Meal expenses are no longer deductible in full. Instead, only 80% of meal (and beverage) expenses can be deducted. All expenses of the meal such as tax, tips, parking, etc. are included under this 80%-Rule. However, transportation to and from a meal is not subject to the reduction.

Example 1

While attending an out-of-town professional meeting, you incur the following unreimbursed expenses for dinner: $40 for meals and beverages, $3 for tax, $1 for coat check, and $6 for tip—a total of $50. The cost of taxi fare (including tip) to and from the restaurant is $7.

The $50 total is subject to the 80%-Rule, but not the taxi fare. Thus, the meal yields a deduction of 80% × $50 = $40 plus the entire $7 taxi fare—a total of $47.

The 80%-Rule is used before application of the 2% of Adjusted Gross Income floor that applies to the total of miscellaneous deductions [cf. the *Miscellaneous Deductions* chapter]. This is illustrated by the following example:

Example 2

An individual's Adjusted Gross Income is $50,000 and his miscellaneous deductions other than travel expenses total $700. In addition, he incurs the following unreimbursed deductible travel expenses during the year:

Transportation:	*$620*
Lodging:	*300*
Laundry:	*50*
	$970
Meals:	*$200*

In computing his travel expenses, he first applies the 80%-Rule to the meal expenses: 80% × $200 = $160. Thus, the total deductible travel expenses come to $970 + $160 = $1,130. His total of all miscellaneous deductions is then $700 + $1,130 = $1,830. However, this is reduced by 2% of Adjusted Gross Income: 2% × $50,000 = $1,000. This produces a net deduction of $1,830 – $1,000 = $830.

The above 2 examples illustrate the principles involved in deducting meal expenses, combined with travel and other job-related expenses. In practice, Form 2106 separates these expenses into 2 columns, Column B for meal and entertainment expenses and Column A for other employee business expenses. At the bottom of the form, the total deduction for employee business expenses is obtained by adding the final Column A total plus 80% of the Column B total. In the body of the form, untaxed reimbursements received from your employer are credited against either Column A or Column B expenses and subtracted from the total *expenses* accordingly. Further details, including examples on how to handle expenses on Form 2106, are contained in Section 1 of the *Miscellaneous Deductions* chapter.

Expenses of Spouse or Other Family Member

When you travel for professional reasons and are accompanied by your spouse or other family members, their expenses are not deductible unless it can be definitely established that their travel has a bona fide business purpose. The performance of incidental services does not satisfy this business purpose requirement. However, if your spouse accompanies you on a business trip, you do not have to split your expenses down the middle. Instead, you can deduct what it would have cost had you traveled alone. For example, if you and your spouse occupy a double room at a hotel which charges $65 for a single room and $80 for a double room, then you may deduct $65 as your lodging cost.

Recordkeeping

You should keep two kinds of records of your travel expenses–receipts and an expense diary. You do not include these records with the tax return you file. Rather, they are kept in case your return is audited.

Expense Diary

Your diary should contain the following:

1. The place or places of your travel

2. The dates of your departure and return home

3. The business reason for your travel

4. A daily list of your deductible expenses

You should list the amount of each separate expenditure (such as the cost of your transportation or lodging). However, each day the cost of your breakfast, lunch, dinner, and other expenses may be grouped together if they are set forth in reasonable categories such as meals, gasoline and oil, cab fares, telephone calls, etc. Tips may be grouped with the cost of the connected service.

You are not required to record amounts your employer pays directly for any ticket or other travel item. However, if you charge these items to your employer (through a credit card or otherwise), then you must make a record of the expenditures.

A receipt, paid bill, or similar evidence is required to support any expenditure of $25 or more and any expenditure for lodging, even if less than $25. The receipt should show the amount, date, place, and type of expenditure and should be sufficiently detailed to show the different elements of the expenditure. For example, a hotel bill should show as separate items, the cost for lodging, telephone calls, meals, etc. A cancelled check together with an appropriate bill will be sufficient. However, a cancelled check alone is inadequate.

If you cannot establish the portion of an expenditure attributable to each person participating in the travel but you have established the amount of the expenditure, it will ordinarily be allocated to each participant on a pro rata basis.

Your records should be timely. You should write down your expenses in your expense diary at or near the time they are incurred. If the record entries are made later when there is a lack of accurate recall, they will not comply with this rule.

The following is a sample of how a diary should look for attending a 2-day professional convention. The format is copied from an official IRS publication.

Date	Item	Place	Amount	Business Purpose
April 1	Airplane fare (round trip Chicago-Dallas)	Dallas	$260.20	Attend Convention of XYZ Assn.
	Meals and tips		35.10	
	Lodging		62.50	
April 2	Meals and tips		28.50	
	Automobile Rental (2 days)		62.00	
	Tips		3.50	

Remark: Pay careful attention to the recordkeeping requirements as illustrated in the above example. Note the **5 different pieces of information required – date, item, place, amount, and business purpose.** If you leave any of these pieces out, your travel expenses could be ruled nondeductible. That's what happened to the taxpayer in the following court case.

Example 3

Mr. Coursey was a manufacturer's representative and traveled extensively for his job. He kept a diary and produced cancelled checks for his lodging expenses. But his expenses were ruled nondeductible because his diaries were not adequate. They did not show the location or the business purpose of his away from home business expenses. Even though the cancelled checks might have established the location of his lodging expenses, the Court said that still would not be good enough. Coursey had presented no evidence indicating the business purpose of his trips. Coursey's failure to write down a few extra words in his diary turned out to be a very expensive mistake. [TC Memo 1974-43]

The substantiation rules are not so strict for local travel as for travel away from home. In particular, the keeping of a contemporaneous diary would not be mandatory if the traveling is done on a regular basis. This would be the case, say, when someone regularly travels between business locations or commutes to a temporary job. This is illustrated in Example 4 of Section. 2

Reimbursed Expenses

You may receive a reimbursement from your employer for travel expenses which you incur. Usually, you are required to give an expense accounting to your employer. If this accounting satisfies the recordkeeping requirements described above, then you do not have to provide any further accounting to the IRS. They will check your employer's records if they wish to see verification of these expenses. If you did not make an adequate accounting to your employer for reimbursed travel expenses or if your expenses exceeded the reimbursement, then you must retain your expense diary and receipts yourself. [Cf. Section 1 of the *Miscellaneous Deductions* chapter for information on how reimbursed expenses are handled on your tax return.]

Your employer may reimburse you on a per diem basis for your combined meals, lodging, and incidental expenses while away from home overnight. If this rate does not exceed $122 for high cost-of-living areas or $85 for other areas, then this will be accepted by the IRS provided the other elements of time, place, and business purpose of the travel are substantiated to the employer. *Incidental Expenses* includes such things as laundry, cleaning and pressing of clothing, and tips for services, such as for waiters and porters. It does not include transportation, taxi fares, or the cost of telephone calls or fax services.

The $122 and $85 per diem rates only apply if you are reimbursed by your employer. If you pay expenses out of your pocket, you cannot use these per diem rates to determine your deduction.

The following is a list of the high cost-of-living areas in the continental U.S. The areas include not just the cities themselves, but also the surrounding metropolitan counties. (For areas outside the continental U.S. and for certain very high cost cities such as New York, the allowable per diem rate is the one used by Federal employees when they travel.)

High Cost-of-Living Areas

California:	Death Valley, Los Angeles, Palm Springs, San Francisco, Santa Barbara
Colorado:	Aspen, Vail
D.C.:	Washington
Georgia:	Atlanta
Illinois:	Chicago
Maryland:	Annapolis, Columbia, Ocean City, Washington Suburbs
Massachusetts:	Andover, Boston, Martha's Vineyard/Nantucket, Plymouth
New Hampshire:	Conway
New Jersey:	Atlantic City, Newark, Ocean City/Cape May, Princeton/Trenton
New York:	New York City, White Plains
Pennsylvania:	Philadelphia
Rhode Island:	Newport
South Carolina:	Hilton Head
Texas:	Dallas/Fort Worth
Virginia:	Washington Suburbs

Your employer might provide you with a per diem rate only for the cost of your meals and incidental expenses. The limit in this case is $34 for high cost meal areas and $26 for other areas. The list of high cost meal areas is somewhat different from the above list of high cost-of-living areas. The high cost meal areas are contained in a table listed later in this Section.

Suppose your employer reimburses you at a rate within the above guidelines and that you provide him with substantiation as to time, place, and business purpose. In this case, there is nothing more for you to do. Your employer should not include such reimbursements in taxable income on your yearend W-2 Form and you do not claim any deduction on your tax return. If your expenses were less than the reimbursement, you wind up with a "profit" of the difference which is not subjected to any tax.

If you receive a per diem rate that is higher than the amount specified by the IRS, then your employer will include the excess in taxable income on your yearend W-2 Form. Note that this applies only to *per diems*. If your employer reimburses you for your *actual* expenses, then there is no taxable income as long as your provide adequate substantiation to your employer.

If your out-of-pocket expenses exceed the reimbursement, then you can claim the difference as a miscellaneous deduction. This is done by listing your total expenses on Form 2106 and then subtracting the amount of the reimbursement as directed on that Form. For a more thorough discussion on handling reimbursed expenses, see Section 1 of the *Miscellaneous* chapter. Also included there is an explanation of the proper use of Form 2106.

There is also a standard reimbursement rate for automobile travel. The IRS will accept a standard reimbursement rate of up to 26 cents per mile for business-related travel. Provided you have made adequate substantiation to your employer, he should not include the reimbursement in taxable income reported on your yearend W-2 Form and you claim no deduction. Section 1 of the *Miscellaneous* chapter contains a more thorough discussion on how to handle reimbursed expenses in more complicated situations.

Under a new 1990 IRS ruling, an employer can sometimes reimburse an employee at a higher tax-free rate than 26 cents per mile. This is done by making estimates of depreciation and operating costs actually incurred. However, the reimbursement must cover at least 5,000 business miles driven by the given employee and satisfy some other requirements. [Rev. Proc. 90-34]

Excess Reimbursement

You may receive a reimbursement from your employer based on a per diem rate in excess of the one's described above. A recent IRS ruling addresses what is to be done in such circumstances. You are not required to return the excess reimbursement. Rather, your employer will report the excess reimbursement as taxable income, included on the "wages" line on your yearend W-2 Form. As such, it will be subjected to income tax and social security withholding.

> **Example 4**
>
> You take a 4-day business trip to Chicago. Instead of keeping track of your meals, lodging, and incidental expenses, you rely upon a $140 per diem reimbursement from your employer.
>
> The $140 per diem exceeds the IRS-approved per diem of $122 by $18, or $72 for the 4-day period. You do not have to return this excess $72 to your employer. Rather, your employer will include this $72 in taxable income by including it in the amount reported as "wages" on your yearend W-2 Form. As such, it will be subjected to income tax and social security withholding. The remaining amount, $122 x 4 = $488, will be included in the non-taxable "Employee information" box on your W-2 Form.

In the above example, no return of the excess reimbursement was required. However, the situation would have been different if you received an advance reimbursement based on an anticipated stay of more than 4 days. In this case, you would be required to return the $140 reimbursement for each day you did not actually stay.

A similar situation applies to the 26 cents per mile reimbursement for auto travel. Reimbursements based on a mileage rate of more than 26 cents do not have to be returned to the employer, but an advance based on mileage not actually traveled do have to be returned.

> **Example 5**
>
> You drive to New York for business purposes, traveling a total round trip distance of 200 miles. Prior to the trip, you received an advance based on an estimated 250 miles at a per mile rate of 30 cents per mile. You must return to your employer the re-

imbursement for the 50 miles not traveled, 50 × $.30 = $15.

For the remaining 200 miles, you received an excess reimbursement of 30 cents - 26 cents = 4 cents per mile, or 200 × .04 = $8. Your employer will include this $8 in taxable income by including it in the amount reported as "wages" on your yearend W-2 Form. The remaining amount, 200 × .26 = $52, will be included in the non-taxable "Employee information" box on your W-2 Form.

Returning Excess Reimbursements

As discussed above, there are circumstances when you must return part of a reimbursement in excess of the amounts allowed by the IRS. This happens when you received per diem travel expenses for days you did not actually travel or a mileage allowance for miles you did not actually drive.

The return of these amounts to your employer must be made in a timely matter. Generally, this means the payment should be made no later than 120 days after your travel expenses were incurred.

If you do not satisfy the requirements for handling reimbursements, the result could be serious. Your employer would be required to include all reimbursements connected with the travel in taxable income on your yearend W-2 Form. You would then have to claim a deduction for these items on Form 2106. If you claim the standard deduction or your other miscellaneous deductions do not exceed the 2% of adjusted gross income floor, this will cost you money. [Cf. Section 1 of the *Miscellaneous* chapter for further information.]

What If You Didn't Apply for Reimbursement?

One of the basic rules of tax policy is that an employee cannot deduct job-related expenses he paid if he could have received a reimbursement from his employer for these expenses. It makes no difference if the employee failed to put in a claim for these expenses. As long as he was entitled to a reimbursement, he cannot claim a deduction on his personal tax return.

With regard to this issue, the IRS pays particular attention to job-related travel expenses. Such expenses are often reimbursed by employers. If there is any reason to believe that an individual could have received a reimbursement, he might be required to provide evidence that he was ineligible to be reimbursed for travel expenses. Otherwise, his deduction might be disallowed.

For this reason, it sometimes pays to file a request with your employer for reimbursement, even if you're convinced the request will be denied. This is particularly true if you have received reimbursement in the past for similar expenses. The difficulty of deducting expenses when there is an indication of possible reimbursability is illustrated by several recent court cases.

In one case, an ROTC teacher at a midwestern college made various trips connected with his employment, many of them to attend enclaves and other activities as faculty advisor to a campus student group. When he claimed a deduction for travel expenses not covered by a reimbursement, the IRS objected. He had made similar trips the prior year for which he received a reimbursement from the college. But for the year in question, he offered no explanation as to why he received no reimbursement. Whether or not he actually received a reimbursement was not the issue. The Court disallowed the deduction because no evidence was presented that the expenses would not have been reimbursed by the college if asked. [Register, TC Memo 1988-390]

In a second case, an employee was entitled to reimbursement for job-related out-of-town travel but not for local travel. When he claimed a travel deduction on his tax return, the IRS objected. The employee's record book was not sufficiently detailed to determine which trips were out-of-town and which were local. Consequently, there was no way to tell to what extent the cost of these trips was eligible for reimbursement. For this reason, the Court ruled out any deduction whatever. [Primas, TC Memo 1988-352]

And in a third case, an engineer set up his own corporation which contracted with the U.S. Department of Energy to perform physical audits on energy conversion facilities. In performing these audits, he incurred $12,167 in travel expenses. Because the Department of Energy did not make advance payments, the engineer paid these expenses out of his own pocket. His corporation could not pay these expenses because it did not have any funds during the year. The Court ruled that the engineer was not entitled to a deduction. The travel expenses were an obligation of the corporation, not the engineer personally. In the Court's words, . . . *"it is clear that petitioner would have been reimbursed had there been available corporation funds. The fact that he was not reimbursed does not change the nature of the expenditures made on behalf of the corporation into ordinary and necessary expenses of petitioner."* [Thomas, TC Memo 1988-505]

What If You Are Missing Records or Receipts?

You are supposed to keep a contemporaneous diary and receipts, as described at the beginning of this section. But, legally speaking, this is not a strict necessity. You are entitled to offer other evidence in support of your deduction, as long as the 5 basic pieces of information (date, item, place, amount, and business purpose) are attested to. For example, the Congressional tax-writing committee specifically noted that *"testimony from a disinterested, unrelated party describing the taxpayer's activities, may be of sufficient probative value that it should not be automatically excluded from consideration."* It also noted that records created at a later date might have some value, but would have far less *"probative value"* than *"written evidence arising at or near the time of the expenditure."*

As a matter of fact, the courts have not been impressed with travel records in which entries were not made in a timely fashion. Four cases illustrate this situation. In the first case, a salesman presented a spiral notebook in which, he claimed, he had made entries on a day to day basis concerning his travel expenses. But the Court took a look at the notebook and promptly threw the case out. The pages were too clean and there was too little wear at the wire ring bindings for a notebook handled frequently. And the ink was suspiciously uniform in color and intensity. [79,002 PH Memo TC]

The second case centered upon the adequacy of a travel diary. In this case, the

Court was convinced that the diary was *"an accurate, contemporaneous record of the date and amounts of expenditures."* But, the Court stated, *"we believe that, in certain instances, the place and business purpose of petitioner's travel were recorded in later years. In such instances, petitioner's diary does not satisfy the adequate records requirement with respect to those elements."* Because of this inadequacy, about 60% of the claimed travel deduction was disallowed. [Benke, TC Memo 1979-195]

The third case illustrates the pitfall of recording suspiciously uniform numbers in the diary. An individual who traveled quite a bit on business presented a diary of his expenses, as required. But for each day he was away during the year, his diary listed meal expenses of exactly $20. The Court found *"it hard to believe that petitioner's expenses remained so perfectly consistent throughout that year."* The Court concluded that the diary simply represented an after-the-fact estimate of expenses rather than a contemporaneous diary of actual expenses incurred. Because of this, it disallowed his meal expenses altogether. [TC Memo 1979-432]

And the fourth case makes it clear that your diary should be handwritten, not typed. The only record which was presented to the court was a neatly-typed statement listing mileage, motel costs, and meal costs. This indicated the entries were not made in a timely fashion and no deduction was allowed. [Johnston, 51 AFTR 2d 83-313]

When some receipts are missing, the matter is not so serious. In the past, IRS agents have been known to disallow a deduction whenever a required receipt is missing. But in recent instructions to its agents, the IRS suggested going a bit easier on this requirement. According to these instructions,

> *"If a taxpayer cannot document precisely the amounts spent for expenses while away from home for a business purpose, examiners may establish that reasonable amounts were spent for such items if the taxpayer can clearly establish the following.*
>
> *(a) Time — Dates of departure and return for each trip away from home, and number of days away from home.*
>
> *(b) Place — Destinations or locality of travel, e.g. name of city or town.*
>
> *(c) Business Purpose — Business reason for travel or nature of business benefit derived or expected to be derived, and*
>
> *(d) Proof that Expenditures were Actually Incurred – A reasonable showing based upon secondary evidence, including oral testimony that out-of-pocket expenses were paid."* [Internal Revenue Manual, Section 4244]

However, despite the liberal wording of item (d), this should not be taken as a go-ahead to ignore the receipt-keeping requirement. IRS agents are only permitted, not required, to allow deductions without the required receipts. And this is only suggested when not too much is missing. If there is substantial disregard of the receipt-keeping rule, the IRS will probably disallow any deductions and perhaps even assess a negligence penalty in flagrant cases.

Standard Per Diem Meal Allowance

There is a standard per diem meal allowance you can use while traveling away from home. You have the option of using this per diem rate or keeping track of your actual expenses. This per diem rate only applies to the cost of meals, not to other travel expenses such as lodging, transportation, etc.

The standard per diem meal allowance is $34 per day in high cost meal areas and $26 per day in other areas. These $34 and $26 figures are the ones you use to compute your total meals-while-away-from-home expenses. After this total is listed on Form 2106, it is subjected to the 80%-reduction factor discussed earlier in this Section.

The $34 and $26 figures apply to 1989 and 1990 tax returns. In an unusual lapse of ordinary procedure, the IRS did not officially announce these figures until several months in 1990 had passed. Those who used lower per diems of $14 or $9 applying in prior years on their 1989 tax returns will have to file amended 1989 returns to take advantage of the higher rates.

The table below gives a list of the high cost meal areas. The areas include not just the cities listed, but also the surrounding metropolitan counties. (This list differs from the one given earlier in this Section of the high cost-of-living areas because not all places with high food costs have high overall living costs.)

High Meal Cost Areas

California:	Death Valley, Los Angeles, Oakland, Palm Springs, Sacramento, San Diego, San Francisco, San Jose, San Luis Obispo, San Mateo, Santa Barbara, Santa Cruz, South Lake Tahoe, Tahoe City, Yosemite
Colorado:	Aspen, Boulder, Denver, Keystone/Silverthorne, Vail
Connecticut:	Hartford, Salisbury
D.C.:	Washington
Florida:	Miami, West Palm Beach
Georgia:	Atlanta
Illinois:	Chicago
Louisiana:	New Orleans
Maryland:	Annapolis, Baltimore, Columbia, Ocean City, Washington Suburbs
Massachusetts:	Andover, Boston, Martha's Vineyard/Nantucket
Michigan:	Detroit
Nevada:	Las Vegas
New Jersey:	Atlantic City, Eatontown, Edison, Newark, Ocean City/Cape May, Princeton/Trenton
New Mexico:	Cloudcroft, Santa Fe
New York:	Monticello, New York City, Saratoga Springs, White Plains
Ohio:	Cleveland
Pennsylvania:	Chester, King of Prussia/Fort Washington, Philadelphia, Valley Forge
Rhode Island:	Newport
South Carolina:	Hilton Head
Texas:	Dallas/Fort Worth, Houston

Virginia: Williamsburg, Washington Suburbs
Washington: Seattle

(For some reason, there is no comparable per diem rate individuals can use for lodging or other expenses. The $122 and $85 per diem rates discussed earlier in the Section only apply to an employer who has a reimbursement plan for his employees. These amounts cannot be automatically claimed on the tax return of an employee or self-employed person.)

On the day that travel begins or ends, the allowance is prorated on the basis of 6-hour periods. For each 6-hour period or portion thereof, you are allowed ¹/₄ of the daily allowance. For example, if you start your trip at 5 a.m. you get the full daily allowance, but if you start at 7 a.m. you get only ³/₄ of the daily allowance for that day.

For a given year, you must either use the standard meal allowance for all travel during the year or else deduct your actual meal expenses throughout the year.

On days for which you receive a travel reimbursement from your employer which is designed to include meal expenses, you cannot use the standard meal allowance. However, such reimbursements do not prevent you from using the standard meal allowance on days for which you are not reimbursed. Also, if you receive a specific per diem meal reimbursement from your employer which falls short of the IRS allowance, you can deduct the difference between the IRS allowance and your employer's allowance. This only applies if the employer allowance is a straight per diem rate not based on an accounting of your actual expenses.

If you use the per diem rate, you still must substantiate the other basic elements for deductible travel – namely time, place, and business purpose. However, if you neglected to keep a diary, then the per diem amounts might be useful.

Example 6

You attended a 3-day professional convention at which you presented a paper. You did not create any diary of your expenses. However, you have receipts for your airplane ticket and your hotel bill. Technically, you have not met the precise recordkeeping requirements for deducting your travel expenses because you have no diary of your expenses. However, you have enough secondary evidence (see the preceding subsection) to establish the time, place and business purpose of your travel. Since you have no record of your meal expenses, you could use the standard allowance of $34 or $26 per day for meals if you wish.

The standard meal allowances are subjected to the same 80%-Rule, described earlier in this section, that applies to meal expenses in general. For example, suppose an individual travels away from home for 10 days, with the standard meal allowance yielding: 10 × $34 = $340. Under the 80%-Rule, the amount actually claimed as a miscellaneous deduction for these meals would be 80% × $340 = $272.

Foreign Travel

The $26 and $34 per diem rates do not apply to Alaska, Hawaii, or any locations outside the U.S. The standard allowance for these areas is 40% of the total Federal per diem rate (which includes lodging) paid government employees when traveling. In many foreign places, this can produce a very high figure. For example, the following would be the meal allowance in various high cost areas: Melbourne $77, Montreal $53, Paris $73, Berlin $65, Tokyo $80, Norway $73, Madrid $88, Stockholm $106, London $74. You should call the IRS to get the Federal per diem amount for a particular foreign location to which you're traveling. You then multiply this amount by 40% to get the per diem meal allowance you can use.

Miscellaneous Travel

The following sections describe special rules that apply to various types of job-related travel. However, don't overlook miscellaneous travel not covered by any of these specific situations. As long as the travel is a non-reimbursable "ordinary and necessary" expense connected with your job, it is deductible [cf. Chapter 1, Section 2].

This is emphasized by several recent court cases. The first concerned a teacher of the handicapped who deducted transportation costs for taking his students on trips to various activities in the community. He was not required to take the students on these trips but that did not matter. According to the Court,

> *"Although there is no proof that Mr. Gudmundsson was obligated by his employer to take the students on these trips, we know of no requirement that there must be an underlying legal obligation to make an expenditure before it can qualify as an 'ordinary and necessary' business expense. . . The arrangement of such activities for his students is in accord with what a teacher of the handicapped might do and the expenses incurred therein are clearly business expenses [and therefore deductible]."* [Gudmundsson, TC Memo 1978-299]

The second case concerned an assistant principal at a high school who was responsible for student discipline and attendance, computer scheduling and grading, student transportation, and other duties. He was expected, although not required, to attend job-related meetings and seminars and to serve on school and civic committees.

During the year, he attended many meetings at different locations at which he discussed the problems which his school and other schools in the county were experiencing. The IRS and the Court both agreed that he was entitled to deduct his transportation costs in attending these meetings. The Court allowed him a $600 deduction, indicating it would have been higher had his recordkeeping been better. [Wilhelm, TC Memo 1978-327]

And a third case involved a Professor of Management and Marketing at a university in the South. During the course of a year, he made about 100 trips by automobile in connection with his professional duties. These included 31 trips to a library 100 miles away which had extensive materials not available in his home town, 44 trips in connection with seminars he ran at a local hotel, 13 trips to the airport to pick up visiting speakers, 2 trips to attend a Board of Regents meeting, and 8 trips to conduct surveys on grocery prices. The Court ruled that all of these trips could be deducted. His total deduction for auto travel during the year amounted to $1,939. [Stearns, TC Memo 1984-97]

Travel to Libraries

Traveling to a library for employment-related purposes is a common occurrence. If the library is located within your general home area, then the rules discussed in Sections 2 and 3 apply. That is, you will be entitled to a deduction if you visit more than one business location during the day, or if the library is an irregular or short-term destination as discussed in Section 3.

On the other hand, if the library (or other business destination) is located outside your general home area, the rules allow you to deduct your transportation costs even if it is the only business activity that day. Such travel falls under the *temporary job away from home* category discussed in Section 4.

However, a recent court case shows that to be deductible, you must be able to point to a business reason for traveling to the out-of-town library. A community college English teacher took courses at a college 160 miles from home. The IRS did not challenge the deduction for traveling to and from the college for days on which he attended class. This was a legitimate educational expense [see the *Expenses of Attending School* chapter].

But he also traveled to the distant college on days he had no class in order to do research in the library. The Court did not allow a deduction for this travel. The only reason the teacher gave for using this particular library was that he was familiar with the layout and it was near his parents' home. According to the Court, there *"were other libraries closer to petitioner's home, that were more extensive in their collection of books and periodicals pertaining to subject matter useful for petitioner's job."* Thus, travel to the library was for *"personal convenience"* rather than for a valid business purpose. [Ginkel, TC Memo 1980-424]

This case offers an important tip to those who travel to a library distant from home. They should have a solid reason why the library was chosen over one closer to home, especially if the closer one has a more extensive collection. For example, the smaller library might have certain materials not found in the larger one. Or, materials in the larger library's collection might typically be off the shelf due to heavy use by faculty and students.

Section 2:
More Than One Job Location

If you work in more than one location during a given day, you can deduct the cost of transportation from one location to another. This applies whether or not you are working for the same employer at both locations or for different employers. You cannot deduct the cost of traveling from your home to the day's first place of employment nor from the final place of employment back home.

Example 1

Atkins is employed at the State University where he is a Professor of Poultry Science. On Monday and Wednesday nights, he goes from the University to the local office of the CROA (Chicken Raisers of America) where he is employed to teach a course in Chicken Management to interested farmers. Along the way, he stops off at a restaurant for dinner. He may deduct the cost of his transportation from the University to the CROA. However, he cannot deduct the cost of dinner because he is not away from home overnight.

Example 2

Baker is a Professor of Computer Science and teaches primarily at the main campus of a State University. However on Tuesday and Thursday, she teaches in the morning at the main campus and in the afternoon she teaches a programming course at a second campus in a different location. She may deduct the cost of transportation from one location to the other. If she stops off at an intermediate point, she deducts what the transportation cost would have been had she traveled directly.

Example 3

Mrs. Chu teaches Chemistry five days a week. On Saturdays she works at a chemical firm. She cannot deduct any transportation costs since she did not visit two different locations during the same day.

Example 4

Friend was a part-time lecturer at various colleges in the Louisville area. He regularly drove between his jobs at the main campus of a local university, a branch location of a different university, and a community college.

Friend was allowed to deduct the $301 he had claimed as a deduction for traveling between these business locations the same day. It did not matter that he didn't keep a contemporaneous diary. He established the deduction by convincing the judge that the traveling took place. Since his trips were made on a regular weekly basis, it was possible to determine the deduction to which he was entitled without reference to a diary.

Example 5

Beards was an associate professor at a Community College in a large northeastern city. The College had 5 buildings located in various parts of the city and she found it necessary to travel from one building to another, usually by taxi, during the course of a day.

Beards was permitted to deduct the cost of traveling from one College building to another the same day. This constituted deductible travel between job locations the same day. [Beards, TC Memo 1984-438]

The above case concerned traveling from one college building to another the same day. Although these buildings were not located on the same "campus," the following case would indicate that travel in such a situation would still be deductible. This case involved travel between different locations on the same Air Force base. But this is the same type of situation as occurs when a college teacher uses his auto to get from one building to another located on the same campus.

Example 6

Brandt was a flight engineer assigned to work at an Air Force base for a period of 44 days. He needed to transport himself from one part of the base to another in connection with the duties he was expected to perform. However, after 2 days, he found the motor pool transportation to be unreliable and rented an automobile for the remainder of his stay.

Brandt was permitted to deduct the cost of his rental automobile. He used the auto to travel from one business location to another. Even though the locations were on the same Air Force base, this made no difference. Because the existing motor pool transportation was inadequate and the Air Force would not reimburse him for his transportation, the Court allowed the deduction. [Brandt, TC Memo 1982-180]

Example 7

Smith drives to his office on the campus of a large University. Later in the morning, he drives several miles to and from a library on the other side of town. In the afternoon, he drives to the airport and back to pick up a visiting faculty member at the airport. None of his travel expenses is reimbursable by the school. The cost of these side trips is a deductible business expense.

Example 8

Kutchinski was a teacher at an Air Force base. Since she had no office at the Air Force base, she set up an office in her home for the preparation of classes and related duties. She was not permitted to deduct the cost of driving between her home and the classroom. The Court ruled her travel to be a non-deductible commuting expense. [Kutchinski, ¶65,043 P-H Memo TC]

Example 9

Lacy was a physician who worked at a medical clinic during the day. He also maintained an office at home which he used for storage of records, bookkeeping, and transcription of medical records in connection with his own medical practice. Lacy attempted to deduct the cost of traveling between his office at home and the clinic where he worked.

The Court denied his deduction. The clinic was the *principal place of business* for his medical practice. His home office was a *secondary* location for this medical practice. When an individual maintains a secondary office at home, travel between his home and his principal place of business is not deductible. [Lacy 55AFTR 2d 85-1273]

Example 10

Davis was employed as a minister for a newly-founded church in a northeastern state. The congregation rented a parsonage adjacent to the church building in which Davis resided. Because the church could not provide Davis with sufficient compensation, he obtained a job teaching at a Bible College in another town. He claimed a deduction for the cost of commuting between his two jobs, one at the church where he lived and the other at the college where he taught.

The Court denied his deduction. His principal place of business was the college where he earned the vast majority of his livelihood. When an individual's residence is located at a minor place of business (in this case the church), the transportation between his residence and his principal place of employment is considered a non-deductible commuting expense. [Davis, TC Memo 1984-302]

As the above 2 examples show, travel between one's home and principal place of business is not deductible, even if some business activity is carried out at home. But, as the next example shows, if one's home is the *principal place of business,* then travel to a secondary business location is deductible.

Example 11

Curphey owned and managed a number of residential rental properties as a side business. His management activities were conducted out of a home office from which he periodically traveled to the various rental properties. Because his home office was the principal place of business for his rental activities, this was considered to be deductible business travel rather than personal commuting. [Curphey, 73 TC No. 61]

If, instead of traveling from one regular job location to another, you go home first, then you cannot deduct any of your transportation expenses. Each trip between home and a regular job location is considered nondeductible commuting. An exception occurs if you travel to a job location outside the general area of your principal place of work.

Example 12

Parker makes several trips during the day between his home and his office at school. His expenses are not deductible – he is commuting each time.

Example 13

Jones works regularly at two different locations in the same city. He drives from home to one of the locations and then back home again. Later, he drives to and from the second location. None of his expenses is deductible. This was spelled out in a court case involving a doctor who drove to and from his office and later drove to and from his hospital. Both of his trips were ruled to be nondeductible commuting. [Shea, TC Memo 1979-303]

Example 14

Chandler was the principal of a high school in the Massachusetts town where he lived. Two nights a week, after returning home for dinner, he drove 37 miles to

Boston where he taught a college accounting course. Since Boston was outside the general location of his home, he could deduct the entire cost of driving from his home to Boston and back. [Chandler, 226 F 2nd 467]

Example 15

A professor taught in a large Texas city during the week. On weekends, he often traveled 150 miles to an out-of-town location in order to oversee a launderette business which he owned. He was permitted to deduct travel expenses connected with his secondary business out-of-town. Since he was away from home overnight, this included meals and lodging in addition to transportation expenses.

Section 3:
Commuting to a Temporary Job Near Home

In prior years, the cost of commuting to a temporary job could be deducted only if the temporary job was located outside the general area of your regular job. But now, due to a surprise 1990 IRS ruling [Rev Rul 90-23], this deduction is available even if the temporary job is in the same general area. However, the restrictions are stricter than for commuting to a temporary job away from home [cf. Section 4].

To qualify for a commuting deduction to a temporary job in the same general area as your regular job, 2 basic conditions must be satisfied.

First, the commuting must be to an *irregular* or *short-term* job site. The IRS defines *short-term* as "*generally a matter of days or weeks.*" This would seem to cover periods of perhaps up to 2 months. (This is much stricter than for commuting to a temporary job away from home where periods of up to a year or more qualify [cf. Section 4].)

Second, in addition to the temporary job, you must have a permanent "business location" where you typically work or perform services on a regular basis.

If the above 2 conditions are satisfied, you can deduct the cost of commuting to the temporary job. If you drive to the job, you can use the standard allowance (26 cents per mile) if you wish [cf. the *Automobile Expense* chapter]. This applies not just to 1990 tax returns, but retroactively to returns for prior years. To get the corresponding deduction for previous years, you would have to file amended tax returns [cf. Section 1 of Chapter 1].

Example 1

Richards is a professor at a State University. During the summer, he teaches a 4-week course at a satellite location in the same city as the regular campus.

Rule: Richards may deduct the cost of commuting to the satellite location. Both the requirements that he have a permanent job and that the job to which he is commuting be temporary are satisfied.

Example 2

Jackson is a teacher at a community college. During one semester, instead of teaching at the community college, he teaches at a different institution located in the same general area.

Rule: Jackson cannot deduct any commuting costs. The semester-long period he is teaching at the different institution is too long to be temporary. (If the second institution were located in a different general area than the community college, then the commuting costs would be deductible as discussed in Section 4.)

Example 3

Trafton is a Professor of Urban Studies in a large city. On days when he does not teach, he travels from his home to various city offices and building sites as part of research he is doing. He also travels occasionally to several libraries in different locations in the city.

Rule: His travels around the city are made on an irregular basis. This means the locations are considered temporary worksites under the rules discussed above. Therefore, his commuting costs to these locations are deductible.

Example 4

Whitworth is a research associate in astronomy at a large university. He spends most of his time in his office, but sometimes travels to an off-campus observatory where the telescope is located. Trips to the observatory are not made weekly, nor do they follow any particular pattern.

Rule: Whitworth cannot deduct the cost of commuting between his home and the observatory. Even though his trips do not follow a regular pattern, the observatory is considered to be a regular place of work, rather than a temporary worksite.

Section 4:
Temporary Job Away From Home

If you have a temporary job *away from home*, then it's easier to qualify for deducting travel expenses. In particular, your temporary job can last up to one year (or more as discussed below) instead of only *days or weeks* for in-town jobs as discussed in the preceding Section. Also, if you live away from home, you get to deduct not just transportation, but also the cost of meals, lodging, and laundry.

The rules in this section apply provided both of the following conditions are satisfied. First, your temporary job must be **located away from home.** Second, the temporary job must qualify as being **temporary** in the eyes of the law.

Job Located Away From Home

You must show that you have some fixed home base in a different location than your temporary job. In unusual circumstances this may hinge on the particular facts involved in your case. But, to take a common example, suppose you have a regular job at which you worked prior to the temporary job and to which you return after the temporary job. Suppose further that you rent your house out during the period you are away (or retain other significant roots with your home base). These two conditions are generally sufficient to establish a fixed home base.

When Is a Job Temporary?

A job is considered temporary if at the time you start, it can be *foreseen to end within a fixed and reasonably short time.* A period of less than one year is considered by the IRS to be a short time for this purpose. For time periods of one year or longer, the matter is not so clear. Prior to 1983, the IRS considered any time periods of this length to be a strong indication that the job was not temporary. Basically, they pretty much held to a one-year cut off policy for deciding whether a job was temporary or not.

But the courts never accepted this one-year principle, stating that only by looking at the facts and circumstances in each case could it be decided whether a job was temporary or not. And in practice, they allowed deductions in a number of cases where the absence exceeded a year in length. In a few cases, they even allowed deductions for temporary stays exceeding 2 years. [Otness, TC Memo 1978-481; Miller, TC Memo 1979-87; Williams, 52 AFTR 2d 83-5929]

In response to these court decisions, the IRS issued a new ruling in 1983 governing temporary jobs away from home [Rev Rul 83-82]. As before, an absence of less than one year qualifies as a short period of time. Absences of 1 year or longer are still *"presumed"* to be too long to be temporary. However, this 1-year presumption may be *"rebutted"* by the taxpayer where the temporary employment lasts for 1 year or more but less than 2 years.

For stays between 1 and 2 years, the following 3 tests are applied:

1. Did you live in and work near your permanent home immediately prior to your temporary job and did you continue to maintain bona fide work contacts (job seeking, leave of absence, on-going business, etc.) back home during your temporary employment?

2. Did you incur duplicate living expenses because you maintained a residence back home?

3. Did a family member (marital or lineal only) live in your permanent home while you were away or did you travel back home frequently to stay at your permanent home?

If you can demonstrate that you satisfy all 3 tests, then your 1-2 year stay is temporary. If you satisfy only 1 of the 3 tests, then the IRS considers your stay not to be temporary. If you satisfy 2 out of the 3 tests, no definite conclusion is reached. In such a case, the IRS would have to consider all the facts and circumstances regarding your stay to determine if you qualify for a temporary position away from home.

If you work away from home for 2 years or more, then your stay is considered by the IRS to be permanent or indefinite in length and does not qualify for the *temporary job away from home* deduction.

One other case where a stay of one year or longer qualifies for deduction is when you reasonably anticipate it will last for less than one year, but because of a change in circumstances it extends up to 2 years (but not longer). In such a case, the above 3-part test does not come into force, but rather the usual rules for stays less than one year are applicable.

Conversely, if your temporary job is scheduled to last for longer than 2 years, but is cut short due to unexpected circumstances, it would not qualify for deduction under the above guideline. According to the IRS, the fact you *anticipated* it would last for more than 2 years disqualifies it from deduction.

Example 1

You work in city A and live there with your family in an apartment. You take an 18-month leave of absence to accept a temporary position in city B. Your family stays behind in city A while you rent an apartment in city B. You visit your family regularly while you are away.

Rule: You have satisfied all 3 tests by (1) being on official leave of absence, (2) incurring duplicate living expenses, and (3) having your family live back home. Thus, your visiting position qualifies for the *temporary job away from home* deduction.

Example 2

Same as Example 1 except that you give up your apartment in city A and your family lives with you in city B.

Rule: You have satisfied only test 1. You did not satisfy test 2, the *duplicate living* test nor test 3, the *family back home* test. Since you have satisfied only 1 out of the 3 tests, your stay does not qualify for deduction under the above IRS guideline.

Example 3

You work in city A and live there with your family in a home which you own. You take an 18-month leave of absence to accept a temporary position in city B. Your family moves with you to city B where you live together in a rented apartment. While away, you rent out your house in city A.

Rule: You have passed test 1 because you were on official leave of absence and have failed test 3 because your family did not remain behind. What about test 2, the duplicate living expense test? The IRS ruling gives no direct guidance as to what this test requires in the way of duplicate expenses except to state that mere storage of furniture does not suffice. However, numerous court cases have discussed the concept of duplicate living expenses in connection with temporary jobs. From these cases, it appears that the maintenance of 2 residences, one back home and one at the temporary post, qualifies as duplicate living expenses. This has been the case even when, as in this example, the house back home is rented out thereby mitigating or eliminating the actual economic loss involved. [cf. Robert J. Henry, *Visiting Professor's Tax Shelter*, Saint Louis University Law Journal, Vol 25, pp 779-811.] This would mean that test 2 is satisfied, placing the temporary position in the 2 out of 3 category. That is, the temporary position is neither automatically qualified nor automatically disqualified under the above tests. Rather, the IRS reserves the right to consider all the facts and circumstances surrounding the temporary job. However, the *facts and circumstances* described above would call for a deduction in this case, even though not explicitly permitted under the ruling.

The advantage an individual has just by knowing about the rules is illustrated by a recent court case.

Court Case

A plumber who was unable to find employment in his home area of Amsterdam, NY accepted a temporary job 142 miles away in Oswego. Upon completion of this temporary job, he was successful in obtaining employment back home in the Amsterdam area. While he was away, he continued paying rent on his Amsterdam apartment which remained occupied by his father. As an informed taxpayer, he knew he would satisfy the conditions of the above ruling as long as his temporary job lasted less than 2 years. Consequently, he arranged his job to last from October 6 of one year to October 4 two years later, a time period less than 2 years. This qualified him to deduct his living expenses for the entire time period away. [Banekatis, TC Memo 1988-474]

Note. The above tests for temporary jobs are guidelines issued by the IRS to express their opinion on the travel deduction rules. However, the Tax Court does not always go along with these guidelines. For example, in one case, a sheet metal worker worked for 26 months at a plant 115 miles from his residence. In another, a pipefitter spent 27 months working on a nuclear power plant away from home. In both cases, the worker's family did not move to the new location, but stayed in its permanent home. Each worker had substantial ties to his permanent home and tried to find work there, rather than remaining at his temporary job. And they each incurred duplicate living expenses, staying in motels or other transient lodging facilities. In both cases, the Tax Court allowed deductions for living expenses at a temporary job away from home. It would not have been reasonable for the workers to uproot their families since they intended to obtain work back home as soon as they could. Considering all the facts in each case, the Court felt a deduction for living expenses while away from home was justified. Although not explicitly addressing itself to the IRS Revenue Ruling 83-82 discussed above, the Court simply chose to ignore the 2-year ceiling contained in that ruling. [Knight, TC Memo 1988-186; Griffin, TC Memo 1988-248]

Despite the above court cases, the IRS has not abandoned its guidelines on temporary jobs away from home. Although legally justified, an individual claiming deductions for a temporary stay exceeding 2 years might still be expected to encounter IRS objection, should his tax return be selected for audit. In such a case, it would probably be necessary to appeal the IRS audit to sustain one's deduction.

Which Expenses Can You Deduct?

If your temporary job is located away from home and you do not return home overnight, then you may deduct the cost of meals, lodging, cleaning and laundry, and commuting between where you obtain your meals and lodging and your temporary job. Your meal expenses are subject to the 80%-Rule discussed in Section 1. That is, you can deduct only 80% of your unreimbursed meal expenses.

You should pay special attention to the new per diem meal rates allowed by the IRS—$34 for high cost areas and $26 for low cost areas [cf. Section 1]. An individual at a temporary position away from home for a full year would be able to claim $34 × 365 = $12,410 in meal expenses for the year. Applying the 80%–reduction factor, his deduction for meals alone would be 80% × $12,410 = $9,928. And to top it off, he wouldn't even have to keep any records of his food costs. (As discussed in Section 1, the per diem meal allowances are much greater in many foreign locations. For example, in London, the $9,928 figure would rise to $21,608.)

In addition to expenses at the location of your temporary job, you can also deduct the initial and final transportation costs of traveling between your permanent home and your temporary residence, as well as the daily commuting between your permanent home and your temporary job, as discussed in Sections 3 and 4.

Temporary Academic Position

Faculty members at academic institutions commonly accept visiting positions at other institutions for a temporary period of time. The following 1979 IRS ruling issued to a college teacher spells out exactly what can be deducted.

IRS Private Letter Ruling #7917044

"You are regularly employed as a professor in the Department of Aeronautics and Astronautics at X University. Y offered you a temporary appointment as a professor in its Aerospace Engineering Department. The appointment which you accepted is of fixed duration commencing October 15, 1978, and ending September 1, 1979. When this temporary appointment terminates, you intend to return to your tenured professorial position at X University.

"In order to discharge your appointment, you will have to travel across country and set up a temporary residence in the vicinity of Y. During the term of the appointment your permanent residence is being rented to unrelated parties.

"In light of these facts you request a ruling finding the following expenses deductible to the extent not reimbursed by your temporary employer:

1. *Travel expenses to and from the temporary work site;*

2. *Local transportation costs at the temporary work site;*

3. *Lodging at the temporary work site;*

4. *Meals at the temporary work site* [now subject to the 80%-Rule described in Section 1–ed.];

5. *Incidental expenses at the temporary work site;*

6. *Travel expenses to and from the temporary work site twice during the appointment (i.e. Christmas and Easter);*

7. *Costs for transportation of personal and professional articles with which to set up housekeeping at the temporary work site.*

"*Although your wife will be accompanying you, no deductions will be claimed for any of the above travel expenses which would be applicable to her.*

"*. . .if your records will establish the recordkeeping and substantiation elements required by [the law], you may claim a deduction for reasonable amounts expended for meals* [now subject to the 80%-Rule-ed.] *and lodging plus other incidental expenses such as laundry you incur as a result of your temporary employment. In addition, your expenses for transportation are deductible to the extent they are reasonable in amount and were incurred in the pursuit of your temporary assignment in going between your place of lodging and place of temporary employment.*

"*In view of these holdings and. . .the regulations you will not be entitled to a deduction for moving expenses.* [Cf. the end of the *Moving Expenses* chapter which explains that moving expenses cannot be claimed in connection with a temporary job.—ed.]

"*The cost of any trips back and forth to the city of your residence are personal expenses and nondeductible under section 262 of the Code. Such travel expenses bear no relation to the execution of your duties at Y, nor in any way benefit your temporary employer. . . .* [However, the initial cost of traveling to the location of the temporary job and the final trip back to the permanent home would be deductible.–ed.] *Similarly, since you will be only temporarily away from your tax home, such expenses as you incur for transportation of personal and professional articles with which to set up housekeeping at Y, are nondeductible personal or living expenses.*"

Example 1

Professor Jones teaches History at a well-known university in Princeton, New Jersey. He takes a leave of absence in order to accept a position as visiting professor at a minor university in New Haven, Connecticut. In September, he drives with his family from Princeton to New Haven to assume his duties there. He returns to Princeton in June. He rents his house in Princeton to a faculty member who was visiting there for the school year. While in New Haven, he and his family live in a rented house five miles from the university he is visiting. He commutes daily by automobile.

Rule: *Professor Jones has taken a temporary position away from home. He can deduct the cost of his transportation between Princeton and New Haven and the cost of his daily commuting between the rented house and his office in New Haven. While in New Haven, he may also deduct his lodging, laundry, and 80% of the cost of his meals. The expenses of his wife and children are non-deductible.*

Example 2

Mr. Black teaches at a special education elementary school in New York City and lives in a nearby suburb. He takes a 10-month leave of absence in order to accept an offer of organizing and setting up a new special education school in New Haven, Connecticut during one school year. He commutes daily from his home in the New York suburbs to his office in New Haven.

Rule: Mr. Black has a temporary position in a different general location than that of his tax home. He deducts his daily commuting costs to and from New Haven. He cannot deduct the cost of meals or other living expenses since he is not away from home overnight.

Example 3. Several Temporary Positions

Professor Brown teaches Physics at a university in Pennsylvania. He accepts a position as a Visiting Professor of Physics at a west coast university in the San Francisco area. He teaches for the academic year plus summer school, his appointment lasting from October 1 through August 30 of the following year. He vacations in Canada during the month of September, after which he travels to a New Mexico university where he has a visiting position in connection with a government funded special semester in his field of expertise. He returns back to his original university to resume his duties for the spring semester.

Professor Brown claims that his tax home is Pennsylvania and that both of his visiting positions qualify as temporary positions. He claims that he is entitled to his transportation costs from Pennsylvania to San Francisco, from New Mexico to Pennsylvania, and what it would have cost him to travel from San Francisco to New Mexico had he traveled directly. In addition, he claims as deductions his cost of lodging, commuting expenses between his temporary homes and temporary jobs, and 80% of the cost of his meals. He does not claim any deduction for expenses incurred while vacationing in Canada.

Rule: Brown's positions in California and New Mexico were both temporary positions away from home. In similar cases (not involving academic personnel), the courts have allowed such deductions.

Example 4. Temporary Position Plus Trip Back Home on Weekends

Professor Dodd's regular job is in Chicago. He takes a 5-month leave of absence to accept a temporary position in St. Louis. His family remains in Chicago. On weekends, he travels back to Chicago to visit his family.

Rule: He is entitled to deduct his living expenses (lodging, commuting, laundry, and 80% of the cost of his meals) while in St. Louis. He cannot deduct his living costs while he is back home in Chicago. However, he may deduct the cost of transportation of returning home for the weekend, provided this cost does not exceed what it would have cost him for food and lodging had he stayed in St. Louis. If the cost of transportation is in excess of this, he may deduct only what he could have deducted for food and lodging in St. Louis.

Example 5

Cass was a Professor of Economics at a university in the East. He accepted an appointment under a "distinguished scholar" program to spend the academic year at a well-known university in Southern California. His stipend qualified as a fellowship grant under the rules that applied at the time.

Cass took a leave of absence from his regular position, rented out his house, and moved—together with his wife, 17-year old son, 11-year old daughter, and dog—out west for the academic year. He was permitted to deduct his living expenses during this stay in California. The issue that arose at trial was how much was spent on food for Professor Cass.

Cass proved by production of receipts that the total food expenses for his family amounted to $4,390. Of this amount, it was agreed that $173 was clearly deductible for lunches Professor Cass ate on campus. Of the remaining $4217, $3307 was for food purchased at the supermarket and $910 for restaurant meals. It was in allocating what part of this $4217 worth of food was consumed by Professor Cass that the dispute arose.

Cass claimed that about $1/3$ of this $4217 was allocable to food that he ate. He testified that making this type of allocation was right up his alley as an economist. His methodology for making the allocation here was to apportion the cost of food for each family member according to that person's body weight.

However, the court did not buy this method. It ruled, *"Petitioner's allocation is, to say the least, creative. However, if it proposes to approach a scientific approximation of the amount of food consumed by each member of the household, it is flawed, e.g., it ignores factors such as the relative metabolic rate of each person. Any parent having a teenage child can attest to the fact that a teenager eats as much as, or more than, the parent regardless of weight.*

"Of course the best proof would be to have receipts directly related to petitioner's own food consumption. Understandably, in a situation such as the one before us now, such a requirement would be onerous. Thus, we will make an estimation which we deem best reflects or approximates the true costs involved. In the absence of proof of a more precise method, we deem it best to employ the simplest approach available. Accordingly, we allocate one-fourth of the total contested food expenses ($4,217) to petitioner, discounting the grocery expenses ($3,307) by 5% to account for dog food. Thus, petitioners may deduct $1,185.91 of the $4,390 food costs as a food expense." (Note that under current law, only 80% of the cost of meals would be deductible.) [Cass, 86TC No. 75]

Example 6. Married People Living Apart

Professor and Professor Lighthouse, a married couple, both have regular teaching positions in cities 400 miles apart. They live in the cities where they work on weekdays but one of them visits the other on weekends. Since neither of their positions is temporary, they are not entitled to deduct any transportation or living expenses. Each person's tax home is considered to be the city where that person works. A weekend trip to visit a spouse is a personal non-deductible activity. However, if one of their positions were temporary and in a different location than the person's permanent home, then expenses as described in Example 4 would be deductible.

Example 7

Mr. and Mrs. Felton moved to a midwestern city where he enrolled as a student at the State university located there. After obtaining his degree, he obtained a position on the faculty of the same university.

Mrs. Felton also enrolled at the university and obtained a master's degree in economics. After teaching part-time for several years in the same locality, she obtained a temporary appointment as a Visiting Lecturer at a university 100 miles away. After 2 years as a Visiting Lecturer, she was promoted to a full-time position on the faculty, as a Lecturer for half a year and then as Assistant Professor upon attainment of her Ph.D. degree.

Mrs. Felton did not move her personal residence. She arranged her schedule so she could spend 5 nights a week back home with her husband, making 2 round trips per week between where she worked and her permanent residence. She rented a room the 2 nights a week she stayed near her job.

Mrs. Felton was permitted to deduct her travel expenses during the 2 years she held a *temporary* position as a Visiting Lecturer. But once she obtained a *permanent* position, her travel expenses were no longer deductible. This was the case even though she prepared classes and did research in the library back home. The Court ruled that the primary reason for her traveling back and forth was for personal rather than business purposes. [Felton, TC Memo 1982-11]

Example 8

An individual sought a ruling from the IRS in the following situation. He was currently doing research and writing from his home. Apparently, he had no other source of employment at the time. He received an appointment as a Visiting Professor for one academic year at a college in a different location. Following his appointment, he expected to return back home.

The IRS ruled that his permanent tax home was where he was currently doing his research and writing. His position as a Visiting Professor constituted a temporary job away from home. Thus, he could deduct his travel expenses, including the cost of commuting, meals [now subject to the 80%-Rule], lodging, and laundry while at his temporary teaching position. [IRS Private Letter Ruling 8449013]

Example 9. Student Working at Summer Job

Hantzsis was a student at a major law school in the Boston area. During the summer of her second year of law school, she accepted a 10-week job as a legal assistant at a New York law firm. While in New York, she rented a small apartment in which she lived. Her husband, a faculty member at a Boston-area university, remained in Boston.

Mrs. Hantzsis viewed her employment in New York as a temporary job away from home. Thus, she claimed a deduction for her transportation between Boston and New York and for meals and lodging while living in New York. The Tax Court allowed the deduction. The amount allowed was surprisingly large — $3,080 just for meals and the rental of a small apartment for the 10 weeks spent in New York.

However, an Appeals Court overruled the Tax Court, disallowing the deduction. It ruled that Boston was not her tax home because she did not work there. Thus she was not entitled to an away-from-home travel deduction while in New York. In order for her to be allowed a deduction, she would need to *"establish the existence of some sort of business relation both to the location she claims as 'home' and to the location of her temporary employment sufficient to support a finding that her duplicative expenses are necessitated by business exigencies."* Presumably, had she held even a part-time job in Boston, her deduction for living expenses in New York would have been allowed. [Hantzsis, 47 AFTR 2d 81-721]

Temporary vs. Indefinite Job

An issue that often arises is whether a job away from home is *temporary* or *indefinite* in length. A *temporary* job is one that is expected to last for a short period of time. An *indefinite* job is one whose expected duration is indeterminate or else a long period of time. Only away-from-home expenses connected with a *temporary* job, not an indefinite job, can qualify for deduction.

Sometimes, a job starts out being temporary, but later becomes indefinite. For example, suppose you accept a position for a temporary period. At the end of this period, an unexpected permanent slot opens up and you accept the position. At that point, your job changes from being temporary to indefinite. If you are *"away-from-home,"* you can deduct your living expenses during the temporary period, but not thereafter. This is illustrated by the following court case.

Example 10

Kaster was a certified welder who worked at various jobs in the northeastern quarter of Ohio and a small portion of northwestern Pennsylvania. He and his family lived in Titusville, 120 miles east of Cleveland, from which he commuted to his various jobsites. He and his family had lived in Titusville their entire lives.

In July, 1981, Kaster obtained work at a nuclear power plant in Perry, Ohio. He expected he would work only two months at the power plant. This was based on his previous work record which showed a large number of short-term jobs during the previous several years. However, the power plant did not advise him of the expected duration of this particular job and Kaster could not know exactly how long his job would last.

Kaster was subject to immediate layoff at any time. Welders were not generally notified that they were to be laid off until the day that the layoff occurred. However, under the *"last hired, first fired"* method of determining layoffs, the longer he worked at that job, the less likely he was to be edged out by a fellow employee in the event of a layoff. In fact, his job lasted for 27 months until November, 1983 before he was laid off.

The IRS agreed that Titusville was Kaster's tax home and that the job at Perry to which he commuted was *away-from-home*. The only question that remained was determining for which period of time the job was temporary and for which period indefinite.

Kaster claimed a deduction on his 1982 tax return for an entire year of commuting between his Titusville home and his job at Perry. His total commuting mileage for the year was 50,000 miles for which he claimed a deduction of $7,178. In order for this claim to be allowed, it would be necessary to determine that his job at Perry was temporary rather than indefinite during the entire 1982 year.

When the IRS audited Kaster's tax return, it allowed a deduction for only part of the year. The IRS said that Kaster's job at Perry was temporary for the first 12 months from July, 1981 to July, 1982. After that, the job became indefinite, ruling out a deduction. But how did the IRS auditor, George Lubic, decide that this was the appropriate cutoff? Most interestingly, it was simply a general policy of Lubic's office to use a one-year standard. According to the Court's written opinion,

> *"Lubic worked in respondent's Erie, Pennsylvania office. This office follows a 'one-year rule' in making determinations as to temporary versus indefinite employment. That is, employment up to one year is considered temporary; if a single employment lasts longer than one year, then the expenses incurred after the end of one year are treated as nondeductible 'commuting' expenses. Lubic's audit report, which followed this one-year rule, was forwarded to respondent's Appeals Office in Pittsburgh, Pennsylvania. This Appeals Office followed the same one-year rule in preparing the notice of deficiency in the instant case. In the notice of deficiency, respondent allowed $4,886.59 of petitioners' claimed deduction and disallowed the remaining $2,291.41."*

The IRS lawyer who prepared the case for trial backed away from the Pennsylvania office's one-year policy. He argued for a denial of any deduction whatsoever for the 1982 tax year. But the judge did not agree. Clearly, the job was temporary for the beginning months because of the expectation it would end shortly. It was reasonable that this expectation would have continued for about a year. After that, the job simply became indefinite in length because its imminent end could no longer be reasonably expected. Thus, the Court accepted the original auditor's determination and allowed a deduction of $4,886.59 for the period through July, 1982. [Kaster, TC Memo 1985-580]

The above case is interesting because of the glimpse it gives of the workings of one particular IRS office. Because of the inherent difficulty of determining whether an impermanent job is *temporary* or *indefinite*, this office apparently adopted a one-year rule in all questionable cases. That is, as long as a permanent tax home was established, a job in a different area would be considered temporary for a period of up to one year, but not thereafter.

As noted above, this one-year policy is not an official position of the IRS. But those in a similar situation should take note of the above case. The fact that one IRS office adopted a one-year policy as a basic test would support the reasonability of considering a similarly impermanent job to be temporary for up to one year, even when no definite end is known in advance.

Duplicate Expenses Test

When in doubt, the Tax Court in recent decisions has referred back to the original justification in allowing deductions for living expenses while at a temporary job away from home, namely to provide relief to those who incur extra *"duplicate living expenses"* because of their situation. When no extra expenses are incurred, the Court is sometimes reluctant to permit a deduction. Another factor the Court has been looking for is secondary evidence such as auto registration, voter registration, bank accounts, etc. which point to where a person considers his permanent home to be. The following court case illustrates both of these considerations.

Example 11

For 5 years, Thomas Crain and his wife lived with his parents in a house in Hot Springs, Arkansas. During this time, he worked as an electrician in various places near Hot Springs, obtaining his job assignments through his union. Then he received an assignment near Baton Rouge, Louisiana which lasted for about 10 months. Despite the impermanence of his job in Louisiana, the Court denied a temporary job-away-from-home deduction.

The Court pointed to the absence of any extra living expenses beyond what would have been normal had they stayed in Hot Springs. During their absence, the Court noted,

"Petitioners did not pay any rent to Thomas' parents, nor did they contribute any money to them for the purchase of groceries, the payment of utility bills, or the payment of other expenses associated with the upkeep of a home. . . .

"The purpose of allowing the deduction of living expenses while a taxpayer is 'away from home' is 'to mitigate the burden of the taxpayer who, because of exigencies of his trade or business, must maintain two places of abode and thereby incur additional and duplicate living expenses. . . .'

"There is no evidence in the record which supports petitioners' contention that they have incurred the requisite increased or duplicate living expenses by maintaining the house [in] Hot Springs, Arkansas."

The Court also noted the extent to which they settled into their new location, stating

"We think it pertinent that in Baton Rouge, Mr. and Mrs. Crain rented and lived in an apartment and maintained an account in a local bank. Mrs. Crain held a Louisiana driver's license, registered to vote in that state, and held a job there during at least part of their stay. Mr.Crain also registered to vote in Louisiana and served as a reserve deputy sheriff in Baton Rouge." [Crain, TC Memo 1985-498]

Travel Expenses While Under a Fellowship Grant

A person at a temporary position away from home might have been paid under a grant qualifying for the $300 per month tax-free treatment described in the *Tax-Free Grants* chapter. Sometimes, the IRS will contend there is no temporary job in such a case. Rather, it claims the taxpayer is simply studying or doing research under a fellowship grant. It makes no difference that tax is paid on that portion of the grant exceeding $300 per month. Since there is no temporary job, the IRS claims there can be no deduction for expenses incurred at a temporary job away from home.

One can counter such an objection by the IRS by claiming that the expenses were incurred as an *educational expense while on temporary leave of absence from one's regular job* (see the *Expenses of Attending School* chapter). Usually, in the process of denying that a job exists, the IRS contends that the grant is provided simply for the educational benefit of the recipient. Thus, the same travel and living expenses that were denied as a *temporary job* deduction can become an *educational expense* deduction. In fact, there is an IRS ruling concerning teachers' sabbaticals which supports this viewpoint [Rev Rul 64-176]. But don't expect the IRS to point this out to you if your deduction is challenged in an audit. You must be prepared to point this out to them.

Exactly how you list your claimed deduction on your tax return could be an important factor. This is underscored by the following 1985 court case.

Example 12

A teacher received a $10,000 grant from the small liberal arts College in the Midwest where he taught. Such grants were awarded after 7 years of employment. The teacher pursued a Ph.D. program at a major University with the grant. During the period he attended the University, he was not employed at the College which provided the grant, nor was he under any obligation to return to the College after he completed his Ph.D. work.

While at the University, he claimed a deduction of $2,006 for his living expenses. The issue arose at trial as to the category under which this deduction was being claimed. Was the deduction being claimed as a *business expense* or an *educational expense*?

The IRS asserted that the teacher was claiming the $2,006 deduction as a *business expense*. If so, it could object to the deduction because the teacher was not ac-

tually employed when the expenses were incurred. To support its assertion, the IRS pointed to the fact that the expenses were claimed on the part of Form 2106, labeled "Employee Business Expenses."

But the teacher asserted that the deduction was being claimed as an educational expense.-As discussed in Section 5 of the Expenses of Attending School chapter, one can deduct educational expenses even while not currently employed, as long as one is considered to be temporarily on leave of absence from his profession. The teacher claimed that the only reason he listed the expenses under the "Employee Business Expenses" section of Form 2106 was that there was no special place for the listing of Educational Expenses on Form 2106.

The judge ruled in favor of the teacher, allowing him to deduct the $2,006 as an educational expense. It agreed that the teacher's claim for a refund hinged on how he had claimed these expenses, i.e. as business expenses or educational expenses. But the teacher had placed the IRS on notice that his deduction was claimed in connection with his education because under the occupation line on Form 2106 he had listed "Scholarship Grant." He had not listed his occupation as "teacher" nor linked the expenses to his job by naming the college where he taught. Since there was no special place for the listing of educational expenses on Form 2106, the teacher had acted sufficiently to identify that the amounts were being deducted as educational expenses connected with his studies rather than as business expenses connected with a job. [Pelowski, DC Ohio, 1985 CCH ¶9217]

Sabbaticals

A sabbatical leave of absence is governed by the same basic rules that apply to temporary jobs as discussed above. Thus, the costs of travel, meals, lodging, commuting, cleaning, and laundry while away from home are generally deductible. This is spelled out by the following IRS ruling:

IRS Private Letter Ruling #7828042

"This is in reply to your letter with enclosures of January 12, 1978, which concerns the treatment, for federal income tax purposes of certain expenses incurred while away from your permanent place of employment on a temporary employment assignment.

"You are regularly employed as a Professor of Industrial Systems Engineering at X University. During your sabbatical you are working for the Federal Government as a Visiting Mathematical Scientist at Y Agency which is located in the metropolitan Washington, D.C., area. This assignment is of fixed duration commencing October 1, 1977, and ending September 29, 1978. Your Department Chairman at X University attests that you are a university employee on temporary government assignment for which you are paid by the University. The government agency where you are temporarily employed then reimburses the University for that part of your salary designated in your Assignment Agreement which is not covered by sabbatical pay and certain sponsored research which you continue to carry out. This latter research is

separately funded under a federal grant program and although you will be working on the project during your temporary employment at Y Agency, the University continues to administer the grant project.

"You have rented out your condominium apartment for part of the time you will be away. During this temporary employment assignment, you are incurring certain expenses which you believe may be deductible for federal income tax purposes. Specifically, you ask whether you may deduct the cost of meals, rental of a temporary apartment, and the cost of commuting between where you obtain your meals, your temporary apartment and Y Agency. Y Agency has paid your round-trip travel expenses between the city of your permanent employment and your temporary post.

". . . Assuming that your appointment with Y Agency is temporary for the term described and that upon expiration of the appointment you will return to your permanent employment at X University, we conclude that while temporarily employed in the metropolitan Washington, D.C. area, you will be traveling away from home for purposes of section 162 of the Code.

"Accordingly, if your records will establish the recordkeeping and substantiation elements required . . ., you may claim a deduction for reasonable amounts expended for meals [now subject to the 80%-Rule] and lodging plus other incidental expenses such as laundry you incur as a result of your temporary employment. In addition, your expenses for transportation are deductible to the extent they are reasonable in amount and were incurred in the pursuit of your temporary assignment in going between your place of lodging and place of temporary employment."

Example 13

A Professor and Chairman of the Department of Anesthesiology at a New York medical school took a 6-month sabbatical from his duties. He spent this period in Washington, D.C., where he served as an unpaid advisor to a Senate subcommittee on health-related issues. He rented an apartment while in Washington and traveled back to New York regularly to take care of certain job-related matters there.

The IRS ruled that he could deduct his living expenses in Washington and his travel back and forth between New York and Washington. According to the IRS, "an appearance or communication by an employee or self-employed individual in connection with legislation or proposed legislation shall be considered to be with respect to legislation of direct interest to such person if the legislation is in the field in which he specializes in his business and if the appearance or communication is made pursuant to an invitation extended to him individually for the purpose of receiving his expert testimony. Expenses incurred by an employee or self-employed individual in connection with such an appearance or communication, including traveling expenses properly allocable thereto, represent ordinary and necessary business expenses and are, therefore, deductible . . . " [IRS Private Letter Ruling 8727010]

Example 14

Michael and Nancy McColloch were both teachers in Colorado—he, an Assistant Professor of Philosophy at a large State university and she, an elementary school teacher at a public school. During one school year, they both took sabbaticals from their respective teaching positions which they spent in Ireland, accompanied by their 4 children.

The IRS did not object to Michael deducting his expenses while on sabbatical. The matter before the Court was whether or not Nancy could deduct hers.

Nancy used her sabbatical to study *"the use of storytelling in elementary curricula of selected high school systems and to learn from Irish storytellers the essentials of their art . . . She chose to take her sabbatical in Ireland because of its rich tradition in storytelling and because many fine storytellers still live there. Further, through the library at Trinity College in Dublin, Mrs. McCulloch had access to an outstanding collection of storytelling literature. In her opinion, Ireland was the best English speaking place to learn storytelling."*

While in Ireland, she spent most weekday mornings at the library, reading collections of stories and books that detailed the importance of storytelling in the elementary school classroom. In the afternoon and evening, in addition to caring for her children, she did more reading and research. In the course of her studies, she prepared an annotated bibliography for use both in a handbook that she was preparing for other teachers and for her Master's thesis.

Upon her return from Ireland, *"Mrs. McCulloch relied heavily on storytelling in her teaching. She told her students stories two to three times each week, and although each story lasted only approximately one-half hour, she used the story as the focal point for many of her lessons. She built handwriting and spelling lessons around the stories and had the children list the adverbs and adjectives that they heard in the stories. She also based some of her social studies lessons on the stories she told.*

"Mrs. McCulloch benefited professionally from her sabbatical in a number of ways. She found that her intensive study of Irish stories enabled her to learn other stories more easily and to relate these stories to her students. As a result of her experience in Ireland, she was able to tell 15 stories well, could learn 50 more at a week's notice and knew hundreds more. In addition, she learned research techniques which enabled her to gain access to stories in Colorado.

"Mrs. McCulloch shared her skills by conducting a workshop and by telling stories in an enrichment program for gifted and talented children. She recommended stories to other teachers and shared with them the bibliography she prepared in Ireland. She also made a videotape which has been used, with impressive results, to train other teachers."

The Court ruled that the primary purpose of her sabbatical was to improve her teaching skills. Thus, she could deduct her travel expenses including her living costs during her stay in Ireland. [McColloch, TC Memo 1988-84]

The above discussion and examples concern sabbaticals during which a teacher studies or does research at a distant location. In such a case, the usual rules for deducting business travel expenses apply. Another type of sabbatical occurs when a teacher travels extensively and claims the travel itself is a form of education. This type of travel is no longer deductible as discussed in Section 8 of this chapter.

The expenses of renting out a home while on sabbatical or other leave of absence are deductible. This is discussed further in Section 4 of the *Homeowners* chapter.

Section 5:
Travel To Look For Employment

You can deduct expenses connected with looking for a new job, whether or not you are successful. However, you can only deduct job-hunting costs if you are looking for work in your current profession. You cannot deduct the expenses of looking for work in a new profession even if you are successful.

If you take a trip to look for a new job in your own profession, then you can deduct all your travel expenses. If the trip combines the search for a job with sightseeing or other personal activity, then you can deduct your travel expenses provided that the **primary purpose** of your trip was to look for a job. Of course, any expense directly connected with your sightseeing activity is not deductible.

> **Example**
> Whitman takes a 2-day trip to New York to interview for a new job. While in New York he rides the Staten Island ferry and does some other incidental sightseeing. He can deduct the entire cost of his trip including transportation, meals, [subject to the 80%-Rule] and lodging. He can't deduct the fare for the Staten Island ferry or other direct sightseeing expenses.

Section 6:
Travel To Professional Conventions

If you attend a convention which is directly connected with your profession, then you may deduct the cost of travel including meals and lodging if you are away from home overnight. This includes professional conventions, conventions of learned societies, union conventions, etc. but not conventions of fraternal organizations. Also excluded now are conventions which provide investment information rather than relate directly to an individual's job or business.

If your spouse accompanies you (and your spouse has no business purpose for being there), you may deduct what it would have cost had you gone alone. Thus, if the hotel rate is $80 for a double and $65 for a single room, you may deduct

$65 as the cost of the room. Likewise, you may deduct 26 cents per mile for your automobile expenses whether or not your spouse travels with you.

For conventions held outside the North American area, it must be "reasonable" for the convention to be held abroad. For example, a foreign convention of an international professional society would qualify, but a convention, say, of the Iowa Engineering Association held in France would not.

Many convention trips include some sightseeing or other personal activity. Section 7 discusses how to treat travel which combines business with personal activities.

Section 7:
Travel Which Combines
Business with Pleasure

A. Travel Within the United States

If your trip was entirely for business, your ordinary and necessary travel expenses may be deducted. If your trip was solely personal, no part of your travel expenses are deductible, even if you engaged in some business activity at your destination.

You may travel to a business destination, and extend your stay for nonbusiness reasons, make a nonbusiness side trip, or engage in other nonbusiness activities. In this case, your travel expenses are deductible only if the trip was related **primarily** to your profession.

Regardless of whether the primary purpose of your trip was business or pleasure, an expense that is properly attributable to a business purpose, such as a registration fee at a professional convention, is deductible.

Whether a trip is primarily for business or is primarily personal in nature depends on the facts and circumstances in each case. However, the length of time spent in business or personal activities is an important factor in determining the primary purpose of the trip.

Example 1

Jones is a Professor of Chemistry at a university in Iowa. He attends the annual convention of the American Chemical Society in San Francisco. The convention consists primarily of papers presented by various members of the society on research in chemistry. Jones attends the convention for five days and spends most of his time during the day attending sessions of the convention. He rides a few cable cars for fun and does some other incidental sightseeing.

Rule: The travel is primarily for business. He may deduct the cost of transportation between Iowa and San Francisco, lodging, and 80% of the cost of meals both while in transit and at the convention. His sightseeing costs are not deductible.

Example 2

Same as in Example 1, except that instead of returning directly from San Francisco to Iowa, Dr. Jones flies to Los Angeles for a day to visit his brother. He then returns to Iowa from Los Angeles.

Rule: Jones can claim that his was primarily a business trip to attend the convention. The side trip to Los Angeles was not his primary purpose in taking the trip. Jones may deduct his lodging and 80% of the cost of meals in San Francisco, plus what the cost of transportation would have been had he traveled directly between Iowa and San Francisco instead of stopping over in Los Angeles. He cannot deduct expenses incurred while in Los Angeles.

Example 3

Mr. Burns teaches high school in Atlanta and travels to St. Louis to attend the convention of the teacher's union to which he belongs. He does little or no sightseeing.

Rule: Travel to union conventions is a legitimate business expense. Therefore his transportation, lodging, and 80% of the cost of his meals while in St. Louis are deductible.

Example 4

Cooper teaches Psychology at a New Mexico high school. After the school term is over, he and his family take a month-long camping trip in California. He leaves his family at Yosemite National Park for two days to attend a meeting of the American Society for Teachers of Psychology in San Francisco.

Rule: His trip was primarily for personal activities connected with his camping trip. However, he may deduct any expenses directly connected with his attendance at the convention. Thus, his living expenses in San Francisco and the cost of transportation between Yosemite and San Francisco are deductible.

B. Travel Outside the United States

Different rules govern travel inside the U.S. and travel outside the U.S. For combined business-with-pleasure travel **inside** the U.S., you may deduct all of your travel expenses (except those specifically connected with personal activities such as sightseeing) as long as you can establish that the primary purpose of your travel was of a business or professional nature.

For combined business-with-pleasure travel **outside** the U.S. where the primary purpose of the travel is for business purposes, you must meet one of the following conditions in order to deduct all of your travel expenses:

1. **You were outside the U.S. a week or less.** In counting the days, do not count the day of departure from the U.S. but do count the day of return to the U.S.

2. **You were reimbursed** by or received a travel expense allowance from your employer (and you are not a managing executive nor related to your employer).

3. **You spent less than 25 per cent of the total time outside the U.S. on non-business activities.**

4. **You had no substantial control over arranging the trip.** You are not considered to have control merely because you have control over timing the trip.

5. **You can establish that a personal vacation was not a major consideration.**

Even if you satisfy one of the above conditions for a trip taken primarily for business, you still cannot deduct for expenses which are strictly personal in nature, such as sightseeing expenses. Similarly, if you extend your stay just to engage in some personal activity, then your living expenses during such an extension are not deductible. However, if you spend time on personal activities during the middle of a business trip, your living expenses during such a period can still be deductible.

Example

You traveled to Paris primarily for business purposes connected with your profession. You left Denver Tuesday and flew to New York. On Wednesday, you flew nonstop from New York to Paris, arriving Thursday morning. Thursday and Friday were spent on business activities and from Saturday until Tuesday you were sightseeing. You flew back to New York, arriving Wednesday afternoon. On Thursday, you flew back to Denver. Since the day of departure from the United States does not count, you were not outside the United States for more than a week. You may deduct what it would have cost you to fly from Denver to Paris, stay there Thursday and Friday, and return on Saturday. The cost of your stay in Paris from Saturday through Tuesday is not deductible since it is not attributable to a business purpose.

However, suppose that your professional activities had temporarily ceased on Friday afternoon, resuming on Monday and Tuesday. In this case, the fact that you spent Saturday and Sunday sightseeing would not disqualify your living expenses during such days from being deductible. You had to stay in Paris during the weekend for the business purpose of being able to continue your professional activities on Monday and Tuesday. Of course, you still cannot deduct your sightseeing expenses.

Allocating Expenses

If you do not meet one of the five conditions listed above for travel outside the U.S. your expenses must be allocated between business and nonbusiness activities. Generally, the amount of your travel expense outside the United States incurred in getting to and from your business destination that is not deductible is determined by multiplying the total travel expenses by the total number of non-business days outside the United States, and dividing the result by the total number of days outside the United States. For this purpose you must count both the day of your departure from, and return to, the United States. The allocation to business or nonbusiness activity is generally made on a day by day basis according to the following rules.

Transportation days. If you travel a reasonably direct route without interruption to your business destination, each day en route outside the United States is considered a business day. If your travel is interrupted by a substantial nonbusiness diversion, or if you do not travel a reasonably direct route, you count as business days only the number of days you would have been outside the United States if you had traveled to your business destination by a reasonably direct route without interruption, using the same means of transportation.

Presence required. Any day that your presence is required in a particular place for a specific and bona fide business purpose is counted as a business day, even though your presence is required for only a part of the day and if during the normal working hours of the day you spend more time in nonbusiness activities than in business activities.

If your principal activity during normal working hours is in pursuit of your business, the day is counted as a business day. Any day that you are prevented from engaging in the conduct of your business as a principal activity because of circumstances beyond your control is also counted as a business day.

Weekends, holidays, and other necessary standby days are counted as business days if they fall between business days. But if they are at the end of your business activity and you remain at your business destination for nonbusiness or personal reasons, they are not business days.

If the nonbusiness activity occurred between the point of departure from the United States and your business destination, you allocate what it would have cost you to travel (including meals and lodging) between the place where your travel outside the United States begins and the place of your nonbusiness activity, and return to the United States, using the same mode of travel as you actually used.

Example

You live in New York and flew to Brussels on Monday, May 31 for professional activities that began at noon Tuesday, June 1, and were over at noon Friday, June 4. That evening you flew to Dublin, Ireland, where you visited with friends until the afternoon of June 17, when you flew home to New York. The primary purpose of the trip was for business purposes. If you had not stopped in Dublin, you would have arrived home the evening of June 4. You were outside the United States more than a week, and you are unable to show that you had no substantial control over arranging the *trip, or that a personal vacation was not a major consideration in making the trip. May 31 through June 4 (5 days) are business days and June 5 through June 17 (13 days) are nonbusiness days. Your expenses while in Dublin are nondeductible. In addition 13/18 of the cost of the round-trip airline fare from New York to Dublin is not deductible. You may deduct the cost of lodging and 80% of the cost of your meals while in Brussels, to the extent they are not lavish or extravagant, all other necessary travel expenses while in Brussels, and that portion of your roundtrip transportation cost (including meals) from New York to Brussels, that exceeds 13/18 of the round-trip plane fare between New York and Dublin.* [IRS Pub. 463]

If the nonbusiness activity was at or beyond your business destination, you would allocate your total travel expenses (including meals and lodging en route) from the place where travel outside the United States began to the place of business activity and return to the United States.

Example

Assume the same facts as in the example above, except that instead of going to Dublin for your vacation, you fly to Venice, Italy, for a vacation, and arrive back in New York on the evening of June 17. (Note that in this example, Venice is further from New York than Brussels, whereas in the preceding example Dublin was closer to New York than Brussels.) You may not deduct any part of the cost of your trip from Brussels to Venice.

You may deduct 5/18 of the round-trip plane fare from New York to Brussels (including 80% of the cost of meals en route), plus lodging and 80% of the cost of your meals while in Brussels to the extent they are not lavish or extravagant, and any other ordinary and necessary business expenses incurred while you were in Brussels. [IRS Pub. 463]

Other allocation method. You may use a different allocation method if it more clearly reflects the proportion of your time spent on business activity.

Converting a Personal Trip Into a Deductible Business Trip

Sometimes, it is possible to convert a trip originally motivated by personal considerations into a deductible business trip. The following court case should prove an inspiration to those who attempt to accomplish this objective.

Example

Habeeb was an assistant professor at a Medical School in the South. For six years in a row, he made an annual trip to Egypt where he visited his mother and other relatives who lived there. The court case involves one of these years when Habeeb claimed that his trip qualified for a tax-deduction because it was made primarily for business purposes. The court opinion describes his trip as follows:

"The trip lasted 45 days and travel was by a chartered flight because it was cheaper. During his stay in Egypt petitioner delivered 5 lectures at the University of Alexandria and 2 lectures at the University of Cairo. These lectures involved subjects within petitioner's expertise, such as 'Antigenicity of Proteins' and 'Chemistry of Antibodies.' The lecture dates span the 14-day period from July 4 to July 18. Petitioner testified that he was invited to give these lectures, but also admitted on cross-examination that he had volunteered his services. He received no compensation or expense reimbursement for such lectures. Petitioner testified that he had numerous discussions with students, professors, and other lecturers while in Egypt for the purpose of exchanging ideas, keeping abreast, reviewing articles, and generally to avoid the isolation which one would experience if one did not travel. Petitioner's testimony on this score was general and nonspecific."

Habeeb had three strikes against him. First, he had volunteered to give the lectures and received no pay or expense reimbursement from the universities he visited. Second, the trip had a strong personal component since he was visiting his mother and other relatives. And third, he spent less than 1/3 of his time, 14 out of 45 days, for business purposes.

In spite of these three negative points, the Court decided that his trip was undertaken primarily for business purposes and therefore a portion of his expenses could be deducted. The written opinion of the Court shows how it reached this conclusion.

"Even though petitioner may have solicited the invitations to lecture, there is no question that he did give the lectures; and additionally, it has been established that petitioner is well-respected for his specialized learning, his writings, and his lectures, and that his lectures helped to maintain that reputation.

"The first question to be answered is whether the trip to Egypt was primarily personal in nature. If so, [IRS regulations] would require disallowance of the travel deduction even though some business activities took place during the trip. Two weeks of the approximate 6-week trip were spent delivering a series of lectures, for which petitioner devoted substantial time and effort in preparation. Even though petitioner might have chosen some other country for some of his lectures had it not been for his mother and father in Egypt, the trip does not, for that reason become 'primarily personal.' It is true that the presence of close relatives at the place of destination may raise a question of disguised personal motive for a trip or series of trips. Cf. William R. Kenney [Dec. 33, 778], 66 T.C. 122 (1976). But if an adequate business justification exists, the fact that trips are repeated to the same destination, where the taxpayer has relatives or friends does not, ipso facto, obliterate the business character of the trip.

"As to the overall time spent on the trip, it is to be noted that petitioner took a 45-day charter flight because it was cheaper. [Although IRS regulations state] that the amount of time spent on personal versus business activities is

'an important factor' in determining primary purpose, it is believed that under the totality of facts and circumstances here present, the trip was taken primarily for the business purpose of maintaining petitioner's reputation in the field of his specialty." [Habeeb, 35 TCM]

Section 8:
Educational Travel

There are two basic types of travel for educational purposes. The first is travel to one or more locations in order to obtain education there. In this case, travel expenses are deductible providing the education qualifies as described in the *Expenses of Attending School* chapter.

The second is travel of a type that the travel itself is of educational value. Travel of this type is no longer deductible.

Example 1
A scholar of French literature travels to Paris to take courses that are offered only at the Sorbonne or to study, doing specific library research that cannot be done elsewhere. Assuming that the cost of his studies is deductible as educational expenses, his associated travel costs are deductible. [Cf. the *Expenses of Attending School* chapter. Also see Sections 3 and 4 of this chapter for other examples where travel expenses connected with research can be deducted as an *employee business expense.*]

Example 2
A French language teacher travels to France in order to improve his general knowledge of the French language and customs. He doesn't spend any significant amount of time doing specific scholarly research or taking classes. His travel is considered to be for personal purposes. Expenses for this type of travel are no longer deductible.

Section 9:
Discount Rates for Teachers

Some hotels and motels offer discounts to teachers who present a faculty ID upon registration. The *Sheraton* chain, in particular, offers an attractive arrangement. At most of its hotels and motels, it offers, subject to availability, a discount of 25% to educators presenting an ID card, pay stub, or other proof of faculty status. In fact, college students get this same 25% discount with presentation of a student ID.

Other hotels give discounts on an individual basis. For example, in New York City, the Roosevelt Hotel gives discounts to college faculty of nearly 50%, depending upon the time of year and day of the week involved. Some Hilton Hotels also offer discounts that range to over 30% off for both teachers and students. And some Marriotts and Quality Inns offer discounts to teachers or to "government employees" which may include teachers who work for the state by teaching in public schools or colleges.

Even if a hotel doesn't have a standard discount policy for teachers, the management often has authority to give a discount. Sometimes, they'll give a teacher their standard corporate discount rate when asked.

Also, most motel and hotel chains give discounts to members of certain "senior citizen" organizations. For example, most Holiday Inns, Howard Johnsons, Quality Inns, Scottish Inns, Ramada Inns, Sheratons, Red Carpet Inns, Master Host Inns, Travelodges, and Econolodges will give a discount to members of the National Retired Teachers Association (NRTA) or American Association of Retired Persons (AARP). While 10% is the typical discount rate, some chains offer well above that. Many Sheratons give 25% off, with occasional promotional campaigns that offer even bigger discounts at some locations. Ramada Inns generally give seniors 25% off while Howard Johnsons give them either 10% to 30% off. And some Marriotts have a limited number of rooms at discounts up to 50% for NRTA or AARP members. Also, most of these motels offer a discount to members of the National Council of Senior Citizens, or to people who can simply show any ID to prove their age is over 55, 60, or 65, depending upon their policy.

Despite their names, memberships in the National Retired Teachers Association and the American Association of Retired Persons are open to those age 50 or over, whether or not they are retired. And the National Council of Senior Citizens is open to anyone who wants to join, irrespective of age. These organizations charge a nominal fee of $12 or less for an annual membership. *[Addresses: NRTA, 1909 K St., N.W., Washington, D.C. 20049; National Council of Senior Citizens, 925 15th St., N.W., Washington, D.C. 20005; AARP, 1909 K St., N.W., Washington, D.C. 20049]*

Another avenue of approach is to ask if the hotel has a "super-saver" or other special discount rate. This can cut the cost by up to 50% or sometimes even more. But some of these discounts aren't advertised or mentioned by the reservation department—you have to know to ask for them. It's a good idea to call the individual hotel for discount information; the 800 operator may not be aware of all the discounts available at each hotel.

Some of the above discount arrangements are subject to *"space availability."* This means that during extra busy periods, discount privileges may be suspended.

If you are renting a car during your trip, ask about discounts there, too. Many Thrifty and Avis Rent-A-Car locations give discounts to members of AARP. Similarly, some Budget Rent-A-Cars give NRTA or AARP discounts and discounts to federal and state government employees. And Hertz offices in some cities give discounts to members of NEA, NRTA, and AARP. Also, some rental car companies give discounts to Federal and State government employees, which may include teachers at publicly supported colleges.

Chapter 22

Miscellaneous Deductions

Section 1:
Basic Rules

This chapter describes the items that can be claimed under the category of *miscellaneous deductions* on Schedule A. As discussed in Section 2, this now includes all deductible job-related expenses. And as discussed in Section 3, *miscellaneous deductions* also include such items as investment-related expenses and expenses connected with tax computation (e.g. the cost of this book).

2% of Adjusted Gross Income (AGI) Floor

There is a 2% of Adjusted Gross Income floor on *miscellaneous deductions*. That is, to determine your deduction for *miscellaneous expenses* on Schedule A, you must subtract 2% of your Adjusted Gross Income (AGI) from the total of your allowable expenses. Schedule A builds in this subtraction (on line 24) in the computation procedure for determining your total itemized deductions.

Example 1

Johnson computes Adjusted Gross Income of $50,000 on his tax return. He has allowable miscellaneous expenses of $1,500. His miscellaneous deduction is computed as follows:

Total Expenses:	$1,500	
less 2% of AGI (2% × $50,000):	− 1,000	
Deduction:	$ 500	(entered on line 24 of Schedule A)

There are a few specialized miscellaneous deductions which escape application of the 2% floor. Included in this category are gambling losses up to gambling winnings, certain expenses for handicapped workers, and jury duty pay turned over to your employer [cf. the end of Section 3].

Where Do You Claim Job-Related Expenses?

Form 2106, *Employee Business Expenses,* is used for reporting your job-related expenses. This form is separated into 2 columns, one for meals and entertainment and the other for the remainder of your expenses. This separation is made so that the 80%-Rule for meals and entertainment [cf. the *Travel* or

Entertainment chapter] can be factored into the computation.

Page 1 of Form 2106 is divided into 3 sections, called "Steps." In Step 1, you report the amounts of your job-related expenses, broken down into several categories as listed on the form.

If your employer **did not reimburse** you for any of your job-related expenses, then you skip Step 2, proceeding directly to Step 3. In Step 3, your total of job-related expenses is computed. The total is then entered as a miscellaneous deduction on line 20 of Schedule A and, when combined with your other miscellaneous deductions, subjected to the 2% of AGI floor as described above.

Reimbursed Expenses

You may have included expenses in Step 1 for which you received a reimbursement from your employer. Your employer is now generally required to report these reimbursements on the yearend W-2 Form he gives you.

There are 2 different ways your employer may report these reimbursements. Either:

Case 1. The **reimbursements are not** included in taxable income on your W-2 Form,

or

Case 2. The **reimbursements are included** in taxable income on your W-2 Form.

Case 1. Reimbursements Not Included in Taxable Income

This is the situation that leads to the most favorable treatment. Reimbursements received from your employer are listed separately on your W-2 Form but are **not included** in the taxable income figure. Or, these reimbursements are simply not listed on your W-2 Form at all.

A. If you **did not** claim any of these expenses as deductions in Step 1 of Form 2106, then you're done. Neither the expenses nor the reimbursements appear on your tax return—producing a net result of zero.

B. If you **did** claim these expenses as deductions in Step 1 of Form 2106, then you list the reimbursements in Step 2 of Form 2106. The reimbursements are then subtracted from the expenses on line 10 of Form 2106—again producing a net result of zero.

Case 1 arises when your employer does not report reimbursements as taxable income received by you. There are 2 requirements that must be satisfied in order for your employer to be able to treat reimbursements this way. First, you must have provided your employer with satisfactory written substantiation for the expenses you incurred. [Cf. Section 1 of the *Travel* chapter for what constitutes satisfactory substantiation.] Second, you must return, in a timely manner, excess reimbursements received for days not traveled or mileage not driven. [Cf. Section 1 of the *Travel* chapter, in particular Examples 4 and 5 along with the surrounding material, for a discussion of this requirement.]

If these 2 conditions are not satisfied, then your employer is supposed to include the reimbursements in your taxable income as discussed in Case 2.

If you have received reimbursements from your employer, be sure to examine your yearend W-2 Form. You'll want to make sure your employer has reported these reimbursements the correct way. Those reimbursements that qualify under the rules described above should not be included as taxable income in the *"Wages"* box on your W-2 Form. If they are, you should request that your employer file an amended W-2 Form correcting the error. (This will produce a reduction in adjusted gross income which can be better than an itemized deduction for reasons discussed above.) Because the reporting rules are new this year, there is an increased likelihood of employer's error.

Case 2. Reimbursements Included in Taxable Income.

As discussed above, there are circumstances under which your employer will report reimbursements you receive for job-related expenses as taxable income on your W-2 Form. In this case, you just claim the expenses as a miscellaneous deduction using Step 1 of Form 2106.

As a miscellaneous deduction, these expenses will be subjected to the 2% of adjusted gross income subtraction that applies, as discussed earlier in this chapter. The disadvantage is that if your total miscellaneous deductions are not sufficiently large, you might get no deduction for these expenses at all. This means you would wind up paying extra tax on the amount of reimbursements received from your employer, without any offsetting deduction. This result was intended by Congress when it changed the law this year. It wanted to treat reimbursement plans harshly in this way if the 2 conditions specified at the end of the Case 1 explanation above were not satisfied.

Example 2

Jones has deductible employee business expenses totaling $1,000, for which he receives a full reimbursement from his employer. None of these expenses is for meals or entertainment.

Case 1. Smith provides an adequate accounting of the expenses to his employer. As a result, Smith's employer does not include the reimbursement as taxable income on the W-2 Form it issues to Smith at yearend.

In this case, there's nothing for Smith to do. He does not claim the expenses on his tax return, nor does the reimbursement show up as taxable income on his tax return—a net result of zero.

Case 2. Smith does not provide an adequate accounting to his employer. As a result, Smith's employer does include the reimbursement as taxable income on Smith's yearend W-2 Form.

In this case, Smith must claim the $1,000 in expenses as a deduction on his own tax return. The expenses are reported on Form 2106 and then claimed as a miscellaneous deduction on line 20 of Schedule A. On Schedule A, this $1,000, when combined with other miscellaneous deductions, is subjected to the 2% of AGI floor that applies. If the 2% floor negates the deduction or if Smith uses the standard deduction, he's out of luck. He winds up with $1,000 in extra taxable income with no offsetting deduction.

Meal and Entertainment Expenses

An extra complication arises from the *80%-Rule* on meal and entertainment expenses. Under this rule, only 80% of these expenses can be claimed as a deduction [cf. the *Travel* and the *Entertainment* chapters].

The IRS handles this by dividing Form 2106 into 2 columns. Column B is used for meal and entertainment expenses, while Column A is used for all other employee business expenses.

The computation procedure given by Steps 1-3, as discussed above, is applied to each column separately. Thus, reimbursements for meal and entertainment expenses are subtracted from the total expenses given in Column B while other reimbursements are subtracted from the total expenses given in Column A. The resulting 2 remainders, one for Column B expenses and one for Column A expenses, appear separately on line 8 of Form 2106.

The bottom line is obtained by adding the Column A result plus 80% of the Column B result. This is the amount you carry over to line 20 of Schedule A as a miscellaneous deduction.

Example 3

Smith has deductible employee business expenses totaling $3,000: $900 for meals and entertainment plus $2,100 of other expenses. His employer has a policy of reimbursing employees for $2/3$ of their expenses. Under this policy, Smith receives a reimbursement of $2,000 ($2/3$ × $900 = $600 for meals and entertainment, plus $2/3$ × $2,100 = $1,400 for other expenses). Because Smith made an adequate accounting to his employer, the employer does not include the reimbursement in taxable income reported on Smith's yearend W-2 Form.

The computation of Smith's employee business expense deduction on Form 2106 proceeds as follows:

	Column A Other than Meals and Entertainment	Column B Meals and Entertainment
Step 1. Expenses:	$2,100	$900
Step 2. Reimbursements not included in taxable income on W-2 Form:	− 1,400	− 600
Step 3. Remainder:	$ 700	$300

Deduction: $700 + (80% × $300) = $940.

Smith transfers the $940 deduction computed above to line 20 of Schedule A. (On Schedule A, this $940, when combined with other miscellaneous deductions, is subjected to the 2% of AGI floor that applies.)

Example 4

Same as Example 3, except that Smith did not make an adequate accounting to his employer. Because of this, the employer includes the $2,000 in taxable income reported on Smith's W-2 Form. As in the Case 2 discussion above, Step 2 of Form 2106 is omitted. Thus, the amounts in Step 3 are equal to amounts in Step 1:

	Column A Other than Meals and Entertainment	Column B Meals and Entertainment
Step 1. Expenses:	$2,100	$900
Step 2. (Omitted)		
Step 3. (Equal to Step 1):	$2,100	$900

Deduction: $2,100 + (80\% \times \$900) = \$2,820$.

Smith transfers the $2,820 deduction computed above to line 20 of Schedule A. On Schedule A, this $2,820, when combined with other miscellaneous deductions, is subjected to the 2% of AGI floor that applies.

The outcome in Example 4 is inferior to that in Example 3 in two ways. First, if Smith cannot use the full miscellaneous deduction as computed in the example, either because of the 2% of AGI floor or because he uses the standard deduction, the result in Example 4 is a disaster. In the absence of any deduction, Smith simply winds up with almost $2,000 in extra taxable income in the Example 4 situation.

Second, even if the deductions are fully usable (because the 2% floor is already exceeded by other miscellaneous expenses), Example 4 produces an inferior result. In Example 3, the net result was a $940 reduction in taxable income produced by the computed deduction. But in Example 4, Smith has $2,000 extra taxable income produced by the reimbursement coupled with a $2,820 deduction—producing a net reduction in taxable income of only $820.

The lesser reduction in taxable income produced in Example 4 is due to the fact that Smith absorbs the full impact of the 80%-reduction factor applying to the $900 expenses for meals and entertainment. In Example 3, only the unreimbursed $300 was subject to this factor on Smith's tax return. (The employer is then stuck with the rest of the 80%-reduction factor when it deducts the reimbursed amounts paid out on its tax return.)

In Example 3, $600 of the reimbursement was applied toward the $900 spent for meals and entertainment because the employer's basic policy was to reimburse 2/3 of all expenses. This meant that Smith had to reduce the remaining unreimbursed $300 by using the 80% factor when computing his total deduction. According to a 1988 IRS regulation, the same type of percentage allocation will be made even if there is no explicit reimbursement policy. Thus, the above example would apply if the same $2,000 reimbursement were received by Smith without any specification as to how the employee calculated this reimbursement amount. [Temp Reg. 1.62-IT(e)]

However, if the employer's policy is to reimburse different categories of expenses differently, then the reimbursement is allocated accordingly. The next example illustrates a situation where the reimbursement could be considered to cover all of the meal and entertainment costs. This is the most favorable situation because there is no 80%-reduction factor that applies to the unreimbursed expenses the employee is allowed to deduct.

Example 5

Parker takes a 4-day business-related trip, incurring meal expenses of $250, lodging expenses of $500, and other travel expenses of $600. Parker's employer reimburses employees for business travel except that meals are limited to $75 per day and lodging to $100 per day. Thus, the total reimbursement is $250 for meals plus $400 + $600 = $1,000 for lodging and other travel expenses, a total of $1,250. Parker's employer does not include this $1,250 reimbursement in taxable income reported on Parker's yearend W-2 Form.

	Column A Other than Meals and Entertainment	Column B Meals and Entertainment
Step 1. Travel Expenses:	$1,100	$250
Additional Expenses:	+ 800	
Total Expenses:	$1,900	$250
Step 2. Reimbursements not included in taxable income on W-2 Form:	– $1,000	– $250
Step 3. Remainder:	$ 900	$ 0

Deduction: $900 + (80% × $0) = $900

Escaping the 2% of AGI Floor

The 2% of AGI floor only affects items claimed as *Miscellaneous Deductions* on Schedule A. It does not apply to items connected with a self-employment activity which can be claimed on Schedule C, *Profit (or Loss) from Business or Profession.* You might be able to claim an item on Schedule C as a *Business Expense* rather than on Schedule A as a *Miscellaneous Deduction.* This might "save" all or part of the deduction from being hit by the 2% floor on miscellaneous deductions.

For example, suppose an employee earns extra income from his own consulting business. Certain items such as books, periodicals, professional dues, etc. may be reasonably attributed to either his regular job or his consulting business. By claiming these items as a business expense on Schedule C instead of as a job-related expense on Schedule A, the 2% of AGI floor is sidestepped. This will lower taxes unless the total of other miscellaneous deductions already exceeds the 2% of AGI floor. (In that case, further miscellaneous deductions will have the same tax-lowering effect as any other deduction.)

To illustrate, suppose an individual's Adjusted Gross Income is $50,000 and he has miscellaneous deductions totaling $1,500. After subtracting 2% of Adjusted Gross Income (2% × $50,000 = $1,000), his deduction on Schedule A is $1,500 − $1,000 = $500. If he has an additional expense of $100 for, say, dues to a professional society, then his miscellaneous expenses would total $1,600 instead of $1,500 and his deduction would be equal to $1,600 − $1,000 = $600. Thus, the extra $100 expense would lower taxable income by an extra $100 ($600 − $500), the same as any other deduction.

However, if he had no other miscellaneous deductions, then claiming the $100 as a miscellaneous deduction would do him no good. The 2% of AGI floor would just reduce the amount to $0. In such a case, claiming the $100 on Schedule C rather than on Schedule A would save the deduction.

Section 2:
Employment Related Expenses

The following employment-related expenses are deductible as *miscellaneous deductions:*

Travel Expenses [cf. Chapter 21]

Auto Expenses [cf. Chapter 10]

Educational Expenses [cf. Chapter 23]

Entertainment Expenses [cf. Chapter 24]

Home Office [cf. Chapter 3]

Research Expenses [cf. Chapter 29]

Books, Supplies, & Equipment [cf. Chapter 2]

Job-Hunting Expenses. These expenses are deductible whether or not you are successful in obtaining a job. However, you must be looking for a job in your same profession, not a different one. An IRS ruling indicates that a part-time teaching position is sufficient to establish membership in a profession. The ruling permitted an attorney who lectured part-time at a law school to deduct the cost of looking for a full-time teaching position. [Rev Rule 78-93]

Deductible expenses include employment agency fees, travel expenses, resume typing costs, job counseling fees, newspapers to check want ads, etc. Also, don't overlook entertainment expenses incurred in your hunt for a job. For example, taking a friend to lunch for the purpose of getting him to help you obtain a job where he works would be deductible, subject to the 80%-Rule described in the *Entertainment* chapter.

Required Physical. You may deduct the cost of a physical examination or TB test which was required by your school. These may be deducted as a business expense if you wish to avoid subjecting them to the 7.5% floor on medical deductions [cf. the *Medical Expenses* chapter].

Payment of Substitute. If your school requires you to pay a substitute teacher when you are absent, then you may deduct this expense. This is covered by an IRS ruling issued to a faculty member at a school with a sabbatical program under which he received full salary during the period of absence. However, the faculty member had to contribute to a fund out of which payments to a substitute were made. The IRS ruled that he could not simply reduce his salary by his payments to the fund and report the difference as income. Instead, he had to report his salary as income and deduct his payments to the substitute fund as a miscellaneous deduction. If he claimed the standard deduction, he would lose out on the deduction for payments to the substitute fund. (The same situation applies if a teacher is required to pay for a bond when taking a sabbatical.) [Rev. Rule 76-286]

Dues to Professional Organizations or Teachers' Unions. Agency shop fees required of a nonmember in lieu of union dues are also deductible.

Extracurricular Activities. Do you travel on school business, coach a school athletic team, sponsor a school organization, visit students' homes, lead student tours, etc.? You can deduct expenses connected with these activities if they are a legitimate part of your profession. *Bar Association dinners?*

Preparing Master's Thesis or Doctoral Dissertation. You may deduct expenses for such things as typing, research, clerical help, etc., which are connected with writing a thesis or dissertation. However, you must qualify under the rules described in the *Expenses of Attending School* chapter.

Telephone Expenses. You can deduct the cost of business-related long distance calls made from your home telephone. You can no longer deduct any portion of the basic monthly service charge for your principal residential telephone [cf. the *Books, Supplies, & Equipment* chapter].

Section 3:
Other Miscellaneous Deductions

In addition to the employment-related expenses discussed in the preceding section, the following items can be claimed as miscellaneous deductions:

Investment Expenses. You can deduct the costs associated with managing your investments. These include safe deposit boxes to store investments, burglar alarms to protect investment items, telephone calls, miscellaneous supplies, investment fees (but not bank fees charged for the privilege of writing checks even on interest-bearing accounts), etc. It also includes travel associated with managing your investments—e.g. to stock brokers for advice, to manage rental property, to place items in your safe deposit box, etc.

Postage. Don't forget to put down a few dollars for the cost of postage connected with your job, investment activities, tax form filing, etc. Even Jimmy Carter didn't overlook this deduction when he was President. His tax return included a $15.53 deduction for the cost of mailing tax records between Georgia and the White House.

Tax Guide. You may deduct the cost of this book and any other book or professional service which aids you in the preparation of your tax return or in tax planning for the future.

Legal Expenses are deductible to the extent they are connected with income-producing investment activities or tax advice. Your lawyer should show a breakdown on his bill indicating the amount of his fees that can be properly claimed as a miscellaneous deduction. (Legal expenses connected with a self-employment business activity are deducted on Schedule C.)

Periodicals. You may deduct magazines, newspapers, etc. connected with your income-producing investment activities. Such publications might include the *Wall Street Journal, Barrons, Forbes Magazine,* etc. For information on how to handle subscription fees for periods longer than one year, see the *Books, Supplies & Equipment* chapter.

IRA & Keogh Fees. You may have an IRA or Keogh Plan which levies a set-up fee or annual maintenance fee. Such a fee can be claimed as a miscellaneous deduction if separately itemized and paid from your personal bank account (rather than paid out of the IRA or Keogh account). On the other hand, brokerage fees for buying and selling securities in the IRA or Keogh Plan are not deductible.

Appraisal fees to value a deductible charitable donation or casualty loss.

Items Exempted from 2% of AGI Floor

There are a few special-purpose items which the law specifies to be miscellaneous deductions **not** subject to the 2% of AGI subtraction. These include:

Impairment-related work expenses incurred by a handicapped individual in order to be able to work. This would include such items as special tools and attendant care services at work.

Deductible gambling losses up to the amount of gambling winnings that are included in taxable income.

Jury duty pay which you are required to turn over to your employer because you are receiving a salary while serving as a juror. Unlike the preceding 3 items which are claimed as a miscellaneous deduction on line 25 of Schedule A, this jury duty pay is claimed as an *adjustment* to *income* on line 30 of Form 1040. You write *"jury pay"* on the dotted line next to line 30.

Deductions connected with certain specialized investment activities— namely, the expenses of short sales, deductions for amortizable premiums on bonds you own, deductions for an unrecovered investment in a terminated annuity, and deductions that arise under the *"claim of right"* doctrine when you return funds that were received erroneously in a prior year.

Chapter 23

Expenses of Attending School

Section 1:
Basic Rules For Deducting
Educational Expenses

The expenses of attending school are deductible provided that certain conditions are satisfied. These conditions are designed to permit an individual to deduct schooling which aids him in his **current** occupation but to rule out schooling which prepares him for a **new** career. For example, a teacher can deduct the cost of a summer refresher course but a college student cannot deduct the cost of education preparing himself for a new career.

When Are the Expenses of Attending School Deductible?
You may deduct the cost of attending school if your attendance is for any one of the following purposes:

(1) Maintaining or improving skills required in your present employment;

(2) Keeping your current employment, status, or salary;

or

(3) Meeting the express requirements of your current employer.

However there are two exceptions. Your expenses **cannot** be deducted if either:

Rule A. The courses are required in order to meet the minimum educational requirements for your employment;

or

Rule B. The education would qualify you for a new trade or business. A change of duties is not considered as being a new trade or business if the new duties involve the same general work that you did previously.

You may have several purposes for attending school. If Rule A or B listed immediately above is among your reasons, then you may not deduct your educational expenses.

There is one further requirement. You must be considered a current member of your profession at the time you incur the educational expenses. This does not mean you must actually be employed at the time. If you were employed prior to the education and intend to resume employment in the same general profession, then your expenses may still be deductible. This is discussed further in Section 5.

Educational Reimbursements Received from Employer

Some employers have a plan under which employees are reimbursed for the cost of courses which they take. As long as the plan meets certain non-discrimination rules, reimbursements for 1990 educational expenses are tax-free, whether or not the education is job-related. There is a ceiling of $5,250 per year on the amount of tax-free educational benefits an employee can receive. This restrictive ceiling does not apply to educational expenses which the employee could have deducted (according to the rules described in this chapter) had he paid the expenses himself. Also, this restrictive ceiling does not generally apply to graduate assistants who receive tax-free aid under a qualified educational reimbursement plan, nor does it apply to non-discriminatory tuition remission plans for faculty dependents.

Exception. Educational reimbursements are not exempt from tax if used for non-job-related graduate level courses of a kind normally taken by an individual pursuing an advanced academic or professional degree (including law, medicine and MBA degrees). However, graduate teaching and research assistants do not have to pay tax on the value of tuition waived by their employers, provided the waiver is not considered to be pay for services rendered [cf. Section 2 of the *Tax-Free Grants* chapter].

The tax status of educational reimbursements you received should be reflected on the W-2 Form received from your employer. That is, the tax-free reimbursements you receive should not be included in taxable income reported by your employer on your yearend W-2 Form. If in doubt, check with the administrator of your reimbursement plan.

Tuition Remission Plans for College Faculty Family Members

Many universities and colleges have plans under which faculty family members receive free college tuition. The value of this fringe benefit is exempt from tax if it is generally applied to all employees on a non-discriminatory basis—not restricted just to faculty members. Otherwise, the value of the free tuition will be included in taxable income.

Also, tuition remission will be considered a tax-free fringe benefit only for education below the graduate level. However, tuition remission at the graduate level can still qualify for tax-free treatment if it falls under the usual fellowship or scholarship rules [cf. the *Tax-Free Grants* chapter]. (Also see the last sentence of the exception above concerning graduate teaching and research assistants.)

Tax-free treatment applies to reciprocal agreements between colleges providing free tuition to children of faculty members attending any of the colleges covered by the agreement. The same is not true if a college has just a unilateral policy of reimbursing tuition for children of its faculty members at any institution the child chooses. According to a 1989 court case, such reimbursements are considered taxable compensation to the faculty member. [Knapp,USTC 89-1].

Tax-Free Savings Bond Tuition Plan

Congress has authorized a tax-free savings plan to provide for future college tuition payments. The vehicle for this plan is the U.S. Series EE Savings Bond. The way it works is this.

You purchase Savings Bonds now and hold them until a later year in which your child attends college. You then cash in the bonds and use the money to pay tuition and required fees. All interest earned on the bonds is excluded from Federal and State taxation. No tax is paid during the years the bonds are accumulating income nor in the year of redemption.

U.S. Series EE Savings Bonds held for at least 5 years pay interest equal to 85% of the rate paid on 5-year U.S. Treasury securities, except that the rate is guaranteed never to fall below 6%. This makes them a fairly decent investment even outside a tax-free tuition plan.

If you purchase these bonds with the intent of making tuition payments, but your child (heaven forbid) decides not to go to college, then you haven't made a big mistake. You can still cash in the bonds, but will have to pay tax on the accumulated interest in the year the bonds are redeemed. However, U.S. Savings Bonds are still exempt from State and local income tax, no matter how the proceeds are used.

To qualify for the exclusion, the purchaser must be at least age 24 at the time of purchase. Bonds purchased by a child or purchased by a parent and later transferred to the child are not eligible. Also, the bonds must actually be purchased—rollovers of Series E Bonds into Series EE Bonds do not qualify.

Under this program, the bonds must be used to pay for tuition (including fees) of the purchaser, his spouse, or his dependents. Thus, bonds purchased by a grandparent (or other relative) will generally be ineligible for the exclusion. To take advantage of the exclusion, a grandparent would have to give the money to the parent so he could purchase the bonds in his name. Married couples must file a joint tax return in the year the bonds are redeemed in order to claim the exclusion.

The interest excluded from tax in the year the bonds are redeemed cannot exceed the cost of tuition (including fees), reduced by any scholarships, fellowships, employer-provided assistance, or any other tuition reduction amounts. The tuition must be for an accredited college, university, junior college, or other qualified post-secondary school. Expenses for other education-related costs such as room, board, or books do not qualify. Also, excluded is tuition for courses on sports, games, or hobbies unless the courses are required as part of a degree or certificate granting program.

If the amount of tuition paid during a year equals or exceeds the amount of bonds redeemed that year, all the interest is excluded from tax.

Example 1

Frank pays $6,000 in 1990 to purchase EE Savings bonds. In a later year, he redeems the bonds for $10,000. (The $10,000 redemption includes the original $6,000 purchase price plus $4,000 in interest.) That same year, he pays $12,000 in college tuition for his child. Since the $12,000 in tuition exceeds the $10,000 in bond redemptions, the entire $4,000 in interest is excluded from tax.

If the amount of tuition and fees is less than the amount of bonds redeemed that year, only a fraction of the interest is excluded from tax. This is the case even if the tuition and fees exceeds the interest earned on the bonds. The reason for this is that the fraction is computed by dividing the tuition and fees by the total amount redeemed. This latter amount includes both interest and principal.

Example 2

Same as Example 1, except that the tuition is only $8,000 instead of $12,000. Since this $8,000 in tuition is less than the total redemption amount of $10,000, only $8,000/$10,000 = 80% of the interest is excludible. Thus Jones excludes 80% x $4,000 = $3,200 of the interest from tax. The remaining $4,000 – $3,200 = $800 is taxable.

Income Limitation

The full benefits described above are available only to those whose *Modified Adjusted Gross Income* does not exceed $40,000 for single persons or $60,000 for married couples filing a joint return. *Modified Adjusted Gross Income* is obtained from adjusted gross income by adding in the following items:

1. Deductible IRA contributions
2. Foreign income excluded from tax
3. The partial exclusion for social security benefits received
4. Adjustments to limitations of passive losses and credits
5. Interest on EE bonds excluded from tax to pay for qualified college tuition and fees.

The $40,000 and $60,000 limitation figures are the ones applying in 1990. These figures will be indexed to increase with inflation for years after 1990. Note that the limitations apply in the year bonds are redeemed to pay for educational expenses. It makes no difference what the income figures are in the year the bonds are purchased.

Phase-Out Ranges

There is a phase-out range above the $40,000 and $60,000 amounts described above where a partial exclusion is permitted. The phase-out ranges are incorporated into the following tables:

	Modified Adjusted Gross Income	Eligibility
Single	Below $40,000	Full Exclusion
	$40,000–$55,000	Partial Exclusion
	Above $55,000	No Exclusion
Married filing jointly	Below $60,000	Full Exclusion
	$60,000–$90,000	Partial Exclusion
	Above $90,000	No Exclusion
Married filing separately		No Exclusion

(Above figures will be adjusted for inflation after 1990)

The way the partial exclusion is computed in the phase-out ranges above is illustrated by the following examples

Example 3

Same as Example 1 except that Frank had modified adjusted gross income on his joint return of $70,000 in the year the bonds are redeemed. This places him into the phase-out range of $60,000 - $90,000 in the above table (We assume a zero inflation rate for purposes of this illustrative example.) Frank's phase-out percentage is equal to ($70,000 - $60,000) ÷ ($90,000 - $60,000) = 33 1/3%. This percentage is applied to the deductible interest figure computed in Example 1. Thus, 33 1/3% x $4,000 = $1,333 of the interest is taxable. The remaining $4,000 - $1,333 = $2,667 is excluded from tax.

Example 4

Same as Example 2 except that Frank's modified adjusted gross income on his joint tax return is $72,000 in the year of redemption. Frank's phase-out percentage is equal to ($72,000 - $60,000) ÷ ($90,000 - $60,000) = 40%. This percentage figure is applied to the deductible interest figure computed in Example 2. Thus, the $3,200 figure is reduced by 40% x $3,200 = $1,280. This means Frank excludes $3,200 - $1,280 = $1,920 of the interest from tax. The remainder of the $4,000 in bond interest, $4,000 - $1,920 = $2,080 is included in taxable income.

Series EE savings bonds can earn interest for any period of time up to 30 years. However, they need to be held at least 5 years in order to guarantee that the full interest rate will be earned. You do not have to specify in advance when you will cash in the bonds. Also, bonds of at least $100 can be partially cashed in, with the remainder continuing on as a savings bond of a reduced amount.

There is a limit of $15,000 (issue price) on the amount of U.S. Savings Bonds that can be purchased by any one individual during a single year.

U.S. savings bonds can be bought at most banks and savings institutions. Also, you can get a brochure on these bonds by writing to *Office of Public Affairs, U.S. Treasury Department, Savings Bonds Division, Washington, D.C. 20226.* The brochure contains an order form for purchasing bonds directly from the government. If you want to know the current interest rate being paid, you can call toll-free 1-800-US BONDS.

Here's a little-known trick when buying a savings bond. Wait until the end of the month to make your purchase. Savings bonds earn interest from the **beginning** of the month of purchase. A savings bond purchased at the end of a month is treated exactly the same as one purchased at the beginning. While waiting until the end of the month to buy a bond, you can earn a month's extra interest in a money-market or other savings account.

State Prepaid Tuition Plans

A number of States have adopted or are considering some type of *prepaid tuition plan*. Under such a plan, the parents generally contribute a certain amount to a state-run trust when their child is young. Later, when the child attends a public (or in some cases private) institution in that State, his tuition costs are covered by the State-run trust. If the child doesn't attend college or goes to a college in a different State, there is usually a refund made of at least the original contribution, plus in some cases, interest on the amount contributed.

The tax advantage that sponsors were hoping would give these plans financial leverage was the fact that non-profit organizations don't have to pay tax on investment earnings. The question of whether a State-run trust under a tuition prepayment plan would come under this general principle had not been previously addressed.

In 1988, the IRS issued a Private Letter Ruling to the State of Michigan answering the basic tax questions involved in the tuition prepayment plan it proposed to set up. The one good piece of news in the ruling was that the parents who made the initial contribution would not pay tax on income earned by the trust. But otherwise, the news was bad.

First, the State-run trust would be taxed on the income it earned, ruining the basic tax angle involved. In addition, when the child did attend college, he would be taxed on the value of the tuition in excess of the original contribution. Thus, the amounts earned by investing the parent's initial contribution would get taxed twice, rather than being exempted from tax. (There might also be a gift tax on the original contribution that would apply only to wealthier individuals who exceed the $600,000 gift and estate tax exemption over their lifetime.)

Because the child would pay tax on the value of the tuition benefits at (presumably) his low tax bracket, the double taxation might not be so prohibitive as to ruin every State's plans. The peace of mind that parents would have in knowing college costs would be covered might be enough of an incentive itself.

Should You Invest in a Prepaid Tuition Plan Now?

If your State offers a prepaid tuition plan that figures to be a good deal, you should seriously consider signing up. Generally speaking, the plan will be a good deal if you can't earn a higher after-tax rate by investing yourself rather than contributing to the plan.

For example, suppose current tuition at public colleges in your State is $1,500 per year. If you can buy into a prepaid tuition plan that guarantees 4 years of college tuition for say, $6,000, then it's a good deal. To do better, you would have to earn an after-tax rate of return averaging more than the average annual inflation rate for college tuition. Considering that this inflation rate has consistently been out-stripping the consumer price index inflation rate, this would be difficult to do.

The above simplified example ignores such things as the tax your child would need to pay when he receives the benefits from the plan as well as any diminution in benefits if your child doesn't attend an in-State college. However, it also ignores the risk-reduction value of such a plan. The peace of mind that comes from knowing future college costs are covered is worth alot to many persons.

Also for some, prepayment of tuition provides the appropriate climate of commitment for encouraging a child in his pre-college academic pursuits.

An important feature to look for is the financial consequences if your child doesn't attend an in-State college. Some plans being proposed would only refund to you the amount of your original contributions, without the addition of any interest. You'd have to be quite sure of your child's future college plans before investing in such a plan.

Other plans offer numerous "outs", depending upon what your child does in the future. An example is the Michigan Plan, already in existence and quite popular in that State. A student who attends an out-of-State college, for example, gets an amount equal to the average tuition charged at Michigan State schools. There's even a refund equal to the lowest tuition charged in Michigan for a child who doesn't attend college. Or, the entire plan can be transferred to other family members (including cousins) who do choose to go to college.

There is a trap in prepaid tuition plans if you anticipate that your child will qualify for financial aid. The U.S. Department of Education ruled in 1990 that amounts invested in the Michigan prepaid tuition plan would be considered assets of the child rather than of the parent. This in turn affects the child's eligibility for Pell Grants and federally backed student loans as follows:

Under federal aid formulas, a student is expected to contribute up to 35% of his assets toward college costs each year. Families are expected to contribute a much smaller percentage of their assets. Thus, contributing to the prepaid tuition plan will reduce the amount of federal aid for a student whose family's financial status qualifies the student for such aid.

It is not yet clear how the above ruling will affect prepaid tuition plans in states other than Michigan. Also, it is possible that the plans in Michigan or other states will be modified to get around this difficulty.

There is also a hidden gift tax trap in tuition prepayment plans. According to a recent IRS private letter ruling, when a parent makes a payment to such a plan, this constitutes a gift to the child. Ordinarily, gifts of up to $10,000 ($20,000 for married couples) per year are automatically exempted from gift tax [cf. the *Estate and Gift Tax* chapter]. But the IRS ruled that this does not apply to tuition prepayments because only gifts of "present interest" (i.e. gifts that can be immediately controlled by the recipient) qualify for the annual $10,000 exclusion.

Also, amounts remitted to a college to pay for tuition are automatically exempted from gift tax. But the IRS rules that payments to the tuition prepayment plan are not the same as payments to the college and do not qualify for this exemption. [IRS Private Letter Ruling 8901027]

Because the tuition prepayments are not covered under the usual annual exemptions, they are counted against and serve to reduce the lifetime $600,000 combined estate and gift tax exemption [cf. the *Estate & Gift Tax* chapter]. However, for those who will not approach this limit, the tuition prepayments will have no gift or estate tax ramifications. Also, it is unclear how the IRS will monitor the gift and estate tax status of relatively small tuition prepayments.

Other College-Savings Plans

Instead of prepaid tuition plans, many States are offering or considering special college tuition bonds, sometimes called *baccalaureate bonds*. These bonds are basically similar to other municipal bonds issued by State and local governments [cf. Section 4 of the *Investing your Money* chapter]. In particular, interest paid on the bonds is exempt from Federal income tax and from State income tax in the State of issue.

However, generally there are special features of these bonds that make them tailor-made for those wishing to save for future tuition payments. First, they are *zero-coupon bonds,* which means that all interest is paid on the date of maturity, like U.S. savings bonds. For example, a parent might purchase a 15-year bond for $1,000 when his child is age 2. On the maturity date 15 years after purchase, the bond would be cashed in for say, $3,500, depending upon the prevailing interest rate. With no tax due, the $3,500 could be used toward making tuition payments (or for some other purpose).

The second feature is that these bonds are easy to purchase directly from the State in reasonably small denominations of $1,000 or less. Ordinary municipal bonds are issued in round lots of $5,000 or more and must be purchased from a commercial broker who charges a commission at the time of purchase.

Note that college tuition bonds do not have the same potential pitfalls as prepaid plans as discussed in the preceding subsection. As long as the bonds remain in the parent's name instead of the child's, there is no gift tax involved, nor are the federal aid formulas negatively impacted.

The basic interest rate on college tuition bonds is set at an appropriate market rate. However, unlike prepaid tuition plans, there is no guarantee that the funds received at maturity will be sufficient to cover tuition. However, what gives some of these tuition bond plans a significant edge are extra features that they provide. The following is a list of some features to look for that appear in some of these plans.

1. Extra Interest. In addition to the interest based on the going market rate, some States pay extra interest when the bond proceeds are used to pay tuition. This can run from an extra interest rate of 1/2% to 4%, or more.

2. Extra Endowment Funds. Some States plan to set up an endowment fund to go along with their tuition bond plan. Money from the endowment fund would supplement tuition payments made from proceeds of the tuition bonds.

3. Extra Financial Aid. Many States have a financial aid program providing loans or grants to college students, based on a needs analysis. To avoid the savings disincentive caused by this needs analysis, some States will exclude, say, the first $25,000 in proceeds from tuition bonds, when computing how much money a family has available to go towards tuition.

4. Indexed Interest Rate. At least one State is considering setting the interest rate on tuition bonds each year to equal the average increase in college costs. This makes it similar to a tuition prepayment plan, except that the student would not be restricted on which school to attend.

As we go to press, tuition savings plans are a "hot" item all over the country. However, many States are still in the planning stage. Some States are awaiting IRS approval while others are waiting to see what type of Federal program, if any, will be passed by Congress. Also, some colleges have tuition prepayment plans of their own. And some colleges have banded together to provide communal tuition prepayment plans. Under this type of plan, the student can choose to attend any one of the colleges and apply amounts in the plan against the tuition. If you know which college your child is likely to attend, you can check with that college to see if there are any prepayment plans which might be of benefit to you. Next year's edition of this Tax Guide will contain more information and guidance on this issue as more details become available.

Section 2:
When Do Educational Expenses
Qualify For Deduction?

Education Which Maintains or Improves Skills
If you incur expenses for education which maintains or improves your professional skills, these expenses are deductible provided they are not disqualified under either the *minimum requirements* of Rule A or the *new trade or business* of Rule B. To qualify, the education must be in subject matter related to your teaching, research, or other professional duties. For example, a German teacher would be allowed to deduct expenses for taking a course in German literature. The education in question may be day courses, refresher courses, vocational courses, research on a dissertation, or any other educational activity. In the following exam-

ple, 2 physical education teachers were recently permitted to deduct a portion of their membership fees in racquetball clubs, because the facilities were used to improve their teaching skills.

Example

A married couple were both physical education teachers at different schools in neighboring cities. They each taught a variety of courses covering different athletic activities, including racquetball and handball.

During the year in question, they paid for memberships in 4 different facilities with racquetball courts. She learned to play racquetball at one of the facilities to which she belonged; she also attended some clinics which taught her how to play racquetball so she could teach the activity to her students.

He already knew how to play racquetball and handball, but he observed clinics in these sports and, from time to time, gave some instruction to students of his who also belonged to the facilities. The clinics were conducted by a professional and he picked up some teaching techniques for use in his classroom. He also played racquetball against handball and vice versa; he used this mixed-sport for a special education class he taught where he matched children with impaired vision (who used a racquet) against those without impaired vision (who used their hands).

The Court ruled that the above activities involved the "maintenance or improvement of skills required in petitioners' employments as physical education teachers. We believe that the business aspect of the foregoing activities predominates over the personal pleasure or general fitness aspect of petitioners' activities at the Facilities."

However, the Court complained that it did "not have any information as to how much of their time at the Facilities was essentially for pleasure or for general physical or mental well-being, rather than being specially connected with their job-related activities." As a result, it allowed a deduction of only $200, 17% of the total cost of the memberships. Had the couple presented better information on which a more favorable allocation could have been made, their deduction would have been higher. [Cohn, TC Memo 1985-480]

The next 1990 court case shows just how impartial the American Judicial System can be. A college teacher who was in prison for murdering his wife took the IRS to Court. He convinced the Court that he should be able to deduct educational expenses incurred by himself and his wife, before she was murdered. And how did he get out of prison to present his case? He didn't. The Tax Court trial judge and IRS lawyers traveled to the prison so the trial could take place there.

Example

Friend was an English teacher, working at several colleges in the Louisville area. His wife, before he murdered her, was also an English teacher. During the year in question, both he and his wife took English courses at a University.

The Court allowed Friend a deduction for the educational expenses of him and his (ex)wife. The courses they took were in the same field as their teaching assignments.

Thus, they were undertaken in order to maintain and improve their respective job skills, and were thus deductible. Apparently, it did not matter that Friend's wife might not have lived long enough to actually make use of the education she received. [Friend, TC Memo 1990-144]

Education which contributes to your general education but is not directly related to your professional duties does not qualify for deduction. For example, a mathematics teacher would not ordinarily be allowed a deduction for taking a course in political science. However, if there is an employment-related reason for you to take courses outside your area of expertise, then your expenses can be deductible. This is illustrated by the following IRS ruling.

Example
Because of shifting enrollments, a college encouraged its faculty members to take courses in the business economics area. In response to this encouragement, a Professor of American History took courses in the Labor and Industrial Relations Program at another institution. The IRS noted that *"surveys have shown that many colleges. . .have been experiencing a decline in the number of History Majors and an increase in the number of Business-Economics Majors."* Thus, his education was sufficiently related to his professional duties to qualify for deduction. [IRS Private Letter Ruling 8030093]

Education Which Maintains Your Current Employment, Status, or Salary

You may deduct expenses for education which meets the express requirements for maintaining your employment, status, or rate of compensation, provided the education does not fall under the *minimum requirements* of Rule A or the *new trade or business* of Rule B. For example, suppose a teacher has already met the minimum requirements for employment but the school board requires that periodic refresher courses or other education be taken to retain employment. Then these expenses are deductible. Similarly, educational expenses are deductible if the education is required in order to avoid demotion or other loss of status. Thus, a teacher can deduct required courses if the requirement is imposed not on the teacher's right to enter the profession (disqualified by Rule A) but on his right to continue in it.

A teacher may be required to obtain further education in order to participate in the normal increases provided by a set salary schedule or by, for example, an across-the-board cost of living increase. Expenses incurred in meeting this type of requirement are deductible.

Education Which Meets the Express Requirements of Your Employer

You may deduct expenses which meet the express requirements of your employer as long as the requirements have been imposed for a bona fide purpose. Again, the education must not fall under the *minimum requirements* of Rule A or the *new trade or business* of Rule B. The requirements must be identifiable. General encouragement alone will not constitute an express requirement. Even if your employer fails to enforce the rule, you can still normally take the deduction.

> **Example**
> From 1953 to 1958, Robertson was an Assistant Professor in the Department of Economics at the University of Nebraska. He had received an M.A. in 1948 and had all the requirements for a Ph.D. except for his doctoral dissertation. At the time he was first appointed, there was no requirement that a staff member have a Ph.D. as a requirement to the granting of tenure. However, in 1958 there was such a policy so Robertson was told that his employment would be terminated unless he obtained a Ph.D. He took a one-year leave of absence in 1958 in order to complete his dissertation.
>
> **Ruling:** Robertson's costs incurred in returning to school to finish his dissertation were deductible. He had met the minimum requirements which were in effect at the time he was appointed and his schooling was for the purpose of maintaining his current employment. [37 TC 1153]

Section 3:
When Are Deductions Disallowed
Under Rule A?

You cannot deduct education which is required in order to meet the minimum requirements for employment in a new job. You may accept a job for which you do not meet the minimum educational qualifications, but you are hired temporarily or provisionally pending fulfillment of those requirements. If you then take courses in order to meet these qualifications (even though you may also qualify under (1), (2), or (3) of Section 1), then you may not deduct your expenses. However, if you meet the minimum educational requirements that are in effect when you are first employed in a job, and those qualifications are raised later, then you may deduct expenses for courses taken to satisfy the new minimum qualifications.

What Are Minimum Educational Requirements?
The IRS has issued the following regulation defining what is meant by minimum educational requirements for teachers.

"The minimum educational requirements for qualification of a particular individual in a position in an educational institution is the minimum level of education (in terms of aggregate college hours or degree) which under the applicable laws or regulations in effect at the time this individual is first employed in such position, is normally required of an individual initially being employed in such a position. If there are no normal requirements as to the minimum level of education required for a position in an educational institution, then an individu-

al in such a position shall be considered to have met the minimum educational requirements for qualification in that position when he becomes a member of the faculty of the educational institution. The determination of whether an individual is a member of the faculty of an educational institution must be made on the basis of the particular practices of the institution. However an individual will ordinarily be considered to be a member of the faculty of an institution if (a) he has tenure or his years of service are being counted toward obtaining tenure; (b) the institution is making contributions to a retirement plan (other than Social Security or a similar program) in respect of his employment; or (c) he has a vote in faculty affairs." [Reg. Sec. 1.162-5(b) (2)]

Example 1

An individual obtained employment in August 1981 as a Professor of Physical Education. At the time, he was enrolled in a doctorate program at a university in a different location. He completed his dissertation about a year later, obtaining his Ph.D. degree in December, 1982. A contingency clause was written into his second year contract to complete the doctorate. However when he was employed, he had already met the minimum requirements for his position as a regular faculty member.

The IRS ruled that he could deduct all his expenses in working toward his doctorate after he became employed. This included tuition as well as *"the reasonable expenses of editing, typing, photocopying, telephone, photography, graphics, mailing, supplies and any reasonable expenses that were incurred as incident to the preparation of [his] doctoral dissertation to obtain [his] graduate doctoral degree."* He was also permitted to deduct his travel expenses, including meals and lodging, for a 2 1/2 month trip back to the institution where he was enrolled in the doctorate program. The trip was needed to enable him to finish some experimental animal work and to use some specialized equipment which was located there. [IRS Private Letter Ruling 8340025]

Example 2

Wilkins, who holds a master's degree, obtains temporary employment as an instructor at a university. He undertakes graduate courses as a candidate for a doctoral degree. He may become a regular faculty member only if he obtains a doctoral degree. He can continue his position as instructor only as long as he shows satisfactory progress towards obtaining that degree.

The graduate courses Wilkins takes are necessary to meet the minimum educational requirements for qualification in his trade or business. Thus the expenditures for these courses are not deductible.

Example 3

Jungreis worked for the University of Minnesota on a part-time basis as a graduate teaching assistant in the zoology department. Since he then had only a Bachelor of Science degree, he was not qualified for a position as a regular faculty member of the University. He was enrolled as a student in the graduate school and was a candidate for a Doctor of Philosophy degree in zoology which was required to qualify him as a regular full-time faculty member. The University required Jungreis to be enrolled as a graduate student before he could be eligible for an appointment as a graduate teaching assistant.

While serving under an appointment as a graduate teaching assistant, he was required to be making satisfactory progress toward a graduate degree to maintain his appointment. The employment as a graduate teaching assistant was a temporary position which terminated upon receipt of the Ph.D.

Jungreis claimed he was entitled to deduct expenses relating to his graduate school education since they were required for him in order to maintain his position as a teaching assistant. He claimed he had already met the minimum requirements, i.e., a bachelor's degree, which were required of him in his current position.

The Tax Court disallowed his deduction. It ruled that the position at an educational institution for which an individual must meet the minimum educational requirements before he can get a deduction is a permanent position on the faculty of the institution. In this case, the minimum education required for permanent employment in the University's zoology department is a Ph.D. Jungreis was enrolled in a program to meet those minimum requirements and hence his expenses were not deductible. [55 TC 581]

Example 4

Damm, after working as a registered civil engineer for 5 years, enrolled in graduate school at a leading California university. He obtained his master's degree and continued as a student in the Ph.D. program for an additional year. He then left school and obtained a job as a lecturer in Engineering at a State college. After several years of full-time teaching, he returned to the university for 2 years and completed his Ph.D. studies. He then returned to teaching, first at the State college for a year and then at a university in the midwest.

When Damm deducted his education expenses for the period he was completing his Ph.D. studies, the IRS objected. It referred back to the Jungreis decision [Example 3], claiming that Damm had not met the minimum requirements for the position of permanent college faculty member, namely the Ph.D. degree.

But the Court did not agree with the IRS, permitting the deduction to stand. It contrasted Damm's situation with that of Jungreis as follows:

> "Jungreis was a teaching assistant, he taught part time, his salary was less than that of the regular faculty members, his work was different from that of regular faculty members, his service did not count toward tenure, and from the outset he could not hold his job for any period unless for that period he was enrolled as a student and making satisfactory progress toward a graduate degree. We concluded that Jungreis was essentially an apprentice, rather than a teacher. Damm, by contrast, was a full-time teacher doing what regular faculty members did in the classroom, he was paid the same as regular faculty members, up to two years of his service could count toward tenure, and his job did not depend on a condition precedent."

The Court also pointed out that the State college

"did not normally require a doctorate degree as a minimum level of educa-tion for lecturers or for faculty members in general. We concluded that Damm, who had already been awarded the baccalaureate degree and the mas-ter's degree, met the minimum educational requirements for lecturers and for faculty members in general at [the State college]. "From the foregoing, we concluded that Damm's educational expenses are not rendered nondeductible by the minimum educational expenses test." [Damm, TC Memo 1981-203]

Section 4:
When are Deductions Disallowed
Under Rule B?

Rule B states that you may not deduct expenses for education which will qual-ify you for a new trade or business. In the case of an employee, a change of du-ties does not constitute a new trade or business if the new duties involve the same type of work that he was formerly doing. Furthermore, all teaching and re-lated duties are considered to involve the same general type of work. For exam-ple, none of the following changes are considered to constitute a new trade or business:

a.   *change from elementary to secondary classroom teacher*
b.   *change from teaching one subject to teaching another*
c.   *change from teaching to guidance counselor*
d.   *change from teacher to principal*

Note that the above does not explicitly state that you can deduct the expenses for education required to make the above changes. It only states that these educa-tion expenses are not automatically excluded from being deductible. However, the following examples taken from government rulings and regulations indicate that expenses undertaken to meet the requirements for such changes are general-ly deductible.

Example 1
Green, who had a master's degree, was an Education Professor at a college. He became eligible for appointment as President of a junior college within the same edu-cational system. The next year, the requirement for this position was raised from a master's degree to a doctorate. In order to be retained on the eligibility list, Green earned a doctorate in education. Note that prior to getting the additional education, Green had met the minimum educational requirements. His appointment as President of a junior college would not be a new trade or business, but merely a change of du-ties in his accustomed type of work. Hence his expenses in obtaining a doctorate were deductible. [Rev. Rul. 68-580]

Example 2

Schwerm was employed as a discussion leader in a local college's adult education program. Discussion topics included family relationships, self-awareness, and coping with problems such as stress, retirement, etc. She enrolled in a graduate program for a master's degree in Educational Psychology. She thought this course of study would aid her in becoming a better discussion leader. After obtaining her master's degree, she entered an internship program to train her to become a school counselor.

The Court ruled she could deduct the expenses of both the master's degree program and the internship program. Even though the internship program was qualifying her for the new position of school counselor, the Court ruled that her positions as discussion leader and school counselor were part of the same trade or business. (In fact, she would perform similar guidance services in both these positions.) [Schwerm, TC Memo 1986-16]

Note that the above examples all show situations in which Rule B did not apply. For teachers, the only case where Rule B is likely to apply is if courses taken were in a completely different field.

Law School Expenses

Rule B eliminates a deduction for education which **qualifies** you for a new trade or profession. It does not matter if you actually make the switch into the new trade or profession. As long as the education enables you to make the switch, a deduction is ruled out. This is best illustrated by a number of cases involving individuals attempting to deduct the expenses of attending law school. In several of these cases, the individual involved did not intend to become a lawyer, but rather to use the law school education in his current profession. But since the education **qualified** him for the new profession of being a lawyer, Rule B prevented a deduction.

One case involved an insurance adjuster who intended to use the legal training in his same line of work [TC Memo 1977-236]. Another case involved a college teacher of mathematics who intended to switch to teaching law, a change of duties which usually qualifies for deduction [Bouchard, TC Memo 1977-273] . A third case involved someone who performed quasi-legal activities for a corporation prior to and after law school [McDermott, 36TCM144] . A fourth case concerned a contracts manager who never took the bar examination and used his law school only to aid in legal negotiations connected with his job [Rehe, TC Memo 1980-316] . A fifth case concerned an Associate Professor of Communication who was studying law because his primary teaching responsibility was a course on the legal aspects of mass communication [IRS Private Letter Ruling 8432028]. And a sixth case, decided in 1990, involved a Philosophy Professor who studied law while on sabbatical [Watkins, TC Memo 1990-206].

In all of the above cases, it was ruled that the profession of being a lawyer was different than the employment they had before. Since their law degree *qualified* them for this new profession, they were not permitted to deduct their educational expenses whether or not they actually entered the new profession.

There was the one lawyer who succeeded in deducting his educational expenses. But he already held a law degree and was a member of the bar. His education consisted of a one-year advanced graduate program in law in the area of his specialty [IRS Private Letter Ruling 7801002].

Section 5:
Temporary vs. Indefinite Absence From Profession

An additional requirement for deductibility is that the education be undertaken when you are a current member of your profession. If you are actively teaching, on vacation, or on a temporary leave of absence, then you are considered to be a current member of the teaching profession. But if you leave your profession for an **indefinite period** of time, then you may not deduct expenses related to that profession. This holds even if you return to the profession at a later date.

If you temporarily leave your profession for a **fixed period** of time to take courses that maintain or improve your skills, then these expenses are eligible for deduction. It is not necessary that you be on official leave of absence or even that you plan to return to the same job. However, you must plan to resume employment in the same field you left.

The IRS had been following the general policy of considering any period exceeding one year, as an indefinite period of time. Thus, education requiring an absence from work for more than a year was considered non-deductible. But the Tax Court has thrown out this one-year policy as being arbitrary and unjustified. In several court cases, they have permitted a deduction for full-time study lasting 2 or 3 years. These cases are discussed below.

Deduction for Graduate School Education
The court cases permitting a deduction for extended periods of education all involved graduate students returning to school after a period of employment. The key to qualifying for deduction was that their education was sufficiently related to their profession. The extended length of time required to complete the education was no barrier.

Example 1
Mrs. H. held a master's degree in the field of nursing education. She held positions first as an Assistant Professor at a community college and then as a consultant to an educational organization. Mrs. H. left her employment to undertake a 3-year doctoral program in nursing education. When she left her job, she did not have any specific intent to return. However, after receiving her doctoral degree, she did in fact return to work for the same educational organization that she had worked for before.

The IRS did not dispute that the education was for the purpose of improving her skills as a nursing educator. However, it maintained that her 3-year absence from the profession ruled out a deduction.

The Court did not agree with the IRS. It found nothing in the law which placed *"an arbitrary limitation on the self-improvement process."* Rather, *"the 3-year period of study was an appropriate period in which to accomplish her educational objective."* [Hitt, TC Memo 1978-66]

Example 2

Over a period of 10 years, Mr. P. was employed by various public school systems in New England. He served as school teacher, curriculum coordinator, and finally principal of an elementary school.

Mr. P. resigned his position as principal and undertook full-time graduate studies in the field of educational administration. He received his Ph.D. three years later. Upon graduation, he wrote letters to various universities, colleges, and school systems seeking employment in a teaching or administrative capacity. However, he met with little success. In spite of continuing his job-seeking efforts for a number of years, he was unable to secure employment except for a few minor part-time positions. In fact, at the time his case came to trial, he was still unemployed.

Mr. P. claimed a deduction for the cost of his schooling. However, the IRS challenged the deduction, reasoning that his extended absence from work meant he was not a member of his profession at the time of his education.

But the Court upheld the deduction. His graduate studies were of definite as opposed to indefinite duration. Moreover, they were directly related to his profession as an educator and educational administrator. The fact that he was unable to obtain a regular job upon graduation was not held against him. To establish that he continued being a member of his profession, it sufficed that he actively pursue employment in that profession, not that he actually obtain employment. [TC Memo 1977-321]

Example 3

Johnson was an Assistant Professor of Nursing at a major public university in Austin, Texas. She took a 2-year leave of absence without pay to pursue a doctorate degree in Educational Foundations at a university in Hawaii.

Johnson sold her home in Texas before moving with her husband to Hawaii where they lived in a rented apartment. After studying for 4 semesters, she returned to Texas where she taught as an Assistant Professor of Nursing as she had done before.

The Tax Court ruled that her living expenses in Hawaii were deductible as educational expenses while temporarily away from home. It agreed with Johnson that the purpose of her attending graduate school was to *"improve her teaching skills so that she would be a better qualified professor"* in Texas.

In its written opinion, the Court addressed the 2 principal objections raised by the IRS—the long period of time she was away and the fact she did not incur duplicate housing expenses since she sold her home in Texas before going to Hawaii.

As for the 2-year period she was away, the Court ruled that this was indeed a temporary absence which did not shift her tax home away from Texas. In the Court's words,

"Studying in a doctoral program is a lengthy process by its very nature. It was not a short refresher course. Nevertheless, we find that it was not of

such substantial duration so as to transfer her place of employment and consequently her 'tax home' from Austin, Texas, to Hawaii."

As for the lack of duplicate living expenses, the Court ruled that this was not determinative, stating

"Granted, she did not incur 'duplicative expenses' when renting an apartment in Hawaii because she had sold her Texas home. However, whether petitioner's expenses were duplicative is not determinative of the issue but rather is only one of many factors which we must weigh in reaching our decision."

Furthermore, Johnson had done a number of things to keep her ties with Texas intact. She and her husband *"maintained a credit union account in Austin while living in Hawaii. They stored all of their personal belongings except for needed clothing and some books in Austin while living in Hawaii. They maintained a post office box in Austin while they lived in Hawaii and they maintained valid Austin public library cards . . ."* Also, they paid taxes on a boat they left docked in Austin while away. All of these factors supported Johnson's claim that Austin remained her tax home while she was temporarily studying in Hawaii. [Johnson, TC Memo 1988-177]

Example 4

For several years, Wyatt was a teacher of secretarial skills in a secondary school in Kansas. From 1963 to 1967 she was employed as a secretary, working for various employers. In March 1967 she accepted an offer to begin teaching again in August 1967. Even though she still had a valid teaching certificate, she took graduate school courses in education in the spring and summer of 1967 preparatory to her resumption of teaching.

Ruling: Wyatt left the teaching profession in 1963 for an indefinite period. At the time she incurred the expenses for her education, she was not engaged in the profession of teaching even though she had accepted a teaching position to begin later. Her expenses were not deductible because they did not improve her skills in the profession she was engaged in at the time she took the courses. [56 TC 517]

If you leave your profession temporarily, you should still list that profession on the *Occupation* line on your tax form. A recent court decision denied an education deduction to a registered nurse who went back to school after a long period of time during which she was unemployed. The denial was based on the Court's conclusion that she was no longer in the nursing profession when she undertook the education. It stated that the fact she did not consider herself a nurse at the time was *"demonstrated by the fact that she listed her occupation on her Federal income tax returns for those years to be that of a student and housewife."* [Cannon, TC Memo 1980-224]

However, you should take care how you fill out the *occupation* line at the top of Form 2106 so that it is clear that you are claiming an *educational deduction* rather than a *job-related travel deduction* [cf. Example 12 in Section 4 of the *Travel* chapter for details].

Court Gives Green Light to Deducting MBA Expenses

The following court case applies to those pursuing advanced degrees in business schools. Often these students have returned to school after a stint in the working world. As this court case shows, the expenses of obtaining education in these circumstances will generally be deductible.

Example 5

Sherman was a civilian employee with the military. He held a managerial job, being in charge of a regional "Plans and Programs Office." He left this employment after two years to attend Harvard University as a candidate for a Master's Degree in Business Administration (MBA). After a two-year period, he received his degree and became Director of Planning and Research in a private corporation.

As in the previous two examples, the IRS asserted first that he had not established any "trade or business" in which he was improving his skills by attending school. And second, his absence from employment beyond one year automatically excluded his deduction in any event.

Once again, the Court sided with the taxpayer against the IRS. Sherman had established himself in a trade or business, namely *"the business of being an employee who was an administrator and planner."* And the MBA program improved his skills in this "business." As in Examples 1 and 2, the Court rejected the one-year limitation placed by the IRS on deductible education. The 2-year program was of fixed duration and entirely reasonable for the purpose of obtaining an MBA degree. [Sherman, TC Memo 1977-301]

Despite the above court cases, the IRS had been stubbornly sticking to its one-year limitation. It had even issued rulings in recent years denying deductions for educational expenses for the sole reason that the schooling exceeded one year—forcing taxpayers to go to court to get a deduction for the expenses of longer-term education.

But in a 1988 Private Letter Ruling, the IRS indicated a possible change of heart. In this ruling, an administrator planned a leave of absence from his job, extending 2 academic years from September, 1987 to May, 1989, in order to pursue a masters degree. He was paid his full salary while at school but received no reimbursements for tuition, fees, or other educational costs. Despite the extended term of the schooling, the IRS ruled that the taxpayer could deduct his educational expenses on his tax returns. [IRS Private Letter Ruling 8813049]

Section 6:
Which Expenses are Deductible?

If your education qualifies for deduction, you may deduct tuition, fees, books, supplies, photocopying, and other related costs (e.g., required physical examination, tutor's fees, etc.). If your education includes writing a thesis or dissertation, then you may deduct associated costs such as typing, research expenses, etc.

Transportation Expenses To and From School

You may deduct transportation expenses for qualified educational activities that you incur in going between:

1. the general area of your principal place of employment and a school located **beyond the general area;**

or

2. your place of employment and a school **within the same general area.** However, if you return home before going to school, you may deduct the expense in going from home to school only to the extent it does not exceed the transportation expense you would have incurred had you gone from work to school.

Example 1

You live and work in Newark, New Jersey, and go to New York City three times a week to attend night classes at a university there. If your educational expenses are deductible, you may deduct your round trip transportation expenses, including tolls and parking fees.

Example 2

You attend night classes at a college located in the same city as your job. (Assume that you can deduct your educational expenses.) You go directly to the college after work. You may deduct the cost of going from your job to the college.

You may not deduct the cost of local transportation between your residence and school on a non-working day. This expense is in the nature of a personal commuting expense.

You cannot deduct transportation between your residence and school during a period of unemployment. This is illustrated by the following court case.

Court Case

An unemployed teacher took college courses, using local transportation to travel the 30 miles between her home and the college. She deducted $1,178 for educational expenses, including $564 for transportation. The IRS allowed the deduction to the extent it covered tuition, fees, and books, but disallowed the $564 travel costs on the grounds they were personal commuting costs.

The Tax Court agreed with the IRS. Since she was unemployed, her travel did not fall into the deductible category described in the preceding example. Also, her schooling was not temporary employment so that the examples in Section 3 of the Travel chapter were inapplicable. The Court simply considered her expenses to serve her personal convenience by allowing her to reside at some distance from her school. Note also that since her education did not require her to be away from home overnight, the provisions of the next subsection do not apply. [Zimmerman 71 TC 34]

Travel Expenses While Away from Home Overnight

Perhaps you attend school out of town to obtain education that qualifies for deduction. In this case, you are governed by the rules for deducting travel expenses as described in the *Travel* chapter. The IRS describes as follows the general situation concerning travel away from home overnight to obtain education:

> *"If you travel away from home primarily to obtain education the expenses of which are deductible, you may deduct your expenditures for travel, meals [subject to the 80%-Rule described in Section 1 of the Travel chapter], and lodging while away from home. However, if you engage in incidental personal activities, such as sightseeing, social visiting, or entertaining, the portion of your expenses attributable to those personal activities are nondeductible.*
>
> *"If your travel away from home is primarily personal, your expenditures for travel, meals and lodging (other than meals and lodging during the time spent on deductible educational pursuits) are not deductible.*
>
> *"An important factor in determining whether a particular trip is primarily personal or primarily to obtain qualifying education is the relative amount of time devoted to personal, as compared with educational activities."* [Reg. Sec. 1.162-5(e)]

Example 1

You work in Newark, New Jersey. You went to Chicago to take a 1-week course, the cost of which is deductible, and while there, you took a sightseeing trip, entertained some personal friends, and took a sidetrip to Pleasantville for a day. Your transportation expenses to Chicago and back are deductible, but your transportation expenses to Pleasantville are not. You may deduct only the meals [subject to the 80%-Rule described in Section 1 of the Travel chapter] and lodging allocable to your educational activities. [IRS Pub. 17]

Example 2

You work in Newark and you went to a university in California to take a course, the cost of which is deductible. The course was one-fourth of a full program of study and you spent the rest of your time on personal activities. Your trip is considered to have been primarily personal unless you can show otherwise. You may not deduct the cost of your transportation to California but you may deduct one-fourth the cost of your meals [reduced further by the 80%-Rule] and lodging while attending the university. [Reg. Sec. 1.162-5(e)2]

If your travel was outside of the United States, see Section 8b of the *Travel* chapter.

Where Do You Deduct Educational Expenses?

Educational expenses incurred by an employee in connection with his job are claimed on Form 2106, *Employee Business Expenses*. The total of expenses computed on Form 2106 is claimed on line 20 of Schedule A as a *miscellaneous deduction,* and when aggregated with other miscellaneous deductions, subjected to a 2% of Adjusted Gross Income floor.

Educational expenses connected with a self-employment activity are claimed on Schedule C. This has the advantage of escaping the 2% floor and being available to those who claim the standard deduction as well as to those who itemize.

Section 1 of the *Miscellaneous Deductions* chapter discusses this in more complete detail. It also shows how to handle the situation where a full or partial reimbursement is received from an employer.

You cannot deduct your educational expenses to the extent you receive a tax-exempt scholarship to defray such expenses. For example, if your educational expenses are $1,500, toward which you receive a $500 scholarship, then your deduction would be $1,500 – $500 = $1,000. [Rev Rul 83-3]

Your break down your educational expenses into categories as provided on Form 2106. Lines 1–3 are used for travel expenses and Line 5 is used for deductible meal expenses. Line 4 is for all other expenses such as tuition, fees, books, etc. You should also keep records and supporting evidence to substantiate each element of expenditure, in case your return is audited.

Further information on the requirements for deducting and keeping records of travel expenses is contained in the *Travel* chapter.

Chapter 24

Entertainment Expenses

Many college teachers entertain as part of their job. They may take a visiting colleague out to lunch or dinner. Or, they may host a dinner or reception in their home in honor of such a visitor. The question then becomes whether or not the expense of such entertainment can be deducted.

There has been no direct guidance on this question in any published court case or IRS ruling. And the basic Tax Code section under which entertainment expenses are deducted offers little illumination. It states only:

"In the case of an individual, there shall be allowed as a deduction all the ordinary and necessary expenses paid or incurred during the taxable year. . . for the production or collection of income."

Thus, to qualify for deduction, entertainment must be an *ordinary and necessary* activity connected with your job. The word *ordinary* refers to an expense connected with a common and accepted practice in your job. For example, a professor could regard the expense of taking a visiting colloquium speaker out to dinner as an ordinary expense if this is typically done on his campus. On the other hand, the expense of treating a class to ice cream cones would not be an ordinary expense because it is not common practice to do so.

The term *necessary* in this context does not have its usual meaning of "compulsory." Here, a necessary expense is one that is *appropriate and helpful* in the conduct of your job.

Employees sometimes have a difficult time convincing the IRS that an entertainment expense qualifies for deduction. The IRS generally expects the employer to pick up the bill for all job-related expenses. Of course, college teachers are in a special category. They often have to dig into their own pockets to pay for job-related items for which an employee in private industry would receive a reimbursement.

The IRS may not always appreciate this fact. However, assistance has come from an unexpected source. President Carter's 1978 Tax Proposal to Congress contained an entire section devoted to entertainment expenses. His exact proposals were not enacted into law, but the explanatory material is of considerable interest. As an illustration of existing law, Carter's message listed examples of entertainment deductions which were allowed in recent audits. And one of these examples is the case of a college professor who was permitted a $1,300 deduction for entertainment expenses. The exact quote is as follows:

Excerpt from the President's 1978 Tax Program

"A university professor received $30,000 in annual salary and, in addition, many of his expenses are reimbursed. His department did not reimburse him for $1,300 spent to entertain visiting professors, but these expenses were deductible on the basis of his department chairman's statement that entertaining visiting professors was required as part of the professor's job. [PH Federal Taxes, Booklet #1252. p. 197]

Of course, President Carter offered the above example, as well as others, to show why existing law should be changed. But his message clearly stated that the law permits such a deduction. Thus, a definite reference has been provided to back up the right of college teachers to deduct their entertainment expenses.

Further details concerning the above example are not available since they were part of a private IRS audit. Neither the President's staff nor the IRS was permitted to give out further information on the professor's audit to us when we inquired. However, a telephone discussion with a high IRS official concerning this matter did offer one piece of further guidance.

The official stated that it was not necessary for there to be an absolute requirement to entertain. As long as the entertainment in question is a general practice in one's institution and is appropriate and helpful to the job, a deduction can be justified. Of course, a statement that such entertainment is required as part of the job would boost one's case. But it is not an absolute requirement.

The *ordinary and necessary* rule discussed above applies to the most common type of business entertaining, namely dining out in a restaurant. This includes having drinks at a bar or cocktail lounge provided there is no distracting floor show or other entertainment. It also includes the cost of *quiet business meals* served to your guests at home.

There is an additional rule that now applies. This rule states that entertainment (including meals and beverages except when traveling away from home) must either (1) be *directly related to the active conduct of the taxpayer's trade or business,* or (2) take place either directly before, at the same time as, or directly after a *substantial and bona fide business discussion* associated with the active conduct of the taxpayer's trade or business. Exactly how this rule will apply to teachers is unclear at this time because there still have not yet been any rulings on this issue. Further details will be contained in future editions of this Tax Guide after more information becomes available.

The above discussion indicates that the cost of hosting a dinner party for an out-of-town visitor can be a deductible entertainment expense. But how about dinner parties attended only by in-town guests? The presumption is that such parties are simply personal gatherings rather than deductible business activities. But a recent court case shows how this presumption might be overcome, namely, by pointing to parties for which no deduction was claimed. A newspaper publisher held dinner parties to which he invited people from politics, business, journalism, publishing, theater, and other fields. He did not have specific business to transact with these individuals. Rather, *"the purpose of the dinners was to provide an opportunity to discuss developments and ideas with people who were prominent in their professions."* The publisher claimed a deduction for about a dozen of these dinner parties. Had these been the only parties given by the publisher, they would have been considered merely social gatherings. But he had hosted many other dinner parties for which no deduction was claimed. Because of this, the Court was able to accept the publisher's contention that the relatively few parties for which he claimed a deduction were business-related rather than being just social gatherings. [Howard, TC Memo 1981-250]

Whose Expenses Can Be Deducted?

When your entertainment activities are deductible, the letter of the law only allows you to deduct your own meal to the extent it exceeds what you would ordinarily have spent. However, in practice, the IRS almost always lets you deduct the full cost of your own meal in addition to that of the person you are entertaining. The IRS also recognizes that when entertaining an out-of-town visitor, it may be impractical to leave out his or her spouse. In such a case, the expenses of the spouse will be deductible also. Furthermore, if your spouse is included because the visitor's spouse is present, these expenses can also be deducted. However, all expenses are subject to the 80%-Rule discussed below.

To be deductible, entertainment expenses should not be reimbursable by the employer. This is illustrated by a 1983 Court case in which an engineer was denied a $122 deduction for lunches and dinners with professional colleagues. The Court agreed that such costs might qualify for deduction. But in this case, the engineer testified that his employer would have reimbursed him for the costs if he had asked. An employee cannot deduct expenses which he pays that his employer would have reimbursed him for. [Narain, TC Memo 1983-701]

80%-Rule for Entertainment Expenses

Entertainment expenses are no longer deductible in full. Instead, only 80% of the cost of entertainment (including meals and beverages) can be deducted. All expenses associated with the entertainment such as tax, tips, parking, etc. are included under this 80%-Rule. However, transportation to and from the place of entertainment is not subject to the 80%-Rule.

Exception. The 80%-Rule does not apply to expenses which are reimbursed by an employer, provided the reimbursement is not included as taxable income on the employee's W2 Form.

The 80%-Rule for entertainment expenses is exactly the same as the 80%-Rule for meal expenses described in Section 1 of the *Travel* chapter. Also see Section 1 of the *Miscellaneous Deductions* chapter which shows how the 80%-Rule is applied when expenses are reported on Form 2106.

Lunch and Dinner

Sometimes, an individual attends lunch or dinner meetings in connection with his professional duties. The cost of attending such meetings can be deductible if they are sufficiently business-related. In one 1982 court case, Example 1 below, the Court even allowed a deduction for luncheon meetings which consisted of discussions of recent journal articles. This court case opens the door for college teachers to deduct for "luncheon meetings" with colleagues organized for similar purposes.

Example 1

Beltran was an anesthesiologist at a hospital in Maryland. He periodically joined a group of other anesthesiologists in "Journal Club" luncheons held at various local restaurants. The purpose of these luncheons was for the anesthesiologists "to discuss the latest professional journals they had read."

The Tax Court ruled that the cost of these luncheons was a legitimate professional expense. Thus, the cost could be claimed as a "business meal" deduction. The court allowed the full amount claimed by the anesthesiologist—about $400 over a two-year period. [Beltran, TC Memo 1982-153]

Example 2

A Vocational Education Coordinator belonged to several vocational organizations which often met over lunch or dinner. The IRS ruled that these meetings were directly related to his professional duties. Therefore, he was entitled to deduct the portion of the cost of any such meal which was in excess of what he would have normally spent. Since he ordinarily simply ate a sack lunch at his school or ate dinner at home, this would cover almost the entire cost of the meals. [IRS Private Letter Ruling 8006004]

While this ruling forced the educational coordinator to subtract what he ordinarily would have spent from the cost of the meals at those meetings, in practice the IRS is not so strict. If a business meal qualifies for deduction, the full cost (subject to the 80%-Rule) will almost always be allowed.

Example 3

Didsbury was a Professor at a college in the East. In addition to his college-related duties, he served on the planning committee of a Society dedicated to the study of world affairs. The Society periodically held conferences and published papers based on these conferences. Didsbury, in addition to participating in the planning of the conferences, helped edit the conference volumes and had some responsibility for obtaining speakers. He received $6,000 in income from the Society-for teaching a course in connection with a conference and for his writing and editing activities.

About once a week, Didsbury met with potential speakers over lunch or dinner to discuss their participation in one of the Society's conferences. He picked up the check each time, but did not receive reimbursement from the Society.

The IRS did not challenge his right to a deduction for the lunches and dinners. These were legitimate expenses connected with his business activity of "Lecture-Writing" for the Society. The issue that arose at trial was the adequacy of the records *he maintained to support his $1,565 entertainment deduction for these meal expenses.*

Didsbury had an adequate collection of receipts, credit card slips, and contemporaneous diary notes to verify the date, amount, and restaurant where each of the meals occurred. However, he did not write down his relationship to the person entertained or the business purpose of the entertainment. Furthermore, he did not always write down the name of the person entertained. In some cases, he just wrote down the initials of the person on the credit card slip and in a few cases had no such notation at all.

However, at the time of trial, he was able to create a listing of the meals, along with the name of the person entertained and an indication of the person's business relationship (e.g. "possible conference participant, conference planning, work draft manuscripts, etc."). This listing was based on his receipts and diary book, plus his own recollections.

The IRS claimed that the documentation was not sufficient because of the lack of contemporaneous recording of all the elements required to substantiate the deduction. However, the Court sided with Didsbury, allowing the entire $1,565 deduction. Didsbury did have contemporaneous records concerning date, place, and amount. And the law permits missing pieces to be substantiated by adequate corroboration. To determine whether the corroboration in this case was adequate, the Court went back to the original Senate committee report explaining the requirements:

"Where the taxpayer fails to maintain adequate records with respect to any of the described aspects of an expense, that aspect must be substantiated by the taxpayer's own statement corroborated by sufficient evidence. The taxpayer's own uncorroborated statement will not constitute substantiation with respect to any such aspect. The evidence required may vary with respect to each aspect of an item claimed as a deduction. Thus, circumstantial evidence, such as the nature of the business activities of the taxpayer and of the person entertained, may be sufficient to corroborate the taxpayer's statement regarding business purpose and business relationship, whereas more direct evidence, such as the testimony of witnesses, would be required to substantiate amount, time, place, date, and description. [S. Rept. No. 1881, 87th Cong., 2d Sess. (1962), 1962-3 C.B. 878.]"

In this case, the Court ruled that Didsbury's listing constituted sufficient alternate evidence of the nature of the "business activities of the taxpayer and the person entertained." It was not simply an "uncorroborated statement." Rather, it was corroborated by the fact it fit with the receipts and other contemporaneous recordkeeping which Didsbury had maintained. [Didsbury, T.C. Memo 1989-1]

Each of the above examples concerned an individual deducting for lunch or dinner meetings with other persons whom he ordinarily did not work with. But what about meetings with co-workers? Can you deduct for lunch or dinner meetings attended just by those whom you regularly see at work? The following court case indicates that the answer is yes, as long as the meetings are not too frequent. Thus, you can't simply use the entertainment deduction to write off all your lunches even if business is always discussed. But occasional lunches with co-workers can qualify for an entertainment expense deduction.

Example 4

Moss was a partner in a law firm in Chicago. The partners and other employees met over lunch at a nearby restaurant each day to give each other advice on handling current matters and to discuss other business. This was the most convenient time to meet since the courts were in recess at this time and all the lawyers would generally be free to attend.

When Moss attempted to deduct his share of the daily lunches, the IRS objected. The Tax Court upheld this objection. It ruled that even though the lunches served a business purpose, the frequency of these lunches meant they became a normal personal expense.

However, 9 of the Tax Court judges signed a concurring opinion that the deduction was only ruled out in this case because of the frequency of the lunches. As the justice who wrote the opinion noted,

"I do not view this opinion as disallowing the cost of meals in all instances where only partners, co-workers, etc. are involved. We have here findings that the partners met at lunch because it was 'convenient' and 'convenient' 5 days a week, 52 weeks a year."

The concurring opinion thus indicates that occasional meetings with co-workers could qualify for the entertainment expense deduction. The line between occasional and regular is not spelled out. That would depend on the particular facts and circumstances.

While only 9 of 19 Tax Court judges signed the concurring opinion, the position of the other 10 is not indicated. Since it is likely that at least one of these 10 would join the other 9 were it necessary to rule on this issue, it is reasonable to treat this as representing the viewpoint of the Tax Court. [Moss. 80 TC No. 57]

Example 4 Continued

Moss appealed to the U. S. Court of Appeals in his district. But the Appeals Court upheld the decision denying the deduction. However, its 1985 written opinion gives additional information as to where to draw the line when deciding the deductibility of lunches with co-workers.

First of all, the purpose of the deduction is to compensate persons who *"spend more money on business meals because they are business meals than they would spend on their meals if they were not working."* Thus, if you are planning to deduct a business lunch, you should go to a more expensive restaurant than the ones to which you ordinarily go. Of course, if you ordinarily bring your own lunch or dine cheaply at the cafeteria where you work, then going out to lunch at a restaurant automatically satisfies this criterion. In the Moss case, they always ate at the same modestly-priced cafe, so there was no evidence that their business lunches were costing them any more than personal lunches would have cost.

Second, the business purpose of lunching together is to provide, in the Court's phrase, *"social lubrication"* conducive to the transacting of business. This extra social lubrication would not ordinarily be needed if you are lunching with an office-mate or someone else you work with closely. On the other hand, discussing business matters with someone you don't know as well might provide the helpful *social lubrication* conducive to the business-related matters being discussed. In the Moss case, the lawyers eating lunch together were part of a small 8-lawyer firm who *"did not need a daily lunch to cement relationships among them."*

And finally, the Appeals Court agreed with the Tax Court that deducting the cost of daily meals was pushing it too far, even had there been more business justification. According to the Court, *"It is all a matter of degree and circumstance (the expense of a testimonial dinner, for example, would be deductible on a morale-building rationale); and particularly of frequency. Daily—for a full year—is too often, perhaps even for entertainment of clients."* [Moss. CA-7 85-1 USTC ¶ 9285 CCH]

Recordkeeping Requirement

You are supposed to record the following information for all entertaining which you claim as a deduction:

(1) The **amount** of each separate item of entertaining, except that incidental items like taxi fares or telephone calls can be aggregated together.

(2) The **date** of the expenditure.

(3) The **place** of entertainment, including the name and location of restaurants where dining occurred.

(4) The **business purpose** of the entertainment. (A sentence or two describing the nature of your business conversation would be appropriate.)

(5) The **occupation** or other information concerning the persons being entertained, including name, title, or other designations sufficient to establish their business relationship to you.

You should record the above information in a timely manner. That is, you should write it down soon after the entertainment occurred, not reconstruct it from memory at a later date.

You must also keep a receipt, cancelled check, or other documentary evidence substantiating any expenditure of $25 or more. You do not have to record information in your record book that duplicates information shown on a receipt as long as your records and receipts compliment each other in an orderly manner.

If your timely-kept records and receipts do not contain all 5 items of information specified above, this does not automatically rule out a deduction. You may be allowed to present other evidence which corroborates your claim as to the missing items. This is more likely to be acceptable in the case of items (4) and (5), than for the first three items. A good illustration of this is provided in Example 3 of this chapter.

Where Do You Deduct Entertainment Expenses?

Unreimbursed entertainment expenses are claimed by employees as an *employee business expense* in column B of Form 2106. The total computed on Form 2106 is carried over to Schedule A where it is claimed as a miscellaneous deduction. The total of miscellaneous deductions is then subjected to the 2% of Adjusted Gross Income floor [cf. Section 1 of the *Miscellaneous Deductions* chapter for information on how to report your expenses on Form 2106]. Self-employed persons claim entertainment expenses on line 24b of Schedule C. (This has the advantage of escaping the 2% floor and being available to those who claim the standard deduction as well as those who itemize.)

An employee who receives a reimbursement that is not included as taxable income on his W-2 Form can simply ignore the reimbursement and expenses for tax purposes, provided the appropriate records are maintained. For situations where a partial or taxable reimbursement is received, see Section 1 of the *Miscellaneous Deductions* chapter.

Chapter 25

Retirement Plans

Section 1:
Introduction

The chances are good that you participate in some sort of retirement plan other than Social Security. This plan may be entirely funded by contributions from your employer or it may be funded by both employer contributions and employee contributions. In almost all cases, contributions required of employees are simply withheld from their paychecks.

In addition to simply providing a savings vehicle for later years, retirement plans are a significant tax-shelter. As explained in Section 3, tax might be avoided on the contributions paid into the plan. And no tax is paid on the annual income earned by funds in the retirement plan. Thus, these funds earn income compounding at a higher effective rate than they could earn in the hands of a taxpaying individual.

To illustrate, compare placing $1,000 into a retirement plan with placing $1,000 into the hands of an individual in the 30% tax bracket (Federal plus State). Let's suppose each $1,000 is invested at 8% interest compounded annually. The retirement plan earns interest at the full 8% rate. But the individual earns a net interest rate of only 5.6% after paying taxes. The $1,000 in the individual's hands would grow to $3,905 after 25 years. But the $1,000 in the retirement plan would grow to $6,848, an increase of 75%.

Section 2:
Payments from Retirement Plans

When you receive annuity payments from your retirement plan, your employer will furnish information concerning the tax status of these payments. A portion of each payment reflecting your own contributions on which you have already paid tax is not subject to further taxation. The remaining portion is taxable. Thus you are taxed when you receive amounts reflecting contributions made by your employer, as well as investment income.

Your employer can compute the tax-free portion of your annuity payments in 2 ways—using either the *General Rule* or the *Simplified General Rule*. The

410

Simplified General Rule is an option announced in a 1989 ruling by the IRS [IR-89-31]. It is not only simpler, but better—generally producing a larger tax-free amount than that produced by the General Rule.

If your employer uses the General Rule, it may pay you to make the computation yourself using the Simplified General Rule. This is done by using the worksheet found in IRS Publication 575, obtainable from the IRS. This rule may generally be used retroactively by filing an amended return within the usual 3-year deadline [cf. Section 1 of Chapter 1]. If your computation produces a different figure than that reported by your employer on Form W-2P, you should attach a statement to your tax return explaining your computation.

The portion of each payment you receive that is exempt from tax is based on your life-expectancy. That is, if you live precisely as long as predicted by the actuarial tables, then the total amounts exempted from tax will be equal to the total contributions you made during the years you worked.

However, if you live beyond the age predicted in the life-expectancy tables, then you must pay tax on the full amount of each annuity payment from that time on. That way, the total amounts exempted from tax will be equal to the total contributions you made.

On the other hand, there is a little known provision that applies if you die before your predicted life expectancy. In that situation, the total amounts you have exempted from tax will be less than your total contributions. The law provides that the difference between these 2 totals can then be deducted on your final tax return for the year in which you die.

Since, mercifully, you won't be filling out this tax return yourself, your spouse or other heirs should be aware of this provision. The amount of this final deduction could be quite large. And there is even a carryback rule that sometimes applies if this final deduction exceeds the taxable income for the year. In such a case, professional assistance will be needed to make the appropriate computation.

Lump-Sum Distributions

If benefits from a retirement plan are paid out in one lump sum after you reach age $59^1/_2$ (or upon your death or disability), then you can choose to apply a special 5-year averaging rule. Essentially, this rule allows you to treat the lump-sum distribution as though it were spread out over a 5-year period and taxes it entirely independent of any other income. The tax on your other income is computed as though you never received any retirement payment.

For example, a $100,000 lump-sum distribution would be taxed at a rate of about 15%. The 5-year averaging rule also applies to lump-sum distributions from Keogh Plans but not from IRAs or Tax-Sheltered Annuities [cf. the *Tax-Sheltered Plans* chapter].

The 5-year averaging rule generally applies only to employees who were plan participants for at least 5 full years prior to the year of distribution. Also, the 5-year averaging rule can be used only once in a lifetime.

In case of death, many retirement plans provide a benefit payment to a beneficiary which also qualifies for the 5-year averaging rule. In such a case, the employee need not have been a plan participant for 5 years.

A distribution cannot qualify for the lump-sum treatment described above unless it constitutes the entire balance to the credit of the employee. The entire distribution need not be made at one time as long as the entire balance is distributed within the same tax year. If an employer maintains several retirement plans of similar type, these may have to be aggregated (i.e. considered to be one plan) when determining if a total distribution has been made.

There is also a special transfer provision of the law which applies to a lump-sum distribution from your retirement plan. A lump-sum distribution received after you leave your job or after you reach age 59$1/2$ can be rolled over, in whole or in part, to another tax-sheltered plan you set up called an Individual Retirement Account (IRA). No tax will be paid until money is paid out from the IRA. Partial distributions of 50% or more of a given pension plan or tax-sheltered annuity received upon leaving your job can generally still qualify for rollover treatment but not for 5-year averaging. You also might be able to transfer the distribution to your new employer's retirement plan if he permits it. Details are discussed in Section 2 of the *Tax-Sheltered Plans* chapter.

Sometimes, a portion of an individual's pension account is used to buy an annuity or other insurance policy before the distribution is made. This policy is then distributed to the individual at the same time the remainder of the balance is distributed in cash. In this situation, the annuity payments are taxed year by year as they are received. Meanwhile, the cash is eligible for 5-year averaging or IRA rollover treatment. However, the 5-year averaging computation may yield a higher tax than if there were no annuity, because the value of the annuity is figured in the determination of which tax bracket to use.

Special Transition Rule for Individuals Born Before 1936

There is a special transition rule for individuals born before 1936. They can choose to apply the prior law 10-year averaging rule using 1986 tax rates if they wish.

The 10-year averaging rule works like the 5-year rule, except that the distribution is taxed as though it were spread out over a 10-year instead of a 5-year period. The 10-year averaging rule is generally better than the 5-year rule for lump-sum distributions up to about $500,000. Above this level, neither averaging rule provides a lower tax than the ordinary tax schedule.

Either 5 or 10-year averaging can be applied to a distribution received upon separation from service, even if the individual is younger than age 59$1/2$. However, the once-in-a-lifetime rule still applies. That is, if either the 5-year or 10-year averaging rule is used on a lump-sum distribution received after 1986, then no use of a special averaging rule is permitted for any future lump-sum distributions.

Pre-1974 Contributions

If you were a participant in your retirement plan before 1974, then you have another option that applies to the *pre-1974 portion* of a lump-sum distribution. This *pre-1974 portion* is determined by multiplying the taxable amount of the distribution by the number of pre-1974 years of participation and dividing by the total number of years of participation. (This amount will be shown on Form 1099-R which you will receive from your employer.) You can then choose to regard the pre-1974 portion as long-term capital gains in the year of distribution and apply 5-year (or 10-year if applicable) averaging to the remainder. Or, you can group the pre-1974 portion with the remaining portion and apply 5-year (or 10-year) averaging to the entire amount. Your choice should be made after computing the consequences of both choices and determining which is the more advantageous in your particular situation.

Only a certain *phase-out percentage* of the pre-1974 portion will qualify for the capital gains treatment described in the preceding paragraph. For 1990, this percentage is 50%; for 1991, 25%

For those who were born before 1936, an extra option is available. They can choose to apply a flat 20% rate to the entire pre-1974 portion, with no phase-out percentage. Either 5-year or 10-year averaging can be applied to the remaining portion of the distribution, as discussed earlier.

The special option for treating the pre-1974 portion of a lump-sum distribution falls under the same once-in-a-lifetime rule that applies to the 5-year averaging option or 10-year averaging option. That is, if any of these 3 options is used for a lump-sum distribution received after 1986, then none of these options can be used for any future lump-sum distributions.

If either 5-year or 10-year averaging is used, the appropriate tax calculations are made on Form 4972.

Extra 10% Tax on Distributions before Age 59 1/2

In general, an individual who receives a distribution from a pension plan prior to reaching age 59 1/2 is subject to an additional "penalty tax" equal to 10% of the taxable portion of the distribution. This 10% tax is in addition to any income tax due on such distributions. However, there is no additional tax on the portion of the distribution that is a return of non-deductible employee contributions.

The 10% penalty tax is waived if either (i) you die and your beneficiaries get the money, (ii) you become disabled, (iii) you leave your job and take your pension entitlement in the form of an annuity payable in equal periodic amounts over a lifetime, (iv) you leave your job after reaching age 55, (v) you use the distribution to pay for medical bills in excess of 7.5% of your adjusted gross income, or (vi) you roll over the distribution tax-free into an IRA.

Due to the complexity of the rules, professional advice should be sought before making any lump-sum distribution decisions. Also, special rules apply if you are covered by a retirement plan of a company of which you are at least a 5% owner. (At presstime, future improvements in the lump-sum distributor rules were being considered.)

Section 3:
Contributions to Retirement Plans

Employer's Contributions

Your employer's contributions to your retirement plan are not taxable at the time the contributions are made, provided (as is usually the case) the IRS has approved the plan as qualifying for this benefit.

Employee's Contributions

An employee's contributions to his retirement plan are taxable. That is, the taxable wages figure reported on his W-2 Form includes his full salary before his contributions to the retirement plan are taken out. He must pay tax based on this full figure and can get no deduction for his contributions to the retirement plan.

This situation is inherently unfair. To illustrate this unfairness, compare the situations of the following two persons:

A earns $52,000 per year. He is required to participate in a retirement plan to which both he and his employer contribute $1,000 per year. Effectively, A's annual salary is $51,000 plus the $2,000 which is contributed to his retirement system.

B, on the other hand, earns an annual salary of $51,000. His retirement plan is entirely funded by his employer who makes a contribution of $2,000 per year. Thus, like A, B has an annual salary of $51,000 plus the $2,000 retirement contribution. The employers of both A & B have precisely the same expense—$53,000 per year.

But there is one important difference. A must pay tax based on his official $52,000 salary while B pays tax only on $51,000. For no good reason, A is required to pay more tax than B. However, when A and B retire, then B must pay tax on the full amount of his retirement pay (see Section 2). A does not have to pay tax on that amount which represents a return of his contributions to the plan. Thus, the net result is A pays tax on the additional $1,000 in the year he earns it while B defers paying tax on his amount until he receives it in the form of retirement benefits. Meanwhile, B has been able to earn interest on the difference for many years. This amount could be multiplied many times over, especially if retirement is far away. In addition, B's tax rate is likely to be lower during retirement than when he is working.

The only distinction in the two situations described above is a semantic one, namely whether contributions are **designated** as being made by the employee or the employer. But Congress has specifically made this semantic distinction the criterion for deduction. The employee must pay tax on any amounts designated as salary even if these amounts are put into a retirement plan as an employee contribution without passing through his hands. However, he does not have to pay tax on amounts put into a qualified retirement plan if these payments are designated as employer contributions.

Private employers are well aware of this distinction. They usually designate all contributions to a retirement plan to be employer contributions. This produces the best tax result for the employee without costing the employer anything extra. In fact, keeping pension plan contributions outside the employee's official salary can even benefit the employer by lowering worker's compensation premiums, social security contributions, and other payments based on salary.

Public institutions are another matter. Their pension plans are often part of a large system established by state or local law. For example, teachers in public institutions typically are covered under the same general retirement plan applying to all state employees. These plans often require contributions to be made both by employer and employee.

Exception. A number of IRS rulings have highlighted an exception to the general rule that employee contributions are included in taxable income. This exception applies when a state or local government retirement plan requires employee contributions but a school district, college education board, or other subdivision agrees to "pick up" the employee contribution. The IRS uses a Congressional committee's report to describe the situation as follows:

> *"However, some state and local government plans designate certain amounts as being employee contributions even though statutes authorize or require the relevant governmental units or agencies to pick up some or all of what would otherwise be the employee's contribution. In other words, the governmental unit pays all or part of the employee's contribution but does not withhold this amount from the employee's salary. In this situation, the portion of the contribution which is 'picked-up' by the government is, in substance, an employer contribution for purposes of Federal tax law, notwithstanding the fact that for certain purposes of State Law the contribution may be designated as an employee contribution. Accordingly,... in the case of a government pick-up plan... the portion of the contribution which is paid by the government, with no withholding from the employee's salary, will be treated as an employer contribution under the tax law."* [H. Rep. 93-807]

A number of IRS rulings have made it relatively easy to qualify under the above pick-up rule. First, the IRS issued a Revenue Ruling stating that pick-up plans need only satisfy the following two criteria:

> *"(1) the employer must specify that the contributions, although designated as employee contributions, are paid by the employer in lieu of contributions by the employee;*

> *and*

> *"(2) the employee must not be given the option of choosing to receive the contributed amounts directly instead of having them paid by the employer to the pension plan."* [Rev. Rul. 81-36]

Then, an IRS Chief Council Memorandum liberalized the interpretation of criteria (2). According to this memorandum, criteria (2)

> *"must not be interpreted to prohibit 'pick-up' of amounts that are, in substance, employer contributions. This rationale suggests that criteria (2) should only be applied to cases in which an employee is considered to have the option to choose to receive the amounts directly rather than having them contributed to a plan because the employee is in fact controlling the amounts and, therefore, the contributions are not, in substance, employer contributions.*
>
> *"An option that would be impermissible under criteria (2) is one in which the employee will currently receive the amounts unless he must annually opt to have these amounts contributed on his behalf to the employer's pension plan. In this case the employee, not the employer, is in fact controlling the contributions."*

But a one-time nonrevocable election whether or not to participate in a pension plan is all right. According to the memorandum,

> *"it is our opinion that the nonexercise of a one-time election to opt out of a plan or the one-time, nonrevocable election to begin early participation in a plan does not vest in the employee enough control of the employer contribution to taint the amounts contributed on the employee's behalf."* [G.C.M. 38820]

For example, under this policy, the IRS issued a private ruling approving a pick-up plan which provided that an employee became a participant when first hired unless he filed a written notice of election not to participate within a 30-day period. [IRS Private Letter Ruling 8209038]

There is no restriction on how the contributions are to be picked up. According to an IRS Private Letter Ruling, *"The employer may pick up these contributions by a reduction in cash salary of the employee or by an offset against future salary increase or by a combination of reduction in salary and offset against a future salary increase."* [IRS Private Letter Ruling 8206146]

As the above discussion indicates, it has become quite easy for governmental units to establish pick-up plans. Essentially, all they need to do is pass the appropriate statute authorizing the pick-up. Practically speaking, this is just a bookkeeping change, costing the employer nothing while saving the employee many hundreds of dollars in taxes. In fact, many pick-up plans involving government employees, including teachers, have been established in States across the country the past few years. Presumably, other States will be giving this no-cost benefit to their employees in the near future.

Special Rules for School Employees

There is another alternative available to schools and certain other non-profit organizations. Instead of qualifying under the usual retirement plan rules, they can set up their retirement plan under the special tax-sheltered annuity regulations that apply only to these types of organizations. [Cf. Section 4 of the *Tax-Sheltered Plans* chapter.] To qualify, the retirement plan must provide that all contributions to the plan are non-transferable and non-forfeitable. This means that amounts credited to the account of an employee cannot be assigned over to someone else nor can they be forfeited because the employee terminates his employment or for any other reason. Also, certain new *non-discrimination* rules apply that require retirement plans not to overly benefit higher-salaried employees when compared with lower-salaried employees.

Under the tax-sheltered annuity regulations, an employee can make an agreement with his employer to reduce his salary by an amount equal to his contribution to the retirement plan. Then, the institution contributes this amount to the retirement plan. The net result is that the employee's contribution is transformed into an employer's contribution. The employee's W2 Form shows the reduced amount as his taxable wages. Since his official salary is reduced, the employee escapes tax on the amount of his contribution to the plan.

Of course, as discussed in Section 2, tax must be paid later when this amount is received in the form of retirement benefits. But in the meantime, the tax that was not paid can be invested to earn interest for many years. In effect, the deferral of tax gives the same benefit as obtaining a long term interest-free loan from the government. Over the long run, this can amount to a substantial benefit.

Private institutions have little trouble qualifying their plans under the tax-sheltered annuity regulations. Public institutions are another matter. Often, their employees are included in the same retirement system that applies to all state employees. These state plans typically require that both the employer and employee contribute to the plan. And, as discussed earlier, amounts designated as being contributed by the employee are included in taxable wages.

However, a court case shows that even if the state retirement system designates amounts as *employee* contributions, this may not rule out a deduction. The administration of the educational organization may be able to *redesignate* these amounts as *employer* contributions, exempting them from tax. This case involved the retirement system applying to employees of the State of North Dakota. According to North Dakota law, both employer and employee were required to contribute 4% of the employee's salary to the state retirement system. The Court ruled that the State Board of Higher Education, under its broad administrative authority, had the power to authorize salary reduction agreements transforming employee contributions into employer contributions, despite the state statute requiring contributions from the employee. [University of North Dakota, 44 AFTR 2d 79-5392]

The TIAA/CREF Retirement System

TIAA and **CREF** (Teachers Insurance and Annuity Association/College Retirement Equities Fund) are a pair of non-profit organizations founded by the Carnegie Foundation. Their basic function is to provide a universal retirement plan which allows faculty members to transfer their retirement plan from one institution to another without losing any benefits.

Most private colleges and a number of public colleges use the TIAA/CREF system as the basic retirement system for their employees. It is also used by a number of other eligible non-profit institutions.

The TIAA/CREF system has recently undergone an overhaul, increasing the array of basic choices that are available to participants. First, CREF inaugurated 2 new funds in 1990. Second, CREF will allow money to be transferred among its funds, and from any of its funds into the TIAA fund or into funds run by employer-approved competing financial organizations. And third, if the employer agrees, CREF accumulations can be received in a lump-sum payout upon termination of employment. These features are discussed below.

Choice of Investments

At the present time, there are the following 5 funds available to participants, one of them run by TIAA and the other 4 run by CREF:

1. TIAA Fund. The TIAA Fund is invested primarily in fixed income securities such as bonds, mortgages, and direct loans to business and industry. The fund operates more like an insurance annuity fund than a mutual fund. That is, your account is credited each year with interest earned by the fund. Money invested when rates are high will continue to earn higher interest than money invested when rates are low. For example, funds invested in 1990 earned 8.25% interest that year, while funds invested in 1982–1985 earned 10% interest in 1990.

By operating in this fashion, TIAA guarantees there will be no loss of principal and that annual interest will never fall below 3%. In fact, the interest rates paid by the fund in recent years have been much higher than this.

2. CREF Stock Fund. This is the basic CREF fund that has been in existence for decades. Money is invested in a wide portfolio of stocks. About 70% of the fund is invested in an indexed portfolio which mirrors the behavior of basic stock market averages. The other 30% is invested in foreign stocks and in domestic stocks selected by the fund managers.

3. CREF Money-Market Fund. This acts like a typical money-market fund [cf. Section 7 of the *Investing Your Money* chapter]. That is, the fund invests in short-term high-quality debt instruments such as U.S. Treasury Bills, certificates of deposit, short-term commercial loans, etc. Money-market funds are the safest type of investment other than short-term securities issued by or guaranteed by the U.S. Government.

4. Bond Market Fund. This new fund, initiated in 1990, invests primarily in investment-grade fixed-income securities. This includes U.S. Government securities, publicly-traded corporate bonds, and mortgage-backed securities which are guaranteed by the U.S. Government or have a sufficiently high investment rating. The Bond Market Fund is run like a mutual fund [cf. Section 5 of the *Investing Your Money* chapter]. The unit value of the fund will fluctuate as the securities in the fund rise and fall in price, and interest earned by the securities in the fund will be credited to the accounts of the investors. There is no guarantee for principal or interest like the one, discussed above, for the TIAA Fund.

5. Social Choice Fund. This new fund, initiated in 1990, invests in a portfolio of stocks and fixed-income securities. According to the prospectus, this fund *"will seek to invest in companies conducting their activities in a manner that recognizes acceptable standards for addressing specified social concerns."* Currently, this fund will not invest in any company which (1) has economic ties to South Africa, (2) has an operation in Northern Ireland which does not follow a code prohibiting religious discrimination, (3) produces nuclear energy, (4) has a significant portion of its business involved in the manufacture of weapons, or (5) produces and markets alcoholic beverages or tobacco products. Currently, the fund is also working on formulating *"practical criteria permitting systematic exclusion of investments in companies that fail to adhere to sound environmental policies and practices."*

You can choose any allocation you want among the above funds. You can have all your money invested in one fund, or specify the percentages if you divide up the money among several funds. The same percentage need not be chosen for each fund. For example, you can have 60% of your money invested in one fund, 30% in another, and 10% in a third.

While most participating organizations will make all of the above funds available to their employees, they do not have to do so. They can prohibit allocations to the CREF Bond Market and/or Social Choice Funds altogether, but may not do so for the CREF Stock or Money-Market Funds.

Transferability

Under the new 1990 rules, you are permitted to transfer funds from one of the CREF funds to the TIAA Fund or to any of the other available CREF funds at any time you choose. The only restriction is that the amount transferred must be at least $1,000. There is even a toll-free Automated Telephone Service (800-842-2252) which you can call to make the transfer. You can also call to change your allocation of future premiums.

Also, TIAA/CREF will now, for the first time, allow you to transfer money out of any of the CREF Funds into any other fund offered by the College (or other non-profit institution) for which you work. However, each College must decide whether and to what extent it will permit this type of transfer.

You will have to check with the personnel office where you work to find out which options are available to you. If the new options are not available, be sure to check whether they have been rejected, or are still under consideration. As of Fall, 1990, only 35% of colleges had made a decision, most of them to allow some or all of the new options. This means some employees will have to wait before they can take advantage of the liberalized new TIAA/CREF rules.

Currently, you are not allowed to transfer money out of the TIAA fund into another fund. However, this is expected to change sometime in the summer of 1991. At that time, TIAA will announce rules under which such transfers can be made. The rules will probably not allow immediate transfer of all of an individual's TIAA account. Rather, it will probably require withdrawal of TIAA funds to take place over, say, a 10-year period. This restriction is required because of the basic setup of the TIAA fund. Investments in TIAA are "locked into" long term investments and large withdrawals could adversely affect the remaining investors. As described above, there is no fluctuating *net asset value* at which to cash out withdrawals as there is with an ordinary mutual fund.

The new transferability options will prove valuable to those who wish to tailor an investment strategy for their retirement funds.

Example

   Mann is 40 years old when he starts participation in the TIAA/CREF system. He wishes to have half of his money in a no-risk investment and the other half in the stock market. As he nears retirement, he wishes to change the mix so he is 75% in the no-risk investment and only 25% in the stock market.

   Mann designates 50% of contributions to be invested in the CREF Stock Fund and the other 50% in the CREF Money Market Fund. The money market fund invests in short-term high-quality securities. This protects it not only from the risk of default, but also from the risk of inflation. (The inflation risk is negated because short-term interest rates track the movement of inflation so your funds will grow in general pace with inflation. This is not the case with either the TIAA Fund or the TIAA Bond Fund which are adversely affected if the inflation rate climbs.)

   After 10 years, let's say the stock market has been kind to Mann. Because of the rise in value, his account in the CREF Stock Market Fund is now worth 2 times the money in his CREF Money Market Fund. To return to his basic investment strategy, he can use a transfer to return to a 50/50 allocation.

   As Mann nears retirement, he can further use the transfer option to work his portfolio towards the 75/25 allocation he desires in retirement.

Cashability

Under the new 1990 rules, CREF will allow participants to withdraw all or part of the accumulated account in a CREF fund upon retirement or terminating employment. However, each employer has the authority to permit or restrict such withdrawals. Many are reluctant to allow full withdrawals, partly out of paternalistic concern that the employee will squander the funds, leaving him with inadequate retirement support.

You will need to check if your employer has made a decision as to what type of lump sum withdrawals, if any, will be permitted under the new TIAA/CREF options. Such withdrawals would come under the rules described in Sections 2 and 4 of the *Tax-Sheltered Plans* chapter. In particular, note there the rules for rolling over funds into an IRA or other plan, and the extra 10% penalty tax that applies to withdrawals before age 59 1/2 in the absence of a rollover.

Contributions to TIAA/CREF are non-transferable and non-forfeitable. Thus, TIAA/CREF satisfies the basic tax-sheltered annuity regulations described above. Most institutions which use the TIAA/CREF system permit their employees to make a reduction-of-salary agreement to shelter their contributions from tax. However, some institutions do not permit such agreements, either because local law does not allow it, because the bookkeeping requirements cannot be met, or for other reasons.

Many institutions permit employees to make tax-sheltered contributions to TIAA/CREF in addition to the regular required contributions to the basic retirement plan. This is the case even if TIAA/CREF is not used for the basic retirement plans. These additional contributions are subject to certain limitations provided for in the law. Details are discussed in Section 4 of the *Tax-Sheltered Plans* chapter.

Some institutions offer their employees a choice between the TIAA/CREF system and a second retirement plan sponsored by the institution. Often, this second plan is a state or local retirement system that applies to all government employees. In such cases, there can be substantial differences between the two plans. The TIAA/CREF system may permit reduction-of-salary agreements to defer tax on employee contributions, while the state or local retirement system may not.

However, this tax advantage could be outweighed by other advantages of the state or local system. Benefits paid by TIAA/CREF are actuarially computed to correspond precisely to the amounts that have been contributed to your account and the investment experience of the funds. But state and local systems are often not based on such actuarial computations. Especially in times of high inflation, governmental pension plans often pay out benefits far more than that which an actuarial computation would yield. This is particularly true when cost-of-living adjustments are provided for.

Often, employees who anticipate changing jobs within a few years will be better off with a plan like TIAA/CREF because it provides for no forfeiture of amounts in the employee's account. This is not the case with many other pension plans. Employees who do not anticipate changing jobs will have to make a careful evaluation of the features of each of the plans being offered to determine which is more favorable in their case.

Retirement Options

Under TIAA, an annuity can be selected which essentially pays a fixed monthly amount until death, based on the size of the employee's account and his age at retirement. Or, an annuity can be chosen which starts at a lower level and increases annually to compensate, roughly, for the increase in the cost of living. A number of options are available to provide that payments continue to a spouse after the death of the employee. Of course, any options which provide payments to a spouse reduce the amount of the original annuity according to the appropriate actuarial computation.

Amounts in CREF are used to purchase a variable annuity upon retirement. Monthly payments are made which vary according to the dividend and interest payments made by the securities and the rise and fall in market value. Options providing benefits to a beneficiary apply to these variable annuities also.

Supreme Court Unisex Ruling

In 1983, the Supreme Court issued a ruling concerning payments from *defined contribution* pension plans. These are pension plans under which each year, money is credited to an individual's account. At retirement, an annuity is purchased based solely on the amount in the individual's account, including investment income earned on the contributions. The plans run by TIAA and CREF are defined contribution plans. Pension plans which promise a certain monthly benefit based on final salary are **not** defined contribution plans.

Historically, two different life-expectancy tables were used to calculate the annuity payments which the funds in an individual's account would purchase— one table for women and the other for men. Since women, on average, live longer than men, their annuity payments would be expected to continue over a longer period of time. Therefore, the monthly payments they received were less than the payments received by men to compensate for the expectation that more payments would be made.

However, the Supreme Court ruled that this policy violated antidiscrimination requirements of the law. As of August 1, 1983, employers must use one unisex mortality table in computing the annuity payments an individual is to receive based on the value of the funds accumulated in his retirement account after this date. That is, there can be no different treatment of men and women as there had been in the past. If women as a class live longer than men, they will simply receive more total benefits than men.

The U.S. Court of Appeals for the Second Circuit extended the Supreme Court ruling to cover all individuals in the TIAA/CREF system retiring after May 1, 1980. It ruled that the pensions of such individuals should be adjusted to conform to a unisex mortality table applied to the entire value of their account. In October, 1984, the Supreme Court declined to review this Court of Appeals decision, thereby letting it stand as law. Although the Second Circuit Court of Appeals only has jurisdiction over a limited geographical area, TIAA/CREF announced that it would apply the decision nationwide. (A separate recent court decision applies to about 50,000 ex-teachers who retired between March 24, 1972 and May 1, 1980 under the TIAA/CREF retirement system. As of January 1, 1986, the dividend portion of their retirement checks is being computed on a unisex basis.)

TIAA/CREF has computed the difference that a switch to unisex mortality tables makes. Pension payments to men generally decrease while pension payments to women generally increase. But the amount of change depends on the type of annuity which is selected.

There are two basic types of annuities—single-life and joint-life annuities. A *single-life annuity* makes payments to the individual until he dies. A *joint-life annuity* continues payments to the surviving spouse until the spouse dies.

Single-life annuities are the ones most affected by the switch to unisex tables. TIAA single-life annuities are lowered $4^1/2\%$ for men and raised $4^1/2\%$ for women. CREF annuities are lowered 8% for men and raised 8% for women.

Single-life annuities can also be chosen which guarantee that payments continue-for 10 or 20 years (to a beneficiary) if the individual dies before that time. For a 10-year guaranteed period, the men's loss/women's gain is $2^1/2\%$ for TIAA and 6% for CREF. For a 20-year guaranteed period, the figures are 1% for TIAA and $2^1/2\%$ for CREF

Joint-life annuities which continue payments to the surviving spouse at the same rate or at a $2/3$ reduction are unaffected by the switch to unisex tables. If annuity payments to the spouse are $1/2$ the payments to the individual, the TIAA change is 2% and the CREF change is $3^{1/2}$%. (All of the above figures are based on an assumption that both husband and wife are 65 years old.)

Those who participate in the TIAA/CREF Retirement System should take note of the above percentage changes when making a selection of payout option. For example, men who select the single-life annuity option are hit the hardest, so from an actuarial point of view this option is the least preferable. The joint-life option is the most favorable with no reduction in benefits if the surviving spouse receives full or $2/3$ benefits.

The opposite is true for women. Under the single-life option, they get an increase in benefits of as much as 8% while under the joint-life option with full or $2/3$ survivor benefits there is no increase.

Of course, non-actuarial considerations may play a larger role in an individual's decision on which payout option to use. For example, a man may still want to choose a straight single-life option if he has no heirs he wishes to provide for. Also, the actuarial tables are based on average life expectancies from which a person may have reason to believe he will deviate. The health, family history, or living habits of an individual may indicate a different life expectancy than average. In such a case, this may point to a particular payout option. For example, the joint-life option is statistically preferable for a female in ill health with a healthy husband even though the single-life option benefits from the switch to unisex mortality tables.

The Supreme Court ruling applies to all defined benefit plans, so they will be affected similarly to TIAA/CREF However, only employer-provided annuities are required to use unisex tables. If a pension plan pays a lump-sum benefit and allows the individual to purchase an annuity from a commercial insurance company of his choice, the Supreme Court ruling does not apply.

It should be pointed out that there is controversy as to why females outlive males on average. It is not known for certain to what degree this is due to biology and to what degree this is due to lifestyle factors such as smoking habits, stress levels, etc. To the extent lifestyle factors play a role, the switch to unisex mortality tables may reflect a more accurate assessment of life expectancy for working women. However, most researchers believe that women do enjoy an inherent biological advantage in life expectancy. Estelle Ramey, a prominent endocrinologist at Georgetown Medical Center, has estimated the inherent longevity difference between women and men to be between 4 and 5 years. Also to be pointed out is that some States now require unisex pricing on commercial annuities or other types of insurance.

Section 4:
Social Security

A major new social security law was passed by Congress in 1983. This law was designed to "rescue" the social security system by increasing taxes and lowering benefits in a variety of different ways, including raising the social security tax, gradually increasing the retirement age, and restricting the cost-of-living benefit increases under certain circumstances. And under this law, the following items are included in the wage base subject to social security tax: deferred compensation, employee contributions to a State retirement plan which are "picked-up" by the employer [cf. Section 3], and amounts paid to a tax-sheltered annuity under a salary reduction plan.

Tax on Social Security Benefits

Congress also subjected social security benefits to income tax. Now, half the social security benefits an individual receives are required to be included in taxable income, provided the individual has total income which exceeds a certain trigger point—$32,000 on joint returns; $25,000 on single returns. (The trigger point for marrieds filing separately who live with their spouses anytime during the year is $0.)

The exact procedure for computing how much is taxed is complex. Here's how it works. Start with Adjusted Gross Income (AGI). Add to this any untaxed interest from municipal bonds. Then add in half the social security benefits. If the total is less than the trigger point, no benefits are taxed. If the total exceeds the trigger point, half this excess is taxed except that no more than half the social security benefits can be subjected to tax in any case.

The obvious effect of this new tax on social security benefits is to lower the net benefit for those who exceed the trigger points. A less obvious but equally strong effect is that for some, an increase in other income triggers a tax on social security benefits. For example, suppose a single person has $22,000 AGI plus $6,000 social security benefits. His AGI + $1/2$ of social security benefits equal $25,000. Since this places him right at the trigger point, no tax is paid on his social security benefits. He simply computes his tax on the $22,000 of Adjusted Gross Income.

But now suppose he earns an extra $3,000 in taxable income, bringing his AGI to $25,000. Now the total of his AGI + $1/2$ of social security benefits equals $28,000. This exceeds the $25,000 trigger point by $3,000, so half this excess, $1/2 \times \$3,000 = \$1,500$ is subjected to tax. He must pay tax on $25,000 + $1,500 = $26,500. Thus, the extra $3,000 in earnings triggers an increase in taxable income of $4,500. In effect, his marginal tax bracket on extra earnings has been increased by 50%!

A similar effect would occur if instead of an extra $3,000 in earnings, he earned an extra $3,000 in tax-exempt income. This would trigger a tax on $1,500 of benefits just as in the preceding computation. Effectively, instead of being totally exempt from tax, half of this "tax-exempt" income is subject to tax.

The taxable amount of social security benefits is reported on line 21b of Form 1040. A worksheet is provided in the instruction booklet accompanying your tax forms for computing this taxable amount.

Note that many States which tie their State income tax computation to the Federal tax computation make an exception in the case of Social Security benefits. In these States, all Social Security benefits are completely exempt from State income tax.

Checking Your Social Security Account

There is a form that you can fill out to obtain a statement which includes an estimate of what your social security benefits will be when you retire. The statement will include a year-by-year breakdown of how much Social Security taxes were credited to your account. You can use this to correct your earnings record if there are inaccuracies. You can obtain this form by calling 1-800-937-2000.

It is recommended that you fill out this form at least once every three years. Otherwise, even if you discover an error, it may be too late to correct it. There are any number of ways your account might have been fouled up. The prudent person will not wait until retirement, when it might be too late, to make sure the proper benefits will be received.

Married women who use their maiden names are especially advised to check their social security records if they had *self-employment* income. Due to a mixup, the IRS has in many cases been using their husbands' last names when sending annual earnings reports to the Social Security System. This means that income may not have been credited to their accounts.

The Social Security Administration has over $60 billion in wages that it has been unable to credit because it can't figure out to whom the wages belong.

Social Security Numbers Required for Children

You are supposed to have social security numbers for children (or other individuals) over age 2 if you wish to claim them as dependents on your tax return. You list these numbers in column (3) of line 6c on Form 1040. Call your local social security office to get application forms.

There's a simple way to get a social security number for a newborn. In most places, you can get the number issued automatically by having a box on the birth record checked. The information will then be sent to the Social Security Administration, which will issue a number within a few months.

If you have applied for but not yet received the required social security numbers by the time you file your tax return, enter *"Applied For"* in column (3) of line 6c. This might spare you an unpleasant letter from the IRS as well as a fine.

Chapter 26

Outside Business Activity

Section 1:
Basic Rules

In addition to your regular job, you or your spouse may have an outside "business" activity, e. g. writing, tutoring, consulting, refereeing, reviewing, art, photography, etc. If this activity produces extra income, it becomes taxable along with the rest of your income. As discussed in Sections 2 and 3, there are a number of ways to ease the tax burden on this outside income.

Of particular note are the remarkable *Defined-Benefit Keogh Plans*. With such Plans, those with self-employment income can often **shelter up to 100% of such income from tax** [cf. Section 3 of the *Tax-Sheltered Plans* chapter for details].

On the other hand, the activity might produce a loss. When a loss is produced, the question arises whether the activity qualifies as a business activity or is simply a hobby. Losses produced by a business activity are fully deductible while losses produced by a hobby are not. Section 4 discusses the rules for deducting losses in more detail.

The methods described in this chapter apply only to income which is earned as a result of your labor. Investment income, income from rents, etc. do not qualify. Furthermore, such income must be self-employment income earned when you are working for yourself or income received from a corporation which you own.

Example

Jones, in addition to his regular job, does consulting work for an industrial company in the city where he lives. He arranges it so that he is not considered an employee of the company for which he works. Rather, he is a self-employed professional contracting out his services. Alternatively, he could form the Jones Consulting Firm (whose only employee is Jones) which contracts with the company for the services of Jones. Actually, the industrial company is quite happy with this arrangement. It doesn't have to pay social security, unemployment insurance, or worker's compensation premiums as it has to do on its regular employees. In fact, Jones' remuneration as a private contractor may be higher than it would be as an employee because of these savings.

What Is an Employee?

You cannot call yourself a private contractor just because you and the party engaging your services agree. There is a definite body of law as to when a person is an employee and when he is a private contractor. The basic definition of an employee is one who performs services subject to control by an employer *"not only as to the result to be accomplished by the work, but also as to the details and means by which that result is accomplished. That is, an employee is subject to the will and control of the employer not only as to what is to be done, but also as to how and when it shall be done."* Of course, the preceding definition is not sufficiently precise to determine borderline cases. There may be specific IRS guidelines which apply in your case. If not, the particular circumstances of your situation will determine your status. You can get a ruling from the IRS in any doubtful situation by filling out a special questionnaire for that purpose.

New IRS Crackdown on Self-Employed Persons

The IRS has a general preference that individuals be labeled *employees* rather than *self-employed persons*. It's easier to tax an employee because both income tax and social security tax are withheld from his paychecks. But self-employed persons are responsible for sending in their tax payments themselves. In fact, studies have shown that underreporting of self-employment income is a significant problem.

As a consequence, the IRS has decided to target individuals who are classifying income as self-employment income when it feels this income might better be classified as wages. Starting in 1991, the IRS is instructing its computers to look for tax returns reporting self-employment income from only one source. That is, it will target tax returns of individuals who have received only one Form 1099 reporting self-employment income.

Generally, payments totalling $600 or more during the year must be reported to the recipient and the IRS on a Form 1099. Thus, an individual with self-employment income exceeding $600 from only one source might find himself targeted by the IRS.

Of course, this targeting device by the IRS is a crude one. As discussed later in this Section, a person can have self-employment income even if it comes only from a single source. And even if income is reclassified, this does not necessarily mean that extra tax will be due, although the tax return may have to be worked over.

To prevent unwanted communications from the IRS, it would be wise to avoid having just one source of self-employment reported to the IRS. If possible, try to earn at least $600 from a second source, so the IRS will receive 2 separate reports of self-employment income.

If you have 2 sources of self-employment income, but one of them amounts to less than $600, there is still something you can do. While only annual payments of $600 or more *must* be reported to the IRS, this does not mean smaller amounts cannot be reported. You can ask payers of amounts less than $600 to file a Form 1099 on you, even though they are not required to do so. This will enable you to get around the IRS targeting program.

Basic Forms of Organization

There are three basic forms of business organizations:

(1) Sole Proprietorship (i.e. Self-Employed)

(2) Partnership

(3) Corporation

(1) Sole Proprietorship (i.e. Self-Employed)

This is how most people in business for themselves operate. It just means you are self-employed. No special form of organization or legal paraphernalia is required. If you are performing services for a fee such as consulting, reviewing, etc. and are not an employee of the party for whom you perform these services, then you are automatically operating a sole proprietorship.

Income and expenses due to self-employment are reported on Schedule C. In addition to income tax, self-employment income is subject to social security tax at the rate of 15.3%. However, there is no social security tax if self-employment income for the year is less than $400. The self-employment social security tax is computed on Schedule SE. However, if an individual has another job which pays at least as much as the social security wage base ($51,300 in 1990), there is no additional social security tax on his self-employment income. As discussed in Chapter 0, this will change in 1991 when the 1.45% medicare portion of the social security tax will apply to income up to $125,000.

New Deduction on 1990 Tax Returns

On 1990 tax returns, there is a new way of handling self-employment earnings. It is important to be aware of this change or the **new 1990 Deduction for Self-Employment Tax** could easily be overlooked.

The change is due to an alteration of the way social security tax is treated. For employees, both the employer and the employee pay 7.65% social security tax on the first $51,300 of 1990 wages—a total rate of 15.3%. The basic rate on self-employment income is 15.3%. While the total rate is 15.3% in each case, there is still a fundamental inequity. The employee pays no income tax on the 7.65% of salary paid by the employer. But the basic rules would subject the self-employed to income tax on the entire amount of his earnings up to $51,300, unreduced by any social security tax paid.

On 1989 tax returns, this inequity was counteracted by a 2% tax credit, reducing the (then) 15.02% rate to 13.02%. But this has now been changed, generally for the better.

On 1990 tax returns, there is a special *adjustment to income* which self-employed persons claim on Line 25 of Form 1040. This adjustment reduces taxable income by one-half of the social security tax on the self-employment income. (The actual computation is made on a worksheet on page 18 of the instruction booklet that accompanies your tax forms.) This basically equalizes the social security treatment of employees and the self-employed because the adjustment is equal to the half of total social security tax payments (paid by the employer) which is not subject to income tax.

As an *adjustment to income* rather than an *itemized deduction,* the deduction for self-employment income can be claimed on line 25 both by those who use the standard deduction as well as by those who itemize their deductions. Adjustments to Income also serve to lower *adjusted gross income,* which can result in increased deductions for medical expenses and miscellaneous expenses [cf. Section 1 of Chapter 1].

(In addition to the deduction on line 25, there is one more technical adjustment required to equalize the treatment of employees and self-employed. On Schedule SE, self-employment income is reduced by 7.65% before calculating the amount of self-employment social security tax due. This technical adjustment compensates for the fact that an employee is not only exempt from income tax on the social security paid by his employer but is also exempt from social security tax on this amount as well. You need not understand this technical adjustment—the computation is made automatically as Schedule SE is filled out.

(2) Partnership

A partnership is similar to a sole proprietorship except that it involves two or more people sharing a business. Each shares in the profits and each is responsible for any liabilities incurred by the business. If one of the partners absconds with all of the company's funds, the remaining partners are personally liable for the debts of the partnership.

(3) Corporation

A corporation is a distinct legal entity which is owned by one or more stockholders. The stockholders have no personal liability by virtue of their ownership. Thus, unlike a partnership, if the company gets into financial difficulties, the stockholders are not required to pay the corporation's liabilities out of their own pockets.

There are two basic types of corporations.

(a) S-Corporation. A corporation with 35 or fewer stockholders may, under certain circumstances, elect S-corporation status. Any profit or loss from the corporation passes directly through to the stockholders as though it were ordinary income from any other source. But the stockholders still benefit from the limited liability protection offered by corporate status.

(b) Regular Corporation. Profits and losses accrue to the corporation itself. The corporation pays tax on any profits. The stockholders pay tax only when they receive dividends or upon the sale or liquidation of the business.

As explained later, more tax-saving benefits are available to regular corporations than to S-corporations or any other form of business organization. However, there are two disadvantages. First, if the business consistently loses money, the stockholders are not always able to get a direct write-off of the losses against their other income. Second, there might be a double taxation involved—first the corporation tax—then the tax on dividends. However, this disadvantage need not always occur. For example, if you are able to pay out all of the profits as salary to yourself, then there is no double taxation since the corporation has no net income.

Consultants

A consultant should have a high degree of independence in his work in order to be considered *self-employed* rather than an *employee* of the firm for which he consults. An illustration of such a situation is contained in a recent IRS ruling. This ruling authorized a consultant to consider himself as self-employed rather than an employee. The IRS noted that he did not have any formal schedule of duties and consulted only on an irregular basis when matters came up in an area in which he had special competence. Also, as the IRS told the consultant, the company *"will not exercise supervision over you in the performance of your consulting duties, nor will it require compliance with detailed orders or instructions."* [IRS Private Letter Ruling 7912055]

At one time, consultants generally had to be available to work for more than one client in order to be considered self-employed. Individuals who agreed to work for only one company were usually considered to be employees of that company. However, some IRS rulings have changed this policy.

In 1982, the IRS issued a ruling concerning an engineer who retired from the company where he worked. Upon retirement, he set up his own laboratory and entered into a consulting contract with the company for which he had worked. His contract precluded him from working for any other company. The IRS ruled that he was a self-employed consultant. The terms of the contract and the nature of his duties were such that he could not be considered an employee of the company. This meant his status was that of a self-employed individual, despite the fact he was not available to perform services for any other company. [Rev. Rule 82-212, IRB 1982-49, p.34]

The policy in the above IRS ruling was upheld by a 1983 Court of Appeals decision. The Court ruled that the proper focus of an inquiry as to self-employment status is *"not upon the number of clients or customers an activity generates but upon the nature of that activity that produced those clients or customers."* In the case at hand, it ruled that an individual had self-employment income even though he was performing services for only one client. [Steffens 83-1 USTC ¶ 9425]

It should be noted that even if consulting activities cannot be considered self-employment, they might still come under the shelter of a corporation owned by the individual. While this requires extra expense and trouble, it could be beneficial in sheltering income from tax. This is discussed later in this chapter.

Technical Service Specialists

The IRS issued a ruling in 1987 that applies to services performed under an arrangement with a *technical service firm*. This type of firm acts as a broker between technical service specialists—engineers, designers, drafters, computer programmers, systems analysts, etc.—and companies who need their services. In the past, such technical service specialists were generally considered to be self- employed independent contractors. This meant they could benefit from Keogh Plans and other advantages accorded self-employed persons, as described in Section 2.

In general, if it is common industry practice to treat a category of workers as self-employed individual contractors instead of employees, then the IRS will go along with this classification as long as the appropriate annual tax-reporting forms have consistently been filed. This is the basis under which the technical service specialists described in the preceding paragraph could classify themselves as self-employed. However, the 1986 Tax Reform Act specifically declared this *common industry practice* principle to no longer apply to such technical service specialists.

With the *common industry practice* umbrella now being denied technical service specialists, most of them will no longer qualify for self-employed status. In general, under the basic rules governing the self-employed/employee distinctions, they will be considered employees, usually of the technical service firm acting as broker [Notice 87-38, IRB 1987-23].

Two recent IRS rulings illustrate the 2 basic different situations that arise. One ruling concerned a systems engineer hired by a technical services firm. While working for one of the firm's clients, he did not perform similar services for others, did not advertise his services elsewhere, and had no investment in equipment which he used. This indicated he was an employee, not a private contractor. [IRS Private Letter Ruling 8903040]

The other ruling was issued to an aeronautical engineer, similarly hired by a technical services firm to serve one of its clients. However, in this case, the engineer did do work for others about half the time during the period he was also working for the client. Furthermore, he had an investment in equipment (computer, drill presses, vertical mill, metal lathe, machinist tool chest, etc.) which he used in his home office. In addition, he represented to the public that he was in business for himself by advertising, maintaining a business listing, sponsoring a sports team in his area, and through the use of business cards, stationery, and checks with his own business name upon them. In this case, the worker was ruled to be a private contractor rather than an employee. [IRS Private Letter Ruling 8830047]

Authors

Income which authors receive is usually considered self-employment income. This is the case even if the individual works at a regular job. For example, the IRS has ruled that income received by a college teacher from writing textbooks is self-employment income when the writing of the books is not part of the basic contract with the college. This IRS ruling, excerpted below, is instructive since it applies to the typical situation encountered by college faculty who do writing on the side.

IRS Revenue Ruling 55-385

"In the instant case, a professor, employed by a State university to perform full-time teaching services at the university, is engaged in sideline activities involving public lecturing and the writing of several books. One of his books is a college textbook which he revises from time to time under contract with the publisher; another is a laboratory manual which he has devised for the use of students at the university where he teaches and which he sells direct to them. He receives royalties from the publisher from the sale of his textbook. During the past year, the publisher made him an advance on his royalties with respect to the preparation of a current revision of the textbook. Although the books and lectures are in the general field of education, they are the result of his own initiative and are not instigated pursuant to his employment contract with the university.

"... In the instant case, it is held that... the royalties and other income received by him from those sideline activities are to be taken into account in computing his net earnings from self-employment."

A basic question is whether an author is in the *trade or business* of writing or has just written a once-in-a-lifetime book. Royalties from writing a book are treated differently depending upon this distinction. Authors in the *trade or business* of writing report their income (and expenses) on Schedule C. This means they are liable for the social security tax on self-employed individuals, as computed on Schedule SE. (However, if they already have income from another job which exceeds the Social Security wage base, $51,300 in 1990, no self-employment social security tax is paid.) However, they can shelter a portion of their net self-employment income by placing it into a Keogh Plan.

Royalties from a *once-in-a-lifetime* book do not count as self-employment income [Rev. Rule 68-498]. Such royalties can be entered on Schedule E, *Rents and Royalties,* with the total of such income being recorded on line 18 of Form 1040. No social security tax is paid on royalties reported on Schedule E. However, such income does not qualify for Keogh Plan tax-sheltering.

To qualify as a "trade or business," the writing of a book should be part of a *continuing and regular* activity. This is illustrated by an IRS ruling issued to a teacher who had written several books. IRS stated that,

"If an individual writes only one book as a sideline and never revises it, he would not be considered to be 'regularly engaged' in an occupation or profession and his royalties therefrom would not be considered net earnings from self-employment. However, when an individual prepares new editions of the book from time to time, and writes other books and materials, such activities reflect the conduct of a trade or business. [IRS Private Letter Ruling 8137103]

A recent court case, however, illustrates that an author need not necessarily have written a previous book to be considered in the trade or business of writing. In this case, a lawyer who moonlighted as a photographer worked on a book of nature photographs. A lower court had agreed with the IRS that the photographer could not already be in the *trade or business* of writing because of his lack of previous work. But the Court of Appeals held that as long as he was engaged in a substantial ongoing activity with a profit-making objective, this constituted a *trade or business.* [Snyder, 49 AFTR 2d 82-1061]

As the above shows, there is no hard and fast rule that determines how royalties must be handled in all cases. In borderline cases, you are best advised to treat the royalties in the manner most advantageous to you. If your other wages do not exceed the social security wage base, then by reporting your royalties on Schedule E instead of on Schedule C as income from a trade or business, you will save on social security taxes. On the other hand, if you want to tax-shelter the income in a Keogh Plan, you would have to report the royalties on Schedule C as income from a trade or business. (Note that, as discussed in Section 3 of the *Tax-Sheltered Plans* chapter, by using a *Defined-Benefit Keogh Plan,* you might actually be able to shelter 100% of this royalty income from tax.)

Work Done While Outside the U.S.

Authors should take particular notice of the foreign earned income exclusion. Under this exclusion, $70,000 or more per year of payments received for writing a book can be totally exempted from tax. This exclusion applies as long as the writing was done outside the U.S., even if the work is published and sold only in the U.S. However, the author must be abroad for at least a year and the payments must occur no later than the year following the year in which the work was performed. See the *Foreign Income* chapter for further details.

Deducting vs. Capitalizing Expenses

Under the 1986 Tax Reform Act, authors were required to *capitalize* expenses incurred in writing a book over the period of time they expected it to be sold using the *income-forecast method* [cf. the 1989 edition of this Tax Guide]. This meant that to make the appropriate allocation, it was necessary to be a forecaster (like a weatherman or perhaps, more appropriately, an astrologer). That is, one had to predict what percentage of income from the book would be produced in each future year it would be sold.

The same rules were applied to artists, photographers, inventors, etc. Under the 1986 Tax Reform Act, they could not just deduct all their expenses in the year these expenses were incurred. Rather, they too had to capitalize these expenses over the period of time during which they received income from sale of the artwork, pictures, inventions, etc.

When waves of protest were made (many by prominent authors and artists), Congress changed the rules back to what they had been. More specifically, writers, photographers, and artists are exempted from the requirement to capitalize their expenses. Instead, they can deduct their business-related expenses in the year these expenses are paid.

This new provision applies not only to future tax returns, but applies retroactively as well. That is, if you capitalized expenses on previous tax returns, you may go back and amend these returns to deduct all expenses in the year paid. Since prior year tax rates were generally higher than they are now, this will produce an overall tax savings for most persons.

The tax-writing committee of Congress makes it clear that this new provision applies specifically only to expenses

* *"paid or incurred by an individual engaged in the business of being a writer, photographer, or artist."*

Thus, for example, inventors would still be required to capitalize their expenses.

For these purposes, *"a writer is defined as any individual whose personal efforts create or may reasonably be expected to create a literary manuscript, musical composition (including any accompanying words), or dance score."* It remains to be seen how the IRS will interpret the phrase *"literary manuscript, musical composition (including any accompanying words), or dance score."* The IRS could interpret this to include any written work, based on the usual definition of *"writer."* Or, it might possibly take a narrower view of the word *"literary manuscript."* For example, it's possible an IRS agent might deem, say, an engineering textbook as not being a *"literary manuscript."* Further information on this issue will be contained in future editions of this Tax Guide as it becomes available.

Under the starred provision above, a photographer can deduct expenses for creating a *photograph, photographic negative, or transparency.* And, an artist is defined as *"any individual whose personal efforts create or may reasonably be expected to create a picture, painting, sculpture, etching, drawing, cartoon, graphic design, or original print edition."*

In a 1989 ruling, the IRS spelled out the key criteria it will use in deciding if the production of an item is considered sufficiently *"artistic"* to qualify expenses to be deducted as incurred. According to this ruling,

"The originality and uniqueness of the item created (or to be created) and the predominance of aesthetic value over utilitarian value of the item created (or to be created) will be considered in determining whether a qualified creative expense is paid or incurred by an artist. Thus, for example, any expense that is paid or incurred in producing jewelry, silverware, pottery, furniture, and other similar household items generally will not be considered as being paid or incurred in the business of an individual being an artist." [Notice 89-67, IRB 1989-24]

The ability to currently deduct instead of capitalize expenses does not apply to any expense paid by an individual in his capacity as an employee. In addition, it does not apply to *"any expense that is related to printing, photographic plates, motion picture films, video tapes, or similar items."*

Profit-Making Intention

One further requirement for the deductibility of expenses is that there be an *intention to make a profit.* Writing a book without expectation of profit is considered a hobby activity and expenses can only be deducted to the extent there is income. However, if there is **intent** to make a profit, expenses can be written off even if income from the book does not cover the expenses. This is discussed in Section 4.

Of course, if expenses are related to one's regular job instead of being incurred to produce a profit-making book, then there is no problem. For example, a professor who incurs research expenses in connection with his job may claim these expenses concurrently as a miscellaneous deduction. It is only when the expenses are incurred to produce a book as a separate business activity that the question of deductibility arises.

An individual whose writing activities produce substantial income might consider incorporating. In effect, the corporation contracts with the publisher to produce a book. After publication, royalties are paid to the corporation which in turn pays out the money in salary and fringe benefits to the author. As discussed later in this section, incorporation can provide certain tax benefits unavailable otherwise.

Assigning Royalties to a Child—A Tax-Reduction Technique

A recent IRS ruling shows how authors who receive royalties from books they have written can shift some of this income to a lower-bracket child, relative, etc. whom they wish to aid financially.

Ordinarily, a person must pay tax on income he earns—e.g. he cannot shift part of his salary to a child to lower his taxes. But once an author has written a book and contracted with a publisher to receive royalty payments, the contract takes on a life of its own. If the author then assigns part or all of the contract over to, say, a child, royalties can be taxed to the child. Since the child will be in a lower (perhaps zero) tax bracket than the parent, this results in a net tax savings. (However, for amounts in excess of $1,000 per year, this income-shifting technique won't work anymore for dependent children under the age of 14. In such a situation, these amounts would be taxed to the parent in any event [cf. Section 5 of Chapter 1].)

In the above ruling, an author entered into an agreement to deliver a manuscript to a publisher. Under the agreement, the publisher was granted the exclusive right to publish the work and take out a copyright in its name. The publisher agreed to publish the work at its expense and to pay royalties on all copies sold.

The author proposed to assign to his child all of his interest in the royalty contract. He asked the IRS if royalties paid under the contract would then be taxed to his child rather than himself.

The IRS ruled in the author's favor. Since he was assigning the contract itself, not simply turning over the royalty payments to his child, the income derived from the contract became taxable to the child rather than to the parent. It was the same as if he had given any other type of property such as stocks or bonds to his child. As long as the income-producing property (in this case the royalty contract) is legally turned over to the child, income from such property can be taxable to the child, not to the parent. [IRS Private Letter Ruling 8444073]

In the above ruling, the author also agreed to later revise the book at the request of the publisher. However, if the author did make such revisions, the IRS said this would be considered rendering personal services to the publisher. Since no additional compensation for the revisions was provided for, a portion of royalty payments received after such revisions were made would be considered *compensation for personal services,* taxable to the author.

Authors (or editors of compiled works of others) who wish to take advantage of the above tax-shifting arrangement should take note of the above distinction between *royalties* and *compensation* when drawing up a contract with a publisher. A contract for the publisher to purchase a manuscript from an author or editor in return for royalties can be transferred to a child, parent, etc. as a tax-shifting maneuver. But to the extent the contract calls for services to be rendered to the publisher rather than a sale of a manuscript, payment for such services is taxable to the one who renders the services.

Also, be sure a publisher you select will be amenable to transferring the contract. If the contract is assignable only with the permission of the publisher and the publisher refuses to go along, you're out of luck. [Miedaner, 81 TC No. 21]

The above income-shifting technique works not just for royalties on a book, but also for royalties from the sale of an invention, musical work, etc. Also, more complicated arrangements can be made than the simple transfer of all royalties to a child described in the above ruling. For example, partial transfers can be made. This is illustrated by a court case in which an inventor sold his invention to a company in return for royalties. He later transferred a 25% interest in the contract each to a son and to a daughter. The Court ruled that royalties from the transferred portion of the contract were taxable to the son and daughter. [Heim v. Fitzpatrick, 262 F 2d 887]

Also, a royalty contract can be transferred to a trust to provide flexibility. The trust, for example, might invest the royalty money, with investment income paid out to a child and taxed to him. The actual funds in the trust could revert at a later time to the original author, inventor, etc. [IRS Private Letter Ruling 8337055]

In the above type of arrangements, take note of the fact that tax-shifting is not generally allowed on amounts used for basic items of support for a minor child such as food, shelter, or clothing. But money spent on extras such as music lessons, summer camp, etc. does not generally fall under this restriction [cf. the *Income-Shifting* chapter for further details]. Also, tax-shifting is not allowed for amounts in excess of $1,000 shifted to a dependent child under age 14 [cf. Section 5 of Chapter 1].

Adjunct Professors

The IRS issued a private letter ruling in 1989 to a university, stating that adjunct professors which it had hired were to be considered employees, rather than private contractors. The university provided all the materials and classroom space necessary for the courses taught by the adjunct professors. And the university established the times the courses were taught, chose the textbooks which were used, and gave instructions on the standards which the teachers were to maintain. Also, the adjunct professors were performing work that was an integral part of the university because the degrees received by the students were awarded by the university, not by the adjunct professors. The students were not private pupils of the teachers, but rather were enrolled in the university. [IRS Private Letter Ruling 8925001]

The above paragraph is only a brief summary of some of the basic circumstances that were extensively detailed in the lengthy ruling issued to the university. While indicative of basic negative IRS thinking on the issue, it does not follow that the same result would necessarily occur in all cases of adjunct professors hired by other universities under different arrangements.

In particular, the university in the ruling had several classes of adjunct professors, one of which it treated as employees. This was a factor in causing the IRS to rule that other adjunct professors, being in the same general situation, should be treated as employees also. This also caused the IRS to deny *"Section 530 Relief,"* which provides that employers who have, over a long period of time, consistently been treating a certain class of individuals as private contractors, can continue to do so if there was a reasonable basis to do so to begin with. A university which has not treated any class of adjunct professors as employees might possibly be able to make a successful *"Section 530 Relief"* argument, depending upon the particular circumstances of the case.

Lecturing Fees and Honorariums

Often, an individual who gives a talk in the field of his expertise will get a small fee or honorarium. Giving an occasional talk will not produce enough income to bother with tax-sheltering. In fact, this would not even be considered a *trade or business* activity so that the income would not qualify for a Keogh Plan.

However, when there are substantial lecturing activities or when the lecturing activities are taken together with other activities such as writing or consulting, then the income becomes self-employment income. This is illustrated by an IRS ruling issued to a teacher-author-lecturer. He had received two $100 honorariums for talks and had received $1,000 from the publication of a book and various newspaper articles. The IRS ruled that the activities, taken together, constituted a *trade or business* activity and the income qualified for Keogh Plan tax-sheltering. [IRS Private Letter Ruling 7904059]

This benefit has not been overlooked by members of Congress. According to the *Washington Post,* at least 40 members of Congress have set up Keogh Plans based on their honoraria income for giving speeches to special interest groups. Even though they must give away amounts exceeding $26,000 for House members or $35,000 for Senators, they can base their contributions on the full amount of honoraria received.

For example, Dan Rostenkowski, chairman of the House tax writing committee, earned $245,000 for giving speeches of which he had to give away about $219,000, keeping $26,000. But he was eligible to contribute the maximum $30,000 contribution limit for regular Keogh Plans based on the full $245,000 of income.

Section 2:
Tax Benefits

Let us suppose you are either self-employed (i.e. a sole proprietor) or else you are the sole stockholder in a corporation which employs you. We assume there are no other employees who work for you or the corporation. Here's a list of some of the benefits which might apply. Certain of these benefits apply only if you incorporate. Others are also available to the self-employed as well.

The importance of fringe benefits such as pension and medical plans lies in their tax-free status. Pure salary or self-employment income is always taxable. But qualifying fringe benefits are not taxed either to you or to the business which pays them. That is, these fringe benefits are not reported as income on your tax return, yet they are taken off as a deduction by the business which pays for them.

1. Tax-Deferred Pension and Profit-Sharing Plans

If you think of private pension or profit-sharing plans as just being a method of forced savings for retirement, then you are missing perhaps the most important element of such plans. In reality, they are among the most powerful tax-saving devices allowed under the current Income Tax Laws. Furthermore, funds placed into such plans do not necessarily have to remain untouched until retirement, but may in some circumstances be withdrawn earlier.

The basic idea behind such plans is described in the *Tax-Sheltered Plans* chapter. Namely, instead of being received as salary and taxed in your highest tax bracket, money can be placed into such plans with no tax paid. The investment income earned by money placed into such plans compounds entirely tax- free until the funds are later drawn out and used for your benefit.

Upon retirement at an age you have specified, money in a pension plan can be used to purchase an annuity or can be withdrawn in a lump sum. (With corporation plans, you may also be able to withdraw all your money plus investment earnings if you cease to work for the corporation or upon dissolution of the corporation.) There is a special averaging rule you can use for computing your tax when all the money in the plan is distributed to you in one lump sum. Using this rule, you can average the money received in a lump sum distribution over a 5-year or 10-year period (depending upon your age), disregarding all other income. The tax on the rest of your income is computed in the usual way without taking into account the lump sum distribution [cf. the *Retirement* chapter].

An example of the value of tax-deferral is contained in Section 1 of the *Tax-Sheltered Plans* chapter. This example shows how one dollar placed in a tax-deferred pension or profit sharing plan can be equal to three dollars or more outside such a plan.

Self-employed persons can set up a tax-sheltered plan called a Keogh Plan. A few years ago, corporation pension plans had more generous limitations than Keogh Plans for the self-employed. However, this disparity has been eliminated. Keogh Plans now have the same contribution limits as regular pension plans [cf. Section 3 of the *Tax-Sheltered Plans* chapter]. Thus, an individual will generally be able to contribute 20% of his 1990 self-employed earned income to a regular Keogh Plan.

Those with self-employment income can actually do much better than this by setting up a *Defined-Benefit Keogh Plan* under the remarkable rules for this special type of plan. Under these rules, they can often **shelter up to 100% of this income from tax** [cf. Section 3 of the *Tax-Sheltered Plans* chapter for further details].

2. Medical Reimbursement Plan

Suppose you set up a corporation which hires you as its employee. The corporation agrees to pay all the medical (including dental) expenses of its employees and their spouses and children. The corporation receives a deduction but you pay no tax on these amounts. Essentially, you are receiving a tax deduction of 100% of the medical expenses you pay for yourself and your family. This is better than the usual medical expense deduction because there is no initial 7.5% exclusion. (In addition to covering medical expenses, a corporation can deduct premiums paid on a disability policy which covers you, the employee.)

A self-employed individual can't be directly covered by this type of medical plan. But he can set up a plan to cover all his other employees (including relatives) and their dependents. Thus, a self-employed person can employ his spouse to help out in the business and set up a medical plan which pays for all medical expenses of his spouse and his spouse's dependents, including himself. He gets a business deduction for the medical expenses paid under the plan but there is no tax to the recipient spouse. In this way, the self-employed person receives the equivalent of a tax deduction for 100% of his family's medical expenses without the ordinary 7.5% exclusion. (The more wages paid to a spouse, the less likely the IRS will try to disallow the arrangement as a sham, should the question arise during an audit. Professional assistance should be obtained to set up such a plan in a valid legal manner.)

Under a special provision in the law, a self-employed individual can deduct 25% of the cost of health insurance purchased in 1990 for himself and his family. (This applies just to health insurance, not ordinary medical expenses.) However, no deduction is allowed if he is covered on a subsidized basis by a health plan of an employer for whom either he or his spouse works. Also, the deduction cannot exceed the net earnings from the individual's self-employment. This deduction is claimed on line 26 of Form 1040.

3. Ability to Escape the 2% of Adjusted Gross Income Floor That Applies to Miscellaneous Deductions

As discussed in the *Miscellaneous Deductions* chapter, a 2% of Adjusted Gross Income floor applies to the total of itemized *miscellaneous deductions* claimed on Schedule A. The *miscellaneous deductions* category includes job-related expenses such as books, supplies, travel, equipment, home office, educational expenses, etc. It also includes expenses connected with tax preparation (e.g. the cost of this Tax Guide) as well as with investment activities.

Self-employed persons can escape this 2% floor to the extent they can treat items as a business deduction on Schedule C connected with their self-employment activity rather than an itemized deduction. For example, a college professor with an outside consulting business might be able to attribute the cost of journals, books, home office, travel to meetings, professional dues, etc. to this consulting business. As such, they could be claimed on Schedule C to escape the 2% of Adjusted Gross Income floor. [See the end of Section 1 of the *Miscellaneous Deductions* chapter for a more complete discussion of this matter.]

Operating in corporate form provides the same benefit as discussed above for self-employed persons. A corporation can deduct as a business expense such items as books, supplies, travel, tax preparation, etc. The 2% floor does not apply to corporation business expenses.

4. Ability to Elect the Standard Deduction and Still Deduct Business Expenses

As an employee, you may deduct expenses connected with your job only if you itemize your deductions. But self-employed persons can subtract their business expenses from their gross income and still claim the standard deduction. If you are the sole owner-employee of a corporation, you still get the same effect because the corporation pays and deducts the expenses. You can still claim the standard deduction on your salary received from the corporation.

5. Benefit of Lower Tax Rate

This benefit applies only to regular corporations. Income can be retained by the corporation instead of being paid out as salary. Tax is then paid at the rate that applies to corporation profits — the first $50,000 of profit is taxed at only 15%, the next $25,000 at 25%. The full 34% corporation tax rate only applies to profits in excess of $75,000. (There is an exception. The lower 15% and 25% rates cannot be used by a *personal service corporation*. This is a corporation engaged in the performance of services in the fields of health, law, engineering, architecture, accounting, actuarial science, the performing arts, or consulting—substantially all the stock of which is owned by its employees.)

6. Tax-Sheltered Accumulation of Funds

Excess funds left in the corporation can benefit from a tax-shelter of their own. Corporations pay only a small tax on dividends received from investments in other corporations. Thus, corporation funds can be used to purchase shares of preferred stock yielding high dividends which are mostly free from tax. There are even special mutual funds geared for corporations to take advantage of this tax shelter.

There is a limit of $250,000 on the amount of funds that can be accumulated by a corporation without having to give a business justification for the accumulation. This limit is reduced to $150,000 for *personal service corporations* [see item 5 above].

The ability to accumulate and tax-shelter funds only applies to corporations involved in an active business. If a corporation receives over 60% of its income from passive sources such as dividends, interest, rents, etc., then the IRS may label it a *personal holding company*. As such, it would be subject to a much higher tax rate than that applying to other corporations.

7. Ability to Delay Tax by Choosing Proper Fiscal Year

Corporations sometimes qualify to use a fiscal year different than the calendar year. This can serve to defer the payment of tax. For example, let's say the corporation qualifies for a fiscal year beginning March 1 and that your salary is paid annually on February 28. Then on February 28, 1991, you receive pay for amounts earned primarily in 1990. If you report this amount on your 1991 return, you have effectively delayed paying tax for almost a year. This enables you to earn a year's worth of interest on the delayed payment.

Disadvantages of Being in Business for Yourself

There are a number of disadvantages in being self-employed or operating under the umbrella of a corporation. Some of these are listed below.

More Forms to Fill Out

Self-employed persons must file an extra form, Schedule C, listing their business income and expenses. Corporations also must file income tax returns of their own. In addition, there are other miscellaneous forms which may have to be filed from time to time.

Legal, Accounting, and Incorporation Fees

There are fees required to incorporate as well as legal or accounting fees. There are do-it-yourself books which will enable you to carry through the incorporation yourself for under $100. However, most people will be well advised to seek professional guidance even if it requires additional fees for advice or services. In addition, you will want professional assistance in setting up medical reimbursement plans or pension and profit-sharing plans even if this assistance is no more than selecting the appropriate standard form to use.

Social Security, Unemployment Taxes, and Worker's Compensation

You may be liable for these taxes depending on your situation.

Caution. We have only briefly touched upon some of the aspects of being in business for yourself to acquaint you with the potential for tax-savings. Especially if you contemplate incorporation, you should consult a lawyer to determine how to take advantage of the tax benefits which apply in your particular case. He can also advise you of any extra conditions you must satisfy. For example, the IRS may require you to have a "business purpose" for incorporating in addition to just the tax benefits involved. Also, restrictions on *personal service corporations* might apply in your case.

However, you should not be overly intimidated by the legal complications.

Businessmen, doctors, and other professionals have learned how to take advantage of the benefits which the law allows and which the general taxpayer subsidizes. If you have an outside source of income, you should explore doing the same for yourself.

Section 3:
Paying Family Members for Assistance

If you have an income-producing outside business activity, then perhaps you can place your children, spouse, or even a live-in friend on the payroll. As discussed below, this might serve to lower the overall amount of taxes that will be paid. The following discussion concerns business activities being operated as a sole proprietorship. The situation is a bit different for corporations because of extra expenses that may be involved.

Payments to Children

One way to lower the taxes due on income produced by an outside business activity is to pay your children for assisting you. You get a deduction for the wages you pay them, while they might pay no tax at all on the amounts received because of the $3,250 standard deduction to which they are entitled.

The IRS has specifically ruled that a parent can deduct payments to a child for services if such services would be deductible if performed by someone else. According to this ruling, *"to do otherwise would be tantamount to penalizing the father for employing his own child, inasmuch as a deduction would be allowable if he employed someone else's child under the same circumstances."* The payments can be for any type of normal services required in a business — cleaning, telephone answering, clerical work, business errands, etc.

A number of court cases illustrate this deduction. For example, a 1984 court case permitted a medical professor a $1,500 per year deduction for payments made to his teenage children. The children performed miscellaneous clerical tasks in connection with a small private practice he ran out of his home [Moriarty, TC Memo 1984-249]. In another case, an engineer paid his children for chores performed in connection with his consulting practice. The IRS objected that the wages violated child labor laws and therefore could not be deducted. But the Court found that these laws were designed to protect children from being hired out to do work in a factory or mercantile establishment where their health or welfare would be imperiled. Since this did not apply in this case, a deduction was allowed [Denman, 48 TC 439]. And in a 1989 court case, a consultant was permitted to deduct salary payments to his children, even though his children failed to include the income on their tax returns. This case is discussed at the end of this chapter.

Not only is the salary of a child working in a parent's business deductible, but it is also exempt from social security tax as long as the child is under age 18. (Nonbusiness wages paid to a child under age 21 are also exempt from social security tax but cannot be deducted by the parent.) However, the salary should be in the form of actual wages. You cannot deduct the value of meals or lodging which you provide to an unemancipated minor child in return for services. [Rev Rule 73-393]

Of course, the IRS sometimes takes a skeptical view of payments made to children because of the potential for abuse. But if the payments are made in a businesslike manner, with suitable records kept, then a deduction should be upheld even if the children are young. This is illustrated by a court case involving a family who owned a mobile home park. The family consisted of the parents plus 3 children with the youngest child being only 7 years old. The children were paid for a variety of chores they performed in the business including cleaning, ground maintenance, answering the telephone, clerical work, and assisting in minor repairs. The Court allowed over $15,000 to be deducted over a 3-year period as being reasonable compensation to the children — including $4,000 for the services performed by the 7-year old. [Eller 77TC#66]

Payments to a Spouse

Payments made to a spouse for services in an outside business can lower the overall tax bill, although not in the same income-shifting way as payments to a child as described above. The reason income-shifting doesn't work is, of course, that payments which are deducted as salary to a spouse become taxable income to that spouse. Thus, on a joint return, there is no change in the amount of tax due.

However, the following provisions in the law can all cause payments to a spouse to lower the overall tax bill.

1. IRA & Keogh Plan Contributions

Each spouse is entitled to contribute up to the first $2,000 of earned income to an IRA [cf. Section 2 of the *Tax-Sheltered Plans* chapter]. If the spouse has no earned income, this opportunity is lost. Also, if you have a Keogh Plan, contributions can be made on behalf of your spouse, based on your spouse's salary.

2. Household Services & Child Care Tax Credit

The expenses to which the household services and child care tax credit is applied cannot exceed the earned income of the spouse with the lower earnings, except when one of the spouses is a full time student [cf. the *Household Services & Child Care* chapter]. Thus, there is generally no tax credit allowed when one spouse has no earned income. In such a situation, placing a spouse on the payroll makes the couple eligible for the tax credit.

The maximum amount of expenses to which the credit can be applied is $2,400 for one qualifying dependent or $4,800 for two or more qualifying dependents. In the latter case, say, paying a spouse $4,800 might allow the couple to claim the maximum credit. This maximum credit depends upon the couple's adjusted gross income — ranging from $1,440 for those with Adjusted Gross Income less than $10,000 to $960 for those with Adjusted Gross Income over $28,000.

3. Obtaining a Full Medical Deduction

Ordinarily, only medical expenses in excess of 7.5% of Adjusted Gross Income are deductible. However, a sole proprietor who employs his spouse can set up a plan to pay all the medical expenses of his spouse (and other employees) and the spouse's dependents (including himself). In this way, he gets a business deduction for 100% of his family's medical expenses with no 7.5% limitation [cf. Section 2 for further details].

Disadvantage

There is also a potential disadvantage to hiring a spouse, namely the extra social security tax that must be paid on the spouse's wages. At one time, wages paid to a spouse in the employ of the other spouse were exempt from social security tax. But now, a spouse's wages earned for working in the other spouse's business are subjected to social security tax, the same as for an unrelated employee. This is usually a disadvantage, but can prove to be a benefit to some spouses who need to accumulate enough quarters of coverage to qualify for social security benefits in their own names.

How Payments Should Be Made

If you want to establish that payments made to a spouse, child, or friend represent pay for services rendered, then you should make the payments in the form of wages. This is illustrated by a 1987 IRS Private Letter Ruling. In this ruling, the wife of a veterinarian worked for her husband, performing such duties as being a receptionist 2 days a week, purchasing office supplies, laundering blankets and towels, and reconciling business bank accounts.

The husband filed a Schedule C for his business earnings. In the years in question, the husband took a deduction for the wife's wages on his Schedule C. The amount of the wages was computed according to the number of hours worked. In each year, a W-2 form was issued to the wife and the income was reported on the couple's joint return. However, no actual payment was made to the wife for her services. Instead, the husband deposited all income from his business into a joint bank account held with the wife.

In his view, the amount representing wages to his wife would end up in the same bank account no matter what. However, this depositing of funds was not sufficient to establish that wages had been paid. The IRS ruled that *"in order for a deduction for wages to be allowed, actual payment must be made, and a deposit into a joint account does not constitute actual payment."* Thus, the husband could not deduct these payments as salary, nor was the wife able to make an IRA contribution based on these payments. [IRS Private Letter Ruling 8707004]

Payments to a Live-In Friend

Support of a live-in friend can be converted into a tax deduction if the friend performs work in a secondary business activity. That's the conclusion the Tax Court reached in a 1983 decision. In this case, a man and woman lived together in a relationship which, in the Court's delicate phrasing, was *"other than platon-*

ic." She assisted him in the acquisition and management of various investments and rental properties which he owned. He, in turn, provided funds for food, shelter, etc. for the household which included himself, his non-platonic friend, her child, and her dog.

The Court ruled that he could deduct $2,500 for the value of the work which she performed. Of course, the $2,500 would have to be reported as taxable income to her as well as social security tax paid on her earnings. But assuming she was in a lower tax bracket than he, a net tax savings would still be achieved. [Bruce, TC Memo 1983-121]

Section 4:
Outside Activities Producing a Loss

An activity such as art, photography, music, writing, etc. might generate expenses in excess of income received. It is desirable to be able to deduct the loss on your tax return. However, to do this, the activity must qualify as a **business activity** as opposed to simply a **hobby.**

What Is a Business Activity?

A **business activity** is one engaged in with the **objective of making a profit.** This does not need to be the only objective or even the most important objective. However, it should be a basic and dominant objective. That is, the activity should be conducted in a manner aimed at making a profit.

It is important to note what the law does not require. When the law was first drafted, the House bill required that the taxpayer show a reasonable expectation of realizing a profit. But this was changed to only require that the activity be engaged in for profit, not that there be a reasonable expectation of making one. For example, the odds might be heavily stacked against a photographer earning enough income to exceed his expenses. But in his own mind he might feel he could buck the odds and earn money at it. As long as he conducted his activities with the intention and expectation of making a profit this would suffice even if others might not expect him to succeed.

The intent to make a profit need not be an immediate one. It is recognized that many business activities result in early losses until the business can become established. This is all right as long as there is an aim to make an overall profit. That is, one should expect that over the period of years the activity is engaged in, the total income will exceed the total expenses.

Note that there is no requirement that the taxpayer not enjoy what he is doing. Just because an activity such as music, art, photography, etc. might be pleasurable does not rule out a deduction.

Presumption in Favor of the Taxpayer

The law contains the following provision: If the activity has produced a profit in any 3 of the preceding 5 years, it will be presumed to be a business activity. Any losses will be deductible.

The IRS can challenge the above presumption if special circumstances are involved. For example, an activity which produced very small profits in 3 years and huge losses the other 2 could be challenged by the IRS.

If the "business" activity has been going on less than 5 years, the above test cannot be applied. Instead, you are permitted to wait until 5 years have passed to see if a profit is produced in at least 3 of the years. If so, then the activity is presumed to have been a business activity for each of the first 5 years of existence.

What Happens if a Profit Is Not Made in 3 Out of the Last 5 Years?

If the above 3 out of 5 year test is not satisfied, this does not mean a business deduction is ruled out. It just means there is no automatic presumption of a business activity. In such a case, the taxpayer must, if challenged, show that the activity is engaged in for profit. (The profit can be expected to come from earnings generated by the activity or from the appreciation in value of assets used in the activity.) The principal indicator is the manner in which the activity is carried out. In case of dispute, the IRS suggests that the following factors be examined in order to determine if an activity is a business activity. [Reg 1.183-2 (b)]:

A. Has the activity been carried out in a businesslike manner, e.g. have appropriate records, receipts, etc. been kept?

B. Does the taxpayer have enough expertise to run a profitable enterprise?

C. Has enough time and effort been expended in carrying on the activity?

D. Has the taxpayer been successful in other business endeavors?

E. What is the past history of profits or losses from the activity?

F. What is the taxpayer's financial status, e.g. does he need to earn a profit or is he looking for a tax writeoff instead?

G. Have there been any profits earned in the past or can assets used in the business be expected to increase in value?

H. Are there significant elements of recreation or pleasure involved?

Note that the above list of factors does not constitute a set of formal criteria. There do not necessarily have to be favorable answers to all or even a majority of them.

If you are trying to qualify a money-losing activity as a business, you should conduct yourself in as businesslike a manner as possible. Any of the following would be helpful:

(1) Establish a separate bank account for the activity.

(2) Advertise your services to the public.

(3) Consult financial or other experts for the purpose of setting up a profitable operation.

(4) Keep businesslike records of income and expenses.

(5) Write down a projection showing how you anticipate future profits.

(6) Operate the activity under a trade name.

(7) Have business cards and stationery printed.

Another thing you can do is time your expenses and income to show a profit for a given year. By turning a profit in 3 out of 5 years, you establish the presumption in your favor.

Activities Never Showing a Profit

As mentioned above, in order to qualify an activity as a business, it is not necessary to actually show a profit — just have the intention of making one. This was dramatically illustrated in the following court case. In spite of 20 straight losing years, a professor's wife established that her artistic activities constituted a business endeavor, enabling her to deduct her losses.

Court Case. Professor's Wife Gets Deduction in Spite of 20 Straight Losing Years

Mrs. C. was the wife of a professor at a well-known university in California. For a period of twenty years, she engaged in artistic activities, mainly painting and sculpture. She devoted a substantial amount of time to these activities and held no other job except as a housewife. She exhibited her work at local galleries several times a year, sent announcements of her shows to a small mailing list, and for a short time even ran a gallery of her own. When dissatisfied with the sale of her paintings, she also began making posters and books with the hope that these items would meet with more commercial success.

However, although she occasionally sold some of her work, at no time during the 20 years did the income from her artwork exceed her expenses. The IRS challenged Mrs. C.'s deduction for the losses produced by her artistic activities. No doubt, the IRS challenge was induced by her 20-year string of losses.

The Court, however, felt that the 20 straight losing years did not rule out a strong profit motive. It examined the case further to see if, despite her actual losses, she had sufficient interest and expectation to show a profit. Referring to the list A-H discussed earlier in this section, the Court noted that the factors A, B, C were in her favor — the businesslike way she maintained records, the training she obtained in art school, and the considerable time and effort she expended on her activities. On the other hand, the financial factors D, E, F, G, and factor H all weighed against her.

But the Court did not feel that her lack of financial success was determinative. After hearing her testimony, it felt she was truly attempting to establish herself as a financially successful artist. Mrs. C. went to considerable effort to sell her works and even to change media to achieve commercial success. As for her losses, it noted that "a history of losses is less persuasive in the art field than it might be in other fields because the archetypical 'struggling artist' must first achieve public acclaim before her serious work will command a price sufficient to pro-

vide her with profit. . . . Petitioner has a relatively large inventory, she had considerable training, she devotes substantial time to her artwork, she has sold some paintings in the past, and is attempting to sell more. It is certainly conceivable, in our view, that she may someday sell enough of her paintings to enable her to recoup the losses which have meanwhile been sustained in the intervening years."

As a result of the above analysis, the Court found her artistic endeavors to be a business activity entitling her to deduct the losses on her tax return.

[68TC 696]

As the above case shows, it is not necessary to show a profit—even if over an extended period of time—to qualify to deduct losses. In fact, it is not even required that any income at all be received. This is illustrated by the following 1987 court case concerning an engineer who attempted to develop an invention in his spare time.

Court Case. Engineer Gets Deduction for Invention That Was Never Produced

Maximoff held a position as Senior Engineer, performing design work for radar warning receivers. During his spare time, he worked on developing a miles per gallon indicator for passenger automobiles. He thought there would be a good market for such a device because of the high price of gasoline. He produced a test set-up combined with a miles per gallon indicator for development purposes.

However, Maximoff encountered unforeseen complexities that would run up the cost of the device. Furthermore, when he contacted General Motors regarding his device, he was told that General Motors had started the development of the same device with a team of engineers. He felt that he would be unable to compete with the corporation's production team. Although he had taken out patents in the past, he did not receive a patent for his miles per gallon indicator. He did not reach a point in development of the device where marketing or sales activity could be realistically attempted. He generated no income from this project.

Maximoff claimed a deduction of $5,747 for expenses connected with his work on the device. This included supplies, postage, rent, telephone, utilities, typing, dues, publications, and auto expenses.

The IRS objected to the deduction, claiming that Maximoff's work on the device was a hobby, rather than a trade or business. According to the Court, the IRS made much of the fact that the project was dropped before the device was fully developed or marketed.

However, the Court regarded this fact as working towards the benefit of Maximoff, not against him. According to the Court opinion, Maximoff

"explained that he dropped the project [after] realizing that he could not compete with General Motors research resources and also that the high cost of the indicator he was developing would prohibit successful marketing. We believe that the abandonment of the project at this point shows that petitioner was interested in a money-making activity rather than just a recreational

hobby or an activity designed to generate tax losses. The record is clear that petitioner was concerned about his future income in view of his uncertain continued employment due to his post-retirement age and was interested in producing some income . . . While no income was generated from this project, this factor is not determinative. Experimental activity may yield little, if any, return during the developmental stages, although it has the potential of producing significant income. Petitioner was involved in the activity of inventing with continuity and regularity during the taxable year in issue as well as subsequently through at least the time of trial. Accordingly, we find petitioner was engaged in a trade or business [and therefore could deduct his expenses].
[Maximoff, TC Memo 1987- 155]

In the next 1989 court case, a professor was able to claim deductions connected with a consulting business he operated on the side, despite the apparent overall lack of profit. In this case, the Court regarded it as a favorable factor that his consulting work was closely related to his university work. This was evidence of expertise that would lead to the expectation that a profit could be achieved.

Court Case

Hutchinson was employed as a Professor at a major state university in the Midwest. He taught courses in management information systems, production, operations research, and quantitative methods.

Hutchinson was an expert in the field of computer applications to the automation of industrial processes. In addition to his university salary, Hutchinson earned income as a consultant to a number of clients, mostly industrial companies. The clients sought assistance from him in exploring the need for an automated computer system design in their businesses.

During the year, Hutchinson had about $20,000 in consulting income. Part of this amount constituted payments for software programs he sold to his clients. The primary program he used in his consulting was a form of artificial intelligence which generated a tailor-made computer program for the client, based on the user's answers to various computer-generated questions.

Hutchinson claimed expenses of over $27,000 incurred in his consulting business. Of this amount, $8,000 was paid to the developer of the basic computer package which he sold as part of his consulting services. The remainder included such items as travel, supplies, books, postage, etc. Also included were payments made to his 2 college-aged sons for helping run time-consuming computer programs and compiling business records.

The basic question to be answered by the Court was whether his consulting activities were truly a separate business activity, undertaken with the objective of making a profit. This would permit him to deduct all his expenses on Schedule C, even if exceeding the income he earned.

Two possible negative factors were the fact that the expenses he claimed exceeded the income received and the intimate connection his university work had with the subject matter on which he consulted. However, the Court ruled that his objective was indeed to make a profit. And the connection between his university work and consulting activities was regarded as a positive, rather than a negative factor. It showed he had the expertise that could be expected to be put to profitable business use. In the Court's words,

> "We conclude that petitioner was engaged in a trade or business. Petitioner devoted large quantities of time and effort to his software consulting and sales business. Petitioner did not merely dabble in software consulting—he approached it in a business-like fashion. Furthermore, his business was integrally related to the courses he taught. . . in that much of the knowledge petitioner gained in the classroom was put to work in his software consulting. . . . Although petitioner finds his activities personally rewarding, his objective was to make a profit."

The other main point of interest was the deductibility of the payments made to Hutchinson's children. The IRS objected that these payments were not fully reflected as income on the children's own tax returns, thereby ruling out a deduction by the father. However, the Court did not agree. The payments to his children were entirely for legitimate services performed in his consulting business, therefore deductible. As to the issue of the lack of inclusion on the children's tax returns, that did not affect the father's return. In the Court's succinct phrasing, that issue *"is not before us today."* [Hutchinson, TC Memo 1989-114]

Chapter 27

Foreign Income

Congress has provided the following important tax break for citizens or residents of the U.S. who work in a foreign country. Income which you earn while outside the U.S. can be excluded from U.S. income tax provided all of the following conditions are met:

(1) The income was *earned income* received for services performed;

(2) The income was for services performed while either:

    a. You were outside the U.S. for at least 330 days out of any period of 12 consecutive months

or

    b. You were a bona fide resident of a foreign country or countries for an uninterrupted period which includes a full calendar year;

(3) Your tax home was in a foreign country;

and

(4) You were not an employee of the United States government or one of its agencies, paid from U.S. government funds.

In (1) above, *earned income* means compensation derived from personal services rendered. This includes wages, salaries, professional fees, and the like. It also includes self-employment income to the extent produced by personal services rather than capital investment. Unearned income such as dividends, interest, alimony, etc. does not qualify, nor do amounts received as a pension or annuity.

To qualify for exclusion, the earned income need not be paid by a foreign institution or company. As long as it is earned while you are outside the U.S., that's all that counts. For example, a bank president was allowed an exclusion under a similar provision in prior law for management services he performed by mail and telephone for his bank while on extended leave abroad. [Rev Rul 72-423, 1972-2 CB 446]

In (2b) above, the residency requirement does not demand that you be outside the U. S. for the full term of foreign residency. Vacations or business trips to the

U.S. or elsewhere do not destroy the period of foreign residency. In fact, the only time condition (2b) would need to be invoked instead of (2a) would be when a foreign stay is interrupted by an extended trip back to the U.S. To establish yourself as a bona fide resident of a foreign country, you should be working there for an indefinite or extended period of time and set up permanent-style quarters for yourself and your family.

In (3) above, the term *tax home* has the same meaning as in Sections 1 and 4 of the *Travel* chapter. That is, your tax home is the location of your principal permanent place of employment. The reason Congress included the tax home condition in addition to Condition (2) was to rule out claiming away-from-home travel expenses in addition to the foreign income exclusion. Since the *tax home* must be in the foreign country to qualify for the foreign income exclusion, it would be a contradiction to claim *away-from-home* expenses in addition.

As discussed in Section 4 of the *Travel* chapter, an IRS ruling [Rev Rul 83-82] addresses the question of whether a person's tax home shifts when he takes a temporary job away from his usual home. According to this ruling, *"If a taxpayer anticipates employment to last for 1 year or more and that employment does, in fact, last for 1 year or more, there is a presumption that the employment is not temporary but rather is indefinite, and that the taxpayer is not away from home during the indefinite period of employment."* (Since the taxpayer would not be *away from home*, his *tax home* would typically shift to the foreign location.)

The ruling goes on to discuss stays lasting between 1 and 2 years. In such cases, the presumption that the tax home shifts can be rebutted *"by the taxpayer"* if he can *"clearly demonstrate"* that he meets the objective factors contained in the 3 tests described in Section 4 of the *Travel* chapter. However, technically, the ruling only refers to the **taxpayer** (not the IRS) being able to **rebut** the one-year presumption. Under this ruling, therefore, any taxpayer ought to be able to use the one-year presumption that his tax home shifts when his employment abroad lasts one year or more. Thus, he could satisfy condition (3), the tax home requirement, for excluding foreign income.

This view is supported by a 1986 Private Letter Ruling. Although such rulings do not carry the force of law and cannot be cited as legal precedent, they do give the thinking of the IRS.

IRS Private Letter Ruling

A history professor took a one-year sabbatical leave from the university where he worked. He traveled to a foreign country in order to do research, the results of which he intended to publish in scholarly journals and in a book he was writing. His stay in the foreign country lasted from June 24, 1984 to June 29, 1985—a period exceeding one year. While on sabbatical, he received money both from the National Endowment for the Humanities (NEH) and from the university where he worked.

The IRS ruled that the research he performed constituted *labor* for which he was being compensated, hence the money he received from both NEH and the university while abroad constituted *earned income*. Thus, Condition (1) on the previous page *was satisfied. Also, NEH regulations specified that recipients of its grants were not classified as employees of the United States so that Condition (4) was satisfied. Condition (2) was clearly satisfied because he was outside the U. S. for the required 330-day period. The only remaining question was whether Condition (3), the tax home requirement, was satisfied.*

The IRS ruled that he did satisfy the tax home requirement. The ruling itself contained no detailed examination of the tax home issue other than a passing reference to Rev. Rul. 83-82 discussed above. The professor clearly intended to return back to his university after his sabbatical year was over, so in that sense he was going to be away only "temporarily." But since his actual stay abroad during which he was doing research exceeded one year, this apparently was sufficient to establish that his tax home shifted to the foreign country during the period he was away.

Since he satisfied all 4 of the foreign income conditions, the IRS ruled that he could exclude from taxable income both the money he received from NEH and from his university while away. [IRS Private Letter Ruling 8619051]

In the above ruling, the professor's research sabbatical actually exceeded one year, if only by 5 days. A stay of exactly one year, however, might be cutting it too close. This is illustrated by a different ruling issued to another teacher. In this ruling, a teacher was planning to take part in an exchange program under which he would teach in the United Kingdom, being paid by his school back in the U.S. The teacher planned to stay in the United Kingdom for only one year, whereupon he would return home to his job in the U.S. The IRS ruled that this one-year stay was too short to shift the tax home from the U.S. to the United Kingdom. [IRS Private Letter Ruling 8452103]

It is also important to note that the IRS ruling concerning tax homes refers to *employment* lasting one year or more. An individual who stayed abroad for more than one year but was considered employed abroad for less than one year might fail the *tax home* test. The professor in the example above was on a research sabbatical so he had no trouble establishing that he was actually working during the entire period abroad. The teacher referred to in the preceding paragraph ran into trouble partly because, while *living* abroad for one year, he did not actually *teach* for the entire one-year period.

It is not so clear what would happen if a person stays in a number of different countries, each stay lasting less than a year, with the total time abroad exceeding one year. It is felt that Congress intended the exclusion to apply in such a case as long as, say, condition (2a) is satisfied by being outside the U.S. the required 330 days. But under the law as written, the IRS might claim that an individual did not stay in any one country long enough to establish a tax home there. Under such an interpretation, the individual would not have established a tax home in a foreign country and would be disqualified under condition (3). Only after further rulings are issued will the intentions of the IRS be known.

Limitation

If you satisfy Conditions (1) — (4) above, you can exclude income earned outside the U.S. up to a maximum of $70,000. If you are not outside the U. S. for the entire year, the $70,000 is prorated according to how many days you were actually away. A separate $70,000 allowance applies to the earned income of your spouse. If your income exceeds this amount, an extra exclusion is provided for certain housing costs.

The exclusion is computed based on when the services were performed. For example, if you receive income in 1991 for services performed outside the U.S. in 1990, you exclude this income on your 1991 tax return, even if you are not outside the U.S. when the payments are received. However, you cannot exclude amounts received two or more calendar years after the services are performed. For example, you can't exclude amounts received in 1992 for services performed in 1990.

If you are planning a stay outside the U.S., you should obtain a copy of Publication 54 from the IRS. This publication will explain the rules governing foreign income in fuller detail and illustrate how to claim the foreign income exclusion on the appropriate form.

Sabbatical Pay

College faculty members often spend their sabbatical abroad. As shown in the earlier example, if their stay in a foreign country lasts more than 1 year, the foreign income exclusion comes into play. However, in some cases, the IRS might argue that sabbatical pay received from one's school while abroad was actually earned in prior years when the individual was teaching in the U.S., thereby disqualifying it from exclusion.

To guard against such IRS challenge, college faculty should submit a proposal to their university stressing the academic work they are going to perform while abroad. Often, colleges treat such proposals as a mere formality. But such a document, when shown to the IRS, can be strong evidence that the sabbatical pay is not a reward for previously performed work, but rather is pay for academic work performed while abroad, thereby possibly qualifying for the foreign earned income exclusion.

An important distinction should be made between two types of sabbaticals. The first is a sabbatical undertaken to study or do research for your own educational development. The second is a sabbatical undertaken to work on publishable research as part of your professional responsibilities. Payments received from your school while on the first type of sabbatical are more open to challenge as having been "earned" in prior years. Payments while on the second type of sabbatical are more likely to be considered as "earned while abroad."

Of course, in real life, the distinction between the two types of sabbaticals is not so clear cut. However, an individual teacher has an opportunity to make this distinction when he applies for sabbatical leave. He should stress the *accomplishment* rather than the *study* aspect of his sabbatical in his official letter to his school requesting a sabbatical leave. This letter then becomes the leading document describing the nature of the sabbatical.

Authors Can Exclude Royalties

Royalties or other payments which an author receives for writing are considered earned income. The situation is similar for artists, composers, inventors, etc. Any payment received for work produced by the personal efforts of these individuals is considered earned income. However, if part of the income is due to capital investment, that part might not be included in earned income. This would not apply, typically, to authors, artists, or composers, but might apply to inventors with significant investment in equipment.

The above represents a terrific opportunity for authors, inventors, etc. to exclude income from tax. For example, suppose an individual plans to write a book. He waits until he is out of the country to do his writing. (In fact, this might be an especially good time to do such writing for, say, a professor on sabbatical or other leave of absence.) If his stay abroad qualifies under the rules in this chapter, payments he receives for his work can be excluded from tax, even though these payments come from an American publisher and the book is sold only in the U.S.

However, note the requirement that to be excluded, payments for work done during a given year must be made no later than the end of the following year. This is a serious restriction, especially for authors who usually have to wait at least a year after they have completed their work before it is published and royalties commence. Hence, an author should try to obtain as much as he can in the way of pre-publication payments. For those planning to write a book while abroad, the willingness to make advance payments qualifying for the earned income exclusion could become an important factor in choosing a publisher.

However, the advance royalties should not be repayable in the event the book does not sell as well as anticipated. Otherwise, the IRS could claim the amounts paid were just loans, not payments for work performed. [IRS Private Letter Ruling 8131016]

Denial of Double Benefits

You cannot claim any deduction or tax credit to the extent attributable to foreign income which is excluded from tax. For example, you can't deduct travel expenses connected with your foreign employment. However, such items as medical expenses, charitable contributions, mortgage interest, etc. would still be deductible.

How to Claim the Foreign Income Exclusion

The foreign income exclusion is elected on Form 2555 which you attach to your tax return. If you submit a suitable statement to your employer that you will qualify for the foreign income exclusion, your employer should not withhold taxes on payments made to you. You can obtain a sample of a suitable statement by writing to the Foreign Operations District, Internal Revenue Service, Washington, D.C. 20225 (Form IO-673).

According to a 1989 court decision, you must be sure to file a tax return containing the proper Form 2555 election to claim the foreign income exclusion.

This is the case even if all your income is excluded from tax. The election can be claimed on an original tax return or on an amended return filed within the allowed 3-year period [cf. Section 1 of Chapter 1]. [Faltesek, 92 TC No. 78]

Note that it is entirely possible for foreign income to be exempt from U.S. income tax as described in this chapter at the same time it is exempt from a foreign country's tax under a treaty with the U.S.

Extension of Time to File

For those who are out of the country on April 15, there is an automatic 2-month extension until June 15 for filing tax returns and paying the tax due. However, this only applies to those whose *tax homes* are in a foreign country. Unlike the 4-month extension that any taxpayer can file for on Form 4868 [cf. Section 1 of Chapter 1], there does not have to be a payment of taxes until the end of the 2-month extension period.

If you have not yet met the 330-day test by the date your tax return is due but expect to do so and thereby owe no tax or receive a refund, you should file for a special extension on Form 2350. This will give you until 30 days after the date on which you meet the 330-day test to file your tax return. Further details on the Foreign Income Exclusion may be found in Publication 54, *Tax Guide for U. S. Citizens Abroad,* obtainable from the IRS.

Other Tax Breaks for Foreign Income
Extra Moving Expense Deduction

If you move to a location outside the United States which is a new *principal place of work,* then you can claim a moving expense deduction as described in the *Moving Expenses* chapter. Note that the limitations on the amounts that can be deducted for foreign moves are substantially higher than for domestic moves. However, you can't deduct moving expenses to a foreign location if your income is excluded from tax according to the rules described above. According to a 1988 court case, moving expenses back to the U.S. can be deducted unless they are *inextricably linked* to the tax-exempt foreign income. In this court case, an individual's deduction was disallowed because of an agreement made with his employer before he left the U.S. that his return moving expenses would be reimbursed upon completion of his foreign assignment. This was a sufficient link between the moving expenses and the foreign income to rule out a deduction. [D.J. Butka, 91 TC No. 13]

Payment of Foreign Taxes

The United States has a number of treaties with foreign countries which generally exempt you from their tax for a period of two to three years, if you are temporarily visiting their country for the purpose of teaching or research. Such countries include Australia, Austria, Belgium, Canada, Denmark, Finland, France, Federal Republic of Germany, Greece, Ireland, Italy, Japan, Luxembourg, Netherlands, New Zealand, Norway, Pakistan, Republic of South Africa, Sweden, Switzerland, and United Kingdom countries.

Chapter 28

Tax-Free Grants

Section 1:
Basic Rules

The 1986 Tax Reform Act changed the tax treatment of scholarship and fellowship grants. There are now two sets of rules, the *old rules* and the *new rules*. The old rules apply to grants *awarded* before August 17, 1986 (even if extending into 1990 or later years). The new rules apply to grants awarded on or after August 17, 1986.

The **old rules** are the ones that applied prior to 1986. These old rules generally allowed degree-candidate students to exempt the full amount of their grants from tax. And, non-degree candidates came under a $300 per month limitation for a lifetime maximum of 36 months on the amounts exempted from income tax [cf. Section 3 for a detailed explanation of these rules]. However, non-degree candidates, as well as degree candidates, received a total exemption from social security tax on the full amount of their scholarships or fellowships, with no $300 per month or 36 month limitation [cf. Section 5].

The **new rules** for grants awarded on or after August 17, 1986 are much more severe. **Degree-candidate** students are only able to exempt from tax amounts used for tuition and related instructional expenses such as fees, books, supplies, and equipment. Amounts that are used for room, board, or other living expenses are subject to income tax. **Non-degree candidates** get no income tax exemption at all under the new rules.

However, the rules for social security tax remain the same under the new rules as under the old. Both degree candidates and non-degree candidates are still exempt from social security tax on the full amount of their scholarship or fellowship grants, no matter when they were awarded.

The exemption from social security tax becomes of particular interest in 1991. In 1990, grant recipients with regular wages exceeding $51,300, the social security wage base, could not be subjected to any additional social security tax no matter what type of extra income was received. But in 1991, income up to $125,000 will be subject to the 1.45% medicare portion of the social security tax [cf. Chapter 0]. This means that virtually all grants will be subject to this tax, unless they qualify as discussed in this chapter [In particular, cf. Section 5].

Definitions

A **scholarship** generally means an amount paid to enable a student to pursue his studies at an educational institution.

A **fellowship** generally means an amount paid to aid an individual in the pursuit of study or research.

The term *scholarship or fellowship* does not include money which is given by a friend or relative, motivated by philanthropic or family considerations. Such a payment, however, will probably qualify to be a tax-free gift.

Some educational institutions participate in a program whereby tuition is not charged for the child of a faculty member at one of the other participating institutions. As discussed in the *Expenses of Attending School* chapter, such tuition remission is generally exempt from tax.

Also, if a grant meets either of the following 2 conditions, it will generally **not** be considered a scholarship and will be taxable income:

(i) The grant is paid as compensation for past, present, or future services; or (ii) the grant is paid to enable you to pursue studies or research primarily for the benefit of the grantor. (These 2 conditions are discussed in more detail in Section 3 which also describes an exception for grants awarded before August 17, 1986, when equivalent services are required of all candidates for a given degree.)

Difference Between a Gift and a Grant

Gifts which you receive are better than grants because they are entirely tax-free, while scholarship and fellowship grants are subject to the limitations described in Sections 2 and 3. But you can't simply call a grant a gift. To be regarded as a gift, you must show that the donor was motivated by family or philanthropic reasons that were directed solely to the recipient. In other words, unless a grant you receive is given by a relative or a charity, you will not be able to treat it as a gift.

Prizes and Awards

Prior to 1987, certain prizes and awards made in recognition of past achievements (e.g. the Nobel Prize, Pulitzer Prize, etc.) were exempt from tax entirely. However, starting in 1987, this exemption has been eliminated, except where the recipient assigns the prize or award to a governmental unit or tax-exempt charitable organization.

IRS Stopped from Harassing Graduate Students

In the late 1980's, about 20,000 graduate students got most unwelcome letters from the IRS. These letters told the students that they owed back taxes, plus interest and penalties, on stipends they received going back to 1984 and 1985. These were stipends the students had thought were tax-free.

Incredibly, many of these stipends satisfied all the conditions specified in an IRS Revenue Ruling [Rev. Rul. 75-280] under which stipends were exempted from tax. This Revenue Ruling, detailed in Section 3, applied to those degree candidates who performed services that were required of all candidates for the same degree, whether or not they received stipends.

Why did the IRS take this action? The basic reason was the way the graduate students handled their stipends on their tax returns. While the colleges reported the stipends on W-2 Forms (with copies sent to the IRS), the students just omitted reporting their stipends on the basic Form 1040 line for wages, salaries, etc.

This made the IRS computers very unhappy. As we have reported in previous issues of this Tax Guide, the IRS has been getting much more efficient with its matching program, under which amounts reported on an individual's tax return are compared with compensation amounts reported on W-2 Forms and dividends, interest, etc. reported on Forms 1099 [cf. Section 9 of Chapter 1]. When the IRS computer found that the students had not reported as income amounts shown on W-2 Forms, it kicked out their returns, sending them to local IRS offices for examination.

Many of these local offices across the country took a hard-line attitude. Ignoring their own Revenue Ruling, they demanded students pay back taxes, plus interest and penalties, on their stipends. It has been reported that when questioned about the inconsistency, some of the local IRS offices pointed to some recent court cases which they felt could be interpreted to override Revenue Ruling 75-280. In fact, a number of Private Letter Rulings issued by the main IRS office during this time were officially approving tax-free treatment of grants because they satisfied Revenue Ruling 75-280. [IRS Private Letter Rulings 8745011; 8750054; 8802062; 8803041]

This caused howls of protest from the graduate students involved and from their colleges and universities. When this unfair treatment of graduate students began to receive more public attention, the IRS did a most unusual thing—it threw in the towel. It announced [IRS News Release 88-65] that it would reimburse students who paid taxes on research and teaching stipends received in 1984 and 1985, as long as they satisfied the basic conditions of Revenue Ruling 75-280. [Cf. Section 3 for a precise statement of these conditions.]

Where to Report a Tax-Free Grant on a Tax Return

The 20,000 graduate students who got harassed by the IRS could have almost certainly avoided trouble if they had handled their stipends as we have advised in annual editions of this Tax Guide for the last 10 years. As spelled out in Section 4, we have warned against creating a discrepancy between amounts reported on a W-2 Form and income reported on line 7 of your Form 1040.

Instead, we advise reporting on line 7 of Form 1040 all income which is shown as wages or other taxable compensation on W-2 Forms you receive from your employer. Then, subtract any amounts that should be tax-free by entering a negative entry on line 22, *Other Income*. This method of handling tax-free income showing up on a W-2 Form is not spelled out in any official IRS instructions (or other Tax Guides we've seen) but has been recommended by the IRS in other similar situations. And in the 10 years we've been recommending similar methods of avoiding the matching program trap (depending upon the layout of the tax return that year), our editorial staff has not received a single letter indicating IRS objection to using this type of reporting procedure. If the 20,000 graduate students who received dunning letters had been properly advised of this reporting method, a lot of trouble (including hiring lawyers, filing Tax Court appeals, borrowing to pay back taxes, or just diverting attention from studies) would have been avoided.

Section 2:
New Rules For Grants Awarded
On Or After August 17, 1986

Degree Candidates

Under the new rules for grants awarded on or after August 17, 1986, students who are candidates for a degree may exempt from tax amounts used for *"qualified tuition* and *related expenses."* This includes tuition and fees required by the school plus books, supplies, and equipment required for courses of instruction. It does not include amounts used for other expenses such as room and board or for optional supplies and equipment. This is illustrated by the following example adapted from one in a proposed IRS regulation. [IRB 1988-28, 35]

> **Example**
>
> On September 1, 1990, A receives a scholarship from University U for academic year 1990-1991. A is enrolled in a writing course at U. Suggested supplies for the writing course in which A is enrolled include a word processor, but students in the course are not required to obtain a word processor. Any amount used for suggested supplies is not an amount used for qualified tuition and related expenses for purposes of this section. Thus, A may not include the cost of a word processor in determining the amount received by A as a qualified scholarship.

It is up to the student to keep records of scholarships or fellowship amounts used for qualified tuition, fees, and required supplies or equipment. These amounts are tax-free; the remainder is taxable income.

The one piece of good news is that scholarship and fellowship grants, to the extent they are taxable, are considered to be **earned income** rather than **unearned income.** As discussed in Section 5 of Chapter 1, tax is due if there is unearned income which exceeds $500. But an individual receiving only earned income up to $3,250 (the amount of the standard deduction for singles) need not even file a tax return.

Exception for Teaching and Research Assistants. The exclusion from income tax does not apply to any portion of amounts received as a scholarship or fellowship grant representing payment for teaching, research, or other services required as a condition for receiving the grant. Such portions are included in taxable income, even if used for tuition or course-related expenses. (Note that this exception applies even if the teaching, research, or other service is required of all candidates for a particular degree. This is contrary to the situation that applies under the old rules.)

If only part of a scholarship or fellowship grant represents payment for services, it is up to the grantor to make the appropriate allocation. According to the IRS.

"Factors to be taken into account in making this allocation include, but are not limited to, compensation paid by

(i) The grantor for similar services performed by students with qualifications comparable to those of the scholarship recipient, but who do not receive scholarship or fellowship grants,

(ii) The grantor for similar services performed by full-time or part-time employees of the grantor who are not students,

and

(iii) Educational organizations, other than the grantor of the scholarship or fellowship, for similar services performed either by students or other employees."

This is illustrated by the following examples adapted from a proposed IRS regulation. [IRS 1988-28]

> **Example**
> *D receives a qualified scholarship from University X. As a condition to receiving the scholarship, D performs services as a teaching assistant for X. Such services are required of all candidates for a degree at X. The amount of D's scholarship from X is equal to the compensation paid by X to teaching assistants who are part-time employees and not students at X. D's scholarship from X represents payment for services. Thus, the entire amount of D's scholarship from X must be included in D's gross income as wages.*

> **Example**
> *E receives a $6,000 scholarship for attending University Y. As a condition to receiving the scholarship, E performs services as a researcher for Y. Other researchers who are not scholarship recipients receive $2,000 for similar services for the year. Therefore, Y allocates $2,000 of the scholarship amount to compensation for services performed by E. Thus, the portion of the scholarship that represents payment for services, $2,000, must be included in E's gross income as wages. However, if E establishes expenditures of $4,000 for qualified tuition and related expenses..., then $4,000 of E's scholarship is excludable from E's gross income as a qualified scholarship.*

The question of whether a stipend is considered payment for services rendered or a scholarship/fellowship grant hinges on whether or not the primary purpose of the grant was for the benefit of the grantor. In the proposed regulation, the IRS spells this out as follows:

"For purposes of this section, a scholarship or fellowship grant represents payment of services when the grantor requires the recipient to perform ser-

vices in return for the granting of the scholarship or fellowship. A require-ment that the recipient pursue studies, research, or other activities primarily for the benefit of the grantor is treated as a requirement to perform services. A requirement that a recipient furnish periodic reports to the grantor for the purpose of keeping the grantor informed as to the general progress of the in-dividual, however, does not constitute the performance of services. A scholar-ship or fellowship grant conditioned upon either past, present, or future teaching, research, or other services by the recipient represents payment for services under this section."

Although stated somewhat ambiguously, the above appears to be the same ba-sic policy as under the old law [cf. Section 3 for a more complete discussion]. That is, teaching is almost always considered to be a service primarily for the benefit of the grantor. And research is also to be considered for the benefit of the grantor if there is a specific project on which the grantor wants the researcher to work.

But freely-chosen research performed essentially for the purpose of writing a dissertation would generally be considered for the primary purpose of aiding the student rather than the grantor. As such, it would be considered a qualified schol-arship or fellowship, tax-free to the extent of amounts spent for tuition, fees, or required books, supplies, equipment, etc.

Tuition Remission Exempt From Tax

Graduate teaching and research assistants often have part or all of their tuition waived. Under a special provision in the law, the value of the tuition waived for such graduate assistants is exempt from tax, provided the remaining monetary stipend is equal to or exceeds fair pay for the services performed.

Example

F is employed as a teaching assistant at University L. F receives a salary from L that represents reasonable compensation for the position of teaching assistant. In addition to salary, F receives a tuition waiver. F includes the salary in gross income. The waiver does not represent payment for services and therefore, is not includable in F's gross income.

Example

Jones receives a research assistantship paying $8,000 for the academic year. In addition to the monetary award, his tuition is waived. As an out-of-state resident, he would have had to pay $5,000 for tuition without such a waiver. Other researchers without research assistantships that include a tuition waiver are paid $10,000 for similar services.

Jones has received $13,000 in money and tuition benefits. Of this, $10,000 is considered taxable income for services rendered. The remaining $3,000 is exempt from tax as a tuition-related scholarship grant.

Non-Degree Candidates

Individuals who are not candidates for a degree lose all income tax exemption under the new rules. Amounts received from grants awarded on or after August 17, 1986 are fully taxable.

However, as discussed in Section 5, the **exemption from social security tax still applies.** As long as the grant satisfies the requirements of being a scholarship or fellowship that applies under prior law [cf. Section 3], the full amount of the grant is excluded from social security tax, no matter when the grant was awarded.

When is a Scholarship or Fellowship Granted?

As discussed above, different rules apply to scholarships or fellowships granted on or after August 17, 1986 than to ones granted before this date. Therefore, it becomes necessary to determine the exact date when a scholarship or fellowship is considered to be *granted*. Rules for making this determination, including the case of multi-year grants, were spelled out by the IRS in a published news release [IRS Notice 87-31, IRB 1987-17]. According to the IRS,

"A scholarship or fellowship is granted when the grantor of the scholarship or fellowship grant either notifies the recipient of the award or notifies an organization or institution acting on the behalf of a specified recipient of the award to be provided to such recipient. If the notification is sent by mail, notification occurs as of the date the notice is postmarked. If evidence of a postmark does not exist, the date of the award letter shall be treated as the notification date... A scholarship or fellowship will be considered granted before August 17, 1986, to the extent that, in a notice of award made before that date, the grantor made a firm commitment to provide the recipient with a fixed cash amount or a readily determinable amount."

Grants awarded before August 17, 1986 which cover a multi-semester or multi-year period still qualify for exemption under the old rules, provided the grant adequately specifies the amounts to be received in the future. The IRS describes this situation as follows:

"If a scholarship or fellowship was granted for a period exceeding one academic period (e. g. semester), amounts received in subsequent academic periods will be treated as granted before August 17, 1986, only if (1) the amount awarded for the first academic period is described in the original notice of award as a fixed cash amount or readily determinable amount, (2) the original notice of award contains a firm commitment by the grantor to provide the scholarship or fellowship amount for more than one academic period, and (3) the recipient is not required to reapply to the grantor in order to receive the scholarship or fellowship grant in future academic periods. A requirement that the recipient file a financial statement on an annual basis to show continuing financial need will not be treated as a requirement to reapply to the grantor."

"*If a scholarship or fellowship satisfying the requirements of the preceding paragraph does not describe the amount to be received in subsequent academic periods as either a fixed cash amount or readily determinable amount, it is presumed that the amount granted before August 17, 1986, to be received in each subsequent academic period is equal to the amount granted for the initial academic period. To the extent that any amount received in a subsequent academic period exceeds the amount received in the initial academic period, the excess amount is treated as a scholarship or fellowship granted after August 16, 1986.*"

The IRS regulations illustrate these rules with the following 3 examples.

Example 1.

On May 1, 1986, A is notified of a scholarship made in the amount of $4,000 annually for four years. The total amount of the scholarship is a fixed cash amount. Thus, the total amount of the scholarship for all four years is exempt from tax under the old rules that applied prior to the 1986 Tax Reform Act.

Example 2.

On May 1, 1986, B is notified of a scholarship that will pay fur B's tuition, room and board for four years. The total amount of the scholarship is readily determinable. Thus, the total amount of the scholarship for all four years is exempt from tax under the old rules that applied prior to the 1986 Tax Reform Act.

Example 3.

On May 1, 1986, C is notified that she is the recipient of a scholarship to attend University X. The scholarship is not conditioned upon the performance of services by C. The notice provides that University X will provide scholarship funds for four years, and specifies that C will receive $5,000 during the first year. C is not required to reapply in order to receive scholarship funds during years 2 through 4. However, the notice does not specify the scholarship funds to be received in years 2 through 4. The $5,000 received in year 1 is treated as granted before August 17, 1986 because this amount is a fixed cash amount described in the notice of award. In addition, because University X has made a specific commitment to provide scholarship funds during years 2 through 4 without requiring C to reapply for the scholarship, an amount equal to $5,000 per year is treated as granted before August 17, 1986 during years 2 through 4. Thus, if C receives $4,000 in year 2, the entire $4,000 is treated as granted before August 17, 1986. If, in year 3, C receives $6,000, only $5,000 of the amount received is treated as granted before August 17, 1986. The additional $1,000 received in year 3 is treated as granted after August 16, 1986. Whether this additional $1,000 is excludable from C's gross income depends upon the amount of qualified tuition and related expenses incurred by C in year 3. Thus, if C's qualified tuition and related expenses for year 3 are $6,000, the entire $6,000 is excludable from C's gross income.

An illustration of how the above regulations work in real-life situations is provided by several recent IRS Private Letter Rulings.

IRS Private Letter Ruling 8848031

In July of 1986 a Ph.D. candidate at a University was awarded a 3-year fellowship grant beginning September 1, 1986. The grant was designed to allow a Ph. D. candidate greater freedom to pursue academic goals. His research was not carried out during the course of any specific project for either the University or the organization which sponsored the grant. His duties under the fellowship grant were simply to carry out the requirements for a Ph.D. degree with no other obligations.

The fellowship grant specified the amounts to be received in each of the three years the grant was in force. The first year amount would increase by $33\frac{1}{3}\%$ for the second year, and by the same amount again for the third year.

The IRS ruled that this grant satisfied all of the conditions required of grants awarded before August 17, 1986. As a result, all amounts received under the grant were exempt both from income tax and from social security tax as well.

IRS Private Letter Ruling 8845008

A graduate student was awarded a research assistantship in 1983. There were no necessary reapplication procedures for continuing the aid throughout the continued enrollment period of the student. In 1988, he sought a ruling as to whether his research assistantship grant remained exempt from tax.

The IRS ruled that the basic pre-August 17, 1986 rules applied as long as the grant continued as described above. Thus, the grant would be exempt from tax if it was made primarily for the benefit of the student, with no substantial quid pro quo services required. This issue was described by the IRS as follows:

> "The research and services you perform as a graduate research assistant are neither in excess of those necessary to satisfy the established degree requirements nor for a party other than the University. Your degree requirements include grading written assignments for a professor for 3-5 hours per week. The grant you received as a research assistant was not made because of past services or conditions upon, or subject to an understanding with respect to, future employment or other requirements, including services in excess of those necessary to satisfy degree requirements. The degree requirements, and the nature and extent of the work that was required of you to satisfy the degree requirements, were reasonably appropriate to the degree you were seeking . . . .
>
> "The payments you receive from the University while serving as a graduate research assistant are paid to you for the primary purpose of furthering your education and training in your own capacity. In addition, the payments are without substantial quid pro quo in terms of services. The 3-5 hours per week of services for a professor do not constitute part-time employment, as these services are required of all degree candidates regardless of whether the candidate receives financial aid. Accordingly, we conclude that the payments you receive are received as a scholarship at an educational organization" [and therefore exempt from tax].

Withholding from Grants

Under the new rules, a scholarship or fellowship grant awarded to a student might be partly tax-exempt and partly taxable. However, making this partition is the duty of the recipient. Neither the grantor nor the school is required to file a form with the IRS reporting on the taxable portion of the grant. And, since such grants are not considered wages, there should be no withholding of income tax or social security on any payments under the grant. Essentially, students are being placed on the honor system with regard to reporting taxable amounts of scholarships or fellowships.

An exception to this rule occurs to the extent amounts received under the grant represent payment for teaching, research, or other services by the student required as a condition for receiving the scholarship or tuition remission. In such a case, the school is required to make the allocation between the taxable and tax-free amounts (as discussed earlier in this Section) and issue an appropriate W-2 Form reporting the amount regarded as wages.

Section 3:
Grants Awarded before August 17, 1986

Scholarship and fellowship grants awarded before August 17, 1986 are subject to the same rules that applied in 1985 and earlier years. Also, as discussed in Section 5, the "old rules" apply when determining whether grants are exempt from social security tax, even for grants awarded after August 17, 1986.

This section contains a description of these "old rules." As discussed in Section 2, these rules apply even if funds from the grant are received on or after August 17, 1986. Under the old rules, scholarship and fellowship grants are exempt from income tax and social security tax, subject to the limitations and provisions in the remainder of this section.

Limitations

If the grant meets either of the following two conditions, it will **not** be considered a scholarship or fellowship and will be taxable income.

(1) The grant is paid as compensation for past, present, or future services. If you are required, as a condition for receiving the grant, to agree to work for the grantor after completing your training, the grant is considered compensation for future services.

or

(2) The grant is paid to enable you to pursue studies or research primarily for the benefit of the grantor. However, if the primary purpose is to further your education and training in your individual capacity, and the amounts do not represent compensation for service, neither the fact that you are required to furnish progress reports to the grantor, nor that the results of your studies or

research may be of some incidental benefit to the grantor shall destroy the tax-free character of the grant.

Exception—Revenue Ruling 75-280

If teaching, research, or other equivalent services are required of all candidates for a particular degree (whether or not recipients of scholarship or fellowship grants), then money received for such services may still be considered a tax-free scholarship or fellowship. According to an IRS ruling [Rev Rul 75-280], a grant will be considered to have been for the primary purpose of benefiting the recipient and hence excludable from gross income if the following conditions are satisfied:

1. The student was a candidate for a degree at an educational institution;

2. The student performed research, teaching, or other services for the institution that satisfied specifically stated requirements for the degree;

3. Equivalent services were required of all candidates for the same degree;

and

4. The work required is reasonably appropriate to the degree.

However, the above conditions will **not** suffice to establish that the grant is excludable from gross income if

A. The student performed services for a party other than the educational institution;

or

B. The grant is made because of past services or conditioned upon future services or other requirements.

If a student performs services in excess of those necessary to satisfy the degree requirements, then amounts received for these excess services are subject to tax. The remainder is tax-free, provided that the student is not required to perform the excess services as a condition to receiving amounts for the regular services required of all candidates for the degree.

Note that Restriction A above only refers to work performed directly for an outside agency. If, for example, a university contracted with an outside agency to provide funds for a research project, and then hired a student to assist in the project, Restriction A would not apply.

Teaching Assistants

If a teaching assistant has met the requirements of the above ruling, then his stipend is tax-free. The IRS based the ruling on the case of a research assistant but specifically stated at the end that the ruling applied to *"amounts received for teaching or other services."*

Note that the equivalent services required of all candidates in condition 3 must actually be **equivalent.** This is illustrated by a 1977 court case in which a teaching assistant in the Classics department attempted to claim that his stipend was a tax-free fellowship because *equivalent* teaching services were required of all Ph.D. candidates in his department. But the Court pointed out that the only stated requirement was that *"a doctoral candidate have 'teaching experience, in order to qualify for the Ph.D. degree in the classics. Neither the amount nor the nature of the required teaching experience is specified in the rule. However, there is nothing in the record to indicate that the rule requires 'all candidates' for the Ph.D. degree in the classics to have the kind or the extent of teaching experience that the [teaching assistant in this case had]."* [Pelz v. U.S., Ct. Clms. No.8-74. 3/23/77]

A similar conclusion was reached in two 1984 court cases which denied tax-exemption to students who held teaching assistantships. In each case, the student's department required some teaching experience to graduate, but not necessarily the same amount required of the teaching assistants. [Tate, TC Memo 1984-206; Zimmerman; TC Memo 1984-207]

The equivalent services must actually be a **requirement,** not just a fact of life. This is illustrated by a 1984 case, affirmed by a 1986 Appeals Court decision, concerning one of 90 teaching assistants in an English Department at a large State University. The fact that all Ph.D. students (except one) were teaching assistants did not suffice because there was *"no formal requirement of the University or the English Department that all such degree candidates teach."* [Sebberson, TC Memo 1984-605; 86-1 USTC]

A teaching assistant who did not meet the *equivalent services required of all candidates* criterion is subject to tax on his grant in almost every case. He has simply received pay for services rendered. It is not sufficient that the University characterize the stipend as a tax-free stipend rather than as taxable pay for services rendered. In the case in the preceding paragraph, the University did not withhold social security tax from the assistants' stipends. Also, the assistants' supervisors testified that the primary purpose of the teaching assistantships was to train the assistants as future teachers. This was not sufficient to convince the Court that the assistants were paid to study rather than to work.

Similarly, a different court case concerned a teaching assistant in the Language Department of a large midwestern University. He received a stipend of $3,580 in return for which he taught several undergraduate Spanish courses. The University provided him with a statement, which he attached to his tax return, characterizing $1,628 of the stipend as a scholarship and the remaining $1,952 as taxable pay. The $1,952 taxable pay figure was calculated by the University to be that amount which *"would have been expended to hire a part-time instructor to perform the teaching services rendered by the petitioner."*

However, the Court ruled that the University's statement did not control the situation. Because substantial services were rendered to the University, it ruled that the primary purpose of the grant was to benefit the grantor rather than the recipient. Therefore, the entire $3,580 stipend represented taxable pay rather than a tax-free scholarship or fellowship.

The fact that the University could have hired part-time instructors for less money than the stipend did not make any part of it tax-free. As the Court ruled,

"It may be true that the stipend from the assistantship was intended to provide petitioner with some financial assistance so that he could continue his studies. He may have been paid more than a part-time instructor would have been. It is certainly within the University's discretion to pay a premium to its own well qualified graduate students. These factors are not inconsistent with what we find to be the primary purpose of the stipend, which was to provide teaching services for the benefit of the Department." [Ellenwood, TC Memo 1982-137]

The above case contrasted with an earlier case involving a teaching assistant in a different department at the same University. In the earlier case, the assistantship was ruled to be exempt from tax. But in that case, equivalent services were required of all candidates for the same degree. Furthermore, the entire assistantship program was geared toward providing teacher training, rather than covering courses for which extra personnel would need to be hired in the absence of an assistantship program. [Steiman, 56 TC 1350]

Research Assistants

Research assistants, in most cases, fall under the above ruling since equivalent research is usually required for all candidates. As long as the requirements of the ruling were satisfied, their grants qualify for tax-free status. [IRS Private Letter Rulings 8240081, 8348045, 8430013, 8405079, 8613005; TC Memo 1980-559]

However, it is not necessary to satisfy the equivalent services test in order to deduct the full amount of the stipend. This is the conclusion of the Tax Court in a case concerning two research assistants in the Department of Economics at a large Midwestern University. One of the assistants was in the Ph.D. program while the other was pursuing a master's degree only. Both of them worked on research projects under the direction of a professor in the Economics Department. Funds for their assistantships came both from the National Science Foundation and from the general research budget of the University.

The Court reasoned that one of the objectives of graduate education at the University was to develop the research skills of its students. These skills cannot be acquired simply by completing the regular course work, but require actual participation in some sort of research project or other similar *creative component*. The Court concluded that the amounts received by the assistants *"were not intended as compensation for services, but rather were intended to facilitate their graduate education."*

The Court pointed to 6 factors which supported its conclusion. First, each assistant derived *"clear and unmistakable educational benefits"* from his research assistantship. Second, they worked longer than the 20 hours per week that was required, without additional compensation. This was *"inconsistent with a true employment relationship where one might reasonably expect to be compensated for overtime."* Third, the review of their research by their Professors was informal and irregular. In substance their Professors *"served more in the capacity of an advisor than a supervisor, and there was a distinct absence of an employer-employee relationship in the traditional sense."* Fourth, the assistants were not required to turn over the results of the research to any persons outside the

Economics Department, nor was there any contractual commitment to perform specific research activities. Fifth, the assistantships were regarded by the University and the students as a means of providing financial aid so the students could complete their studies. And sixth, *"many of the trappings associated with an employment relationship"* were absent in this case. The University did not contribute to a health plan, made no Worker's Compensation or Unemployment Insurance contributions, did not withhold social security or taxes, etc.

The IRS objected that the research services provided by the assistants went beyond what was required of graduate students who were not research assistants so they did not meet the *equivalent services* test. But the Court found this objection to be groundless. Although satisfying the equivalent services test is *sufficient* to establish the deductibility of an assistantship as described earlier in this section, it is not necessary to satisfy this requirement. Here, the Court found that the payments received by the research assistants were only educational in nature and were *"not intended to compensate petitioners for services rendered as an employee or any other capacity."* This meant that none of the stipend was wages, but rather the entire amount was a tax-exempt scholarship or fellowship. It did not matter whether or not equivalent services were required of all candidates for the same degree. [Langley and O'Riley, TC Memo 1982-460]

Even if a research assistant did some teaching, he can still get an exemption for a stipend covering just his research activities. This is illustrated by the following IRS Private Letter Ruling issued to a Mechanical Engineering Ph.D. candidate:

IRS Private Letter Ruling 8451053

"... The information submitted discloses that you are an instructor and a candidate for the degree of Ph. D. in the Mechanical Engineering Department at X. You have been awarded a research grant through X, by the ***** covering a period of approximately one year beginning September 15, 1983. During this time you will perform research at a ***** research center as a portion of your dissertation research for the Ph.D. degree. You have indicated that the research that you perform for X satisfies a specifically stated requirement and that equivalent services are required of all candidates for the same degree. The research will not be performed in your capacity as an instructor at X.

"Your research is to be performed under the guidance of a 'principal investigator' that has been approved by *****. The grantee is required to submit to the grantor semi-annual status reports and a final technical report during the course of the grant. The research performed is not carried out during the course of a specific project of the grantor and the grant is not awarded based on past or future services to be rendered by you to X or *****.

"Based upon the information submitted we conclude that the stipend that you receive from ***** under the research grant will be excludable from gross income under section 117(a) of the Code. . ."

Typically, universities will provide statements for research or teaching assistants to attach to their income tax returns for the purpose of claiming total or partial tax-free status for their stipends. These statements should be geared toward showing that the stipend falls within the requirements of the revenue ruling described earlier. The following is an example of what such a statement might include in the case of a research assistant. This statement is tailored to the specific language of the ruling.

TO WHOM IT MAY CONCERN:

During the calendar year 19_____, _____
                                                    name of student
served as a Research Assistant in the Department of _____ at

_____from _____ to_____. He was

paid a stipend of $_____ for his services. The funds were

derived from _____.
                                         description of grant/contract

During the above period of time,

(1) The above student was a candidate for the degree of _____;

(2) He performed research for the above institution which satisfied then existing specifically stated requirements for the degree; and

(3) Equivalent services were required of all candidates for the degree.

Also, pursuant to receiving any of the above stipend,

(1) He did not perform services in excess of those necessary to satisfy degree requirements;

(2) Services were not performed for any party other than the above named institution;

(3) The grant was not made because of past services nor was it conditioned on, or subject to an understanding with respect to future employment or other requirements, including services in excess of those necessary to satisfy degree requirements; and

(4) The degree requirements, and the nature and extent of the work that is approved as satisfying the degree requirements are reasonably appropriate to the above degree.

In accordance with Revenue Ruling 75-280 and the above facts, the stipend is excludable from gross income as a scholarship or fellowship under Section 117 of the Internal Revenue Code before amendment by the 1986 Tax Reform Act.

The statement should also include a verification that the grant was awarded before August 17, 1986 according to the criteria described in the preceding section. This is especially important because under the new rules, Revenue Ruling 75-280 no longer applies. That is, for grants awarded on or after August 17, 1986, the fact that equivalent services are required of all degree recipients will not suffice to exempt amounts received after 1986 from tax [cf. Section 2].

Note: If the university omits any of the above information, the grant recipient should attach his own statement providing the missing information.

Interns and Residents

Interns and residents are seldom able to claim that the money they receive is a scholarship or fellowship. Their stipends are considered to be pay for services rendered to the hospital where they work. This has been the case even when stipends have covered a portion of the residency program during which no clinical services were performed [Kersten, TC Memo 1984-204]. Exceptions have occurred in programs which are not strictly medical in nature (e.g. hospital administration, psychology), where the recipients performed no substantial services for the institutions where they performed their internships. [IRS Private Letter Rulings 8206079, 8238054]

Disadvantages of Fellowships

There are two possible advantages for graduate students in having their stipends labeled as taxable pay rather than tax-free fellowships. The first advantage concerns the special negative income tax feature of the law called the *earned income credit* [cf. Chapter 1]. This credit applies to those who maintain a household for a child and earn under $20,264. In particular, for those who earn under $6,810, the credit is equal to 14% of *earned income*. Thus, $6,810 received as taxable pay could generate a $943 rebate from the government. But a tax-free fellowship would not be earned income and would therefore generate no earned income credit.

The other possible advantage in having a stipend labeled as taxable pay is that a graduate student who then cannot find a job might qualify for unemployment compensation. Whether or not unemployment compensation applies to graduate students depends upon State and federal laws applicable at the time. However, being unemployed right after being supported by tax-free fellowship money would almost certainly not qualify.

Non-Degree Candidates

If you are not a candidate for a degree, your scholarship or fellowship grant awarded before August 17, 1986 is subject to three further restrictions.

(1) A maximum of $300 per month may be excluded from taxable income. The remainder is subject to income tax (but not Social Security tax as discussed in Section 5). In addition to the $300 exclusion, you do not have to pay tax on allowances specifically designated for travel, research, equipment, etc., provided these allowances are actually used for their intended purposes.

(2) During your lifetime, you are limited to a total of 36 months (not necessarily consecutive) during which you are eligible for this tax-free treatment.

(3) The money must be received from a governmental agency or qualifying educational, religious, charitable, scientific, or literary organization. However, a grant given a teacher by his own school is generally taxable because of the employee-employer relationship between them. (This does not necessarily apply to grants which come from a qualifying organization that are merely administered by the school.)

Amounts Specifically Designated for Expenses

As indicated in (1) above, amounts specifically designated for travel, research, equipment, etc. are totally exempt from tax provided they are spent for their intended purposes. You do not apply the $300 per month limitation to these amounts.

The "specific designation" requirement does not mean that the grant itself specify the amounts to be spent for which purposes. As long as the purpose of the grant is indicated and the grant is intended to cover expenses connected with this purpose, the "specific designation" requirement is met. A good way to show that the grant is intended to cover certain expenses is to show that these expenses were itemized in your application and that the amount of the grant was based on this itemization. [Rev Rul 69-367]

What If Less Than $300 Per Month Is Excluded?

The 36-month limitation in (2) applies whenever an individual has received an amount which was either excluded or excludable from his gross income for any prior 36 months. For example, if an individual received $200 per month for three years, his exclusion period would be exhausted. Even though he did not make use of the maximum $300 exclusion, he would no longer be entitled to any further income tax exclusion.

What If You Were Eligible but Failed to Claim the Exclusion?

You lose out. If there have been 36 months during which you were eligible to exclude any scholarship or fellowship grants as a non-degree candidate, then you are ineligible for further exclusion. It makes no difference whether or not you actually claimed the exclusion. In fact, one statistics professor was denied an exclusion because he admitted that he had received some kind of grant a number of years earlier which might have qualified for the exclusion. If so, this would have put him over the 36-month limit. He did not claim the exclusion for this grant but he could not prove that he was ineligible to claim such exclusion. [Wijsman, 54 TC 1539]

Grants Received While Outside the U.S.

If payments from a grant were received while outside the U.S., it might be better to consider the payments as wages for services rendered, rather than as a scholarship or fellowship. Wages can qualify for **total** exemption from income tax under the rules applying to foreign earned income [cf. the *Foreign Income* chapter]. Scholarships and fellowships, on the other hand, run the risk of being disqualified from the foreign income exemption by the IRS as not being *earned income*.

Can the Receipt of a Tax-Free Grant Rule Out a Travel Deduction?

Sometimes the following situation arises. A person receives a grant to study or do research at a location away from home. When he uses the $300 per month fellowship exclusion and claims a deduction for travel expenses while away from home, the IRS objects. Since there were no job-related wages, the IRS claims no job-related expenses can be deducted. This objection can be countered by asserting that the travel expenses were *educational expenses* rather than *business expenses*. This is discussed more fully at the end of Section 3 of the *Travel* chapter.

What Kinds of Grants Qualify for Tax-Free Treatment?

Whether or not a grant qualifies for tax-free treatment depends upon the **primary purpose** of the grant. In order to be tax-deductible, the primary purpose of a grant must be *to further the education and training of the recipient in his individual capacity*. On the other hand, if the primary purpose is *for the benefit of the grantor,* then the grant is taxable.

In practice, the determination of the *primary purpose* of a grant can be difficult to make. The courts have given little guidance on how to decide this question. They simply have stated that this determination must be made *"on a case by case basis by considering the particular facts and circumstances"* concerning the grant in question.

The IRS and the courts have issued a number of rulings on specific grants, deciding in each case whether or not the grant qualifies for tax-free status. Due to the individual nature of each type of grant, it is not possible to foretell with accuracy how grants will be ruled upon. The finest of differences may cause one grant to be ruled taxable and another tax-free. Furthermore, the result might be the exact opposite of what would be reasonably expected by most people.

This is illustrated by two IRS rulings concerning grants from the National Endowment for the Humanities. The first ruling concerned a grant made to junior college professors *"to increase their understanding of the subjects they teach and to improve their teaching ability."* The second ruling concerned a grant to a professor of English literature so he could *"study the interaction of the sciences and literature with a view toward writing a book on the taxpayer's conclusion."* If anything, the first grant would seem to better qualify under the tax-free criterion of furthering *the education and training of the recipient in his individual capacity.* The second grant would seem more likely to yield a concrete result that could be regarded as *benefiting the grantor.*

But the IRS ruled just the opposite. It decided that the first grant was taxable because a non-exclusive right to reproduce publishable matter arising from the grant made the grant primarily for the benefit of the grantor. The second grant did not have this feature and was ruled to qualify for tax-free treatment.

Following are excerpts from these two rulings.

IRS Ruling 1

"The taxpayer, who was not a candidate for a degree, was the recipient of a fellowship grant by the National Endowment for the Humanities, a governmental agency. The announced purpose of the grant program was to enable junior college professors, chosen on the basis of their ability as teachers and interpreters of the humanities, to increase their understanding of the subjects they teach and to improve their teaching ability. Each applicant was to specify his proposed area of study and to explain its contribution to his development as a teacher and interpreter of humanistic knowledge and to a better understanding of matters of current national concern, or of other matters of significance to humanistic knowledge and the quality of national life.

"... The grantor reserved a nonexclusive license to use and reproduce for government purposes, without payment, any publishable matter, including copyrighted matter, arising out of the taxpayer's activities.

" . . . Based on the above it is concluded that the grant is made primarily for the benefit of the grantor because of the right retained by the grantor, in the form of a nonexclusive license, to any materials resulting from the recipients research.

"A further indication that the objectives of the grant program were not solely focused on the experience to be gained by the recipients is shown by the grantor's evaluation of each applicant's ability as an interpreter of the humanities, and of the contribution to be made by the proposed area of study to a better understanding of matters of current national concern, or of other matters of significance to humanistic knowledge and the quality of national life.

"Accordingly, in the instant case, the amounts received by the taxpayer from the National Endowment for Humanities grant are not excludable on the taxpayer's gross income under the provisions of section 117(a) of the Code, but are includible in his gross income under section 61 as compensation for services." [Rev. Rul. 74-95, 1974-1 CB 39]

IRS Ruling 2

" . . . The taxpayer, who was not a candidate for a degree, applied for and was granted a lump-sum grant for two months from the National Endowment for the Humanities, a governmental agency. The taxpayer was a professor of English literature and proposed to spend the two-month grant period studying the interaction of the sciences and literature with a view towards writing a book on the taxpayer's conclusions.

"As a condition to receiving the grant the taxpayer was to devote two full consecutive months during the summer to the study and research for which the grant was awarded. The taxpayer was not permitted to accept a teaching assignment, undertake another major activity, or enroll in a degree program during the two-month period and was prohibited from applying the work done during that period toward any future degree. The taxpayer was not required to publish the results of the study but was free to do so without restriction. If the taxpayer chose to publish the results of the study, the grantor requested, but did not require, a copy of the publication and advance notice *thereof so that it could consider issuing a public information release or cooperating in a joint release.*

"... In this case, the grant was paid to enable the taxpayer to pursue a program of independent study. The grantor reserved no publication rights. Since the grant was awarded solely to further the education of the taxpayer, it was for the taxpayer's benefit and not for the benefit of the grantor. Further, there was no employment relationship between the grantor and the taxpayer previous to or at the time of the grant, nor was there any obligation on the part of the taxpayer to accept employment or otherwise perform services after acceptance of the grant.

"Accordingly, in the instant case, the grant received from the National Endowment for the Humanities is excludable from the taxpayer's gross income as a fellowship grant.

"This case is distinguishable from [the preceding ruling] which holds that amounts received as a grant from the National Endowment for the Humanities are not excludable from the taxpayer's gross income. . . [In that ruling], the grantor reserved a nonexclusive license to use and reproduce for government purpose, without payment, any publishable matter, including copyrighted matter arising out of the taxpayer's activities, and the objectives of the program under which the grant was awarded were not solely focused on the experience to be gained by the recipients. [Rev Rul 76-351, IRB 1976-38 p. 6]

In IRS Ruling 1 above, the nonexclusive right of the grantor to use and reproduce the results of the research disqualified the grant from tax-free treatment. In fact, two private rulings show that the IRS has latched onto this seemingly minor point as a deciding criterion. Both grants were provided by governmental agencies to support independent research in the humanities. One grant was awarded to a doctoral candidate and the other to an established researcher who had already obtained his degree. But the wording of both grants contained the fatal clause granting the government a nonexclusive right to use the results of the research without paying royalties. And in both rulings, the IRS declared that this alone was enough to rule out tax-free treatment for the grants. [IRS Private Letter Rulings 8021120 and 8008056]

NSF Grants

The preceding ruling offers a good example of a common type of grant received by college professors. Namely, the grant provides funds for the professor to do research in his specialty.

For scientists, the most common grant of this type comes from the NSF (National Science Foundation). The Tax Court has, on the two occasions when the issue came to trial, denied a deduction for NSF research grants. In 1977, the Tax Court ruled against a computer scientist. In an ironic twist, the computer scientist's expertise and the fact that his work was considered valuable were used against him by the court. (A similar conclusion was reached in a different case involving a mathematics professor. In that case, the grant proposal specified that the recipient would spend 1/3 of his time during the academic year on the project funded by the grant, such services to be paid by the university. This linking of the work performed under the summer grant and his ordinary academic-year work was a decidedly negative factor. [Carroll, 60 TC 96]) But in 1978, the IRS issued a private ruling to a scientist giving him permission to deduct his NSF grant. Although the IRS ruling was devoid of detailed reasoning, it is worthwhile to take a look at the two grants in question.

1977 Court Case — Deduction for NSF Grant Denied

A professor of Computer Science applied for and received an NSF grant to work on the development of a new kind of programming language. As is the usual case, the grant was actually awarded to the university, with the professor as principal investigator. Funds from the grant were used to pay him for a 6-month period when he was on sabbatical.

The professor claimed that he was entitled to exclude $300 per month from taxable income, a total of $1,800 for the 6 months involved. But the Court denied his claim. It appeared to be influenced by 3 major considerations.

First, it pointed out that the grant actually covered a longer period of time than the 6-month period during which direct payments were received from the grant. Over this longer period of time, the professor was to be working on the same project as part of his regular duties as a Computer Science professor and paid his normal salary from university funds. This indicated to the Court that the payments should not be considered as a fellowship. It stated,

> ". . . it was not the intent of Congress that grants which were in effect continuing salary payments to the recipient while on leave from his regular job be considered as fellowship grants. Here, part of petitioner's regular job and part of the activity he undertook during the school year while he was performing his other functions at the university was research on the project for which NSF had made a grant. When he went on sabbatical leave and pursued this research full-time instead of part-time, the nature of his research work was unchanged. He was still pursuing the research as a part of his work as a professor and in accordance with the NSF grant."

Second, the Court seemed impressed by the usefulness of the research. Ironically, this worked against the professor because it meant that NSF and the university would receive "benefit" from the research. The Court stated,

> "NSF seeks to further research which it finds to be in the public interest. Because it found that the research proposal by the petitioner met that standard, NSF made funds available to support such research. The university is interested in encouraging the members of its faculty to perform research, and for that reason it undertook to administer the grant made by NSF and to make its facilities available for the performance of such research."

Finally, the Court held the professor's experience and competence against him. The fact that he was already an expert in the field was evidence the grant was not for the purpose of providing him with training or education. It stated that since he

> "had so many years of work in the area with which his research dealt, it is not even shown by this record that his education was enhanced by the research he did. In any event, in this case the facts as a whole show that the funds were made available for petitioner's project because NSF wished to have it performed by him, and that the payments made to petitioner from the NSF funds were for the services he performed on the research project. Here, an essential element of having the research proposal approved was the qualifications of petitioner to perform the important research he had outlined. The grant was made to support the proposed research which NSF determined should be performed."

1978 IRS Ruling — Deduction Allowed for NSF Grant

A scientist solicited an official opinion from the IRS as to whether his NSF grant qualified for deduction. In response, the IRS issued him a private letter ruling. This private ruling does not set legal precedent, but since the IRS attempts to be consistent in its interpretation of the law, it is still of considerable interest. As is customary, the IRS ruling is published with all mention of taxpayer's name or other identifying information deleted. With this exception, the entire IRS ruling is reproduced below.

IRS Private Letter Ruling 7817011

We are writing in reply to a letter dated July 8, 1977, submitted on your behalf by — and prior correspondence. You request a ruling regarding the treatment for federal income tax purposes of amounts received by you under the circumstances described below.

You received a grant from the National Science Foundation for research in your field. The grant was established for the purpose of recognizing and encouraging the work of younger scientists whose capabilities and accomplishments show exceptional promise of significant future achievements. Your grant is administered by Princeton University.

At the time you received the grant, you were on the faculty of_____. Since the beginning of the grant period, you have been on leave from your faculty position. You teach no classes and participate in no administrative duties. You have no schedule other than that which you set for yourself, and you receive no supervision from the University.

You choose your own research problems, however, when you publish the results of your work, you are required to acknowledge the support of the National Science Foundation. You must also publish a "disclaimer" that the views presented are your own and not those of the National Science Foundation. You are not required to submit any reports of the progress of your work to the University or the National Science Foundation.

You request a ruling that the amounts you receive are excludable from your gross income as a fellowship grant pursuant to section 117 of the Internal Revenue Code of 1954.

Section 61 of the Code defines gross income as all income from whatever source derived unless specifically excluded by law.

Section 117(a) of the Code provides that gross income does not include any *amount received as a scholarship at an educational organization or as a fellowship grant.*

Section 117(b)(2)(B) of the Code provides that in the case of an individual who is not a candidate for a degree at an educational organization, the amount of the scholarship or fellowship grant excluded in any taxable year shall be limited to an amount equal to $300 times the number of months for which the recipient received amounts under the scholarship or fellowship grant during such taxable year, except that no exclusion shall be allowed after the recipient has been entitled to exclude under this section for a period of 36 months (whether or not consecutive) amounts received as a scholarship or fellowship grant while not a candidate for a degree at an educational institution.

In Biederdorf v. Commissioner, 60 T.C. 114 (1973), the United States Tax Court held that a postdoctoral fellowship grant awarded to a licensed physician and funded by the National Institutes of Health was excludable from the recipient's gross income. Seventy-five to eighty percent of his time was spent performing research which was of only incidental value to the grantor, and there was no requirement for future employment services as a condition for receiving the grant. A similar result was reached in Bailey v. Commissioner, 60 T.C. 447 (1973).

Revenue Ruling 58-498, 1958-2 C.B. 47, provides that amounts paid as grants to high school and college teachers to attend summer institutes for science are excludible from the recipients' gross income pursuant to the limitations of section 117 of the Code. The grantees were not affiliated with the National Science Foundation (the grantor) nor did they incur any independent obligation to any educational institution by accepting the stipend.

Based upon our analysis of the authorities cited above and the information submitted by you, we conclude that you may exclude from your gross income amounts received under your grant, subject to the limitations of section 117(b) (2) (B) of the Code.

A copy of this ruling should be attached to your income tax return when it is filed.

A copy of this letter is being sent to your representative pursuant to the power of attorney on file with this office.

As the above discussion indicates, the deductibility of a research grant is often a borderline question which can be decided in either direction, depending upon who does the deciding. However, an instructive pattern has emerged from the recent cases on this issue.

First, let us compare the Court Case above in which a deduction was denied to a Computer Science Professor with IRS Ruling 2 described earlier in which tax-free treatment was approved for a Professor of English. The difference seems to lie mostly in the more specific nature of the Computer Science proposal than the English proposal. The grant to the English Professor was awarded for the purpose of *"study with a view towards writing a book."* There was no mention of any concrete results that it was hoped would be attained. The NSF grant to the Computer Science Professor, on the other hand, was made on the basis of a specific research proposal to develop a particular type of programming language.

The court felt that NSF *"wished to have the research performed"* and therefore received *benefit* from the research.

It is also interesting to compare the two NSF Grants discussed above. The first grant was awarded to an established scientist by NSF in order to *"further research which it finds to be in the public interest."* Because of the existing expertise of the researcher and the desired end product of the research, the grant was considered to be for the primary purpose of *benefiting the grantor* rather than *furthering the education and training of the recipient.*

The second NSF grant, on the other hand, had the stated purpose of *"recognizing and encouraging the work of younger scientists whose capabilities and accomplishments show exceptional promise of significant future achievements."* In this case, the purpose of *furthering the education and training of the recipient in his individual capacity* predominated over the purpose of benefiting the grantor.

Two 1983 examples illustrate that when asked to rule, the IRS generally looks for some special feature of the grant which will make it fully taxable.

In the first of these rulings, the IRS denied tax-exemption for a research grant received by a professor at an unnamed college. This research grant provided not just summer support, but also provided 1/4 support during the academic year so that the professor could receive a reduced teaching load to carry on his research. The ruling was devoid of detailed reasoning. However, the fact that the grant covered not just the summer months but also part of the regular academic year was clearly a negative factor—indicating the grant was more in the nature of pay for services rendered than for the educational benefit of the recipient. [IRS Private Letter Ruling 8336021]

The second ruling concerned a summer-only NSF grant to a professor for 2/9 of his academic year salary. Under this grant, however, the NSF retained the right to receive a portion of royalties from copyrights produced during the life of the grant and for 3 years thereafter. The grant also gave the NSF the rights to patentable inventions arising from work done under these grants. As discussed earlier in this section, the retention of rights by the grantor to work produced under a grant is an important indicator to the IRS that the grant is for the purpose of benefiting the grantor rather than the recipient. Hence, it ruled that this NSF grant did not qualify for tax-free treatment. [IRS Private Letter Ruling 8337049]

The above discussion indicates that the official IRS policy on tax-free grants is to be tough about allowing tax-free treatment. In fact, 4 more recent IRS Private Letter Rulings have all denied tax exemptions for various NSF grants with no obvious special features which were awarded to college faculty members. In each case, the IRS ruled that the grant was primarily for the benefit of the grantor (NSF) rather than the recipient. In 3 of these rulings, the IRS used the following same language (including reference to a 1970 court case, *Turem vs. Commissioner,* it uncovered) describing why it considered the grant to *"benefit"* the NSF:

> *"A grant in support of basic research is made because the National Science Foundation decides that the results of the research are desired and in the public interest. A grant for basic research sets forth the budget to be followed, including the allocation of the amounts to be paid as salary to the*

principal investigator and others working on the project. On the other hand, a fellowship grant is always made to an individual and is awarded to enhance the applicant's competence. Although a recipient of a fellowship grant may engage in research as an incident of his study and development, the objective of the grant is to further his study and not to achieve the research.

"In Turem v. Commissioner, *54 T.C. 1494 (1970), the court found that governmental grants resulted in grantor benefit by inducing recipients to engage in educational activity beneficial to governmental agencies in the attainment of their objectives, even though the general public was expected to be the ultimate beneficiary of the petitioner's education. Thus, Turem stands for the proposition that grantor benefit need not be in the form of monetary gain or services rendered directly to the grantor."* [IRS Private Letter Rulings 8521084, 8521029, 8524071, 8528012]

The above discussion suggests that grant recipients are wise to avoid formal confrontation with the IRS, if possible. (Be sure to read Section 4 on the most inconspicuous way to claim the tax-free portion of your grant.) However, the basic legal situation remains. That is, each grant is judged separately on its merits as to whether or not it is primarily for the benefit of the grantor or the recipient.

How to Obtain Tax-Free Treatment for a Grant

As the above discussion indicates, there are no rigid rules to apply which will determine whether or not a grant is deductible. Even the Court has admitted that the tax status of a grant must be decided *"on a case by case basis by considering the facts and circumstances"* in the given situation. However, the above discussion suggests how to improve the chances of obtaining tax-free status for a grant. Namely, the **study** aspect of the research should be stressed as opposed to the **result** aspect. Funds for study tend to be regarded as benefiting the recipient while funds to obtain specific results tend to be regarded as benefiting the grantor.

Scientists, especially, should be aware of the above distinction in order to properly protect their deduction. An individual whose NSF grant is challenged may wish to present a copy of IRS Private Letter Ruling 7817011 reproduced above to support his case, even if the particulars of his situation differ somewhat from that in the ruling. A given IRS examining officer may or may not perceive a difference between two relatively similar situations.

Because the deductibility of a grant is a judgment call, most recipients of grants awarded before August 17, 1986 will probably want to go ahead and treat their grants as qualifying for tax-free treatment on their 1990 tax returns. The risk of challenge by the IRS is usually outweighed by the expected tax benefit.

Grants Requiring Future Services

A grant should not be conditioned upon the performance of future services. For example, if a faculty member accepted a grant which requires him to return to his school after the grant period is over, then this would disqualify the grant from tax-free status. This fact was emphasized in several court cases and IRS rulings. [IRS Private Letter Rulings 7828044, 7907079, 8439055, 8439086, TC Memo 1978-449]

Sabbatical Grants

Money which a teacher received from an employer while on a sabbatical is usually not considered to be a tax-free grant. The direct employer-employee relationship that exists between the grantor and the grantee in most cases leads the IRS to consider such money to be a form of compensation for services rendered. However, if the grant is supplied by an outside organization, then the grant qualifies for the $300 per month tax-free treatment as described in this section. The following 1986 IRS Private Letter Ruling illustrates this situation.

IRS Private Letter Ruling 8601039

"This is in reply to your letter of September 3, 1985, requesting a ruling that a stipend that you receive from X is a fellowship grant within the meaning of section 117(a) of the Internal Revenue Code.

"The information submitted discloses that during the period August 15, 1985 to August 14, 1986, you will be on sabbatical from your position as a member of the faculty of Y. The sabbatical is not a requirement for continued employment at Y. During the above-described period, you will be receiving an amount equal to one-half of your normal, annual salary from Y which you acknowledge represents taxable income for federal income tax purposes.

"During this same period, however, you will be receiving a stipend from X under a Visiting Scientist fellowship which is being treated as a postdoctoral fellowship by X.

"You were awarded this fellowship after you submitted a research proposal to X. The only responsibilities to X are to complete the project as outlined in the proposal, and to file a mid-term and final progress report to X. While you may engage in other research projects during the year, such activities are at your discretion and you are free to conduct your research as you see fit. Your sponsor at X is acting as your official contact with X and will offer advice when necessary. He is not acting in a supervisory capacity. Your only obligation to Y is to file a report on your research activities at the end of your sabbatical.

"X's description of the program provides that fellows will be selected for the importance of the work they propose—its contribution to their field, and to the fulfillment of their intellectual promise—provided such work can be undertaken successfully in X's facilities and a member of X's professional research staff is available for collaboration and assistance. X is an organization which is an instrumentality of the United States. . . .

"Rev. Rul. 58-222, 1958-1 C.B. 54, holds that the amount received from a college by a member of its teaching staff (on sabbatical leave) while engaged in research in his particular field of interest does not constitute a scholarship or fellowship grant within the meaning of section 117 of the Code. The amount so received is includible in the member's gross income as compensation.

"Rev. Rul. 58-222 further holds that the amount received by such member from a private (tax-exempt) foundation while engaged in such research is excludable from his gross income as a fellowship grant to the extent provided by section 117 of the Code. Any amount received by him which is specifically des-

ignated to cover expenses for travel (including meals and lodging while travel-ing and an allowance for travel of his family), research, clerical help, or equip-ment incident to the fellowship grant, is excludable from gross income to the extent that it is used for such purposes.

"Based upon the information submitted, and the representations made, we conclude that the stipend that you receive from X is excludable from your gross income under section 117(a) of the Code subject to the limitation of sec-tion 117(b) (2) [discussed at the beginning of Section 1—ed.].

"It is further concluded that any amount received from X designated for travel, clerical help, or equipment incident to the grant, is excludable from gross income to the extent that it is used for such purposes. . . . "

Exceptions

There are exceptions when money received from an employer might qualify for tax-free treatment. The following 1985 court case shows that a grant from one's employer can qualify as a tax-free grant if there are truly no strings attached.

Court Case

Pelowski, a teacher at a small liberal arts college in the Midwest, received a $10,000 grant from the college. Such grants were awarded after 7 years of employ-ment. Pelowski used the grant to pursue a Ph.D. program at a major University in a neighboring state.

No strings were attached to the grant. Pelowski had no obligation to return to the college where he had taught. The college did not select the curriculum for his Ph.D. thesis. While studying at the University, he was on leave of absence but not employed at the college, nor did he receive any benefits from the college. No progress reports were given to his former employer.

The Court ruled that based on the above facts, the $10,000 grant did not repre-sent compensation for past, present, or future services. Nor were the studies primari-ly for the benefit of the college. Rather, the $10,000 was ruled to be a tax- exempt scholarship grant. [Pelowski, DC Ohio, 1985 CCH ¶ 9217]

Section 4:
How to Claim the Income Tax Exemption

Ideally, the W-2 form which you receive from your employer should not in-clude any amounts received under a tax-free grant. Since the grant is not pay for services rendered, the **full amount** of the grant is supposed to be excluded from *Wages* on your W-2 form. (An **exc**eption occurs when a portion of the grant is paid for services rendered, in which case such portion should be included on your W-2 form.) You would then report any portion of the grant subject to tax as *Other Income* on line 22 of Form 1040.

However, institutions often tend to be conservative and treat all grants issued to their faculty members as wages, even though this can cost both you and the institution extra social security tax. This means the entire amount received under the grant will be included as taxable income on the W-2 form which you receive at the end of the year. In this case, the official procedure calls for you to subtract the tax-free amount of the grant from the figure shown on your W-2 form and report the difference on the *Wages* line of your tax return.

However, this procedure has caused numerous grant recipients a lot of trouble because it has flagged their tax returns for audit [cf. the end of Section 1]. The IRS has a "Matching Program" to verify that the amount reported on W-2 forms matches the amount reported as *Wages* on an individual's tax return. If the figures do not match, the return will be singled out for examination. This can result not only in the tax-free status of the grant being called into question, but also other items as well [cf. Section 9 of Chapter 1].

If the W-2 form sent to you by your employer includes amounts which qualify as a tax-free grant, the following procedure is best. Report the full amount shown on your W-2 form as *Wages* on your tax return. Then list the tax-free amount of your grant as a negative amount on line 22, *Other Income*. The net tax result will be the same as if you had omitted the tax-free amount of the grant from your total wages, but you won't have stirred up the IRS computer by creating an arithmetical discrepancy. The listing of negative amounts on line 22 is a procedure suggested by the IRS in similar situations.

Note that there are two additional advantages to including tax-free grants in taxable income and then subtracting these amounts on line 22. First, you cannot be accused of fraud for failing to report income. Second, you have subjected the question of your grant's tax status to the statute of limitations.

You should attach a statement to your return showing the amounts received and the letter of award to you or other description of the grant. If you received any specific allowances for travel, research expenses, etc., these should be listed separately along with a statement showing the use to which these allowances were applied.

Section 5:
Exemption from Social Security Tax

A grant which qualifies for exemption from income tax under the rules described in the preceding sections is also exempt from social security tax. (As discussed on the first page of this chapter, the social security tax exemption becomes of particular importance in 1991 because of the 1.45% medicare tax applying to income up to $125,000 [cf. Chapter 0]. This exemption from social security tax still applies to grants issued on or after August 17, 1986. It does not matter that the grant may be subject to income tax under the new law. The 1986 Tax Reform Act only affects the *income tax* treatment of grants, not the *social security* treatment.

This social security tax exemption applies to the **entire amount of the grant** and is unaffected by the $300 per month and 36 total-months limitations described in Section 3 for awards issued to non-degree candidates prior to August 17, 1986. For example, such a non-degree candidate who received a $2,000 per month grant for 2 months would be able to exclude $300 × 2 = $600 of this grant from income tax. But the entire $4,000 would be exempt from social security tax.

The exemption from social security tax is spelled out in a number of IRS rulings. The reasoning in these rulings goes as follows:

Under the old rules discussed in Section 3, a grant qualified for partial tax-free treatment if the *primary purpose* of the grant was to further the education and training of the recipient in his individual capacity, rather than being for the benefit of the grantor. This meant that the money received under the grant was not classified as *wages*. And social security tax is only levied against *wages,* not against any other type of income even if this income is subject to income tax. [IRS Private Letter Rulings 7929051, 7929066, and 8047019]

The exemption from social security tax on the entire amount of the grant can be worth a substantial amount of money. For example, a person earning $2,000 per month under a 12-month grant would save about $1,800 in social security taxes, a substantial tax-free benefit. (However, if a person's other income already exceeds the social security wage base, above which no additional social security tax is withheld, then there would be no social security tax savings.)

Recipients of grants qualifying for tax-free treatment should request that the institution administering the grant withhold no social security taxes. In fact, if the grant qualifies for tax-free treatment, the institution is legally required to do this.

Refund of Prior Social Security Tax

If social security (also known as FICA) was withheld on money you received from a grant which qualified for tax-free treatment, then you are entitled to a refund of the amounts withheld. This situation is covered in a ruling which describes the exact procedure to follow to obtain the refund. This ruling was issued to an individual who received a grant on which social security was incorrectly withheld. Since many individuals are in the same situation, we quote the relevant portion of this ruling in its entirety.

IRS Private Letter Ruling 8109026

"... *We conclude that the stipend you receive is excludable from gross income to the extent of $300.00 per month for the number of months of the internship, not to exceed the 36 month limitation of Code section 117(b) (2) (B).*

"*Because FICA payments have been withheld on this amount, you are entitled to a recovery.*

"*Section 31. 6402 (a)-2 (a) of the Employment Tax Regulations provides that any person who pays to the district director more than the correct amount of employee tax under section 3101 or employer tax under section 3111 of the Federal Insurance Contributions Act (FICA) may file a claim for refund of the overpayment or may claim a credit for the overpayment. The employer may file a claim for refund on Form 843 or take a credit for the overpayment on any subsequent return. Claims filed by an employer for refund, credit, or abatement of employee tax collected from an employee must include a statement by the employee that the employer has repaid him/her the amount of the overcollection or has obtained the employee's written consent to the allowance of the refund or credit. If the claim for credit or refund is for a calendar year prior to the calendar year in which the claim is made, the employer must obtain a statement that the employee has not and will not claim a refund or credit of the amount of the overcollection. This is the preferable method for recovery.*

"If the employer does not correct the error, the employee may file a claim for refund or credit of an overcollection of FICA tax where: (1) the employer collects more than the correct amount of employee social security tax and pays it to the district director, and (2) the employee has not claimed reimbursement through credit against, or refund of, his income tax (or if so claimed, the claim has been rejected), and (3) the employee does not receive reimbursement in any manner from such employer and does not authorize the employer to file a claim and receive refund or credit. The employee may file a claim for refund of the overpayment on Form 843. Each employee who makes such a claim must submit along with the claim a statement setting forth (a) the extent, if any, to which the employer has reimbursed the employee in any manner for the overcollection, and (b) the amount, if any, of credit or refund of such overpayment collected by the employer. If the employee is unable to obtain the employer's statement, the employee must make the statement to the best of his knowledge and belief and include an explanation of his inability to obtain the statement from the employer.

"The statement to accompany an employer's and employee's claim for credit or refund of employee tax under section 3101 or employer tax under section 3111 made with respect to payments erroneously reported on a return as wages paid to an employee must include (1) the identification number of the employer, (2) the name and account number of the employee, (3) the period covered by the return, (4) the amount of payments actually reported as wages for the employee, and (5) the amount of wages which should have been reported for the employee. No particular form is prescribed for making such statement, but if printed forms are desired, Form 941c may be used."

Although not mentioned in the above ruling, the 3-year statute of limitations applies to the filing of a refund claim. That is, the refund claim generally should be filed within 3 years of the date the employer filed the erroneous social security withholding tax form with the government.

In addition to not taking out any social security tax, the employer should not have withheld any income tax either, even if part of the grant is subject to income tax. This can be corrected by having the employer reimburse the employee for any amounts incorrectly withheld during the same calendar year. After the end of the year, overwithholding of income tax is corrected only by filing the usual income tax return on which the appropriate refund is calculated.

Chapter 29

Research Expenses of College Teachers

Section 1:
Deduction for Research Expenses

College teaching is one of the most misunderstood professions that exists to-day. Most people do not understand the difference between the job of teaching elementary or high school and that of teaching college. They do not understand that many college teachers must do more than just teach their classes, consult with students, and serve on administrative committees. College teachers are expected to keep abreast of advances in their field by reading journals, attending seminars, traveling to conventions, etc. Furthermore, in many colleges and universities, faculty members are required to be scholars in their own right. They must do original research and communicate their results by publishing articles in journals, writing books, giving colloquium and seminar talks, corresponding with colleagues, discussing topics with their fellow teachers and graduate students, etc.

College teachers often incur expenses in doing their research. They may spend money on attending meetings in their specialty, subscribing to journals, buying books, buying equipment or supplies, etc.

Fortunately, the tax regulations now specifically recognize the integral part that research plays in the duties of many professors. This was not always the case. For example, in one 1962 case, the Tax Court denied a deduction to a Professor of English at a distinguished college in California. The professor had claimed a deduction for expenses incurred doing research on *Translators and Translations into English from 1475 to 1640*. The court ruled that the purpose of his research activity was "to increase his prestige as a scholar" and not to fill a requirement of his job. Since he was already tenured, he did not have to perform this research to keep his job. For this reason, his expenses were ruled nondeductible. [Davis, 38 TC 175]

However, in 1963, the IRS issued an important ruling which is excerpted below. This ruling declared that a college professor can deduct expenses he incurs in connection with his research, provided this research is expected of him in his capacity as a professor. He does not have to show that he will be fired or suffer a salary decrease if he does not do the research.

Special IRS Ruling on Professors' Research
(Revenue Ruling 63-275)

"*Advice has been requested concerning the deductibility for Federal income tax purposes of research expenses, including traveling expenses incurred by college and university professors in their capacity as educators.*

"*The facts presented are that the duties of a professor, with or without tenure, encompass not only the usual lecture and teaching duties but also the communication and advancement of knowledge through research and publication. Appointments are commonly made to college and university faculties with the expectation that the individuals will carry on independent research in their fields of competence and will put that research to use in advancing the body of learning in that area by teaching, lecturing, and writing. It is customary, therefore, for professors to engage in research for the above purposes. Where the research is undertaken with a view to scholarly publication, the expenses for such purposes can not usually be considered to have been incurred for the purpose of producing a specific income-producing asset.*

"*Based on the facts presented, it is held that research expenses, including traveling expenses properly allocable thereto, incurred by a professor for the purpose of teaching, lecturing, or writing and publishing in his area of competence, as a means of carrying out the duties expected of him in his capacity as a professor and without expectation of profit apart from salary, represent ordinary and necessary business expenses incurred in that capacity and are, therefore, deductible. The responsibility rests with each professor to show that the amounts claimed are reasonable in relation to the research performed and that the research is in his area of competence; that is, that the research directly relates to the general field in which the professor is performing services as an educator.*"

The above ruling applies to college faculty members whose duties include research. However, for others in a position where research is not part of their professional responsibilities, deductions may be disallowed. In one case, for example, a high school physics teacher was not permitted to deduct the cost of a trip taken to do research on solar eclipses. The Court held that he failed to show that this research was related to his job of teaching high school physics. [Feldman, TC Memo 1967-91]

If a professor's research leads to profit such as the writing of a book, then of course he may not take a double deduction for his expenses. That is, he cannot deduct his expenses under this chapter on Schedule A and also deduct the same expenses on Schedule C as business expenses incurred in the production of his book.

What Research Expenses Are Deductible?

(a) **Travel.** As the above ruling expressly states, you may deduct travel costs connected with your research activities. The rules governing travel expenses described in the *Travel* chapter apply here. Thus, you may deduct not only the cost of transportation, but also of lodging, laundry, and 80% of the cost of meals while away from home overnight.

> ### Example: Sabbatical to Do Research
>
> Jones is a Professor of Art History at a major university in California. He is one of the world's leading experts on the history of Albanian lithography. Jones spends his sabbatical year at Princeton and returns home after the year is over. During his absence, he rents out his California home. While at Princeton, he does research in the history of Modern Albanian lithography and uses Princeton's special collection of Albanian lithographs. He also collaborates with several other scholars in his field who are on the Princeton faculty.
>
> Jones is entitled to deduct travel expenses connected with his sabbatical at Princeton. This includes not only his transportation costs between California and New Jersey, but also such living expenses as lodging, laundry, and commuting costs while away from California, plus 80% of the cost of his meals. The same deduction and recordkeeping rules apply as for any type of travel expense. See the Travel chapter for details, including Section 4 which contains examples of teachers at a temporary position away from home.

(b) Home Office or Laboratory. If you use a home office or laboratory for research, or other professional duties, check the *Home Office* chapter. You might be able to deduct a portion of your house expenses such as rent, depreciation, utilities, etc.

(c) Books, Equipment, and Supplies.

(d) Publication Costs. You can deduct expenses incurred in getting material published. This is confirmed by a Tax Court case concerning a research associate. He had a number of articles published in scientific journals at no cost to himself. But he wrote one paper he couldn't get published, apparently because it criticized work by another prominent researcher. So the research associate published the work himself at a cost of $1,400 for 1,000 copies.

The IRS refused to allow a deduction for the $1,400 spent on publishing the paper. It argued that since research papers are customarily published at no expense to the author, the cost involved in publishing the paper himself was not an "ordinary and necessary" business expense.

However, the Court allowed the deduction, calling the IRS reasoning too narrow. It stated,

> "We are satisfied that petitioner's employer expected (although it did not require) its research associates to communicate the results of their research. To be sure, petitioner's employer anticipated that such communication would be accomplished through publication in scientific journals without cost to the author. However, the facts herein indicate, albeit not with crystal clarity, that with respect to the particular article in question, the normal channel of com-

munication was not available to petitioner because the article contained critical comment of a person who was in a position to control its acceptance for publication. Such being the case, petitioner's only viable alternative to discharge his reasonably perceived responsibility to disseminate the results of his work was to finance personally the publication thereof. In this respect, he was in a position not unlike the handicapped person who, because of his handicap, is required to incur an expense which nonhandicapped persons similarly situated would not customarily incur."

However, the Court did not allow a deduction for the cost of mailing a different paper to experts in his field because he could have had his employer pay for these mailing costs. An employee is not entitled to deduct expenses for which he could have been reimbursed by his employer. [77,199 P-H Memo TC]

(e) Miscellaneous Expenses. Be on the alert for other deductible expenses you incur in connection with your research activities such as telephone calls, clerical help, special laboratory apparel, etc.

Example

Rottman is a Professor of American History at a university in Washington, D.C. He is the author of a number of books and papers on recent American history. Rottman teaches in the mornings and spends many of his afternoons doing research at the Library of Congress and the Smithsonian Institution. He also spends time tape-recording interviews with ex-government officials in connection with his research. He has an office at home which he uses for his book writing activities.

Rottman can deduct the expenses he incurs in connection with his research activities. This may include travel expenses, home office expenses, and incidental costs for such things as photocopying, tapes, supplies, etc. He also may be able to claim deductions for his tape recorder, typewriter, home office furniture, etc. (cf. the *Travel, Home Office,* and *Depreciation* chapters).

There is another item which Rottman can deduct. He can pay his children or spouse for assisting him in his research (e.g., transcribing tapes, typing, filing etc.). This then becomes a deductible business expense as discussed in the next subsection.

Paying Your Children or Spouse for Assistance

Suppose your children assist you with your research activities. Perhaps they perform clerical work, clean laboratory equipment, help you conduct a survey, etc. If you had paid another person for these services, then you would have been able to deduct their salaries as a business expense. Under these circumstances, you can pay your children a reasonable salary and deduct this amount as a business expense. This will lower the overall tax bill since your children are in a lower (often zero) tax bracket.

Similarly, you can pay your spouse for assistance in your research activities. This will not bring the payments into a lower bracket but may still lower the overall tax due because of the effects of the IRA deduction, the child care tax credit, and the ability to set up a tax-deductible medical plan for your family. [Cf. Section 3 of the *Outside Business Activity* chapter.]

Where Do You Deduct Your Research Expenses?

Research expenses are treated the same as other business expenses. Employees report their job-related expenses on Form 2106. These expenses then become a miscellaneous deduction on Schedule A which, when combined with other miscellaneous deductions, is subject to a 2% of Adjusted Gross Income floor [cf. the *Miscellaneous Deductions* chapter]. Self-employed individuals report all their income and expenses on Schedule C.

Section 2:
Research Tax Credit

This credit generally applies when costs for research and experimentation in a given year exceed the average costs for these items in previous years. The actual computation of the credit is somewhat complicated and can be accomplished by referring to IRS Publication 572, available from your local IRS office.

What Kind of Research Expenses Qualify for the Credit?

The **research tax credit** is meant to apply to research and experimentation *"performed in a field of laboratory science (such as physics or biochemistry), engineering or technology."* The research must be undertaken for the purpose of discovering information that is technological in nature. It must relate to a new or improved function, performance, reliability, or quality; research relating to style, taste, cosmetic, or seasonal design factors does not qualify.

Specifically excluded is research in connection with literary, historical, or similar projects. Also excluded is research in the social sciences (including economics, business management, and behavioral sciences), arts, or humanities.

The credit applies to costs for the development or improvement of a pilot model, product, formula, invention, or similar property. It does not apply to the cost of management or consumer surveys, routine improvements of existing products, production planning, engineering follow-through during production, or routine data collection.

The costs of developing new or significantly improved computer software can qualify for the credit. The software should relate to research or production that is technological in nature. Software for bookkeeping, payroll, personnel management, etc. does not qualify. Also, the software should be innovative, involve significant economic risk, and not be commercially available from an outside source.

The following expenses qualify for the credit: (i) wages or self-employment earned income, (ii) supplies used in the conduct of the research, and (iii) payments for computer time.

Land or property of a character subject to the allowance for depreciation does not qualify. Also excluded are the costs of activities indirectly connected with the research such as bookkeeping, quality control, market testing, routine data collection, etc., and expenses for research conducted outside the U.S.

Who Can Claim the Research Credit?

The credit can only be claimed by the taxpayer on whose behalf the research is conducted. It cannot be claimed by an individual for research activities performed for another party, whether *"funded by any grant, contract, or otherwise."* This would apparently rule out the credit for expenses incurred by an employee conducting research in connection with his job. (But if substantial rights in the research are retained by the taxpayer, expenses qualify for the credit except to the extent the taxpayer is entitled to payment for performing the research.)

However, research expenses connected with an outside activity would qualify. The activity must be an ongoing business activity undertaken with the aim of making a profit, rather than just a hobby [cf. the *Outside Business Activity* chapter]. For example, research expenses connected with inventing a new or improved product would qualify as long as the aim is to make money by bringing the product to market. The research must be performed in connection with an existing business. Expenses paid to develop a product the sale of which would constitute a new trade or business don't qualify for the credit.

A taxpayer can also deduct the cost of qualified research expenses he contracts with another party to perform on his behalf for business purposes. In this case, 35% of the cost of the contract is deemed to be overhead not qualifying for the credit.

Chapter 30

Alternative Minimum Tax

Under our basic tax system, individuals are entitled to reduce their taxable income by using various deductions, credits, exclusions, etc. which apply. A consequence of this system is that some wealthy individuals with high incomes can wind up paying little or no income tax. In fact, newspapers have periodically run stories on the number of people with income over $1,000,000 who legally pay no tax whatever.

Congress has been sensitive to this issue. Many taxpayers have been displeased with a system under which they paid sizable chunks of their earnings in taxes while some millionaires paid nothing. To remedy this situation, Congress added an extremely complex provision, the *alternative minimum tax,* as part of the 1986 Tax Reform Act.

Most people can simply ignore this provision. It is aimed only at those with an unusually large amount of tax writeoffs or shelters. In fact, individuals with less than $30,000 in deductions, exemptions, and tax losses are automatically excused from this provision.

In more detail, if you need to check that the alternative minimum tax does not apply to you, first add up your minimum tax *preferences* and *adjustments*. These include:

1. State and local taxes deducted on Schedule A.

2. Personal exemptions.

3. Miscellaneous deductions exceeding 2% of your adjusted gross income.

4. Your medical expense deduction on Schedule A (after the 7.5% subtraction) up to a maximum of 2.5% of your adjusted gross income.

5. Your deduction on Schedule A for property given to charity to the extent it exceeds what you paid for the property.

6. Tax-exempt interest on private activity bonds issued after August 7, 1986.

7. The "bargain element" of certain incentive stock options when exercised by an employee.

8. Interest you were able to deduct in computing your regular tax solely because of the phase-in rules described in the *Interest* chapter.

9. Interest claimed on Schedule A on a mortgage, taken out after June 30, 1982 on a primary or second residence, to the extent it was not used to purchase, build, or substantially rehabilitate the residence. (For mortgages refinanced after June 30, 1982, for an amount in excess of your original mortgage, only the interest on this excess counted.)

10. Certain excess subtractions from taxable income produced by tax-shelter type investments in oil, gas, minerals, farming, real estate, etc.

11. A portion of your deduction for depreciation that is considered *excessively accelerated.*

12. Deferred amounts resulting from installment sales of either (i) real estate used in a trade or business, or (ii) rental real estate when the sales price exceeds $150,000.

You are exempt from the alternative minimum tax if the total of the above items on a joint tax return is less than $30,000. Above this amount, it's possible the alternative minimum tax will apply. However, for taxable income exceeding about $35,000, this $30,000 floor is higher.

If you are not exempt from the alternative minimum tax, you need to seek professional assistance. Essentially what happens is that the sum of your regular taxable income plus the above items is subject to a flat 21% tax, replacing the income tax computed in the regular way. (In 1991, the 21% rate will rise to 24%.)

However, tax computations and planning become quite complex when the alternative minimum tax is involved. The above is only a brief sketch of the actual rules designed to alert those with unusually large deductions, exclusions, etc. to the existence of the alternative minimum tax.

An individual may be ensnared by the alternative minimum tax because of an unusual situation in only one year. If so, the tax result may not be so bad. It may be possible to recapture the extra tax on later years' tax returns by use of a special tax credit that applies in this situation.

APPENDIX

SAMPLE TAX RETURN

The following sample tax return is intended to illustrate the full spectrum of professional deductions. It is not meant to represent a "typical" tax return.

Form **1040** Department of the Treasury—Internal Revenue Service
U.S. Individual Income Tax Return 19**90**

For the year Jan.–Dec. 31, 1990, or other tax year beginning _____, 1990, ending _____, 19__ | OMB No. 1545-0074

Label (See Instructions on page 8.)

Use IRS label. Otherwise, please print or type.

Your first name and initial: HOWARD M.   Last name: DAVIDSON

Your social security number: 111 22 3333

If a joint return, spouse's first name and initial: SUSAN J.   Last name: DAVIDSON

Spouse's social security number: 555 66 7777

Home address (number and street). (If you have a P.O. box, see page 9.): 1234 RUST AVE.   Apt. no.

City, town or post office, state, and ZIP code. (If you have a foreign address, see page 9.): PITTSBURGH, PA 15219

For Privacy Act and Paperwork Reduction Act Notice, see Instructions.

Presidential Election Campaign (See page 9.)

Do you want $1 to go to this fund? . . . . Yes ☐   **No** ☒
If joint return, does your spouse want $1 to go to this fund? ☒ Yes ☐   No

Note: Checking "Yes" will not change your tax or reduce your refund.

Filing Status

Check only one box.

1. ☐ Single. (See page 10 to find out if you can file as head of household.)
2. ☒ Married filing joint return (even if only one had income)
3. ☐ Married filing separate return. Enter spouse's social security no. above and full name here. ▶ _____
4. ☐ Head of household (with qualifying person). (See page 10.) If the qualifying person is your child but not your dependent, enter this child's name here. ▶ _____
5. ☐ Qualifying widow(er) with dependent child (year spouse died ▶ 19__). (See page 10.)

Exemptions (See Instructions on page 10.)

6a ☒ **Yourself** If your parent (or someone else) can claim you as a dependent on his or her tax return, do not check box 6a. But be sure to check the box on line 33b on page 2
b ☒ **Spouse**

No. of boxes checked on 6a and 6b: **2**

c **Dependents:**

(1) Name (first, initial, and last name)	(2) Check if under age 2	(3) If age 2 or older, dependent's social security number	(4) Dependent's relationship to you	(5) No. of months lived in your home in 1990
CARL A. DAVIDSON	X		SON	12
JENNY B. DAVIDSON		123 45 6789	DAUGHTER	12

If more than 6 dependents, see Instructions on page 11.

No. of your children on 6c who:
• lived with you **2**
• didn't live with you due to divorce or separation (see page 11)

No. of other dependents on 6c

d If your child didn't live with you but is claimed as your dependent under a pre-1985 agreement, check here ▶ ☐
e Total number of exemptions claimed

Add numbers entered on lines above ▶ **4**

Income

Attach Copy B of your Forms W-2, W-2G, and W-2P here.

If you do not have a W-2, see page 8.

Attach check or money order on top of any Forms W-2, W-2G, or W-2P.

7	Wages, salaries, tips, etc. (attach Form(s) W-2)	7	72170
8a	**Taxable** interest income (also attach Schedule B if over $400)	8a	948
b	**Tax-exempt** interest income (see page 13). DON'T include on line 8a 8b 4,822		
9	Dividend income (also attach Schedule B if over $400)	9	681
10	Taxable refunds of state and local income taxes, if any, from worksheet on page 14	10	514
11	Alimony received	11	
12	Business income or (loss) (attach Schedule C)	12	5013
13	Capital gain or (loss) (attach Schedule D)	13	(1,856)
14	Capital gain distributions not reported on line 13 (see page 14)	14	
15	Other gains or (losses) (attach Form 4797)	15	
16a	Total IRA distributions 16a	16b Taxable amount (see page 14)	16b
17a	Total pensions and annuities 17a	17b Taxable amount (see page 14)	17b
18	Rents, royalties, partnerships, estates, trusts, etc. (attach Schedule E)	18	
19	Farm income or (loss) (attach Schedule F)	19	
20	Unemployment compensation (insurance) (see page 16)	20	
21a	Social security benefits . 21a	21b Taxable amount (see page 16)	21b
22	Other income (list type and amount—see page 16)	22	
23	Add the amounts shown in the far right column for lines 7 through 22. This is your **total income** ▶	23	77,470

Adjustments to Income

(See Instructions on page 17.)

24a	Your IRA deduction, from applicable worksheet on page 17 or 18 24a		
b	Spouse's IRA deduction, from applicable worksheet on page 17 or 18 24b		
25	One-half of self-employment tax (see page 18) . . 25 383		
26	Self-employed health insurance deduction, from worksheet on page 18 26		
27	Keogh retirement plan and self-employed SEP deduction *D.B.* 27 5,013		
28	Penalty on early withdrawal of savings 28		
29	Alimony paid. Recipient's SSN ▶ _____ 29		
30	Add lines 24a through 29. These are your **total adjustments** ▶	30	5,396

Adjusted Gross Income

31 Subtract line 30 from line 23. This is your **adjusted gross income**. If this amount is less than $20,264 and a child lived with you, see page 23 to find out if you can claim the "Earned Income Credit" on line 57 . . . . ▶ | 31 | 72,074

Form 1040 (1990)   Page **2**

Tax Compu-tation	32	Amount from line 31 (adjusted gross income)	32	72,074

Tax Compu-tation

If you want IRS to figure your tax, see Instructions on page 19.

33a Check if: ☐ **You** were 65 or older ☐ Blind; ☐ **Spouse** was 65 or older ☐ Blind.
Add the number of boxes checked above and enter the total here . . . . . ▶ 33a ☐

b If your parent (or someone else) can claim you as a dependent, check here . . . ▶ 33b ☐

c If you are married filing a separate return and your spouse itemizes deductions, or you are a dual-status alien, see page 19 and check here . . . . ▶ 33c ☐

34 Enter the larger of:
• Your **standard deduction** (from the chart (or worksheet) on page 20 that applies to you), **OR**
• Your **itemized deductions** (from Schedule A, line 27).
If you itemize, attach Schedule A and check here. . ▶ ☒

34		28,194
35	Subtract line 34 from line 32	43,880
36	Multiply $2,050 by the total number of exemptions claimed on line 6e	8,200
37	**Taxable income.** Subtract line 36 from line 35. (If line 36 is more than line 35, enter -0-.) . . .	35,680
38	Enter tax. Check if from: a ☒ Tax Table, b ☐ Tax Rate Schedules, or c ☐ Form 8615 (see page 21) (If any is from Form(s) 8814, enter that amount here ▶ d _____ .) . . .	5,771
39	Additional taxes (see page 21). Check if from: a ☐ Form 4970 b ☐ Form 4972 . . .	
40	Add lines 38 and 39 . . . . ▶	5,771

Credits

(See Instructions on page 21.)

41	Credit for child and dependent care expenses (attach Form 2441)	41	853
42	Credit for the elderly or the disabled (attach Schedule R) . . .	42	
43	Foreign tax credit (attach Form 1116)	43	
44	General business credit. Check if from: a ☐ Form 3800 or b ☐ Form (specify) _____ .	44	
45	Credit for prior year minimum tax (attach Form 8801) . . .	45	

46	Add lines 41 through 45	853
47	Subtract line 46 from line 40 (If line 46 is more than line 40, enter -0-.) . . . . ▶	4,918

Other Taxes

48	Self-employment tax (attach Schedule SE)	84
49	Alternative minimum tax (attach Form 6251)	
50	Recapture taxes (see page 22). Check if from: a ☐ Form 4255 b ☐ Form 8611 . .	
51	Social security tax on tip income not reported to employer (attach Form 4137) . .	
52	Tax on an IRA or a qualified retirement plan (attach Form 5329)	
53	Advance earned income credit payments from Form W-2	
54	Add lines 47 through 53. This is your **total tax** . . . . ▶	5,002

Payments

Attach Forms W-2, W-2G, and W-2P to front

55	Federal income tax withheld (if any is from Form(s) 1099, check ▶ ☐)	55	5,194
56	1990 estimated tax payments and amount applied from 1989 return	56	
57	**Earned income credit** (see page 23)	57	
58	Amount paid with Form 4868 (extension request)	58	
59	Excess social security tax and RRTA tax withheld (see page 24)	59	
60	Credit for Federal tax on fuels (attach Form 4136) . . .	60	
61	Regulated investment company credit (attach Form 2439) . .	61	

62	Add lines 55 through 61. These are your **total payments** . . . . ▶	5,194

Refund or Amount You Owe

63	If line 62 is more than line 54, enter amount **OVERPAID** . . . . ▶	192
64	Amount of line 63 to be **REFUNDED TO YOU** . . . . ▶	192
65	Amount of line 63 to be **APPLIED TO YOUR 1991 ESTIMATED TAX** ▶	65
66	If line 54 is more than line 62, enter **AMOUNT YOU OWE.** Attach check or money order for full amount payable to "Internal Revenue Service." Write your name, address, social security number, daytime phone number, and "1990 Form 1040" on it.	66
67	Estimated tax penalty (see page 25)	67

Sign Here

Keep a copy of this return for your records.

Under penalties of perjury, I declare that I have examined this return and accompanying schedules and statements, and to the best of my knowledge and belief, they are true, correct, and complete. Declaration of preparer (other than taxpayer) is based on all information of which preparer has any knowledge.

Your signature	*Howard M. Davidson*	Date 4/10/91	Your occupation COLLEGE TEACHER
Spouse's signature (if joint return, BOTH must sign)	*Susan J. Davidson*	Date 4/10/91	Spouse's occupation THERAPIST

Paid Preparer's Use Only

Preparer's signature ▶	Date	Check if self-employed ☐	Preparer's social security no.
Firm's name (or yours if self-employed) and address ▶		E.I. No.
		ZIP code

500

Schedule A—Itemized Deductions

(Schedule B is on back)

▶ Attach to Form 1040. ▶ See Instructions for Schedules A and B (Form 1040).

OMB No. 1545-0074

1990

Attachment
Sequence No. **07**

Name(s) shown on Form 1040

HOWARD M. & SUSAN J. DAVIDSON

Your social security number

111 22 3333

Medical and Dental Expenses		Caution: *Do not include expenses reimbursed or paid by others.*			
	1	Medical and dental expenses. (See page 27 of the Instructions.)	1	6283	
	2	Enter amount from Form 1040, line 32 .	2	72,074	
	3	Multiply the amount on line 2 by 7.5% (.075). Enter the result . .	3	5406	
	4	Subtract line 3 from line 1. Enter the result. If less than zero, enter -0- ▶	4		877
Taxes You Paid	5	State and local income taxes	5	3107	
	6	Real estate taxes	6	938	
(See Instructions on page 27.)	7	Other taxes. (List—include personal property taxes.) ▶	7		
	8	Add the amounts on lines 5 through 7. Enter the total . . . . ▶	8		4045
Interest You Paid	9a	Deductible home mortgage interest paid to financial institutions and reported to you on Form 1098. Report deductible points on line 10 . .	9a	6333	
(See Instructions on page 27.)	b	Other deductible home mortgage interest. (If paid to an individual, show that person's name and address.) ▶			

		---	9b		
	10	Deductible points. (See Instructions for special rules.) . . .	10		
	11	Deductible investment interest (attach Form 4952 if required). (See page 28.)	11	428	
	12a	Personal interest you paid. (See page 28.) 12a 1256			
	b	Multiply the amount on line 12a by 10% (.10). Enter the result .	12b	126	
	13	Add the amounts on lines 9a through 11, and 12b. Enter the total . . . . ▶	13		6887
Gifts to Charity		Caution: *If you made a charitable contribution and received a benefit in return, see page 29 of the Instructions.*			
(See Instructions on page 29.)	14	Contributions by cash or check	14	2813	
	15	Other than cash or check. (You **MUST** attach Form 8283 if over $500.)	15	280	
	16	Carryover from prior year	16		
	17	Add the amounts on lines 14 through 16. Enter the total . . . . . . ▶	17		3093
Casualty and Theft Losses	18	Casualty or theft loss(es) (attach Form 4684). (See page 29 of the Instructions.) . ▶	18		
Moving Expenses	19	Moving expenses (attach Form 3903 or 3903F). (See page 30 of the Instructions.). ▶	19		3575
Job Expenses and Most Other Miscellaneous Deductions	20	Unreimbursed employee expenses—job travel, union dues, job education, etc. (You **MUST** attach Form 2106 if required. See Instructions.) ▶......................	20	10,669	
(See Instructions on page 30 for expenses to deduct here.)	21	Other expenses (investment, tax preparation, safe deposit box, etc.). List type and amount ▶ SAFE DEPOSIT BOX 53 TAX GUIDE 29, INVESTMENT PUBLICATIONS 290 TRAVEL TO BROKER 83, POSTAGE 24, IRA FEE 10	21	489	
	22	Add the amounts on lines 20 and 21. Enter the total . . .	22	11,158	
	23	Enter amount from Form 1040, line 32 . . 23 72,074			
	24	Multiply the amount on line 23 by 2% (.02). Enter the result . .	24	1,441	
	25	Subtract line 24 from line 22. Enter the result. If less than zero, enter -0-. . . . ▶	25		9,717
Other Miscellaneous Deductions	26	Other (from list on page 30 of Instructions). List type and amount ▶			

		--- ▶	26		
Total Itemized Deductions	27	Add the amounts on lines 4, 8, 13, 17, 18, 19, 25, and 26. Enter the total here. Then enter on Form 1040, line 34, the **LARGER** of this total or your standard deduction from page 20 of the Instructions . . . . ▶	27		28,194

For Paperwork Reduction Act Notice, see Form 1040 Instructions.

Schedule A (Form 1040) 1990

501

Schedules A&B (Form 1040) 1990

OMB No. 1545-0074   Page **2**

Name(s) shown on Form 1040. (Do not enter name and social security number if shown on other side.)

Your social security number

Schedule B—Interest and Dividend Income

Attachment
Sequence No. **08**

Part I
Interest
Income

(See
Instructions
on pages 13
and 30.)

If you received more than $400 in taxable interest income, or you are claiming the exclusion of interest from series EE U.S. savings bonds issued after 1989 (see page 31), you must complete Part I. List ALL interest received in Part I. If you received more than $400 in taxable interest income, you must also complete Part III. If you received, as a nominee, interest that actually belongs to another person, or you received or paid accrued interest on securities transferred between interest payment dates, see page 31.

Interest Income		Amount	
1 Interest income. (List name of payer—if any interest income is from seller-financed mortgages, see Instructions and list that interest first.) ▶			
Note: If you received a Form 1099-INT, Form 1099-OID, or substitute statement, from a brokerage firm, list the firm's name as the payer and enter the total interest shown on that form.	*U.S. TREASURY NOTE*		*240*
	CITIZENS S. & L.		*46*
	FIDELITY BANK		*124*
	CREDIT UNION		*218*
	EXXON BONDS	1	*320*

2 Add the amounts on line 1. Enter the total		2	*948*
3 Enter the excludable savings bond interest, if any, from Form 8815, line 14. Attach Form 8815 to Form 1040		3	
4 Subtract line 3 from line 2. Enter the result here and on Form 1040, line 8a . . ▶		4	*948*

Part II
Dividend
Income

(See
Instructions on
pages 13 and
31.)

If you received more than $400 in gross dividends and/or other distributions on stock, you must complete Parts II and III. If you received, as a nominee, dividends that actually belong to another person, see page 31.

Dividend Income		Amount	
5 Dividend income. (List name of payer—include on this line capital gain distributions, nontaxable distributions, etc.) ▶			
	GENERAL MOTORS		*450*
Note: If you received a Form 1099-DIV, or substitute statement, from a brokerage firm, list the firm's name as the payer and enter the total dividends shown on that form.	*VANGUARD MONEY MARKET FUND*		*231*
		5	

6 Add the amounts on line 5. Enter the total		6	*681*
7 Capital gain distributions. Enter here and on Schedule D* . .	7		
8 Nontaxable distributions. (See the Inst. for Form 1040, line 9.) .	8		
9 Add the amounts on lines 7 and 8. Enter the total		9	
10 Subtract line 9 from line 6. Enter the result here and on Form 1040, line 9 . . . ▶		10	*681*

* If you received capital gain distributions but do not need Schedule D to report any other gains or losses, see the Instructions for Form 1040, lines 13 and 14.

Part III
Foreign
Accounts
and
Foreign
Trusts

(See
Instructions
on page 31.)

If you received more than $400 of interest or dividends, OR if you had a foreign account or were a grantor of, or a transferor to, a foreign trust, you must answer both questions in Part III.

		Yes	No
11a At any time during 1990, did you have an interest in or a signature or other authority over a financial account in a foreign country (such as a bank account, securities account, or other financial account)? (See page 31 of the Instructions for exceptions and filing requirements for Form TD F 90-22.1.)			X
b If "Yes," enter the name of the foreign country ▶			
12 Were you the grantor of, or transferor to, a foreign trust that existed during 1990, whether or not you have any beneficial interest in it? If "Yes," you may have to file Form 3520, 3520-A, or 926			X

For Paperwork Reduction Act Notice, see Form 1040 Instructions.

Schedule B (Form 1040) 1990

502

SCHEDULE C
(Form 1040)

Department of the Treasury
Internal Revenue Service

Profit or Loss From Business
(Sole Proprietorship)
Partnerships, Joint Ventures, Etc., Must File Form 1065.
▶ Attach to Form 1040 or Form 1041. ▶ See Instructions for Schedule C (Form 1040).

OMB No. 1545-0074

1990

Attachment
Sequence No. **09**

Name of proprietor
HOWARD M. DAVIDSON

Social security number (SSN)
111 22 3333

A Principal business or profession, including product or service (see Instructions)
CONSULTING

B Enter principal business code
(from page 2) ▶

C Business name and address ▶ ....
(include suite or room no.)

D Employer ID number (Not SSN)

E Accounting method: (1) ☐ Cash (2) ☐ Accrual (3) ☐ Other (specify) ▶ ....

F Method(s) used to
value closing inventory: (1) ☐ Cost (2) ☐ Lower of cost (3) ☐ Other (attach (4) ☒ Does not apply (if
or market explanation) checked, go to line H)

	Yes	No
G Was there any change in determining quantities, costs, or valuations between opening and closing inventory? (If "Yes," attach explanation.)		X
H Are you deducting expenses for business use of your home? (If "Yes," see Instructions for limitations.)		X
I Did you "materially participate" in the operation of this business during 1990? (If "No," see Instructions for limitations on losses.)	X	
J If this is the first Schedule C filed for this business, check here ▶ ☐		

Part I Income

1 Gross receipts or sales. *Caution: If this income was reported to you on Form W-2 and the "Statutory employee" box on that form was checked, see the Instructions and check here* ▶ ☐	1	15,257
2 Returns and allowances	2	
3 Subtract line 2 from line 1. Enter the result here	3	15,257
4 Cost of goods sold (from line 38 on page 2)	4	
5 Subtract line 4 from line 3 and enter the **gross profit** here	5	15,257
6 Other income, including Federal and state gasoline or fuel tax credit or refund (see Instructions)	6	
7 Add lines 5 and 6. This is your **gross income** ▶	7	15,257

Part II Expenses

8 Advertising	8	470	**21** Repairs and maintenance	21	
9 Bad debts from sales or services (see Instructions)	9		**22** Supplies (not included in Part III)	22	631
10 Car and truck expenses (attach **Form 4562**)	10		**23** Taxes and licenses	23	1246
11 Commissions and fees	11	620	**24** Travel, meals, and entertainment:		
12 Depletion	12		**a** Travel	24a	292
13 Depreciation and section 179 expense deduction (not included in Part III) (see Instructions)	13		**b** Meals and entertainment 108		
14 Employee benefit programs (other than on line 19)	14		**c** Enter 20% of line 24b subject to limitations (see Instructions) 22		
15 Insurance (other than health)	15	962	**d** Subtract line 24c from line 24b	24d	86
16 Interest:			**25** Utilities	25	
a Mortgage (paid to banks, etc.)	16a		**26** Wages (less jobs credit)	26	
b Other	16b	1116	**27a** Other expenses (list type and amount):		
17 Legal and professional services	17	600	POSTAGE: 42		
18 Office expense	18	3359	SECRETARIAL: 228		
19 Pension and profit-sharing plans	19		XEROXING: 61		
20 Rent or lease (see Instructions):			TELEPHONE: 348		
a Vehicles, machinery, and equip.	20a		DELIVERY SERVICE 183		
b Other business property	20b		**27b** Total other expenses	27b	862

28 Add amounts in columns for lines 8 through 27b. These are your **total expenses** ▶	28	10,244
29 Net profit or (loss). Subtract line 28 from line 7. If a profit, enter here and on Form 1040, line 12. Also enter the net profit on Schedule SE, line 2 (statutory employees, see Instructions). If a loss, you MUST go on to line 30 (fiduciaries, see Instructions).	29	5,013

30 If you have a loss, you MUST check the box that describes your investment in this activity (see Instructions).
If you checked 30a, enter the loss on Form 1040, line 12, and Schedule SE, line 2 (statutory employees, see Instructions). If you checked 30b, you MUST attach **Form 6198**.

30a ☐ All investment is at risk.
30b ☐ Some investment is not at risk.

For Paperwork Reduction Act Notice, see Form 1040 Instructions.

Schedule C (Form 1040) 1990

SCHEDULE SE
(Form 1040)

Department of the Treasury
Internal Revenue Service

Social Security Self-Employment Tax

▶ See Instructions for Schedule SE (Form 1040).

▶ Attach to Form 1040.

OMB No. 1545-0074

1990

Attachment
Sequence No. **17**

Name of person with **self-employment** income (as shown on Form 1040)	Social security number of person with **self-employment** income ▶
HOWARD M. DAVIDSON	111 22 3333

Who Must File Schedule SE

You must file Schedule SE if:

● Your net earnings from self-employment were $400 or more; **OR**

● You were an employee of an electing church or church-controlled organization that paid you wages (church employee income) of $100 or more;

AND

● Your wages (subject to social security or railroad retirement tax) were less than $51,300.

Exception: If your only self-employment income was from earnings as a minister, member of a religious order, or Christian Science practitioner, AND you filed **Form 4361** and received IRS approval not to be taxed on those earnings, DO NOT file Schedule SE. Instead, write "Exempt–Form 4361" on Form 1040, line 48.

For more information about Schedule SE, see the Instructions.

Note: *Most people can use the short Schedule SE on this page. But, you may have to use the longer Schedule SE on the back.*

Who MUST Use the Long Schedule SE (Section B)

You must use Section B if ANY of the following apply:

● You elect the "optional method" to figure your self-employment tax (see Section B, Part II, and the Instructions);

● You are a minister, member of a religious order, or Christian Science practitioner and you received IRS approval (from **Form 4361**) not to be taxed on your earnings from these sources, but you owe self-employment tax on other earnings;

● You had church employee income of $100 or more that was reported to you on Form W-2;

● You had tip income that is subject to social security tax, but you did not report those tips to your employer; OR

● You were a government employee with wages subject ONLY to the 1.45% Medicare part of the social security tax (Medicare qualified government wages) AND the total of **all** of your wages (subject to social security, railroad retirement, or the 1.45% Medicare tax) plus **all** your earnings subject to self-employment tax is **more** than $51,300.

Section A—Short Schedule SE (Read above to see if you must use the long Schedule SE on the back (Section B).)

1	Net farm profit or (loss) from Schedule F (Form 1040), line 36, and farm partnerships, Schedule K-1 (Form 1065), line 15a	1	
2	Net profit or (loss) from Schedule C (Form 1040), line 29, and Schedule K-1 (Form 1065), line 15a (other than farming). See Instructions for other income to report.	2	*5013*
3	Combine lines 1 and 2. Enter the result	3	*5013*
4	Multiply line 3 by .9235. Enter the result. If the result is less than $400, **do not** file this schedule; you do not owe self-employment tax. . . . . ▶	4	*4630*
5	Maximum amount of combined wages and self-employment earnings subject to social security or railroad retirement (tier 1) tax for 1990	5	$51,300 00
6	Total social security wages and tips (from Form(s) W-2) and railroad retirement compensation (tier 1). **Do not** include Medicare qualified government wages on this line	6	*50,750*
7	Subtract line 6 from line 5. Enter the result. If the result is zero or less, **do not** file this schedule; you **do** not owe self-employment tax. . . . . ▶	7	*550*
8	Enter the **smaller** of line 4 or line 7	8	*550*
9	Rate of tax	9	×.153
10	**Self-employment tax.** If line 8 is $51,300, enter $7,848.90. Otherwise, multiply the amount on line 8 by the decimal amount on line 9 and enter the result. Also enter this amount on Form 1040, line 48. **Note:** *Also enter one-half of this amount on Form 1040, line 25.*	10	*84*

For Paperwork Reduction Act Notice, see Form 1040 Instructions.

Schedule SE (Form 1040) 1990

504

SCHEDULE D
(Form 1040)

Department of the Treasury
Internal Revenue Service

Capital Gains and Losses

(And Reconciliation of Forms 1099-B for Bartering Transactions)
▶ Attach to Form 1040. ▶ See Instructions for Schedule D (Form 1040).
▶ For more space to list transactions for lines 2a and 9a, get Schedule D-1 (Form 1040).

OMB No. 1545-0074

1990

Attachment
Sequence No. **12A**

Name(s) shown on Form 1040

HOWARD M. & SUSAN J. DAVIDSON

Your social security number

111 : 22 : 3333

1 Enter the total sales of stocks, bonds, other securities, and real estate transactions reported to you for 1990 on Forms 1099-B and 1099-S (or on substitute statements). If this total is not the same as the total of lines 2c and 9c, column (d), attach a statement explaining the difference. (Do not include on this line amounts from Form 1099-S if you reported them on another form or schedule.) **See Instructions for line 1** . . . . | 1 | 34,031

Part I Short-Term Capital Gains and Losses—Assets Held One Year or Less

(a) Description of property (Example, 100 shares 7% preferred of "Z" Co.)	(b) Date acquired (Mo., day, yr.)	(c) Date sold (Mo., day, yr.)	(d) Sales price (see Instructions)	(e) Cost or other basis (see Instructions)	(f) LOSS If (e) is more than (d), subtract (d) from (e)	(g) GAIN If (d) is more than (e), subtract (e) from (d)

2a Stocks, Bonds, Other Securities, and Real Estate. Include Form 1099-B and 1099-S Transactions. See Instructions.

(a)	(b)	(c)	(d)	(e)	(f)	(g)
100 SH. ABC	11/7/89	9/1/90	3473	8612	5139	
300 SH. DEF	2/4/90	6/14/90	7824	7311		513

2b Amounts from Schedule D-1, line 2b (attach Schedule D-1) .

2c Total of All Sales Price Amounts.
Add column (d) of lines 2a and 2b . . . . ▶ 2c | 11297

2d Other Transactions (Do NOT include real estate transactions from Forms 1099-S. Report them on line 2a.)

3 Short-term gain from sale or exchange of your home from Form 2119, line 10 or 14c . | 3
4 Short-term gain from installment sales from Form 6252, line 22 or 30 . . . . | 4
5 Net short-term gain or (loss) from partnerships, S corporations, and fiduciaries. . | 5
6 Short-term capital loss carryover from 1989 Schedule D, line 29 . . . . . . | 6
7 Add lines 2a, 2b, 2d, and 3 through 6, in columns (f) and (g) . . . . | 7 (5139) | 513
8 **Net short-term gain or (loss).** Combine columns (f) and (g) of line 7 . . . . | 8 (4626)

Part II Long-Term Capital Gains and Losses—Assets Held More Than One Year

9a Stocks, Bonds, Other Securities, and Real Estate. Include Form 1099-B and 1099-S Transactions. See Instructions.

(a)	(b)	(c)	(d)	(e)	(f)	(g)
100 SH. XYZ	4/3/86	6/13/90	3121	2410		711
200 SH. MNL	3/8/89	3/10/90	6174	6786	612	
LAND	12/6/87	1/14/90	13,439	10,768		2671

9b Amounts from Schedule D-1, line 9b (attach Schedule D-1) .

9c Total of All Sales Price Amounts.
Add column (d) of lines 9a and 9b . . . ▶ 9c | 22734

9d Other Transactions (Do NOT include real estate transactions from Forms 1099-S. Report them on line 9a.)

10 Long-term gain from sale or exchange of your home from Form 2119, line 10 or 14c . | 10
11 Long-term gain from installment sales from Form 6252, line 22 or 30. . . . . | 11
12 Net long-term gain or (loss) from partnerships, S corporations, and fiduciaries . . | 12
13 Capital gain distributions . . . . | 13
14 Gain from Form 4797, line 7 or 9 . . . . | 14
15 Long-term capital loss carryover from 1989 Schedule D, line 36 . . . . . . | 15
16 Add lines 9a, 9b, 9d, and 10 through 15, in columns (f) and (g). . . . . . . | 16 (612) | 3382
17 **Net long-term gain or (loss).** Combine columns (f) and (g) of line 16. . . . . | 17 | 2770

For Paperwork Reduction Act Notice, see Form 1040 Instructions.

Schedule D (Form 1040) 1990

Schedule D (Form 1040) 1990   Attachment Sequence No. 12A   Page 2

Name(s) shown on Form 1040. (Do not enter name and social security number if shown on other side.)   Your social security number

Part III   Summary of Parts I and II

18	Combine lines 8 and 17, and enter the net gain or (loss) here. If the result is a gain, **stop here** and also enter the gain on Form 1040, line 13	18	(1856)
19	If line 18 is a (loss), enter here and as a (loss) on Form 1040, line 13, the **smaller** of:		
a	The (loss) on line 18; **or**		
b	($3,000) or, if married filing a separate return, ($1,500)	19	(1856)

Note: *When figuring whether line 19a or 19b is* **smaller**, *treat both numbers as if they were positive.*

Go on to Part IV if the loss on line 18 is more than $3,000 ($1,500, if married filing a separate return), OR if taxable income on Form 1040, line 37, is zero.

Part IV   Capital Loss Carryovers from 1990 to 1991

Section A.—Carryover Limit

20	Enter taxable income from Form 1040, line 37. **(If Form 1040, line 37 is zero, see Instructions for amount to enter.)**	20	
	Note: *For lines 21 through 36, enter all amounts as positive numbers.*		
21	Enter the loss on line 19	21	
22	Enter the amount on Form 1040, line 36	22	
23	Combine lines 20, 21, and 22. If zero or less, enter -0-	23	
24	**Carryover Limit.** Enter the **smaller** of line 21 or line 23	24	

Section B.—Short-Term Capital Loss Carryover to 1991
(Complete this section only if there is a loss on both line 8 and line 19. Otherwise, go on to Section C.)

25	Enter the loss on line 8	25		
26	Enter the gain, if any, on line 17	26			
27	Enter the amount on line 24	27			
28	Add lines 26 and 27	28		
29	**Short-term capital loss carryover to 1991.** Subtract line 28 from line 25. If zero or less, enter -0- . .	29		

Section C.—Long-Term Capital Loss Carryover to 1991
(Complete this section only if there is a loss on both line 17 and line 19.)

30	Enter the loss on line 17	30		
31	Enter the gain, if any, on line 8	31		
32	Enter the amount on line 24	32			
33	Enter the amount, if any, on line 25	33			
34	Subtract line 33 from line 32. If zero or less, enter -0-	34		
35	Add lines 31 and 34	35		
36	**Long-term capital loss carryover to 1991.** Subtract line 35 from line 30. If zero or less, enter -0- . .	36		

Part V   Election Not to Use the Installment Method (Complete this part only if you elect out of the installment method and report a note or other obligation at less than full face value.)

37	Check here if you elect out of the installment method . . . . ▶ ☐	
38	Enter the face amount of the note or other obligation . . . . ▶	
39	Enter the percentage of valuation of the note or other obligation . . . . ▶	

Part VI   Reconciliation of Forms 1099-B for Bartering Transactions
(Complete this part if you received one or more Forms 1099-B or substitute statements reporting bartering income.)

Amount of bartering income from Form 1099-B or substitute statement reported on form or schedule

40	Form 1040, line 22	40	
41	Schedule C (Form 1040)	41	
42	Schedule D (Form 1040)	42	
43	Schedule E (Form 1040)	43	
44	Schedule F (Form 1040)	44	
45	Other form or schedule (identify) (if nontaxable, indicate reason—attach additional sheets if necessary): ------------------------------ ------------------------------ ------------------------------	45	
46	Total (add lines 40 through 45)	46	

Note: *The amount on line 46 should be the same as the total bartering income on all Forms 1099-B and substitute statements received for bartering transactions.*

506

Form **2106**	**Employee Business Expenses**	OMB No. 1545-0139
Department of the Treasury Internal Revenue Service	▶ See separate Instructions. ▶ Attach to Form 1040.	1990 Attachment Sequence No. **54**

Your name HOWARD M. DAVIDSON	Social security number 111 22 3333	Occupation in which expenses were incurred COLLEGE TEACHER

Part I Employee Business Expenses and Reimbursements

STEP 1   Enter Your Expenses

		Column A Other Than Meals and Entertainment	Column B Meals and Entertainment
1 Vehicle expense from line 22 or line 29	1	491	
2 Parking fees, tolls, and local transportation, including train, bus, etc. . .	2	261	
3 Travel expense while away from home overnight, including lodging, airplane, car rental, etc. **Do not** include meals and entertainment . . .	3	3465	
4 Business expenses not included on lines 1 through 3. **Do not** include meals and entertainment	4	5319	
5 Meals and entertainment expenses. (See the separate Instructions.) . .	5		1416
6 Add lines 1 through 5 and enter the **total expenses** here	6	9536	1416

Note: If you were not reimbursed for any expenses in Step 1, skip line 7 and enter the amount from line 6 on line 8.

STEP 2   Enter Amounts Your Employer Gave You For Expenses Listed In STEP 1

7 Enter amounts your employer gave you that were **not** reported to you in Box 10 of Form W-2. Include any amount reported under code "L" in Box 17 of your Form W-2. (See Instructions.)	7		

STEP 3   Figure Expenses To Deduct on Schedule A (Form 1040)

8 Subtract line 7 from line 6	8	9536	1416

Note: If **both columns** of line 8 are zero, **stop here.** If column A is less than zero, report the amount as income and enter -0- on line 10, column A. See the separate Instructions for how to report.

9 Enter 20% (.20) of line 8, Column B	9		283
10 Subtract line 9 from line 8	10	9536	1133

11 Add the amounts on line 10 of both columns and enter the total here. **Also enter the total on Schedule A (Form 1040), line 20.** (Qualified performing artists and individuals with disabilities, see the separate Instructions for special rules on where to enter the total.) . . . . ▶ | 11 | 10 669

For Paperwork Reduction Act Notice, see the separate Instructions.   Form **2106** (1990)

Part II Vehicle Expenses (See Instructions to find out which sections to complete.)

Section A.—General Information		(a) Vehicle 1	(b) Vehicle 2
12	Enter the date vehicle was placed in service **12**	6 /13/ 88	/ /
13	Total mileage vehicle was used during 1990 . . . . **13**	17,261 miles	miles
14	Miles included on line 13 that vehicle was used for business . . **14**	1,888 miles	miles
15	Percent of business use (divide line 14 by line 13) **15**	11 %	%
16	Average daily round trip commuting distance **16**	23 miles	miles
17	Miles included on line 13 that vehicle was used for commuting . **17**	5,750 miles	miles
18	Other personal mileage (add lines 14 and 17 and subtract the total from line 13). **18**	9,623 miles	miles

19 Do you (or your spouse) have another vehicle available for personal purposes? . . . . ☒ Yes ☐ No

20 If your employer provided you with a vehicle, is personal use during off duty hours permitted? . . ☐ Yes ☐ No ☒ Not applicable

21a Do you have evidence to support your deduction? ☒ Yes ☐ No. **21b** If "Yes," is the evidence written? ☒ Yes ☐ No

Section B.—Standard Mileage Rate (Use this section only if you own the vehicle.)

22	Multiply line 14 by 26¢ (.26). Enter the result here and on line 1. (Rural mail carriers, see the separate Instructions.). **22**		491

Section C.—Actual Expenses		(a) Vehicle 1		(b) Vehicle 2	
23	Gasoline, oil, repairs, vehicle insurance, etc.. . . . . . . **23**				
24a	Vehicle rentals. **24a**				
b	Inclusion amount **24b**				
c	Subtract line 24b from line 24a . **24c**				
25	Value of employer-provided vehicle (applies only if 100% annual lease value was included on Form W-2. See Instructions.) . **25**				
26	Add lines 23, 24c, and 25 . . . **26**				
27	Multiply line 26 by the percentage on line 15 . . . . **27**				
28	Enter amount from line 38 below . **28**				
29	Add lines 27 and 28. Enter total here and on line 1. . . . . . . **29**				

Section D.—Depreciation of Vehicles (Use this section only if you own the vehicle.)		(a) Vehicle 1		(b) Vehicle 2	
30	Enter cost or other basis. (See Instructions.) **30**				
31	Enter amount of Section 179 deduction. (See Instructions.) . . **31**				
32	Multiply line 30 by line 15. (See Instructions if you elected the Section 179 deduction.) . . . **32**				
33	Enter depreciation method and percentage. (See Instructions.) . **33**				
34	Multiply line 32 by the percentage on line 33. (See Instructions.) . . **34**				
35	Add lines 31 and 34 . . . . . **35**				
36	Enter the limitation amount from the table in the line 36 instructions. **36**				
37	Multiply line 36 by the percentage on line 15. . . . . **37**				
38	Enter the **smaller** of line 35 or line 37. Also enter it on line 28 above. **38**				

508

Form **2441**

Department of the Treasury
Internal Revenue Service

Child and Dependent Care Expenses

▶ Attach to Form 1040.

▶ See separate Instructions.

OMB No. 1545-0068

1990

Attachment
Sequence No. **21**

Name(s) shown on Form 1040

HOWARD M. & SUSAN J. DAVIDSON

Your social security number

III 22 3333

- If you are claiming the child and dependent care credit, complete Parts I and II below. But if you received employer-provided dependent care benefits, first complete Part III on the back.
- If you are not claiming the credit but you received employer-provided dependent care benefits, only complete Part I, below, and Part III on the back.

Part I Persons or Organizations Who Provided the Care—You must complete this part. (See the Instructions. If you need more space, attach a statement.)

1	(a) Name	(b) Address (number, street, city, state, and ZIP code)	(c) Identifying number (SSN or EIN)	(d) Amount paid (see Instructions)
	TOTS DAY CARE	4567 W. IRON AVE. PITTSBURGH, PA 15219	987654321	4263

2 Add the amounts in column (d) of line 1 and enter the total. . . . . **2** | 4,263

Note: *If you paid cash wages of $50 or more in a calendar quarter to an individual for services performed in your home, you must file an employment tax return. Get Form 942 for details.*

Part II Credit for Child and Dependent Care Expenses

3 Enter the number of qualifying persons who were cared for in 1990. (See the Instructions for the definition of qualifying persons.) **Caution:** *To qualify, the person(s) must have shared the same home with you in 1990* . . . . ▶ | **3** | 2

4 Enter the amount of **qualified** expenses you incurred and actually paid in 1990. See the Instructions to find out which expenses qualify. **Caution:** *If you completed Part III on page 2, do not include on this line any excluded benefits shown on line 25* . . . . **4** | 4263

5 Enter $2,400 ($4,800 if you paid for the care of two or more qualifying persons) . . . . **5** | 4,800

6 If you completed Part III on page 2, enter the **excluded benefits**, if any, from line 25 . . . . **6**

7 Subtract line 6 from line 5 and enter the result. (If the result is zero or less, skip lines 8 through 13. Enter zero on line 14, and go to line 15.) . . . . **7** | 4800

8 Compare the amounts on lines 4 and 7. Enter the **smaller** of the two amounts here . . . . . **8** | 4263

9 You **must** enter your earned income. (See the Instructions for the definition of earned income.) . . **9** | 55,763

10 If you are married filing a joint return, you **must** enter your spouse's earned income. (If your spouse was a full-time student or disabled, see the Instructions for the amount to enter.). . . . . . . **10** | 21,420

11 If you are married filing a joint return, compare the amounts on lines 9 and 10. Enter the **smaller** of the two amounts here . . . . **11** | 21,420

12 • If you are married filing a joint return, compare the amounts on lines 8 and 11. Enter the **smaller** of the two amounts here.
• All others, compare the amounts on lines 8 and 9. Enter the **smaller** of the two amounts here. . . . . **12** | 4,263

13 Enter the decimal amount from the table below that applies to the **adjusted gross income** on Form 1040, line 32 . . . . **13** | x .20

If line 32 is:		Decimal amount is:	If line 32 is:		Decimal amount is:
Over—	But not over—		Over—	But not over—	
$0	—10,000	.30	$20,000	—22,000	.24
10,000	—12,000	.29	22,000	—24,000	.23
12,000	—14,000	.28	24,000	—26,000	.22
14,000	—16,000	.27	26,000	—28,000	.21
16,000	—18,000	.26	28,000		.20
18,000	—20,000	.25			

14 Multiply the amount on line 12 by the decimal amount on line 13 and enter the result . . . . . **14** | 853

15 Multiply any child and dependent care expenses for 1989 that you paid in 1990 by the decimal amount that applies to the adjusted gross income on your 1989 Form 1040, line 32, or Form 1040A, line 14. Enter the result. (You must complete Part I and attach a statement. See the Instructions.) . **15**

16 Add the amounts on lines 14 and 15. See the Instructions for the amount of credit you can claim . **16** | 853

For Paperwork Reduction Act Notice, see separate Instructions.

Form **2441** (1990)

Form **3903**	**Moving Expenses**	OMB No. 1545-0062
Department of the Treasury Internal Revenue Service	▶ Attach to Form 1040. ▶ See separate Instructions.	**19**○**90** Attachment Sequence No. **62**

Name(s) shown on Form 1040	Your social security number
HOWARD M. & SUSAN J. DAVIDSON	111 22 3333

1 Enter the number of miles from your **old** home to your **new** workplace . . . . **1** | **297**
2 Enter the number of miles from your **old** home to your **old** workplace . . . . **2** | **24**
3 Subtract line 2 from line 1. Enter the result (but not less than zero) . . . . ▶ **3** | **273**

If line **3** is 35 or more miles, complete the rest of this form. If line **3** is less than 35 miles, you may not deduct your moving expenses. This rule does not apply to members of the armed forces.

Part I Moving Expenses

Section A.—Transportation of Household Goods
4 Transportation and storage for household goods and personal effects . . . . **4** | **1834**

Section B.—Expenses of Moving From Old To New Home

5 Travel and lodging **not** including meals . . . . **5** | **181**

6 Total meals . . . . **6** | **82**

7 Multiply line 6 by 80% (.80) . . . . **7** | **66**

8 Add lines 5 and 7 . . . . **8** | **247**

Section C.—Pre-move Househunting Expenses and Temporary Quarters (for any 30 days in a row after getting your job)

9 Pre-move travel and lodging **not** including meals . . . . **9** | **245**

10 Temporary quarters expenses **not** including meals **10**
11 Total meal expenses for both pre-move househunting and temporary quarters . . . . **11** | **79**

12 Multiply line 11 by 80% (.80) . . . . **12** | **63**

13 Add lines 9, 10, and 12 . . . . **13** | **308**

Section D.—Qualified Real Estate Expenses

14 Expenses of (check one): **a** ☒ selling or exchanging your old home; or
                             b ☐ if renting, settling an unexpired lease . . . **14** | **573**
15 Expenses of (check one): **a** ☒ buying your new home; or
                             b ☐ if renting, getting a new lease . . . . **15** | **613**

Part II Dollar Limits

16 Enter the amount from line 13 . . . . **16** | **308**

17 Enter the **smaller** of line 16 or $1,500 ($750 if married filing a separate return, and at the end of 1990 you lived with your spouse who also started work during 1990) . . . . **17** | **308**

18 Add lines 14, 15, and 17 . . . . **18** | **1494**

19 Enter the **smaller** of line 18 or $3,000 ($1,500 if married filing a separate return, and at the end of 1990 you lived with your spouse who also started work during 1990) . . . . **19** | **1494**

20 Add lines 4, 8, and 19. This is your moving expense deduction. **Enter here and on Schedule A (Form 1040), line 19.** (Note: *Any payments your employer made for any part of your move (including the value of any services furnished in kind) should be included on Form W-2. Report that amount on Form 1040, line 7. See Reimbursements in the Instructions.*) . . . . ▶ **20** | **3575**

For Paperwork Reduction Act Notice, see separate Instructions. | Form **3903** (1990)

Form **4562**	**Depreciation and Amortization**	OMB No. 1545-0172
Department of the Treasury Internal Revenue Service	**(Including Information on Listed Property)** ▶ See separate instructions. ▶ Attach this form to your return.	19**90** Attachment Sequence No. **67**

Name(s) shown on return	Identifying number
HOWARD M. & SUSAN J. DAVIDSON	III-22-3333

Business or activity to which this form relates

Part I Election To Expense Certain Tangible Property (Section 179) (Note: *If you have any "Listed Property," also complete Part V.)*

1 Maximum dollar limitation (see instructions)	1	$10,000
2 Total cost of section 179 property placed in service during the tax year (see instructions)	2	3,535
3 Threshold cost of section 179 property before reduction in limitation	3	$200,000
4 Reduction in limitation—Subtract line 3 from line 2, but do not enter less than -0-	4	0
5 Dollar limitation for tax year—Subtract line 4 from line 1, but do not enter less than -0-	5	10,000

(a) Description of property	(b) Cost	(c) Elected cost	
6 7 YR.: BOOKS, CALCULATOR, TYPEWRITER	705	705	

7 Listed property—Enter amount from line 26	7	2,830	
8 Total elected cost of section 179 property—Add amounts in column (c), lines 6 and 7	8	3,535
9 Tentative deduction—Enter the lesser of line 5 or line 8	9	3,535
10 Carryover of disallowed deduction from 1989 (see instructions)	10	
11 Taxable income limitation—Enter the lesser of taxable income or line 5 (see instructions)	11	10,000
12 Section 179 expense deduction—Add lines 9 and 10, but do not enter more than line 11	12	3,535
13 Carryover of disallowed deduction to 1991—Add lines 9 and 10, less line 12 ▶	13		

Note: *Do not use Part II or Part III below for automobiles, certain other vehicles, cellular telephones, computers, or property used for entertainment, recreation, or amusement (listed property). Instead, use Part V for listed property.*

Part II MACRS Depreciation For Assets Placed in Service ONLY During Your 1990 Tax Year (Do Not Include Listed Property)

(a) Classification of property	(b) Mo. and yr. placed in service	(c) Basis for depreciation (Business use only—see instructions)	(d) Recovery period	(e) Convention	(f) Method	(g) Depreciation deduction
14 General Depreciation System (GDS) (see instructions):						
a 3-year property						
b 5-year property						
c 7-year property						
d 10-year property						
e 15-year property						
f 20-year property						
g Residential rental property			27.5 yrs.	MM	S/L	
			27.5 yrs.	MM	S/L	
h Nonresidential real property			31.5 yrs.	MM	S/L	
			31.5 yrs.	MM	S/L	
15 Alternative Depreciation System (ADS) (see instructions):						
a Class life					S/L	
b 12-year			12 yrs.		S/L	
c 40-year			40 yrs.	MM	S/L	

Part III Other Depreciation (Do Not Include Listed Property)

16 GDS and ADS deductions for assets placed in service in tax years beginning before 1990 (see instructions).	16	312
17 Property subject to section 168(f)(1) election (see instructions)	17	
18 ACRS and other depreciation (see instructions)	18	750

Part IV Summary

19 Listed property—Enter amount from line 25	19	32
20 Total—Add deductions on line 12, lines 14 and 15 in column (g), and lines 16 through 19. Enter here and on the appropriate lines of your return. (Partnerships and S corporations—see instructions) . .	20	4,629
21 For assets shown above and placed in service during the current year, enter the portion of the basis attributable to section 263A costs (see instructions).	21	

For Paperwork Reduction Act Notice, see page 1 of the separate instructions.   Form **4562** (1990)

Form 4562 (1990)   Page **2**

Part V | Listed Property.—Automobiles, Certain Other Vehicles, Cellular Telephones, Computers, and Property Used for Entertainment, Recreation, or Amusement

If you are using the standard mileage rate or deducting vehicle lease expense, complete columns (a) through (c) of Section A, all of Section B, and Section C if applicable.

Section A.—Depreciation (Caution: *See instructions for limitations for automobiles.*)

22a Do you have evidence to support the business use claimed? ☒ Yes ☐ No | 22b If "Yes," is the evidence written? ☒ Yes ☐ No

(a) Type of property (list vehicles first)	(b) Date placed in service	(c) Business use percentage	(d) Cost or other basis	(e) Basis for depreciation (business use only)	(f) Recovery period	(g) Method/ Convention	(h) Depreciation deduction	(i) Elected section 179 cost
23 Property used more than 50% in a trade or business:								
COMPUTER	10/90	90 %	3144	2830				2830
		%						
		%						
24 Property used 50% or less in a trade or business:								
VIDEO CAMERA	9/87	40 %	962	385	12-YR	S/L–	32	
		%				S/L–		
		%				S/L–		

25 Add amounts in column (h). Enter the total here and on line 19, page 1 . . . . | 25 | 32
26 Add amounts in column (i). Enter the total here and on line 7, page 1 . . . . | 26 | 2830

Section B.—Information Regarding Use of Vehicles—*If you deduct expenses for vehicles:*
- Always complete this section for vehicles used by a sole proprietor, partner, or other "more than 5% owner," or related person.
- If you provided vehicles to your employees, first answer the questions in Section C to see if you meet an exception to completing this section for those vehicles.

	(a) Vehicle 1		(b) Vehicle 2		(c) Vehicle 3		(d) Vehicle 4		(e) Vehicle 5		(f) Vehicle 6	
27 Total business miles driven during the year (DO NOT include commuting miles) . .												
28 Total commuting miles driven during the year												
29 Total other personal (noncommuting) miles driven												
30 Total miles driven during the year—Add lines 27 through 29												
	Yes	No	Yes	No	Yes	No	Yes	No	Yes	No	Yes	No
31 Was the vehicle available for personal use during off-duty hours?												
32 Was the vehicle used primarily by a more than 5% owner or related person? . . .												
33 Is another vehicle available for personal use?												

Section C.—Questions for Employers Who Provide Vehicles for Use by Their Employees
(*Answer these questions to determine if you meet an exception to completing Section B.* Note: *Section B must always be completed for vehicles used by sole proprietors, partners, or other more than 5% owners or related persons.*)

	Yes	No
34 Do you maintain a written policy statement that prohibits all personal use of vehicles, including commuting, by your employees?		
35 Do you maintain a written policy statement that prohibits personal use of vehicles, except commuting, by your employees? (See instructions for vehicles used by corporate officers, directors, or 1% or more owners.)		
36 Do you treat all use of vehicles by employees as personal use?		
37 Do you provide more than five vehicles to your employees and retain the information received from your employees concerning the use of the vehicles?.		
38 Do you meet the requirements concerning qualified automobile demonstration use (see instructions)?		

Note: *If your answer to 34, 35, 36, 37, or 38 is "Yes," you need not complete Section B for the covered vehicles.*

Part VI | **Amortization**

(a) Description of costs	(b) Date amortization begins	(c) Amortizable amount	(d) Code section	(e) Amortization period or percentage	(f) Amortization for this year
39 Amortization of costs that begins during your 1990 tax year:					
40 Amortization of costs that began before 1990.			40		
41 Total. Enter here and on "Other Deductions" or "Other Expenses" line of your return			41		

SUPPLEMENT # 1

JOB-RELATED TRAVEL EXPENSES AWAY FROM HOME OVERNIGHT
(FORM 2106, PART I, LINES 3 AND 5)

1. Sabbatical at University of Arizona to do
   research: February 1-April 30.

Meals		$1135
Round-trip airplane fare	$ 406	
Lodging	1412	
Cleaning and laundry	146	
Daily bus fares between temporary home and school	170	

2. Trip to attend meeting of American
   Physics Society: Oct. 10-Oct. 16 in
   Los Angeles, Cal.

Meals and Entertainment		213
Round-trip airplane fare	458	
Lodging	341	
Taxi fares	35	

3. Trip to interview for new job in same
   line of work: Jan. 7-Jan. 9 in Miami, Fla.

Meals		68
Round-trip airplane fare	356	
Lodging	126	
Airport Limousine	15	

TOTAL OTHER THAN MEALS & ENTERTAINMENT
(FORM 2106, PART I, LINE 3) $3465

    TOTAL MEALS & ENTERTAINMENT
    (FORM 2106, PART I, LINE 5) $1416

SUPPLEMENT # 2

JOB-RELATED EXPENSES-OTHER THAN FOR TRAVEL, MEALS,
   & ENTERTAINMENT (FORM 2106, PART I, LINE 4)

A. Books & Equipment:

Listed Property (Form 4562, Part V)

1. Home computer (including peripherals)
    used 90% for job-related research:

       Date of purchase: 10/13/90
       Purchase price: $3144
       Expensing deduction: 90% x $3144 . . . . $2830
       (Included on Form 4562, Line 7)

2. Video camera, required by employer,
    purchased 9/14/87 for $962 used
    40% for job-related purposes:

       Depreciation deduction using 12-year
       listed property table percentage (8.33%)
       for item in fourth year of use:
       Basis for Depreciation:
         $962 x 40% = $385
       Deduction for 1990: $385 x 8.33% . . .   32
       (Included on Form 4562, Line 19)

Non-listed Property Purchased in 1990:

1. Books $382
2. Calculator   36
3. Typewriter . . . .   <u>287</u>

       Expensing Deduction   705
       (Form 4562, Line 6)

Non-Listed Property Purchased in 1987-1989 . .   312
    (Depreciation included on Form 4562, Line 16)
Non-Listed Property Purchased Before 1987: . .   112
    (Depreciation included on Form 4562, Line 18) <u>   </u>

TOTAL DEDUCTION FOR
  JOB-RELATED BOOKS & EQUIPMENT $3991

SUPPLEMENT # 2 (continued)

B. Educational Expenses:

Expenses connected with attending seminar
in Advanced Mechanics at University of
Pittsburgh to learn new material for use
in job-related research. (This seminar
was not needed to meet the minimum
requirements for holding my job nor was
it part of a program qualifying for a
new job.):

```
Tuition . . . . . . . . . . . . . . . . . .   $640
Textbook  . . . . . . . . . . . . . . . .       35
Supplies  . . . . . . . . . . . . . . . .       10
Laboratory Fee  . . . . . . . . . . . . .       30

TOTAL EDUCATIONAL EXPENSES . . . . . . . . .   $715
```

C. Other Expenses:

```
Dues to National Education Association . . . .   $ 60
Dues to A.A.U.P. . . . . . . . . . . . . . . .     80
Dues to American Physics Society . . . . . . .     50
Subscriptions to professional journals . . . .    184
Supplies used in teaching--paper, pens,
   record book, etc. . . . . . . . . . . . . .    146
Laboratory apparel (including cleaning)  . . .     75
Laboratory equipment . . . . . . . . . . . . .     57
Required physical exam . . . . . . . . . . . .     40
Payment to substitute teacher  . . . . . . . .    165
Employment agency fee to obtain job  . . . . .    350

TOTAL "OTHER EXPENSES" . . . . . . . . . . . .  $1207


GRAND TOTAL (FORM 2106, PART I, LINE 4)  . . .  $5319
```

SUPPLEMENT # 3

SCHEDULE C DEDUCTION

1. Home Office (1 room of 6 room house)

   Home Expenses:
Mortgage interest	$9224
Property taxes	1511
Heating oil	1130
Electricity for light and air conditioning	981
Homeowner's insurance	156
Cleaning service	1775
Repair of furnace	230

   $15,007

   Home expenses attributable to office:
   1/6 x $15,007 . . . . $2501
   Plus: Painting the office 220
          *Depreciation 638

   TOTAL HOME OFFICE DEDUCTION
   (SCHEDULE C, LINE 18) $3359

   *Depreciation Calculation:
   Purchase price of house (excluding land): $63,830
   Date of purchase: 1/18/85
   Basis of home office: 1/6 x $63,830 = $10,638
   Depreciation deduction for 1990:
          6% x $10,638 = $638

   (Depreciation included on Form 4562, Line 18)

516

SUPPLEMENT # 4

JOB-RELATED AUTO MILEAGE (FORM 2106, LINE 14)

1. Travel between two different jobs:
   18 miles per week for 20 weeks . . .   360 miles

2. Travel to temporary job away from
   home in city 51 miles from home:
   2 weeks x 3 days/week x 102 miles .   612

3. Travel to attend seminar on Advanced
   Mechanics   514

4. Travel to libraries to do research . .   282

5. Travel to pick up official visitors
   at airport   120

   TOTAL . . . .   1888 miles

INDEX

INDEX
(Boldface indicates primary reference)

Abortions 118
Accelerated depreciation method....... 92-99
Accident
    insurance.. 294
    loss from........:........................... 288-294
Acquisition debt............................ 149-154
Acupuncture................................ 117, 124
Adjunct Professors 436-437
Adjusted gross income..................... 15-17
Adjustments to income **15-17**, 28,
              209,233, 321,376,428-429
Air cleaner.. 121
Air conditioners................................... 104
    medical deduction for 121-122
Airplanes 325, 328
Alcoholics Anonymous 124
Alimony.................................. 28, **319-322**
    IRAs based on................................. 216
Allergies 120-121
Alternative minimum tax 493-494
Amending tax returns 19-20, 302-303
Annuities
    retirement.................................. 410-413
    tax sheltered......................45, 225-226,
         233-244, 412, 416-423
    withholding on................................. 317
Apartment buildings 88, 99-104
Appliances 169
Appraisal fees...................................... 376
Artistic activities 426, 433-434
    loss-producing 445-450
Aspirin... 119
Assessments.................................... 159-160
Athletic events, tickets to.............. 125-126
Athletic wear 54
Audits 45-47, **295-313**
Authors 66-68, 75, 83, 226-233,
        324, 351, 426, 428-429,
        431-436, 445-450, 455
    new deduction for..................... 428-429
Automobile **175-189**, 326,
         330-332, 337-342,
         347-353, 360, 374
    accident.. 289
    charitable use 127-128, 296
    depreciation 88-99, 179-189
    expensing option..................... 179-189

garage rent 180, 185
insurance.................... 179-180, 185, 294
interest............... l06-107, 114, 180, 188
license 185, 187-188, 196, 296
logs, mileage............................ 176-178
medical use 119-120, 122
mileage rate 26, **119-120**, **128**,
      175, **179**, 180, 185-187, **285**,
      296, 330-332, 342, 360
operating expenses 179-180, 185-187
parking fees............... 179-180, 185-187
recordkeeping 176-179
registration fee.. 179, 187-188, 196, 296.
rental...................................... 328, 367
repairs 179-180, 185, 188
sampling techniques
    for expenses........................... 177-178
taxes.................. 179, 187-188, 196, 296
telephone 89-90, 94-99
towing expenses 180
used for moving........................ 285-286
washing... 185
Averaging, income (see Income averaging)
Awards 458
Babysitting
    expenses 28, **138-148**, 246-247
    paid by employer....................... 145-146
Baccalaureate bonds 386-387
Basic rules..15-48
Basis................................103, 165, 167-168
Bedroom used as home office............64-65,
        71-73
Bill of rights, taxpayer 304-305
Bills, U. S. Treasury 262-265
Birth control pills and devices............. 118
Boats... 107
    as second home 149
Bonds
    baccalaureate 386-387
    college tuition............ 381-384, 386-387
    interest on 109-110
    mutual funds 274-278
    savings 191-192, 381-384, 386-387
    tax-free municipal.............. 41, 110-111,
        265-266, 275-277, 282
    transfer tax on 197
    trusts.. 277

U. S. Treasury 262-265
Books 49, **52**, 61-62, 374,
      398, 439-440, 489
  depreciation 49, 52, 61-62, 88-99
  donated to charity 135-137
  expensing 49,52, 88-92
  purchased in the past 61-62
Brackets, tax 17
Briefcases 52
Broker reports to IRS 257-258
Brokerage fees 258
Burglar alarm 375
Business, outside 75-76, **426-450**,
      491-492
  losses from 445-450
Business expenses 45, 47, 368-378,
      439-440
Business interest 109, 188
Business school (see MBA expenses)
Cafeteria plans 246-247
Calculators 55, 78-79,88-99
Camera 49-51,55-56, 88-99
Camp, summer 142
Capital gains tax 13, 45, 47, **256-259**
  on home 87, 161-169
  on mutual funds 271-273
Capitalizing expenses 433-434
Cash management accounts 279-282
Casualty losses 15, 35, **288-294**
Cellular telephone 50-51, 89-90, 94-99
Chairs 55
Charity
  contributions to 37, **125-137**,
      252, 254-255, 296
  recordkeeping 129-133, 137
  travel for 26, 127-128, 296
Check, payment by 44, 112-114
Checking accounts
  fees 279
  interest-paying 276, 278-282
Child
  custody 321-322
  dependent 15-19, 23-24,
      28-33, 321-322
  giving money to 33
  income received by 28-33
  loans to 194-195
  lowering your tax 190-195
  medical expenses. 31
  paying for assistance 193,**442-444**,
      450, 490-491
  shifting income to 33, 190-195,
      435-436, 442-444

social security number for 425
support 191-193, 319-322
tax-return **28-33**
trips taken by 141-142
Child care tax credit 16, 28, 35,
      138-148, 443
Childbirth classes 120
Church, contributions to 125-137
Cigarette tax 196
Cleaning (also see Laundry) 54, 79,
      82-85
  house 138-148
Clothing 54
  given to charity 132-135
Cohabitation 19, 444-445
Cohan rule 42
College, contributions to 125-137
College education
  deduction for 379-401
  loans for 107-108, 114
  prepaid tuition plans 381-386
  tuition bonds 381-384, 386-387
  tuition savings plans 381-387
College event tickets 125-126
Collision insurance 294
Commissions, real estate 162, 285
Commuting 326, 338-343,
      347-353, 356-357
  to school 399
Composers 434
Computation of tax 15-17
Computers 49-51, **55-60**, 88-99
Condominium (see Home)
Consulting 75-76, 84-85, 109,
      226-233, 373, **426-450**
Contributions
  charitable 37, **125-137**,
      252, 254-255, 296
Conventions 324, 328,
      336-337, **359-360**
Corporations 428-430, 438-442
Cosmetic surgery 124
County taxes (see State and local taxes)
Credit cards
  interest 107, 114
  payment by 44-45
Credits (see Tax Credits)
CREF (see TIAA/CREF)
Crutches 118
Day care **138-148**, 246-247
  paid by employer 145-146
  reporting requirement 147-148
Debt-ceiling on home 150-154

Decorating 79
Deductions 15-17
  average claimed by taxpayers 301
Deferred compensation plans......... 244-246
  borrowing from............................... 245
Deficit Reduction Act 9-13
Defined-Benefit Keogh plans............. 202,
                                 229-231, 439
Dental expenses 117
Dentures 118
Dependent..... 15-19, 23-24, 28-33, 321-322
  parent....................................... 18, 25-26
  tax return of 28-33
Depreciation.................................. **88-105**
  5-year recovery class.......... 88-89, 92-99
  7-year recovery class......... 88-89, 92-99
  accelerated method 92-99
  apartment building................. 88, 99-104
  automobile..................... 88-99, 179-189
  basis 103
  books 88-99
  calculators...................................... 88-99
  camera 88-99
  computers 59, 88-99
  double declining balance method 93
  entertainment items............ 89-90, 94-99
  equipment....................................... 88-99
  expensing option 88-90, 91-92,
                                          179-189
  40%-rule 98-99
  furniture......................... 88-94, 169-170
  home............................... 78, 81-85, 88,
              99-105, 164-165, 170-171
  items purchased late in the year 97-99
  items used part of the year..... 97-99, **103**
  land 100
  listed property **89-90,** 94-99
  prescribed (PRE) method.................. 93
  real estate class 88, 99-105
  rental property 88, 99-104
  research items 88-99
  straight-line method.......................92-98
  telephones...................... 89-90, 94-99
  typewriters.....................................88-99
  video equipment.................89-90, 94-99
Desk..55
Diet program...................... 120-121, 123
Dinner meetings...............................402-409
  80%-rule...404
Disability, payroll deductions for 197
Disability income 18, 124
Dissertation expenses..... 375, 390-391, 398
Dividend reinvestment plan 193-194
Dividends...................................... 109-110

reporting on tax return....... 15, 22-23, 46
shifting tax on........................... 190-195
withholding on 316
Divorce.......................... 117, 147, **318-323**
Doctor bills 116-117
Donations (see Contributions)
Driver's license 196
Drought, damage from.................. 289-290
Drugs... 119
Dues to unions or professional
  societies... 375
Earned income 13, 28-30, 460
Earned income credit 23-24, 472
Educational expenses ... 107-108, 114, 118,
            122-123, 140-144, 245, 295-296,
            324, 355-356, 366, **379-401**, 439
  tuition savings plans 381-387
Educational materials, miscellaneous 62
Educational reimbursements from
  employer 380
80%-rule for meal expenses **326-327**,
            337, 347-352, 368, 371-373, 404
Electricity (see Utilities)
Electronic filing of tax return.................. 20
Employee, definition of 427-428
Employment agency fees 374
Entertainment expenses 368-374,
                                 402-409
  80%-rule 368, 371-373, 404
Entertainment items 89-90, 94-99
Equipment 49-51, **55-56**, 78, 88-99,
                        439,472-473,489
  medical 121-124
Estate tax....................... 167, **248-255**, 386
Estimated tax................................. 316-317
Exchange students 126
Exemptions 15-19
  of dependent child 28
Exercise.. 123
  equipment.................................. 121-122
Expensing option 88-92
  items converted to personal use.......... 92
Extension of time to file........................ 22
Exterminators 82
Extracurricular activities 375
Eyeglasses.. 118
Face lifts... 124
Family members, hiring............... 442-445,
                        450,490-491
Fees 216
Fellowships....... 47, 355-356, 401, **457-486**
Film 52
Fire, damage from............................... 289
Fiscal year 441

5-year withdrawal rule 215-216
Flexible spending accounts 246-247
Flood, damage from 289
Food 368-374
   at business meetings 402-409
   80%-rule **326-327**, 336,
           347-352, 368, 371-373, 404
   per diem rate 329-331, **335-337**, 347
   special diet 120-121, 123
   while away from home 284-285,
           325-337, 347-352,
           356-364, 489
Foreign income 337, 347, 433,
           451-456, 473-474
   moving expenses 287
Forms
   (also see Sample Tax Forms
   at end of book)
Form 843 485
Form 942 146-147
Form 1040-ES 316
Form 1040X 20, 222
Form 1099 .... 37, 45-47, 257-258,
           427-428, 459
Form 1099-G 200
Form 1099-R 224,413
Form 1099-S 166
Form 2106 .... 25, 46, 175, 178,
           324, 327, 332, 356, 368-371,
           397, 400-401, 409, 491
Form 2119 .... 47, 166
Form 2120 18
Form 2210 316
Form 2350 456
Form 2440 124
Form 2441 .... 20, 145, 147
Form 2688 22
Form 3903 287
Form 4506 20
Form 4562 .... 49, 51-52, 61,
           89, 92, 94, **104**, 175, 178
Form 4684 294
Form 4782 286
Form 4868 .... 22, 456
Form 4952 109
Form 4972 413
Form 5500 229
Form 5500-EZ 229
Form 8283 133
Form 8332 .... 318, 321-322
Form 8582 262
Form 8606 210
Form 8615 30-31

Form 8814 32-33
Form 8822 20
Form IO-673 455
Form W-2 .... 297, 459, 466, 483-484
Form W-4 314-317
Form W-10 148
   401(k) plans 244-245
   borrowing from 245
403(b) plans 233-244
40%-rule for depreciation 98-99
Freeze, damage from 288-289
Furniture 49, 55, 78-79,
           83, 88-94, 169-170
Gambling losses 368, 376
Gas (see Utilities)
Gasoline 179-180, 185
Gasoline tax 196
Gifts 458
   tax on 167, **248-255**, 385-386
   to minors 190-191
Gold coins, IRA purchase of 219
Graduate assistants 47, 391-392,
           457-472, 483-486
   tuition remission 462
Graduate school education 390-398
Grants, tax-free 47, 355-356,
           401, **457-486**
   awarded after August 16, 1986
        .... 460-466, 483-486
   awarded before August 17, 1986
        466-486
   earned income 460
   National Endowment
      for the Humanities 474-476
   NSF 476-481
   non-degree candidates 463, 466-486
   received outside the U. S. 473-474
   reporting on your return 459-460,
           483-484
   sabbatical 477-478, 482-483
   social security tax on 457, 463,
           466, 484-486
   summer 475-476, 480
Hair, removal and transplants 124
Handicapped, aids for the 123-124
Handicapped workers,
   expenses of 368, 376
Head of household 25-26, 33, 318
Health insurance 116, 118
Health spas 123
Hearing aids 118
Hiring a child or spouse 193
Hobby 445-450

Home
  acquisition debt.......................... 149-154
  adjusted sales price................... 163-164
  capital gains on sale 87, **161-169**
  cleaning 138-148
  debt ceiling on 150-154
  depreciation 78, 81-85, 88,
    99-105, 164-165, 170-171
  equity loans 106-107, 114, **149-155**
  fix-up costs before sale 163
  improvements 41, 103-104, 151,
    153, 161-162
  insurance 82-85, 169-170
  interest, mortgage..........82-85, 106-107,
    114, **149-159**, 169-174, 494
  joint ownership 167-169, 251
  mobile 107, 149
  owner's expenses...................... **149-174**
  passive interest 108-109, 169
  recordkeeping 41
  refinancing of 150-154, 156, 494
  renting to others.............. 36, 42, 99-104,
    149-150, 163, **169-174**,
    259-262
  renting to relatives 174
  repairs 82-85, 103-104, 162-163
  sale of 47, 87, **160-169**, 296
  second........................ 106-107, 149-150
  settlement charges........................... 161
  taxes 82-85, 149, **159-170**
  transfer taxes 161-162, 197
Home computers 49-51, **55-60**, 88-99
Home office......... **63-87**, 439-440, 489-490
  carryover of losses................. 42, 85-86
  depreciation............... 78, 81-85, 99-105
  items used in.............................. 78-79
  losses on 83-86
  research, used for..................... 63, 66-68
  travel to and from 80-81
  used by 2 persons 74-75
  used for separate activities 74-75
Homeowner's expenses **149-174**
Honorariums................................ 226, 437
Hotel (see Lodging)
House (see Home)
Household services, tax credit for.......... 16,
    28, 35, **138-148**, 443
Housekeeper, tax credit for 138-148
Housing, free or low rent 47-48
Humidifier.. 121
Hurricane, damage from...................... 289
Ice, damage from.................................289
Improvements on house..........41, 103-104,
    151, 153, 161-162

Imputed interest 194- 195
Income
  earned 28-30, 460
  foreign 433, 473-474
  received by child........................ 28-33
  unearned 28-33, 190
Income averaging for lump-sum
  distributions...................... 224-227, 230,
    232-233, **411-413**
Income shifting 33, **190-195**,
    435-436, 442-445
Income tax, state and local............... 26-27,
    196-201
Incorporation 428-430, 438-442
Individual retirement account (see IRAs)
Inherited property ... 167-168, 248-255, 259
Insects, damage from 288
Installment sale 259, 494
Insulin.. 119
Insurance................................. 60, 293-294
  automobile................. 179-180, 185, 294
  home.............................. 82-85, 169-170
  life... 250-251
  medical... 118
Interest........... 41, 45-46, **106-115**, 493-494
  acquisition debt on home 149-154
  automobile......... 106-107, 114, 180, 188
  business.. 188
  consumer loan............................ 107-108
  debt ceiling on home 150-154
  discount loans 156-157
  home-equity loan.................... 106-107,
    114, **149-155**
  imputed 194-195
  investment.................. **109-110**, 111-114
  late payment charge 26
  margin.............................. 109-110, 115
  mortgage on home..82-85, 106-107, 114,
    149-159, 169-174
  on checking accounts......... 276, 278-282
  on credit cards............................ 107, 114
  on homes 106-107, 114, **149-159**
  on loans to relatives........... 108, 194-195
  on portfolio income 109-114
  on rental property 108-109, 115,
    259-262
  on stock purchases 109-110, 114-115
  on student loans 107-108, 114
  on taxes owed 107-108
  paid to relative 108
  passive 108-109, 115, 169, 259-262
  personal **106-108**, 110-111, 172
  phase-in rules 493
  points **155-156**, 162

reporting on tax return....... 15, 22-23, 46
shifting tax on............................ 190-195
tax-free......... 41, 265-266, 275-277, 282
tax-sheltered................ 190-195, 202-247
30-day rule.................................. 112-113
tracing rule.................................. 111-113
trade or business 109
withholding...................................... 316
Interest-free loans 194-195
Interns 472
Investing your money **256-282**
Investment expenses............................ 375
Investment income,
  shifting tax on............................ 190-195
Investment interest.......... **109-110**, 111-114
Investment plan, stock 193-194
Investments 256-282
IRAs............................ 28, 35-36, 42, 111,
            203, **204-226**, 232-233,
            237-238, 321, 376, 443
  5-year withdrawal rule............... 215-216
  beneficiary................................. 223-224
  borrowing from.......................... 220-221
  distributions from 211-216
  dividing contributions between spouses
            205-208, 213-214
  early withdrawal........................ 214-216
  fees... 216-217
  non-deductible contributions to 204,
            209-215
  rollovers into **224-226**, 237-238, 412
  switching funds.......................... 219-220
  tainted spouse rule 205-206
  withdrawals 211-216
IRS (see Audit)
IRS bill of rights 304-305
IRS matching program 45-47, 297-298
IRS private rulings 310-313
IRS telephone assistance 21
Itemized deductions, average. 301
Itemizing deductions 15-17
Job-hunting expenses 359, 374
Job-related expenses 368-375
Joint ownership..................... 167-169, 251
Joint return 26-27, 33-36, 38-41
  placing spouse's name first 23
Joint tenancy 167-169, 251
Journals 52-53
  donated to charity 135-137
Jury duty 376
Keogh plans 45, 111, **226-233**, 376,
            411-412, 431-433, 437-439, 443
  defined-benefit 202, **229-231**, 439
  early withdrawal 231-232

Laboratory clothing 54, 490
Lamps 55
Land 100
Landscaping 79
Late payment charges 26, 108, 149
Laundry while away from
  home 325, 327,
            347-352, 356-357, 489
Law school 394-395
Lawn care. 79
Leave of absence........................... 343-359
  rental of home during 169-174
  to obtain education 395-398
Lecturing fees....................................... 437
Legal expenses............. 162, 169-170, 285,
            295, 323, 376
Libraries, travel to 175, 337-338
Licenses 185, 187-188, 196, 296
Life insurance 250-251
Limited partnerships 108, 259-262
Listed property.......... 42, **49-51**, 61, 89-90,
            94-99, 186-187
Loans (see Interest)
Local taxes (see State and local taxes)
Lodging.............. 284-285, 325, 327-329,
            347-352, 355-364, 489
  discounts for teachers 366-367
Log........................... 50, 176-178, 327-329
Loss, passive 259-262
Loss produced by outside activity ..445-450
Lump-sum distributions from retirement
  plans 224-227, 230, 232-233,
            237-238, 251, **411-413**, 420
Lunch, business-related 374, **402-409**
  80%-Rule................. 368, 371-373, 404
MBA expenses 398
Magazines 53-54, 376
Maid, tax credit for 138-148
Maiden name on joint return 23
Mailing in your tax return 19
  electronic filing 20
Management Fees 258, 267-269
Maps... 52
Margin interest....................... 109-110, 115
Married couples
  filing joint returns 23,
            26-27, 33-36, 38-41
  filing separate returns 26-27,
            33-41, 46
  joint ownership by............. 167-169, 251
  living apart 351
  order of names on tax return 23
Matching program, IRS 45-47
Meals (see Food)

Medical expenses 26, 31, 36-37,
          116-124, 203, 217, 234,
     245-247,322, 374, 439, 444
  getting around 7.5% floor 31-32, 43,
          116-117, 230-231, 439, 444
Medical reimbursement plan......... 439, 444
Medicare tax...12
Medicine.. 119
Mileage rate for auto travel 26, **119-120**,
          128, 175, **179**, 180, 185-187,
          285, 296, 330-332, 342, 360
  charitable.. 128
  medical 119-120
  moving 285
Minimum tax................................ 493-494
Miscellaneous
  deductions......................... 15, 35,37, 52,
          62, 86, 89, 175, 203,
     217, 258-279, 324, **368-377**,
     401, 439-440, 491, 493
  educational materials 62, 398
  supplies 62
2% floor on deductions............... 35, 43-44,
          368-374, 376-377
Mistakes commonly made 25-27
Mobile home 107, 149
Money-market accounts................. **278-282**
Money-market funds 23, 46,
          274-275, **280-282**
Mortgage payments
  deducting an extra
     month's interest 158
  interest portion 82-85, 106-107,
          114, **149-159**, 169-174, 494
  late payment charge........................... 26
Motels (see Lodging)
Motor club membership........................ 185
Moving expenses . 15, 46, 86, **283-287**, 456
Moving, notifying the IRS 20
Multiple support agreement 18
Municipal bond......... 41, 110-111, **265-266**
  funds......................... 267, **275-277**, 282
  trusts... 277
Municipal taxes (see State and local taxes)
Mutual funds............. 46, **267-278**, 280-282
  advertising 268-270
  bonds 274-278
  comparing.................................. 268-270
  directory of no-load 267, 275
  fees.. 267-270
  hidden fees.................................. 267-270
  management fees...................... 267-270
  money-market............... 23, 46, 274-275,
          280-282

newspaper listing 268
no-load 267-270, 274-275
reports to IRS........................... 257-258
tax-free...................... 267, 275-277, 282
taxes on.................................... 271-273
12b-l funds 267
National Science Foundation 476-481
Necessary business expense................... 24
Negative income tax 23-24
Negligence penalty, appeal of.............. 309
New trade or business, education to qualify
  for 379, 393-395
Newspapers 53-54, 376
1990 Deficit Reduction Act.................9-13
Notes, U. S. Treasury 262-265
NOW accounts 279, 282
Nursery school 138, 140-141
Nursing homes 118-119
Nursing services..................................... 117
Office at home (see Home Office)
Ombudsman 21
Ordinary expense 24
Orthopedic shoes 118
Outside business activity 75-76,
          226-233, **426-450**, 491-492
Painting 82
Paper...52
Parent, shifting income 190-195,
          435-436, 442-444
Parent, support of........................ 18, 25-26
  tax return of dependent...................28-33
Parking fees.................... 179-180, 185, 187
Partnerships.................................428-429
Passive activities..... 108-109, 115, **259-262**
Passive losses........................... 42, 259-262
Passport fee 196
Payroll taxes......................... 197, 484-486
Penalty....................... 26, 108, 158
Pencils 52
Pens 52
Pension plans (see Retirement plans)
Per diem travel rate 329-331,
          335-337, 347
Periodicals 52-53, 376
  donated to charity 135-137
Personal interest **106-108**, 110-111, 172
Personal property tax 187-188, 196
Phase-out
  of interest deduction 493
  of passive loss deductions................ 261
Photography 49-51, 55-56, 426,
          432-434, 445-450
Physical examinations 117, 374
Physical therapy 117

Pictures.. 79
Plants.. 79
    damage to 288-289, 292-293
Podiatrists.. 117
Points charged on loan... **155-156**, 162, 285
Portfolio interest 109-114
Postage 376
Prepaid tuition plans 381-386
Prepayment penalty on loan 158
Prescribed (PRE) depreciation method ... 93
Private contractor........... 427-431, 436-437
Private IRS rulings........................ 310-313
Private school 122-123, 142-144
Prizes 458
Problems Resolution Officer 21
Professional society dues 375
Profit-sharing plans 438-439
Projectors... 55
Property taxes 82-85, 149, **159-161**,
        169-174, 187-188, 196, 200-201
Psychologist fees 117
Publication costs 489-490
Publications 52-53
    donated to charity 135-137
Radios... 55
Rainstorm, damage from............... 288-289
Real estate
    commissions 162, 285
    passive investment in 108, 115,
                                259-262
    transfer tax on 197
Recordation tax, real estate.... 161-162, 285
Record books.. 52
Recordkeeping 41-43
Records, phonograph............................. 52
Recovery exclusion........................ 198-199
Reduction-in-salary agreements ... 233-234,
                        239, 417, 420
Refereeing 226, 426
Refinancing of home...... **150-154**, 156, 494
Refund of state taxes..................... 198-200
Reimbursable expenses 25
Reimbursed expenses 329-333, **368-373**
Reimbursement for educational expenses
    380
Religious orders, members of 48
Religious organizations, contributions to
    125-137
Rent 81
Rental of home............ 36, 42, 99-104, 108,
    115, 149-150, 163, **169-174**, 259-262
Repairs............... 82-85, 103-104, 162-163,
                    179-180, 185, 188

Research assistants .. 47, 457-472, 483-486
    tuition remission 462
Research done at home 63, 66-68
Research expenses 88-89, 175,
                337-338, 365, 374, 398,
                433, 473, **487-492**
    special ruling for college teachers 488
Research grants 47, 457-486
Research tax credit........................ 491-492
Residents 472
Retired persons.................................... 367
Retirement home fees 118-119
Retirement plans **410-425**
    borrowing from......................... 114-115
    cafeteria plans......................... 246-247
    deferred compensation 244-247
    defined-benefit 202, **229-231**, 439
    early death................................... 411
    individual retirement account
    (IRA). 35-36, 42, 203, **204-226**,
                232-233, 237-238, 412, 443
    Keogh p l ans 45, **226-233**,
                431-433, 437-439, 443
    lump-sum distributions from.... 224-227,
                230, 232-233, 237-238,
                251, **411-413**, 420
    payments from.......................... 410-413
    penalty for early distribution from.... 413
    rollovers into IRAs **224-226**,
                        237-238, 412
    tax-sheltered annuities........ 45, 225-226,
                233-234, 412, 416-423
    withholding on payments 317
Reviewing 226
Ring, damage to 289-291
Rollovers into IRAs **224-226**,
                        237-238, 412
Roundoff.. 21-22
Royalties 190-195, 226, 431-436, 455
    shifting to child or parent 435-436
Rulings, private IRS...................... 310-313
Sabbatical 343-359, 477-478,
                        482-483, 489
    foreign 452-454
    rental of home during 169-174
Safe deposit box 375
Safety equipment 54
Sales tax 196-197
Sampling technique............ 51, 54, 177-178
Savings, investing your................. 202-247,
                                256-282
Savings bond............................... 191-192
    used for tuition 381-384, 386-387

Savings plans, tax-free.................... 202-247
Schedules
  A........................... 15, 17, 61, 82, 84-86,
          89, 92, 107, 109-110, 116, 126,
          158-159, 172-174, 175, 180,
          188, 197, 217, 287, 294, 295-296,
          324, 368-374, 376, 401,
          409, 439, 488, 491
  B....................................... 22-23, 32, 46
  C.................... 16, 25, 28, 61, 79, 85, 87,
          89, 109, 175, 188, 233, 324,
          373-374, 376, 378, 401, 409,
          428, 432-433, 440, 441, 488, 491
  D................................. 47, 256-259, 297
  D-1 257
  E... 169, 432-433
  SE 428-429, 432
Scholarships........................... 47, 355-356,
          457-472, 483-486
School
  contributions to......................... 125-137
  expenses of attending 118, 122-123,
          140-144, 295-296, 355-356, **379-401**
School-related trips........................ 141-142
Second home................................. 149-150
Self-employed persons 16, 23, 28,
          71-76, 84-86, 226-233, 324,
          425, **426-450**, 491-492
  audit selection............................ 427-428
  new 1990 deduction for............. 428-429
Seminars, travel to................................. 338
Senior citizens 367
SEP 228
Separate tax returns 26-27, **33-41**, 46
Separated couples 147, **318-323**
Sheet music 52
Ship, travel by 325
Shoes, orthopedic 118
Sick pay..124
Silver coins, IRA purchase of 219
Simplified Employee Pension (SEP) 228
Slides.. 52
Small case tax court...................... 309-310
Smog, damage from 289
Snowstorm, damage from 289
Social lubrication test................... 407-408
Social security........................12, **424-425**,
          428-429, 432, 444
  checking your account 23, 425
  error in crediting payments................. 23
  excess withheld................................... 16
  household workers.................... 146-147
  income tax on 36, 424-425
  number for child 425

number of spouse............................... 26
overpayment of 16
tax on grants 457, 463, 466, **484-486**
tax on tax-sheltered annuities 239
Software... 59-60
Sole proprietorship.............................. 428
Spouse.. 205-208
  listing on tax return............................23
  paying for assistance 193, 443-444,
          490-491
  retirement plan for...... 205-208, 213-214
Standard deduction 15-16, **27-28**,
          44, 209, 440
Staples 52
State and local taxes 26-27,
          196-201, 296-301
  interest paid on 107-108
  penalty paid on................................ 108
Stock investment plan................... 193-194
Stock options 493
Stockbroker.......................... 257-258, 375
  fees...258
Stocks bought on margin 109-110, 115
  interest paid on 109-110, 115
  transfer tax on 197
Storm, damage from 289
Straight-line depreciation
  method....................................92-98
Students 18, 23-24, 47, 315, 379-401
  exchange 126
  living expenses at summer job.......... 352
  loans to 107-108, 114
Substitute teacher, payment to 375
Summer camp.. 142
Summer jobs.. 315
Supplemental retirement annuity
  (SRA).. 238-239
Supplies................................ 52, 62, 78-79,
          374, 398, 439-440, 489
Support, legal definition of 18, 192-193
Support of child 18, 191-193, 319-322
Supreme Court unisex decision 239,
          421-423
Swimming.. 121-123
Tainted spouse rule 205-206
Tape.. 52
Tape recorders 49-51, 55
Tax brackets 17
Tax court, small case 309-310
Tax credits 16, 28
  child care 16, 28, 35, **138-148**, 443
  earned income...................... 23-24, 472
  elderly 16
  household services **138-148**, 443

private school 142-144
research....................................... 491-492
social security overwithholding 16
Tax deferral 202-247, 438-439, 441
Tax guides..................................... 376, 439
Tax home......... 325-326, 343-359, 451-453
Tax rates 17
Tax returns, obtaining from IRS 20-21
Tax-sheltered annuities 45, 225-226,
233-244, 412, 416-423
borrowing from................................. 236
withdrawals from 225-226, 234-239
Tax-sheltered plans 45, **202-247**
Tax shelters................... 190-195, 259-262,
410, 438-442, 494
Tax tables........................... 9-12, 17, 25-26
Taxable income................................. 15-16
Taxes
automobile 179, 187-188, 196, 296
capital gains on home 47, **161-169**
disability 197
estate 167, **248-255**
estimated 316-317
Federal 296
gift 167, **248-255**
income, state and local 196-201
interest paid on 107-108
payroll 197, 484-486
personal property 187-188
property 81-85, 149, **159-161**,
169-174, 187-188, 196, 200-201
recordation, real estate....... 161-162, 296
refunds.....................................198-200
sales 196-197
state and local................26-27, **196-201**,
296, 301, 493
transfer, bond 197
transfer, real estate 197, 285, 296
transfer, stocks 197
utility.. 296
Taxi fares 325-326, 328
Taxpayer bill of rights................... 304-305
Teaching assistants 47, 391-392,
457-472, 483-486
tuition remission 462
Technical service specialists.......... 430-431
Telephone............. 50-51, **54-55**, 78, 89-90,
94-99, 325, 375, 490
assistance from IRS 21
Temporary job 324, 342-359
moving to....................................... 287
rental of home during 169-174
Tenancy-by-the-entireties 251
Tenancy-in-common 251

Tenancy, joint 167-169, 251
Termites, damage from 82, 288
Theft losses.. 291
Thesis, expenses of writing................. 375,
390-391, 398
30-day purchase rule..................... 112-113
TIAA/CREF.................................... **417-423**
investment options..................... 418-419
retirement system 417-423
tax-sheltered annuities............... 238-239
transfer privileges 419-420
withdrawals from...................... 420-421
Tickets.. 125-126
Tips... 326, 328
Title fees.. 162
Tolls 179-180, 185, 187
Tornado, damage from........................ 289
Towing expenses.................................. 180
Trade or business interest 109
Transfer taxes......... 161-162, 197, 285, 296
Transportation (see Travel)
Travel...................... **324-367**, 439-440
airplane fares............................. 325, 328
automobile 119-120, 122, 128,
175-189, 326, 330-332,
337-342, 347-353, 360, 367
away from home overnight....... 324-337,
343-367, 400
between job locations 324, 326,
337-342
charitable 26, 127-128, 296
children's.................................. 141-142
combining business with
pleasure................................... 360-366
commuting 326, 338-343, 347-353,
356-357, 399
convention.. 324, 328, 336-337, **359-360**
deduction without receipts 333-335
difference between travel and
transportation 325
education related............... 324, 355-356
366, 391, 399-400
extracurricular activities 375
foreign 337, 347, 358, 361-366
from home office 80-81
funds from grants.....................473-483
hotel discounts for teachers 366-367
leave of absence........................ 343-359
log.. 327-329
medical-related 26, 116, 119-120, 122
miscellaneous 337-338
moving.. 283-287
ocean liner.................................... 325
per-diem rate 329-331, 335-337, 347

recordkeeping....... 42, 327-329, 333-335
reimbursement............ 329-333, 368-373
retired persons................................. 367
sabbatical.................................. 343-359
second job location.... 324, 326, 337-342
senior citizens 367
ship.. 325
spouse, expenses of........................... 327
taxi fares 325-326, 328
temporary job 324, 342-359
to attend meetings...................... 337-338
to do research 175, 337-338, 488-490
to libraries........................... 175, 337-338
to look for a house..................... 285-286
to look for a job..................... 359, 374
to pick up visitors............................. 338
to seminars....................................... 338
to stock brokers............................... 375
train fares 325
vacation 141-142, 360-367
yearend strategies 44
Treasury Securities, U.S. **262-265**, 282
Trees, damage to............ 288-289, 292-293
Trips taken by child 141-142
Trucks 88-89
Trusts.................................. 192, 254, 436
Tuberculosis test.................................... 374
Tuition 140-144, 245, 398
bonds.......................... 381-384, 386-387
free for faculty dependents........ 380-381
medical portion of 118, 122-123
remission plans.................. 380-381, 462
savings bond.............. 381-384, 386-387
savings plans............................. 381-387
Tutoring 75, 226, 398, 426
Typewriter 55, 78-79, 88-99
Typing.................................... 374-375, 426

Unallowable items 295-296
Underpayment penalty 108
Unearned income 190
of dependent................................. 28-33
Unemployment compensation.............. 472
Unemployment fund, contribution to ... 197
Uniform Gifts to Minors Act . 190-191, 254
Uniform Transfer to Minors Act........... 191
Uniforms 54, 127
Union dues 375
Unisex mortality tables 239, 421-423
University, contributions to 125-137
U.S. Savings bonds 191-192
used for tuition........................... 381-384
U. S. Treasury Securities **262-265**, 282
Utilities................................ 78, 82-85, 169
late payment fee 107
Utility taxes....................................... 296
Vacation trips................. 141-142, 360-367
Vacuum cleaners...................................... 82
Vandalism, loss from 289
Vasectomies 118
Video equipment 49-51, 89-90, 94-99
W-2 Form.............. 297, 459, 466, 483-484
W-4 Form...................................... 314-317
Wages 15, 483-485
Water (see Utilities)
Weight reduction program 123
Wheelchair............................ 118, 123-124
Whiskey 121
Wills.. 253
Withholding 314-317
on grants 466, 483-486
state and local tax 197-199
Work-related expenses 368-375
Workers' Compensation...................... 124
Yearend strategies............. **43-45**, 114, 158